LORD BOLINGBROKE

THE

WORKS

GREGG INTERNATIONAL PUBLISHERS LIMITED

Kneller pinx.ᵗ   T. A. Dean, sculp.

HENRY ST JOHN,

LORD VISCOUNT BOLINGBROKE.

Engraved by permission, from the Picture in the possession of the Earl of Egremont.

THE

WORKS

OF

LORD BOLINGBROKE.

WITH

A LIFE,

PREPARED EXPRESSLY FOR THIS EDITION,

CONTAINING ADDITIONAL INFORMATION RELATIVE
TO HIS PERSONAL AND PUBLIC CHARACTER,

SELECTED FROM THE BEST AUTHORITIES.

IN FOUR VOLUMES.

VOL. I.

PHILADELPHIA:

CAREY AND HART

1841.

S.B.N. - GB: 576.53004.2

Republished in 1969 by Gregg International Publishers Limited
1 Westmead, Farnborough, Hants., England

Printed in offset by Anton Hain KG, Meisenheim/Glan
Western Germany

PREFACE.

In the composition of a Biography of Lord Bolingbroke for the American publishers, the meagre outlines sketched by Goldsmith, in the Life which was prefixed to Mallet's Edition, have been filled up with materials derived from various sources, some of which were, at the time, inaccessible to, and others were not made use of by, this ever pleasing but commonly indolent writer. Of these, the chief are two articles in the *Edinburgh Review*, the last of which is generally attributed to Lord Brougham; and one in the *Quarterly*, which contains extracts from the *Marchmont Papers;* and, also, the *Memoirs of Lord Bolingbroke*, by Mr. Cooke. Occasional use has been made of a small volume entitled *Memoirs of the Life and Ministerial Conduct, &c., of Lord Bolingbroke;* and of the article *St. John*, in the *Biographia Britannica*, from the latter of which Goldsmith chiefly drew both the details and reflections for his sketch.

Accuracy and impartiality have been studied in the following Biography, more than elegance and that labored eulogy, which so often defeats its purpose. The quick genius and diversified attainments of the author and the statesman, have not been allowed to cast a glare over the vices of the man and the specious hollowness of the pretended philosopher. The Life of Bolingbroke ought to be regarded, and in this light it is exhibited on the present occasion, as a warning but not an example; as a lurid meteor rather than a guiding star.

CONTENTS.

VOL. I.

THE LIFE

HENRY ST. JOHN,

LORD VISCOUNT BOLINGBROKE.

THERE are some characters that seem formed by nature to take delight in struggling with opposition, and whose most agreeable hours are passed in storms of their own creating.   The subject of the present memoir was perhaps of all others the most indefatigable in raising himself enemies, to show his power in subduing them; and was not less employed in improving his superior talents, than in finding objects on which to exercise their activity. His life was spent in a continued conflict of politics, and as if that was too short for the combat, he has left his memory as a subject of lasting contention.

It is indeed no easy matter to preserve and acknowledge impartiality, in talking of a man so differently regarded on account of his political, as well as his religious principles.   Those whom his politics may please, will be sure to condemn him for his religion; and on the contrary, those most strongly attached to his theological opinions, are the most likely to decry his politics.   On whatever side he is regarded, he is sure to have opposers, and this was perhaps what he most desired, having from nature a mind better pleased with the struggle than the victory.

HENRY ST. JOHN, Lord Viscount BOLINGBROKE, was born in the year 1678, at Battersea in Surrey, at a seat that had been in the possession of his ancestors for ages before.   His family was of the first rank, equally conspicuous for its antiquity, dignity, and large possessions.   Mabel, a female descendant of William de St. John, who held a post in the army of the Conqueror, at the time of the Norman invasion, married Adam de Post, who was descended from the barons of Basing, in Hampshire; a title which had been enjoyed by the latter anterior to the Conquest. The heir of Adam de Post took the maternal name of St. John, which was retained by his issue. But the importance of this family did not depend on antiquity alone, even with the added lustre of wealth. It is found, in a succession of ages to have produced warriors, patriots, and statesmen, some of whom were conspicuous for their loyalty, and others for their defending the rights of the people. Henry's grandfather, Sir Walter St. John, of Battersea marrying one of the daughters of lord chief justice St. John, who, as all know, was strongly attached to the republican party, the subject of the present memoir was brought up in his family, and consequently imbibed the first principles of his education amongst the dissenters. Stress has been laid by more than one biographer on the probably injurious effects produced on the boy St. John, by his being subjected to the rigid discipline and mistaken zeal of his first teacher, Daniel Burgess. There are not wanting some who are disposed even to attribute his subsequent debaucheries and religious infidelity to the violence of reaction from these early injudicious restraints. But in the case of St. John, as in the reputed analogous one of Voltaire, who was said, but erroneously, to have acquired a contempt for religion from the rigid observances imposed on him by his first teachers, the Jesuits, much greater importance must be attributed to the manner in which the period of adolescence was spent, and to the temptations then offered in the way of worldly pleasure, without the correctives of parental example and virtuous associates. That both Bolingbroke and Voltaire would be averse from engaging in polemics, and manifest a decided distaste for controversial and dogmatical theology, may be readily understood; but their scepticisim in religious matters must be sought for in other sources than in such a one as that commonly assigned. Nor is justice done to Burgess in describing him, as Goldsmith has done, to have been a fanatic of a very peculiar kind; he was at once possessed of zeal and humor, and was as well known for the archness of his conceits as for the furious obstinacy of his principles. His quaint style of exhorting from the pulpit is illustrated, indeed, by a passage of a sermon, in which the preacher, after having inveighed against pernicious doctrines, and enumerated many kinds thus continued; "But above all other pernicious doctrines, beware, my beloved, of the thorough-paced doctrine; that doctrine I mean, which, coming in at one ear, paces straight through the head and out at the other ear." It is well known that Burgess had been employed many years as a private teacher to the sons of nobility and gentry, first in England and then in Ireland, whither he went in 1667, at the particular solicitation of the Earl of Orrery, lord president of Munster. In private society, it appears that, to all the strictness of the puritan he joined a cheerful and even facetious style of discourse—a quality which certainly could not be said to unfit him for procuring the good will and respect of his pupils. St. John himself, when speaking afterwards of the annoying tasks imposed on him at this time, says: " I was obliged, while yet a boy, to read over the commentaries of Dr. Manton, whose pride it was to have made a hundred and nineteen sermons on the hundred and nineteenth psalm." It must be admitted that Dr. Manton and his sermons were not likely to prevail much on one, who was, perhaps, the most sharp-sighted in the world at discovering the absurdities of others, however he might have been guilty of exhibiting many of his own: but, as to the disgust he felt at this kind of study, we cannot be insensible to the truth of the remark, that, it is just as probable a boy would not have entertained much less dislike to a voluminous history, if he were obliged to read it when he wished to be idle.

Although the prejudices or the wishes of his grandmother were consulted in the selection of a teacher, it does not follow, indeed there is no proof, that great, if any, pains were taken to inculcate him with the doctrines of the dissenters. Sir Walter St. John, the grandfather, was a thorough, though a moderate churchman, a term used by English writers to designate a member of, or an adherent to, the Protestant Episcopal church. He repaired the church at Battersea more than once, erected an entire new gallery, and endowed a charity school, all at his own expense. Hence it is probable, that young St. John, when he left home for the public school at Eton, belonged nominally to the church of England. From his father's example, he could not be supposed to derive either zeal or knowledge on this important matter. The elder St. John is represented by Swift to be " a man of pleasure, that walks the mall, and frequents St. James's coffee-house and the chocolate houses."

At Eton, St. John became the school associate of Robert Walpole, who was his senior by two years, and between whom and himself was early displayed a mutual dislike, in which we may trace the origin of the bitter and personal hostility that was afterwards manifested in their strife for political ascendency and distinction. " The parts of Mr. St. John, " says Mr. Coxe, " were more lively and brilliant; those of Walpole more steady and solid. Walpole was industrious and diligent, because his talents required application; St. John was negligent, because his quickness of apprehension rendered less labor necessary." These characteristics prevailed in both throughout life.

It is not known how long he remained at Eton, from which he was removed to Christ Church College, Oxford, where wider scope was furnished for the development of his intellect and the attainment of learning. His genius and understanding were seen and admired in both these seminaries, but his love of pleasure had so much the ascendency, that he seemed contented rather with the consciousness of his own great powers, than their exertion. However, his friends, and those who knew him most intimately, were thoroughly sensible of the extent of his mind; and when he left the university, he was considered as one who had the fairest opportunity of making a shining figure in active life.

If inquiry were instituted as to the precise extent of his classical education at Eton and Oxford, it would be discovered that he there laid the foundation of one, which, as in the case of all others who have shone as scholars, he afterwards completed. But, as remarked by one of our contemporary authorities, his attention was more bestowed upon the remains of Rome than of Athens. He was extensively and thoroughly acquainted with Latin writers, as indeed his frequent quotation of passages little known may show. With Greek literature he seems not to have been familiar; nor can the reader of his works fail to perceive, that his style is not redolent of the flowers which grow in the more vigorous climate of the Attic school. (*Edinburgh Review*, No. CXLIII.)

Nature seemed not less kind to him in her external embellishments, than in adorning his mind. With the graces of a handsome person, and a face in which dignity was happily blended with sweetness, he had a manner of address that was very engaging. His vivacity was always awake, his apprehension quick, his wit refined, and his memory amazing: his subtlety in thinking and reasoning was profound, and all these talents were adorned with an elocution that was irresistible.

To the assemblage of so many gifts from nature, it was expected that art would soon give her finishing hand; and that a youth begun in excellence would soon arrive at perfection: but such is the perverseness of human nature, that an age which should have been employed in the acquisition of knowledge, was dissipated in pleasure; and instead of aiming to excel in praiseworthy pursuits, St. John seemed more ambitious of being thought the greatest rake about town. In this state of disorder he was not without his lucid intervals; and even while he was noted for keeping Miss Gumley, the most expensive prostitute in the kingdom, and bearing the greatest quantity of wine without intoxication, he still despised his paltry ambition. "The love of study," says he, "and desire of knowledge, were what I felt all my life; and though my genius, unlike the demon of Socrates, whispered so softly, that very often I heard him not in the hurry of these passions with which I was transported, yet some calmer hours there were, and in them I hearkened to him." These secret admonitions were indeed very few, since his excesses were well remembered in after days. I have spoken to an old man, says Dr. Goldsmith, who assured me that he saw St. John and another of his companions run naked through the Park, in a fit of intoxication; but then it was a time when public decency might be transgressed with less danger than at present.

During this period, as all his attachments were to pleasure, so his studies only seemed to lean that way. His first attempts were in poetry, in which he discovers more wit than taste, more labor than harmony in his versification. We have a copy of his verses prefixed to Dryden's Virgil, complimenting the poet, and praising his translation. There is another not so well known, prefixed to a French work, published in Holland, by the Chevalier de St. Hyacinth, entitled, *le Chef d' Œuvre d' un Inconnu.* This preformance is a humorous piece of criticism upon a miserable old ballad, and Bolingbroke's compliment, though written in English, is printed in Greek characters, so that at the first glance it may deceive the eye, and be mistaken for real Greek. There are two or three things more of his composition in poetry, which have appeared since his death, but which neither do honor to his parts nor his memory.

St. John travelled on the continent about this period, but whether this was enjoined on him with a view of enlarging his observation of men and things, and of thus completing a liberal education; or of detaching him from dissolute associates and expensive pleasures, which drew too heavily on his father's purse, we are not well informed. It is conjectured, for want of positive data, that he passed two years abroad; but it is certain, that during the period of his travels he acquired such a knowledge of the French language, as to enable him to write and speak it with perfect ease; an accomplishment which was found to be of signal service to him in his subsequent public career, and is said to have been the cause of his not losing office in one of the intrigues of Harley for that purpose. He was the only one of the ministry who understood and wrote French, and who was able to keep up the necessary correspondence in the negotiations then pending with France. Though still young, and a devotee of pleasure in all its aspects, he seems, on his return to England, to have sought more intently than before for an increase of those "calmer hours" in which he might gratify the love of study, and the desire of knowledge, that he professed, and no doubt truly, to have felt all his life. With such aspirations, St. John would the more incline to the wish of his friends that he should form a matrimonial connection: and, accordingly, a selec-

tion was made for him, in the person of the daughter and co-
heiress of Sir Henry Winchescomb. This lady was a descendant from the famous Jack of Newbury, who, though but a
clothier in the reign of Henry VIII, was able to entertain the
king and all his retinue in the most splendid manner. The
marriage took place in 1700, when St. John was but twenty-two
years of age. It was one of mere convenience, and, like all
such arrangements was attended with little happiness. The most
substantial result was the accession of a large fortune, estimated
at forty thousand pounds, to his own patrimony. Indifference
could not well be converted into love, or, in its place, permanent
esteem, when the husband was imperious and inconstant, and the
wife obstinate and jealous: his indiscretions, perhaps vices, could
not be arrested by her outbreaks of temper and bitter reproaches.
They parted by mutual consent, both equally displeased; he
complaining of the obstinacy of her temper, she of the shame-
lessness of his infidelity. A great part of her fortune some time
after this event, on the occasion of his attainder, was given back
to her; but as the family estates were settled upon him, he enjoyed them after her death, when his attainder was reversed.

But, however determined the lady was, not to submit to the
infidelities of her husband, there is a good reason for believing
that their separation was not followed by enduring resentment on
either side; and that the reconciliation was of such a nature as to
admit of forgiveness, if not a return of affection. In 1716, two
years after the first disgrace and exile of St. John, (then Lord
Bolingbroke,) we find his lady corresponding with Swift to
whose acquaintance she was probably introduced by her husband, and using this remarkable expression: "As to my temper, if it is possible, I am more insipid and dull than ever, except in some places, and there I am little fury, especially if they
dare mention my dear lord without respect, which sometimes
happens. I have not yet seen her grace, [the Duchess of
Ormond,] but design it in a day or two; we have kept a constant
correspondence, ever since our misfortunes; and her grace is
pleased to call me sister. " The Duke of Ormond had also been
obliged to fly his country, and was then under an act of attainder
for conspiracy to bring in the Pretender, as successor to Queen
Anne, and to the exclusion of the Elector of Hanover. In another letter dated August 4th of the same year, Lady Bolingbroke says, "I hope one time or other his majesty [George I]
will find my lord has been misrepresented, and by that means he
may be restored to his country once more with honor; or else,
however harsh it may sound out of my mouth, I had rather wear
black. These are my real sentiments."

Having taken a resolution to quit the allurements of pleasure for the stronger attractions of ambition, soon after his marriage he procured a seat in the house of commons, in being elected for the borough of Wotton-Basset, in Wiltshire. His father had served several times for the same place. Besides his natural endowments and his large fortune, he had other very considerable advantages that gave him weight in the senate, and seconded his views of preferment. His grandfather Sir Walter St. John was still alive, and that gentleman's interest was so great in his own county of Wilts, that he represented it in two parliaments in a former reign. His father, also, was then the representative for the same, and the interest of his wife's family in the house was very extensive. Thus St John took his seat with many accidental helps, but his chief and great resource lay in his own extensive abilities.

At that time the whig and the tory parties were strongly opposed in the house, and pretty nearly balanced. In the latter years of King William, the tories, who from every motive were opposed to the court, had been gaining popularity, and now began to make a public stand against their competitors. Robert Harley, afterwards Earl of Oxford, a staunch and confiremd tory, was in the year 1700 chosen speaker of the house of commons, and was continued in the same upon the accession of Queen Anne, the year ensuing. Bolingbroke had all along been bred up, as was before observed, among the dissenters, his friends leaned to that persuasion, and all his connections, including his grandfather and father, were of the whig interest. However, either from principle, or from perceiving the tory party to be gaining ground, while the whigs were declining, he soon changed his connections, and joined himself to Harley, for whom he then had the greatest esteem: nor did he bring him his vote alone, but his opinion; which even before the end of his first session he rendered very considerable, the house perceiving even in so young a speaker the greatest eloquence, united with the profoundest discernment. The year following he was again chosen for the same borough, and persevering in his former attachments, he gained such an authority and influence in the house, that it was thought proper to reward his merit; accordingly, on the 10th of April, 1704, he was appointed Secretary at War, and of the marines, his friend Harley having a little before been made Secretary of State.

The tory party being thus established in power, it may easily be supposed that every method would be used to depress the whig interest, and to prevent it from rising; yet so much justice was done even to merit in an enemy, that the Duke of Marlborough, who might be considered as the head of the opposite party, was supplied with all the necessaries for carrying on the

war in Flanders with vigor; and it is remarkable, that the greatest events of his campaigns, such as the battles of Blenheim and
Ramillies, and several glorious attempts made by the duke to
shorten the war by some decisive action, fell out while St. John
was secretary at war.   In fact, he was a sincere admirer of that
great general, and avowed it upon all occasions to the last moment of his life: he knew his faults, he admired his virtues, and
had the boast of being instrumental in giving lustre to those
triumphs, by which his own power was in a manner overthrown.

As the affairs of the nation were then in as fluctuating a state
as at present, Harley, after maintaining the lead for above three
years, was in his turn obliged to submit to the whigs, who once
more became the prevailing party, and he was compelled to resign the seals.   The friendship between him and Bolingbroke
seems at this time to have been sincere and disinterested; for
the latter chose to follow his fortune, and the next day resigned
his employments in the administration, following his friend's
course and setting an example at once of integrity and moderation.   As an instance of this, when his coadjutors, the tories, were
carrying a violent measure in the house of commons, in order to
bring the princess Sophia into England, Bolingbroke so artfully
opposed it, that it dropped without a debate.   For this his moderation was praised, but perhaps at the expense of his sagacity.

For some time the whigs seemed to have gained a complete
triumph, and upon the election of a new parliament, in the year
1708, St. John was not returned.   The interval which followed
of above two years, he employed in the severest study; and this
recluse period he ever after used to consider as the most active
and serviceable of his whole life.   But his retirement was soon
interrupted, by the prevailing of his party once more; for the
whig parliament being dissolved in the year 1710, he was again
chosen, and Harley being made chancellor, and under-treasurer
of the exchequer, the important post of Secretary of State was
given to our author, in which he discovered a degree of genius
and assiduity, that perhaps have never been known to be united
in one person to the same degree.

The English annals scarcely produce a more trying juncture,
or one that required such various abilities to regulate.   He was
then placed in a sphere, where he was obliged to conduct the
machine of state, struggling with a thousand various calamities:
a desperate and enraged party, whose characteristic it is said to
be to bear none in power but themselves; a war conducted by
an able general, his professed opponent, and whose victories
only tended to render him every day more formidable; a foreign
enemy, possessed of endless resources, and seeming to gather
strength from every defeat; an insidious alliance, that wanted

only to gain the advantages of victory, without contributing to the expenses of the combat; a weak declining mistress, who was led by every report, and seemed ready to listen to whatever was said against him; still more, a gloomy, indolent, and suspicious colleague, who envied his power, and hated him for his abilities: these were a part of the difficulties, that St. John had to struggle with in office, and under which he was to conduct the treaty of peace of Utrecht, which was considered as one of the most complicated negotiations that history can afford. But nothing seemed too great for his abilities and industry: he set himself to the undertaking with spirit; and began to pave the way to the intended treaty, by making the people discontented at the continuance of the war. For this purpose he employed himself in drawing up accurate computations of the numbers of our own men, and that of foreigners employed in its destructive progress. He even wrote in the *Examiner* and other periodical papers of the times, showing how much of the burden rested upon England, and how little was sustained by those who falsely boasted their alliance. By these means, and after much debate in the house of commons, the queen received a petition from parliament, showing the hardships the allies had put upon England in carrying on this war, and consequently how necessary it was to apply relief to so ill-judged a connection. It may be easily supposed that the Dutch, against whom this petition was chiefly levelled, did all that was in their power to oppose it; many of the foreign courts also, with which England had any transactions, were continually at work to defeat the minister's intentions. Memorial was delivered after memorial; the people of England, the parliament, and all Europe were made acquainted with the injustice and the dangers of such a proceeding. Notwithstanding all this, Bolingbroke went on with steadiness and resolution, and although the attacks of his enemies at home might have been deemed sufficient to employ his attention, yet he was obliged at the same time that he furnished materials to the press in London, to prepare instructions to all the ministers and ambassadors abroad, who would do nothing but in pursuance of his directions. As an orator, in the senate he exerted all his eloquence; he stated all the great points that were brought before the house; he answered the objections that were made by the leaders of the opposition; and all this with such success, that even his enemies while they opposed his power, acknowledged his abilities. Indeed, such were the difficulties he had to encounter, that we find him acknowledging, himself, some years after, that he never looked back on this great event passed as it was, without a secret emotion of mind; when he compared the vastness of the undertaking and the importance of the success, with the means em-

ployed to bring it about, and with those which were enlisted
to frustrate his intentions.

While he was thus industriously employed, he was not without
the rewards that deserved to follow such abilities, joined to so
much assiduity. In July, 1712, he was created Baron St.
John, of Lidyard Tregoze, in Wiltshire, and Viscount Bolingbroke, by
e last of which titles he is now generally known, and is likely
to be talked of by posterity: he was also the same year appointed lord lieutenant of the county of Essex. By the titles of
Tregoze and Bolingbroke, he united the honors of the elder and
younger branches of his family; and thus transmitted into one
channel, the opposing interests of two races, which had been distinguished, one for their loyalty to king Charles I, the other for
their attachment to the parliament that opposed him. It was
afterwards his boast, that he steered clear of the extremes for
which his ancestors had been distinguished, having kept the
spirit of freedom of the one, and acknowledged the subordination
characteristic of the other.

Here we shall suspend, for a while, the narrative of his life, in
order to convey, on competent authority, some ideas of the peculiar and shining merits of Bolingbroke, additional to those furnished in the last few pages by the pen of Goldsmith. We cannot, for
this purpose, do better than borrow the description of the man,
the minister, and the orator, as given by his friend Swift, in
the following language: " It happens to very few men in any
age or country to come into the world with so many advantages
of nature and fortune as the late secretary Bolingbroke: descended from the best families in England, heir to a great patri-
monial estate, of a sound constitution, and a most graceful,
amiable person: but all these, had they been of equal value,
were infinitely inferior in degree to the accomplishments of his
mind, which was adorned with the choicest gifts that God has
yet thought fit to bestow upon the children of men, a strong
memory, a clear judgement, a vast range of wit and fancy, a
thorough comprehension, an invincible eloquence, with a most
agreeable elocution. He had well cultivated all these talents
by travel and study; the latter of which he seldom omitted, even
in the midst of his pleasures, of which he had indeed been too
great and criminal a pursuer; for, although he was persuaded to
leave off intemperance in wine, which he did for some time to
such a degree that he seemed rather abstemious; yet he was
said to allow himself other liberties, which can by no means be
reconciled to religion or morals; whereof I have reason to believe
he began to be sensible. But he was fond of mixing pleasure
and business, and of being esteemed excellent at both, upon
which account he had a great respect for the characters of Alci-

biades and Petronius, especially the latter, whom he would gladly be thought to resemble. His detractors charged him with some degree of affectation, and perhaps not altogether without grounds, since it was hardly possible for a young man with half the business of the nation upon him, and the applause of the whole, to escape some tincture of that infirmity. He had been early bred to business, was a most artful negotiator, and perfectly understood foreign affairs. But what I have often wondered at in a man of his temper, was his prodigious application whenever he thought it necessary; for he would plod whole days and nights, like the lowest clerk in an office. His talent of speaking in public, for which he was so very much celebrated, I know nothing of, except from the information of others: but understanding men of both parties have assured me, that in this point, in their memory and judgment, he was never equalled."

We cannot forbear from introducing additional and more recent yet in some respects more convincing testimony of Bolingbroke's oratorical powers, presented, if we are not mistaken, by one who is himself one of the greatest masters of the art in our own day. The passages occur in an article entitled *Walpole and his Contemporaries,* in a number of the Edinburgh Review, already quoted, and which, we believe, is from the pen of Lord Brougham himself:—

" Few men, whose public life was so short, have filled a greater space in the eyes of the world during his own times than Lord Bolingbroke, or left behind them a more brilliant reputation. Not more than fifteen years elapsed between his first coming into parliament and his attainder, during not more than ten of these years was he brought before the public in the course of its proceedings; and yet, as a statesman and an orator, his name ranks among the most famous in our history, independently of the brilliant literary reputation which places him among the best classics of our Augustan age. Much of his rhetorical fame may certainly be ascribed to the merit of his written works; but had he never composed a page, he would still have come down to our times as one of the most able and eloquent men of whom this country could boast.

" They who look down upon even the purely ethical and purely metaphysical writings of Bolingbroke, would do well to show us any statesman or any orator, except perhaps Cicero, who in any age has brought to the senate the same resources of moral science, which even the failures of Bolingbroke, as a professed author on these subjects, prove him to have possessed; and it is hardly necessary to remark how vast an accession of force to his eloquence, whether in its argumentative, its pathetic, or its declamatory department, would have been gained by even far less skill, capacity, or practice, than he had as a moral philosopher, a student of the nature of the mind, or an expert logician.

" Accordingly, when all these accomplishments joined to his strong natural sagacity, his penetrating acuteness, his extraordinary quickness of apprehension, a clearness of understanding, against which sophistry set itself up in vain, as the difficulties of the most complicated subjects in vain opposed his industry and his courage, with a fancy rich, lively, various beyond that of most men, a wit exuberant and sparkling, a vehemence of passion belonging to his whole temperament, even to his physical powers, came to be displayed before the assembly which he was to address, and when the mighty '*armentaria cœli*' were found under the command of one whose rich endowments of mind and whose ample stores of acquired virtue, resided in a person of singular grace, animated a countenance at once beautiful and expressive, and made themselves heard in the strains of an unrivalled voice, it is easy to comprehend how vast, how irresistible must have been their impression."

" But all agree in describing the external qualities (so to speak) of his oratory as perfect. A symmetrical, beautiful and animated countenance, a noble and dignified person, a sonorous and flexible voice, action graceful and correct, though unstudied, gave an inexpressible charm to those who witnessed his extraordinary displays as spectators or critics, and armed his eloquence with resistless effect over those whom it was intended to sway, or persuade, or control. If the concurring accounts of witnesses, and the testimony to his merits borne by his writings, may be trusted, he must be pronounced to stand, upon the whole, at the head of modern orators. There may have been more measure and matured power in Pitt, more fire in the occasional bursts of Chatham, more unbridled vehemence, more intent reasoning in Fox, more deep-toned declamation in passages of Sheridan, more learned imagery in Burke, more wit and humor in Canning; but, as a whole, and taking in all rhetorical gifts, and all the orator's accomplishments, no one, perhaps hardly the union of several of them, can match what we are taught by tradition to admire in Bolingbroke's spoken eloquence, and what the study of his works makes us easily believe to be true."

Mr. Pitt's opinion of Bolingbroke's oratory was strongly expressed when, in conversation with some friends about the *desiderata* most to be lamented, and one said the lost books of Livy, another those of Tacitus, a third a Latin tragedy, he at once declared for " A speech of Bolingbroke," a thing unhappily not on record.

Bolingbroke being thus raised very near the summit of power, began to perceive more nearly the defects of him who was placed there. He began to find that Harley, now Lord Oxford, whose party he had followed, and whose person he had esteemed, was by no means so able or so industrious as he supposed him to be. He now began from his heart to renounce the friendship which he once had for his coadjutor; and to imagine him treacherous, mean, indolent, and invidious; he was inclined even to ascribe his own promotion to Oxford's hatred, and to suppose that he was sent up to the house of lords, only to render him contemptible. These suspicions were partly true, and partly suggested by Bolingbroke's own ambition: being sensible of his own superior importance and capacity, he could not bear to see another take the lead in public affairs, when he knew they owed their chief success to his own management. In a letter to Lord Strafford, the English ambassador at the Hague, dated July 23, 1712, Bolingbroke writes: "It would ill become the friendship I profess to you if I did not naturally own what passes in my soul upon this subject, and confess to you, what I will do to no one else, that my promotion was a mortification to me. In the house of commons, I may say, that I was at the head of business, and I must have continued so, whether I had been in court or out of court. There was, therefore, nothing to flatter my ambition in removing from thence, but giving me the title which had been many years in my family, and which reverted to the crown about a year ago, by the death of the last of the elder house." He thought himself to be as fully entitled to an earldom as his associate Harley, forgetting that the latter was his senior by seventeen years, had seen longer parliamentary service, and was now prime minister. There were, also, about this time, some new knights of the garter to be made; Harley was one of these; Bolingbroke thought himself equally entitled to that distinction, but did not obtain it. Whatever might have been his motives, whether of contempt, hatred, or ambition, it is certain that an irreconcilable breach began between these two leaders of their party; their mutual hatred was so great, that even their own common interest, the vigor of their negotiations, and the safety of their friends, were entirely sacrificed to it. It was in vain that Swift, who was admitted into their counsels, urged the unreasonable impropriety of their disputes; and that while they were thus at variance within the walls, the enemy were making irreparable breaches without. Bolingbroke's antipathy was so great, that even success would have been hateful to him, if Lord Oxford were to be a partner. He abhorred him to that degree, that he could not bear to be joined with him in any case; and even some time after, when the lives of both were aimed at, he could not think of concerting measures with him for their mutual safety, preferring even death itself to the appearance of a temporary friendship.

Nothing could have been more weak and injudicious, than the mutual animosities of these two statesmen at this juncture; and it may be asserted with truth, that men who are unable to suppress or conceal their resentments upon such a trying occasion, were unfit to take the lead in any measures, be their industry or their abilities ever so great.   In fact, their dissensions were soon found to involve not only them, but their party in utter ruin; their hopes had for some time been declining, the whigs were daily gaining ground, and the queen's death soon after totally destroyed all their schemes with their power, just at the juncture when Bolingbroke had procured the dismission of his rival, and his own nomination to be first minister.

Upon the accession of George I to the throne, in 1714, dangers began to threaten the late ministry on every side: whether they had really intentions of bringing in the Pretender, or whether the whigs made it a pretext for destroying them, was then uncertain; but the king very soon began to show, that they were to expect neither favor nor mercy at his hands. After his landing at Greenwich, when the court came to wait upon him, and Lord Oxford among the number, he studiously avoided taking any notice of him, and testified his resentment by the caresses he bestowed upon the members of the opposite faction.   A regency had been sometime before appointed to govern the kingdom, and Addison was made secretary.   Bolingbroke still maintained his place of State Secretary, but subject to the contempt of the great, and the insults of the mean.   The first step taken by them to mortify him, was to order all letters and packets directed to the Secretary of State, to be sent to Mr. Addison; so that Bolingbroke was in fact removed from his office, that is, the execution of it, in two days after the queen's death.   But this was not the worst, for his mortifications were continually heightened, by the daily humiliation of waiting at the door of the apartment where the regency sat, with a bag in his hand, and being all the time, as it were, on purpose, exposed to the insolence of those who were tempted by their natural malevolence, or who expected to make their court to those in power by abusing him.

Upon this sudden turn of fortune, when the seals were taken from him, he went into the country, and having received a message from court, to be present when the seal was taken from the door of the secretary's office, he excused himself; alleging, that so trifling a ceremony might as well be performed by one of the under secretaries, but at the same time requested the honor of kissing the king's hand, to whom he testified the utmost submission. This request, however, was rejected with disdain; the king had been taught to regard him as an enemy, and he threw himself entirely on the whigs for safety and protection.

The new parliament, mostly composed of whigs, met the 17th of March; and in the king's speech from the throne, many inflaming hints were given, and many methods of violence chalked out to the two houses. "The first steps (says Lord Bolingbroke, speaking on this occasion) in both were perfectly answerable; and, to the shame of the peerage be it spoken, I saw at that time several lords concur to condemn in one general vote, all that they had approved in a former parliament by many particular resolutions. Among several bloody resolutions proposed and agitated at this time, the resolution of impeaching me of high treason was taken; and I took that of leaving England, not in a panic terror, improved by the artifices of the Duke of Marlborough, whom I knew even at that time too well to act by his advice or information, in any case, but on such grounds as the proceedings which soon followed sufficiently justified, and such as I have never repented building upon. Those who blamed it in the first heat, were soon after obliged to change their language: for what other resolution could I take? The method of prosecution designed against me, would have put me out of a condition immediately to act for myself, or to serve those who were less exposed than me, but who were however in danger. On the other hand, how few were there on whose assistance I could depend, or to whom I would, even in these circumstances be obliged. The ferment in the nation was wrought up to a considerable height; but there was at that time no reason to expect that it could influence the proceedings in parliament, in favor of those who should be accused: left to its own movement, it was much more proper to quicken than slacken the prosecution; and who was there to guide its motions? The tories, who had been true to one another to the last, were a handful, and no great vigor could be expected from them: the whimsicals, disappointed of the figure which they hoped to make, began indeed to join their old friends. One of the principal among them, namely, the earl of Anglesea, was so very good as to confess to me, that if the court had called the servants of the late queen to account, and stopped there, he must have considered himself as a judge, and acted according to his conscience, on what should have appeared to him: but that war had been declared to the whole tory party, and that now the state of things was altered. This discourse needed no commentary, and proved to me, that I had never erred in the judgment I made of this set of men. Could I then resolve to be obliged to them, or to suffer with Oxford? As much as I still was heated by the disputes, in which I had been all my life engaged against the whigs, I would sooner have chosen to owe my security to their indulgence, than to the assistance of the whimsicals: but I thought banishment, with all her train of evils, preferable to either."

Such was the miserable situation to which he was reduced upon this occasion, that of all the number of his former flatterers and dependents scarce one was found remaining. Every hour brought fresh reports of his alarming situation, and the dangers which threatened him and his party on all sides. Prior, who had been employed in negotiating the treaty of Utrecht, was come over to Dover, and had promised to reveal all he knew. The Duke of Marlborough planted his creatures round his lordship, who artfully endeavored to increase the danger; and an impeachment was actually preparing in which he was accused of high treason. It argued therefore no great degree of timidity in his lordship, to take the first opportunity to withdraw from danger, and to suffer the first boilings of popular animosity, to quench the flame that had been raised against him: accordingly, having made a gallant show of despising the machinations against him, having appeared in a very unconcerned manner at the playhouse in Drury-lane, and having bespoken another play for the night ensuing; having subscribed to a new opera that was to be acted some time after, and talked of making an elaborate defence, he went off that same night in disguise to Dover, as a servant to Le Vigne, a messenger belonging to the French king; and there one William Morgan, who had been a captain in General Hill's regiment of dragoons, hired a vessel, and carried him over to Calais, where the governor attended him in his coach, and carried him to his house with all possible distinction.

The news of Lord Bolingbroke's flight was soon known over the whole town; and the next day, a letter from him to Lord Lansdowne, was handed about in print, to the following effect:

"My Lord:—I left the town so abruptly, that I had no time to take leave of you or any of my friends. You will excuse me, when you know that I had certain and repeated informations, from some who are in the secret of affairs, that a resolution was taken by those who have power to execute it, to pursue me to the scaffold. My blood was to have been the cement of a new alliance, nor could my innocence be any security, after it had once been demanded from abroad, and resolved on at home, that it was necessary to cut me off. Had there been the least reason to hope for a fair and open trial, after having been already prejudged unheard by two houses of parliament, I should not have declined the strictest examination. I challenge the most inveterate of my enemies to produce any one instance of a criminal correspondence, or the least corruption of any part of the administration in which I was concerned. If my zeal for the honor and dignity of my royal mistress, and the true interest of my country, has anywhere transported me to let slip a warm or ungarded expression, I hope the most favorable interpretation will be put upon it. It is a comfort that will remain with me in all my misfortunes, that I served her majesty faithfully and dutifully, in that especially which she had most at heart, relieving her people from a bloody and expensive war, and that I have also been too much an Englishman, to sacrifice the interest of my country to any foreign ally; and it is for this crime only that I am now driven from thence. You shall hear. more at large from me shortly. Yours, &c."

No sooner was it universally known that he had retired to France, than his flight was construed into a proof of his guilt; and his enemies accordingly set about driving on his impeachment with redoubled alacrity. Mr. afterwards Sir Robert Walpole and finally Earl of *Orford*, who had suffered a good deal by his attachment to the whig interest during the former reign, undertook to bring in and conduct the charge against him in the house of commons. Walpole now retorted on Bolingbroke for the injuries which he had suffered from the hands of the latter, who, a few years before, in the period of tory ascendency, was one of the leaders of that accusation, which resulted in a vote of the throne declaring Walpole to have been guilty of a high breach of trust and notorious corruption, and sentencing him to expulsion, and to imprisonment in the Tower. Bolingbroke's impeachment consisted of six articles, which Walpole read to the house, in substance as follows: First, That whereas the Lord Bolingbroke had assured the Dutch ministers, that the queen his mistress would make no peace but in concert with them, yet he had sent Mr. Prior to France, that same year, with proposals for a treaty of peace with the French monarch, without the consent of the allies. Secondly, That he advised and promoted the making a separate treaty of convention with France, which was signed in September. Thirdly, That he disclosed to M. Menager, the French minister at London, this convention, which was the preliminary instructions to her majesty's plenipotentiaries at Utrecht. Fourthly, That her majesty's final instructions to her plenipotentiaries, were disclosed by him to the Abbé Guatier, who was an emissary of France. Fifthly, That he disclosed to the French the manner how Tournay in Flanders might be gained by them. And lastly, That he advised and promoted the yielding up Spain and the West Indies to the Duke of Anjou, then an enemy to her majesty. These were urged by Walpole with great vehemence, and aggravated with all the eloquence of which he was master. He challenged any person in behalf of the accused, and asserted, that to vindicate were in a manner to share his guilt. In this

universal consternation of the tory party, none was for some
time seen to stir; but at length General Ross, who had received
favors from his lordship, boldly stood up, and said that he wondered that no man more capable was found to appear in defence
of the accused.   However, in attempting to proceed, he hesitated
so much that he was obliged to sit down, observing, that he
would reserve what he had to say to another opportunity.   It
may easily be supposed, that the whigs found no great difficulty
in passing the vote for Bolingbroke's impeachment through the
house of commons.   It was brought into that house on the 10th
of June, 1715, and was sent up to the house of lords on the 6th
of August ensuing; in consequence of which he was attainted by
them of high treason on the 10th of September.

   Although this sentence was by many considered at the time to
be unjust, and an evidence of the violence of party, yet subsequent revelations prove, beyond doubt, that both Lord Oxford,
who remained in England to brave his accusers, and Bolingbroke
who fled, had been guilty both of treachery to the allies before
the peace of Utrecht, and of treason against their own country,
in fostering designs to bring in the Pretender, or Chevalier, as he
is often called, the son of James II, after the death of his sister
Anne, the reigning queen.   As on the turn given to those questions, will greatly depend Lord Bolingbroke's character for probity as a statesman, and patriotism as a Briton, we must not let
the occasion pass without giving the heads of evidence that cannot fail, we fear, to be regarded by impartial minds, as unequivo-
cally condemnatory.   And first, respecting his design to bring in
the Pretender.   The documents on this head are the Memoirs of
Marshal Berwick, and collections made by Sir James Mackintosh
for his history of England, during his residence in Paris in 1814.
Extracts have been made from these latter, by a writer in the
Edinburgh Review, in a notice of Cooke's Memoirs of Lord
Bolingbroke.   The volumes to which he refers, chiefly consist
of the correspondence of Torcy with Guatier, a private agent of
France, resident in London; and with D'Aumont and D'Iberville,
who came to England in public capacities after the peace of
Utrecht.   They also contain numerous letters from the Pretender, and from the Duke of Berwick, both of whom corresponded
with Torcy, the French minister for foreign affairs, on the matters of interest to the Pretender.   Many of the letters of D'Aumont and D'Iberville are addressed directly to the French king.
We must on the present occasion abridge even the summary of
the reviewer.

   Guatier had been attached to Marshal Tallard, when the latter came as ambassador, after the peace of Ryswick.   He formed
at this time a connection with Lord Jersey, who had married a

Roman Catholic, and with Prior, who had been secretary of embassy with Lord Jersey at Paris. On the breaking out of the war for the Spanish succession, Guatier was allowed to remain in England, and though secretly in the pay of France, he had the address to get himself employed in the chapel of count Gallas, ambassador from the archduke Charles, who was recognised by England as king of Spain. It was by the agency of this person, that Lord Oxford (Harley) carried on his secret correspondence with the French minister, and also made his verbal communications to the Pretender, and to the Duke of Berwick, to whom Guatier had been recommended by Torcy, as one on whom they might have reliance. Guatier remained in England, until the queen's death, and of course after the treaty of Utrecht, in constant correspondence with Oxford and Bolingbroke. Passing over the proofs of Oxford's implication in a treasonable plot to bring in the Pretender, we find in Mackintosh's note book an assertion, that the first introduction of Bolingbroke into the secret negotiation, was during the illness of Oxford, after the latter had been stabbed by Guiscard, (1711.) The correspondence of Guatier contains frequent reference to the part taken by Bolingbroke, in the designs for insuring the succession of the Pretender to the throne. But the most decisive proofs of his eager participation in these machinations, are afforded by his confidential conversations with D'Iberville, who was charged with the affairs of France in England, after the departure of the Duc d'Aumont. One condition insisted on by both Oxford and Bolingbroke was, that the Pretender should abjure, at least in form, the catholic religion, and avow himself to be a protestant. To this proposal, the weak, but conscientious prince steadily refused his assent. In illustration of the duplicity of the English ministry at this time, we may state, that, whilst Bolingbroke, as secretary of state, was demanding the expulsion of the Pretender from the territories of the Duke of Lorraine, it furnished the latter with pretexts for a refusal.

On the dismissal of Oxford, brought about as we have already stated, through the intrigues of Bolingbroke, Guatier consoled himself and his employers at the French court, with the thought, that the latter is to become the leader in the ministry, and he adds expressions made use of by Bolingbroke, himself, in evidence of his continued regard for the exiled prince, and a desire to promote his return. Some strong measures were on the eve of execution, in furtherance of this intention; but they were frustrated by the death of the queen. On the day after this event, Bolingbroke assured D'Iberville, that measures had been so well taken, that in six weeks more, things would have been placed on such a footing, as to leave no fears for the result.

The apologist of Bolingbroke may adduce, in reply to these

charges of treasonable intention, which are proved by the above correspondence, that Bolingbroke in 1713, the year before the death of the queen, had issued a proclamation, offering five thousand pounds reward to any person who should apprehend the Pretender upon his landing in any part of Great Britain, an intention which this prince was said then seriously to entertain. Bolingbroke also brought in a bill to put an effectual stop in future, to attempts at enlisting soldiers for the service of the Pretender. This bill was received in Parliament with great favor; and its penalties were extended to all who should engage in the service of any foreign prince, without the consent of the queen, signified under her sign manual. On the same side is likewise Bolingbroke's positive denial, of his having been engaged in the treasonable manner now too distinctly proved against him. The passage occurs in his letter on the state of parties at the accession of George I, annexed to his "*Patriot King.*" "Whatever anecdotes you have been told, and whatever prepossessions you have had, take these facts for undoubted truths, that there were no designs on foot, during the last four years of queen Anne's reign, to set aside the House of Hanover, and to place the crown on the head of the Pretender, nor any party formed for this fugitive at the time of the death of that princess. I deny the fact absolutely, and I have the better title to expect credit, because it could not be true without my knowledge, or at least suspicion of it."

On summing up the evidence, so clear and direct, of Bolingbroke's guilt on the one side, and the collateral testimony in his favor, by his own denial on the other, we are forced to the following conclusion, expressed by the admirer and eulogist of his genius and oratory in the passages already transcribed. " Upon the schemes in which he was engaged for restoring the Stuarts, undoing the work of the revolution, exposing the civil and religious liberties of the country to the most imminent peril, and effecting this change through the horrors of civil war, possibly aggravated by foreign invasion, there can no doubt whatever exist." While the queen was alive, Oxford and Bolingbroke mutually blamed each other for the neglect of efficient measures in favor of the Pretender. After her death, Bolingbroke gave vent in bitter terms to his indignation against Oxford, as the sole cause of the failure of their schemes; and when told that the latter threatened to be his accuser, he replied, that Oxford had more to fear from him than he from Oxford.

Regarding the other charge against Bolingbroke and his associates in the ministry, of treachery to the allies, by which these powers were forced into the treaty of Utrecht, and France was left, after having been beaten fourteen years, with the prize of victory· in her hands, Mr. Cooke in his " *Memoirs of Lord*

Bolingbroke," admits, that in separating England from her allies, in taking a part with the enemy, and in negotiating a separate peace, this minister acted a treacherous part. Although the contemporaries of Bolingbroke could produce no direct evidence of his guilt, they had no doubt that the systematic violations of honor and good faith, which marked the whole course of the negotiation, had their origin in a design to set aside the act of settlement and to bring in the Pretender. It was difficult to imagine, why the English ministers should place themselves in this new and reversed position, with respect to France and to their former allies, if they had no other object in view but peace. it was, therefore, suspected, that they had some secret and ulterior design, in which the friendship of France might be of use, and to which the allies, and particularly the Dutch must be disinclined. The writer in the Edingburgh Review, (No. CXXVI,) whose language and argument we are here adopting, gives accumulative proofs of the falsehood and treachery of the English ministry to their allies, during the years 1711 and 1712. They began with a wanton and useless attempt at deception. On the 12th—23d January 1711, Bolingbroke wrote to Buys, Pensionary of Amsterdam, that to obtain a good peace, the first advances must come from the enemy, though he had despatched the Abbé Guatier ten days before, with a message from the English ministry, to Torcy, proposing a renewal of negotiation. In disregard of mutual engagements between the English and Dutch governments, made on the April following, that no negotiations should be entered into by either party, without the knowledge and concurrence of the other, Bolingbroke sent Prior (the Poet) privately to Paris in July, with proposals which were to be kept secret from the allies. The grand Pensionary Heinsius, was afterwards told, that proposals of peace had come from France, but that the queen had refused to enter into a separate treaty, and had desired to have specific terms transmitted to her, which could be laid before her allies, while the fact was concealed, that the first advances had been made by England, and that Prior had been the bearer of specific proposals to the French.

" After several conferences in London, private articles in favor of England were signed by Menager, on the 27th of September, and 8th of October, and accepted by Bolingbroke and Dartmouth, the two Secretaries of State, on behalf of their mistress. General propositions for the allies were at the same time presented, which were transmitted to Holland, while the private articles were kept secret. In the midst of this duplicity, Bolingbroke had the effrontery to complain of the Dutch for manifesting a want of confidence in his sincerity, and both he and Oxford boast of the honesty of their proceedings." In December Bolingbroke desired Lord

Raby (who was made Earl Strafford at this period), the English minister at the Hague, to assure Buys, that neither Spain nor the Indies should be allotted to any prince of the House of Bourbon, though the contrary had been tacitly, and by implication, settled with Menager in the preceding October; and so secret was this determination kept, that it was not communicated to the English plenipotentiaries at Utrecht till after the conferences had been opened.   As the negotiations advanced, the impatience of the English ministry for peace, and their undisguised partiality for France, became every day more apparent.   In spite of the remonstrances of their own plenipotentiaries, they hurried on the conclusion of a definite treaty, with a precipitancy which left many of the articles intended for the particular benefit of England undigested and useless.   Their treaty of commerce, in particular was so defective, that it was rejected by the House of Commons. In the affair of Tournay, their conduct was little short of treason. While still at war, they privately suggested to the French government pretext for insisting on the cession of that important place to France, though at an earlier stage of the negotiation, Louis had consented to leave it in possession of the Dutch, as an essential part of their barrier."

The defeat of a division of Eugene's army at Denain, was owing to the separation of the English from the allied troops. And, soon after, to desertion of the cause was added treachery, in Ormond, the successor of Marlborough in the command of the English army, having apprised Villars, by intelligence communicated through Bolingbroke, and by him to Torcy, that Eugene entertained the project of surprising either Nieuport or Furnes; measures were taken accordingly by the French commander to prevent its success.

That peace was the true policy of England, is not now contested; it is of the means adopted, and the sacrifice of national honor to procure it, that we find so much cause for censure. The delay in the negotiation, notwithstanding the uncommon labors of Bolingbroke to bring it to a successful termination, gave rise to a resolution of the ministry, which displays both its eagerness for peace, and the confidence placed in his abilities.   It was determined to send his lordship incognito to France in 1712, to remove, as his instructions expressed it, "all difficulties and differences, that might obstruct the general suspension of arms between England and France from taking place, or settling the treaty of peace in such a course, as might bring it to a happy and speedy conclusion."   Accordingly, he set out for Dover on the second of August, accompanied by Prior and the Abbé Guatier. The next day he landed at Calais, and according to the historians of that period, his whole journey to Paris was not less marked with high respect, than his arrival in that city. In his first letter from Fontainbleau, addressed to the other secretary Lord Dartmouth, he informs him, that he took all possible precaution to conceal his name, and to avoid all sort of ceremony, by stopping to refresh himself as little as possible; and when he did stop, by choosing to do it out of the great towns. His care was, however, in a great measure, fruitless; and the authorities did their utmost, in the places through which he passed, to show their respect to his royal mistress, so that he arrived at least as much fatigued with compliments, as tired with his journey. Having accomplished the object of his mission with much address and firmness, he took leave of the king of France, August 27th, receiving from his majesty a diamond ring valued at about 4000 pounds sterling. He left Mr. Prior at Paris, to take care of some private affairs still under negotiation, and resumed the management of affairs at home. It was, afterwards, made a matter of grave complaint by his enemies, and the fact was represented to the queen in strong colors, that he should have been at the opera in Paris, one evening when the Pretender was also present, although the latter was in another part of the house from that in which Bolingbroke was seated.

We now resume the thread of our narrative. Bolingbroke finding all hopes cut off at home, began to think of improving his wretched fortune upon the continent. He had left England with a very small fortune, and his attainder totally cut off all resources for the future. In this depressed situation, he began to listen to some proposals which were made him by the Pretender, who was then residing at Barr, in France, and who was desirous of admitting Bolingbroke into his secret councils. A proposal of this nature had been made to him shortly after his arrival at Paris, and before his attainder at home; but while he had yet any hopes of succeeding in England, he absolutely refused, and made the best application his ruined fortune would permit, to prevent the extremity of his prosecution.

He had for some time waited for an opportunity of determining himself, even after he found it vain to think of making his peace at home. He let his Jacobite friends in England know that they had but to command him, and he was ready to venture in their service the little all that remained, as frankly as he had exposed all that was gone. At length, (says he, talking of himself,) these commands came, and were executed in the following manner. The person who was sent to me, arrived in the beginning of July 1715, at the place I had retired to in Dauphiné. He spoke in the name of all the friends whose authority could influence me; and he brought me word that Scotland was not only ready to take arms, but under some sort of dissatisfaction to be withheld from beginning; that in England the people were exasperated against the government to such a degree, that far from wanting to be encouraged, they could not be restrained from insulting it on every occasion; that the whole tory party was become avowedly Jacobites; that many officers of the army, and the majority of the soldiers, were well affected to the cause; that the city of London was ready to rise, and that the enterprises for seizing of several places, were ripe for execution; in a word, that most of the principal tories were in a concert with the Duke of Ormond: for I had pressed particularly to be informed whether his grace acted alone, or if not, who were his council; and that the others were so disposed, that there remained no doubt of their joining as soon as the first blow should be struck. He added, that my friends were a little surprised, to observe that I lay neuter in such a conjuncture. He represented to me the danger I ran, of being prevented by people of all sides from having the merit of engaging early in this enterprise, and how unaccountable it would be for a man, impeached and attainted under the present government, to take no share in bringing about a revolution so near at hand, and so certain. He entreated that I would defer no longer to join the Chevalier, to advise and assist in carrying on his affairs, and to solicit and negotiate at the court of France, where my friends imagined that I should not fail to meet a favorable reception, and from whence they made no doubt of receiving assistance in a situation of affairs so critical, so unexpected, and so promising. He concluded, by giving me a letter from the Pretender, whom he had seen in his way to me, in which I was pressed to repair without loss of time to Comercy; and this instance was grounded on the message which the bearer of the letter had brought me from England. In the progress of the conversation with the messenger, he related a number of facts, which satisfied me as to the general disposition of the people; but he gave me little satisfaction as to the measures taken to improve this disposition, for driving the business on with vigor, if it tended to a revolution, or for supporting it to advantage if it spun into a war. When I questioned him concerning several persons whose disinclination to the government admitted no doubt, and whose names, quality, and experience were very essential to the success of the undertaking, he owned to me that they kept a great reserve, and did at most but encourage others to act by general and dark expressions. I received this account and this summons ill in my bed; yet important as the matter was, a few minutes served to determine me. The circumstances wanting to form a reasonable inducement to engage, did not excuse me; but the smart of a bill of attainder tingled in every vein, and I looked on my party to be under oppression, and to call for my assistance. Besides which, I considered first that I should be certainly informed, when I conferred with the Chevalier, of many particulars unknown to this gentleman; for I did not imagine that the English could be so near to take up arms as he represented them to be, on no other foundation than that which he exposed.

It has been said in a preceding part of this narrative, " that no sooner was it universally known that he (Bolingbroke) had retired to France, than his flight was construed into a proof of his guilt." With sorrow for the tarnished fame of this brilliant, but erratic statesman, we can see no other construction which could be put upon such an act. That, from the height of power in England, with the fairest prospects before him, he should be reduced within a few months to the condition of an attainted exile, was a state of things which, whilst it would render him suspected by impartial men, was not yet beyond the possibility of satisfactory explanation. But when we learn, in addition, that in one short year he was Secretary of State to Queen Anne, and Secretary of State to the Pretender, this fact carries with it his decisive and unmitigated condemnation. The case is stated with force and legal precision in the article from which we have already borrowed, in the 143d number of the Edinburgh Review, and which we attribute to Lord Brougham himself. " It is not often that a guilty person can make an honest-looking, worthy defence, not seldom that the excuses offered by suspected culprits work their own conviction. But never yet did any one, when charged with a crime, draw the noose around his own neck more fatally than Bolingbroke did, when he resorted to so wretched an explanation of the act, which, unexplained, was a confession—the flight from his accusers. If that act, standing alone, was fatal to the supposition of his innocence, the defence of it was, if possible, more decisive to his condemnation."

" A statesman, professing inviolable attachment to the Revolution Settlement, is accused of treasonable correspondence with the exiled family; he flies, and because he has been, as he alleges, falsely accused of that offence, he immediately proceeds to commit it. Suppose he made the only feasible excuse for running away from his accusers—that the public prejudices against him were so strong as to deprive him of all chance of a fair trial—did he not know that all such prepossessions are in their nature, in the nature of the people, in the nature of truth and justice, temporary, and pass away? Then would not innocence, if acting under the guidance of common sense, and an ordinary knowledge of mankind, have waited more or less patiently, more or less tranquil, for the season of returning calm, when justice might be surely expected? But could any thing be more inconsistent with all the supposition of innocence than instantly to commit the offence in question, because there was a delay of justice, through popular prejudice, prevailing?"

The Revolution Settlement had obtained Bolingbroke's delibe-rate (official and public) approbation; yet against this settlement he declares war. It was established, and could only be upset by civil commotion, and probably required the aid of foreign inva-sion to overthrow it. "To darken the face of his native land with these greatest of all plagues, he willingly consented, that he might take his revenge on his enemies, and trample upon them, to be raised to power under the restored dynasty of the bigoted and tyrannical Stuarts!"

Having for some time debated with himself, and taken his re-solution, he lost no time in repairing to the Pretender at Comer-cy, and took the seals of that nominal king, as he had formerly those of his potent mistress. But this was a terrible falling off indeed; and the very first conversation he had with this weak projector, gave him the most unfavorable expectations of future success. He talked to me (says his lordship) like a man who ex-pected every moment to set out for England or Scotland, but who did not very well know for which; and when he entered into the particulars of his affairs, I found, that concerning the former, he had nothing more circumstantial or positive to go upon, than what I have already related. But the Duke of Ormond had been for some time, I cannot say how long, engaged with the Chevalier: he had taken the direction of this whole affair, as far as it related to England, upon himself, and had received a commission for this purpose, which contained the most ample powers that could be given. But still, however, all was unsettled, undetermined, and ill understood. The duke had asked from France a small body of forces, a sum of money, and a quantity of ammunition; to the first part of the request he received a flat denial, but was made to hope that some arms and some ammunition might be given. This was but a very gloomy prospect; yet hope swelled the depressed party so high that they talked of nothing less than an instant and ready revolution. It was their interest to be secret and industrious; but, rendered sanguine by their passions, they made no doubt of subverting a government with which they were angry, and gave as great an alarm, as would have been imprudent at the eve of a general insurrection.

Such was the state of things when Bolingbroke arrived to take up his new office at Comercy; and although he saw the deplora-ble state of the party with which he was embarked, yet he re-solved to give his affairs the best complexion he was able, and set out for Paris, in order to procure from that court the necessary succors for his new master's invasion of England. But his re-ception and negotiations at Paris, were still more unpromising

than those at Comercy, and nothing but absolute infatuation seemed to dictate every measure taken by the party. He there found
a multitude of people at work, and every one doing what seemed
good in his own eyes; no subordination, no order, no concert.
The Jacobites had wrought one another up to look upon the success of the present designs, as infallible: every meeting-house
which the populace demolished, as he himself says, every little
drunken riot which happened, served to confirm them in these
sanguine expectations; and there was hardly one among them
who would lose the air of contributing by his intrigues to the restoration, which he took for granted would be brought about in
a few weeks. Care and hope, says our author very humorously,
sate on every bushy Irish face; and those who could read and
write, had letters to show, and those who had not arrived to this
pitch of erudition, had their secrets to whisper. No sex was excluded from this ministry; Fanny Oglethorpe kept her corner in
it, and Olive Trant, a woman of the same mixed reputation, was
the great wheel of this political machine. The ridiculous correspondence was carried on with England by people of like importance, and who were busy in sounding the alarm in the ears of
an enemy, whom it was their interest to surprise. By these
means, as he himself continues to inform us, the government of
England was put on its guard, so that before he came to Paris,
what was doing had been discovered. The little armament made
at Havre de Grace, which furnished the only means to the Pretender of landing on the coasts of Britain, and which had exhausted the treasury of St. Germains, was talked of publicly. The
Earl of Stair, the English minister at that city, very soon discovered its destination, and all the particulars of the intended invasion; the names of the persons from whom supplies came, and
who were particularly active in the design, were whispered about
at tea-tables and coffee-houses. In short what by the indiscretion of the projectors, what by the private interests and ambitious
views of the French, the most private transactions came to light;
and such of the more prudent plotters, who supposed that they
had trusted their heads to the keeping of one or two friends, were
in reality at the mercy of numbers. Into such company, exclaims
our noble writer, was I fallen for my sins. Still however, he
went on, steering in the wide ocean without a compass, till the
death of Louis XIV and the arrival of the Duke of Ormond at
Paris, rendered all his endeavors abortive: yet notwithstanding
these unfavorable circumstances, he still continued to despatch
several messages and directions for England, to which he received
very evasive and ambiguous answers. Among the number of
these, he drew up a paper at Chaville, in concert with the Duke
of Ormond, Marshal Berwick, and De Torcy, which was sent to

England, just before the death of the King of France, representing that France could not answer the demands of their memorial,
and praying directions what to do. A reply to this came to him
through the French Secretary of State, wherein they declared
themselves unable to say anything, till they saw what turn affairs
would take on the death of the king, which had reached their
ears. Upon another occasion, a message coming from Scotland
to press the Chevalier to hasten their rising, he despatched a messenger to London to the Earl of Mar, to tell him that the concurrence of England in the insurrection, was ardently wished and
expected: but instead of that nobleman's waiting for instructions,
he had already gone into the Highlands, and had there actually
put himself at the head of his clans. After this, in concert with
the Duke of Ormond, he despatched one Mr. Hamilton, who got
all the papers by heart, for fear of a miscarriage, to their friends
in England, to inform them, that though the Chevalier was destitute of succor, and all reasonable hopes of it, yet he would land
as they pleased, in England or Scotland, at a minute's warning,
and therefore they might rise immediately after they had sent
despatches to him. To this message Mr. Hamilton returned very
soon, with an answer given by Lord Landsdowne, in the name
of all the persons privy to the secret, that since affairs grew daily
worse, and would not mend by delay, the malcontents in England had resolved to declare immediately, and would be ready
to join the Duke of Ormond on his landing; adding, that his person would be as safe in England as in Scotland, and that in every
other respect it was better he should land in England; that they
had used their utmost endeavors; and hoped the western counties
would be in a good posture to receive him, and that he should
land as near as possible to Plymouth. With these assurances the
duke embarked, though he had heard before of the seizure of
many of his most zealous adherents, of the dispersion of many
more, and the consternation of all; so that upon his arrival at
Plymouth, finding nothing in readiness, he returned to Brittany.
In these circumstances, the Pretender himself sent to have a vessel got ready for him at Dunkirk, in which he went to Scotland,
leaving Lord Bolingbroke all this while at Paris, to try if by any
means some assistance might not be procured, without which all
hopes of success were at an end. It was during his negotiation
upon this miserable proceeding, that he was sent for by Mrs.
Trant, (a woman who had some time before ingratiated herself
with the Regent of France, by supplying him with mistresses
from England,) to a little house in the *Bois de Boulogne,* where
she lived with Mademoiselle Chaussery, an old superannuated
waiting-woman belonging to the regent. By these he was acquainted with the measures they had taken for the service of the

Duke of Ormond, although Bolingbroke, who was actual secretary to the negotiation, had never been admitted to a confidence in their secrets. He was, therefore, a little surprised at finding such mean agents employed without his privity, and very soon found them utterly unequal to the task. He quickly withdrew himself in consequence, from such wretched auxiliaries, and the regent himself seemed pleased at his defection.

In the mean time the Pretender set sail from Dunkirk for Scotland, and though Bolingbroke had all along perceived that his cause was hopeless and his projects ill designed; although he had met with nothing but opposition and disappointment in his service, yet he considered that this of all others was the time he could not be permitted to relax in the cause. He now therefore neglected no means, forgot no argument which his understanding could suggest, in applying to the court of France: but his success was not answerable to this industry. The king of France, not able to furnish the Pretender with money himself, had written some time before his death to his grandson the king of Spain, and had obtained from him a promise of forty thousand crowns. A small part of this sum had been received by the queen's treasurer at St. Germains, and had been sent to Scotland, or employed to defray the expenses which were daily making on the coast: at the same time Bolingbroke pressed the Spanish ambassador at Paris, and solicited the minister at the court of Spain. He took care to have a number of officers picked out of the Irish troops which served in France, gave them their routes, and sent a ship to receive and transport them to Scotland. Still, however, the money came in so slowly, and in such trifling sums, that it turned to little account; and the officers were on their way to the Pretender. At the same time he formed a design of engaging French privateers in the expedition, which were to have carried whatever should be necessary to send to any part of Britain in their first voyage, and then to cruize under the Pretender's commission. He had actually agreed for some, and had it in his power to have made the same bargain with others: Sweden on one side, and Scotland on the other, could have afforded them retreats; and if the war had been kept up in any part of the mountains, this armament would have been of the utmost advantage. But all his projects and negotiations failed, by the Pretender's precipitous return, who was not above six weeks in his expedition, and flew out of Scotland even before all had been tried in his defence.

The expedition being in this manner totally defeated, Bolingbroke now began to think that it was his duty as well as interest, to save the poor remains of the disappointed party. He never had any great opinion of the Pretender's success before he set

off; but when this adventurer had taken the last step which it
was in his power to make, our secretary then resolved to suffer
neither him nor the Scotch, to be any longer bubbles of their
own credulity, and of the scandalous artifices of the French
court.   In a conversation he had with the marshal D'Huxelles,
he took occasion to declare that he would not be the instrument
of amusing the Scotch; and since he was able to do them no
other service, he would at least inform them of what little dependence they might place upon assistance from France.   He
added, that he would send them vessels, which with those already on the coast of Scotland, might serve to bring off the Pretender, the earl of Mar, and as many others as possible.   The
marshal approved his resolution, and advised him to execute it
as the only thing which was left to do; but in the mean time the
Pretender landed at Gravelines, and gave orders to stop all vessels bound on his account to Scotland.   Bolingbroke saw him the
morning after his arrival at St. Germains, and was received by
him with open arms.

As soon as Bolingbroke heard of his return, he went, as it
was the secretary's business, to acquaint the French court with
it, by which he was recommended to advise the Pretender to
proceed to Bar with all possible diligence; and in this measure
Bolingbroke entirely concurred.   But the Pretender himself was
in no such haste; he had a mind to stay some time at St. Germains, and in the neighborhood of Paris, and to have a private
meeting with the regent: he accordingly sent Bolingbroke to
solicit this meeting, who exerted all his influence in the negotiation.   He wrote and spoke to the marshal D'Huxelles, who
answered him by word of mouth and by letters, refusing him by
both, and assuring him that the regent said the things which
were asked were puerilities, and swore he would not see him.
The secretary, no ways displeased with his ill success, returned
with this answer to his master, who acquiesced in this determination, and declared he would instantly set out for Lorraine; at
the same time assuring Bolingbroke of his firm reliance on his
integrity.

However, the Pretender, instead of taking post for Lorraine,
as he had promised, went to a little house in the *Bois de Boulogne*, where his female ministers resided, and there continued
for several days, seeing the Spanish and Swedish ministers, and
even the regent himself.   It might have been in these interviews
that he was set against his new secretary, and taught to believe
that he had been remiss in his duty, and false to his trust: be this
as it may, a few days after, the Duke of Ormond came to see
Bolingbroke, and having first prepared him for the surprise, put
into his hands a note directed to the duke, and a little scrip of

paper directed to the secretary; they were both in the Pretender's hand writing, and dated as if written by him on his way to Lorraine: but in this Bolingbroke, who knew the place of his present residence, was not to be deceived. In one of these papers the Pretender declared that he had no further occasion for the secretary's service, and the other was an order to him to give up the papers in his office; all which he observes, might have been contained in a letter-case of a moderate size. He gave the duke the seals, and some papers which he could readily come at; but for some others, in which there were several insinuations under the Pretender's own hand, reflecting upon the duke himself, these he took care to convey by a safe hand, since it would have been very improper that the duke should have seen them. As he thus gave up without scruple all the papers which remained in his hands, because he was determined never to make use of them, so he declares he took a secret pride in never asking for those of his own which were in the Pretender's hands; contenting himself with making the duke understand, how little need there was to get rid of a man in this manner, who only wanted an opportunity to get rid of the Pretender and his cause. In fact, if we survey the measures taken on the one side, and the abilities of the man on the other, it will not appear any way wonderful that he should be disgusted with a party, who had neither principle to give a foundation to their hopes, union to advance them, or abilities to put them in motion.

Bolingbroke being thus dismissed from the Pretender's service, he supposed that he had got rid of the trouble and the ignominy of so mean an employment at the same time; but he was mistaken; he was no sooner rejected from the office, than articles of impeachment were preferred against him, in the same manner as he had before been impeached in England, though not with such effectual injury to his person and fortune. The articles of his impeachment by the Pretender were branched out into seven heads, in which he was accused of treachery, incapacity, and neglect. The first was, That he was never to be found by those who came to him about business; and if by chance or stratagem they got hold of him, he affected being in a hurry, and by putting them off to another time, still avoided giving them any answer. The second was, That the Earl of Mar complained by six different messengers, at different times, before the Chevalier came from Dunkirk, of his being in want of arms and ammunition, and prayed a speedy relief; and though the things demanded were in my lord's power, there was not so much as one pound of powder in any of the ships, which by his lordship's directions parted from France. Thirdly, the Pretender himself, after his arrival, sent general Hamilton to inform him, that his want of arms and ammunition was such, that he should be obliged to leave Scotland, unless he received speedy relief; yet Lord Bolingbroke amused Mr. Hamilton twelve days together, and did not introduce him to any of the French ministers, though he was referred to them for a particular account of affairs; or so much as communicated his letters to the queen, or any body else. Fourthly, The count Del Castel Blanco had for several months, at Havre, a considerable quantity of arms and ammunition, and did daily ask his lordship's orders how to dispose of them, but never got any instructions. Fifthly, The Pretender's friends at the French court, had for some time past no very good opinion of his lordship's integrity, and a very bad one of his discretion. Sixthly, At a time when many merchants in France would have carried privately any quantity of arms and ammunition into Scotland, his lordship desired a public order for the embarkation, which being a thing not to be granted, is said to have been done in order to urge a denial. Lastly, The Pretender wrote to his lordship by every occasion after his arrival in Scotland; and though there were many opportunities of writing in return, yet from the time he landed there, to the day he left it, he never received any letter from his lordship. Such were the articles, by a very extraordinary reverse of fortune, preferred against Lord Bolingbroke, in less than a year after similar articles were drawn up against him by the opposite party at home. It is not easy to find out what he could have done, thus to disoblige all sides; but he had learned by this time, to make out happiness from the consciousness of his own designs, and to consider all the rest of mankind as uniting in a faction to oppress virtue.

But though it was mortifying to be thus rejected on both sides, yet he was not remiss in vindicating himself from all. Against these articles of impeachment, therefore, he drew up an elaborate answer, in which he vindicates himself with great plausibility. He had long, as he assures us, wished to leave the Pretender's service, but was entirely at a loss how to conduct himself in so difficult a resignation; but at length, says he, the Pretender and his council disposed of things better for me than I could have done for myself. I had resolved, on his return from Scotland, to follow him till his residence should be fixed somewhere; after which, having served the tories in this, which I looked upon as their last struggle for power, and having continued to act in the Pretender's affairs, till the end of the term for which I embarked with him, I should have esteemed myself to be at liberty, and should, in the civilest manner I was able, have taken my leave of him. Had we parted thus, I should have remained in a very strange situation all the rest of my life; on one side, he would have thought that he had a right on any future occasion to call

me out of my retreat, the tories would probably have thought
the same thing, my resolution was taken to refuse them both,
and I foresaw that both would condemn me; on the other side,
the consideration of his having kept measures with me, joined to
that of having once openly declared for him, would have created
a point of honor by which I should have been tied down, not
only from ever engaging against him, but also from making my
peace at home. The Pretender cut this Gordian knot asunder
at one blow; he broke the links of that chain which former engagements had fastened on me, and gave me a right to esteem
myself as free from all obligations of keeping measures with him,
as I should have continued if I had never engaged in his interest.

It is not to be supposed that one so very delicate to preserve
his honor, would previously have basely betrayed his employer:
a man conscious of acting so infamous a part, would have undertaken no defence, but let the accusations, which could not mate-
rially affect him, blow over, and wait for the calm that was to
succeed in tranquillity. He appeals to all the ministers with
whom he transacted business, for the integrity of his proceedings
at that juncture; and had he been really guilty, when he opposed
the ministry after his return to England, they would not have
failed to brand and detect his duplicity. The truth is, that he,
perhaps, was the most disinterested minister at that time in the
Pretender's court; as he had spent great sums of his own money
in his service, and never would be obliged to him for a farthing,
in which case he believes that he stood alone. His integrity is
much less impeachable on this occasion than his ambition; for
all the steps he took may be fairly ascribed to his displeasure at
having the Duke of Ormond and the Earl of Mar treated more
confidentially than himself. It was his aim always to be fore-
most in every administration, and he could not bear to act as a
subaltern, in so paltry a court as that of the Pretender.

The charge of having neglected the interests of the Pretender,
and done less than he ought to further the attempt in 1715, made
against him by the thoughtless zeal, the gross ignorance, the foolish presumption of the Jacobites; and against which is almost
entirely confined his defence of himself, in his celebrated, and for
composition justly celebrated, " Letter to Sir William Wyndham," was plainly groundless, in the opinion of Lord Brougham
—(*Edin. Rev.*) It was likely, indeed, to be groundless; for the
interests of Bolingbroke, all the speculations of his ambition, all
the revengeful passions of his nature, were enlisted to make him
zealous in good earnest for the success of the rebellion; and to
aid that enterprise, however much he might despair of it, he

exerted his utmost resources of intrigue, of solicitation, of argument.

But regarding his final abandonment of the Pretender, his conduct exhibits the same selfishness, the same vindictiveness, irrespective of either justice or of generous devotion, which had marked his opposition to the government at home. "Because the Parliament of the Brunswicks attainted him when he confessed his guilt by his flight, he joined the standard of the Stuarts. It was covered with irremediable defeat, and he resolved to quit it. But, meanwhile, the master into whose service he came as a volunteer, chose to take another minister; therefore, Bolingbroke deserted him when his misfortunes were much more unquestionable than his ingratitude. The pivot of all his actions, by all that he urges in his own behalf, was his individual, private, personal interest. To this consideration all sense of principle was sacrificed, all obligation of duty subjected; whatever his revenge prompted, whatever his ambition recommended, that he deemed himself justified in doing, if not called upon to do." A severe, but a true opinion, this, of my Lord Bolingbroke by my Lord Brougham.

At all periods of his exile, he still looked towards home with secret regret; and had taken every opportunity to apply to those in power, either to soften his prosecutions, or lessen the number of his enemies at home. In accepting his office under the Pretender, he made it a condition to be at liberty to quit the post whenever he should think proper; and being now disgracefully dismissed, he turned his mind entirely towards making his peace in England, and employing all the unfortunate experience he had acquired to undeceive his tory friends, and to promote the union and quiet of his native country. It was not a little favorable to his hopes, that about this time, though unknown to him, the Earl of Stair, ambassador to the French court, had received full power to treat with him whilst he was engaged with the Pretender; but yet had never made him any proposals, which might be considered as a gross insult. But when the breach with the Pretender was universally known, the earl sent one Monsieur Saludin, a gentleman of Geneva, to Lord Bolingbroke, to communicate to him his majesty King George's favorable disposition to grant him a pardon; and his own earnest desire to serve him as far as he was able. This was an offer by much too advantageous for Bolingbroke in his wretched circumstances to refuse; he embraced it, as became him to do, with all possible sense of the king's goodness, and of the ambassador's friendship. They had frequent conferences shortly after upon the subject. The turn which the English ministry gave the matter, was to enter into a treaty to reverse his attainder, and to stipulate the conditions on which this act of grace should be granted him: but this method of negotiation he would by no means submit to; the notion of a treaty shocked him, and he resolved never to be restored, rather than go that way to work. Accordingly he opened himself without any reserve to Lord Stair, and told him, that he looked upon himself obliged in honor and conscience, to undeceive his friends in England, both as to the state of foreign affairs, as to the management of the Jacobite interest abroad, and as to the characters of the persons; in every one of which points he knew them to be most grossly and most dangerously deluded. He observed that the treatment he had received from the Pretender and his adherents, would justify him to the world in doing this. That, if he remained in exile all his life, he might be assured that he would never have more to do with the Jacobite cause, and that if he were restored, he would give it an effectual blow, in making that apology which the Pretender had put him under a necessity of making. That in doing this, he flattered himself that he should contribute something towards the establishment of the king's government, and to the union of his subjects. He added, that if the court thought him sincere in those professions, a treaty with him was unnecessary; and if they did not believe so, then a treaty would be dangerous to him. The Earl of Stair, who has also confirmed this account of Lord Bolingbroke's, in a letter to Mr. Craggs, readily came into his sentiments on this head, and soon after the king approved it upon their representations: he accordingly received a promise of pardon from George I, who, on the 2d of July 1716, created his father Baron of Battersea, in the county of Surry, and Viscount St. John. This seemed preparatory to his own restoration; and instead of prosecuting any farther ambitious schemes against the government, he rather began to turn his mind to philosophy; and since he could not gratify his ambition to its full extent, he endeavored to learn the arts of despising it. The variety of distressful events that had hitherto attended all his struggles, at last had thrown him into a state of reflection, and this produced, by way of relief, a *Consolatio Philosophica,* which he wrote the same year, under the title of " Reflections upon Exile." In this piece, in which he professes to imitate the manner of Seneca, he, with some wit, draws his own picture, and represents himself as suffering persecution, for having served his country with abilities and integrity. A state of exile thus incurred, he very justly shows to be rather honorable than distressful; and indeed, there are few men who will deny, but that the company of strangers to virtue, is better than the company of enemies to it. Besides this philosophical tract, he also wrote this

year several letters, in answer to the charge laid upon him by
the Pretender and his adherents; and the following year he drew
up a vindication of his whole conduct with respect to the tories,
in the form of a letter to Sir William Wyndham.

Nor was he so entirely devoted to the fatigues of business, but
that he gave pleasure a share in his pursuits. He had never
much agreed with the lady he first married, and after a short co-
habitation, they separated, and lived ever after asunder. She,
therefore, remained in England, upon his going into exile, and
by proper application to the throne, was allowed a sufficient
maintenance to support her with becoming dignity. She did
not long survive his first disgrace; and upon his becoming a
widower, he began to think of trying his fortune once more,
in a state which was at first so unfavorable. For this purpose he cast his eye on the widow of the Marquis of Villette,
and niece to the famous Madame de Maintenon; a young lady of
great merit and understanding, possessed of a very large fortune,
but incumbered with a long and troublesome law-suit. He had
passed some time at her chateau at Marcilly, ostensibly, in aiding her to devise schemes of architectural improvement; but
with the effect, as might have been anticipated, of affecting her
reputation. They were privately married in the month of May,
1720, at Aix la Chapelle. Bolingbroke was fortunate in his
union with his second wife, for whom he ever manifested affectionate regard. In proportion as he stood, from increasing years
forlorn in the world, he felt more strongly her kindness, her attachment, and tender fidelity. She certainly looked up to him
as the first of human beings. She died about two years before
his lordship. To *La Source*, a small estate near Orleans which
he had purchased the year before his marriage, he now retired,
and gave up his time to improving, with all the aid of taste and
art, its natural beauties. The banks of the Loiret, at the origin
of which river was his estate, and from which circumstance it
derived its name, were visited by the most distinguished in
France for genius and acquirements. Among the number was
Voltaire, who speaks in raptures of the spot, adding, that he
found in its illustrious proprietor all the erudition of England
with all the politeness of France. In the company of this very
sensible woman, he passed his time in France, and sometimes at
the capital, till the year 1723, in which, after the breaking up of
the parliament, his majesty was pleased to grant him a pardon
as to his personal safety, but as yet neither restoring him to his
family inheritance, his title, nor a seat in parliament.

To obtain this favor had been the governing principle of his
politics for some years before; and upon the first notice of his
good fortune, he prepared to return to his native country, where,

however, his dearest connections were either dead, or declared themselves suspicious of his former conduct in support of their party. It is observable, that Bishop Atterbury, who was banished at this time, for a supposed treasonable correspondence in favor of the tories, was set on shore at Calais, just when Lord Bolingbroke arrived there, on his return to England. So extraordinary a reverse of fortune, could not fail of strongly affecting that prelate, who observed, with some emotion, that he perceived himself to be exchanged: he presently left it to his auditors, to imagine whether his country was the loser or the gainer by such an exchange.

The restoration of Lord Bolingbroke was the work of the Duchess of Kendall, mistress of George I; and Walpole, in obedience to the express commands of the king, supported the act, just as we before found Bolingbroke committing his treasons with the Pretender, in connivance with Queen Anne. The whole appears to have been a state intrigue, in which the respective parties performed their share with very little of that openness and candor which govern the affairs of private life. Bolingbroke's crime was, we fear, not an uncommon one: he paid court to every party and every individual who could serve his cause; and he succeeded so far as to compel his original prosecutor (Walpole) to become his advocate against his will; but as the latter did not fulfil the whole of Bolingbroke's expectations, their mutual aversion remained in its pristine state, and remained during their respective lives. Bolingbroke has drawn an overcharged picture of Walpole: the relations of Walpole have since endeavored to repay him in the same manner.

He might freely complain that positive injustice was done to him by a protracted display of lenity, without his receiving the substantial advantages which could alone give it value in his own eyes, or make it available for the conduct of others. The fact of his being reconciled with the king in 1716–17, after he abandoned the cause of the Pretender, was known at the time, both in London and Paris. The Duc de Saint Simon, in his attractive *Memoires* (t. xv, p. 230), writes under the head of the year 1717 "It was at this time that Viscount Bolingbroke was received but still secretly, into favor; and that Stair (the English ambassador) had orders to announce the circumstance to the regent, and to request that the latter would henceforth look upon him as a subject whom the king of England honored with his protection." But yet, notwithstanding this positive assurance on the part of the sovereign, no steps were taken to carry it into practice. The opposition of the minister (Walpole) was too powerful, and was, as we have seen, at last only overcome by the Duchess of Kendall's adopting the cause of the illustrious

exile.   The immediate agent in this transaction was Bolingbroke's new wife, who, for reasons connected with her tenure
and enjoyment of property in England, found it necessary to
visit that country; she having resumed her widow's title, before
setting out.   She soon succeeded, with the the aid of Lord Harcourt, who still retained his friendship for his old coadjutor, in
regaining possession of her property, which, on the first intelligence of her marriage, was declared by her agent to belong to
Lord Bolingbroke, and in consequence of his attainder to revert
to the crown.   Her success in her own affairs, and the knowledge which she acquired of the state and bearing of parties,
encouraged her to engage warmly in her husband's restoration.
Through Lord Harcourt she gained access to the Duchess of
Kendall, who was notoriously rapacious and corrupt; and she
succeeded, by bribing this person with a sum of 11,000 pounds,
in attaching her to Bolingbroke's interest.   Walpole still vehe-
mently opposed his pardon at all, in a speech at the Council
Board, in which he is said to have made use of this strong expression:—" May his attainder never be reversed, and may his
crimes never be forgotten."   When, finally, this minister, who
had diverted so long the king alone, from any definite action on
the subject, saw that he could not resist the king, after his mistress, the Duchess of Kendall, was made a party to the discussion, he found means to reduce the favor to its smallest possible
value.   Bolingbroke was assured of his personal safety only,
with permission to live in England: but he was not restored to
his family inheritance, to his title, nor to his seat in parliament.
   It was doubtless in allusion to the return of Bolingbroke to
England, and the banishment of Atterbury thence, that Pope
wrote the following passage, which occurs in a letter to Swift:
" The Lord Bolingbroke is now returned, as I hope, to take me,
with all his other hereditary rights.   It is sure my ill fate, that
all those whom I most loved, and with whom I most lived, must
be banished.   After both of you left England, my constant host
was the Bishop of Rochester.   Sure, this is a nation which is
cursedly afraid of being overrun with too much politeness; and
we cannot regain one great genius, but at the expense of another."
   The first stay of the restored exile in his native country was
of short duration: finding the times not propitious for any
further attempt to regain his original position, as holder of property and a peer, he returned to France, and was soon after
attacked with a fever, for the entire recovery from which, he
visited Aix la Chapelle, and drank the mineral waters there.
This disease was speedily followed by a fit of the gout.
   Bolingbroke remained in France about two years after the

termination of his compulsory exile; mainly, we must suppose, because his restricted income would not allow of his living in England in a style, either at all approaching to that which he once exhibited, or commensurate with even his more moderate wishes at this time. But he was not idle in urging by all the means in his power, for further favors from the crown, viz: the restoration of his title and estates. He had, however, notwithstanding the positive promise of the king, and the implied one of the ministry, the mortification to find his claims continually evaded: we cannot, therefore, wonder at or blame him, for giving utterance in his letters, in terms of indignant complaint, to the bad faith of both king and ministers, for breaking their word with him. The chief obstacle now, as heretofore, to the accomplishment of his wishes was the persevering and hostile opposition of Walpole, whose interest was still all powerful, as his hatred was inveterate. Policy, indeed, not less than passion, dictated this course against his old rival, whom he would naturally be averse to see invested with the power of once more agitating parliament, if not of convulsing the country. At length, however, the persevering efforts of Bolingbroke's friends, backed by the Dnchess of Kendall, were so far successful, as to induce, it may be said, compel Walpole to report favorably on the petition which the attainted peer had presented, praying for leave to bring in a bill. But the one introduced by Walpole, as the ministerial leader in the commons, and which (after a stormy debate) was carried, allowing Bolingbroke to enjoy the family inheritance that was settled upon him, fell far short, in its scope and objects, of the wishes and expectations of the petitioner. This measure was adopted in May, 1725. Walpole's rejection of the clause introduced by Lord William Paulet, to disqualify Bolingbroke from sitting in either house of parliament, deceived nobody; the minister made it certain, as far, at least, as depended on the expressed will of the king and his counsel, that the petitioner should never more be admitted to any share of power.

Bolingbroke's own disappointment and chagrin are expressed in a letter to his friend, Sir William Wyndham: "Here I am then," says he, "two-thirds restored, my person safe, (unless I meet hereafter with harder treatment than even that of Sir Walter Raleigh,) and my estate, with all the property I have acquired or may acquire, secured to me. But the attainder is kept carefully and prudently in force, lest so corrupt a member should come again into the House of Lords, and his bad leaven should sour that sweet and untainted mass."

Soon availing himself of his restricted privileges, he became the purchaser of a seat of Lord Tankerville's, at Dawley, near

Uxbridge, in Middlesex, and of course, not far from London, where he settled with his lady, and laid himself out for the enjoyment of rural pleasures; since, in his opinion, the more glorious ones of ambition were denied him.

With this resolution he began to improve his new purchase in a very peculiar style, giving it all the air of a country farm, and adorning even his hall with all the implements of husbandry. We have a sketch of his way of living in this retreat, in a letter from Pope to Swift, who omits no opportunity of representing his lordship in the most amiable points of view. This letter is dated from Dawley, the country farm above-mentioned, and began thus:—"I now hold the pen for my Lord Bolingbroke, who is reading your letter between two haycocks; but his attention is somewhat diverted, by casting his eyes on the clouds, not in admiration of what you say, but for fear of a shower. He is pleased with your placing him in the triumvirate, between yourself and me; though he says he doubts he shall fare like Lepidus, while one of us runs away with all the power, like Augustus, and another with all the pleasure, like Antony. It is upon a foresight of this, that he has fitted up his farm, and you will agree that this scheme of retreat is not founded upon weak appearances. Upon his return from Bath, he finds all peccant humors are purged out of him; and his great temperance and economy are so signal, that the first is fit for my constitution, and the latter would enable you to lay up so much money as to buy a bishopric in England. As to the return of his health and vigor, were you here, you might inquire of his hay-makers; but as to his temperance, I can answer, that, for one whole day, we have had nothing for dinner but mutton-broth, beans and bacon, and a barn-door fowl. Now his lordship is run after his cart, I have a moment left to myself to tell you, that I overheard him yesterday agree with a painter for two hundred pounds, to paint his country-hall with rakes, spades, prongs, &c., and other ornaments, merely to countenance his calling this place a FARM." What Pope here says of engagements with a painter, was shortly after executed; the hall was painted accordingly in black crayons only, so that at first view it brought to mind the figures often seen scratched with charcoal, or the smoke of a candle, upon the kitchen walls of farm-houses. The whole, however, produced a most striking effect, and over the door, at the entrance into it, was this motto, SATIS BEATUS RURIS HONORIBUS. His lordship seemed to be extremely happy in this pursuit of moral tranquillity: and in the exultation of his heart could not fail of communicating his satisfaction to his friend Swift. "I am in my own farm," says he, "and here I shoot strong and tenacious roots: I have caught hold of the earth, to use a gardener's phrase, and neither my enemies nor my friends will find it an easy matter to transplant me again."

There is not, perhaps, a stronger instance in the world than his lordship, that an ambitious mind can never be fairly subdued, but will still seek for those gratifications which retirement can never supply. All this time he was mistaken in his passion for solitude, and supposed that to be the child of philosophy, which was only the effects of spleen: it was in vain that he attempted to take root in the shade of obscurity; he was originally bred in the glare of public occupation, and he secretly once more wished for transplantation. He was only a titular lord, not having been thoroughly restored; and, as he was excluded from a seat in the house of peers, he burned with impatience to play a part in that conspicuous theatre. Impelled by this desire, he could no longer be restrained in obscurity, but once more, in 1726, entered into the bustle of public business, and, disavowing all obligations to the minister, he embarked in the opposition against him, in which he had several powerful coadjutors. He was now resolved to shake that power, which endeavored to obstruct the increase of his own. Taking, therefore, his part in the opposition with Pulteney, the " Great Commoner," while the latter engaged to manage the house of commons, Bolingbroke undertook to enlighten the people; and, accordingly, he soon distinguished himself by a multitude of pieces, written during the latter part of the reign of George the First, and likewise in the beginning of that which succeeded. These were conceived with great vigor and boldness; and now, once more engaged in the service of his country, though disarmed, gagged, and almost bound, as he declared himself to be, yet he resolved not to abandon his cause, as long as he could depend on the firmness and integrity of those coadjutors, who did not labor under the same disadvantages with himself. His letters in a paper called the Craftsman, were particularly distinguished in this political contest; and though several of the most expert politicians of the times joined in this paper, his essays were peculiarly relished by the public. Besides this work, he published several other separate pamphlets, which were afterwards reprinted in the second edition of his works, and which were very popular in their day. Among the light political papers of this kind, a series of letters, published under the title of the "*Occasional Writer*," had great vogue. The first of these, written in January, 1727, is declared by Mr. Cooke to be one of the finest specimens of caustic irony in our language.

Of the kind of warfare carried on by Bolingbroke at this

time against Sir Robert Walpole, his son Horace speaks in the
following terms:—" Craftsmen, pamphlets, libels, combinations
were showered on or employed for years against the prime
minister, without shaking his power or ruffling his temper, and
Bolingbroke had the mortification of finding his rival had abilities to maintain his influence against the mistresses of two kings,
with whom his antagonist had plotted in vain to overturn him."
This is a partial and an unfair view of the relative temper and
conduct of the two antagonist parties. The Duchess of Kendall
was, it is true, entirely in Bolingbroke's interest, and decidedly
opposed to Walpole. Lady Suffolk, the first mistress of George
II, was also won over to favor the pretensions of the former,
although the king himself was never favorably inclined towards
him. The duchess, as we are told by Horace Walpole, had
actually prevailed on George I to see Bolingbroke secretly in
his closet. "That intriguing Proteus, aware that he might not
obtain an audience long enough to efface former prejudices, and
make sufficient impression on the king against Sir Robert, and
in his own favor, went provided with a long memorial, which
he left in the closet, and begged his majesty to peruse coolly at
his leisure. The king kept the paper, but no longer than till he
saw Sir Robert, to whom he delivered the poisoned remonstrance." George II, it is said, parted with Lady Suffolk, on the
Princess Amelia informing him that the mistress had interviews
with Lord Bolingbroke.

The other part of the allegation of Horace Walpole is not so
well founded. Bolingbroke's alliance with Pulteney, his being
the trusted adviser of the parliamentary conduct of Wyndham,
and the undoubted and extensive influence which he exerted
over the people in his political writings, must all have contributed not a little to shake the popularity of Sir Robert Walpole, and to hasten his downfall. As a specimen of the distor-
tion of fact, by the friends and adherents of either of these two
rivals, when speaking of the other, the following narrative, related by Horace Walpole, will suffice:—" Bolingbroke at his
return could not avoid waiting on Sir Robert to thank him, and
was invited to dine with him at Chelsea: but, whether tortured
at witnessing Walpole's serene frankness and felicity, or suffo-
cated with indignation and confusion at being forced to be
obliged to one whom he hated and envied, the first morsel he
put into his mouth was near choking him, and he was reduced
to rise from the table and leave the room for some minutes. I
never heard of their meeting more." If every case of imperfect
deglutition were to be paraded as an instance of the person, at
the time, being under the influence of some malignant passion,
the records of evil would be singularly enlarged.

This political warfare continued for ten years, during which time he labored with great strength and perseverance, and drew up such a system of politics, as some have supposed to be the most complete now existing. But, as upon all other occasions, he had the mortification once more to see those friends desert him, upon whose assistance he most firmly relied, and all that web of fine-spun speculation actually destroyed at once by the ignorance of some and the perfidy of others. He then declared that he was perfectly cured of his patriotic frenzy; he fell out not only with Pulteney for his selfish views, but with his old friends the tories, for abandoning their cause as desperate, averring that the faint and unsteady exercise of parts on one side, was a crime but one degree inferior to the iniquitous misapplication of them on the other. But he could not take leave of a controversy in which he had been so many years engaged, without giving a parting blow, in which he seemed to summon up all his vigor at once, and where, as the poet says,

Animam in vulnere posuit.

This inimitable piece is entitled, " *A Dissertation on Parties,*" and of all his masterly pieces it is in general esteemed the best.

The work is comprehended in nineteen letters, and was, like most of his other political pieces in the period which we have been describing, first printed in the Craftsman. It was the closing effort of Bolingbroke, in a contest in which he won unequalled success as a writer, but without any fruits for himself personally, as a politician. The sentiments contained in it form, says Mr. Cooke, a bitter commentary upon those which he so ostentatiously avowed in his letter to Sir William Wyndham. Then he considered a devotion to his party a sufficient apology for treason against his country. Then, he ranked himself among those whom he afterwards censured as men who mean little more than to make a private court at the public expense; who choose to be the instruments of a bad king rather than to be out of power, and who are often so wicked that they would prefer such a service to that of the best of kings: now, he considers that very party spirit which he then avowed as a merit, to be a complaint and grief among good men, a domestic weakness, and a national disgrace. The reflection with which these remarks are concluded, implying suspicion of "the candor of the patriotic philosopher" in this his later work, is not, we think, just to its author. That time should have enlarged his knowledge of the true operations and bearings of party, and age have so far abated his early and passionate onesidedness as to have merged selfishness in an honest desire for the public good, may not unreasonably be expected from a

man whose reasoning powers were so acute as those of Bolingbroke, and whose perceptions of right, though clouded at first by
the lust of power and afterwards by the feeling of revenge, could
not be extinguished.

In another point of view, this Dissertation will merit the careful study of the reader, not only for its "abounding in acute, sagacious, and often profound reflections, with forcible arguments,
much happy illustration," but for its plainly bearing in many
passages the impress of the "extraordinary oratorical powers"
of Bolingbroke, "and which, if spoken, must have produced an
indescribable effect."

Another series of letters which appeared also in the Craftsman, was upon the History of England, written under the signa-
ture of *Humphrey Oldcastle.* Several of these were so annoying to the ministers by their pungent and apposite satire,
that they vented their rage in prosecutions against the pub-
lisher. Mr. Cooke judiciously remarks, in reference to the
merit of this performance, "The just opinions he had formed of
our constitution, and the soundness of his views of public policy
were in these letters made apparent; and the reader of them
must acknowledge that so far at least, as theoretical knowledge
can qualify, Bolingbroke had the highest claims to the reputation
of an able statesman." During the appearance of these letters,
the Craftsman had an immense sale, which far exceeded even
that of the Spectator. The dedication is to Sir Robert Walpole,
then Earl of Orford, and was written in the ironical strain of the
Occasional Writer.

Having finished his "Dissertation," which was received with
the utmost avidity, he resolved to take leave not only of his enemies and friends, but even of his country; and in this resolution, in
the year 1735, he once once retired to France, where he looked to
his native country with a mixture of anger and pity, and upon
his former professing friends, with a share of contempt and indignation. I expect little, says he, from the principal actors that
tread the stage at present. They are divided not so much as it
seemed, and as they would have it believed, about measures.
The true division is about their different ends. Whilst the minister was not hard pushed, nor the prospect of succeeding to
him near, they appeared to have but one end, the reformation of
the government. The destruction of the minister was pursued
only as a preliminary, but of essential and indisputable necessity,
to that end: but when his destruction seemed to approach, the
object of his succession interposed to the sight of many, and the
reformation of the government was no longer their point of view.
They had divided the skin, at least in their thoughts, before they

had taken the beast. The common fear of hastening his downfall for others, made them all faint in the chase. It was this, and this alone, that saved him, and put off his evil day.

Such were his cooler reflections, after he had laid down his political pen, to employ it in a manner that was much more agreeable to his usual professions, and his approaching age. He had long devoted the few hours he could spare to subjects of a more general and important nature to the interests of mankind; but as he was frequently interrupted by the alarms of party, he made no great progress in his design. Still, however, he kept it in view, and he makes frequent mention in his letters to Swift, of his intentions to give metaphysics a new and useful turn. I know, says he, in one of these, how little regard you pay to writings of this kind; but I imagine, that if you can like any, it must be those that strip metaphysics of all their bombast, keep within the sight of every well constituted eye, and never bewilder themselves, whilst they pretend to guide the reason of others.

The resolution of Bolingbroke to retire once more to France could not, of course, be allowed to pass without comment, and for want of a knowledge of the true cause, surmises were indulged in. Of these, one was to the purport, that he had gone once more to join the Pretender; another, that he was driven away by an attack made upon him by Sir Robert Walpole, in a speech in the house of commons. The first supposition gained little credence at the time, and is not supported by any circumstance which has come to light since. The second merits more notice, but not in the sense in which it is examined by Mr. Cooke. With the latter we can readily refuse assent to a belief, that the speech simply as a piece of indignant, or even vindictive declamation could work on the sensibility of so veteran a politician, practised partisan, and controversialist, as to drive him into exile in order to conceal his humiliation if not his shame. But, as suggested by a writer in the *Quarterly Review* (No. cviii), the speech might have acquired power over the feelings and movements of the person against whom it was aimed, both by the spirit of practical hostility which it avowed, and the knowledge of Bolingbroke's guilty practices, which, to his own conscience, it might reveal. It was the *moral* and *political* force, and not the mere cleverness of the speech to which its effects should be attributed. One passage in it may have borne harder on Bolingbroke than others, or even his friends were aware. Walpole's speech is a reply to the celebrated one of Sir William Wyndham, in which that able parliamentary orator supposes a case of a minister misleading his sovereign, corrupting the people, and plundering the nation for his own benefit; the whole picture intended, however, and it was so understood, to apply to Walpole himself. The latter, in place of defending himself or attacking the speaker, follows in the same style, of giving a supposed picture; but it was soon known to be meant for the friend and adviser of Wyndham, and the leader, in fact, of his party, Bolingbroke himself. Wyndham's attack on Walpole is generally known and has been often quoted. The reply of the latter, in an attack on Bolingbroke, is less familiar to the reader, who will not be displeased at our introducing its most pointed passages on this occasion. After speaking of the declamatory invectives in which the leaders of the opposite party were so fond of indulging, and adverting to some of the terms employed by Wyndham, the minister proceeds thus:

"But now, sir, let me too suppose—and the house being cleared, I am sure no person that hears me can come within the description of the person I am to suppose. Let us suppose in this, or in some other unfortunate country, an anti-minister who thinks himself a person of so great and extensive parts, and of so many eminent qualifications, that he looks upon himself as the only person in the kingdom capable to conduct the public affairs of the nation, and therefore christening every other gentleman who has the honor to be employed in the administration, by the name of blunderer. Suppose this fine gentleman lucky enough to have gained over to his party some persons really of fine parts, of ancient families and of great fortunes, and others of desperate views arising from disappointed and malicious hearts; all these gentlemen, with respect to their political behavior, moved by him and by him solely; all they say, either in private or public, being only a repetition of the words he has put into their mouths, and a spitting out of that venom which he has infused into them; and yet we may suppose this leader not really liked by any even of those who so blindly follow him, and hated by all the rest of mankind. We will suppose this anti-minister to be in a country where he really ought not to be, and where he could not have been but by an effect of too much goodness and mercy; yet endeavoring with all his might and all his art to destroy the fountain from whence that mercy flowed. In that country let us suppose him continually contracting friendships and familiarities with the ambassadors of those princes who, at the time happen to be most at enmity with his own: and if at any time it should happen to be for the interest of any of those foreign ministers to have a secret divulged to them which might be highly prejudicial to his native country, as well as to all its friends, I suppose this foreign minister applying to him and he answering, I will get it you; tell me but what you want, I will endeavor to procure it for you! Upon this he puts a speech or two in the mouths of some of his creatures, or some of his new converts; what he wants is moved for in parliament; and when so reasonable a request as this is refused, suppose him, and his creatures and tools by his advice, spreading the alarm over the whole nation, and crying out; ' Gentlemen our country is at present involved in many dangerous difficulties, all which we would have extricated you from, but a wicked minister and a corrupt majority refused us the proper materials, and upon this scandalous victory this minister becomes so insolent as to plume himself in defiances.' Let us further suppose this anti-minister to have travelled, and at every court where he was thinking himself the greatest minister, and making it his trade to betray the secrets of every master he ever served. I could carry my suppositions a great deal further, and I may say I mean no person now in being; but if we can suppose such a one, can there be imagined a greater disgrace to human nature than such a wretch as this?"

The surmise which might be made from reading that part of Walpole's speech relating to Bolingbroke's intriguing with the ambassadors from foreign powers, that the latter had actually passed the limits not merely of patriotic duty but of law, and that his illegal practices were known to the minister at this time, is greatly strengthened by reference to some parts of the Marchmont papers which were not known either to the writer in the ' Biographia' or to Goldsmith. Bolingbroke in one of his letters to Lord Marchmont, dated July 24th, 1746, states: "I did not leave England in 1735, till *some schemes which were then on the loom,* though they never came into effect, made me *one too many even to my most intimate friends.*" *March. Pap.* ii, 350.

This scheme, continues the Quarterly Review, from which we derive the above extract, seems to us to be a decisive admission that the flight from England was the consequence of some political *schemes,* the discovery of which placed him in personal danger, and in some degree involved his most intimate friends; and the intelligent and well informed editor of the Marchmont Papers explains this passage by the following note.

" He had been so marked by Sir Robert Walpole as caballing with *foreign ministers against his own country,* in 1734, tha Mr. Pulteney and the other heads of the opposition recommended him to leave England, which he did in 1735, on seeing that the ministers were strong in the new parliament." *March. Pap.* ii, 350.

Pope, whose letter to Swift on this subject has been introduced by Goldsmith in the Life, probably knew the truth, but thought as he says, " that it ought to be, if possible, concealed:" his excuse of the noble exile's intended literary leisure, *vacare literis,* was friendly and natural.

Plausible as is this view of the cause of Bolingbroke's second
abandonment of England, we cannot resist the belief that the
state of his pecuniary affairs contributed not a little to this step.
Bearing very strongly upon the subject, and if not entirely eluci-
dating it, is a letter of his to Sir William Wyndham, which
none of the biographers of Bolingbroke seem to have noticed.
From it we should be led to suppose that the secession was not
as compulsory as must have been the case agreeably to the
opinion held by the Quarterly Review.   It is dated, March
18th, 1736.   The first part is on the gloomy prospect that England will not be better governed: he then proceeds to speak of himself and of his private affairs as follows: " If I could have retired
from the world with quiet, decency and some degree of dignity
at home, I should have chosen it; but since that could not be,
and since nothing shall ever call me out of retreat again, but the
necessity of self defence, or such public confusion in my own
country as may set me on a level with every other man in acting
for her, one of which I believe, and the other of which I hope
will not happen, it is probable in the highest degree, that I shall
never return to look among you.   This, applied to my private
affairs, decides, you see, for selling my estate at Dawley as soon
as I can.   I do not desire, you know, to sell it at any extravagant rate; but I would not willingly undersell it very much to
one of those who may want to take advantage of the necessity
they may guess I am in of selling; nor easily yield to the contrariety of my fortune, that may render it hard for me, when it
would not be for any other man, to sell at a fair price."   The
construction, which will be most naturally put upon the words
" the necessity they may guess I am in of selling," is that the
writer was in some pecuniary straits, which would render a sale
of his property highly desirable, though not actually compulsory.
The concluding part of the sentence is somewhat enigmatical: it
may refer either to his uniform hard fate or ill fortune, or to some
recent and serious yet unexplained difficulty in which he is involved.
But a passage in a subsequent part of this letter shows, as we have
already remarked, that his absence was not compulsory, and was
little likely to have been forced on him by the fear of accusation
for traitorous manœuvres.   He had just before been speaking of
the ways in which he hoped to be able to dispose of his property,
and then adds: " If neither of these can be done this summer, I
shall feel a reasonable uneasiness, and be exposed to future inconveniences, that will disturb all the quiet of my life; for although I do not wish to live like Aristippus, I cannot live like
Diogenes.   In this case there will remain but one thing for me to
do, which I shall do, though very unwillingly, and that will be *to
go into England before the end of the summer*, set Dawley and

all I have there to sale, make the most of it, content myself with that, whatever it be, and return *free from cares of all kinds* to my foreign hermitage?" This, it must be admitted, is not the language of a man whose movements were governed by a knowledge, that the minister and the attorney-general had the power to molest him if he returned to England, or *à fortiori* before he left that country. In confirmation also of this view of ours we find that he actually revisited his native land, as he had promised to do, and for the purpose which he indicates in the letter above quoted. Dawley brought him twenty-six thousand pounds: a sum it has been alleged more than sufficient to release him from his difficulties.

Bolingbroke's feelings and opinions as well as his character, during his second exile, are delineated in his letters to Sir William Wyndham, published in Coxe's Appendix to the Life of Sir Robert Walpole, and which we have placed at the conclusion of the present memoir.

But he was far from suffering, even in solitude, his hours to glide away in torpid inactivity. That active restless disposition still continued to actuate his pursuits; and having lost the season for gaining power over his contemporaries, he was now resolved upon acquiring fame from posterity. He had not been long in his retreat at Chanteloup, when he began a course of letters on the study and use of history, for the use of a young nobleman, (Lord Cornbury.) In these he does not follow the methods of St. Real and others who have treated on this subject, and who make history the great fountain of all knowledge; he very wisely confines its benefits, and supposes them to consist in deducing general maxims from particular facts, more than in illustrating maxims by the application of historical passages. In mentioning ecclesiastical history, he gives his opinion very freely upon the subject of the divine original of the sacred books, which he supposes to have no such foundation. This new system of thinking, which he had always propagated in conversation, and which he now began to adopt in his more labored compositions, seemed no way supported either by his acuteness or his learning. He began to reflect seriously on these subjects too late in life, and to suppose those objections very new and unanswerable, which had been already confuted by thousands. "Lord Bolingbroke," says Pope, in one of his letters, "is above trifling; when he writes of any thing in this world, he is more than mortal. If ever he trifles, it must be when he turns divine." Very appropriate, also, is the remark in reference to this very work, in the "*Memoirs of the Life and Ministerial Conduct, &c., of Lord Viscount Bolingbroke,*" viz: " I should be sorry that you took your politics from priests; but I should be in more pain if I thought you in any danger of receiving your religion from a politician." Bolingbroke was not calculated by education, conduct, prior reading or study, and frame of mind, for treating so important a subject as the origin of the sacred writings. How greatly it is to be regretted that, in place of this immature and discreditable production, he did not give the world his projected history of Europe, from the year 1659, that of the peace of the Pyrenees, to 1713, that of the peace of Utrecht.

In the mean time, as it was evident, that a man of his active ambition, in choosing retirement when no longer able to lead in public, must be liable to ridicule in assuming a resigned philosophical air, he, in order to obviate this censure, addressed a letter to Lord Bathurst, upon the true use of retirement and study; in which he shows himself still able and willing to undertake the cause of his country, whenever its distresses should require his exertion. "I have," he says, "renounced neither my country, nor my friends; and by friends, I mean all those, and those alone, who are such to their country. In their prosperity, they shall never hear of me; in their distress, always. In that retreat wherein the remainder of my days shall be spent, I may be of some use to them, since even from thence I may advise, exhort, and warn them." Bent upon this pursuit only, and having now exchanged the gay statesman for the grave philosopher, he shone forth with distinguished lustre. His conversation took a different turn from what had been usual with him, and, as we are assured by Lord Orrery, who knew him, it united the wisdom of Socrates, the dignity and ease of Pliny, and the wit of Horace.

His mode of life in France, at this time, is described by Pope to be " divided between study and exercise; for he still reads or writes five or six hours a day, and hunts generally twice a week. He has the whole forest of Fontainebleau at his command, with the king's stables and dogs." " I never saw him in stronger health, or in better humor with his friends, or more indifferent and dispassionate as to his enemies." He had built a pavilion in a garden belonging to the abbey of Sêns, which retreat he represents in one of his letters to be the scene of all his literary labors at this time.

But it was Bolingbroke's fate never to pass a long period in the same kind of pursuit, nor to present himself long in the same guise before the world. By the death, in 1742, of his father, he Viscount St. John, at the advanced age of ninety, he was placed in possession of the family estate, which he was empowered by act of parliament to inherit. This event necessarily occasioned his return to England, and gave him such an accession of fortune as to enable him to remain, and to live in a manner conformable with his wishes and tastes. In the same year in which

Bolingbroke returned to England, Walpole ceased to be prime minister. We have already intimated the probable share which the former had in the downfall of his rival, and need not recur to the subject. But, although his revenge may have been gratified by this occurrence, he gained little personally. Time was hardly allowed to ascertain how far he would have been willing to accept, or his old associates in the opposition who were become the dominant party, to offer office to him, or additional title, before they lost their own popularity and influence by a mixed display of selfishness and timidity. Walpole was dead, and Pulteney soon became politically so, by allowing himself to be removed from the House of Commons to that of the Peers, with the title of the Earl of Bath. Of him Walpole used to say, that he feared his tongue more than another man's sword. But far different were the emotions of the ex-minister, now Earl of Oxford, when he first met his once formidable rival in the upper house; and truly might he say, as far as Pulteney was concerned: "My Lord of Bath, you and I are now the two most insignificant men in the kingdom." It was in reference to Pulteney, who, at the instance of Walpole was compelled to take out a patent for the earldom, which had been promised him at the formation of the new ministry, that the latter used the expression, of his having turned the key upon his rival; intimating thereby, that the door of the cabinet was never to be unlatched for him. The result verified the prediction, or rather was in harmony with the intention.

Bolingbroke now in possession of the old family seat at Battersea, resolved, according to some accounts of his life, to spend the remainder of his days in philosophical retirement. But, however sincere he may have been in such often announced resolutions, he had not yet reached the time when he could abstain from manifesting a lively interest, and taking, moreover, an active part in public questions, and political intrigues connected with them. In the summer of 1743 we find him writing from France, a visit to which country was said to be connected with some pecuniary difficulties at home. Pope seems ever to have had a poor opinion of the domestic economy and management of his noble friend, who, the poet said, would never be worth three thousand pounds.

In the letters from Argeville, the politician and the agriculturist, says Mr. Cooke, are strangely mingled. The notice of the battle of Dettingen, and some dark observations upon a political intrigue which we are now unable to explain, are directly succeeded by an earnest request for a consignment of a quantity of acorns, and for the necessary instructions as to their culture. The evacuation of Germany, and the designs of the Queen of Hungary, are discussed in almost the same sentence with the excellences of the red Virginia oak. After a visit to Aix la

Chapelle, for the relief of the rheumatism, he returned to England. In the summer of the following year he again visited France, where he had still kept up an establishment. This was now broken up, and he took a final leave of the country in which so large a portion of his life had been spent.

His first production after his settlement at Battersea, written with political views and for political effect, was the "Idea of a Patriot King." It was composed ostensibly for the instruction of Frederick, Prince of Wales, heir apparent of George II, but who was fated never to reach the throne. It is not probable that, if he had lived, he would have conferred either credit upon his political teacher, or lustre on his reign. He was weak, vicious and false. According to Lord Brougham, (*Edin. Rev.*), Bolingbroke's "Idea of a Patriot King," certainly differed from his idea of a patriot subject. The duty of the former, according to the author, required a constant sacrifice of his own interests to the good of his country, the duty of the latter he considered to be a constant sacrifice of his country to himself. The one was bound on no account ever to regard either his feelings or his tastes, the interests of his family or the powers of his station; the other was justified in regarding his own gratification, whether of caprice or revenge, or ambition, as the only object of his life. Between the ruler and his subjects there was in this view no kind of reciprocity; for all the life of real sacrifice spent by the one was to be repaid by a life of undisturbed and undisguised self-seeking in the other." The remainder of the critique is in the same spirit.

It would appear, from the biographers of Bolingbroke, as if after the year 1744, when he quitted France for ever, that he really practised the secluded life which he had so often affected. His advanced age, and increasing infirmities, his disappointment at the turn of his own fortunes, and loss of confidence in the integrity, if he ever gave them credit for it, and at any rate in the ability of his political associates and coadjutors, to purify the corruption in government, and renovate the decayed state, might all be supposed adequate causes for his seclusion and determined abstinence from interfering any more in public life. But from the temperament of the man, and the very constitution of his mind, he was ever impelled to continue his former courses as a political manager—advising and exhorting where he could no longer lead, and aiding to pull down, though without the power of rebuilding after his own fashion, and according to his own views and theory. He was still, as is shown by the Marchmont Papers, "busy and deep in all the intrigues of that most intriguing period,"—the six or seven years preceding his death. On the 6th of November, 1744, we find him "conferring with Mr. Pitt for maintaining and extending a coalition of parties, and stating

to Lord Marchmont, that he found Mr. Pitt so haughty and impracticable that he was obliged to remind him, that as to the
existing coalition, 'neither Lord Chesterfield nor Mr. Pitt had
formed it, but *he* (Bolingbroke) himself.'"—*Marchmont Papers*,
I, 72. Nor was it in domestic intrigues alone that he busied
himself. " Dec. 25th, 1744—Lord Bolingbroke told me (Marchmont) that Lord Chesterfield had been with him this morning,
and had talked to him of our situation as to foreign affairs, and
that he wanted to see me about them."—*Ibid.* 93.

" Again, in February, 1746, (and indeed *passim*,) we find
Bolingbroke very busy about the short-lived Barteret ministry,
(*Ibid.* 173,) and we have in the same work an important letter
from him so late as July, 1746,—(to a passage of which we have
already referred for another purpose)—in which he says: ' I did
not leave England in 1735, till some schemes, which were then
in the loom—though they never came to effect—made me one
too many even to my most intimate friends; and *I have not left
off, since I came to resettle here,* advising and extending, till
long after you saw it was to no purpose.'"—*Marchmont Papers*,
II, 356.

" And though of course a man of seventy would every year
rapidly lose some of his vivacity and eagerness in public affairs,
we have letters of his down to the eve of his decease, which
prove that he still took a lively interest in the business of the
political world."—*Quart. Rev.*, No. cviii.

The peace of Aix la Chapelle, in 1748, was made an occasion
by Bolingbroke for his resuming his pen, and giving to the public, in the following year, his last work, "*Some Reflections upon
the Present State of the Nation, principally with regard to
her Taxes and her Debts, and on the Causes and Consequences
of them.*" The subject so ably discussed in this treatise has lost
none of its interest since that time, indeed must be regarded as
of increased importance, even though we might not estimate it
in the ratio of the increase of the main topic—the national debt.
The language which the author held at that time was certainly
not prophetic, although both the political economist and the
patriot may wish that the warning it conveyed had been since
attended to; as where he says: " Nothing but the speedy diminution of our national debts, can secure us effectually against con-
tingent effects, that may be of fatal consequence. Upon this the
future prosperity and safety of this country depend." This work,
however, was never finished. Its completion, at first interrupted
by the death of Lady Bolingbroke, was prevented subsequently
by the increasing infirmities, and the painful malady which terminated the life of the author himself.

In February, 1750, Bolingbroke writes from London, to his

friend Lord Marchmont, "It is true that I have been these two
months in the town, much out of order myself, and yet not on
my own account, but on that of a poor woman, who is come, I
think, to die here. It is impossible to describe the torment she
has endured these many months, and the weakness to which she
is reduced by a slow but almost continual fever at this time. A
man who thinks and feels as I do, can find no satisfaction in the
present scene; and I am about to lose one who has been the
comfort of my life, in all the melancholy scenes of it, just at a
time when the present is most likely to continue and to grow
daily worse."

In the following month he writes to the same correspondent:
"You are very good to take any share in this affliction, which
has lain upon me so long, and which still continues, with the fear
of being increased by a catastrophe I am little able to bear.

"Resignation, my lord, is a principal duty in my system of
religion. Reason shows that it ought to be willing, if not cheerful, but there are passions and habitudes in human nature which
reason cannot entirely subdue. I should be even ashamed not
to feel them in the present case, though I am resigned to the
condition of humanity and the usual course of things.

"I shall never retire so as to deny myself to my friends, however useless they may be to me, and I much more so to them.
But there are few whom I esteem such, and I have been long
saying to myself what I told you once old Victor said to me,
'Je deviens tous les ans de plus en plus isolé dans ce monde.'
From your lordship I hope I never shall be separated: by my
affection I never shall.

"You will forgive me, my lord, if I make use of another hand,
rather than to defer my answer to you: a strong affection which
rheumatic pains have left on the nerves deprives me often of the
power to exert it in writing."

This, except a letter of mere compliment dictated upon the
birth of an heir to the Earl of Marchmont, is the last letter, according to Mr. Cooke, we have of Bolingbroke's. It would be
manifest injustice to the subject of this memoir, if, in giving a
slight sketch, from his biographer, of the wife of Bolingbroke,
who died on the 18th March, 1750, we were to omit to mention
that, on the testimony of all his friends, his tenderness and affection to her were exemplary. Among the illustrious persons who
sought the society of her husband, she was equally celebrated for
her conversational talents, and the ease and elegance of her manners. No violence of temper embittered their union. Lady Bolingbroke was as amiable as she was graceful, and the husband
found those failings treated as subjects of repartee by her which
he had before heard urged in a tone of angry reproach. Many
specimens are recorded of her vivacity; and although she never

acquired sufficient skill in the English language to speak it habitually, yet she perfectly understood it when spoken by others.
Her remarks were generally in French; but their justice and
smartness when called forth by the peculiarities of her husband's
friends, caused them to be frequently repeated or translated.

Lady Bolingbroke was buried in the family vault of the St.
Johns, in Battersea church, where the following inscription, written by her husband, may yet be seen.

In this vault
Are interred the Remains of
MARY CLARA DES CHAMPS DE MARSILLY;
Marchioness of Villette and Viscountess of Bolingbroke.
Born of a noble family,
Bred in the Court of Louis XIV,
She reflected a lustre on the former
By the superior accomplishments of her mind:
She was an ornament to the latter
By the amiable dignity and grace of her behaviour.
She lived
The honor of her own sex,
The delight and admiration of ours.
She died
An object of imitation to both,
With all the firmness that Reason,
With all the resignation that Religion
Can inspire.

In addition to the solitariness and privation caused by the
death of his wife, this event subjected him to vexatious annoy-
ances, involving questions relating both to her property and character. Her nearest kindred in France commenced a suit in the
French court for the recovery of the property she had possessed,
as a widow, under the plea that no marriage had taken place
between her and Bolingbroke. The result of the first trial was
unfavorable to him; but ultimately, through the exertions of his
friend and the friend of his wife, the Marquis de Martignon, an
appeal made to the parliament of Paris resulted in a reversal of
the former sentence, and a restoration of the money which had
been seized in consequence of it by Montmorier, the original
claimant. This last event did not occur till after Bolingbroke's
death; and it was not, therefore, reserved for him to see the fair
fame of his lady, which had been aspersed by the first suit, vindicated to the satisfaction of their common friends and the world
at large.

His own mortal career was now drawing to a close; the evening of his life was reached, and not without much pain and suffering was it allowed to terminate in the night of death. Visitors distinguished by their rank, or by their genius, their learning and taste, still resorted to Battersea, eager to continue the acquaintance or to hear the eloquent discourses on men and things of its noble owner. Among these, Frederick, Prince of Wales, is mentioned, as having often sought and obtained advice from Bolingbroke, to whom he was said to be strongly attached, if indeed he were capable of any such feeling, and on whom it has been alleged he would have conferred the office of prime minister in the event of his own accession to the throne. This intercourse led to an intimacy with Mallet, the under secretary of the prince; a person who, by blind obedience and unsparing flattery to Bolingbroke, succeeded in becoming legatee of the works of the distinguished statesman and author.

Lord Chesterfield had long been on terms of intimacy and confidence with the aged and suffering invalid, and from his letters we can glean some particulars respecting the fatal disease and last days of the latter. He had been for several months laboring under a cruel, and to appearance, an incurable disorder —a cancer in his face, which was making daily progress; and the empirical treatment to which he submitted on the occasion, not only hastened his end, but also exposed him to the most excruciating tortures. Lord Chesterfield saw him for the last time before his tortures began. Though the unhappy patient, as well as his friend, expected then that he would recover, and accordingly desired him not to come again till his cure was completed, yet still he took leave of him in a manner which showed how much he was affected. He embraced the earl with tenderness, and said, " God, who placed me here, will do what he pleases with me hereafter, and he knows best what to do. May he bless you."

In one of the earl's letters to a lady in Paris, he says: " I frequently see our friend Bolingbroke, but I see him with great concern. A humor he has long had in his cheek proves to be cancerous, and has made an alarming progress of late. Hitherto it is not attended with pain, which is all he wishes, for as to the rest he is resigned. Truly, a mind like his, so far superior to the generality, would have well deserved that nature should have made an effort in his favor as to the body, and given him an uncommon share of health and duration."

The last scene is thus lamented, in a letter to the same lady: "Are you not greatly shocked, but I am sure you are, at the dreadful death of our friend Bolingbroke? The remedy has hastened his death, against which there was no remedy; for his cancer was not topical, but universal, and had so infected the whole mass of his blood, as to be incurable. What I most lament is, that the medicines put him to exquisite pain; an evil I dread much more than death, both for my friends and myself. I lose a warm, an amiable and instructive friend. I saw him a fortnight before his death, when he depended upon a cure, and so did I; and he desired I would not come any more till he was quite well, which he expected he would be in ten or twelve days. The next day the great pains came on, and never left him till within two days of his death, during which he was insensible. What a man! what eloquence! His passions, which were strong, were injurious to the delicacy of his sentiments; they were apt to be confounded together, and often wilfully. The world will do him more justice now than in his lifetime."

Lord Bolingbroke died on the 15th of December, 1751, in the seventy-fourth year of his age. As already intimated, his death was hastened by the violent applications of a boastful quack, to whose treatment he had submitted himself. It is somewhat singular, that his great rival or rather enemy, Walpole, was killed by a pretender of the same description. May we, not uncharitably, suppose, that as both of these distinguished men have been accustomed to see, if not practice, (to a great extent,) political quackery, they thought they might have recourse to medical with equal impunity, if not success; but they so far overlooked the difference in the two cases; that, whereas in the first, they were the dispensers; in the latter, they consented to be the takers of nostrums.

In another respect, Bolingbroke was consonant with himself to the last, and those principles which he had all along avowed, he confirmed with his dying breath, having given orders that none of the clergy should be permitted to visit him in his latest moments.

His body was interred in Battersea church, with those of his ancestors; and a marble monument erected to his memory, with the following excellent inscription, written by himself, and the original of which is still extant, in the British Museum.

Here lies
HENRY ST. JOHN,
In the Reign of Queen Anne
Secretary of War, Secretary of State, and
Viscount Bolingbroke.
In the Days of King George I, and King George II,
Something more and better.
His attachment to Queen Anne,
Exposed him to a long and severe Persecution;
He bore it with Firmness of Mind.

He passed the latter Part of his Time at home,
The enemy of no national Party;
The Friend of no Faction.
Distinguished under the Cloud of Proscription,
Which had not been entirely taken off,
By Zeal to maintain the Liberty,
And to restore the ancient Prosperity
Of Great Britain.

In this manner lived and died Lord Bolingbroke; ever active, never depressed, ever pursuing fortune, and as constantly disappointed by her. In whatever light we view his character, we shall find him an object rather more proper for our wonder, than our imitation; more to be feared than esteemed, and gaining our admiration without our love. His ambition ever aimed at the summit of power, and nothing seemed capable of satisfying his immoderate desires, but the liberty of governing all things without a rival. With as much ambition, as great abilities, and more acquired knowledge than Cæsar, he wanted only his courage to be as successful: but the schemes his head dictated, his heart often refused to execute; and he lost the ability to perform, just when the great occasion called for all his efforts to engage.

The same ambition that prompted him to be a politician, actuated him as a philosopher. His aims were equally great and extensive in both capacities: unwilling to submit to any rival in the one, or any authority in the other, he entered the fields of science, with a thorough contempt of all that had been established before him, and seemed willing to think every thing wrong, that he might show the force of his genius in the reformation. It might have been better for his quiet, as a man, if he had been content to act as a subordinate character in the state; and it had certainly been better for his memory as a writer, if he had aimed at doing less than he attempted. Wisdom, in morals, like every other art or science, is an accumulation which numbers have contributed to increase; and it is not for one single man to pretend, that he can add more to the heap than the thousands that have gone before him. Such innovations more frequently retard than promote knowledge; their maxims are more agreeable to the reader, by having the gloss of novelty to recommend them, than those which are trite, only because they are true. Such men are, therefore, followed at first with avidity, nor is it till after some time that their disciples begin to find their error. They often, though too late, perceive that they have been following a speculative inquiry, while they have been leaving a practical good; and while they have been practising the arts of doubting, they have been losing all firmness of principle which might tend to estab-

lish the rectitude of their private conduct. As a moralist, therefore, Lord Bolingbroke, by having endeavored at too much,
seems to have done nothing: but as a political writer, few can
equal, and none can exceed him. As he was a practical politician, his writings are less filled with those speculative illusions
which are the result of solitude and seclusion. He wrote them
with a certainty of their being opposed, sifted, examined, and
reviled; he therefore took care to build them up of such materials as could not be easily overthrown: they prevailed at the
times in which they were written; they still continue to the admiration of the present age, and will probably last forever.

Some additional sketches of his conduct as a statesman, of his
intimacies with men of letters and genius, and of his personal character, will now come in, not unaptly, in completion of the entire
picture of Bolingbroke. Passages of his public life have been
already introduced in this narrative, and some of them explained
and criticised in a manner not at all complimentary to his fame.
But whilst truth requires an exhibition of this nature, let us not,
at the same time, omit to mention, that although Bolingbroke,
then Mr. St. John, participated in the advantages to his party
from the intrigues and treachery of Harley, by which Godolphin
and Marlborough, the whig leaders, lost their influence at court,
we have no direct evidence of his active participation in these
measures. When secretary of war, he supplied the great duke
with abundant succors abroad, and defended his conduct at
home. It was, as we already stated in a preceding page, during
the administration of St. John, that the duke achieved some of
his most glorious exploits. The former introduced and carried
through the commons the bill which conferred Woodstock upon
the duke, and perpetuated it in his family. Nor did St. John,
when his associate, Harley, was dismissed from office, attempt,
which he might readily have done, with the base political morality of the day, any compromise with the whigs, through their
true leader, Marlborough; but he immediately resigned, and took
his place with his tory friends in the opposition. In the intrigues
which were carried on after his secession from office, he is not,
as far as we know, accused of taking any part; and, indeed, his
whole conduct in parliament during the period which intervened
between his retirement and the dissolution, was marked by a
moderation which was quite unexpected by his late colleagues.

The period that followed the dissolution of this parliament,
and in which he was left out of the house of commons, was
spent by the ex-secretary in study and preparation for a brilliant
exhibition of intellectual power, when he should again be called
on to act a responsible part in public life. The intrigues of Harley were fast preparing for such a result, and, ere long, St. John

was induced to take office, as secretary of state, with and under
his former associate. If, on a former occasion, he effectually
and zealously supported the war, or at least the great duke in
his conduct of it, he now, in conjnnction with his colleagues in
the ministry, displayed an equal ardor in procuring a peace.
Happy would it have been for his reputation if the steps which
he took to bring about' so desirable a consummation, had not,
also, been marked by treachery to former and still admitted
allies, and practices of treasonable tendency against the constitu-
tutional laws of his native country. On these we have already
animadverted, and shall not again dwell; except just to suggest
one excuse for the conduct both of Bolingbroke and Oxford, in
their secret measures to bring in the Pretender, which, although
it does not abate the enormity of the wrong intended to the nation, will, if admitted, go far to free them from treachery to the
queen, their sovereign. It is the strong probability that their
correspondence with the French court, and messages to the Pretender, were with the connivance and implied concert of Anne
herself, who, if her feelings alone could have determined the
question, would have preferred her brother for her successor,
to the Princess Sophia of Hanover, or the elector George, son of
the latter, who afterwards ascended the throne, as the first
sovereign which England had of the house of Brunswick.

Among the means taken by Bolingbroke, whilst he was negotiating with signal ability abroad, and eloquently expounding
and defending his party in the house of commons at home, was
to enlist a portion of the periodical press in his favor. The chief
paper employed for this purpose was the Examiner, to which
he was himself a frequent contributor, and to the other writers,
in which he commonly furnished the information and arguments
required for them to work on. He was himself not nice in the
terms he used when speaking of his political adversaries; as, for
instance, in a letter to the Examiner, in reference to the Duchess
of Marlborough's attempt to prevent the queen from forming
the new (tory) ministry, he speaks of " subjection to the will of
an arbitrary junto, and to the caprice of an insolent woman;"
adding, " Unhappy nation! which expecting to be governed by
the best, fell under the tyranny of the worst of her sex. But
now, thanks be to God, that fury who broke loose to execute
the vengeance of heaven on a sinful people, is restrained, and
the royal hand is reached out to chain up the plague." Yet was
Bolingbroke little inclined to allow any undue license to the
writers in the opposition. In a letter to the Earl of Stafford,
July 23d, 1712, this passage occurs: " It is a melancholy consideration, that the laws of the country are too weak to punish
effectually these factious scribblers, who presume to blacken the

brightest characters, and to give even scurrilous language to those who are in the first degrees of honor. This, my lord, among others, is a symptom of the decayed condition of our government, and serves to show how fatally we mistake licentiousness for liberty. All I could do was to take up Hurt, the printer, to send him to Newgate, and to bind him over upon bail to be prosecuted; this I have done: and if I can arrive at legal proof against the author, Ridpath, (editor of the Flying Post,) he shall have the same treatment."

In a letter to the queen, written about this time, he informs her majesty that he had discovered the author of another scandalous libel; and adds, " he will make the thirteenth I have seized, and the fifteenth I have found out." One of these libellers was Dr. Hare, Canon Residentiary of St. Paul's and afterwards bishop of Chichester, whom he frequently calls the Duke of Marlborough's " stupid chaplain." On the 23d of October, fourteen booksellers, printers, or publishers, whom Mr. St. John had apprehended, appeared at the bar of the Court of the Queen's Bench, for sundry libels, but, at the request of the attorney-general, they were dismissed on their recognizances till the last day of term. Bolingbroke was grievously offended at these libellers, who, if they had written for his own party, would have been called its literary supporters. Were the writings on both sides now before the public, it would probably be found, that, although the suppressive arm of power was on one side, the "scurrilous language" was pretty equally divided. So much easier is it to recommend than to practise philosophical forbearance; an ease manifested in the conduct of those, too, who, like a Bolingbroke, a Frederick of Prussia, and a Voltaire, were most eloquent against intolerance of all kinds, and apparently most intent in favor of freedom of opinion. With the secretary were associated, as writers in the Examiner, his political and personal friends, Swift, Prior, and Atterbury. Opposed to them, and advocates and expounders of the whig cause, we find recorded the names of a Walpole, an Addison, and a Steele, whose contributions appeared in the *Whig Examiner* and the *Censor*. So great was the effect produced by the letter of St. John in the Examiner, a passage from which we have already quoted, that Somers, Earl Cowper, who still held the seals, thought it necessary to answer it in the *Tatler*, a sure proof this of the extensive influence which periodical writing on politics must have acquired over the minds of the English public at that time. The susceptibility to be impressed by this means is still retained, and is every now and then acted on with powerful results.

The only public measure which St. John originated and directly superintended, was the expedition against Quebec. His anxiety for the success of this favorite measure of his, is evident in his correspondence at the time. In a letter' to Mr. Drummond, he writes:—" I am glad to find that, whatever guesses curious people may make, there yet appears no more light into the secret of Mr. Hill's expedition. As that whole design was formed by me, and the management of it singly carried on by me, you will easily imagine that I have a sort of paternal concern for the success of it." The armament consisted of a strong squadron of ships under Sir Hivenden Walker; and a troop of 5000 men, commanded by Brigadier Hill, the brother of Mrs. Masham. By a series of disasters, some depending on the elements, some on the mismanagement of the leaders, this expedition ended in disaster and disgrace. Its fate is said to have quickened the determination of the ministry to agree with the French court on the preliminaries of peace.

From the large share which Bolingbroke had in bringing about the peace of Utrecht, and his known and admitted influence in the cabinet at this time, much of the responsibility of the character and results of that important measure must necessarily rest on him. With all his reading and philosophy, and his knowledge of the natural rights, and of the laws of nations, he does not seem to have raised himself, in the least, above the level of the cold, calculating and heartless diplomacy of the most ordinary and selfish minds of his age. He exerted himself to secure for England the profit and the eternal infamy of the *Assiento* treaty, by a stipulation in which a company, chartered by the English government, should enjoy the exclusive privilege of importing every year, for thirty years, four thousand eight hundred slaves, into the West Indies from Africa, on the condition, that a moderate fixed duty upon each slave should be paid to the Spanish government. The queen had insisted on the Assiento contract, with a view in part of augmenting her own funds, by reserving one quarter of the proceeds of this trade to herself.

If the Assiento contract shows Bolingbroke to have been deficient in high and practical philanthropy, the conduct of the English government, through his agency, to the Catalans, is evidence of his disregard, both of the principles of public justice and of liberty. The people of Catalonia had been instigated and encouraged by the English government, to take sides with the Archduke in his attempts to gain the Spanish crown, and at the same time to assert their prescriptive and long established privileges, in opposition to Philip V. But, notwithstanding all this, they were abandoned by the treaty of Utrecht, without a single word, or still more a pledge being stipulated in their favor. Worse than this again, Bolingbroke threatened to employ English ships against them. In his private letters, he treats this

people as rebels to their lawful sovereign; and in his public
despatches, he urges the king of Spain, to hasten the conclusion
of peace with Portugal, that he might be enabled more speedily
to chastise and reduce to obedience the Catalans.

Bolingbroke, with an exception soon to be noticed, was more
fortunate in his literary, than in his political connections. The
reader will have learned already the confidential intercourse between him and Swift and Pope; in his letters and correspondence
with whom, much may be gleaned relating to his chequered fortunes, as well as his opinions and tastes. The views of this triumvirate in political affairs were nearly the same, and their aims
were, probably, not far different. Bolingbroke wanted power,
and Swift promotion; Pope's wishes are less obvious. He so
frequently professes contentment with his situation, and contempt
for all that the world can bestow, that we are under the necessity of believing him to have been an associate of the others from
friendship, and from a dislike of whom and of what they disliked. His religion stood in the way of secret favor, and he was
surely unreasonable, if with an income of 800 pounds, he did not
think himself " passing rich." Nothing, however, is more evident, than the lofty opinion these correspondents had of each other,
and the consciousness, not unfrequently repeated, that they were
enabled to look down upon the pitiful concerns of this world,
with the wisdom and indifference of superior beings.

Of these two associates, Swift was the oldest, and in many
respects the ablest. Bolingbroke's first interview with him appears to have taken place on November 11th, 1710, when he
invited Swift to dine with him; but the latter appears to have
formed no very high opinion of his new acquaintance at this
time, and expresses his surprise, that the office of Secretary of
State should be filled by a young fellow hardly thirty. He complains too of having been treated with the cant of the court.

Their intimacy, however, increased rapidly, and in their inter-
change of sentiments we find the same opinion, reciprocally, of
their sufferings and unmerited neglect, and the same affected
philosophy in despising the objects of their ambition. Bolingbroke appears, indeed, to have captivated Swift, who was, in an
uncommon degree, hard to be pleased. In one of the Exami-
ners, dated February 1st, 1711, not three months after their first
interview, the young statesman was characterised by his new
friend, as one " who from youth applying those admirable talents
of nature, and improvements of art, to public business, grew
eminent in court and parliament, at an age when the generality
of mankind is employed in trifles and folly. It is to be lamented,
that he has not yet procured himself a busy, important counte-

nance, nor learned that profound part of wisdom, to be difficult of access. Besides, he has clearly mistaken the true use of books, which he has thumbed and spoiled with reading, when he ought to have multiplied them on his shelves, not like a great man of my acquaintance, who knew a book by the back, better than a friend by the face, although he had never conversed with the former, and often with the latter."

But as this character was written for the public, and in a paper in which Bolingbroke was concerned, the reader may, perhaps, derive more satisfactory proof of Swift's esteem from what he says in one of his confidential communications. In the Journal to Stella, November 1711, he gives the following pleasing and animated character: "I think Mr. St. John the greatest young man I ever knew: wit, capacity, beauty, quickness of apprehension, good learning, and an excellent taste; the best orator in the House of Commons, admirable conversation, good nature, and good manners; generous, and a despiser of money. His only fault is, talking to his friends in way of complaint of too great a load of business, which looks a little like affectation; and he endeavors too much to mix the fine gentleman and man of pleasure with the man of business. What truth and sincerity he may have, I know not. He is now but thirty-two, and has been secretary above a year."

That Swift did not afterwards discover any deficiency of truth and sincerity in Bolingbroke's character, may perhaps be inferred from their intimacy continuing during the whole of his life. Bolingbroke, when in exile, carried on a correspondence with him, and assured him, that among all the losses which he had sustained, none affected him more sensibly than that of Swift's company and conversation. At this time (1711) he wishes to represent himself and his correspondent, as "two men who are out of the world, and who do not care a farthing to return to it again!" But the best evidence of Swift's continued high esteem for Bolingbroke, is found in the more elaborately drawn character of the latter, which was introduced in an earlier part of this memoir, and which originally appeared in Swift's celebrated pamphlet, "An Inquiry into the Behavior of the Queen's last Ministry." The writer could not be supposed to be biassed by any consideration of present, or even future dependency on, or favor from the subject of his description, who was then in exile, under the most adverse circumstances for his fame and recovery of power; at the same time, it will have been seen, that in this character, Swift's friendship did not sway him, so as to cause concealment of the objectionable part of Bolingbroke's conduct, and the representation he has given is, probably, on that account, more to be depended on, than the looser assertions of the friends of the Walpole party, who seem inclined to deprive him of every thing valuable in genius and morals.

In the correspondence of Bolingbroke, Swift and Pope, it must be acknowledged, there is an appearance of affectation, which has brought a general suspicion on their sincerity, and an overvaluing of their consequence, that will certainly not now be allowed; although a similar feeling of importance of self and friends, is continually witnessed in those who associate much together in a club or society, for the discussion of literature or science, of the arts or political economy.   With respect to friendship and sincerity, Bolingbroke has some remarks deserving of consideration, in a letter to Swift, dated March, 1719; "The truest reflection, and, at the same time, the bitterest satire, which can be made on the present age, is this: that to think as you think, will make a man pass for romantic.   Sincerity, constancy, and tenderness, are rarely to be found.   They are so much out of use, that the man of mode imagines them to be out of nature. We meet with few friends; the greatest part of those who pass for such, are, properly speaking, nothing more than acquaintance: and no wonder, since Tully's maxim is certainly true, that friendship can subsist *non nisi inter bonos*.   At that age of life, when there is balm in the blood, and that confidence in the mind which the innocency of our own heart inspires, the experience of other men's destroys, I was apt to confound my acquaintance and my friends together," &c.

In all this, we have the sentiments of a man of experience, and of more moral feeling than we should have expected from one, whom it has been the fashion to represent as uniformly profligate, and whom we know to have studied himself, after his fashion, into infidelity.   Yet in these sentiments, it would be hard to suppose him insincere.   He doubtless felt what he expressed at the moment; but he ought to have reflected, that he brought upon himself some of those sufferings which are out of the common occurrences of life.   The unfaithful friends to whom he alludes were political friends, who had embraced the safer side, while he was an exile, useless and abandoned by his country.

To this favorite subject of friendship, he again recurs in a letter written in 1721, assuring his correspondent, that there is more pleasure and more merit too, in cultivating friendship than in taking care of the state.   Fools and knaves are generally best fitted for the last; and none but men of sense and virtue are capable of the other.   Several years after this (1727), when at Dawley, he exclaims, "would to God my whole life could be divided in the same manner, two-thirds to friendship, one-third to myself, and not a moment to the world."   And yet, nearly

the whole of his life, from this period, to the end of Sir Robert
Walpole's administration, was a struggle to subvert the measures
of that minister.

Pope appears to have been introduced to Bolingbroke by Swift,
before his lordship was compelled to fly from impeachment. He
was ten years younger than Bolingbroke, and, it is well known,
looked up to him as to a preceptor—his "guide, philosopher
and friend." Their friendship was soon cemented by an intimate
correspondence, when Bolingbroke was abroad, and was renewed by mutual and frequent visits to Twickenham and Dawley. The coincidence, however, between their political principles, was sometimes apparently interrupted by Pope's more impartial regard and candid praise of some individuals of the opposite party. In particular he is said to have greatly offended
Bolingbroke by his high encomium on Lord Oxford, in the epistle
to that nobleman. But Swift had done the same justice to Oxford on many occasions, and, what is very singular, maintained
an equal intimacy with both, which we do not find that Bolingbroke resented, although he sometimes mentioned Oxford to
Swift with the usual contempt which he never could conceal.
In this, Swift acted with a consistency and manliness, which
must, if any thing could, have made him beloved by both. He
thought, we may infer, much higher of the morals and integrity
of Oxford, than he did of those of his antagonist; yet in their
mutual bickerings, he often blames Oxford, and entirely acquits
Bolingbroke. In his first letter to Bolingbroke, after the queen's
death, dated August 7, 1714, he says, " I will swear for no man's
sincerity, much less that of a minister of state: but thus much I
have said, whenever it was proper, that your lordship's proposals
were always the fairest in the world, and I faithfully delivered
them as I was empowered," &c.

Pope's obligations to Bolingbroke for the principles of his
unrivalled ethical poem, the *Essay on Man*, are freely acknowledged by the author; but of the extent to which he availed
himself of the philosophical precepts of the latter in the composition of this work, there is great difference of opinion. The truth
of the case is probably most nearly reached by Johnson, when,
as he tersely expresses it in his life of the poet, " The Essay
plainly appears the fabric of a poet; what Bolingbroke supplied
could be only the first principles; the order, illustration and embellishments, must be all Pope's." By some, it has been said
that Pope gave the obnoxious philosophy, which he received
from his friend, such a turn and coloring in his poem as to make
it a real vindication of the ways of Providence to man. Others,
again, having had their mental vision quickened, and the subject
placed before them in a different light, by the criticism of Crousaz,

who exposed the tendency of many passages in it to natural as contrasted with if not in opposition to revealed religion, were not slow in accusing Bolingbroke of having deceived Pope. The imputation of the want of candor cast on the former can only adhere by imputing a want of knowledge to the latter, and that the poet was so poor a metaphysician as to be unacquainted with the full scope and tendency of doctrines which were handed over to him, in order that they might receive, at his hands, their poetical garb and a lustre of exhibition to which they were not entitled. It is not probable either that Pope had not philosophical acumen enough to enable him to see the bearing of a few ethical maxims and abstract ideological propositions, or that he was not suspicious of the want of adaptation of his noble friend's philosophy to the requirements of good morals and the wants of taste purified by religion. Critics and essayists, in their eagerness to condemn Bolingbroke for his share in this literary undertaking, have not, we fear, paid attention to the exposition of the subject, as narrated by himself in a letter to his friend Swift: " Does Pope talk to you of the noble work which, at my instigation, he has begun in such a manner, that he must be convinced by this time, I judged better of his talents than he did? The first Epistle, which considers man relatively to the whole system of universal being: the second, which considers him in his own habitation, in himself: and the third, which shows how a universal cause works to oue end, but works by various laws; how man and beast, and vegetable, are linked in a mutal dependency, parts necessary to each other, and necessary to the whole; how human societies were formed; from what springs true religion and true policy are derived; how God has made our greater interests and our plainest duty indivisibly the same: these three epistles are finished. The fourth he is now intent upon. It is a noble subject; he pleads the cause of God, I use Seneca's expression, against that famous charge which atheists in all ages have brought—the supposed unequal dispensations of Providence, a charge which I cannot heartily forgive you divines for admitting. You admit it indeed for an extreme good purpose, and you build on this admission the necessity of a future state of rewards and punishments; but if you should find that this future state will not account for God's justice in the present state, which you give up, in opposition to the atheist, would it not have been better to defend God's justice in this world, against these daring men, by irrefragable reasons, and to have rested the other point on revelation? I do not like concessions made against demonstration, repair or supply them how you will. The Epistles I have mentioned will compose a first book; the plan of the second is settled. You will not understand, by what I have said, that Pope will go so deep into the argument, or carry it so far, as I have hinted." If the above sketch be taken as evidence, it will not be easy to convict Bolingbroke of passing off counterfeit philosophy on Pope: nor can we find cause for censure, still less for lavish abuse of ethics, a part of which teaches us, " how God has made our greatest interests and our plainest duty indivisibly the same." On a review of the subject, and taking the *animus* or intention of Bolingbroke, as conveyed in the preceding letter, in connection with the impression really and commonly produced on the mind of the well intentioned and unprejudiced reader, as set forth by Johnson on this point, when he says: " So little was any evil tendency discovered, that, as innocence is unsuspicious, many read it [the poem] for a manual of piety," we shall have small cause of thanks for the pene-trative perception of Crousaz, in detecting hidden evils, or for the ingenious pleadings of Warburton, to show, that the poet was innocent, and really meant, not that which he did say, but that which his advocate afterwards said for him.

Better service, in the opinion of some critics, was rendered by Bolingbroke to Pope, whose genius he certainly estimated very accurately, when he suggested the imitation of the First Satire of the Second Book of Horace. In the opening lines of the imitation of the First Epistle of Horace, there occurs the well known apostrophe —

> "St. John, whose love indulged my labor past,
> Matures my present and shall bound my last!"

expressive of the obligations that he felt himself to be under to Bolingbroke, whom he invokes also in the beginning of the *Essay on Man*, in a strain of friendly expostulation and re-gard.

> " Awake, my St. John! leave all meaner things
> To low ambition and the pride of kings."

Their sentiments for each other have all the appearance, all the warm and affectionate expressions of the tenderest and most lasting friendship. Pope, in one of his letters to Richardson the artist, who had painted Bolingbroke, avers, " that posterity will, through the means of that portrait, see the man whom it will for ages honor, vindicate and applaud, when envy is no more, and when (as I have already said in the essay to which you are so partial),

> "The sons shall blush their fathers were his foes."

To Aaron Hill he says, with still more fervency: " My Lord Bo-lingbroke is yet with me; more properly, I yet belong to him, body as well as mind, for my mind is every where his." It would be difficult to believe, if our evidence of the fact were not so full and clear, that such reciprocal professions could end in the bitterness of resentment, and that at a time when resentment, even among vulgar minds, is accounted unnatural; when Bolingbroke had just wiped away the tears he shed over his dying friend, and when Pope could no longer answer for himself. Does not this remind us of Bolingbroke's quotation, that friendship exists *non nisi inter bonos. (Additions to the life of Lord Bolingbroke.)* The cause of offence, as known to many of our readers, was in Pope having had printed secretly, and without the remotest knowledge of the fact by its author, an edition of " *The Patriot King,*" of fifteen hundred copies, in addition to a few impressions, which last were all that he was requested and authorised to have struck off, for distribution among the friends of Bolingbroke, and by his directions. This suspicious act of Pope's was only revealed after his death, by the printer whom he had employed, and who brought and resigned to Bolingbroke, as to the right owner, the entire edition of his work. The latter, with great indignation, made a fire in the yard, and delivered the whole to the flames. " Hitherto," says Johnson, " nothing had been done which was not naturally dictated by resentment of violated faith—resentment more acrimonious, as the violator had been more loved or more trusted. But here the anger might have stopped—the injury was private, and there was little danger from the example."

Bolingbroke, however, was not yet satisfied; his thirst of vengeance incited him to blast the memory of the man over whom he had wept in his last struggles; and he employed Mallett, another friend of Pope's, to tell the tale to the public, with all its aggravations. Warburton, whose heart was warm with his legacy, interposed, and endeavored to show, with great appearance of reason, that the irregularity of his conduct proceeded wholly from his zeal for Bolingbroke, who might perhaps have destroyed the pamphlet, which Pope thought it his duty to preserve even without its author's approbation. We shall close the notice of this topic by the judicious remark, in the *Additions to the Life*, &c.. on a careful examination of the whole matter, candor will probably decide, that Pope's conduct was suspicious, and that Bolingbroke's resentment was unmanly. He was now, however, in years, and his passions, under supposed injury, rather unmanageable.

Reference has been already made to the visit which Bolingbroke, during his residence in France, received from Voltaire, and the admiration expressed by the latter for his distinguished host. The obligations of the French author were largely increased when, some years after, he visited England, to solicit subscriptions to his poem, the " *Henriade,*" and procured, through the active patronage of Bolingbroke, a list of distinguished names and the more substantial encouragement of a sum of money, which may be regarded as the foundation of his large fortune, Many hints and corrections are said to have been furnished by Bolingbroke to Voltaire for the " *Henriade.*"

We may mention in this place, as evincing Bolingbroke's love of letters, even in the turmoil of public life, and the intrigues of parties, his formation of the "Brothers' Club." In a letter to the Earl of Orrery, in 1711, the time that he was Secretary of State, he writes: "I must, before I send this letter, give your lordship an account of a club which I am forming, and which, as light as the design may seem to be, I believe will prove to be of real service. We shall begin to meet in a small number; and that will be composed of some who have wit and learning to recommend them; of others who from their own situations or from their relations have power and influence; and of others who, from accidental reasons may be properly taken in. The first regulation proposed, and that which must be most invariably kept, is decency. None of the extravagance of the Kit Cat, none of the drunkenness of the Beafsteak, is to be endured. The improvement of friendship and the encouragement of letters are to be the two great ends of our society.

St. John's anticipations, as we learn from Mr. Cooke, were fully verified: this society, under the name of the Brothers' Club, continued for some time to restrain the outburst of those elements of disunion with which the Harley ministry was so rife. To be a member of this club was esteemed a distinguished honor. They addressed each other as "brother," and we find their ladies in their correspondence claiming to be enrolled as sisters. The members were the Dukes of Ormond, Shrewsbury, Beaufort; the Earls of Oxford, Arran, Jersey, Orrery, Bathurst; Lords Harley, Duplin, Masham; Sir Sobert Raymond, Sir William Wyndham, Colonel Hill, Colonel Desney, St. John, Granville, Arbuthnot, Prior, Swift, and Friend.

It would be unjust to both the parties if we were to omit recording the intimacy between Bolingbroke, then in his early manhood, an admitted genius and a notorious rake, with Dryden, whose fame had reached maturity, but who was not insensible either to the poetical flattery, or to the more prosaic yet more useful patronage and active kindness of his young friend. Pope in a letter to Dr. Arbuthnot, states, that his Lordship was the patron, the friend, and the protector, of that great poet in the decline of his age, though not of his parts; for the very last poems of Dryden are his best.

His patronage and assistance were also extended to Prior, Gay, and Thomson. The two latter were, it is true, only known to him at a period when his political influence was gone and his power every way of befriending less. Gay inscribed his Pastorals to Lord Bolingbroke. In describing, in his Prologue, the people whom he saw at court, he says:—

> There saw I St. John, sweet of mien,
> Full steadfast both to Church and Queen,
> With whose fair name I'll deck my strain—
> St. John right courteous to the swain.

Dr. King addressed a poetical welcome to him on his return from his mission to France; and to his patronage, we are told, is due the "Blenheim" of John Phillips. "Nor should it be forgotten," continues Mr. Cooke, "as an honorable instance of the triumph of the love of literature over party feeling, that when Addison's Cato was first produced, Bolingbroke took his friends to the house, and rewarded Booth liberally for his representation of the hero. Spence, who relates this anecdote, adds, that this circumstance contributed much to the success of the play."

The varied attainments of Bolingbroke are generally admitted, and they have been more than once referred to in this Memoir. He spoke Italian with ease and purity, and his perfect skill in French drew from Voltaire the acknowledgment that he had never heard the language spoken with more power and accuracy.

The concluding topic, or that on the private life and personal character of the subject of this Memoir, cannot be displayed in stronger relief than by our borrowing the vigorous pen of Lord Brougham (*Ed. Rev.* No. cxliii), which traces in somewhat harsh lines; but, upon the whole, the sketch will, we believe, be found to be a correct portrait of the man, whose political and literary merits had been so well described by the same philosophical artist.

Of Bolingbroke's private life and personal qualities, as apart from his public and political, little needs be added. He who bore the part in affairs which we have been contemplating, could not easily have been a man of strict integrity or of high principle in any relation of life. There may have been nothing mean or sordid in his nature—an honesty seldom tried in persons of his station, may have been proof against the common temptations to which it was exposed—the honor which worldly men make their god may have found in him a submissive worshipper, but the more exalted and nobler qualities of the soul were not likely to be displayed by one whose selfish propensities were grafted in public life, at the cost of all that statesmen most regard in public character, and little reliance can be placed either on the humanity, or the self-control, or the self-respect of one whose passions are his masters, and hurry him on to gratification at all the hazards that virtue can encounter. Accordingly, his youth was a course of unrestrained and habitual indulgence. In a libertine age he was marked as among the most licentious. Even his professed panegyrist, Dean Swift, makes no defence of this part of his life, and only ventures to suggest that he had lived long enough to regret and repent of it.   Sir William Wyndham, too, fell into such courses, carried away by his example, and seduced by the charms of his society; and they who have written of him ascribe his early dissipation to the ascendency of such a Mentor.   That he survived this usurper of the passions many years, and became more quiet in his demeanor during the calmness of his blood, is perhaps more the result of physical causes than any great eulogy of his returning virtues or any manifestation of his penitence.

That his feelings, however, when left to their natural course, unperverted by evil associates, nor hurried by evil propensities, were kind and generous, there is sufficient proof.   The marriage which in early youth he first contracted, was one of accident and of family arrangement: like all such unions it was attended with little happiness.   The second wife was one of his choice; to her his demeanor was blameless, and he enjoyed much comfort in her society.   His attachment to his friends was warm and zealous; and they cultivated and looked up to him with a fervor which can ill be expressed by such ordinary words as esteem, or respect or even admiration.   Yet even in this relation, the most attractive in which he appears to us, his proud temper got the better of his kinder nature, and he persecuted the memory of Pope, whom living he had loved so well, with a rancor hardly to be palliated, certainly not to be vindicated by the paltry trick to which that great poet and little man had lent himself, in an underhand publication of the manuscripts confided to his care.

His spirit was high and manly; his courage, personal and political, was without a stain.   He had no sordid propensities; his faults were not mean or paltry; they were both in his private and his public life on a large scale, creating, for the most part, wonder or terror rather than scorn or contempt—though his conduct to the Pretender approached near an exception to this remark; and the restless impatience with which he bore his long exclusion from the great stage of public affairs, and the relentless vengeance with which he, in consequence of this exclusion, pursued Walpole as its cause, betokened any thing rather than greatness of soul.

That the genius which he displayed in the senate, his wisdom, his address, and his resources in council, should, when joined to fascinating manners and literary accomplishments, have made him shine in society without a rival, can easily be comprehended. So great an orator, so noble a person in figure and demeanor—

one so little under the dominion of the principle which makes men harsh, and the restraints which tend to render their manners formal—was sure to captivate all superficial observers, and even to win the more valuable applause of superior minds. To do that which he did so well, naturally pleased him; to give delight was itself delightful; and he indulged in the more harmless relaxations of society, long after he had ceased to be a partaker in the less reputable pleasures of polished life. He probably left as high a reputation behind him among the companions of his maturer years for his social qualities, which remained by him to the last, as he had gained with those who remembered the eloquence that in his earlier days had shook the senate, or the policy and intrigues that had also shaken the monarchy itself. The dreadful malady under which he long lingered and at length sunk—a cancer in the face—he bore with exemplary fortitude, a fortitude drawn from the natural resources of his vigorous mind, and unhappily not aided by the consolation of any religion; for having early cast off the belief in revelation, he had substituted in its stead a dark and gloomy naturalism, which did not even admit of those glimmerings of hope as to futurity, not untasted by the wiser of the heathens.

Such was Bolingbroke; and as such he must be regarded by impartial posterity, after the virulence of party has long subsided, and the view is no more intercepted either by the rancor of political enmity, or by the partiality of adherents, or by the fondness of friendship. Such too is Bolingbroke, when the gloss of trivial accomplishments is worn off by time, and the lustre of genius itself has faded beside the simple and transcendent light of virtue. The contemplation is not without its uses. The glare of talents and success is apt to obscure defects which are incomparably more mischievous than any intellectual powers can be either useful or admirable. Nor can a lasting renown—a renown that alone deserves the aspirations of a rational being—ever be built upon any foundations save those which are laid in an honest heart and a firm purpose, but conspiring to work out the good of mankind. That renown will be as imperishable as it is pure.

The last Will and Testament of the late Right Honorable Henry St. John, Lord Viscount Bolingbroke.

In the name of God, whom I humbly adore, to whom I offer up perpetual thanksgiving, and to the order of whose providence I am cheerfully resigned: This is the Last Will and Testament of me, Henry Saint John, in the reign of Queen Ann, and by her grace and favor Viscount Bolingbroke, after more than thirty years proscription, and after the immense losses I have sustained by unexpected events in the course of it; by the injustice and treachery of persons nearest to me; by the negligence of friends; and by the infidelity of servants. As my fortune is so reduced at this time, that it is impossible for me to make such disposition, and to give such ample legacies as I always intended, I content therefore to give as follows:

My debts, and the expenses of my burial in a decent and private manner at Battersea, in the vault where my last wife lies, being first paid, I give to William Chetwynd of Stafford, Esq., and Joseph Taylor of the Inner-Temple, London, Esq., my two assured friends, each of them one hundred guineas, to be laid out by them, as to each of them shall seem best, in some memorial, as the legacy of their departed friend; and I constitute them executors of this my will. The diamond ring which I wear upon my finger, I give to my old and long approved friend the Marquis of Matignon, and, after his decease, to his son the Count de Gace, that I may be kept in the remembrance of a family whom I love and honor above all others.

Item, I give to my said executors, the sum of four hundred pounds in trust to place out the same in some of the public funds, or government securities, or any other securities, as they shall think proper, and to pay the interest or income thereof to Francis Arboneau, my valet-de-chambre, and Ann his wife, and the survivor of them; and after the decease of the survivor of them, if their son John Arboneau shall be living and under the age of eighteen years, to pay the said interest or income to him, until he shall attain his said age, and then to pay the principal money, or assign the securities for the same to him; but if he shall not be living at the decease of his father and mother, or shall afterwards die before his said age of eighteen years, in either of the said cases, the said principal sum of four hundred pounds, and the securities for the same, shall sink into my personal estate, and be accounted part thereof.

Item, I give to my two servants, Marianne Tribon, and Remi Charnet commonly called Picard, each one hundred pounds; and to every other servant living with me at the time of my decease, and who shall have lived with me two years or longer, I give one year's wages more than what shall be due them at my death.

And whereas I am the author of the several books or tracts following, viz:

Remarks on the History of England, from the Minutes of Humphrey Oldcastle. In twenty-four letters.

A Dissertation upon Parties. In nineteen letters, to Caleb Danvers, Esq.

The Occasional Writer. Numb. 1, 2, 3.

The Vision of Camilick.

An Answer to the London Journal of December 21, 1728, by John Trot.

An Answer to the Defence of the Inquiry into the Reasons of the Conduct of Great Britain.

A final Answer to the Remarks on the Craftsman's Vindication.

All which books or tracts have been printed and published; and I am also the author of

Four Letters on History, &c.

Which have been privately printed, and not published; but I have not assigned to any person or persons whatsoever the copy, or the liberty of printing or reprinting any of the said books, or tracts or letters: Now I do hereby, as far as by law I can, give and assign to David Mallet, of Putnam in the County of Surry, Esquire, the copy and copies of all and each of the beforementioned books or tracts, and letters, and the liberty of reprinting the same. I also give to the said David Mallet, the copy and copies of all the manuscript books, papers, and writings, which I have written or composed, or shall write or compose, and leave at the time of my decease. And I further give to the said David Mallet, all the books which, at the time of my decease, shall be in the room called my library.

All the rest and residue of my personal estate, whatsoever and wheresoever, I give to my said executors: and hereby revoking all former wills, I declare this to be my last will and testament. In witness whereof, I have hereunto set my hand and seal the twenty-second day of November, in the year of our Lord one thousand seven hundred and fifty-one.

HENRY SAINT JOHN, BOLINGBROKE.

Signed, sealed, published, and declared, by the said testator, as and for his last will and testament, in the presence of

OLIVER PRICE.
THOMAS HALL.

Proved at London, the fifth day of March, 1752, before the worshipful Robert Chapman, doctor of laws and surrogate, by the oaths of William Chetwynd and Joseph Taylor, Esquires, the executors named in the will, to whom administration was granted, being first sworn duly to administer.

WILLIAM LEGARD, ⎫
PETER ST. ELOY, ⎬ *Deputy Registers.*
HENRY STEVENS. ⎭

March, 1752.

So soon as it was publicly known that Mallet had acquired the property of Lord Bolingbroke's works, Lord Hyde, to whom, as Lord Cornbury, the Letters upon History had been addressed, wrote the legatee a letter, in which he dissuaded him from publishing that part of the work containing the " Reflections on Sacred History," of which hitherto a few copies only had been printed for some of Bolingbroke's friends. But Mallet excused himself from a compliance with this wish, on the plea, that he could not, without being unfaithful to his trust, omit or alter any thing in those works which Lord Bolingbroke had prepared for the press; and adds, that he will publish no other. The work in question remains therefore, not so much an injury to religion as an evidence of the shallow reasoning of its author, and a kind of involuntary expiation for the wrong intended. Its publication in this sense may serve to induce in others, for the sake of their own reputation, if not of the peace and happiness of their fellow men, greater caution in sending forth to the world, or even committing to writing, their crude speculations on a subject of such vital importance as religion. By a strange contradiction, not uncommon in the so called philosophical school, men are found, who, whilst they ridicule the idea of persons having written and acted under inspiration from on high, behave as if they themselves were thus inspired: for, unless it were conceded that they had knowledge on so difficult a subject as revealed religion, either by intuition or inspiration, it is impossible, that is, of course, without a miracle, that in the state of unpreparedness in which they take up and discuss the subject, they could explain its difficulties or elucidate its mysteries. They do not approach it in the spirit of impartiality, nor pursue it with the pains-taking, which even their pagan teachers tell them to be so necessary for reaching the truth.

The MSS. from which Mallet's edition of Bolingbroke's works was printed, were presented to the British Museum by the widow of the former.

———————

The character of Lord Bolingbroke will be still farther illustrated by the following letters, addressed, during his second retirement to France, to his friend, Sir William Wyndham. It is left to the perspicacity of the reader, to discrimininate between the professions of the statesman and ardent party politician, and the real opinions of the man.

Lord Bolingbroke to Sir William Wyndham.

March the 18th, 1736.

DEAR SIR WILLIAM:—I answer yours of the 4th, 6th, and 22d of February. If corruption will be the bane of our constitution, and that the continuance of it must be so even the corrupt cannot doubt; and if nothing can put a stop to this gangrene, but a conjuncture wherein the crown shall have little to ask, and a minister who will scorn this odious and abominable expedient of government shall be in power, as you think; *desperandum est de republica;*—I shall carry the weight of this affliction to my grave, and nothing will in the least lighten the burden, unless a perfect indifference to all that can happen, if this be to happen, can lighten it; or the comfortable reflection that I did, in a low and perhaps no very effectual part, but the only part I could act, all that was in my power to prevent the ruin. I once thought that there was another remedy to this fatal evil, a remedy which might constantly palliate, and, by redoubling the doses in a favorable crisis, radically cure the distemper. But perhaps I was mistaken; or perhaps there is not patience and perseverance enough for the one, nor vigor or perseverance enough for the other, in the minds of men. Both come to the same point. For it is as much a mistake to depend upon that which is true, but impracticable at a certain time, as to depend on that which is neither true, nor practicable at any time.

But no more of this. Since I can be no longer of use to my particular friends, and to my country, I must live to myself; and I thank the Author of human and all other nature, that I am able to do so with the utmost contentment. I can drudge away my life in business, when my judgment and my sentiment concur in approving it; or I can trifle away my time in pleasure, when opportunity and example seduce me, and no strong call summons me from it. But I can and I always could do, what I will express in Latin better than English would express it, *me mihi vindicare.* I am now at an age when this is to be done for the last time: two acts are over at least; and the farce, you know, consists but of three.

Upon this foundation I will speak to you about my private affairs; for though I have mentioned all the particulars that occurred to me, necessary to be mentioned at present, in my letter to Mr. Corry, which you will see to be sure, yet there are some other more general and ruling considerations, that I must explain to you. If I could have retired from the world with quiet, decency, and some degree of dignity at home, I should have chosen it; but since that could not be, and since nothing shall ever call me out of retreat again, but the necessity of self-defence, or such public confusion in my own country as may set me on a level with every other man in acting for her, one of which I believe, and the other of which I hope will not happen, it is probable in the highest degree, that I shall never return to live among you. This, applied to my private affairs, decides, you see, for selling my estate at Dawley as soon as I can. I do not desire, you know, to sell it at any extravagant rate; but I would not willingly undersell it very much to one of those, who may wait to take advantage of the necessity they may guess I am in of selling; nor easily yield to the contrariety of my fortune, that may render it hard for me, when it would not be for any other man, to sell at a fair price. I will add two other considerations, that decide on the same side very strongly in my mind: they are these: a revenue fully sufficient, and secured without risk or trouble, is an article of vast importance in the life I propose to lead; and such a revenue I can have whenever Dawley is sold as I propose to sell it. A settlement of all my affairs, not only for my own life, but for those that will be concerned in them after my death, is another point on which my mind is very intent; and the more so, because I judge without either fear or spleen, upon my word, that my life will not be long. Now, this settlement cannot be made either as definitively or as effectually as I desire, until Dawley be sold.

When I examine myself, and consider my affairs and circumstances in this light, you may be sure I am under the pangs of impatience till this transaction be finished; but upon the whole matter, thus I simplify my thoughts, and thus I resolve. If, by luck better than I expect, you can sell for me as I desired, sell without hesitation: if the opportunity of doing it hangs off, let upon the hints given in my letter to Mr. Corry. If neither of these can be done this summer, I shall feel a reasonable uneasiness, and be exposed to future inconveniences, that will disturb all the quiet of my life; for though I do not wish to live like Aristippus, I cannot live like Diogenes. In this case, there will remain but one thing for me to do, which I shall do, though very unwillingly, and that will be to go into England before the end of the summer, set Dawley and all I have there to sale, make the most I can of it, content myself with that, whatever it be, and return free from cares of all kinds to my foreign hermitage. This, my friend, is the sum total of my thoughts, and the result of all my reflections. Upon this foot act for me, and let me hear from you as frequently as you see occasion, or have the opportunity.

* * * * * * *

Dean Swift had begun a history of the four last years of the.

queen's reign. I saw it some years ago, and disliked it. Many mistakes were in it, and I thought it a party pamphlet, not a history. I spoke my mind freely to Pope, to whom you will do me a pleasure to talk about this work. I think I took the copy away, that it might not go into the world as it was; and if I did so, that copy remains among some papers, that I have laid by carefully and safely in England.

Lord Bolingbroke to Sir William Wyndham.

June the 9th, 1737.

*　　*　　*　　*　　*　　*　　*

DEAR SIR WILLIAM:—Since du Noquet is to send you this letter by no conveyance that is not extremely sure, I will speak openly to you on one part of yours. It has been plain to me for some years, that nothing but the hand of fate could shake the men who domineer over you. I am afflicted at it, because the principles and methods of government will not be changed, nay, cannot by them; and because, if any thing can be demonstrated in politics by reason, and be supported by the authority of example, it is this: that these principles and methods of government must impoverish the nation to a degree ruinous and insupportable, with consequences, some of which are easily foreseen, and others as certain, though not equally obvious. I am afflicted at it, because the long continuance of these principles and methods of government, which have been continued long already, must wear the true notions of the English constitution out of the heads, and the true spirit of it out of the hearts of men: and because it is evident, that the consequence of this must be, a little sooner or later, either falling into national confusion, the seeds of which, very thick sown, are not so hard to point out; or submitting tamely and silently to indirect, which is in many respects worse than direct tyranny, and which leads inevitably to it. The word tyranny is not too strong; for whenever will prevails constantly and without control or account, the will of a prince or the will of a minister, whatever forms are preserved, tyranny is established. I am piqued at it, because this could never happen; nay, the progress toward it could never have been such as we have seen, and see; if there had not been industrious, active, impudent perseverance, for bold or resolute, are words too good, on one side, and negligent, uncertain, timid opposition on the other. Do not imagine, that to think in this manner is to presage, like a splenetic man, evils that will never happen; think rather, that he who is out of the fray, sees the progress of it in every part, and foresees, upon the whole, the event of it better than he who is in it can. How many measures have been pursued or neglected in my time, and almost in my time,* the consequences of which pursuit or neglect are felt severely at this hour; and yet these consequences, when they were foretold, passed among honest intelligent men, as contingencies too uncertain to be opposed to immediate expediency; or as the dreams of melancholy persons, or as the artful misrepresentations of the ill-affected.

You say, my friend, that the affair of the prince alarmed the minister purely because of the state of the king's health in that point of time. I believe so: but I beleive likewise, that this affair would have alarmed, and done more than alarm him, in whatever state the king's health had been, if it had been the first measure of a scheme of conduct wisely formed, and concerted among all those that stand in opposition to the present administration. If a scheme of conduct had been formed and concerted to follow this measure, in the case of losing as well as carrying the question, I incline to believe you would have carried it; for nothing gives success like hope, and nothing gives hope like the assurance of having a good second game to play. I applaud extremely the prudence and dignity, with which his royal highness conducted himself, as well as the firmness he has shown since; the marks of duty he gives to his parents, and the coldness of the good breeding he exercised towards their servants, and I suppose towards those of his own who voted against him. The rest of his behaviour, his taking dutifully what is given him, the assurances he gives that he will not treat for more, that he will not ask for more, is too finely spun for my gross sight; it will keep him where he is, you where you are, and Walpole where he is. It affords, indeed, an example of most polite moderation; but I do not imagine the persons he and you have to do with capable of being won by such amiable proceedings; and for the minister, he is not such a changeling as to think this circumstance unpleasant, or to disquiet himself about resentments, against which he has so much time and so many means to provide. I am apt to believe, that he would think the circumstance much more unpleasant, and have more disquietude about future events, if the prince was at this time retired to Southampton house: for instance, if he lived there, with all the economy of a private nobleman, and was surrounded with friends that might adorn the court of a prince; if his language and his conduct expressed the utmost personal duty to his parents, and yet the freedom of a British subject. Those among you who imagine, that a contrary conduct carries terror with it, and will produce overtures of reconciliation, are

* So in the original.

like Picherol, in Rabelais, who sauntered about at the city gate, and did nothing but inquire whether the storks, for they were to bring with them all kinds of good fortune, were coming; or like the bowing dean, who waits on foot in the dust or the dirt the arrival of his patron, who is to promote him to a bishopric.

I could not help saying thus much to you in the freedom, the confidence, and the warmth of friendship, and therefore you will excuse it. Interest, personal interest I mean, I have none in any of these affairs; for, however they turn, my situation will be the same; and, I dare say, you do me the justice to be persuaded, that, if it was in my power to alter it, I would not, after all that has passed, neither by the means of my enemies nor of my friends. I look often back on the parts I have acted, and on the events of my life: in the former I discern many mistakes, but no iniquity; no one step was not directed originally, or brought immediately to the true interests of my country. This consciousness takes away all regrets as to the events of my life, since the worst of them have been owing to things that I should do again, upon the whole, if I was again in the same circumstances, though not quite in the same manner in some cases. If I live, I will continue a year or two more as I am, perhaps longer, for other persons' sake, not for my own. But if my Lord St. John lives longer, and Dawley is not soon sold pretty well, I shall have a just reason for doing what I desire to do, that is, for retiring absolutely from the world, and into a sort of life, where, free from care of all kinds, I shall live by myself, and to myself, and be lost to mankind before I cease to be one of their number.   *   *   *

Lord Bolingbroke to Sir William Wyndham.

October the 13th, 1737.

I writ to you very lately, dear Sir William, and having heard from Calais, that my letter was sent safely into England, I suppose it come safely by this time to your hands. This shall be forwarded with more precaution still; for I shall not forbear saying, in answer to yours of the 13th of the last month, things very unfit for the inspection of clerks of the post-office. Though I am informed very irregularly, and very imperfectly of what passes in the island of Great Britain, yet, by what I have heard, it seemed plain to me, that an entire rupture between the father and the son has been long unavoidable. I have therefore waited to see what the immediate occasion or pretence of this rupture would be; for I always believed the counsellors of his royal highness would think it of great importance to render this not only plausible, but popular.

I thought, that such an occasion or pretence might have been founded on the proceedings of last winter: but I saw things at a distance, and they who saw them nearer judged otherwise. The settlement on the princess was not then made; this and other reasons might concur to make them judge and act as they did at that time. But I am at a loss to find the plausibility or the popularity of the present occasion of rupture. He hurries his wife from court when she is on the point of being delivered of her first child. His father swells, struts, and storms. He confesses his rashness, and asks pardon in terms of one who owns himself in the wrong. Beside that all this appears to me boyish, it is purely domestic; and there is nothing, as far as I can discern, to interest the public in the cause of his royal highness. But notwithstanding this, extreme severity on the other side, and the prejudices of mankind against those who exercise this severity, may have, perhaps, that effect. I think truly they will have it, if the prince shows, upon this occasion, firmness in his character, and decency in his behaviour; one without any mixture of humor, or air of obstinacy; the other without any thing low, or, if I may say so, unprincely. The resolution he has taken to pay his debts, and to live like a man of quality who has a good estate, deserves great commendation; there is honor, sense, and dignity in it. He may build on this foundation great reputation; and great reputation is great power, especially in one of his rank. If it was not so, my friend, it would scarcely be worth our esteem; since popular fame is strictly and truly, what a man weak enough to be fond of it, even for its own sake called it, *fama consensu stultorum improborumque excitata.*

As little as I concern myself at present, and shall do the rest of my life, in these affairs, and in their consequences, I could not help saying thus much, in answer to the account you give me of the scene that passed while you were at London, and all I shall add is this: it gave you inwardly, I suppose, much the same emotion as a scene of Tom Thumb would have done. But you are too wise not to know, that they who are on the stage must keep the countenance their parts require in a tragi-comical farce, while they who are in the pit may laugh their fill. " *Nous mourions de rire, si nous ne mourions pas de faim,*" was the burden of a French song during the great distress of this country in the last war that Louis the Fourteenth waged.

It occurs often to me, when I think of the state of our own country, of the characters of persons, and of the conduct of affairs, it is impossible to have any concern for Britain, and not to lament the near approach of general beggary and slavery that threaten her; for I think the latter must and will go hand in hand

with the former. And though I have as little of the spirit of
party about me, as any man living, which you know to be true,
yet I cannot forbear saying, that these are the fruits of those principles of foreign and domestic policy, that a number of men who
called themselves Whigs, and who lived on the credit of that
name, and on the folly and obstinacy of those who called themselves by another, began to plant almost half a century ago, and
have continued to plant and to propagate ever since. The progress of both was covered long from public sight by a specious
veil that dazzled the vulgar: but the progress has been so gross,
and the veil has been worn so thin, of late years, that he must be
stark blind who has not seen it. I fear it is seen; and if it was
not, there would be room to hope, though effectual remedies were
yet unattempted; if it is, all hope seems to be cut off. The patient who knows his distemper, and chooses rather to bear it than
to go through the remedy, is incurable.

You say, that the monopoly of money in a few hands discloses
itself manifestly. Is not power engrossed in a few hands as well
as wealth? Things are brought to this pass. While you have
weak princes on the throne, some cabal or other will draw the
whole wealth of the nation, and the whole power of the state,
to itself. Whenever you have an able prince there, he will soon
find means of being, directly or indirectly, the proprietor of
both.   *   *   *   *   *   *   *

Lord Bolingbroke to Sir William Wyndham.

February 3d, 1738.

Yours of the 28th and 31st of December have come safely to
my hands, as I hope that this will come to yours. I thank you
very much for the clear state you represent to me of things that
must affect the friends I love, and the country I love, to a great
degree, and which concern me therefore in this respect, though
they do so in no other. I cannot wonder that the same man,
who has so often, nay so constantly, sacrificed the national interest to his avarice, his ambition, and his fears, should sacrifice to
his passions the peace of his master's family, and take that opportunity to make this master declare a proscription against all
those who oppose his minister; for those general words in the
message include you all, and mean no less. But I am surprised
he should so directly, and so personally, push things to extremity
against one, who may be his master some time or other. Since
he has done so, he opens a scene that may be tragical to him, if
it is well acted; and surely it may be well acted, when the principal actor is so well disposed. The French have a proverb,

which is true in private life, *Que la bonne compagnie chasse la mauvaise.* Inverted it would be true likewise, *Que la mauvaise chasse la bonne:* but in this case, it should seem the good may have the advantage if they please, since the others have only his habit for them, and since his reflection is against them, and makes him ashamed of them. A multitude of prompters will confound the actor, and destroy all consistency of behaviour and conduct; but is it impossible then to prompt by concert, and, since his confidence is well placed, to prevail on him to listen to no other prompting? The very aggravation of his little defects by some people at this time should be the strongest proof imaginable to him of the necessity of correcting them. In short when I consider what use I have seen and see actually made of very uncouth characters, I am not without hopes, that a good use may be made of this. When I speak of prompting by concert, I do not mean a concert so extended as must be formed in some cases; I mean a concert of a few intimately united with those in whom his greatest confidence is placed. Such a concert, conducting his conduct with wisdom, industry, firmness and perseverance, would make his cause as powerful as you wish it, and still more popular, as you think it cannot fail of being.

I am of your mind, that the queen's death must make a great alteration in the inward state of things at court; but this will not decide in iavor of the public; nor indeed any thing less than the power of developing to the public the mystery of one of the weakest and wickedest administrations that ever was. Such a concert, with such a person to figure at the head of it, might bring this about. I know what will be objected; the different characters and views of the men who must concur in bringing this about, and the supposed impossibility of prevailing in these days against a man who has the purse in his hands. I saw much of the first when I was among you; and I lamented the want of that which you now have, a centre of union, a superior authority among yourselves, under whose influence men of different characters and different views will be brought to draw better together, and your measures being more systematical, your efforts will be far stronger—I hope irresistible. The other objection I heard every day made, or insinuated, during the latter part of the time I was in Britain; and I must suppose it was urged as a reason for submitting to the little tyrant who has domineered so long over you; because nothing can be more absurd in the mouths of men who do not submit, but continue to act against him. For if it is impossible to stem the tide of corruption, and prevail against the man who holds the purse, it is absurd to make the attempt, and more absurd to persist in it. But I saw then, or thought I saw that it was not his own strength, but the purse alone that supported him, and I hope you will see this verified by his fall.

* * * * *

I return to mention a thing I forgot above. I love the chancellor much, and I should therefore be very sorry to see him become the crutch of a battered minister. If he has engaged to a certain degree with the Pelhams, and if the Duke of Newcastle's breach with Walpole is irreconcileable, why should not these circumstances be improved? Why should not you cultivate such a coalition, being in friendship with one lately, and having old habitudes with the other? Adieu, my friend; I am to you, and to all that belong to you, as sincerely devoted as the heart of man can make him.

Lord Bolingbroke to Sir William Wyndham.

(July the 23d, 1739.) I have settled myself in the same habitation, after more than two months of silly and teasing negotiation, and after apprehending more than once, that I should have no settlement at all. My lease is for the life of a widow, or the term of a widowhood. She will not marry, I think, because she would lose by it the best part of a small revenue; and though she be younger than I am, she is old enough not to be courted for her beauty. The tranquillity you wish me, my dear Sir William, I think I shall have; my mind is tempered for it. Fewer things give me regret, fewer fear; and the objects that could principally affect me with trouble are at a distance: I see them imperfectly, I hear them faintly.

I have not been, nor am, in the way of political information; but, as far as I know, there is no reason to alter the opinion I was of in England, concerning the part this government would act, if the obstinacy of Spain drove things to a rupture, and you took up arms purely to repel usurpation, injuries, and insults, and to assert a plain and incontestible right, which the French claim as well as you, to a free and independent navigation. It is said that your ministers ask to negotiate with Spain, under the cardinal's mediation,* and that he accepts it. I dare to say he would not suffer this right on the part of France to be made a matter of treaty. But if you will make it such on your part, it is not a mediator's duty to hinder you. The great augmentation of your land forces makes no impression: people wonder what you mean. He that should say, you have an invasion to fear, would be laugh-

---

* This assertion was ungrounded: France offered her mediation, but England rejected it.

ed at almost as much as he that should say, you meant to chase *guarda costas* with horse, foot, and dragoons. What then do your government mean? I believe you or I could answer the question better than any foreign politician.

The account you gave me in yours of a conversation with our friend [Pulteney] did not surprise me; it only renewed an affliction I have often felt on the same account; for, though I love the man, though I look on myself to be perfectly indifferent to him, the step* he was so fond of, and grew tired of so soon, is the only one that you could take of any meaning or tendency; if it is supported decently, but strongly, soberly, but resolutely, it must have a good effect. If it is not supported so, the case will be as bad, with a little more dishonor to particular men, as if it had not been taken. In one case, and in the other, the plain and necessary consequence would have been, or is, to leave the honor, interest, and constitution of their country at the mercy of an avowed faction, with the most profligate man in the nation at the head of it. Such a remonstrance as he mentioned would be, no doubt, a proper, one of the properest measures, that could be taken to justify and support the secession. But what then does he mean by saying, it would ruin the Whig party? The Whig faction it might break; and what has he, and you, and every honest man, meant by the opposition you have carried on, and by your coalition, but to break the Whig and Tory faction both? The whole body of the Whigs must be reunited, he says; and this great measnre of the city remonstrance must be executed by the Tories alone. I forbear any remarks on a discourse as wild as a dream. Surely, a man of his parts must be fascinated, as you say, to talk in such a style. I hear he has talked of something he expects from me; but I have desired he may be told that I will write nothing. He thought my very name and presence in England did hurt. What hurt then would the bare suspicion do, that a paper, designed to explain and justify the secession, and to point out the true end of it, came from me? Since you are all separated, I am willing to hope, that it is to hold separately the same language, and to pursue the same measures at once in different places; and that your separation will continue no longer than is necessary for this purpose. Any thing of the kind you expect will have its effect, perhaps, more strongly after the minds of men are so prepared; and I need say nothing of it to you here, because you will hear of it another way; and I think no one but you should hear of it any way, till it appears without any possible notices of the quarter from whence it comes.

I own to you that this fresh mark of uniformity of sentiment

* The secession.

and steadiness of conduct in a certain person,* gives me great pleasure, and the more because the attack was made by surprise: keep him right for his sake, for your own, and for your country's sake. In all events the weight of that person must be greater every day, if he confirms, in the opinion of mankind, his character of steadiness and truth. Adieu, dear sir; take this to be the speech of a departed friend, who writes to you from another world, who had some experience of the world, and who takes no farther interest in it, beside that of a concern for his living friends.

Of all the causes of your present public misfortunes, which are easy to be traced, a principal one is this: The Whigs have always looked on the protestant succession, and the Tories on the restoration of the Stewarts, as sure means to throw the whole power of the government into the hands of one or the other of them and to keep it there. I am confident the latter would have found themselves deceived: the former were encouraged and confirmed by the weak conduct of my Lord Oxford; by the characters of the late and present king, different indeed, but suited to their purpose, and by the absurd behaviour of the Tories, which no experience can cure. Thus party has become faction, distinguished no longer by principle, whatever may be represented, but by personal attachments. Had great men been at the head of the ruling faction, your liberties had been lost without a chance to save them. Their characters would have imposed, and a successful administration might have hindered men from seeing the invasions made on liberty. Walpole's character could impose on no man. All the power and all the wealth of Britain has not been able to deck him out with a little dignity, nor to procure him common respect. A narrow capacity, good as far as it extends, but confined to the lowest and worst arts, to the tricks of domestic government, has rendered his administration one of the wickedest and weakest, the most hateful and the most contemptible, that our nation ever saw; and thus many chances to redeem yourselves from his tyranny, and to restore good government, have been created: the last, that which I hope still subsists, is the fairest that any infatuated minister could give against himself. His mal-administration appeared so flagrant, that faction could not save him without avowing faction. You pulled off the mask; at least you showed mankind the turpitude of this proceeding, and you appealed to the nation; for your secession is such an appeal, or it is the most pompous nothing I ever saw or heard of. To go back from this, would be to admit what you have appealed against. For your own sakes, and for the sake of your country, you must go forward. You may do so by the strongest and

* The Prince of Wales.

most irreproachable measures; you may bring the dispute to fix on this single point, the personal interest of Walpole, in the eyes of the whole kingdom.   If you persist, it must rest there at last, and there is not a man of spirit left in Britain, if it can rest there long.

Lord Bolingbroke to Sir William Wyndham.

November the first, 1739.

Geraldino having no more a share in despatching the couriers between London and Calais, I conclude du Nocquet will be able to convey my letters safely by them, or by the sloops, and that I may venture to write the more freely, as well as more frequently, to you, my dear friend.   You heard from me some time ago, and you have doubtless the letter I writ, and the papers I sent to that valuable, or rather invaluable young man, Polwarth.   A great deal of what is there contained will be out of date, if it be true that your resolution is taken of returning to the house, as I hear from my neighborhood that it is.   Concerning this resolution I presume nót to decide; all I can say is, that the tranquillity of the summer prepared me to expect it.   I see some concomitant resolutions, that may have been taken at the same time, which, if they go together, and are executed alike, may support the honor of the secession, and promote a crisis, necessary, in my opinion, and that I believe of every thinking man, to save your country from ruin of every kind, from absolute beggary, and the most abject servitude.

There are other things contained in those papers, which will not be out of date, even if this resolution be taken.   You must mate the insolence, aud stop, at least, if you cannot punish, the treachery of Walpole.   I scruple not to use the word treachery, for he is a changeling, if he is not a traitor to Britain. If you cannot do one of these, you are undone.   I do not mean as a party; that consideration is too low for such conjuncture, bnt as a nation.   I do not see your state so near as you do, but have the mortification to hear every man I see express contempt for a country they have been used to respect, and even to fear.   I have been asked many times within this month, how it came to pass, that we suffered ourselves to be insulted and pirated upon so many years together by the Spaniards: and to be bantered all the while by the trifling clauses in treaties, made by ministers who did not dare at that time to make a single reprisal. We took the Fleuron; France immediately made reprisals, very justly, and has brought our court to redeem their folly with their money; for this capture costs you, I believe, £5000. France and you are not at war for this. France has disputes frequently with Spain, particularly about territory and encroachments in the island of St. Domingo. Has France borne the least insult, the least invasion, the least menace from the Spaniards, without opposition or reprisal? Not one; and yet the amity between the two crowns subsists so well, that your ministers seem afraid of it. From these instances, and others, men argue, unanswerably, that how little soever Walpole may think it for his interest to engage in a war, he might have reconciled, some years ago, his interest and that of his country, if he had not been resolved not only to postpone the latter to the former, but to give it up.

I have been asked, what is meant by the great armaments made in Britain, which they say are absurd, whether the ministers mean a war or not? a war with Spain, that is. For if the meaning be to give the law to the people of Great Britain, not to the Spaniards, augmentation of land forces are necessary to do it effectually, and the *eclat* of a great fleet to cover the design. In short, I should afflict and tire you, if I repeated the twentieth part of what I have heard on this subject. I will conclude, therefore, this head by telling you what I take to be a great truth, that there is not a man of sense, who does not think you betrayed by a minister, who is, on what motives he best knows, in a concert with your adverse party, and who does not rather despise than pity you for bearing it.

Your parliament being to meet in about three weeks, I conclude this letter will find you returned to London, where I wish you health and success: half this wish will be enough for me; my private affairs are as much broken as they can be, and I neither take nor will take any share in public affairs. What have I then to do with success? but I have still something to do with health, and even of that I have often been deprived of late. Almost all the warm sentiments of the heart are dead in me except that of friendship; and if I take any concern for what passes in the world, it is on the account of my friends, whom I think friends to their country, and not on my own. Adieu, dear Wyndham; I embrace you and yours with a heart that will be devoted to you as long as it beats.

Lord Bolingbroke to Sir William Wyndham.

(November the 18th, 1739.) Yours of the 23d of September, O. S. is come safe to my hands. The common style and matter of epistolary correspondence would want an apology indeed, if it was employed between you and me: our confidence in each other's friendship needs none of what the French call *petits devoirs* to support it; and I would no more write to you about trifles, than I would write seriously to a coquette or a *petit maître*.

I felt much concern in reading your letter; if the spirit of the gentlemen is subdued, and they are grown indifferent about the preservation of the British constitution, *conclamatum est.* A people cannot be saved against their will; and Walpole, or your kinsman, may use them like the slaves they are, and deserve to be. It gives me some pleasure, amidst all my real grief, to think that the man of that country whom I love the best has done his utmost to save it. This gives me pleasure; and believe me, dear Sir William, it will give you a pleasure to your latest hour, which they who conspire to ruin their country never knew. I see a glimpse of light, through all this darkness, in the hope you have, that you shall keep one person steady to the principles of his and your late conduct. If you cannot save your country, do not drop your protest against the men and the measures that ruin it.

I say nothing to you about foreign affairs; what I could say about them relatively to Britain, I have said in former letters. Never nation was so bantered, so imposed upon, and so lied, as yours. They who lied so impudently, when the Spanish treaty of Vienna was made, in order to have a pretence for arming at home, and keeping foreign troops in pay, may lie again with the same view, and the same success; though I think it impossible they shall procure any better information than that you mention, to color what they advance. Nothing can be, I dare say, more foreign to the present politics of all the councils of Europe, except those of his holiness, or perhaps the queen of Spain, than the cause of the Pretender; and yet this trite expedient may be again employed. Dan. Pulteney used to say, that the Pretender would never subdue us, but his name would.

I thank you for sending me the account wherein I am mentioned for a correspondence with persons I never heard of before. I have desired a friend, who is going to Paris, to take such notice of it as it deserves to my Lord Waldegrave; and to add, that though he and I know how much these idle reports of invasions are to be despised, yet as we have seen them politically employed for many purposes, and may see them so again, I promise his lordship that if my name be mingled in any of them, I will instantly repair to Paris to receive his orders, as little as I care to leave my retreat, and go from thence to London, as fast as post-horses can carry me to Paris, and winds waft me from thence. You will do me a favor, my friend, to speak in the same style, if an occasion that deserves it offers.

My health has tottered a good deal since I came last into this country, but begins, I think, to strengthen, though we be in the decline of the year, and though the season be more remarkable for epidemical distempers than any that has been known.

You are now to be sure in town, and you see what you have

to expect for the public—little good, I fear; but much honor to yourself, and to those gentlemen who backed you in the measure you took last session, and who will pursue with you the ends of it. The eyes of mankind are upon you. Let me hear from you, at least of you. As retired as I am, and as indifferent as I am grown, I look abroad with curiosity and impatience to learn what becomes of the wealth, honor, and liberty of a country I must always love, in this decisive moment. We are told here that Lord Harrington is to be general of the marines, and Horace secretary of state; and that the latter and Sir John Norris are to be made peers. These promotions, the hundred-gun ships you put into commission, and the horse and dragoons you raise, may well frighten Spain. Adieu. I am most faithfully and entirely yours; my kindest wishes and best respects attend all yours.

1740.

Lord Bolingbroke to Sir William Wyndham.

(New-year's day, 1740.) I cannot begin the year better than by writing to you, and therefore will send this letter to take its chance for a passage at Calais, without waiting for another conveyance. I make no reflections on the contents of your letter of the 11th of November, because I can make none but what you make yourself in it. You are in a melancholy scene: but I am sure you experience now that advantage, which a virtuous conduct alone can procure. When our conduct has not been such, if we fail of success, we fail of all: but when it has been such, we are sure to gain something—more ease. Inward contentment enhances public joy. In the other, it makes some amends for the want of it. What shall I say further to you, my friend? When men are so far from acting on generous, noble, and wise principles, that they avow the most ungenerous and the meanest, and pride themselves in the most foolish, they neither can be served, nor deserve to be so: and the greatest sacrifice a good man can make to the public, is, for the sake of the public, not to break with them.

The two young men you name have not only the principles, but the flame of public virtue, and it is for that I admire and love them. When these principles are in the head alone, they are notions, principles from which to reason, and they serve oftener to judge of the conduct of others, than to influence our own. But when they are in the heart too, they become sentiments, principles of action, and they unite the powers of the whole man in pursuit of every laudable purpose. I write to the lord, make my best compliments to the other. May you find more to walk steadily with you and them in those paths, which wisdom, not cunning, points out; for as they direct to different means, they direct to different ends. I have seldom known a cunning man an honest man, and as seldom a wise man a knave. I am persuaded, that our cunning men will be the bubbles of their cunning, and that the measure, so full of good purposes as they pretend, will serve only to unmask them of their patriotism, and show the true visage of faction that lies behind it. But be this as it will, if the constitution of Britain can be saved, and the weak and wicked administration altered, you are just in the way to bring this about on the principles laid down, and according to the solemn engagements taken twelve or fourteen years ago. If one must perish, and the other subsist, no matter under whose name or direction. May you, and those who concur with you, have the virtue of which I doubt not, and then you will have the honor to be the last of Britons. I wish for you as I wish for myself. I judge for you and of you, as I judge for myself and of myself, how little soever the unthinking, trifling part of mankind may discern it.

The British constitution of government is at a great crisis, which must turn either to life or death. The disease cannot be long borne. God knows whether the remedies can. When I recall to my mind the several causes, and the gradual progress of their effects, which have brought us into this state, I am ready to apply to our times what Livy said of his: *Ad hæc tempora, quibus nec vitia nostra, nec remedia pati possumus, perventum est.* On this supposition I think myself happy to be what I am, a stranger in my own country, a sojourner in a foreign land. You ought to think yourself still happier, not because you have escaped a great part of the losses I have sustained, and the troubles I have gone through, but because you are still in a condition to speak and act in defence of the noblest cause a virtuous man can undertake. Adieu, my friend. May the providence of God protect and favor you, and such as you, and I doubt not but this will be, if in truth the Supreme Being does govern the moral world by the interposition of particular providences!

Lord Bolingbroke to Sir William Wyndham.

(January 25, 1740.) Since I writ to you not very long ago, your letter of the 25th November and 4th December came to my hands. My dear Sir William, I inclined to think many years ago, and have been confirmed in the opinion for some time, that the great end and visible progress which has been made towards the destruction of the British constitution, and the extinction of the spirit of it, has not been owing so much to the shifts of a minister in distress, or in fear of being so, as it has been to a formed design and established system. The men in power have pursued it, and many of those out of power have only waited the opportunity of pursuing it. This is infamous, but it is not strange; there is no need of great acuteness to discover, that no ministers can govern long in Britain, unless they govern well, while the constitution maintains any degree of purity and vigor: nor that it is much more easy, as well as profitable to govern ill than well. From hence the system, which has been almost avowed in words, and which has been so very emphatically in actions, whose declarations are many times as explicit, and always more sure, than those that are contained in words. That such a system should be formed or adopted by faction, nay by contrary factions, I am not surprised; but what surprises me is, that any man, or faction of men in power, should wantonly sacrifice the honor and interest of their country to those of another, in a case where they can reap no conceivable private advantage by it, and where they might, by a contrary conduct, have confirmed themselves in power, and acquired some degree of public approbation, without the least discomposure of their original scheme.

I agree, that if any private job was to be done, or connived at, against the national interest, and in favor of some other to which the prince on the throne might be supposed affectionate, Sir Robert would not fail to make his court. This we have seen. But how can it be supposed in the present case, that the prince on the throne should think it his interest to favor Spain at the expense of Great Britain, unless Sir Robert has persuaded him that it is so? But then the question returns, why has he persuaded him? He may think that Philip II is on the throne of Spain; that an invincible armada will invade his kingdom; that the Pretender is actually in it; and that a formidable party, composed of all Sir Robert's enemies, is ready to take arms against the establishment. But his minister knows, I believe, that Philip V is on the throne of Spain; he must have heard something, even from Wager, of the weakness of the maritime forces of Spain; his brother may have informed him that the Pretender is at Rome; and as he is well enough apprised of the state of things at home, he must know that the jacobite party in Britain is an unorganised lump of inert matter, without a principle of life or action in it; capable of mobility, perhaps, but more capable of divisibility, and utterly void of all power of spontaneous motion.

I said that Walpole might, by a contrary conduct, have confirmed his authority, and have acquired some degree of public approbation. I think I said right; for though it has been said and thought, and thought perhaps by himself, that authority would be more divided in case of a war, and the event of a war might influence the state of things at home to his prejudice, yet it is evident he had nothing of this kind to fear. After negotiating his country into a necessity of making war, and then endeavoring to prevent it by the most scandalous, and in him the most impudent treaty that ever was made, he is continued, with as much authority as ever, at the head of the administration of the government, and the direction of this very war is by consequence left to him. What then is it that ties up his hands? Spain may be hurt, and cruelly hurt, many ways: why is not one stroke given, no nor aimed to be given? Why does he not endeavor to shut those mouths by his efforts in a war, that were opened against him by his negotiations? I could ask many questions of this kind, but I protest I could answer none of them, unless I supposed him a pensioner of Spain, or a silly, as well as a proud and obstinate creature, so silly as not to see his advantage, which every man, even in this country, sees for him; so proud and obstinate, that he determines, after having escaped vengeance for perverting the intentions of parliament by his negotiations in consequence of them, to deserve it still more by disappointing the hopes of the nation by a languid war.

And is this, my dear friend, the man in favor of whom the spirit of inquiry ought to *subside*, when he gives greater occasion for it by his manner of beginning the war, than he did even by that of concluding the negotiations, if in truth he has concluded them? Is this the man, the machine of whose power *no one is likely to have reputation enough to shake?* Is this the awful man, against whom little intrigues, warily carried on, must be alone employed? Is this the man, the hero, whom the king of terrors alone can subdue? If this man be so great, how little must others be! A European dwarf may appear a giant, but it must be at Lilliput.

The papers you mention may expose again to public view the turpitude of your minister; and the more that is shown, the more will the turpitude of those who will, and need not, bear him, be shown too. You are, however, in the right, to publish the part you and P. design to publish; and I shall be obliged to you, if you please to direct that it may be sent me. Make my best and kindest compliments to P. I rejoice in his fame, and I applaud your intimacy with him. Believe me, it is no small service to the commonwealth, to fan such fires as his. He is in the right to profit of your experience and judgment; and you are in the right to profit of his activity and vigor. Every age has something to lend to another. It is no small satisfaction to me to hear, that your fit of the gout is over; as much concern as I have for you personally, and no man has or can have more, even this concern increases as the want the public has of your assistance increases daily.   I thank you for making my compliments to the gentlemen you mention, and on the occasion you refer to.   On any other occasion, I believe, I have very few compliments to make in the country where you are.   No matter for that.   My affection for the British nation and government is founded on principles, that the injustice, the ingratitude, and treachery of particular men cannot shake; and I have often had the pleasure, such as it is, of observing some persons, while they imagined that they hid their game from me, and made use of me, against my intention, to serve their particular ends, who in truth hid nothing from me, and of whom I made some use, more in several cases than they intended, to serve the general and national end.   Adieu, my friend.

THE WORKS

OF

HENRY ST. JOHN,

LORD VISCOUNT BOLINGBROKE.

A LETTER

SIR WILLIAM WINDHAM.

I was well enough acquainted with the general character of mankind, and in particular with that of my own countrymen, to expect to be as much out of the minds of the tories during my exile, as if we had never lived and acted together. I depended on being forgot by them, and was far from imagining it possible that I should be remembered, only to be condemned loudly by one half of them, and to be tacitly censured by the greatest part of the other half. As soon as I was separated from the Pretender and his interest, I declared myself to be so, and I gave directions for writing into England what I judged sufficient to put my friends on their guard against any surprise concerning an event which it was their interest, as well as mine, that they should be very rightly informed about.

As soon as the Pretender's adherents began to clamor against me in this country, and to disperse their scandal by circular letters every where else, I gave directions for writing into England again. Their groundless articles of accusation were refuted, and enough was said to give my friends a general idea of what had happened to me, and at least to make them suspend the fixing any opinion till such time as I should be able to write more fully and plainly to them myself. To condemn no person unheard is a rule of natural equity, which we see rarely violated in Turkey, or in the country where I am writing: that it would not be so with me in Great Britain, I confess that I flattered myself. I dwelt securely in this confidence, and gave very little attention to any of those scurrilous methods, which were taken, about this time, to blast my reputation. The event of things has shown, that I trusted too much to my own innocence, and to the justice of my old friends.

It was obvious, that the chevalier and the Earl of Mar hoped to load me with the imputation of treachery, incapacity, or neglect; it was indifferent to them of which. If they could ascribe to one of those their not being supported from France, they imagined that they should justify their precipitate flight from Scotland, which many of their fastest friends exclaimed against; and that they should varnish over that original capital fault, the drawing the highlanders together in arms at the time and in the manner in which it was done.

The Scotch, who fell at once from all the sanguine expectations with which they had been soothed, and who found themselves reduced to despair, were easy to be incensed: they had received no support whatever, and it was natural for them rather to believe, that they failed of this support by my fault, than to imagine their general had prevailed on them to rise in the very point of time when it was impossible that they should be supported from France, or from any other part of the world. The Duke of Ormond, who had been the bubble of his own popularity, was enough out of humor with the general turn of affairs to be easily set against any particular man. The emissaries of this court, whose commission was to amuse, had imposed upon him all along, and there were other busy people who thought to find their account in having him to themselves. I had never been in his secret whilst we were in England together: and from his first coming into France he was either prevailed upon by others, or, which I rather believe, he concurred with others to keep me out of it. The perfect indifference I showed whether I was in it or no, might carry him from acting separately, to act against me.

The whole tribe of Irish and other papists were ready, to seize the first opportunity of venting their spleen against a man, who had constantly avoided all intimacy with them; who acted in the same cause but on a different principle, and who meant no one thing in the world less than raising them to the advantages which they expected.

That these several persons, for the reasons I have mentioned, should join in a cry against me, is not very marvellous: the contrary would be so to a man who knows them as well as I do.— But that the English tories should serve as echoes to them, nay more, that my character should continue doubtful at best amongst you, when those who first propagated the slander are become ashamed of railing without proof, and have dropped the clamor, this I own that I never expected, and I may be allowed to say, that as it is an extreme surprise, so it shall be a lesson to me.

The whigs impeached and attainted me. They went farther —at least in my way of thinking that step was more cruel than all the others—by a partial representation of facts, and pieces of facts, put together as it best suited their purpose, and published to the whole world, they did all that in them lay to expose me for a fool, and to brand me for a knave. But then I had deserved this abundantly at their hands, according to the notions of party-justice. The tories have not indeed impeached nor attainted me; but they have done, and are still doing something very like to that which I took worse of the whigs, than the impeachment and attainder: and this, after I had shown an inviolable attachment to the service, and almost an implicit obedience to the will of the party; when I am actually an outlaw, deprived of my honors, stripped of my fortune, and cut off from my family and my country for their sakes.

Some of the persons who have seen me here, and with whom I have had the pleasure to talk of you, may, perhaps, have told you, that far from being oppressed by that storm of misfortunes in which I have been tossed of late, I bear up against it with firmness enough, and even with alacrity. It is true, I do so: but it is true likewise, that the last burst of the cloud has gone near to overwhelm me. From our enemies we expect evil treatment of every sort, we are prepared for it, we are animated by it, and we sometimes triumph in it: but when our friends abandon us, when they wound us, and when they take, to do this, an occasion where we stand the most in need of their support, and have the best title to it, the firmest mind finds it hard to resist.

Nothing kept up my spirits when I was first reduced to the very circumstances I now describe, so much as the consideration of the delusions under which I knew that the tories lay, and the hopes I entertained of being able soon to open their eyes, and to justify my conduct. I expected that friendship, or if that principle failed, curiosity at least would move the party to send over some person, from whose report they might have both sides of the question laid before them. Though this expectation be founded in reason, and you want to be informed at least as much as I do to be justified, yet I have hitherto flattered myself with it in vain. To repair this misfortune, therefore, as far as lies in my power, I resolve to put into writing the sum of what I should have said in that case: these papers shall lie by me till time and accidents produce some occasion of communicating them to you. The true occasion of doing it, with advantage to the party, will probably be lost: but they will remain a monument of my justification to posterity. At worst if even this fails me, I am sure of one satisfaction in writing them; the satisfaction of unburdening my mind to a friend, and of stating before an equitable judge the account, as I apprehend it to stand, between the tories and myself. " Quantam humano concilio efficere potui, circumspectis rebus meis omnibus, rationibusque subductis, summam seci cogitationum mearum omnium, quam tibi si potero breviter exponam."

It is necessary to my design that I call to your mind the state of affairs in Britain from the latter part of the year one thousand seven hundred and ten, to the beginning of the year one thousand seven hundred and fifteen, about which time we parted. I go no farther back, because the part which I acted before that time, in the first essays I made in public affairs, was the part of a tory, and so far of a piece with that which I acted afterwards. Besides, the things which preceded this space of time had no immediate influence on those which happened since that time; whereas the strange events which we have seen fall out in the king's reign were owing in a great measure to what was done, or neglected to be done, in the last four years of the queen's. The memory of these events being fresh, I shall dwell as little as possible upon them. It will be sufficient that I make a rough sketch of the face of the court, and of the conduct of the several parties during that time. Your memory will soon furnish the colors which I shall omit to lay, and finish up the picture.

From the time at which I left Britain I had not the advantage of acting under the eyes of the party which I served, nor of being able from time to time to appeal to their judgment. The gross of what happened has appeared, but the particular steps which led to those events have been either concealed or misrepresented. Concealed from the nature of them, or misrepresented by those with whom I never agreed perfectly, except in thinking that they and I were extremely unfit to continue embarked in the same bottom together. It will, therefore, be proper to descend, under this head, to a more particular relation.

In the summer of the year one thousand seven hundred and ten the queen was prevailed upon to change her parliament and her ministry. The intrigue of the Earl of Oxford might facilitate the means, the violent prosecution of Sacheverel, and other unpopular measures might create the occasion, and encourage her in the resolution: but the true original cause was the personal ill usage which she received in her private life, and in some trifling instances of the exercise of her power; for indulgence in which she would certainly have left the reins of government in those hands, which had held them ever since her accession to the throne.

I am afraid that we came to court in the same dispositions as all parties have done; that the principal spring of our actions was to have the government of the state in our hands; that our principal views were the conservation of this power, great employments to ourselves, and great opportunities of rewarding those who had helped to raise us, and of hurting those who stood in opposition to us. It is however true, that with these considerations of private and party interest, there were others intermingled which had for their object the public good of the nation, at least what we took to be such.

We looked on the political principles which had generally prevailed in our government from the revolution in one thousand six hundred and eighty-eight to be destructive of our true interest, to have mingled us too much in the affairs of the continent, to tend to the impoverishing our people, and to the loosening the bands of our constitution in church and state. We supposed the tory party to be the bulk of the landed interest, and to have no contrary influence blended into its composition. We supposed the whigs to be the remains of a party, formed against the ill designs of the court under king Charles the Second, nursed up into strength and applied to contrary uses by king William the Third, and yet still so weak as to lean for support on the presbyterians and the other sectaries, on the bank and the other corporations, on the Dutch and the other allies. From hence we judged it to follow, that they had been forced, and must continue so, to render the national interest subservient to the interest of those who lent them an additional strength, without which they could never be the prevalent party. The view, therefore, of those amongst us who thought in this manner, was to improve the queen's favor, to break the body of the whigs, to render their supports useless to them, and to fill the employments of the kingdom down to the meanest with tories. We imagined that such measures, joined to the advantages of our numbers and our property, would secure us against all attempts during her reign; and that we should soon become too considerable, not to make our terms in all events which might happen afterwards: concerning which, to speak truly, I believe few or none of us had any very settled resolution.

In order to bring these purposes about, I verily think that the persecution of dissenters entered into no man's head. By the bills for preventing occasional conformity and the growth of schism, it was hoped that their sting would be taken away. These bills were thought necessary for our party interest, and besides were deemed neither unreasonable nor unjust. The good of society may require that no person should be deprived of the protection of the government on account of his opinions in religious matters, but it does not follow from hence that men ought to be trusted in any degree with the preservation of the establishment, who must, to be consistent with their principles, endeavor the subversion of what is established. An indulgence to consciences, which the prejudice of education and long habits have rendered scrupulous, may be agreeable to the rules of good policy and of humanity: yet will it hardly follow from hence, that a government is under any obligation to indulge a tender-

ness of conscience to come; or to connive at the propagating of
these prejudices, and at the forming of these habits. The evil
effect is without remedy, and may therefore deserve indulgence;
but the evil cause is to be prevented, and can, therefore, be entitled to none. Besides this, the bills I am speaking of, rather
than to enact anything new, seemed only to enforce the observation of ancient laws; which had been judged necessary for the
security of the church and state, at a time when the memory of
the ruin of both, and of the hands by which that ruin had been
wrought, was fresh in the minds of men.

The bank, the East-India company, and in general the moneyed
interest, had certainly nothing to apprehend like what they
feared, or affected to fear from the tories, an entire subversion of
their property. Multitudes of our own party would have been
wounded by such a blow. The intention of those, who were
the warmest, seemed to me to go no farther than restraining
their influence on the legislature, and on matters of state; and
finding at a proper season means to make them contribute to the
support and ease of a government, under which they enjoyed
advantages so much greater than the rest of their fellow subjects,
The mischievous consequence which had been foreseen and foretold too, at the establishment of those corporations, appeared
visibly. The country gentlemen were vexed, put to great expenses and even baffled by them in their elections: and among
the members of every parliament numbers were immediately or
indirectly under their influence. The bank had been extravagant enough to pull off the mask, and when the queen seemed
to intend a change in her ministry, they had deputed some of
their members to represent against it. But that which touched
sensibly, even those who were but little affected by other considerations, was the prodigious inequality between the condition
of the moneyed men and of the rest of the nation. The proprietor of the land, and the merchant who brought riches home
by the returns of foreign trade, had during two wars bore the
whole immense load of the national expenses; whilst the lender
of money, who added nothing to the common stock, throve by
the public calamity, and contributed not a mite to the public
charge.

As to the allies, I saw no difference of opinion among all those
who came to the head of affairs at this time. Such of the tories
as were in the system abovementioned, such of them as deserted
soon after from us, and such of the whigs as had upon this occasion deserted to us, seemed equally convinced of the unreasonableness and even of the impossibility of continuing the war on
the same disproportionate foot. Their universal sense was that
we had taken, except the part of the States General, the whole

burden of the war upon us, and even a proportion of this; while
the entire advantage was to accrue to others: that this had appeared very grossly in one thousand seven hundred and nine and
one thousand seven hundred and ten, when preliminaries were
insisted upon, which contained all that the allies, giving the
greatest loose to their wishes, could desire, and little or nothing
on the behalf of Great Britain: that the war, which had been
begun for the security of the allies, was continued for their grandeur; that the ends proposed when we engaged in it might have
been answered long before, and therefore that the first favorable
occasion ought to be seized of making peace; which we thought
to be the interest of our country. and which appeared to all mankind, as well as to us, to be that of our party.

These were in general the views of the tories, and for the part
I acted in the prosecution of them, as well as of all the measures
accessory to them, I may appeal to mankind. To those who had
the opportunity of looking behind the curtain I may likewise appeal for the difficulties which lay in my way, and for the particular discouragements which I met with. A principal load of
parliamentary and foreign affairs in their ordinary course, lay
upon me: the whole negotiation of the peace and of the troublesome invidious steps preliminary to it, as far as they could be
transacted at home, were thrown upon me. I continued in the
house of commons during that important session which preceded
the peace; and which, by the spirit shown through the whole
course of it, and by the resolutions taken in it, rendered the conclusion of the treaties practicable. After this I was dragged into
the house of lords in such a manner, as to make my promotion a
punishment, not a reward, and was there left to defend the treaties
almost alone.

It would not have been hard to have forced the Earl of Oxford
to use me better. His good intentions began to be very much
doubted of: the truth is, no opinion of his sincerity had ever taken
root in the party; and which was worse, perhaps, for a man in
his station, the opinion of his capacity began to fall apace. He
was so hard pushed in the house of lords, in the beginning of one
thousand seven hundred and twelve, that he had been forced, in
the middle of the session, to persuade the queen to make a promotion of twelve peers at once; which was an unprecedented
and invidious measure, to be excused by nothing but the necessity, and hardly by that. In the house of commons his credit was
low, and my reputation very high. You know the nature of that
assembly: they grow, like hounds, fond of the man who shows
them game, and by whose halloo they are used to be encouraged.
The thread of the negotiations, which could not stand still a moment without going back, was in my hands: and before another

man could have made himself master of the business, much time wulod have been lost, and great inconveniences would have followed.   Some, who opposed the court soon after, began to waver then: and if I had not wanted the inclination, I should have wanted no help to do mischief.   I knew the way of quitting my employments and of retiring from court when the service of my party required it: but I could not bring myself up to that resolution, when the consequence of it must have been the breaking of my party, and the distress of the public affairs.   I thought my mistress treated me ill, but the sense of that duty which I owed her came in aid of other considerations, and prevailed over my resentment.   These sentiments, indeed, are so much out of fashion, that a man who avows them is in danger of passing for a bubble in the world: yet they were, in the conjuncture I speak of, the true motives of my conduct, and you saw me go on as cheerfully in the troublesome and dangerous work assigned me as if I had been under the utmost satisfaction.   I began, indeed, in my heart to renounce the friendship, which till that time I had preserved inviolable for Oxford.   I was not aware of all his treachery, nor of the base and little means which he employed then, and continued to employ afterwards, to ruin me in the opinion of the queen and every where else.   I saw, however, that he had no friendship for any body, and that with respect to me, instead of having the ability to render that merit which I endeavored to acquire an addition of strength to himself, it became the object of his jealousy, and a reason for undermining me.   In this temper of mind I went on, till the great work of the peace was consummated, and the treaty signed at Utrecht: after which a new and more melancholy scene for the party, as well as for me, opened itself.

I am far from thinking the treaties, or the negotiations which led to them, exempt from faults.   Many were made no doubt in both, by those who were concerned in them, by myself in the first place: and many were owing purely to the opposition they met with in every step of their progress.   I never look back on this great event, passed as it is, without a secret emotion of mind; when I compare the vastness of the undertaking, and the importance of its success, with the means employed to bring it about, and with those which were employed to traverse it.   To adjust the pretensions and to settle the interest of so many princes and states, as were engaged in the late war, would appear, when considered simply and without any adventitious difficulty, a work of prodigious extent.   But this was not all.   Each of our allies thought himself entitled to raise his demands to the most extravagant height.   They had been encouraged to this, first by the engagements which we had entered into with several of them;

with some to draw them into the war, with others to prevail on them to continue it; and secondly, by the manner in which we had treated with France in seventeen hundred nine and ten. Those who intended to tie the knot of the war as hard, and to render the coming at a peace as impracticable as they could, had found no method so effectual as that of leaving every one at liberty to insist on all he could think of, and leaving themselves at liberty, even if these concessions should be made, to break the treaty, by ulterior demands. That this was the secret, I can make no doubt after the confession of one of the plenipotentiaries* who transacted these matters, and who communicated to me and to two others of the queen's ministers an instance of the Duke of Marlborough's management at a critical moment, when the French ministers at Gertrudenberg, seemed inclinable to come into an expedient for explaining the thirty-seventh article of the preliminaries, which could not have been refused. Certain it is, that the king of France was at that time in earnest to execute the article of Philip's abdication: and therefore the expedients for adjusting what related to this article would easily enough have been found, if on our part there had been a real intention of concluding. But there was no such intention: and the plan of those who meant to prolong the war was established among the allies, as the plan which ought to be followed whenever a peace came to be treated. The allies imagined that they had a right to obtain at least every thing which had been demanded for them respectively: and it was visible that nothing less would content them. These considerations set the vastness of the undertaking in a sufficient light.

The importance of succeeding, in the work of the peace, was equally great to Europe, to our country, to our party, to our persons, to the present age, and to future generations. But I need not take pains to prove what no man will deny. The means employed to bring it about were in no degree proportionable. A few men, some of whom had never been concerned in business of this kind before, and most of whom put their hands for a long time to it faintly and timorously, were the instruments of it. The minister who was at their head showed himself every day incapable of that attention, that method, that comprehension of different matters, which the first post in such a government as ours requires in quiet times. He was the first spring of all our motion by his credit with the queen, and his concurrence was necessary to every thing we did by his rank in the state. And yet this man seemed to be sometimes asleep and sometimes at play. He neglected the thread of business, which was carried on for this reason with less despatch and less advantage in the proper channels, and he

* Buys, pensionary of Amsterdam.

kept none in his own hands. He negotiated indeed by fits and
starts, by little tools and indirect ways: and thus his activity
became as hurtful as his indolence; of which I could produce
some remarkable instances. No good effect could flow from such
a conduct. In a word, when this great affair was once engaged,
the zeal of particular men in their several provinces drove it forward, though they were not backed by the concurrent force of
the whole administration, nor had the common helps of advice till
it was too late, till the very end of the negotiations: even in
matters, such as that of commerce, which they could not be supposed to understand. That this is a true account of the means
used to arrive at the peace, and a true character of that administration in general, I believe the whole cabinet council of that time
will bear me witness. Sure I am, that most of them have joined
with me in lamenting this state of things whilst it subsisted, and
all those who were employed as ministers in the several parts of
the treaty felt sufficiently the difficulties which this strange management often reduced them to. I am confident they have not
forgotten them.

If the means employed to bring the peace about were feeble,
and in one respect contemptible, those employed to break the
negotiation were strong snd formidable. As soon as the first
suspicion of a treaty's being on foot crept abroad into the world,
the whole alliance united with a powerful party in the nation to
obstruct it. From that hour to the moment the congress of
Utrecht finished, no one measure possible to be taken, was omitted to traverse every advance that was made in this work, to intimidate, to allure, to embarrass every person concerned in it.
This was done without any regard either to decency or good
policy: and from hence it soon followed, that passion and humor
mingled themselves on each side. A great part of what we did
for the peace, and of what others did against it, can be accounted for on no other principle. The allies were broke among themselves before they began to treat with the common enemy. The
matter did not mend in the course of the treaty: and France and
Spain, but especially the former, profited of this disunion.

Whoever makes the comparison, which I have touched upon,
will see the true reasons which rendered the peace less answerable to the success of the war than it might, and than it ought to
have been. Judgment has been passed in this case, as the different
passions or interests of men have inspired them. But the real
cause lay in the constitution of our ministry, and much more in
the obstinate opposition which we met with from the whigs and
from the allies. However, sure it is that the defects of the peace
did not occasion the desertions from the tory party which happened about this time, nor those disorders in the court which immediately followed.

Long before the purport of the treaties could be known, those whigs who had set out with us, in seventeen hundred and ten, began to relapse back to their party.   They had among us shared the harvest of a new ministry, and like prudent persons they took measures in time to have their share in that of a new government.

The whimsical, or the Hanover tories, continued zealous in appearance with us, till the peace was signed.   I saw no people so eager for the conclusion of it.*   Some of them were in such haste, that they thought any peace would be preferable to the least delay, and omitted no instances to quicken their friends who were actors in it.   As soon as the treaties were perfected and laid before the parliament, the scheme of these gentlemen began to disclose itself entirely.   Their love of the peace, like other passions, cooled by enjoyment.   They grew nice about the construction of the articles, could come up to no direct approbation, and, being let into the secret of what was to happen, would not preclude themselves from the glorious advantage of rising on the ruins of their friends and of their party.

The danger of the succession, and the badness of the peace, were the two principles on which we were attacked.   On the first, the whimsical tories joined the whigs, and declared directly against their party.   Although nothing is more certain than this truth, that there was at that time no formed design in the party, whatever views some particular men might have, against his majesty's accession to the throne.   On the latter and most other points, they affected a most glorious neutrality.

Instead of gathering strength, either as a ministry or as a party, we grew weaker every day.   The peace had been judged with reason to be the only solid foundation whereupon we could erect a tory system: and yet when it was made we found ourselves at a full stand.   Nay, the very work which ought to have been the basis of our strength, was in part demolished before our eyes, and we were stoned with the ruins of it.   Whilst this was doing, Oxford looked on, as if he had not been a party to all which had passed; broke now and then a jest, which savored of the inns of court and the bad company in which he had been bred: and on those occasions, where his station obliged him to speak of business, was absolutely unintelligible.

Whether this man ever had any determined view besides that of raising his family is, I believe, a problematical question in the world.   My opinion is, that he never had any other.   The conduct of a minister, who proposes to himself a great and noble object, and who pursues it steadily, may seem for a while a riddle to the world; especially in a government like ours, where

* Hanmer's Letter.

numbers of men different in their characters and different in their interests are at all times to be managed: where public affairs are exposed to more accidents and greater hazards than in other countries; and where, by consequence, he who is at the head of business will find himself often distracted by measures which have no relation to his purpose, and obliged to bend himself to things which are in some degree contrary to his main design.— The ocean which environs us is an emblem of our government: and the pilot and the minister are in similar circumstances. I seldom happens, that either of them can steer a direct course, and they both arrive at their port by means which frequently seem to carry them from it. But as the work advances, the conduct of him who leads it on with real abilities clears up, the appearing inconsistencies are reconciled, and when it is once consummated, the whole shows itself so uniform, so plain, and so natural, that every dabbler in politics will be apt to think he could have done the same. But on the other hand, a man who proposes no such object, who substitutes artifice in the place of ability, who instead of leading parties and governing accidents is eternally agitated backwards and forwards by both, who begins every day something new, and carries nothing on to perfection, may impose a while on the world: but a little sooner or a little later the mystery will be revealed, and nothing will be found to be couched under it but a thread of pitiful expedients, the ultimate end of which never extended farther than living from day to day. Which of these pictures resembles Oxford most, you will determine. I am sorry to be obliged to name him so often; but how is it possible to do otherwise, while I am speaking of times wherein the whole turn of affairs depended on his motions and character?

I have heard, and I believe truly, that when he returned to Windsor in the autumn of seventeen hundred and thirteen, after the marriage of his son, he pressed extremely to have him created Duke of Newcastle or Earl of Clare: and the queen presuming to hesitate on so extraordinary a proposal, he resented this hesitation in a manner which little became a man who had been so lately raised by the profusion of her favors upon him. Certain it is, that he began then to show a still greater remissness in all parts of his ministry, and to affect to say, that from such a time, the very time I am speaking of, he took no share in the direction of affairs, or words to that effect.

He pretended to have discovered intrigues which were set on foot against him, and particularly he complained of the advantage which was taken of his absence, during the journey he made at his son's marriage, to undermine him with the queen. He is naturally inclined to believe the worst, which I take to be a certain mark of a mean spirit and a wicked soul: at least I am sure that the contrary quality, when it is not due to weakness of understanding, is the fruit of a generous temper, and an honest heart. Prone to judge ill of all mankind, he will rarely be seduced by his credulity; but I never knew a man so capable of being the bubble of his distrust and jealousy. He was so in this case, although the queen, who could not be ignorant of the truth, said enough to undeceive him. But to be undeceived, and to own himself so, was not his play. He hoped by cunning to varnish over his want of faith and of ability. He was desirous to make the world impute the extraordinary part, or to speak more properly, the no part which he acted with the staff of treasurer in his hand, to the queen's withdrawing her favor from him, and to his friends abandoning him: pretences utterly groundless, when he first made them, and which he brought to be real at last. Even the winter before the queen's death, when his credit began to wane apace, he might have regained it; he might have reconciled him self perfectly with all his ancient friends, and have acquired the confidence of the whole party. I say he might have done all this; because I am persuaded that none of those I have named were so convinced of his perfidy, so jaded with his yoke, or so much piqued personally against him as I was: and yet if he would have exerted himself in concert with us, to improve the few advantages which were left us, and to ward off the visible danger which threatened our persons and our party, I would have stifled my private animosity, and would have acted under him with as much zeal as ever. But he was incapable of taking such a turn. The sum of all his policy had been to amuse the whigs, the tories, and the jacobites, as long as he could, and to keep his power as long as he amused them. When it became impossible to amuse mankind any longer, he appeared plainly at the end of his line.

By a secret correspondence with the late Earl of Halifax, and by the intrigues of his brother, and other fanatical relations, he had endeavored to keep some hold on the whigs.

The tories were attached to him at first by the heat of a revolution in the ministry, by their hatred of the people who were discarded, and by the fond hopes which it is easy to give at the setting out of a new administration. Afterwards he held out the peace in prospect to them, and to the jacobites, separately, as an event which must be brought about before he could effectually serve either. You cannot have forgot how things which we pressed were put off, upon every occasion, till the peace: the peace was to be the date of a new administration, and the period at which the millennary year of toryism should begin. Thus were the tories at that time amused: and since my exile I

have had the opportunity of knowing certainly and circumstantially that the jacobites were treated in the same manner,
and that the Pretender was made, through the French minister,
to expect that measures should be taken for his restoration, as
soon as the peace had rendered them practicable. He was to
attempt nothing, his partisans were to lie still, Oxford undertook
for all.

After many delays, fatal to the general interest of Europe,
this peace was signed, and the only considerable thing which he
brought about afterwards was the marriage I have mentioned
above: and by it an accession of riches and honor to a family
whose estate was very mean, and whose illustration before this
time I never met with any where but in the vain discourses
which he used to hold over claret. If he kept his word with
any of the parties above mentioned, it must be supposed that he
did so with the whigs; for as to us we saw nothing after the
peace but increase of mortification and nearer approaches to
ruin. Not a step was made towards completing the settlement
of Europe, which the treaties of Utrecht and Radstat left imperfect; towards fortifying and establishing the tory party;
towards securing those who had been the principal actors in this
administration against future events. We had proceeded in a
confidence that these things should immediately follow the conclusion of the peace: he had never, I dare swear, entertained a
thought concerning them. As soon as the last hand was given
to the fortune of his family, he abandoned his mistress, his friends,
and his party, who had borne him so many years on their shoulders: and I was present when this want of faith was reproached
him in the plainest and strongest terms by one of the honestest*
men in Britain, and before some of the most considerable tories.†
Even his impudence failed him on this occasion; he did not so
much as attempt an excuse.

He could not keep his word which he had given the Pretender
and his adherents, because he had formed no party to support
him in such a design. He was sure of having the whigs against
him if he made the attempt, and he was not sure of having the
tories for him.

In this state of confusion and distress, to which he had reduced himself and us, you remember the part he acted. He
was the spy of the whigs, and voted with us in the morning
against those very questions which he had penned the night before with Walpole and others. He kept his post on terms which
no man but he would have held it on, neither submitting to the

---

* Lord Trevor.
† Duke of Ormond, Lord Anglesey, Lord Harcourt, and myself in Oxford's
lodgings in St. James's house.

queen, nor complying with his friends. He would not, or he
could not act with us, and he resolved that we should not act
without him, as long as he could hinder it. The queen's health
was very precarious, and at her death he hoped by these means
to deliver us up, bound as it were hand and foot, to our adversaries. On the foundation of this merit he flattered himself that
he had gained some of the whigs, and softened at least the rest
of the party to him. By his secret negotiations at Hanover, he
took it for granted that he was not only reconciled to that court,
but that he should under his present majesty's reign have as
much credit as he had enjoyed under that of the queen. He
was weak enough to boast of this, and to promise his good
offices voluntarily to several, for no man was weak enough to
think them worth being solicited. In a word, you must have
heard that he answered to Lord Dartmouth and to Mr. Bromley,
that one should keep the privy seal, and the other the seals of
secretary; and that Lord Cowper makes no scruples of telling
how he came to offer him the seals of chancellor. When the
king arrived, he went to Greenwich with an affectation of pomp
and of favor. Against his suspicious character, he was once in
his life the bubble of his credulity: and this delusion betrayed
him into a punishment, more severe in my sense than all which
has happened to him since, or than perpetual exile; he was
affronted at the manner in which he was presented to the king.
The meanest subject would have been received with goodness,
the most obnoxious with an air of indifference; but he was received with the most distinguishing contempt. This treatment
he had in the face of the nation. The king began his reign, in
this instance, with punishing the ingratitude, the perfidy, the
insolence which had been shown to his predecessor. Oxford
fled from court covered with shame, the object of the derision of
the whigs, and of the indignation of the tories.

The queen might, if she had pleased, have saved herself from
all those mortifications she met with during the last months of
her reign, and her servants and the tory party from those misfortunes which they endured during the same time; perhaps
from those which they have fallen into since her death. When
she found that the peace, from the conclusion of which she expected ease and quiet, brought still greater trouble upon her;
when she saw the weakness of her government, and the confusion of her affairs increase every day; when she saw her first
minister bewildered and unable to extricate himself or her; in
fine, when the negligence of his public conduct, and the sauci-
ness of his private behavior had rendered him insupportable to
her, and she took the resolution of laying him aside, there was
a strength still remaining sufficient to have supported her govern-

ment, to have fulfilled in great part the expectations of the tories,
and to have constituted both them and the ministers in such a
situation as would have left them little to apprehend.   Some
designs were indeed on foot which might have produced very
great disorders: Oxford's conduct had given much occasion to
them, and with the terror of them, he endeavored to intimidate
the queen.   But expedients were not hard to be found, by which
those designs might have been nipped in the bud, or else by which
the persons who promoted them, might have been induced to lay
them aside.   But that fatal irresolution inherent to the Stuart
race hung upon her.   She felt too much inward resentment to
be able to conceal his disgrace from him: yet after he had made
this discovery, she continued to trust all her power in his hands.
No people were ever in such a condition as ours continued to
be from the autumn of one thousand seven hundred and thirteen,
to the summer following.   The queen's health sunk every day.
The attack which she had in the winter at Windsor, served as a
warning both to those who wished, and those who feared her
death, to expect it.   The party which opposed the court had
been continually gaining strength by the weakness of our administration: and at this time their numbers were vastly increased,
and their spirit was raised by the near prospect of the succession
taking place.   We were not at liberty to exert the strength we
had.   We saw our danger, and many of us saw the true means
of avoiding it: but whilst the magic wand was in the same
hands, this knowledge served only to increase our uneasiness;
aud whether we would or no, we were forced with our eyes
open to walk on towards the precipice.   Every moment we became less able, if the queen lived, to support her government:
if she died, to secure ourselves.   One side was united in a common view, and acted upon a uniform plan; the other had really
none at all.   We knew that we were out of favor at the court
of Hanover, that we were represented there as jacobites, and
that the elector, his present majesty, had been rendered publicly
a party to that opposition, in spite of which we made the peace:
and yet we neither had taken, nor could take, in our present circumstances, any measures to be better or worse there.   Thus we
languished till the twenty-seventh of July one thousand seven
hundred and fourteen, when the queen dismissed the treasurer.
On the Friday following, she fell into an apoplexy, and died on
Sunday the first of August.

You do me, I dare say, the justice to believe, that whilst this
state of things lasted, I saw very well, how little mention soever
I might make of it at the time, that no man in the ministry, or
in the party, was so much exposed as myself.   I could expect
no quarter from the whigs; for I had deserved none.   There

were persons amongst them for whom I had great esteem and
friendship; yet neither with these nor with any others had I preserved a secret correspondence, which might be of use to me in
the day of distress: and besides the general character of my
party, I knew that particular prejudices were entertained against
me at Hanover. The whigs wanted nothing but an opportunity
of attacking the peace, and it could hardly be imagined that they
would stop there. In which case, I knew that they could have
hold on no man so much as myself: the instructions, the orders,
the memorials had been drawn by me, the correspondence relating to it in France, and every where else, had been carried on
by me; in a word, my hand appeared to almost every paper
which had been writ in the whole course of the negotiation.
To all these considerations I added that of the weight of personal resentment, which I had created against myself at home
and abroad: in part unavoidably by the share I was obliged to
take in these affairs; and in part, if you will, unnecessarily by
the warmth of my temper, and by some unguarded expressions
for which I have no excuse to make, but that which Tacitus
makes for his father-in-law, Julius Agricola: " *honestius puta-
bam offendere quam odisse.*"

Having this prospect of being distinguished from the rest of
my party in the common calamity, by severer treatment, I might
have justified myself, by reason and by great authorities too, if I
had made early provision, at least to be safe, when I should be
no longer useful. How I could have secured this point, I do not
think fit to explain, but certain it is that I made no one step towards it. I resolved not to abandon my party by turning whig,
or, which is worse a great deal, whimsical, not to treat separately
from it. I resolved to keep myself at liberty to act on a tory
bottom. If the queen disgraced Oxford and continued to live
afterwards, I knew we should have time and means to provide
for our future safety: if the queen died and left us in the same
unfortunate circumstances, I expected to suffer for and with the
tories, and I was prepared for it.

The thunder had long grumbled in the air, and yet when the
bolt fell, most of our party appeared as much surprised as if they
had no reason to expect it. There was a perfect calm and universal submission through the whole kingdom. The Chevalier
indeed set out as if his design had been to gain the coast and to
embark for Great Britain, and the court of France made a merit
to themselves of stopping him and obliging him to return. But
this, to my certain knowledge, was a farce acted by concert, to
keep up an opinion of his character, when all opinion of his
cause seemed to be at an end. He owned this concert to me at
Bar, on the occasion of my telling him that he would have found

no party ready to receive him, and that the enterprise would have been to the last degree extravagant. He was at this time far from having any encouragement: no party, numerous enough to make the least disturbance, was formed in his favor. On the king's arrival the storm arose. The menaces of the whigs, backed by some very rash declarations, by little circumstances of humor which frequently offend more than real injuries, and by the entire change of all the persons in employment, blew up the coals.

At first many of the tories had been made to entertain some faint hopes that they would be permitted to live in quiet. I have been assured that the king left Hanover in that resolution. Happy had it been for him and for us if he had continued in it; if the moderation of his temper had not been overborne by the violence of party, and his and the national interest sacrificed to the passions of a few. Others there were among the tories who had flattered themselves with much greater expectations than these, and who had depended, not on such imaginary favor and dangerous advancement as was offered them afterwards, but on real credit and substantial power under the new government. Such impressions on the minds of men had rendered the two houses of parliament, which were then sitting, as good courtiers to king George as ever they had been to queen Anne. But all these hopes being at once and with violence extinguished, despair succeeded in their room.

Our party began soon to act like men delivered over to their passions, and unguided by any other principle; not like men fired by a just resentment and a reasonable ambition to a bold undertaking. They treated the government like men who were resolved not to live under it, and yet they took no one measure to support themselves against it. They expressed, without reserve or circumspection an eagerness to join in any attempt against the establishment which they had received and confirmed, and which many of them had courted but a few weeks before: and yet in the midst of all this bravery, when the election of the new parliament came on, some of these very men acted with the coolness of those who are much better disposed to compound than to take arms.

The body of the tories being in this temper, it is not to be wondered at, if they heated one another, and began apace to turn their eyes towards the Pretender: and if those few, who had already engaged with him, applied themselves to improve the conjuncture and endeavored to list a party for him.

I went about a month after the queen's death, as soon as the seals were taken from me, into the country, and whilst I continued there I felt the general disposition to jacobitism increase daily among people of all ranks; among several who had been con-

stantly distinguished by their aversion to that cause.   But at my
return to London in the month of February or March one thousand seven hundred and fifteen, a few weeks before I left England,
I began for the first time in my whole life to perceive these general dispositions ripen into resolutions, and to observe some regular
workings among many of our principal friends, which denoted a
scheme of this kind.   These workings, indeed, were very faint,
for the persons concerned in carrying them on did not think it
safe to speak too plainly to men who were, in truth, ill disposed
to the government, because they neither found their account at
present under it, nor had been managed with art enough to leave
them hopes of finding it hereafter; but who at the same time had
not the least affection for the Pretender's person, nor any principle favorable to his interest.

This was the state of things when the new parliament, which
his majesty had called, assembled.   A great majority of the
elections had gone in favor of the whigs; to which the want
of concert among the tories had contributed as much as the vigor
of that party, and the influence of the new government.   The
whigs came to the opening of this parliament full of as much violence as could possess men who expected to make their court, to
confirm themselves in power, and to gratify their resentments by
the same measures.   I have heard that it was a dispute among the
ministers how far this spirit should be indulged, and that the king
was determined or confirmed in a determination, to consent to the
prosecutions, and to give the reins to the party by the representations that were made to him, that great difficulties would arise
in the conduct of the session, if the court should appear inclined to
check this spirit, and by Mr. W——'s undertaking to carry all
the business successfully through the house of commons if they
were at liberty.   Such has often been the unhappy fate of our
princes: a real necessity sometimes, and sometimes a seeming
one, has forced them to compound with a part of the nation at
the expense of the whole; and the success of their business for one
year has been purchased at the price of public disorder for many.

The conjuncture I am speaking of affords a memorable instance
of this truth.   If milder measures had been pursued, certain it
is, that the tories had never universally embraced jacobitism.
The violence of the whigs forced them into the arms of the
Pretender.   The court and the party seemed to vie with one
another which should go the greatest lengths in severity: and
the ministers, whose true interest it must at all times be to calm
the minds of men, and who ought never to sct the examples of
extraordinary inquiries or extraordinary accusations, were upon
this occasion the tribunes of the people.

The council of regency, which began to sit as soon as the

queen died, acted like a council of the holy office. Whoever looked on the face of the nation saw every thing quiet; not one of those symptoms appearing which must have shown themselves more or less at that moment, if, in reality, there had been any measures taken during the former reign to defeat the protestant succession. His majesty ascended the throne with as little contradiction and as little trouble, as ever a son succeeded a father in the possession of a private patrimony. But he, who had the opportunity, which I had till my dismission, of seeing a great part of what had passed in that council, would have thought that there had been an opposition actually formed, that the new establishment was attacked openly from without, and betrayed from within.

The same disposition continued after the king's arrival. This political inquisition went on with all the eagerness imaginable in seizing of papers, in ransacking the queen's closet, and examining even her private letters. The whigs had clamored loudly, and affirmed in the face of the world, that the nation had been sold to France, to Spain, to the Pretender: and whilst they endeavored in vain, by very singular methods, to find some color to justify what they had advanced without proof, they put themselves under an absolute necessity of grounding the most solemn prosecution on things whereof they might indeed have proof, but which would never pass for crimes before any judges, but such as were parties at the same time.

In the king's first speech from the throne, all the inflaming hints were given, and all the methods of violence were chalked out to the two houses. The first steps in both were perfectly answerable: and to the shame of the peerage be it spoken, I saw at that time several lords concur to condemn, in one general vote, all that they had approved of in a former parliament by many particular resolutions. Among several bloody resolutions proposed and agitated at this time, the resolution of impeaching me of high treason was taken: and I took that of leaving England, not in a panic terror improved by the artifices of the Duke of Marlborough, whom I knew even at that time too well to act by his advice or information in any case, but on such grounds as the proceedings which soon followed sufficiently justified, and as I have never repented building upon. Those who blamed it in first heat were soon after obliged to change their language; for what other resolution could I take? The method of prosecution designed against me would have put me immediately out of condition to act for myself, or to serve those who were less exposed than me, but who were, however, in danger. On the other hand, how few were there on whose assistance I could depend, or to whom I would, even in those circumstances, be obliged?

The ferment in the nation was wrought up to a considerable height; but there was at that time no reason to expect that it would influence the proceedings in parliament in favor of those who should be accused. Left to its own movement, it was much more proper to quicken than slacken the prosecutions: and who was there to guide its motions? The tories who had been true to one another to the last were an handful, and no great vigor could be expected from them. The whimsicals, disappointed of the figure which they hoped to make, began, indeed, to join their old friends. One* of the principal amongst them was so very good as to confess to me, that if the court had called the servants of the late queen to account, and had stopped there, he must have considered himself as a judge; and have acted according to his conscience on what should have appeared to him: but that war had been declared to the whole tory party, and that now the state of things was altered. This discourse needed no commentary, and proved to me, that I had never erred in the judgment I made of this set of men. Could I then resolve to be obliged to them, or to suffer with Oxford? As much as I still was heated by the disputes in which I had been all my life engaged against the whigs, I would sooner have chose to owe my security to their indulgence, than to the assistance of the whimsicals: but I thought banishment, with all her train of evils, preferable to either. I abhorred Oxford to that degree, that I could not bear to be joined with him in any case. Nothing perhaps contributed so much to determine me as this sentiment. A sense of honor would not have permitted me to distinguish between his case and mine own: and it was worse than death to lie under the necessity of making them the same, and of taking measures in concert with him.

I am now come to the time at which I left England, and have finished the first part of that deduction of facts which I proposed to lay before you. I am hopeful, that you will not think it altogether tedious or unnecessary: for although very little of what I have said can be new to you, yet this summary account will enable you with greater ease to recall to your memory the passages of those four years, wherewith all that I am going to relate to you has an immediate and necessary connection.

In what has been said I am far from making my own panegyric. I had not in those days so much merit as was ascribed to me: nor since that time have I had so little as the same persons allowed me. I committed without dispute many faults, and a greater man than I can pretend to be, constituted in the same

---

* Earl of Anglesey. I told the fact to the Bishop of Rochester that night or the next day.

circumstances, would not have kept clear of all: but with respect to the tories I committed none. I carried the point of party honor to the height, and sacrificed every thing to my attachment to them during this period of time. Let us now examine whether I have done so during the rest.

When I arrived in France, about the end of March one thousand seven hundred and fifteen, the affairs of England were represented to me in another light than I had seen them in, when I looked upon them with my own eyes a very few weeks before. I found the persons, who were detached to speak with me, prepared to think that I came over to negotiate for the Pretender: and when they perceived that I was more ignorant than they imagined, I was assured by them, that there would be suddenly a universal rising in England and Scotland. The leaders were named to me, their engagements specified, and many gentlemen, yourself among others, were reckoned upon for particular services, though I was certain you had never been treated with. From whence I concluded, and the event has justified my opinion, that these assurances had been given on the general characters of men, by such of our friends as had embarked sooner, and gone farther than the rest.

This management surprised me extremely. In the answers I made, I endeavored to set the mistake right: to show that things were far from the point of maturity imagined; that the Chevalier had yet no party for him, and that nothing could form one but the extreme violence which the whigs threatened to exercise. Great endeavors were used to engage me in this affair, and to prevail on me to answer the letter of invitation sent me from Bar. I alleged, as it was true, that I had no commission from any person in England, and that the friends I left behind me were the only persons who could determine me, if any could, to take such a step. As to the last proposition, I absolutely refused it.

In the uncertainty of what would happen, whether the prosecutions would be pushed, which was most probable, in the manner intended against me, and against others, for all of whom except the Earl of Oxford, I had as much concern as for myself; or whether the whigs would relent, drop some, and soften the fate of others; I resolved to conduct myself so as to create no appearance which might be strained into a pretence for hard usage, and which might be retorted on my friends when they debated for me, or when they defended themselves. I saw the Earl of Stair, I promised him that I would enter into no jacobite engagements, and I kept my word with him. I wrote a letter to Mr. Secretary Stanhope, which might take off any imputation of neglect of the government; and I retired into Dauphiné to remove the objection of residence near the court of France.

This retreat from Paris was censured in England, and styled a desertion of my friends and of their cause: with what foundation let any reasonable man determine. Had I engaged with the Pretender before the party acted for him, or required of me that I should do so, I had taken the air of being his man; whereas I looked on myself as theirs: I had gone about to bring them into his measures; whereas, I never intended, even since that time, to do any thing more than to make him act conformably to their views.

During the short time I continued on the banks of the Rhone, the prosecutions were carried on at Westminster with the utmost violence, and the ferment among the people had risen to such a degree, that it could end in nothing better, it might have ended in something worse, than it did. The measures which I observed at Paris had turned to no account; on the contrary, the letter which I wrote to Mr. Secretary Stanhope was quoted as a base and fawning submission: and what I intended as a mark of respect to the government, and a service to my friends, was perverted to ruin me in the opinion of the latter. The act of attainder, in consequence of my impeachment, had passed against me, for crimes of the blackest dye: and among other inducements to pass it, my having been engaged in the Pretender's interest was one. How well founded this article was has already appeared; I was just as guilty of the rest. The correspondence with me was, you know, neither frequent nor safe. I heard seldom and darkly from you, and though I saw well enough which way the current ran, yet I was entirely ignorant of the measures you took, and of the use you intended to make of me. I contented myself, therefore, with letting you all know that you had but to command me, and that I was ready to venture in your service the little which remained, as frankly as I had exposed all which was gone. At last your commands came, and I shall show you in what manner I executed them.

The person who was sent to me arrived in the beginning of July, one thousand seven hundred and fifteen at the place where I was. He spoke in the name of all the friends whose authority could influence me, and he brought me word that Scotland was not only ready to take arms, but under some sort of dissatisfaction to be withheld from beginning; that in England the people were exasperated against the government to such a degree, that far from wanting to be encouraged, they could not be restrained from insulting it on every occasion; that the whole tory party had become avowedly jacobite; that many officers of the army, and the majority of the soldiers were very well affected to the cause; that the city of London was ready to rise, and that the enterprises for seizing of several places were ripe for execution: in a

word, that most of the principal tories were in concert with the
Duke of Ormond, for I had pressed particularly to be informed
whether his grace acted alone, or if not, who were his council;
and that the others were so disposed that there remained no doubt
of their joining as soon as the first blow should be struck. He
added, that my friends were a little surprised to observe that I lay
neuter in such a conjuncture. He represented to me the·danger
I ran of being prevented by people of all sides from having the
merit of engaging early in this enterprise; and how unaccountable
it would be for a man impeached and attainted under the present
government to take no share in bringing about a revolution so
near at hand and so certain. He entreated that I would defer
no longer to join the Chevalier; to advise and assist in carrying
on his affairs, and to solicit and negotiate at the court of France,
where my friends imagined that I should not fail to meet with a
favorable reception, and from whence they made no doubt of
receiving assistance in a situation of affairs so critical, so unexpected, and so promising. He concluded by giving me a letter
from the Pretender, whom he had seen in his way to me, in which
I was pressed to repair without loss of time to Commercy: and
this instance was grounded on the·message which the bearer of
the letter had brought me from my friends in England. Since
he was sent to me, it had been more proper to have come directly
where I was: but he was in haste to make his own court, and
to deliver the assurances which were entrusted to him. Perhaps,
too, he imagined that he should tie the knot faster on me by ac
quainting me that my friends had actually engaged for themselves
and me, than by barely telling me that they desired I would
engage for myself and them.

In the progress of the conversation he related a multitude of
facts, which satisfied me as to the general disposition of the people;
but he gave little satisfaction as to the measures taken for improving this disposition; for driving the business with vigor if it
tended to a revolution, or for supporting it with advantage if it
spun into a war. When I questioned him concerning several
persons whose disinclination to the government admitted of no
doubt, and whose names, quality, and experience were very essential to the success of the undertaking, he owned to me, that
they kept a great reserve, and did at most but encourage others
to act, by general and dark expressions.

I received this account and this summons ill in my bed: yet
important as the matter was, a few minutes served to determine
me. The circumstances wanting to form a reasonable inducement to engage did not escape me. But the smart of a bill of
attainder tingled in every vein: and I looked on my party to be
under oppression, and to call for my assistance. Besides which

I considered first that I should certainly be informed, when I conferred with the Chevalier, of many particulars unknown to this
gentleman; for I did not imagine that you could be so near to take
arms, as he represented you to be, on no other foundation than
that which he exposed: and secondly, that I was obliged in honor
to declare, without waiting for a more particular information of
what might be expected from England; since my friends had
taken their resolution to declare, without any previous assurance
of what might be expected from France.   This second motive
weighed extremely with me at that time: there is, however, more
sound than sense in it, and it contains the original error, to which
all your subsequent errors, and the thread of misfortunes which
followed, are to be ascribed.

My resolution thus taken, I lost no time in repairing to Commercy. The very first conversations with the Chevalier answered in no degree my expectations: and I assure you, with great
truth, that I began, even then, if not to repent of my own rashness, yet to be fully convinced both of yours and mine.

He talked to me like a man who expected every moment to
set out for England or Scotland, but who did not very well know
for which: and when he entered into the particulars of his affairs,
I found that concerning the former he had nothing more circumstantial nor positive to go upon than what I had already heard.
The advices that were sent from thence contained such assurances
of success, as it was hard to think that men, who did not go upon
the surest grounds, would presume to give. But then these assurances were general, and the authority seldom satisfactory. Those
which came from the best hand were verbal, and often conveyed
by very doubtful messengers; others came from men whose fortunes were as desperate as their counsels; and others came from
persons whose situations in the world gave little reason to attend
to their judgment in matters of this kind.

The Duke of Ormond had been for some time, I cannot say
how long, engaged with the Chevalier. He had taken the direction of this whole affair, as far as it related to England, upon
himself, and had received a commission for this purpose, which
contained the most ample powers that could be given. After this
one would be apt to imagine, that the principles on which the
Pretender should proceed, and the tories engaged in this service,
had been laid down; that a regular and certain method of correspondence had been established; that the necessary assistances
had been specified, and that positive assurances had been given
of them. Nothing less. In a matter as serious as this, all was
loose and abandoned to the disposition of fortune. The first
point had never been touched upon. By what I have said above
you see how little care was taken of the second: and as to the

third, the duke had asked a small body of regular forces, a sum of money, and a quantity of arms and ammunition. He had been told in answer by the court of France, that he must absolutely despair of any number of troops whatever, but he had been made in general to hope for some money, some arms, and some ammunition: a little sum had, I think, been advanced to him. In a case so plain as this, it is hard to conceive how any man could err. The assistances demanded from France at this time, and even greater than these, will appear, in the sequel of this relation, by the sense of the whole party, to have been deemed essentially necessary to success. In such an uncertainty, therefore, whether even these could be obtained, or rather with so much reason to apprehend that they could not, it was evident that the tories ought to have lain still. They might have helped the ferment against the government, but should have avoided with the utmost care the giving any alarm, or even suspicion of their true design, and have resumed or not resumed it as the Chevalier was able or not able to provide the troops, the arms, the money, &c. Instead of which, those who were at the head of the undertaking, and therefore answerable for the measures which were pursued, suffered the business to jog merrily on. They knew, in general, how little dependence was to be placed on foreign succor, but acted as if they had been sure of it: while the party were rendered sanguine by their passions, and made no doubt of subverting a government they were angry with, both one and the other made as much bustle, and gave as great alarm, as would have been imprudent even at the eve of a general insurrection. This appeared to me to be the state of things, with respect to England, when I arrived at Commercy.

The Scots had long pressed the Chevalier to come amongst them, and had of late sent frequent messages to quicken his departure, some of which were delivered in terms much more zealous than respectful. The truth is, they seemed in as much haste to begin as if they had thought themselves able to do the work alone; as if they had been apprehensive of no danger but that of seeing it taken out of their hands, and of having the honor of it shared by others. However, that which was wanting on the part of England was not wanting in Scotland: the Scots talked aloud, but they were in a condition to rise. They took little care to keep their intentions secret, but they were disposed to put those intentions into immediate execution, and thereby to render the secret no longer necessary. They knew upon whom to depend for every part of the work, and they had concerted with the Chevalier even to the place of his landing.

There was need of no great sagacity to perceive how unequal such foundations were to the weight of the building designed to

be raised on them.   The Scots, with all their zeal and all their
valor, could bring no revolution about, unless in concurrence with
the English: and among the latter, nothing was ripe for such an
undertaking but the temper of the people, if that was so.   I
thought, therefore, that the Pretender's friends in the north should
be kept from rising, till those in the south had put themselves in
a condition to act; and that, in the meanwhile, the utmost endeavors ought to be used with the king of France to espouse the
cause; and that a plan of the design, with a more particular spe-
cification of the succors desired, as well as of the time when, and
the place to which they should be conveyed, ought to be written
for: all which, I was told by the Marshal of Berwic, who had
the principal direction at that time of these affairs in France, and
I dare say very truly, had been often asked, but never sent.   I
looked on this enterprise to be of the nature of those which can
hardly be undertaken more than once, and I judged that the success of it would depend on timing, as near as possible together,
the insurrection in both parts of the island, and the succors from
hence.   The Pretender approved this opinion of mine.   He instructed me accordingly: and I left Lorain, after having accepted
the seals much against my inclination.   I made one condition
with him.   It was this: that I should be at liberty to quit a station which my humor and many other considerations made me
think myself very unfit for, whenever the occasion upon which
I engaged was over, one way or other: and I desire you to remember that I did so.

  I arrived at Paris towards the end of July one thousand seven
hundred and fifteen.   You will observe that all I was charged
with, and all by consequence that I am answerable for, was to
solicit this court, and to dispose them to grant us the succors
necessary to make the attempt, as soon as we should know certainly from England in what it was desired that these succors
should consist, and whither they should be sent.   Here I found
a multitude of people at work, and every one doing what seemed
good in his own eyes: no subordination, no order, no concert.
Persons concerned in the management of these affairs upon former occasions, have assured me this is always the case.   It might
be so to some degree; but I believe never so much as now.   The
jacobites had wrought one another up to look on the success of
the present designs as infallible.   Every meeting-house which
the populace demolished, every little drunken riot which happened, served to confirm them in these sanguine expectations:
and there was hardly one amongst them who would lose the air
of contributing by his intrigues to the restoration, which he took
it for granted would be brought about without him in a very
few weeks.

Care and hope sat on every busy Irish face. Those who could write and read had letters to show, and those who had not arrived to this pitch of erudition had their secrets to whisper. No sex was excluded from this ministry. Fanny Oglethorp, whom you must have seen in England, kept her corner in it, and Olive Trant was the great wheel of our machine.

I imagine that this picture, the lines of which are not in the least too strong, would serve to represent what passed on your side of the water at the same time. The letters which came from thence seemed to me to contain rather such things as the writers wished might be true, than such as they knew to be so; and the accounts which were sent from hence were of the same kind. The vanity of some, and the credulity of others supported this ridiculous correspondence, and I question not but very many persons, some such I have known, did the same thing from a principle which they took to be a very wise one: they imagined that they helped by these means to maintain and to increase the spirit of the party in England and France. They acted like Thoas, that turbulent Ætolian, who brought Antiochus into Greece: "quibus mendaciis de rege, multiplicando verbis copias ejus, erexerat multorum in Græcia animos; iisdem et regis spem inflabat, omnium votis eum arcessi." Thus were numbers of people employed under a notion of advancing the business, or from an affectation of importance, in amusing and flattering one another, and in sounding the alarm in the ears of an enemy, whom it was their interest to surprise. The government of England was put on its guard: and the necessity of acting, or of laying aside with some disadvantage all thoughts of acting for the present, was precipitated before any measures necessary to enable you to act had been prepared or almost thought of.

If his majesty did not, till some short time after this declare the intended invasion to parliament, it was not for want of information. Before I came to Paris, what was doing had been discovered. The little armament made at the Havre which furnished the only means the Chevalier then had for his transportation into Britain, which had exhausted the treasury of St. Germains, and which contained all the arms and ammunition that could be depended upon for the whole undertaking, though they were hardly sufficient to begin the work even in Scotland, was talked of publicly. A minister less alert and less capable than the Earl of Stair would easily have been at the bottom of the secret; for so it was called, when the particulars of messages received and sent, the names of the persons from whom they came, and by whom they were carried, were whispered about at tea-tables and in coffee-houses.

In short; what by the indiscretion of people here, what by the rebound which came often back from London, what by the private interests and ambitious views of persons in the French court, and what by other causes unnecessary to be examined now, the most private transactions came to light: and they who imagined that they trusted their heads to the keeping of one or two friends, were in reality at the mercy of numbers. Into such company was I fallen, for my sins: and it is upon the credit of such a mob-ministry, that the tories have judged me capable of betraying a trust, or incapable of discharging it.

I had made very little progress in the business which brought me to Paris, when the paper so long expected was sent, in pursuance of former instances, from England. The unanimous sense of the principal persons engaged was contained in it. The whole had been dictated word for word to the gentleman who brought it over by the Earl of Mar, and it had been delivered to him by the Duke of Ormond. I was driving in the wide ocean without a compass, when this dropped unexpectedly into my hands. I received it joyfully, and I steered my course exactly by it. Whether the persons from whom it came pursued the principles, and observed the rules which they laid down as the measures of their own conduct and of ours, will appear by the sequel of this relation.

This memorial asserted, that there were no hopes of succeeding in a present undertaking, for many reasons deduced in it without an immediate and universal rising of the people in all parts of England upon the Chevalier's arrival, and that this insurrection was in no degree probable unless he brought a body of regular troops along with him: that if this attempt miscarried, his cause and his friends, the English liberty and government, would be utterly ruined: but if by coming without troops he resolved to risk these and every thing else, he must set out so as not to arrive before the end of September, O. S., to justify which opinion many arguments were urged. In this case twenty thousand arms, a train of artillery, five hundred officers with their servants, and a considerable sum of money were demanded: and as soon as they should be informed, that the Chevalier was in condition to make this provision, it was said that notice should be given him of the places to which he might send, and of the persons who were to be trusted. I do not mention some inconveniences which they touched upon arising from a delay. Because their opinion was clearly for this delay, and because they could not suppose that the Chevalier would act, or that those about him would advise him to act, contrary to the sense of all his friends in England. No time was lost in making the proper use of this paper. As much of it as was fit to be shown to this court was translated into French and laid before the King of

France. I was now able to speak with greater assurance, and in some sort to undertake conditionally for the event of things.

The proposal of violating treaties so lately and so solemnly concluded, was a very bold one to be made to people, whatever their inclinations might be, whom the war had reduced to the lowest ebb of riches and power. They would not hear of a direct and open engagement, such as the sending of a body of troops would have been, neither would they grant the whole of what was asked in the second plan. But it was impossible for them or any one else to foresee how far those steps which they were willing to take, well improved, might have encouraged or forced them to go. They granted us some succors, and the very ship in which the Pretender was to transport himself was fitted out by Depine d'Anicant at the king of France's expense. They would have concealed these appearances as much as they could; but the heat of the whigs and the resentment of the court of England might have drawn them in. We should have been glad indirectly to concur in fixing these things upon them: and in a word, if the late king had lived six months longer, I verily believe there had been war again between England and France. This was the only point of time when these affairs had, to my apprehension, the least reasonable appearance even of possibility: all that preceded was wild and uncertain: all that followed was mad and desperate. But this favorable aspect had an extreme short duration. Two events soon happened, one of which cast a damp on all we were doing, and the other rendered vain and fruitless all we had done. The first was the arrival of the Duke of Ormond in France, the other was the death of the king.

We had sounded the duke's name high. His reputation and the opinion of his power were great. The French began to believe, that he was able to form and to head a party; that the troops would join him; that the nation would follow the signal whenever he drew his sword; and the voice of the people, the echo of which was continually in their ears, confirmed them in this belief. But when in the midst of all these bright ideas they saw him arrive, almost literally alone, when, to excuse his coming, I was obliged to tell them, that he could not stay; they sunk at once from their hopes: and that which generally happens happened in this case; because they had had too good an opinion of the cause, they began to form too bad a one. Before this time, if they had no friendship for the tories, they had at least some consideration and esteem. After this, I saw nothing but compassion in the best of them, and contempt in the others.

When I arrived at Paris, the king was already gone to Marly, where the indisposition which he had begun to feel at Versailles increased upon him. He was the best friend the Chevalier had:

and when I engaged in this business, my principal dependence was on his personal character. This failed me to a great degree: he was not in a condition to exert the same vigor as formerly. The ministers who saw so great an event as his death to be probably at hand, a certain minority, an uncertain regency, perhaps confusion, at best a new face of government and a new system of affairs, would not, for their own sakes, as well as for the sake of the public, venture to engage far in any new measures. All I had to negotiate by myself first, and in conjunction with the Duke of Ormond soon afterwards, languished with the king. My hopes sunk as he declined, and died when he expired. The event of things has sufficiently shown, that all those which were entertained by the duke and the jacobite party under the regency were founded on the grossest delusions imaginable. Thus was the project become impracticable before the time arrived, which was fixed by those who directed things in England, for putting it in execution.

The new government of France appeared to me like a strange country; I was little acquainted with the roads. Most of the faces I met with were unknown to me, and I hardly understood the language of the people. Of the men who had been in power under the late reign, many were discarded, and most of the others were too much taken up with the thoughts of securing themselves under this, to receive applications in favor of the Pretender. The two men who had the greatest appearance of favor and power were d'Aguessau and Noailles. One was made chancellor, on the death of Voisin, from attorney general; and the other was placed at the head of the treasury. The first passes for a man of parts, but he never acted out of the sphere of the law: I had no acquaintance with him before this time; and when you consider his circumstances and mine, you will not think it could be very easy for me to get access to him now. The latter I had known extremely well while the late king lived: and from the same court principle, as he was glad to be well with me then, he would hardly know me now. The minister* who had the principal direction of foreign affairs I lived in friendship with, and I must own to his honor, that he never encouraged a design, which he knew that his court had no intention of supporting.

There were other persons, not to tire you with farther particulars upon this head, of credit and influence, with whom I found indirect and private ways of conversing: but it was in vain to expect any more than civil language from them, in a case which they found no disposition in their master to countenance, and in favor of which they had no prejudices of their own. The pri-

* M. d'Huxelles.

vate engagements into which the Duke of Orleans had entered
with his majesty, during the life of the late king, will abate of
their force as the regent grows into strength, and would soon
have had no force at all if the Pretender had met with success:
but in these beginnings they operated very strongly.   The air
of this court was to take the counterpart of all that had been
thought right under Louis the Fourteenth. " Cela resemble trop
à l'ancien système," was an answer so often given, that it became
a jest, and almost a proverb.   But to finish this account with a
fact which is incredible, but strictly true; the very peace, which
had saved France from ruin, and the makers of it, were become
as unpopular at this court, as at the court of Vienna.

The Duke of Ormond flattered himself in this state of things,
that he had opened a private and sure channel of arriving at the
regent, and of bending him to his purposes.   His grace and I
lived together at this time in a house which one of my friends
had lent me.   I observed that he was frequently lost, and that he
made continual excursions out of town, with all the mysterious
precaution imaginable. I doubted at first, whether these intrigues
related to business or pleasure.   I soon discovered with whom
they were carried on, and had reason to believe that both were
mingled in them.   It is necessary that I explain this secret to you.

Mrs. Trant, whom I have named above, had been preparing
herself for the retired abstemious life of a Carmelite,* by taking
a surfeit of the pleasures of Paris; when a little before the death
of the queen, or about that time, she went into England.   What
she was entrusted, either by the Chevalier, or any other person,
to negotiate there, I am ignorant of, and it imports not much to
know.   In that journey she made or renewed an acquaintance
with the Duke of Ormond.   The scandalous chronicle affirms,
that she brought with her, when she returned into France, a
woman, of whom I have not the least knowledge, but who was
probably handsome; since without beauty, such a merchandise
would not have been saleable, nor have answered the design of
the importer: and that she made this way her court to the regent.
Whatever her merit was, she kept a correspondence. with him,
and put herself upon that foot of familiarity, which he permits all
those who contribute to his pleasures to assume.   She was placed
by him, as she told me herself, where I found her some time after
that which I am speaking of, in the house of an ancient gentlewoman, who had formerly been maid of honor to Madame, and
who had contracted at court a spirit of intrigue, which accompanied her in her retreat.

* She used to pretend a resolution of turning nun.   She is since married to
the Duke of Bouillon's brother, who was too much dishonored by his former
life, to be so even by this scandalous match.

These two had associated to them the abbé de Tesieu, in all the political parts of their business; for I will not suppose that so reverend an ecclesiastic entered into any other secret. This abbé is the regent's secretary; and it was principally through him that the private treaty had been carried on between his master and the Earl of Stair in the king's reign. Whether the priest had stooped at the lure of a cardinal's hat, or whether he acted the second part by the same orders that he acted the first, I know not. This is sure, and the British minister was not the bubble of it, that whilst he concerted measures on one hand to traverse the Pretender's designs, he testified on the other all the inclination possible to his service. A mad fellow, who had been an intendant in Normandy, and several other politicians of the lowest form, were at different times taken into this favorite junto.

With these worthy people his grace of Ormond negotiated, and no care was omitted on his part to keep me out of the secret. The reason of which, so far as I am able to guess at, shall be explained to you by and by. I might very justly have taken this proceeding ill, and the duke will not find in my whole conduct towards him any thing like it: I protest to you very sincerely I was not in the least moved at it.

He advanced not a step in his business with these sham ministers; and yet imagined that he got daily ground. I made no progress with the true ones, but I saw it. These, however, were not our only difficulties. We lay under another, which came from your side, and which embarrassed us more. The first hindered us from working forward to our point of view, but the second took all point of view from us.

A paper was sent into England just before the death of the king of France, which had been drawn by me at Chaville, in concert with the Dukes of Ormond and Berwic, and with Monsieur de Torcy. This paper was an answer to the memorial received from thence. The state of this country was truly represented in it: the difference was fixed between what had been asked and what might be expected from France, and upon the whole it was demanded what our friends would do, and what they would have us to do? The reply to this came through the French secretary of state to our hands. They declared themselves unable to say any thing, till they should see what turn affairs would take on so great an event as the death of the king, the report of which had reached them.

Such a declaration shut our mouths and tied our hands. I confess I knew neither how to solicit, nor what to solicit; this last message suspending the project on which we had acted before, and which I kept as an instruction constantly before my eyes. It seemed to me uncertain, whether you intended to go on, or whether your design was to stifle as much as possible all past transactions; to lie perfectly still; to throw upon the court the odium of having given a false alarm, and to wait till new accidents at home, and a more favorable conjuncture abroad, might tempt you to resume the enterprise. Perhaps this would have been the wisest game you could have played: but then, you should have concerted it with us who acted for you here. You intended no such thing, as appeared afterwards: and therefore, those who acted for the party at London, whoever they were, must be deemed inexcusable for leaving things on the foot of this message, and giving us no advice fit to be depended upon for many weeks. Whilst preparations were to be made, and the work was to be set a going by assistance from hence, you might reasonably expect to hear from us, and to be determined by us: but when all hopes of this kind seemed to be gone, it was your part to determine us, and we could take no resolution here, but that of conforming ourselves to whatever should come prescribed from England.

Whilst we were in this condition, the most desperate than can be imagined, we began to receive verbal messages from you that no more time was to be lost, and that the Chevalier should come away. No man was, I believe, ever so embarrassed as I found myself at that time. I could not imagine that you would content yourselves by loose verbal messages, after all that had happened, to call us over, and I know by experience how little such messages are to be depended on. For soon after I engaged in these affairs, a monk arrived at Bar, despatched, as he affirmed, by the Duke of Ormond, in whose name he insisted that the Chevalier should hasten into Britain, and that nothing but his presence was wanting to place the crown on his head. The fellow delivered his errand so positively, and so circumstantially, that the resolution was taken at Bar to set out, and my rendezvous to join the Chevalier was appointed me. This method to fetch a king with as little ceremony as one would invite a friend to supper, appeared somewhat odd to me, who was then very new in these affairs. But when I came to talk with the man, for by good luck he had been sent for from Bar to Paris, I easily discerned that he had no such commission as he pretended to, and that he acted of his own head. I presumed to oppose the taking any resolution upon his word, though he was a monk; and soon after we knew from the Duke of Ormond himself, that he had never sent him.

This example made me cautious, but that which determined my opinion was, that I could never imagine, without supposing you all run mad, that the same men who judged this attempt unripe for execution, unless supported by regular troops from France, or at least by all the other assistances which are enumerated above, while the design was much more secret than at present, when the king had no fleet at sea, nor more than eight thousand men dispersed over the whole island, when we had the good wishes of the French court on our side, and were sure of some particular assistances, and of a general connivance; that the same men, I say, should press for making it now without any other preparation, when we had neither money, arms, ammunition, nor a single company of foot, when the government of England was on its guard, national troops were raised, foreign forces sent for, and France, like all the rest of the continent, against us. I could not conceive such a strange combination of accidents as should make the necessity of acting increase gradually upon us, as the means of doing so were taken from us.

Upon the whole matter, my opinion was, and I did not observe the Duke of Ormond to differ from me, that we should wait till we heard from you, in such a manner as might assure us of what you intended to do yourselves, and of what you expected from us, and that in the meanwhile we should go as far as the little money which we had, and the little favor which was shown us would allow, in getting some embarkations ready on the coast.

Sir George Byng had come into the road of Havre, and had demanded by name several ships which belonged to us, to be given up to him. The regent did not think fit to let him have the ships; but he ordered them to be unloaded, and their cargoes were put into the king's magazines. We were in no condition to repair the loss: and therefore, when I mention embarkations, you will please to understand nothing more than vessels to transport the Pretender's person, and the persons of those who should go over with him. This was all we could do, and this was not neglected.

We were thus employed, when a gentleman arrived from Scotland to represent the state of that country, and to require a definitive answer from the Chevalier, whether he would have the insurrection to be made immediately, which they apprehended they might not be able to make at all, if they were obliged to defer it much longer. This gentleman was sent instantly back again, and was directed to let the persons he came from know, that the Chevalier was desirous to have the risings of his friends in England and Scotland so adjusted, that they might mutually assist each other, and distract the enemy; that he had not received a final answer from his friends in England, but that he was in daily expectation of it; that it was very much to be wished, that all attempts in Scotland could be suspended till such time as the English were ready; but that if the Scots were so

pressed that they must either submit or rise immediately, he was
of opinion they should rise, and he would make the best of his
way to them.

What this forwardness in the Scots, and this uncertainty and
backwardness in the English must produce, it was not hard to
foresee; and therefore, that I might neglect nothing in my power
to prevent any false measure, as I was conscious to myself that
I had neglected nothing to promote true ones, I despatched a
gentleman to London, where I supposed the Earl of Mar to be,
some days before the message I have just spoken of was sent to
Scotland. I desired him to make my compliments to Lord Mar,
and to tell him from me, that I understood it to be his sense, as
well as the sense of all our friends, that Scotland could do
nothing effectually without the concurrence of England, and
that England would not stir without assistance from abroad:
that he might assure himself no such assistance could be depended upon, and that I begged of him to make the inference
from these propositions. The gentleman went, but upon his
arrival at London, he found that the Earl of Mar was already
set out to draw the Highlanders into arms. He communicated
his message to a person* of confidence, who undertook to send
it after his lordship, and this was the utmost which either he or
I could do in such a conjuncture.

You were now visibly departed from the very scheme which
you had sent us over, and from all the principles which had been
ever laid down. I did what I could to keep up my own spirit as
well as the spirits of the Chevalier and of all those with whom I
was in correspondence: I endeavored even to deceive myself. I
could not remedy the mischief, and I was resolved to see the conclusion of the perilous adventure. But I own to you, that I
thought then, and that I have not changed my opinion since, that
such measures as these would not be pursued, by any reasonable
man, in the most common affairs of life. It was with the utmost astonishment that I saw them pursued, in the conduct of
an enterprise which had for its object nothing less than the dispositions of crowns, and for the means of bringing it about
nothing less than a civil war.

Impatient that we heard nothing from England, when we expected every moment to hear that the war was begun in Scotland; the Duke of Ormond and I resolved to send a person† of
confidence to London. We instructed him to repeat to you the
former accounts, which we had sent over, to let you know how
destitute the Chevalier was, either of actual support, or even of

---

* Mr. Lewis, who belonged to the Earl of Oxford.
† Mr. Ezechiel Hamilton: he got all the papers by heart.

reasonable hopes, and to desire that you would determine whether he should go to Scotland, or throw himself on some part of the English coast. This person was farther instructed to tell you, that the Chevalier being ready to take any resolution at a moment's warning, you might depend on his setting out the instant he received your answer: and therefore, that to save time, if your intention was to rise, you would do well to act immediately, on the assurance that the plan you prescribed, be it what it would, should be exactly complied with. We took this resolution the rather, because one of the pacquets which had been prepared in cypher, to give you an account of things which had been put above three weeks before into Monsieur de Torcy's hands, and which by consequence we thought to be in yours, was by this time sent back to me by this minister, I think open, with an excuse that he durst not take upon him to forward it.

The person despatched to London returned very soon to us, and the answer he brought was,* that since affairs grew daily worse, and could not mend by delay, our friends in England had resolved to declare immediately, and that they would be ready to join the Chevalier on his landing: that his person would be as safe there as in Scotland, and that in every other respect, it was better that he should land in England; that they had used their utmost endeavors, and that they hoped the western counties were in a good posture to receive him. To this was added, a general indication of the place he should come to, as near to Plymouth as possible.

You must agree, that this was not the answer of men who knew what they were about. A little more precision was necessary in dictating a message, which was to have such consequences: and especially since the gentleman could not fail to acquaint the persons he spoke with, that the Chevalier was not able to carry men enough to secure him from being taken up, even by the first constable. Notwithstanding this, the Duke of Ormond set out from Paris, and the Chevalier from Bar. Some persons were sent to the north of England, and others to London, to give notice that they were both on their way. Their routes were so ordered, that the Duke of Ormond was to sail from the coast of Normandy some days before the Chevalier arrived at St. Malo, to which place the duke was to send immediate notice of his landing; and two gentlemen acquainted with the country, and perfectly well known to all our friends in those parts, were despatched before, that the people of Devonshire and Somersetshire, who were, we concluded, in arms, might be ap-

---

* Lansdown gave this answer in the name of all the persons privy to the secret.

prised of the signals which were to be made from the ships, and might be ready to receive the duke.

On the coast of France, and before his embarkation, the duke heard that several of our principal friends had been seized, immediately after the person who came last from them had left London; that the others were all dispersed, and that the consternation was universal. He embarked notwithstanding this melancholy news; and, supported by nothing but the firmness of his temper, he went over to the place appointed: he did more than his part, and he found that our friends had done less than theirs. One of the gentlemen who had passed over before him, and had traversed part of the country, joined him on the coast, and assured him that there was not the least room to expect a rising. In a word, he was refused a night's lodging in a country which we had been told was in a good posture to receive the Chevalier, and where the duke expected that multitudes would repair to him.

He returned to the coast of Britany after this uncomfortable expedition, where the Chevalier arrived about the same time from Lorain. What his grace proposed by the second attempt, which he made as soon as the vessel could be refitted, to land in the same part of the island, I profess myself to be ignorant. I wrote him my opinion at the time, and I have always thought, that the storm in which he had like to have been cast away, and which forced him back to the French coast, saved him from a much greater peril, that of perishing in an attempt as full of extravagant rashness, and as void of all reasonable meaning, as any of those adventures which have rendered the hero of La Mancha immortal.

The Chevalier had now but one of these two things left him to do, one was to return to Bar, the other was to go to Scotland, where there were people in arms for him. He took this last resolution. He left Britany where he had as many ministers as there were people about him, and where he was eternally teased with noisy disputes about what was to be done, in circumstances in which no reasonable thing could be done. He sent to have a vessel got ready for him at Dunkirk, and he crossed the country as privately as he could.

Whilst all these things passed, I remained at Paris, to try, if by any means some assistance might be at last procured; without which it was evident, even to those who flattered themselves the most, that the game was up.

No sooner was the Duke of Ormond gone from Paris, on the design which I have mentioned, and Mrs. Trant, who had accompanied him part of the way, returned, but I was sent for to a little house at Madrid in the Bois de Boulogne, where she lived with Mademoiselle de Chaussery, the ancient gentlewoman with whom the Duke of Orleans had placed her.   These two persons opened to me what had passed whilst the Duke of Ormond was there, and the hopes they had of drawing the regent into all the measures necessary to support the attempts which were making in favor of the Chevalier.

By what they told me at first, I saw that they had been trusted; and by what passed in the course of my treating with them, it appeared that they had the access which they pretended to.   All which I had been able to do by proper persons and in proper methods, since the king of France's death, amounting to little or nothing, I resolved, at last, to try what was to be done by this indirect way.   I put myself under the conduct of these female managers, and without having the same dependence on them as his grace of Ormond had, I pushed their credit and their power as far as they reached, during the time I continued to see them. I met with smoother language and greater hopes than had been given me hitherto.   A note signed by the regent, supposed to be written to a woman, but which was to be explained to be intended for the Earl of Mar, was put into my hands to be sent to Scotland.   I took a copy of it, which you may see at the end of these papers.*   When Sir John Areskine came to press for succor, the regent was prevailed upon by these women to see him, but he carried nothing real back with him, except a quantity of gold, part of the money which we had drawn from Spain, and which was lost with the vessel in a very odd manner on the Scotch coast.   The Duke of Ormond had been promised seven or eight thousand arms, which were drawn out of the magazines, and said to be lodged, I think at Compeigne.   I used my utmost efforts, that these arms might be carried forward to the coast, and I undertook for their transportation: but all was in vain; so that the likelihood of bringing any thing to effect in time appeared to me no greater than I had found it before I entered into this intrigue.

I soon grew tired of a commerce, which nothing but success could render tolerable, and resolved to be no longer amused by the pretences, which were daily repeated to me, that the regent had entertained personal prejudices against me, and that he was insensibly, and by degrees, to be dipped in our measures; that both these things required time, but that they would certainly be brought about, and that we should then be able to answer all the expectations of the English and the Scotch.   The first of these pretences contained a fact, which I could hardly persuade myself to be true, because I knew very certainly that I had never

* This note has not been found among the author's papers.

given his royal highness the least occasion for such prejudices: the second was a work which might spin out into a great and uncertain length. I took my resolution to drive what related to myself to an immediate explanation, and what related to others to an immediate decision, not to suffer any excuse for doing nothing to be founded on my conduct, nor the salvation, if I could hinder it, of so many gallant men as were in arms in Scotland, to rest on the success of such womanish projects. I shall tell you what I did on the first head now, and what I did on the second hereafter in its proper place.

The fact, which it is said the regent laid to my charge, was a correspondence with Lord Stair, and having been one night at his house, from whence I did not retire till three in the morning. As soon as I got hold of this, I desired the Marshal of Berwic to go to him. The marshal told him from me, that I had been extremely concerned, to hear in general, that I lay under his displeasure; that a story, which it was said he believed, had been related to me; that I expected the justice which he could deny to no man of having the accusation proved, in which case I was contented to pass for the last of human kind, or of being justified if it could not be proved. He answered, that such a story had been related to him by such persons as he thought would not have deceived him; that he had been since convinced, that it was false, and that I should be satisfied of his regard for me: but that he must own that he was very uneasy to find that I, who could apply to him through the Marshal d'Huxelles, could choose to treat with Mrs. Trant, and the rest; for he named all the cabal, except his secretary, whom I had never met at Mademoiselle Chaussery's. He added, that these people teased him at my instigation, to death, and that they were not fit to be trusted with any business. He applied to some of them the severest epithets. The Marshal of Berwic replied, that he was sure I should receive the whole of what he had been pleased to say with the greatest satisfaction; that I had treated with these persons much against my will; and finally, that if his royal highness would not employ them, he was sure I would never apply to them. In a conversation which I had, not long after with him, he spoke to me in much the same terms as he had done to the marshal. I went from him very ill edified as to his intentions of doing anything in favor of the Chevalier; but I carried away with me this satisfaction, that he assigned me, from his own mouth, the person through whom I should make my applications to him, and through whom I should depend on receiving his answers; that he disavowed all the little politic clubs, and had commanded me to have no more to do with them.

Before I resume the thread of my narration, give me leave to

make some reflection upon what I have been last saying to you.
When I met with the Duke of Ormond at his return from the
coast, he thought himself obliged to say something to excuse his
keeping me out of a secret, which during his absence I had been
let into. His excuse was, that the regent had exacted from him
that I should know nothing of the matter. You will observe,
that the account which I have given you seems to contradict this
assertion of his grace, since it is hard to suppose, that if the
regent had exacted that I should be kept out of the secret, these
women would have dared to have let me into it; and since it is
still harder to suppose, that the regent would make this express
condition with the Duke of Ormond, and the moment the duke's
back was turned, would suffer these women to tease him from
me, and to bring me answers from him. I am, however, far
from taxing the duke with affirming an untruth. I believe the
regent did make such a condition with him, and I will tell you
how I understand all this little management, which will explain
a great deal to you. This prince, with wit and valor, has joined
all the irresolution of temper possible, and is, perhaps, the man
in the world the least capable of saying no to your face. From
hence it happened, that these women, like multitudes of other
people, forced him to say and do enough to give them the air of
having credit with him, and of being trusted by him. This
drew in the Duke of Ormond, who is not, I dare say, as yet undeceived. The regent never intended from the first, to do anything, even indirectly, in favor of the jacobite cause. His interest
was plainly on the other side, and he saw it. But then, the same
weakness in his character carried him, as it would have done his
great uncle Gaston in the same case, to keep measures with the
Chevalier. His double trimming character prevailed on him to
talk with the Duke of Ormond: but it carried him no farther. I
question not but he did on this occasion, what you must have
observed many men to do. We not only endeavor to impose on
the world, but even on ourselves. We disguise our weakness,
and work up in our minds an opinion that the measure which
we fall into by the natural or habitual imperfection of our character, is the effect of a principle of prudence, or of some other
virtue. Thus the regent, who saw the Duke of Ormond, because he could not resist the importunity of Olive Trant, and
who gave hopes to the duke, because he can refuse nobody,
made himself believe that it was a great strain of policy to blow
up the fire, and to keep Britain embroiled. I am persuaded that
I do not err in judging that he thought in this manner; and here
I fix the reason of his excluding me out of the commerce which
he had with the Duke of Ormond, of his affecting a personal
dislike of me, and of his avoiding any correspondence with me

upon these matters; till I forced myself in a manner upon him, and he could not keep me any longer at a distance without departing from his first principle, that of keeping measures with every body. He then threw me, or let me slide, if you will, into the hands of these women, and when he found that I pressed him hard that way too, he took me out of their hands and put me back again into the proper channel of business, where I had not been long, as you will see by and by, before the scene of amusement was finished.

Sir John Areskine told me, when he came from the first audience that he had of his royal highness, that he put him in mind of the encouragement which he had given the Earl of Mar to take arms. I never heard anything of this kind, but what Sir John let drop to me. If the fact be true, you see that the Scotch general had been amused by him with a witness. The English general was so in his turn, and while this was doing, the regent might think it best to have him to himself. Four eyes comprehend more objects than two, and I was a little better acquainted with the characters of people, and the mass of the country, than the Duke, though this court had been at first a strange country to me in comparison of the former.

An infinity of little circumstances concurred to make me form this opinion, some of which are better felt than explained, and many of which are not present to my memory. That which had the greatest weight with me, and which is, I think decisive, I will mention. At the very time when it is pretended, that the regent treated with the Duke of Ormond, on the express condition that I should know nothing of the matter; two persons* of the first rank and greatest credit in this court, when I made the most pressing instances to them in favor of the Chevalier, threw out in conversation to me, that I should attach myself to the Duke of Orleans, that in my circumstances I might want him, and that he might have occasion for me. Something was intimated of pensions, and establishment, and of making my peace at home. I would not understand this language, because I would not break with the people who held it: and when they saw that I would not take the hints, they ceased to give them.

I fancy that you see by this time the motives of the regent's conduct. I am not, I confess, able to explain to you those of the Duke of Ormond's: I cannot so much as guess at them. When he came into France I was careful to show him all the friendship, and all the respect possible. My friends were his, my purse was his, and even my bed was his. I went further, I did all those

* Marshal d'Huxelles, Marshal d'Effiat: twenty-five thousand pounds offered by the last.

things which touch most sensibly people who have been used to pomp. I made my court to him, and haunted his levee with assiduity. In return to this behavior, which was the pure effect of my good will, and which no duty that I owed his grace, no obligation that I had to him, imposed upon me; I have great reason to suspect, that he went at least half way in all that was said or done against me. He threw himself blindly into the snare which was laid for him, and instead of hindering, as he and I, in concert, might have done, those affairs from languishing, in the manner they did several months, he furnished this court with an excuse for not treating with me, till it was too late to play even a saving game; and he neither drove the regent to assist the Chevalier, nor to declare that he would not assist him; though it was fatal to the cause in general, and to the Scotch in particular, not to bring one of the two about.

It was Christmas one thousand seven hundred and fifteen before the Chevalier sailed for Scotland. The battle of Dunblain had been fought, the business of Preston was over; there remained not the least room to expect any commotion in his favor among the English; and many of the Scotch, who had declared for him, began to grow cool in the cause. No prospect of success could engage him in this expedition, but it was become necessary for his reputation. The Scotch on one side spared not to reproach him; I think unjustly, for his delay; and the French on the other were extremely eager to have him gone. Some of those who knew little of British affairs imagined, that his presence would produce miraculous effects. You must not be surprised at this. As near neighbors as we are, ninety-nine in a hundred among the French are as little acquainted with the inside of our island as with that of Japan. Others of them were uneasy to see him skulking about in France, and to be told of it every hour by the Earl of Stair. Others again imagined, that he might do their business by going into Scotland, though he should not do his own: that is, they flattered themselves, that he might keep a war for some time alive, which would employ the whole attention of our government: and for the event of which they had very little concern. Unable, from their natural temper, as well as their habits, to be true to any principle, they thought and acted in this manner, whilst they affected the greatest friendship to the king, and whilst they really did desire to enter into new and more intimate engagements with him. Whilst the Pretender continued in France they could neither avow him nor favor his cause: if he once set his foot on Scotch ground, they gave hopes of indirect assistance: and if he could maintain himself in any corner of the island, they could look upon him,* it

---

* Discourse of Abbé d'Estrees, afterwards Archbishop of Cambray.

was said, as a king. This was their language to us. To the British minister they denied, they foreswore, they renounced; and yet the man* of the best head in all their councils, being asked by Lord Stair what they intended to do, answered before he was aware, that they pretended to be neuters. I leave you to judge, how this slip was taken up.

As soon as I received advice that the Chevalier was sailed from Dunkirk, I renewed, I redoubled all my applications. I neglected no means, I forgot no argument which my understanding could suggest to me. What the Duke of Ormond rested upon, you have seen already; and I doubt very much whether Lord Mar, if he had been here in my place, would have been able to employ measures more effectual than those which I made use of. I may, without any imputation of arrogance, compare myself on this occasion with his lordship, since there was nothing in the management of this affair above my degreee of capacity; nothing equal, either in extent or difficulty, to the business which he was a spectator of, and which I carried on, when we were secretaries of state together under the late queen.

The king of France, who was not able to furnish the Pretender with money himself, had written some time before his death to his grandson, and had obtained a promise of four hundred thousand crowns from the king of Spain. A small part of this sum had been received by the queen's treasurer at St. Germain's, and had been either sent to Scotland, or employed to defray the expenses which were daily making on the coast. I pressed the Spanish ambassador at Paris, I solicited, by Lawless, Alberoni, at Madrid; and I found† another more private and more promising way of applying to him. I took care to have a number of officers picked out of the Irish troops, which serve in that country; their routes were given them, and I sent a ship to receive and transport them. The money came in so slowly and in such trifling sums, that it turned to little account, and the officers were on their way when the Chevalier returned from Scotland.

In the summer, endeavors had been used to prevail on the king of Sweden to transport from Gottenburg the troops he had in that neighborhood into Scotland, or into the north of England. He had excused himself, not because he disliked the proposition, which, on the contrary, he thought agreeable to his interest, but for reasons of another kind. First, because the troops at hand for this service consisted in horse, not in foot, which had been asked, and which were alone proper for such an expedition: secondly, because a declaration of this sort might turn the Protestant princes of the empire, from whose offices he had still some

---

* Mar. d'Huxelles.   † Marquis Monti.

prospect of assistance, against him: and thirdly, because although he knew that the king of Great Britain was his enemy, yet they were not in war together, nor had the latter acted yet a while openly enough against him to justify such a rupture. At the time I am speaking of, these reasons were removed by the king of Sweden's being beat out of the empire, by the little consequence which his management of the Protestant princes was to him, and by the declaration of war which the king, as elector of Hanover, made.   I took up this negotiation therefore again.   The regent appeared to come into it.   He spoke fair to the Baron de Spar, who pressed him on his side, as I pressed him on mine, and promised, besides the arrears of the subsidy due to the Swedes, an immediate advance of fifty thousand crowns for the enterprise on Britain.   He kept the officer who was to be despatched, I know not how long, booted; sometimes on pretence, that in the low state of his credit he could not find bills of exchange for the sum, and sometimes on other pretences, and by these delays he evaded his promise.   The French were very frank in declaring, that they could give us no money, and that they would give us no troops. Arms, ammunition, and connivance, they made us hope for. The latter, in some degree, we might have had, perhaps; but to what purpose was it to connive, when, by a multitude of little tricks, they avoided furnishing us with arms and ammunition, and when they knew that we were utterly unable to furnish ourselves with them?   I had formed the design of engaging French privateers in the Pretender's service.   They were to have carried whatever we should have to send to any part of Britain in their first voyage, and after that to have cruised under his commission. I had actually agreed for some, and it was in my power to have made the same bargains with others.   Sweden on one side, and Scotland on the other, would have afforded them retreats: and if the war had been kept up in any part of the mountains, I conceive the execution of this design would have been of the greatest advantage to the Pretender.   It failed, because no other part of the work went on.   He was not above six weeks in his Scotch expedition, and these were the things I endeavored to bring to bear in his absence.   I had no great opinion of my success before he went; but when he had made the last step which it was in his power to make, I resolved to suffer neither him nor the Scotch to be any longer bubbles of their own credulity, and of the scandalous artifice of this court.   It would be tedious to enter into a longer narrative of all the useless pains I took.   To conclude, therefore; in a conversation which I had with the M. d'Huxelles, I took occasion to declare, that I would not be the instrument of amusing the Scotch; and that since I was able to do them no service, I would at least inform them, that they must flatter them-

selves no longer with hopes of succor from France. I added, that
I would send them vessels, which, with those already on the
coast of Scotland, might serve to bring off the Pretender, the Earl
of Mar, and as many others as possible. The marshal approved
my resolution, and advised me to execute it, as the only thing
which was left to do. On this occasion he showed no reserve;
he was very explicit, and yet, in this very point of time, the promise of an order was obtained, or pretended to be obtained, from
the regent, for delivering those stores of arms and ammunition
which belonged to the Chevalier, and which had been put into
the French magazines, when Sir George Byng came to Havre.
Castel Blanco is a Spaniard, who married a daughter of Lord
Melford, and who under that title set up for a meddler in English
business. I cannot justly tell whether the honor of obtaining this
promise was ascribed to him, to the junto in the Bois de Boulogne, or to any one else. I suppose they all assumed a share of
the merit. The project was, that these stores should be delivered
to Castel Blanco; that he should enter into a recognisance to carry
them to Spain, and from thence to the West Indies; that I should
provide a vessel for this purpose, which he should appear to hire
or buy; and that when she was at sea she should sail directly for
Scotland. You cannot believe that I reckoned much on the effect
of this order: but accustomed to concur in measures, the inutility
of which I saw evidently enough, I concurred in this likewise.
The necessary care was taken, and in a fortnight's time the ship
was ready to sail, and no suspicion of her belonging to the Chevalier, or of her destination, was gone abroad.

As this event made no alteration in my opinion, it made none
in the despatches which I prepared and sent to Scotland. In
them I gave an account of what was in negotiation. I explained
to him what might be hoped for in time, if he was able to maintain himself in the mountains without the succors he demanded
from France. But from France I told him plainly, that it was
in vain to expect the least part of them. In short, I concealed
nothing from him. This was all I could do to put the Chevalier and his council in a condition to judge what measures to
take: but these despatches never came to his hands. He was
sailed from Scotland just before the gentleman, whom I sent,
arrived on the coast. He landed at Graveline about the twenty-
second of February, and the first orders he gave, were to stop
all the vessels which were going on his account to the country
from whence he came.

I saw him the morning after his arrival at St. Germain's, and
he received me with open arms. I had been, as soon as we
heard of his return, to acquaint the French court with it. They
were not a little uneasy, and the first thing which the M. d'Hux-

elles said to me upon it was, that the Chevalier ought to proceed
to Bar with all the diligence possible, and to take possession of
his former asylum before the Duke of Lorrain had time to desire
him to look out for a residence somewhere else: nothing more
was meant by this proposal, than to get him out of the dominions of France immediately.   I was not in my mind averse to it
for other reasons.   Nothing could be more disadvantageous to
him than to be obliged to pass the Alps, or to reside in the papal
territories on this side of them.   Avignon was already named
for his retreat in common conversation, and I know not whether
from the time he left Scotland, he ever thought of any other.   I
imagined, that by surprising the Duke of Lorrain we should furnish that prince with an excuse to the king, and to the emperor;
that we might draw the matter into length, and gain time to
negotiate some other retreat than that of Avignon for the Chevalier.   The duke's good will there was no room to doubt of, and
by what the Prince of Vaudemont told me at Paris some time
afterwards, I am apt to think we should have succeeded.   In all
events it could not be wrong to try every measure, and the Pretender would have gone to Avignon with much better grace,
when he had done, in the sight of the world, all he could to
avoid it.

I found him in no disposition to make such haste: he had a
mind, on the contrary, to stay sometime at St. Germain's and in
the neighborhood of Paris, and to have a private meeting with
the regent.   He sent me back to Paris to solicit the meeting.   I
wrote, I spoke to the Marshal d'Huxelles, I did best to serve him
in his own way.   The marshal answered me by word of mouth,
and by letter.   He refused me by both.   I remember he added
this circumstance, that he found the regent in bed, and acquainted him with what the Chevalier desired; that the regent
rose up in a passion, said that the things which were asked were
puerilities, and swore that he would not see him.   I returned
without having been able to succeed in my commission: and I
confess I thought the want of success on this occasion no great
misfortune.

It was two or three o'clock on the Sunday or Monday morning when I parted from the Pretender.   He acquiesced in the
determination of the regent, and declared that he would instantly
set out for Lorrain : his trunks were packed, his chaise was
ordered to be at the door at five, and I sent to Paris to acquaint
the minister that he was gone.   He asked me how soon I should
be able to follow him, gave me commissions for some things,
which he desired I should bring after him: and in a word, no
Italian ever embraced the man he was going to stab with greater
show of affection and confidence.

Instead of taking post for Lorrain, he went to the little house in the Bois de Boulogne, where his female ministers resided; and there he continued lurking for several days, and pleasing himself with the air of mystery and business, whilst the only real business, which he should have had at that time, lay neglected. He saw the Spanish and Swedish ministers in this place. I cannot tell, for I never thought it worth asking, whether he saw the Duke of Orleans: possibly he might. To have been teased into such a step, which signified nothing, and which gave the cabal an air of credit and importance, is agreeable enough to the levity of his royal highness's character.

The Thursday following the Duke of Ormond came to see me, and after the compliment of telling me, that he believed I should be surprised at the message he brought, he put into my hands a note to himself, a little scrip of paper directed to me, and drawn in the style of a justice of peace's warrant. They were both in the Chevalier's hand writing, and they were dated on the Tuesday, in order to make me believe that they had been written on the road and sent back to the duke: his grace dropped in our conversation, with great dexterity, all the insinuations proper to confirm me in this opinion. I knew at this time his master was not gone, so that he gave me two very risible scenes, which are frequently to be met with when some people meddle in business; I mean that of seeing a man labor with a great deal of awkward artifice to make a secret of a nothing, and that of seeing yourself taken for a bubble, when you know as much of the matter as he who thinks that he imposes on you.

I cannot recollect precisely the terms of the two papers. I remember that the kingly laconic style of one of them, and the expression of having no farther occasion for my service, made me smile. The other was an order to give up the papers in my office; all which might have been contained in a letter-case of a moderate size. I gave the duke the seals, and some papers which I could readily come at. Some others, and indeed all such as I had not destroyed, I sent afterwards to the Chevalier: and I took care to convey to him, by a safe hand, several of his letters, which it would have been very improper the duke should have seen. I am surprised he did not reflect on the consequence of my obeying his order literally. It depended on me to have shown his general what an opinion the Chevalier had of his capacity. I scorned the trick, and would not appear piqued, when I was far from being angry. As I gave up, without scruple, all the papers which remained in my hands, because I was determined never to make any use of them; so I confess to you, that I took a sort of pride in never asking for those of mine, which were in the Pretender's hands: I contented myself with

making the duke understand how little need there was to get rid
of a man in this manner, who had made the bargain which I
had done at my engagement, and with taking this first opportunity to declare, that I would never more have aught to do with
the Pretender, or his cause.

That I might avoid being questioned and quoted in the most
curious and the most babbling town in the world, I related what
had passed to three or four of my friends, and hardly stirred
abroad during a fortnight, out of a little lodging which very few
people knew of. At the end of this term, the Marshal of Berwic
came to see me, and asked me what I meant, to confine myself
to my chamber, when my name was trumpeted about in all the
companies of Paris, and the most infamous stories were spread
concerning me. This was the first notice I had, and it was soon
followed by others. I appeared immediately in the world, and
found there was hardly a scurrilous tongue which had not been
let loose on my subject, and that those persons whom the Duke
of Ormond and the Earl of Mar must influence, or might silence,
were the loudest in defaming me.

Particular instances wherein I had failed were cited; and as it
was the fashion for every jacobite to affect being in the secret,
you might have found a multitude of vouchers to facts, which,
if they had been true, could in the nature of them be known to
very few persons.

This method of beating down the reputation of a man by noise
and impudence, imposed on the world at first, convinced people
who were not acquainted with me, and staggered even my
friends. But it ceased in a few days to have any effect against
me. The malice was too gross to pass upon reflection. These
stories died away almost as fast as they were published, for this
very reason, because they were particular.

They gave out, for instance, that I had taken to my own use,
a very great sum of the Chevalier's money, when it was notorious that I had spent a great sum of my own in his service; and
never would be obliged to him for a farthing, in which case, I
believe, I was single. Upon this head it was easy to appeal to
a very honest gentleman, the queen's treasurer, at St. Germain's,
through whose hands, and not through mine, went the very little
money which the Chevalier had.

They gave out, that whilst he was in Scotland, he never heard
from me, though it was notorious that I sent him no less than
five expresses during the six weeks which he consumed in this
expedition. It was easy, on this head, to appeal to the persons,
to whom my despatches had been committed.

These lies, and many others of the same sort which were
founded on particular facts, were disproved by particular facts,

and had not time, at least at Paris, to make any impression. But the principal crime with which they charged me then, and the only one which since that time they have insisted upon, is of another nature. This part of their accusation is general, and it cannot be refuted without doing what I have done above, deducing several facts, comparing these facts together, and reasoning upon them; nay, that which is worse is, that it cannot be fully refuted without the mention of some facts, which, in my present circumstances, it would not be very prudent, though I should think it very lawful for me, to divulge. You see that I mean the starving the war in Scotland, which it is pretended might have been supported, and might have succeeded, too, if I had procured the succors which were asked, nay, if I had sent a little powder. This the jacobites, who affect moderation and candor, shrug their shoulders at: they are sorry for it, but Lord Bolingbroke can never wash himself clean of this guilt; for these succors might have been obtained, and a proof that they might, is, that they were so by others. These people leave the cause of this management doubtful, between my treachery and my want of capacity. The Pretender, with all the false charity and real malice of one who sets up for devotion, attributes all his misfortunes to my negligence.

The letters which were written by my secretary above a year ago into England, the marginal notes which have been made since to the letter from Avignon, and what is said above, have set this affair in so clear a light, that whoever examines, with a fair intention, must feel the truth, and be convinced by it. I cannot, however, forbear to make some observations on the same subject here. It is even necessary that I should do so in the design of making this discourse the foundation of my justification to the tories at present, and to the whole world in time.

There is nothing which my enemies apprehend so much as my justification, and they have reason. But they may comfort themselves with this reflection, that it will be a misfortune, which will accompany me to my grave, that I suffered a chain of accidents to draw me into such measures and such company; that I have been obliged to defend myself against such accusations and such accusers; that by associating with so much folly, and so much knavery, I am become the victim of both; that I was distressed by the former, when the latter would have been less grievous to me, since it is much better in business to be yoked to knaves than fools, and that I put into their hands the means of loading me like the scape-goat with all the evil consequences of their folly.

In the first letters which I received from the Earl of Mar, he wrote for arms, for ammunition, for money, for officers, and all

things, frankly, as if these things had been ready and I had engaged to supply him with them, before he set up the standard at
the brae of Mar; whereas our condition could not be unknown to
his lordship, and you have seen that I did all I could to prevent
his reckoning on any assistance from hence.   As our hopes at
this court decreased, his lordship rose in his demands: and at the
time when it was visible that the regent intended nothing less
than even privately and indirectly to support the Scotch, the Pretender and the Earl of Mar wrote for regular forces and a train
of artillery; which was in effect to insist that France should enter
into a war for them.   I might in answer to the first instances
have asked Lord Mar, what he did in Scotland? and what he
meant by drawing his countrymen into a war at this time? or at
least upon this foot?   He who had dictated not long before a
memorial, wherein it was asserted, that to have a prospect of
succeeding in this enterprise, there must be an universal insurrection, and that such an insurrection was in no sort probable, unless
a body of troops was brought to support it?   He who thought
that the consequence of failing, when the attempt was once made,
must be the utter ruin of the cause, and the loss of the British
liberty?   He who concurred in demanding as a *pis-aller*, and the
least which could be insisted on, arms, ammunition, artillery,
money, and officers?   I say, I might have asked what he meant
to begin the dance when he had not the least assurance of any
succor, but on the contrary, the greatest reason imaginable to
believe this affair was become as desperate abroad by the death
of the most christian king, as it was at home by the discovery
of the design, and by the measures taken to defeat it?

Instead of acting this part, which would have been wise, I
took that which was plausible.   I resolved to contribute all I
could to support the business, since it was begun.   I encouraged
his lordship as long as I had the least ground for doing so, and I
confirmed the Pretender in his resolution of going to Scotland,
when he had nothing better left him to do.   If I have any thing
to reproach myself with, in the whole progress of the war in Scotland, it is having encouraged Lord Mar too long.   But on the
other hand, if I had given up the cause, and had written despond-
ingly to him, before this court had explained itself as fully as the
Marshal d'Huxelles did in the conversation which is mentioned
above, it is easy to see what turn would have been given to such
a conduct.

The true cause of all the misfortunes which happened to the
Scotch, and to those who took arms in the north of England, lies
here; that they arose without any previous certainty of foreign
help, in direct contradiction to the scheme which their leaders
themselves had formed.   The excuse which I have heard made

for this, is, that the act of parliament for curbing the Highlanders was near to be put in execution; that they would have
been disarmed and entirely disabled from rising at any other time,
if they had not rose at this.   You can judge better than I of the
validity of this excuse.   It seems to me, that, by management,
they might have gained time, and that even when they had been
reduced to the dilemma supposed, they ought to have got together under pretence of resisting the infractions of the union,
without any mention of the Pretender, and have treated with
the government on this foot.   By these means they might probably have preserved themselves in a condition of avowing their
design when they should be sure of being backed from abroad:
at the worst, they might have declared for the Chevalier, when
all other expedients failed them.   In a word, I take this excuse
not to be very good, and the true reason of this conduct, to have
been the rashness of the people, and the inconsistent measures
of their heads.

But admitting the excuse to be valid, it remains still an undeniable truth, that this is the original fountain from whence all
those waters of bitterness flowed, which so many unhappy people have drunk of.   I have said already, that the necessity of acting was precipitated before any measures to act with success had
been taken, and that the necessity for doing so seemed to increase
as the means of doing so were taken away.   To whom is this to
be ascribed?   Is it to be ascribed to me, who had no share in
these affairs, till a few weeks before the Duke of Ormond was
forced to abandon England, and the discovery of the intended
invasion was published to parliament and to the world? or is it
to be ascribed to those who had from the first been at the head
of this undertaking.

Unable to defend this point, the next resort of the jacobites is
to this impudent and absurd affirmation, that notwithstanding the
disadvantages under which they took arms, they should have
succeeded, if the indirect assistances, which were asked from
France, had been obtained: nay, that they should have been able
to defend the Highlands, if I had sent them a little powder.   Is
it possible that a man should be wounded with such blunt weapons?   Much more than powder was asked for from the first, and
I have already said, that, when the Chevalier came into Scotland,
regular troops, artillery, &c., were demanded.   Both he and the
Earl of Mar judged it impossible to stand their ground, without
such assistance as these.   How scandalous then must it be deemed,
that they suffer their dependents to spread in the world, that for
want of a little powder I forced them to abandon Scotland?   The
Earl of Mar knows that all the powder in France would not have
enabled him to stay at Perth as long as he did, if he had not had

another security: and when that failed him, he must have quitted the party, if the regent had given us all that he made some of us expect.

But to finish all that I intend to say on a subject which has tired me, and perhaps you; the jacobites affirm, that the indirect assistances which they desired might have been obtained: and I confess, that I am inexcusable if this fact be true. To prove it, they appeal to the little politicians of whom I have spoken so often. I affirm, on the contrary, that nothing could be obtained here to support the Scotch, or to encourage the English. To prove the assertion, I appeal to the ministers with whom I negotiated, and to the regent himself, who, whatever language he may hold in private with other people, cannot controvert with me the truth of what I advance. He excluded me formerly, that he might the more easily avoid doing any thing; and perhaps he has blamed me since, that he might excuse his doing nothing. All this may be true, and yet it will remain true, that he would never have been prevailed upon to act directly against his interest in the only point of view which he has, I mean the crown of France, and against the unanimous sense of all his ministers. Suppose that in the time of the late queen, when she had the peace in view, a party in France had implored her assistance, and had applied to Margery Fielding, to Israel, to my Lady Oglethorpe, to Dr. Battle, and Lieutenant-general Stewart; what success do you imagine such applications would have had? The queen would have spoke them fair, she would speak otherwise to nobody: but do you imagine she would have made one step in their favor? Olive Trant, Magny, Mademoiselle Chaussery, a dirty Abbé Brigault, and Mr. Dillon, are characters very apposite to these; and what I suppose to have passed in England is not a whit more ridiculous that what really passed here.

I say nothing of the ships which the jacobites pretend that they sent into Scotland, three weeks or a month after the Pretender was returned. I believe they might have had my Lord Stair's connivance then, as well as the regent's. I say nothing of the order which they pretend to have obtained, and which I never saw, for the stores that were seized at Havre to be delivered to Castel Blanco. I have already said enough on this head, and you cannot have failed to observe, that this signal favor was never obtained by these people, till the Marshal d'Huxelles had owned to me, that nothing was to be expected from France, and that the only thing which I could do was to endeavor to bring the Pretender, the Earl of Mar, and the principal persons who were most exposed, off: neither he nor I imagining that any such would be left behind.

When I began to appear in the world, upon the advertisements which my friends gave me of the clamor that was raised against me, you will easily think I did not enter into so many particulars as I have done with you.   I said even less than you have seen, in those letters which Brinsden wrote into England, in March and April was twelve-month; and yet the clamor sunk immediately.   The people of consideration at this court beat it down, and the court of St. Germain's grew so ashamed of it, that the queen thought fit to purge herself of having had any share in encouraging the discourses which were held against me, or having been so much as let into the secret of the measure which preceded them.   The provocation was great, but I resolved to act without passion.   I saw the advantage the Pretender and his council, who disposed of things better for me than I should have done for myself, had given me: but I saw likewise, that I must improve this advantage with the utmost caution.

As I never imagined that he would treat me in the manner he did, nor that his ministers could be weak enough to advise him to it, I had resolved, on his return from Scotland, to follow him till his residence should be fixed somewhere or other: after which, having served the tories in this, which I looked upon as their last struggle for power, and having continued to act in the Pretender's affairs till the end of the term for which I embarked with him, I should have esteemed myself to be at liberty, and should, in the civilest manner I was able, have taken my leave of him. Had we parted thus, I should have remained in a very strange situation during the rest of my life: but I had examined myself thoroughly—I was determined, I was prepared.

On one side he would have thought that he had a sort of right on any future occasion to call me out of my retreat; the tories would probably have thought the same thing: my resolution was taken to refuse them both, and I foresaw that both would condemn me.   On the other side, the consideration of his keeping measures with me, joined to that of having once openly declared for him, would have created a point of honor, by which I should have been tied down, not only from ever engaging against him, but also from making my peace at home.   The Chevalier cut this Gordian knot asunder at one blow.   He broke the links of that chain, which former engagements had fastened on me, and gave me a right to esteem myself as free from all obligations of keeping measures with him, as I should have continued if I had never engaged in his interest.   I took therefore, from that moment, the resolution of making my peace at home, and of employing all the unfortunate experience I had acquired abroad, to undeceive my friends, and to promote the union and the quiet of my country.

The Earl of Stair had received a full power to treat with me, whilst I was engaged with the Pretender, as I have been since informed. He had done me the justice to believe me incapable to hearken, in such circumstances, to any proposals of that kind: and as much friendship as he had for me, as much as I had for him, we entertained not the least even indirect correspondence together during that whole time. Soon afterwards he employed a person* to communicate to me the disposition of his majesty to grant me my pardon, and his own desire to give me, on this occasion, all the proofs he could of his inclination in my favor. I embraced the offer, as it became me to do, with all possible sense of the king's goodness, and of his lordship's friendship.† We met, we talked together, and he wrote to the court on the subject. The turn which the ministers gave to this matter was, to enter into a treaty to reverse my attainder, and to stipulate the conditions on which this act of grace should be granted me.

The notion of a treaty shocked me. I resolved never to be restored rather than go that way to work, and I opened myself without any reserve to Lord Stair. I told him that I looked on myself to be obliged in honor and in conscience to undeceive my friends in England, both as to the state of foreign affairs, as to the management of the jacobite interest abroad, and as to the characters of persons: in every one of which points I knew them to be most grossly and most dangerously deluded. That the treatment I had received from the Pretender and his adherents would justify me to the world in doing this: that if I remained in exile all my life, he might be assured that I would never more have to do with the jacobite cause; and that if I was restored, I should give it an effectual blow, in making that apology which the Pretender has put me under a necessity of making: that in doing this I flattered myself, that I should contribute something to the establishment of the king's government, and to the union of his subjects; but that this was all the merit which I could promise to have: that if the court believed these professions to be sincere, a treaty with me was unnecessary for them; and that if they did not believe them so, a treaty with them was dangerous for me: that I was determined in this whole transaction to make no one step which I would not own in the face of the world; that in other circumstances it might be sufficient to act honestly, but that in a case as extraordinary as mine, it was necessary to act clearly, and to leave no room for the least doubtful construction.

The Earl of Stair, as well as Mr. Craggs, who arrived soon after in France, came into my sense. I have reason to believe

* Saladin of Geneva, then at Paris.

† There will be added, at the end of this relation, an original letter from the Earl of Stair to Mr. Craggs, giving a full account of the transaction here mentioned.

that the king has approved it likewise, upon their representations, since he has been pleased to give me the'most gracious assurances of his favor. What the effect of all this may be, in the next, or in any other session, I know not: but this is the foot on which I have put myself, and on which I stand at the moment I write to you. The whigs may continue inveterate, and by consequence frustrate his majesty's good intentions towards me; the tories may continue to rail at me, on the credit of such enemies as I have described to you in the course of this relation: neither the one nor the other shall make me swerve out of the path which I have traced to myself.

I have now led you through the several stages which I proposed at first, and I should do wrong to your good understanding as well as to our mutual friendship, if I suspected that you could hold any other language to me than that which Dolabella uses to Cicero. "Satisfactum est jam a te vel officio vel familiaritati; satisfactum etiam partibus." The king, who pardons me, might complain of me, the whigs might declaim against me, my family might reproach me for the little regard which I have shown to my own and to their interest; but where is the crime I have been guilty of towards my party and towards my friends? In what part of my conduct will the tories find an excuse for the treatment which they have given me? As tories, such as they were when I left England, I defy them to find any. But here lies the sore, and, tender as it is, I must lay it open. Those amongst them, who rail at me now, are changed from what they were, or from what they professed themselves to be, when we lived and acted together. They were tories then, they are jacobites now. Their objections to the course of my conduct whilst I was in the Pretender's interest are the pretence; the true reason of their anger is, that I renounce the Pretender for my life. When you were first driven into this interest, I may appeal to you for the notion which the party had. You thought of restoring him by the strength of the tories, and of opposing a tory king to a whig king. You took him up as the instrument of your revenge and of your ambition. You looked on him as your creature, and never once doubted of making what terms you pleased with him. This is so true, that the same language is still held to the catechumens in jacobitism. Were the contrary to be avowed even now, the party in England would soon diminish. I engaged on this principle, when your orders sent me to Commercy, and I never acted on any other. This ought to have been part of my merit towards the tories, and it would have been so if they had continued in the same dispositions. But they are changed, and this very thing is become my crime. Instead of making the Pretender their tool, they are his. Instead of having in view to restore him on their own terms, they are laboring to do it without any terms; that is, to speak properly, they are ready to receive him on his. Be not deceived: there is not a man on this side of the water who acts in any other manner. The church-of-England jacobite and the Irish papist seem, in every respect, to have the same cause. Those on your side of the water, who correspond with these, are to be comprehended in the same class: and from hence it is, that the clamor raised against me has been kept up with so much industry, and is redoubled on the least appearance of my return home, and of my being in a situation to justify myself.

You have seen already what reasons the Pretender, and the several sorts of people who compose his party here, had to get rid of me, and to cover me to the utmost of their power with infamy. Their views were as short in this case as they are in all others. They did not see at first, that this conduct would not only give me a right, but put me under a necessity of keeping no farther measures with them, and of laying the whole mystery of their iniquity open. As soon as they discovered this, they took the only course which was left them, that of poisoning the minds of the tories, and of creating such prejudices against me whilst I remained in a condition of not speaking for myself, as will, they hope, prevent the effect of whatever I may say when I am in a condition of pleading my own cause. The bare apprehension, that I shall show the world that I have been guilty of no crime, renders me criminal among these men: and they hold themselves ready, being unable to reply either in point of fact or in point of reason, to drown my voice in the confusion of their clamor.

The only crimes I am guilty of, I own. I own the crime of having been for the Pretender, in a very different manner from those with whom I acted. I served him as faithfully, I served him as well as they, but I served him on a different principle. I own the crime of having renounced him, and of being resolved never to have to do with him as long as I live. I own the crime of being determined sooner or later, as soon as I can, to clear myself of all the unjust aspersions which have been cast upon me; to undeceive by my experience as many as I can of those tories who may have been drawn into error, and to contribute, if ever I return home, as far as I am able, to promote the national good of Britain without any other regard. These crimes do not, I hope, by this time appear to you to be of a very black dye. You may come, perhaps, to think them virtues, when you have read and considered what remains to be said; for before I conclude, it is necessary that I open one matter to you which I could not weave in sooner without breaking too much the thread of my narration.

In this place, unmingled with anything else, it will have, as it deserves to have, your whole attention.

Whoever composed that curious piece of false fact, false argument, false English, and false eloquence, the letter from Avignon, says, that I was not thought the most proper person to speak about religion. I confess I should be of his mind, and should include his patrons in my case, if the practice of it was to be recommended: for surely it is unpardonable impudence to impose by precept what we do not teach by example. I should be of the same mind, if the nature of religion was to be explained, if its mysteries were to be fathomed, and if this great truth was to be established, that the church of England has the advantage over all our churches in purity of doctrine, and in wisdom .of discipline. But nothing of this kind was necessary. This would have been the task of reverend and learned divines. We of the laity had nothing more to do than to lay in our claim, that we could never submit to be governed by a prince who was not of the religion of our country. Such a declaration could hardly have failed of some effect towards opening the eyes and disposing the mind even of the Pretender. At least, in justice to ourselves, and in justice to our party, we who were here ought to have made it, and the influence of it on the Pretender ought to have become the rule of our subsequent conduct.

In thinking in this manner I think no otherwise now than I have always thought: and I cannot forget, nor you neither, what passed when a little before the death of the queen, letters were conveyed from the Chevalier to several persons, to myself among others. In the letter to me, the article of religion was so awkwardly handled, that he made the principal motive of the confidence we ought to have in him to consist in his firm resolution to adhere to popery. The effect which this epistle had on me was the same which it had on those tories to whom I communicated it at that time; it made us resolve to have nothing to do with him.

Sometime after this I was assured by several, and I make no doubt but others have been so too, that the Chevalier at the bottom was not a bigot. That whilst he remained abroad and could expect no succor, either present or future, from any princes but those of the Roman catholic communion, it was prudent, whatever he might think, to make no demonstration of a design to change: but that his temper was such, and he was already so disposed, that we might depend on his compliance with what should be desired of him, if he ever came amongst us, and was taken from under the wing of the queen his mother. To strengthen this opinion of his character, it was said that he had sent for Mr. Lesley over; that he allowed him to celebrate the church-of-England service in his family, and that he had promised to hear what this divine should represent on the subject of religion to him. When I came abroad, the same things, and much more, were at first insinuated to me, and I began to let them make impression upon me, notwithstanding what I had seen under his hand. I would willingly flatter myself, that this impression disposed me to incline to jacobitism, rather than allow that the inclination to jacobitism disposed me easily to believe what, upon that principle, I had so much reason to wish might be true. Which was the cause, and which the effect, I cannot well determine: perhaps they did mutually occasion each other. Thus much is certain, that I was far from weighing this matter as I ought to have done, when the solicitation of my friends and the persecution of my enemies precipitated me into engagements with the Pretender.

I was willing to take it for granted, that since you were as ready to declare, as I believed you at that time, you must have had entire satisfaction on the article of religion. I was soon undeceived: this string had never been touched. My own observation, and the unanimous report of all those who from his infancy have approached the Pretender's person, soon taught me how difficult it is to come to terms with him on this head, and how unsafe to embark without them.

His religion is not founded on the love of virtue and the detestation of vice; on a sense of that obedience which is due to the will of the Supreme Being; and a sense of those obligations which creatures formed to live in a mutual dependence on one another lie under. The spring of his whole conduct is fear. Fear of the horns of the devil and of the flames of hell. He has been taught to believe, that nothing but a blind submission to the church of Rome, and a strict adherence to all the terms of that communion, can save him from these dangers. He has all the superstition of a capuchin; but I found on him no tincture of the religion of a prince. Do not imagine that I loose the reins to my imagination, or that I write what my resentments dictate: I tell you simply my opinion. I have heard the same description of his character made by those who know him best; and I conversed with very few among the Roman catholics themselves, who did not think him too much a papist.

Nothing gave me from the beginning so much uneasiness as the consideration of this part of his character, and of the little care which had been taken to correct it. A true turn had not been given to the first steps which were made with him. The tories, who engaged afterwards, threw themselves, as it were, at his head. He had been suffered to think that the party in England wanted him as much as he wanted them. There was no

room to hope for much compliance on the head of religion, when
he was in these sentiments, and when he thought the tories too
far advanced to have it in their power to retreat: and little dependence was at any time to be placed on the promises of a man
capable of thinking his damnation attached to the observance,
and his salvation to the breach of these very promises.   Something, however, was to be done: and I thought that the least
which could be done was, to deal plainly with him, and to show
him the impossibility of governing our nation by any other expedient, that by complying with that which would be expected
from him as to his religion.   This was thought too much by the
Duke of Ormond and Mr. Lesley; although the duke could be
no more ignorant than the minister, how ill the latter had been
used, how far the Chevalier had been from keeping the word
which he had given, and on the faith of which Mr. Lesley had
come over to him.   They both knew, that he not only refused to
hear himself, but that he sheltered the ignorance of his priests,
or the badness of his cause, or both, behind his authority, and
absolutely forbid all discourse concerning religion.   The duke
seemed convinced that it would be time enough to talk of religion to him when he should be restored, or, at soonest, when
he should be landed in England; that the influence under which
he had lived being at a distance, the reasonableness of what we
might propose, joined to the apparent necessity which would
then stare him in the face, could not fail to produce all the effects
which we could desire.

To me this whole reasoning appeared fallacious.   Our business was not to make him change appearances on this side of the
water, but prepare him to give those which would be necessary on the other: and there was no room to hope that if we
could gain nothing on his prejudices here, we should be able to
overcome them in Britain.   I would have argued just as the
Duke of Ormond and Lesley, if I had been a papist; and I saw
well enough that some people about him, for in a great dearth
of ability there was cunning to be met with, affected nothing
more than to keep off all discourse of religion.   To my apprehension it was exceeding plain that we shonld find, if we were
once in England, the necessity of going forward at any rate
with him, much greater than he would find that of complying
with us.   I thought it an unpardonable fault to have taken a
formal engagement with him, when no previous satisfaction had
been obtained on a point, at least as essential to our civil as to
our religious rights; to the peace of the state, as to the prosperity
of the church: and I looked on this fault to be aggravated by
every day's delay.   Our silence was unfair, both to the Chevalier, and to our friends in England.   He was induced by it to

believe, that they would expect far less from him, than we knew they expected: and they were confirmed in an opinion of his docility, which we knew to be void of all foundation.   The pretence of removing that influence, under which he had lived, was frivolous, and should never have been urged to me, who saw plainly, that according to the measures pursued by the very persons who urged it, he must be environed in England by the same people that surrounded him here; and that the court of St. James's would be constituted, if ever he was restored, in the same manner as that of St. Germain's was.

When the draught of a declaration, and other papers which were to be dispersed in Great Britain, came to be settled, it appeared that my apprehension and distrust were but too well founded.   The Pretender took exception against several passages, and particularly against those, wherein a direct promise of securing the churches of England and Ireland was made.   He was told, he said, that he could not in conscience make such a promise: and, the debate being kept up a little while, he asked me with some warmth, why the tories were so desirous to have him, if they expected those things from him which his religion did not allow?   I left these drafts by his order with him, that he might consider and amend them.   I cannot say that he sent them to the queen to be corrected by her confessor and the rest of her council: but I firmly believe it.   Sure I am, that he took time sufficient to do this; before he sent them from Bar where he then was, to Paris whither I was returned.   When they were digested in such a manner as satisfied his casuists, he made them be printed: and my name was put to the declaration, as if the original had been signed by me.   I had hitherto submitted my opinion to the judgment of others; but on this occasion I took advice from myself.   I declared to him, that I would not suffer my name to be at the bottom of this paper.   All the copies which came to my hands I burnt, and another was printed off, without any countersigning.

The whole tenor of the amendments was one continued instance of the grossest bigotry; and the most material passages were turned with all the jesuitical prevarication imaginable. As much as it was his interest, at that time, to cultivate the respect which many of the tories really had for the memory of the late queen, and which many others affected as a farther mark of their opposition to the court, and to the whig party; as much as it was his interest to weave the honor of her name into his cause, and to render her, even after her death, a party to the dispute; he could not be prevailed upon to give her that character which her enemies allowed her, nor to make use of those expressions in speaking of her, which by the general manner of

their application, are come to be little more than terms of respect
and words of form, proper in the style of public acts. For
instance:

She was called in the original draught "his sister of glorious
and blessed memory." In that which he published, the epithet
of "blessed" was left out. Her eminent justice and her exemplary piety were occasionally mentioned. In lieu of which, he
substituted a flat, and in this case an invidious expression, "her
inclinations to justice."

Not content with declaring her neither just nor pious in this
world, he did little less than declare her damned in the other,
according to the charitable principles of the church of Rome.

"When it pleased Almighty God to take her to himself," was
the expression used in speaking of the death of the queen. This
he erased, and instead thereof inserted these words: "when it
pleased Almighty God to put a period to her life."

He graciously allowed the universities to be nurseries of loyalty, but did not think that it became him to style them "nurseries of religion."

Since his father passes already for a saint, and since reports
are encouraged of miracles, which they suppose to be wrought
at his tomb, he might have allowed his grandfather to pass for a
martyr; but he struck out of the draught these words: "that
blessed martyr who died for his people," which were applied to
King Charles the First, and would say nothing more of him than
that "he fell a sacrifice to rebellion."

In the clause which related to the churches of England and
Ireland, there was a plain and direct promise inserted of "effectual provision for their security; and for their re-establishment in
all those rights which belong to them." This clause was not
suffered to stand, but another was formed, wherein all mention
of the church of Ireland was omitted, and nothing was promised
to the church of England but the security, "and re-establishment
of all those rights, privileges, immunities, and possessions, which
belong to her," and wherein he had already promised, by his
declaration of the twentieth of July, to secure and "protect all
her members."

I need make no comment on a proceeding so easy to be understood. The drift of these evasions, and of this affected obscurity
is obvious enough, at least it will appear so by the observations
which remain to be made.

He was so afraid of admitting any words which might be construed into a promise of his consenting to those things, which
should be found necessary for the present or future security of
our constitution, that in a paragraph where he was made to say,
that he thought himself obliged to be solicitous for the prosperity

of the church of England, the word prosperity was expunged; and we were left by this mental reservation to guess what he was solicitous for? It could not be for her prosperity, that he had expunged. It must, therefore, be for her destruction, which, in his language, would have been styled, her conversion.

Another remarkable proof of the same kind is to be found towards the conclusion of the declaration. After having spoke of the peace and flourishing estate of the kingdom, he was made to express his readiness to concert with the two houses such further measures as should be thought necessary for securing the same to future generations. The design of this paragraph you see. He and his council saw it too, and therefore the word " securing" was laid aside, and the word "leaving" was inserted in lieu of it.

One would imagine, that a delaration corrected in this manner might have been suffered to go abroad without any farther precaution. But these papers had been penned by protestants, and who could answer that there might not still be ground sufficient from the tenor of them to insist on every thing necessary for the security of that religion? The declaration of the twentieth of July had been penned by a priest of the Scotch college, and the expressions had been measured so as to suit perfectly with the conduct which the Chevalier intended to hold, so as to leave room to distinguish him upon future occasions, with the help of a little pious sophistry, out of all the engagements which he seemed to take in it. This orthodox paper was therefore to accompany the heretical paper into the world, and no promise of moment was to stand in the latter, unless qualified by a reference to the former. Thus the church was to be secured in the rights, &c., which belong to her. How? No otherwise than according to the declaration of the month of July. And what does that promise? Security and protection to the members of this church in the enjoyment of their property. I make no doubt, but Bellarmine, if he had been the Chevalier's confessor, would have passed this paragraph thus amended. No engagement whatever taken in favor of the church of Ireland, and a happy distinction found between securing that of England and protecting her members. Many a useful project for the destruction of heretics, and for accumulating power and riches to the see of Rome, has been established on a more slender foundation.

The same spirit reigns through the whole. Civil and religious rights are no otherwise to be confirmed, than in conformity to the declaration of July; nay, the general pardon is restrained and limited to the terms prescribed therein.

This is the account which I judged too important to be omitted, and which I chose to give you all together. I shall surely be justified at present in concluding, that the tories are grossly deluded in their opinion of this prince's character, or else that they sacrlfice all which ought to be esteemed precious and sacred among men, to their passions.   In both these cases I remain still a tory, and am true to the party.   In the first I endeavor to undeceive you by an experience purchased at my expense and for your sakes: in the second, I endeavor to prevail on you to reverl to that principle from which we have deviated.   You never intended, whilst I lived amongst you, the ruin of your country; and yet every step, which you now make towards the restoration you are so fond of, is a step towards this ruin.   No man of sense, well informed, can ever go into measures for it, unless he thinks himself and his country in such desperate circumstances, that nothing is left them but to choose, of two ruins, that which they like best.

The exile of the royal family, under Cromwell's usurpation, was the principal cause of all those misfortunes in which Britain has been involved, as well as of many of those which have happened to the rest of Europe, during more than half a century.

The two brothers, Charles and James, became then infected with popery to such degrees, as their different characters admitted of.   Charles had parts, and his good understanding served as an antidote to repel the poison.   James, the simplest man of his time, drank off the whole chalice.   The poison met, in his composition, with all the fear, all the credulity, and all the obstinacy of temper proper to increase its virulence, and to strengthen its effect.   The first had always a wrong bias upon him; he connived at the establishment, and indirectly contributed to the growth of that power, which afterwards disturbed the peace, and threatened the liberty of Europe so often: but he went no farther out of the way.   The opposition of his parliaments, and his own reflections stopped him here.   The prince and the people were indeed mutually jealous of one another, from whence much present disorder flowed, and the foundation of future evils was laid: but his good and his bad principles combatting still together, he maintained, during a reign of more than twenty years, in some tolerable degree, the authority of the crown, and the flourishing state of the nation.   The last, drunk with superstitious and even enthusiastic zeal, ran headlong into his own ruin, whilst he endeavored to precipitate ours.   His parliament and his people did all they could to save themselves by winning him.   But all was vain; he had no principle on which they could take hold.   Even his good qualities worked against them, and his love of his country went halves with his bigotry.   How he succeeded we have heard from our fathers.   The revolution of one thousand six hundred and eighty-eight saved the nation and ruined the king.

Now the Pretender's education has rendered him infinitely less fit than his uncle, and at least as unfit as his father, to be king of Great Britain. Add to this, that there is no resource in his understanding. Men of the best sense find it hard to overcome religious prejudices, which are of all the strongest; but he is a slave to the weakest. The rod hangs like the sword of Damocles over his head, and he trembles before his mother and his priest. What, in the name of God, can any member of the church of England promise himself from such a character? Are we by another revolution to return into the same state from which we were delivered by the first? Let us take example from the Roman catholics, who act very reasonably in refusing to submit to a protestant prince. Henry the Fourth had at least as good a title to the crown of France as the Pretender has to ours. His religion alone stood in his way, and he had never been king if he had not removed that obstacle. Shall we submit to a popish prince, who will no more imitate Henry the Fourth in changing his religion, than he will imitate those shining qualities which rendered him the honestest gentleman, the bravest captain, and the greatest prince of his age? Allow me to give a loose to my pen for a moment on this subject. General benevolence and universal charity seem to be established in the Gospel as the distinguishing badges of Christianity. How it happens I cannot tell; but so it is, that in all ages of the church the professors of Christianity seem to have been animated by quite a contrary spirit. Whilst they were thinly scattered over the world, tolerated in some places, but established nowhere, their zeal often consumed their charity. Paganism, at that time the religion by law established, was insulted by many of them; the ceremonies were disturbed, the altars thrown down. As soon as by the favor of Constantine their numbers were increased, and the reins of government were put into their hands, they began to employ the secular arm, not only against different religions, but against different sects which arose in their own religion. A man may boldly affirm that more blood has been shed in the disputes between Christian and Christian, than has ever been drawn from the whole body of them in the persecutions of the heathen emperors; and in the conquest of the Mahometan princes. From these they have received quarter, but never from one another. The Christian religion is actually tolerated among the Mahometans, and the domes of churches and mosques arise in the same city. But it will be hard to find an example, where one sect of Christians has tolerated another which it was in their power to extirpate. They have gone farther in these later ages: what was practised formerly has been taught since. Persecution has been reduced into system, and the disciples of the meek and humble Jesus have avowed a tyranny, which the most barbarous conquerors never claimed. The wicked subtility of casuists has established breach of faith with those who differ from us, as a duty in opposition to faith, and murder itself has been made one of the means of salvation. I know very well that the reformed churches have been far from going those cruel lengths, which are authorised by the doctrine as well as example of that of Rome—though Calvin put a flaming sword on the title of a French edition of his institute, with this motto, " Je ne suis point venu mettre la paix, mais l'epée:" but I know likewise, that the difference lies in the means, and not in the aim of their policy. The church of England, the most humane of all of them, would root out every other religion, if it was in her power. She would not hang and burn; her measures would be milder, and therefore, perhaps, more effectual.

Since then there is this inveterate rancor among Christians, can any thing be more absurd, than for those of one persuasion to trust the supreme power, or any part of it, to those of another? Particularly, must it be reputed madness in those of our religion, to trust themselves in the hands of Roman catholics? Must it not be reputed impudence in a Roman catholic to expect that we should? he who looks upon us as heretics, as men in rebellion against a lawful, nay a divine authority, and whom it is therefore meritorious by all sorts of ways to reduce to obedience. There are many, I know, among them who think more generously, and whose morals are not corrupted by that which is called religion: but this is the spirit of the priesthood, in whose scale that scrap of a parable, "Compel them to come in," which they apply as they please, outweighs the whole decalogue. This will be the spirit of every man who is bigot enough to be under their direction: and so much is sufficient for my present purpose.

During your last session of parliament, it was expected that the whigs would attempt to repeal the occasional bill. The same jealousy continues; there is, perhaps, foundation for it. Give me leave to ask you, upon what principle we argued for making this law, and upon what principle you must argue against the repeal of it. I have mentioned the principle in the beginning of this discourse. No man ought to be trusted with any share of power under a government, who must, to act consistently with himself, endeavor the destruction of that very government. Shall this proposition pass for true, when it is applied to keep a presbyterian from being mayor of a corporation? and shall it become false when it is applied to keep a papist from being king? The proposition is equally true in both cases, but the argument drawn from it is just so much stronger in the latter, than in the former case, as the mischiefs which may result from the power and influence of a king, are greater than those which can be wrought

by a magistrate of the lowest order. This seems to my apprehension to be argumentum ad hominem, and I do not see by
what happy distinction a jacobite tory could elude the force of it.

It may be said, and it has been urged to me, that if the Chevalier was restored, the knowledge of his character would be our
security; "habet fœnum in cornu:" there would be no pretence
for trusting him, and by consequence it would be easy to put such
restrictions on the exercise of the regal power as might hinder
him from invading or sapping our religion and liberty. But this
I utterly deny. Experience has shown us how ready men are
to court power and profit; and who can determine, how far either
the tories or the whigs would comply, in order to secure to themselves the enjoyment of all the places in the kingdom? Suppose,
however, that a majority of true Israelites should be found, whom
no temptation could oblige to bow the knee to Baal; in order to
preserve the government on one hand, must they not destroy it
on the other? The necessary restrictions would in this case be so
many, and so important, as to leave hardly the shadow of a monarchy, if he submitted to them; and if he did not submit to them,
these patriots would have no resource left but in rebellion. Thus,
therefore, the affair would turn, if the Pretender was restored. We
might, most probably, lose our religion and liberty by the bigotry
of the prince, and the corruption of the people. We should have
no chance of preserving them, but by an entire change of the
whole frame of our government, or by another revolution. What
reasonable man would voluntarily reduce himself to the necessity
of making an option among such melancholy alternatives?

The best which could be hoped for, were the Chevalier on the
throne, would be, that a thread of favorable accidents, improved
by the wisdom and virtue of parliament, might keep off the evil
day during his reign. But still the fatal cause would be established, it would be entailed upon us, and every man would be
apprised, that sooner or later the fatal effect must follow. Consider a little what a condition we should be in, both with respect
to our foreign interest and our domestic quiet, whilst the reprieve
lasted, whilst the Chevalier or his successors made no direct
attack upon the constitution.

As to the first, it is true, indeed, that princes and states are
friends or foes to one another, according as the motives of ambition drive them.   These are the first principles of union and division amongst them.   The protestant powers of Europe have
joined, in our days, to support and aggrandise the house of Austria, as they did in the days of our forefathers, to defeat her designs, and to reduce her power; and the most Christian king
of France has more than once joined his councils, and his
arms too, with the councils and arms of the most Mahometan

emperor of Constantinople. But still there is, and there must continue, as long as the influence of the papal authority subsists in Europe, another general, permanent, and invariable division of interests. The powers of earth, like those of heaven, have two distinct motions. Each of them rolls in his own political orb, but each of them is hurried at the same time round the great vortex of his religion. If this general notion be ust, apply it to the present case. Whilst a Roman catholic holds the rudder, how can we expect to be steered in our proper course? His political interest will certainly incline him to direct our first motion right; but his mistaken religious interest will render him incapable of oing it steadily.

As to the last, our domestic quiet; even whilst the Chevalier and those of his race concealed their game, we should remain in the most unhappy state which human nature is subject to—a state of doubt and suspense. Our preservation would depend on making him the object of our eternal jealousy, who, to render himself and his people happy, ought to be that of our entire confidence.

Whilst the Pretender and his successors forbore to attack the religion and liberty of the nation, we should remain in the condition of those people who labor under a broken constitution, or who carry about them some chronical distemper. They feel a little pain at every moment, or a certain uneasiness, which is sometimes less tolerable than pain, hangs continually on them, and they languish in the constant expectation of dying, perhaps, in the severest torture.

But if the fear of hell should dissipate all other fears in the Pretender's mind, and carry him, which is frequently the effect of that passion, to the most desperate undertakings; if among his successors a man bold enough to make the attempt should arise, the condition of the British nation would be still more deplorable. The attempt succeeding, we should fall into tyranny; for a change of religion could never be brought about by consent; and the same force that would be sufficient to enslave our consciences would be sufficient for all the other purposes of arbitrary power. The attempt failing, we should fall into anarchy; for there is no medium when disputes between a prince and his people are arrived at a certain point; he must either be submitted to, or deposed.

I have now laid before you even more than I intended to have said when I took my pen; and I am persuaded, that if these papers ever come to your hands, they will enable you to cast up the account between party and me. Till the time of the queen's death it stands, I believe, even between us. The tories distinguished me by their approbation, and by the credit which I had amongst them; and I endeavored to distinguish myself in their service, under the immediate weight of great discouragement, and with the no very distant prospect of great danger.   Since that time the account is not so even, and I dare appeal to any impartial person, whether my side in it be that of the debtor.   As to the opinion of mankind in general, and the judgment which posterity will pass on these matters, I am under no great concern. "Suum cuique decus posteritas rependit."

FROM THE EARL OF STAIR,

HIS MAJESTY'S AMBASSADOR AT PARIS,

TO JAMES CRAGGS, JUNIOR, ESQ.

(Secret Letter.*)

MONSIEUR:—Vous avés vu par ma depêche l'état de la negotiation.   J'ai à present à vous parler, en particulier, de Bolingbroke. Je l'ai vu chés moi le jour après l'arrivée de Mr. Pitt: et nous avons eu ensemble une conversation d'une heure et demie; dont la substance est, que lui, Bolingbroke, renttroit, du meilleur de son cœur, dans son devoir envers son roi et sa patrie; et que rien au monde étoit capable de le détacher de cette resolution, quand même sa majesté ne trouveroit pas à propos de lui faire grace. Qu'il étoit prêt, de ce moment, à s'employer avec moi dans ce païs-ici pour le service du roi, si je croyois qu'il y pouvoit être utile à quelque chose; et qu'il me communequeroit tout ce qui viendroit à sa connoissance qui me pourroit être de quelque usage, et qu'il m'aideroit volontiers de toutes les lumieres qu'il pourroit avoir acquises par ses habitudes ici.

Il me dit, que je sçavois bien, par son caractere, qu'il ne faisoit pas les choses à demi; qu'en rentrant en son devoir il se proposoit de servir le roi et sa patrie avec zèle et avec affection.   Que pour cet effet, il se croiroit obligé, par toutes les obligations du devoir, de la reconnoissance, de l'honneur et de l'interêt même, d'informer le roi de tout ce que son experience lui pourroit suggérer d'utile pour le service de sa majesté, pour l'affermissement de la tranquillité publique, et pour prévenir tous les projets qui se pourront former en faveur de ses ennemis.   Qu'il feroit tout ce qui dependroit de lui de faire rentrer les toris qui ont embrassé le

---

* This letter, which, with several more private and secret letters, had been returned to Lord Stair by his correspondent, was communicated to the editor of these papers, some time ago, by a relation of his lordship: and it is copied here, exactly, from the original in his own handwriting.

parti du prétendant dans leur devoir, en leur faisant voir quelle
espece d'homme le prétendant étoit; et qu'ils se trompoient s'ils
croyoient qu'ils pourroient avoir de la seuréte avec lui ou pour
leur liberté ou pour leur réligion.   Que pour pouvoir faire cela,
il étoit necessaire, même pour le service du roi, que lui, Bolingbroke; ne fût pas perdu de reputation, qu'il ne passât pas pour
délateur.

Il insista beaucoup sur cet article.   "Ce que je propose de
faire, me dit-il, est digne d'un honnête homme, convaincu de son
erreur et touché d'un vrai répentir; c'est ce que je ferai haute-
ment et à la face de l'univers: et permettés-moi d'ajouter, que
c'est un service réel que je rendrai au roi et à ma patrie.   Mais
de consentir à trahir des particuliers, ou à trahir des particuliers,
ou à révéler ce qui m'a été confié, ce seroit me deshonnorer à
jamais."

Je ne dois pas oublier à vous dire, qu'outre son éloignement
pour le prétendant, il m'a temoigné beaucoup de dépit contre la
France: et je suis sûr qu'il me parloit sincerement.

Je serai bien-aise d'être instruit au plutôt touchant les intentions du roi à son égard, et de ce que je dois lui promettre au nom
de sa majesté; afin qu'il puisse être en état de se rétirer de ce païs-
ici, où j'appréhende qu'il ne fait pas bon pour lui.

Pour moi; je vous avoue franchement, que je crois qu'il m'a
parlé dans la sincérité de son cœur; qu'il est resolu de faire son
mieux pour abattre le parti du prétendant, et pour le déraciner
tout-à-fait si cela dependoit de lui: et il me paroit certain, qu'il n'y
a personne qui puisse nuire au prétendant au point qu'il le peut
faire.

A la fin de nôtre conversation, il me serra la main, et me dit:
"Mi lord, si l'on me fait la justice de croire que mes professions
sont sinceres, plus ils menagent ma réputation, plus ils font le service du roi.   Si au contraire ils me soupçonnent de ne pas mar-
cher droit, ils auront raison d'exiger de moi des conditions que
j'aurai en même tems raison, comme un honnête homme, dé ré-
fuser.   Les difficultés que je fais de promettre trop, peuvent servir de garans que je tiendrai ce à quoi je m'engage. En tout cas,
le tems et ma conduite uniforme convaincront tout le monde de
la droiture de mes intentions: et il vaut mieux attendre ce tems
avec patience, quelque long qu'il puisse être, que d'arriver avec
precipitation à son but en sortant du grand chemin de l'honneur
et de la probité."

REFLECTIONS UPON EXILE.*

MDCCXVI.

DISSIPATION of mind, and length of time, are the remedies to which the greatest part of mankind trust in their afflictions. But the first of these works a temporary, the second a slow, effect: and both are unworthy of a wise man. Are we to fly from ourselves that we may fly from our misfortunes, and fondly to imagine that the disease is cured because we find means to get some moments of respite from pain? Or shall we expect from time, the physician of brutes, a lingering and uncertain deliverance? Shall we wait to be happy till we can forget that we are miserable, and owe to the weakness of our faculties a tranquillity which ought to be the effect of their strength? Far otherwise. Let us set all our past and our present afflictions at once before our eyes.† Let us resolve to overcome them, instead of flying from them, or wearing out the sense of them by long and ignominious patience. Instead of palliating remedies, let us use the incision-knife and the caustic, search the wound to the bottom, and work an immediate and radical cure.

The recalling of former misfortunes serves to fortify the mind against later. He must blush to sink under the anguish of one wound, who surveys a body seamed over with the scars of many, and who has come victorious out of all the conflicts wherein he received them. Let sighs, and tears, and fainting under the lightest strokes of adverse fortune, be the portion of those unhappy people whose tender minds a long course of felicity has enervated: while such as have passed through years of calamity bear up, with a noble and immovable constancy, against the heaviest. Uninterrupted misery has this good effect, as it continually torments, it finally hardens.

Such is the language of philosophy: and happy is the man who acquires the right of holding it. But this right is not to be acquired by pathetic discourse. Our conduct can alone give it us: and

* Several passages of this little treatise are taken from Seneca; and the whole is writ, with some allusion to his style and manner: quanquam non omnino temere sit, quod de sententiis illius queritur Fabius," &c. Eras. De sen. jud.

† Sen. De con. ad Hel.

therefore, instead of presuming on our strength, the surest method is to confess our weakness, and, without loss of time, to apply ourselves to the study of wisdom. This was the advice which the oracle gave to Zeno,* and there is no other way of securing our tranquillity amidst all the accidents to which human life is exposed. Philosophy has, I know, her *thrasos*, as well as war: and among her sons many there have been, who, while they aimed at being more than men, became something less. The means of preventing this danger are easy and sure. It is a good rule, to examine well before we addict ourselves to any sect: but I think it is a better rule, to addict ourselves to none. Let us hear them all, with a perfect indifferency on which side the truth lies: and, when we come to determine, let nothing appear so venerable to us as our own understandings. Let us gratefully accept the help of every one who has endeavored to correct the vices, and strengthen the minds of men; but let us choose for ourselves, and yield universal assent to none. Thus, that I may instance the sect already mentioned, when we have laid aside the wonderful and surprising sentences, and all the paradoxes of the Portique, we shall find in that school such doctrines as our unprejudiced reason submits to with pleasure, as nature dictates, and as experience confirms. Without this precaution, we run the risk of becoming imaginary kings, and real slaves. With it, we may learn to assert our native freedom, and live independent on fortune.

In order to which great end, it is necessary that we stand watchful, as sentinels, to discover the secret wiles and open attacks of this capricious goddess before they reach us.† Where she falls upon us unexpected, it is hard to resist; but those who wait for her, will repel her with ease. The sudden invasion of an enemy overthrows such as are not on their guard; but they who foresee the war, and prepare themselves for it before it breaks out, stand, without difficulty, the first and the fiercest onset. I learned this important lesson long ago, and never trusted to fortune even while she seemed to be at peace with me. The riches, the honors, the reputation, and all the advantages which her treacherous indulgence poured upon me, I placed so, that she might snatch them away without giving me any disturbance. I kept a great interval between me and them. She took them, but she could not tear them from me. No man suffers by bad fortune, but he who has been deceived by good. If we grow fond of her gifts; fancy that they belong to us, and are perpetually to remain with us, if we lean upon them, and expect to be considered for them; we shall sink into all the bitterness of grief, as soon as these false and transitory benefits pass away, as soon

* Diog. Laert.   † Sen. De con. ad. Hel.

as our vain and childish minds, unfraught with solid pleasures, become destitute even of those which are imaginary.   But, if we do not suffer ourselves to be transported by prosperity, neither shall we be reduced by adversity.   Our souls will be of proof against the dangers of both these states: and, having explored, our strength, we shall be sure of it; for in the midst of felicity, we shall have tried how we can bear misfortune.

It is much harder to examine and judge, than to take up opinions on trust; and therefore the far greatest part of the world borrow, from others, those which they entertain concerning all the affairs of life and death.*   Hence it proceeds that men are so unanimously eager in the pursuit of things, which, far from having any inherent real good, are varnished over with a specious and deceitful gloss, and contain nothing answerable to their appearances.†   Hence it proceeds, on the other hand, that, in those things which are called evils, there is nothing so hard and terrible as the general cry of the world threatens.   The word *exile* comes indeed harsh to the ear, and strikes us like a melancholy and execrable sound, through a certain persuasion which men have habitually concurred in.   Thus the multitude has ordained.   But the greatest part of their ordinances are abrogated by the wise.

Rejecting therefore the judgment of those who determine according to popular opinions, or the first appearances of things, let us examine what exile really is.‡   It is, then, a change of place; and, lest you should say that I diminish the object, and conceal the most shocking parts of it, I add, that this change of place is frequently accompanied by some or all of the following inconveniences: by the loss of the estate which we enjoyed, and the rank which we held; by the loss of that consideration and power which we were in possession of; by a separation from our family and our friends; by the contempt which we may fall into; by the ignominy with which those who have driven us abroad, will endeavor to sully the innocence of our characters, and to justify the injustice of their own conduct.

All these shall be spoken to hereafter.   In the meanwhile, let us consider what evil there is, in change of place, abstractedly and by itself.

To live deprived of one's country is intolerable.§   Is it so? How comes it then to pass that such numbers of men live out of their countries by choice?   Observe how the streets of London

---

* Dum unusquisque mavult credere, quam judicare, nunquam de vita judicatur, semper creditur.   Sen. De vita beat.
† Sen. De con. ad Hel.
‡ Sen. De con. ad Hel.
§ Sen. De con. ad Hel.

and of Paris are crowded. Call over those millions by name, and ask them one by one, of what country they are: how many will you find, who, from different parts of the earth, come to inhabit these great cities, which afford the largest opportunities, and the largest encouragement, to virtue and to vice? Some are drawn by ambition, and some are sent by duty; many resort thither to improve their minds, and many to improve their fortunes; others bring their beauty, and others their eloquence, to market. Remove from hence, and go to the utmost extremities of the east or the west: visit the barbarous nations of Africa, or the inhospitable regions of the north: you will find no climate so bad, no country so savage, as not to have some people who come from abroad and inhabit there by choice.

Among numberless extravagances which have passed through the minds of men, we may justly reckon for one that notion of a secret affection, independent of our reason, and superior to our reason, which we are supposed to have for our country; as if there were some physical virtue in every spot of ground, which necessarily produced this effect in every one born upon it.

"—— Amor patriæ ratione valentior omni."*

As if the heimvei was an universal distemper, inseparable from the constitution of a human body, and not peculiar to the Swiss, who seem to have been made for the mountains, as their mountains seem to have been made for them.† This notion may have contributed to the security and grandeur of states. It has therefore been not unartfully cultivated, and the prejudice of education has been with care put on its side. Men have come in this case, as in many, from believing that it ought to be so, to persuade others, and even to believe themselves that it is so. Procopius relates that Abgarus came to Rome, and gained the esteem and friendship of Augustus to such a degree, that this emperor could not resolve to let him return home: that Abgarus brought several beasts, which he had taken one day in hunting, alive to Augustus: that he placed in different parts of the circus some of the earth which belonged to the places where each of these animals had been caught; that as soon as this was done, and they were turned loose, every one of them ran to that corner where his earth lay: that Augustus, admiring their sentiment of love for their country which nature has graved in the hearts of beasts, and struck by the evidence of the truth, granted the request which Abgarus immediately impressed upon him, and allowed, though with regret, the tetrarch to return to Edessa. But this tale deserves just as much credit as that which follows

* Ov. De Ponto, El. iv.   † Card. Benti. Let.

in the same place, of the letter of Abgarus to Jesus Christ, of our Saviour's answer, and of the cure of Abgarus. There is nothing, surely, more groundless than the notion here advanced, nothing more absurd. We love the country in which we are born, because we receive particular benefits from it, and because we have particular obligations to it: which ties we may have to another country, as well as to that we are born in; to our country by election, as well as to our country by birth. In all other respects, a wise man looks upon himself as a citizen of the world: and, when you ask him where his country lies, points, like Anaxagoras, with his finger to the heavens.

There are other persons, again, who have imagined that as the whole universe suffers a continual rotation, and nature seems to delight in it, or to preserve herself by it, so there is in the minds of men, a natural restlessness, which inclines them to change of place, and to the shifting their habitations.* This opinion has at least an appearance of truth, which the other wants; and is countenanced, as the other is contradicted, by experience. But, whatever the reasons be, which must have varied infinitely in an infinite number of cases, and an immense space of time; true it is in fact, that the families and nations of the world have been in a continual fluctuation, roaming about on the face of the globe, driving and driven out by turns. What a number of colonies has Asia sent into Europe! The Phœnicians planted the coasts of the Mediterranean sea, and pushed their settlements even into the ocean. The Etrurians were of Asiatic extraction; and, to mention no more, the Romans, those lords of the world, acknowledged a Trojan exile for the founder of their empire. How many migrations have there been, in return to these, from Europe into Asia? They would be endless to enumerate; for, besides the Æolic, the Ionic, and others of almost equal fame, the Greeks, during several ages, made continual expeditions, and built cities in several parts of Asia. The Gauls penetrated thither too, and established a kingdom. The European Scythians overran these vast provinces, and carried their arms to the confines of Egypt. Alexander subdued all from the Hellespont to India, and built towns, and established colonies to secure his conquests, and to eternise his name. From both these parts of the world Africa has received inhabitants and masters; and what she has received she has given. The Tyrians built the city, and founded the republic of Carthage; and Greek has been the language of Egypt. In the remotest antiquity we hear of Belus in Chaldea, and of Sesostris planting his tawny colonies in Colchos: and Spain has been, in these latter ages, under the dominion of the Moors. If we

* Sen. De con. ad Hel.

turn to Runic history, we find our fathers, the Goths, led by
Woden and by Thor, their heroes first, and their divinities afterwards, from Asiatic Tartary into Europe: and who can assure us
that this was their first migration? They came into Asia perhaps
by the east, from that continent to which their sons have lately
sailed from Europe by the west: and thus, in the process of three
or four thousand years, the same race of men have pushed their
conquests and their habitations round the globe: at least this
may be supposed as reasonably as it is supposed, I think, by
Grotius, that America was peopled from Scandinavia. The
world is a great wilderness, wherein mankind have wandered
and jostled one another about from the creation. Some have removed by necessity and others by choice. One nation has been
fond of seizing what another was tired of possessing: and it
will be difficult to point out the country which is to this day in
the hands of its first inhabitants.

Thus fate has ordained that nothing shall remain long in the
same state: and what are all these transportations of people but
so many public exiles? Varro, the most learned of the Romans,
thought, since Nature* is the same wherever we go, that this
single circumstance was sufficient to remove all objections to
change of place, taken by itself, and stripped of the other inconveniences which attend exile. M. Brutus thought it enough
that those who go into banishment cannot be hindered from carrying their virtue along with them. Now, if any one judge that
each of these comforts is in itself insufficient, he must, however,
confess that both of them joined together, are able to remove the
terrors of exile. For what trifles must all we leave behind us be
esteemed, in comparison of the two most precious things which
men can enjoy, and which, we are sure, will follow us wherever
we turn our steps, the same nature, and our proper virtue?† Believe me, the providence of God has established such an order in
the world, that of all which belongs to us the least valuable parts
can alone fall under the will of others. Whatever is best is
safest; lies out of the reach of human power; can neither be given
nor taken away. Such is this great and beautiful work of nature,
the world. Such is the mind of man, which contemplates and
admires the world whereof it makes the noblest part. These are
inseparably ours, and as long as we remain in one we shall enjoy
the other. Let us march, therefore intrepidly wherever we are led
by the course of human accidents. Wherever they lead us, on
what coast soever we are thrown by them, we shall not find ourselves absolutely strangers. We shall meet with men and women,
creatures of the same figure, endowed with the same faculties,

---

* Sen. De con. ad Hel.   † Ibid.

and born under the same laws of nature. We shall see the same virtues and vices, flowing from the same general principles, but varied in a thousand different and contrary modes, according to that infinite variety of laws and customs which is established for the same universal end, the preservation of society. We shall feel the same revolution of seasons, and the same sun and moon* will guide the course of our year. The same azure vault, bespangled with stars, will be every where spread over our heads. There is no part of the world from whence we may not admire those planets which roll, like ours, in different orbits round the same central sun; from whence we may not discover an object still more stupendous, that army of fixed stars hung up in the immense space of the universe, innumerable suns whose beams enlighten and cherish the unknown worlds which roll around them: and whilst I am ravished by such contemplations as these, whilst my soul is thus raised up to heaven, it imports me little what ground I tread upon.

Brutus,† in the book which he wrote on virtue, related that he had seen Marcellus in exile at Mitylene, living in all the happiness which human nature is capable of, and cultivating, with as much assiduity as ever, all kinds of laudable knowledge. He added, that this spectacle made him think that it was rather he who went into banishment, since he was to return without the other, than the other who remained in it. O Marcellus, far more happy when Brutus approved thy exile, than when the commonwealth approved thy consulship! How great a man must thou have been to extort admiration from him who appeared an object of admiration even to his own Cato! The same Brutus reported further, that Cæsar overshot Mitylene, because he could not stand the sight of Marcellus, reduced to a state so unworthy of him. His restoration was at length obtained by the public intercession of the whole senate, who were dejected with grief to such a degree, that they seemed all upon this occasion to have the same sentiments with Brutus, and to be suppliants for themselves rather than for Marcellus.‡ This was to return with honor; but surely he remained abroad with greater, when Brutus could not resolve to leave him, nor Cæsar to see him; for both of

---

* Plut. Of Banishment. He compares those who cannot live out of their own country, to the simple people who fancied that the moon of Athens was a finer moon than that of Corinth.
——— labentem cœlo quæ ducitis annum.—Virg. Georg.
† Sen. De con. ad Hel.
‡ Marcellus was assassinated at Athens, in his return home, by Chilo, an old friend, and fellow-soldier of his. The motive of Chilo is not explained in history. Cæsar was suspected. But he seems to be justified by the opinion of Brutus.

them bore witness of his merit.   Brutus grieved, and Cæsar
blushed to go to Rome without him.

Q. Metellus Numidicus had undergone the same fate some
years before, while the people, who are always the surest instruments of their own servitude, were laying, under the conduct of
Marius, the foundation of that tyranny which was perfected by
Cæsar.   Metellus alone, in the midst of an intimidated ·senate,
and outrageous multitude, refused to swear to the pernicious laws
of the tribune Saturninus.   His constancy became his crime, and
exile his punishment.   A wild and lawless faction prevailing
against him, the best men of the city armed in his defence, and
were ready to lay down their lives, that they might preserve so
much virtue to their country.   But he, having failed to persuade,
thought it not lawful to constrain.   He judged, in the frenzy of
the Roman commonwealth, as Plato judged in the dotage of the
Athenian.   Metellus knew, that if his fellow-citizens amended,
he should be recalled; and if they did not amend, he thought he
could be nowhere worse than at Rome.   He went voluntarily
into exile, and wherever he passed he carried the sure symptom
of a sickly state, and the certain prognostic of an expiring commonwealth.   What temper he continued in abroad will best appear by a fragment of one of his letters, which Gellius,* in a
pedantic compilation of phrases used by the annalist, Q. Claudius,
has preserved for the sake of the word *fruniscor.* "Illi vero omni
jure atque honestate interdicti: ego neque aqua neque igne careo:
et summa gloria fruniscor." Happy Metellus! happy in the
conscience of thy own virtue! happy in thy pious son, and in that
excellent friend who resembled thee in merit and in fortune!

Rutilius had defended Asia against the extortions of the pub-
licans, according to the strict justice of which he made profession,
and to the particular duty of his office.   The Equestrian order
were upon this account his enemies, and the Marian faction was
so of course, on account of his probity, as well as out of hatred
to Metellus.   The most innocent man of the city was accused of
corruption.   The best man was prosecuted by the worst—by
Apicius; a name dedicated to infamy.†   Those who had stirred
up the false accusation sat as judges, and pronounced the unjust
sentence against him.   He hardly deigned to defend his cause,
but retired into the East, where that Roman virtue which Rome
could not bear, was received with honor.‡   Shall Rutilius now
be deemed unhappy, when they who condemned him are, for that
action, delivered down as criminals to all future generations?

* Lib. xvii, cap. 2.
† There was another Apicius, in the reign of Tiberius, famous for his glut-
tony; and a third in the time of Trajan.
‡ Sen. L. De prov. cap. 3.

when he quitted his country with greater ease than he would suffer his exile to finish? when he alone durst refuse the dictator Sylla, and being recalled home, not only declined to go, but fled farther off?

What do you propose, it may be said, by these examples, multitudes of which are to be collected from the memorials of former ages? I propose to show that as change of place, simply considered, can render no man unhappy, so the other evils which are objected to exile, either cannot happen to wise and virtuous men; or, if they do happen, cannot render them miserable. Stones are hard, and cakes of ice are cold: and all who feel them, feel them alike.* But the good or the bad events, which fortune brings upon us, are felt according to what qualities we, not they, have. They are in themselves indifferent and common accidents, and they acquire strength by nothing but our vice or our weakness. Fortune can dispense neither felicity nor infelicity unless we cooperate with her. Few men who are unhappy under the loss of an estate, would be happy in the possession of it: and those who deserve to enjoy the advantages which exile takes away, will not be unhappy when they are deprived of them.

It grieves me to make an exception to this rule; but Tully was one so remarkably, that the example can neither be concealed nor passed over. This great man, who had been the saviour of his country, who had feared, in the support of that cause, neither the insults of a desperate party, nor the daggers of assassins, when he came to suffer for the same cause, sunk under the weight. He dishonored that banishment which indulgent providence meant to be the means of rendering his glory complete. Uncertain where he should go, or what he should do, fearful as a woman, and froward as a child, he lamented the loss of his rank, of his riches, and of his splendid popularity. His eloquence served only to paint his ignominy in stronger colors. He wept over the ruins of his fine house which Clodius had demolished: and his separation from Terentia, whom he repudiated not long afterwards, was perhaps an affliction to him at this time. Every thing becomes intolerable to the man who is once subdued by grief.† He regrets what he took no pleasure in enjoying, and overloaded already, he shrinks at the weight of a feather. Cicero's behaviour, in short, was such, that his friends, as well as his enemies, believed him to have lost his senses.‡ Cæsar beheld, with a secret satisfaction, the man, who had refused to be his lieutenant, weeping under the rod of Clodius. Pompey hoped to find some excuse

---

* Plut. on Exile.

† Mitto cætera intolerabilia. Etenim fletu impedior. L. iii, Ad Atic. ep. 10.

‡ Tam sæpe, et tam vehemeter objurgas, et animo infirmo esse dicis. Ibid.

for his own ingratitude in the contempt which the friend, whom he had abandoned, exposed himself to. Nay, Atticus judged him too meanly attached to his former fortune, and reproached him for it. Atticus, whose great talents were usury and trimming, who placed his principal merit in being rich, and who would have been noted with infamy at Athens, for keeping well with all sides, and venturing on none:* even Atticus, blushed for Tully, and the most plausible man alive assumed the style of Cato.

I have dwelt the longer on this instance, because, whilst it takes nothing from the truth which has been established, it teaches us another of great importance. Wise men are certainly superior to all the evils of exile. But in a strict sense he, who has left any one passion in his soul unsubdued, will not deserve that appellation. It is not enough that we have studied all the duties of public and private life, that we are perfectly acquainted with them, and that we live up to them in the eye of the world: a passion that lies dormant in the heart, and has escaped our scrutiny, or which we have observed and indulged as venial, or which we have perhaps encouraged, as a principle to excite and to aid our virtue, may one time or other destroy our tranquillity, and disgrace our whole character. When virtue has steeled the mind on every side, we are invulnerable on every side: but Achilles was wounded in the heel. The least part, overlooked or neglected, may expose us to receive a mortal blow. Reason cannot obtain the absolute dominion of our souls by one victory. Vice has many reserves, which must be beaten; many strongholds, which must be forced; and we may be found of proof in many trials, without being so in all. We may resist the severest, and yield to the weakest attacks of fortune. We may have got the better of avarice, the most epidemical disease of the mind, and yet be slaves to ambition.† We may have purged our souls of the fear of death, and yet some other fear may venture to lurk behind. This was the case of Cicero. Vanity was his cardinal vice.‡ It had, I question not, warmed his zeal, quickened his industry, animated

---

* Plut. Vit. Solon.

† Seneca says the contrary of all this, according to the Stoical system, which however he departs from on many occasions. " Si contra unam quamlibet partem fortunæ satis tibi roboris est, idem adversus omnes erit.—Si avaritia dimisit, vehementissima generis humani pestis, moram tibi ambitio non faciet. Si ultimum diem, &c. De con. ad Hel.

Non singula vitia ratio, sed pariter omnia prosternit. In universum semel vincitur. Ibid.

Nec audacem quidem timoris adsolvimus: ne prodigem quidem avaritia liberamus. De Benef. L. iv, c. 27.

Qui autem habet vitium unum, habet omnia. Ibid. L. v, c. 15.

‡ In animo autem gloriæ cupido, qualis fuit Ciceronis, plurimum potest. Vel. Pat. L. i.

the love of his country, and supported his constancy against Cati-
line: but it gave to Clodius an entire victory over him.   He was
not afraid to die, and part with estate, rank, honor, and every
thing which he lamented the loss of: but he was afraid to live
deprived of them.   " Ut vivus hæc amitterem."*   He would probably have met death on this occasion with the same firmness
with which he said to Popilius Lænus, his client and his mur-
derer: "Approach, veteran, and, if at least thou canst do this well,
cut off my head."   But he could not bear to see himself, and to
be seen by others, stripped of those trappings which he was accustomed to wear.   This made him break out into so many shameful expressions.   " Possum oblivisci qui fuerim? non sentire qui
sim? quo caream honore? qua gloria?"   And speaking of his
brother—"Vitavi ne viderim; ne aut illius luctum squaloremque
aspicerem, aut me, quem ille florentissimum reliquerat, perditum
illi afflictumque offerrem."†   He had thought of death, and prepared his mind for it.   There were occasions too where his vanity
might be flattered by it.   But the same vanity hindered him in
his prosperous estate from supposing such a reverse as afterwards
happened to him.   When it came, it found him unprepared, it
surprised him, it stunned him; for he was still fond of the pomp
and hurry of Rome, "fumum et opes, strepitumque Romæ," and
unweaned from all those things which habit renders necessary,
and which nature has left indifferent.

We have enumerated them above, and it is time to descend
into a more particular examination of them.   Change of place
then may be borne by every man.   It is the delight of many.
But who can bear the evils which accompany exile?   You who
ask the question can bear them.   Every one who considers them
as they are in themselves, instead of looking at them through
the false optic which prejudice holds before our eyes.   For what?
you have lost your estate: reduce your desires, and you will perceive yourself to be as rich as ever, with this considerable advantage to boot, that your cares will be diminished.   Our natural and real wants‡ are confined to narrow bounds, whilst those
which fancy and custom create are confined to none.   Truth lies
within a little and certain compass, but error is immense.   If we
suffer our desires therefore to wander beyond these bounds, they
wander eternally.   " Nescio quid curtæ semper abest rei."   We

* Ep. ad Attic. L. iii. ep. 3, 7, 10, et passim.

† L. iii, ep. 10, ad Attic.

‡ Naturalia desideria finita sunt; ex falsa opinione nascentia ubi desinant
non habent, nullus enim terminus falso est.   Sen. Ep. 16.

Excerp. ex. Lib. Sen. falsely so called.

Si ad naturam vives, nunquam eris pauper; si ad opinionem, nunquam dives.
Exiguum natura desiderat, opinio immensum.   Sen. Ep. 16.

become necessitous in the midst of plenty, and, our poverty increases with our riches. Reduce your desires, be able to say with the apostle of Greece, to whom Erasmus was ready to address his prayers, "quam multus ipse non egeo!" banish out of your exile all imaginary, and you will suffer no real wants. The little stream which is left will suffice to quench the thirst of nature, and that which ˙cannot be quenched by it, is not your thirst, but your distemper; a distemper formed by the vicious habits of your mind, and not the effect of exile. How great a part of mankind bear poverty with cheerfulness, because they have been bred in it, and are accustomed to it?* Shall we not be able to acquire by reason and by reflection, what the meanest artisan possesses by habit? Shall those who have so many advantages over him, be slaves to wants and necessities of which he is ignorant? The rich, whose wanton appetites neither the produce of one country, nor of one part of the world, can satisfy, for whom the whole habitable globe is ransacked, for whom the caravans of the east are continually in march, and the remotest seas are covered with ships; these pampered creatures, sated with superfluity, are often glad to inhabit an humble cot, and to make a homely meal. They run for refuge into the arms of frugality. Madmen that they are, to live always in fear of what they sometimes wish for, and to fly from that life which they find it luxury to imitate! Let us cast our eyes backward on those great men who lived in the ages of virtue, of simplicity, of frugality, and let us blush to think that we enjoy in banishment more than they were masters of in the midst of their glory, in the utmost affluence of their fortune. Let us imagine that we behold a great dictator giving audience to the Samnite ambassadors, and preparing on the hearth his mean repast with the same hand which had so often subdued the enemies of the commonwealth, and borne the triumphal laurel to the capitol. Let us remember that Plato had but three servants,† and that Zeno had none.‡ Socrates, the reformer of his country, was

* Sen De con. ad Hel.

† Plato's will, in Diog. Laer. mentions four servants, besides Diana, to whom he gave her freedom.

Apuleius makes his estate consist in a little garden near the Academy, two servants, a patten for sacrifices, and as much gold as would serve to make ear-rings for a child.

‡ Zeno was owner of a thousand talents when he came from Cyprus into Greece, and he used to lend his money out upon ships at a high interest. He kept, in short, a kind of insurance office. He lost this estate perhaps when he said, "recte sane agit fortuna, quæ nos ad philosophiam impellit." Afterwards he received many and great presents from Antigonus. So that his great frugality and simplicity of life, was the effect of his choice, and not of necessity. Vid. Dio. Laer.

maintained, as Menenius Agrippa, the arbiter of his country was buried by contribution.* While Attilius Regulus beat the Carthaginians in Africa, the flight of his ploughman reduced his family to distress at home, and the tillage of his little farm became the public care. Scipio died without leaving enough to marry his daughters, and their portions were paid out of the treasury of the state; for sure it was just that the people of Rome should once pay tribute to him, who had established a perpetual tribute on Carthage. After such examples shall we be afraid of poverty? Shall we disdain to be adopted into a family which has so many illustrious ancestors? shall we complain of banishment for taking from us what the greatest philosophers, and the greatest heroes of antiquity never enjoyed?

You will find fault, perhaps, and attribute to artifice, that I consider singly misfortunes which come all together on the banished man, and overbear him with their united weight. You could support change of place if it was not accompanied with poverty, or poverty if it was not accompanied with the separation from your family and your friends, with the loss of your rank, consideration, and power, with contempt and ignominy. Whoever he be who reasons in this manner, let him take the following answer. The least of these circumstances is singly sufficient to render the man miserable who is not prepared for it, who has not divested himself of that passion upon which it is directed to work. But he who has got the mastery of all his passions, who has foreseen all these accidents, and prepared his mind to endure them all, will be superior to all of them, and to all of them at once as well as singly. He will not bear the loss of his rank, because he can bear the loss of his estate: but he will bear both, because he is prepared for both; because he is free from pride as much as he is from avarice.

You are separated from your family and your friends. Take the list of them, and look it well over. How few of your family will you find who deserve the name of friends? and how few among these who are really such? Erase the names of such as ought not to stand on the roll, and the voluminous catalogue will soon dwindle into a narrow compass. Regret, if you please, your separation from this small remnant. Far be it from me, whilst I declaim against a shameful and vicious weakness of mind, to proscribe the sentiments of a virtuous friendship. Regret your separation from your friends: but regret it like a man

---

* Diog. Laer. Vit. Soc. quotes Aristoxenus for affirming that Socrates used to keep a box, and lived upon the money which was put into it: " Posita igitur arcula, colligisse pecuniam quæ daretur; consumpta autem ea, rursus posuisse."

who deserves to be theirs. This is strength, not weakness of mind; it is virtue, not vice.

But the least uneasiness under the loss of the rank which we held is ignominious. There is no valuable rank among men, but that which real merit assigns. The princes of the earth may give names, and institute ceremonies, and exact the observation of them; their imbecility and their wickedness may prompt them to clothe fools and knaves with robes of honor, and emblems of wisdom and virtue: but no man will be in truth superior to another, without superior merit; and that rank can no more be taken from us, than the merit which establishes it. The supreme authority gives a fictitious and arbitrary value to coin, which is therefore not current alike in all times and in all places; but the real value remains invariable, and the provident man, who gets rid as fast as he can of the drossy piece, hoards up the good silver. Thus merit will not procure the same consideration universally. But what then? the title to this consideration is the same, and will be found alike in every circumstance by those who are wise and virtuous themselves. If it is not owned by such as are otherwise, nothing is however taken from us; we have no reason to complain. They considered us for a rank which we had; for our denomination, not for our intrinsic value. We have that rank, that denomination no longer, and they consider us no longer: they admired in us what we admired not in ourselves. If they learn to neglect us, let us learn to pity them. Their assiduity was importunate: let us not complain of the ease which this change procures us: let us rather apprehend the return of that rank and that power, which, like a sunny day, would bring back these little insects, and make them swarm once more about us. I know how apt we are, under specious pretences, to disguise our weakness and our vices, and how often we succeed not only in deceiving the world, but even in deceiving ourselves. An inclination to do good is inseparable from a virtuous mind, and therefore the man, who cannot bear with patience the loss of that rank and power which he enjoyed, may be willing to attribute his regrets to the impossibility which he supposes himself reduced to of satisfying this inclination. But let such an one know, that a wise man contents himself with doing as much good as his situation allows him to do; that there is no situation wherein we may not do a great deal; and that when we are deprived of greater power to do more good, we escape at the same time the temptation of doing some evil.*

The inconveniences, which we have mentioned, carry nothing along with them difficult to be borne by a wise and virtuous man;

---

* Sen. De con. ad. Hel.

and those which remain to be mentioned, contempt and ignominy, can never fall to his lot. It is impossible that he who
reverences himself should be despised by others: and how can
ignominy affect the man who collects all his strength within himself, who appeals from the judgment of the multitude to another
tribunal, and lives independent of mankind and of the accidents
of life? Cato lost the election of prætor, and that of consul; but
is any one blind enough to truth to imagine that these repulses
reflected any disgrace on him?   The dignity of those two
magistracies would have been increased by his wearing them.
They suffered, not Cato.

   You have fulfilled all the duties of a good citizen; you have
been true to your trust, constant in your engagements, and have
pursued the interest of your country without regard to the enemies you created, and the dangers you run. You severed her
interest, as much as lay in your power, from those of her factions;
and from those of her neighbors and allies too, when they became different.   She reaps the benefit of these services, and you
suffer for them.   You are banished, and pursued with ignominy,
and those whom you hindered from triumphing at her expense,
revenge themselves at yours.   The persons, in opposition to
whom you served, or even saved the public, conspire and accomplish your private ruin.   These are your accusers, and the
giddy ungrateful crowd your judges.   Your name is hung up in
the tables of proscription, and art joined to malice endeavors to
make your best actions pass for crimes, and to stain your character.   For this purpose the sacred voice of the senate is made
to pronounce a lie, and those records, which ought to be the
eternal monuments of truth, become the vouchers of imposture
and calumny.   Such circumstances as these you think intolerable,
and you would prefer death to so ignominious an exile.   Deceive not yourself.   The ignominy remains with them who per-
secute unjustly, not with him who suffers unjust persecution.
"Recalcitrat undique tutus."   Suppose that in the act which
banishes you, it was declared that you have some contagious
distemper, that you are crooked, or otherwise deformed.   This
would render the legislators ridiculous.*   The other renders
them infamous.   But neither one nor the other can affect the
man, who in a healthful well-proportioned body enjoys a conscience void of all the offences ascribed to him.   Instead of such
an exile, would you compound, that you might live at home in
ease and plenty, to be the instrument of blending these contrary
interests once more together, and of giving but the third place to
that of our country?   Would you prostitute her power to the

* The dialogue between Cicero and Philiscus.   Dion. Cass. L. xxxviii.

ambition of others, under the pretence of securing her from imaginary dangers, and drain her riches into the pockets of the meanest and vilest of her citizens, under the pretence of paying her debts? If you could submit to so infamous a composition, you are not the man to whom I address my discourse, or with whom I will have any commerce: and if you have virtue enough to disdain it, why should you repine at the other alternative? Banishment from such a country, and with such circumstances, is like being delivered from prison. Diogenes was driven out of the kingdom of Pontus for counterfeiting the coin, and Stratonicus thought that forgery might be committed in order to get banished from Scriphos. But you have obtained your liberty by doing your duty.

Banishment, with all its train of evils, is so far from being the cause of contempt, that he who bears up with an undaunted spirit against them, while so many are dejected by them, erects on his very misfortunes a trophy to his honor: for such is the frame and temper of our minds, that nothing strikes us with greater admiration than a man intrepid in the midst of misfortunes. Of all ignominies an ignominious death must be allowed to be the greatest; and yet where is the blasphemer who will presume to defame the death of Socrates?[*] This saint entered the prison with the same countenance with which he reduced thirty tyrants, and he took off ignominy from the place: for how could it be deemed a prison when Socrates was there? Phocion was led to execution in the same city. All those who met the sad procession, cast their eyes to the ground, and with throbbing hearts bewailed, not the innocent man, but Justice herself, who was in him condemned. Yet there was a wretch found, for monsters are sometimes produced in contradiction to the ordinary rules of nature, who spit in his face as he passed along. Phocion wiped his cheek, smiled, turned to the magistrate, and said, "admonish this man not to be so nasty for the future."

Ignominy then can take no hold on virtue;[†] for Virtue is in every condition the same, and challenges the same respect. We applaud the world when she prospers; and when she falls into adversity we applaud her. Like the temples of the gods, she is venerable even in her ruins. After this must it not appear a degree of madness to defer one moment acquiring the only arms capable of defending us against attacks which at every moment we are exposed to? Our being miserable, or not miserable, when we fall into misfortunes, depends on the manner in which we enjoyed prosperity. If we have applied ourselves betimes to the study of wisdom, and to the practice of virtue, these evils

* Sen. De con. ad Hel.　　　　　† Ibid.

become indifferent; but if we have neglected to do so, they become necessary. In one case they are evils, in the other they are remedies for greater evils than themselves. Zeno* rejoiced that a shipwreck had thrown him on the Athenian coast: and he owed to the loss of his fortune, the acquisition which he made of virtue, of wisdom, of immortality. There are good and bad airs for the mind, as well as for the body. Prosperity often irritates our chronical distempers, and leaves no hopes of finding any specific but in adversity. In such cases banishment is like change of air, and the evils we suffer are like rough medicines applied to inveterate diseases. What Anacharsis† said of the vine, may aptly enough be said of prosperity. She bears the three grapes of drunkenness, of pleasure, and of sorrow: and happy it is if the last can cure the mischief which the former work. When afflictions fail to have their due effect, the case is desperate. They are the last remedy which indulgent Providence uses: and if they fail, we must languish and die in misery and contempt. Vain men! how seldom do we know what to wish or to pray for? When we pray against misfortunes, and when we fear them most, we want them most. It was for this reason that Pythagoras forbid his disciples to ask any thing in particular of God. The shortest and best prayer which we can address to him, who knows our wants, and our ignorance in asking, is this: "Thy will be done."

Tully says, in some part of his works, that as happiness is the object of all philosophy, so the disputes among philosophers arise from their different notions of the sovereign good. Reconcile them in that point, you reconcile them in the rest. The school of Zeno placed this sovereign good in naked virtue, and wound the principle up to an extreme beyond the pitch of nature and truth. A spirit of opposition to another doctrine, which grew into great vogue while Zeno flourished, might occasion this excess. Epicurus placed the sovereign good in pleasure. His terms were wilfully, or accidentally mistaken. His scholars might help to pervert his doctrine, but rivalship inflamed the dispute; for in truth there is not so much difference between stoicism reduced to reasonable intelligible terms, and genuine orthodox epicurism, as is imagined. The felicis animi immota tranquillitas, and the voluptas of the latter are near enough akin: and I much doubt whether the firmest hero of the Portique would have borne a fit of the stone, on the principles of Zeno, with greater magnanimity and patience than Epicurus did, on those of his own philosophy.‡ However, Aristotle took a mid-

* Diog. Laert.   † Sen.
‡ Compare the representations made so frequently of the doctrine of volupty taught by Epicurus, with the account which he himself gives in his

dle way, or explained himself better, and placed happiness in
the joint advantages of the mind, of the body, and of fortune.
They are reasonably joined; but certain it is, that they must not
be placed on an equal foot.   We can much better bear the privation of the last, than of the others; and poverty itself, which
mankind is so afraid of, " per mare pauperiem fugiens, per saxa,
per ignes," is surely preferable to madness, or the stone, though
Chrysippus* thought it better to live mad, than not to live!   If
banishment, therefore, by taking from us the advantages of fortune, can not take from us the more valuable advantages of the
mind and the body, when we have them; and if the same accident is able to restore them to us, when we have lost them,
banishment is a very slight misfortune to those who are already
under the dominion of reason, and a very great blessing to
those who are still plunged in vices which ruin the health both
of body and mind.   It is to be wished for, in favor of such as
these, and to be feared by none.   If we are in this case, let us
second the designs of Providence in our favor, and make some
amends for neglecting former opportunities by not letting slip the
last.   " Si nolis sanus, curres hydropicus."   We may shorten the
evils which we might have prevented, and as we get the better
of our disorderly passions, and vicious habits, we shall feel our
anxiety diminish in proportion.   All the approaches to virtue are
comfortable.   With how much joy will the man, who improves
his misfortunes in this manner, discover that those evils, which
he attributed to his exile, sprung from his vanity and folly, and
vanish with them!   He will see that, in his former temper of
mind, he resembled the effeminate prince who could drink† no
water but that of the river Choaspes, or the simple queen, in
one of the tragedies of Euripides, who complained bitterly, that
she had not lighted the nuptial torch, and that the river Ismenus
had not furnished the water at her son's wedding.   Seeing his
former state in this ridiculous light, he will labor on with pleasure towards another as contrary as possible to it; and when he
arrives there, he will be convinced by the strongest of all proofs,
his own experience, that he was unfortunate because he was
vicious, not because he was banished.

If I was not afraid of being thought to refine too much, I
would venture to put some advantages of fortune, which are due
to exile, into the scale against those which we lose by exile.
One there is which has been neglected even by great and wise

letter to Menoceus, of the sense wherein he understood this word.   Vid.
Diog. Laer.
    * In his third book of Nature, cited by Plutarch, in the treatise on the
contradictions of the Stoics.
    † Plut. On Banishment.

men. Demetrius Phalereus, after his expulsion from Athens, became first minister to the king of Egypt; and Themistocles found such a reception at the court of Persia, that he used to say his fortune had been lost if he had not been ruined. But Demetrius exposed himself, by his favor under the first Ptolemy, to a new disgrace under the second: and Themistocles, who had been the captain of a free people, became the vassal of the prince he had conquered. How much better is it to take hold of the proper advantage of exile, and to live for ourselves, when we are under no obligation of living for others? Similis, a captain of great reputation under Trajan and Adrian, having obtained leave to retire, passed seven years in his retreat, and then dying, ordered this inscription to be put on his tomb: that he had been many years on earth, but that he had lived only seven.* If you are wise, your leisure will be worthily employed, and your retreat will add new lustre to your character. Imitate Thucydides in Thracia, or Xenophon in his little farm at Scillus. In such a retreat you may sit down, like one of the inhabitants of Elis, who judged of the Olympic games, without taking any part in them. Far from the hurry of the world, and almost an unconcerned spectator of what passes in it, having paid in a public life what you owed to the present age, pay in a private life what you owe to posterity. Write as you live, without passion; and build your reputation as you build your happiness, on the foundations of truth. If you want the talents, the inclination, or the necessary materials for such a work, fall not however into sloth. Endeavor to copy after the example of Scipio at Linternum.— Be able to say to yourself,

> "Innocuas amo delicias doctamque quietem."

Rural amusements, and philosophical meditations, will make your hours glide smoothly on; and if the indulgence of Heaven has given you a friend like Lælius, nothing is wanting to make you completely happy.

These are some of those reflections which may serve to fortify the mind under banishment, and under the other misfortunes of life, which it is every man's interest to prepare for, because they are common to all men:† I say they are common to all men: because even they who escape them are equally exposed to them. The darts of adverse fortune are always levelled at our heads. Some reach us, some graze against us, and fly to wound our neighbors. Let us therefore impose an equal temper on our minds, and pay without murmuring the tribute which we owe to humanity. The winter brings cold, and we must freeze.—

* Xiphil.   † Sen. Ep. 107.

The summer returns with heat, and we must melt. The incle-
mency of the air disorders our health,'and we must be sick.—
Here we are exposed to wild beasts, and there to men more
savage than the beasts: and if we escape the inconveniences and
dangers of the air and the earth, there are perils by water and
perils by fire. This established course of things it is not in our
power to change; but it is in our power to assume such a greatness of mind as becomes wise and virtuous men; as may enable
us to encounter the accidents of life with fortitude, and to conform
ourselves to the order of nature, who governs her great kingdom,
the world, by continual mutations. Let us submit to this order,
let us be persuaded that whatever does happen ought to happen,
and never be so foolish as to expostulate with nature. The best
resolution we can take is to suffer what we cannot alter, and to
pursue, without repining, the road which Providence, who directs
every thing, has marked out to us: for it is not enough to follow;
and he is but a bad soldier who sighs, and marches on with re-
luctancy. We must receive the orders with spirit and cheerfulness, and not endeavor to slink out of the post which is assigned
us in this beautiful disposition of things, whereof even our sufferings make a necessary part. Let us address ourselves to God,
who governs all, as Cleanthes did in those admirable verses,
which are going to lose part of their grace and energy in my
translation of them.

> Parent of nature! Master of the world!
> Where'er thy Providence directs, behold
> My steps with cheerful resignation turn.
> Fate leads the willing, drags the backward on.
> Why should I grieve, when grieving I must bear?
> Or take with guilt, what guiltless I might share?

Thus let us speak, and thus let us act. Resignation to the will
of God is true magnanimity. But the sure mark of a pusillani-
mous and base spirit, is to struggle against, to censure the order
of Providence, and, instead of mending our own conduct, to set
up for that of correcting our Maker.

THE OCCASIONAL WRITER.

Fidens animi atque in utrumque paratus.—VIRG.

INSCRIBED TO THE PERSON, TO WHOM ALONE IT CAN BELONG.

MOST NOBLE SIR:

I AM one, whose ambition it hath been, ever since I came into the world, to distinguish myself as a writer; in which, I fairly confess, I had not only the view of raising my reputation but that of establishing my fortune. A prospect, which seemed very reasonable in a time of general peace and universal affluence; in an age so particularly polite, that it is even the fashion to appear knowing in all the elegant arts and sciences; and that, to whatever branch of them a genius shall think fit to turn himself, he is sure it will be to one that is in vogue.

The first essays of my pen made a good deal of noise in the world: they filled foreign journals, and were translated into several languages. The Sorbonne, and both our mother Universities, returned me thanks for having reconciled several disputes and solved several difficulties in chronology and history, which had perplexed the learned world, from the impartial Eusebius, down to the circumstantial Prideaux: my philosophical Poems were received with the greatest applause; and it is well known, that if the gay part of the world read my Anti-Lucretius for amusement, the gravest divines have not disdained to borrow arguments from it in their disputes with the materialists.

Animated by such success, in one part of my aim, I proceeded with indefatigable labor, till continual disappointments, in the other, rendered me at length more indifferent to that imaginary good, applause, and less patient of that real evil, want. I began then to compare my condition with that of several great authors both ancient and modern; and finding upon the comparison that they had not been better treated than myself, I was soon led by my reflections to discover the true reason of our ill fortune in the world; I was soon convinced that they and I had been on a wrong pursuit; that ministers of state pay no respect to the brightest talents, when they are misapplied, and esteem all talents to be so, which are not wholly employed about the present time, and principally dedicated to the service of their administration; neither can I say this proceeding is unjust, how much soever I suffer by it.

If we write for posterity, we must not complain that the care of rewarding our merit is left to posterity; and if we neglect to serve the state, those, who are appointed to preside over it, break no rule of equity when they neglect us. Spencer has been amply recompensed by posterity for his Fairy Queen; but the wise treasurer Burleigh declined the payment of an hundred pounds, which Queen Elizabeth ordered him, and left this admirable poet to starve. Had Spencer applied himself to more serious studies, had he excelled in physics, in metaphysics, or even in the first philosophy, or in theology, instead of excelling in wit and poetry, the "amabiles insaniæ" of Horace, his usage would have been the same no doubt. Even the greatest productions of these studies are but trifles in the account of a consummate statesman, and may properly enough be distinguished from the others in his sense, by the title of " insaniæ severiores."

Our English ministers, to their honor be it spoken, have at all times proceeded upon this admirable principle; the most excellent sermons, the most elaborate treatises, have not been sufficient to procure the advancement of some divines, whilst a sorry pamphlet or a spiritual libel has raised others to the highest dignities of the church. As it has fared with mere divinity, so has it fared with mere eloquence: as one never caused the divine, so the other never caused the lawyer to be distinguished. But we know that if either of them be employed in a court cause, he never fails of making his fortune. The same fate has attended writers of another kind; the celebrated Tattlers, and Spectators, had no reward except from booksellers and fame. But when those authors made the discovery I have made, and applied their talents better, in writing the Englishman and the Freeholder, one was soon created a knight, and the other became secretary of state. In short, without enumerating any more instances, I may confidently affirm, that this has been the case from the days of Burleigh to this time; how much sooner it began to be so, I hope, sir, you will not give me the leisure to inquire.

From the moment I resolved to become a state-writer, I mentally devoted myself to your service: and I do it now in this public and most solemn manner. Employ me, sir, as you please; I abandon myself entirely to you; my pen is at your disposition, and my conscience in your keeping. Like a lawyer, I am ready to support the cause, in which, give me leave to suppose that I shall be soon retained, with ardor; and, if occasion be, with subtility and acrimony. Like a Swiss, I will behave myself with equal boldness and fidelity; my pen is my fortune, and I think it as honorable to offer it, as offer my sword, without inquiring in a general battle, or in private skirmishes, at what relation or friend I strike. I cancel at once all former obligations and friendship, and will most implicitly follow your instructions in panegyric on yourself and friends, in satire on your adversaries, in writing for or against any subject; nay, in writing for or against the same subject, just as your interest, or even your passions, may render it expedient.

I am not ignorant that when Carneades offered to argue for virtue, and then against it, Cato proposed to drive that great philosopher and orator out of Rome. But Cato was a man of narrow principles, and of too confined an understanding. He considered virtue abstractedly, without any regard to time, to place, and to that vast variety of conjunctures, which happens in the course of human affairs. In common life, morality is no doubt necessary, and therefore legislators have been careful to enforce the practice of it; but whenever morality clashes with the interest of the state, it must be, and it always has been laid aside. These are my opinions: and it is a great comfort to my conscience to find them confirmed by the practice of some reverend persons, whose examples ought to be of greater weight with me, than that of a wretched pagan. I shall therefore show myself neither squeamish nor whimsical in pursuing the enterprise to which I offer my services, but shall remain firmly persuaded, that all the moral vices, I may be occasionally guilty of in so good a course, will be exalted into political virtues.

After this plain and honest account which I have given of myself, it may be allowed me to say, that you cannot find a person better qualified for your service, or more worthy to be listed, among those who draw their pens in your cause, and of whom I am willing to hope that you have a greater and an abler body in reserve, than you have hitherto judged proper to bring into the field.

It is evident that a minister, in every circumstance of life, stands in as much need of us public writers as we of him. In his prosperity he can no more subsist without daily praise than we without daily bread, and the farther he extends his views, the more necessary are we to his support. Let him speak as contemptuously of us as he pleases, for that is frequently the manner of those who employ us most, and pay us best, yet it will fare with his ambition as with a lofty tree, which cannot shoot its branches into the clouds, unless its root work into the dirt, from which it rose, on which it stands, and by which it is nourished.

If a minister falls into adversity, shall he take up the pen in his own defence? would not the case be as deplorable for him to be left to write as for a prince to be left to fight in his own quarrel? Believe me, sir, whenever fortune abandons you, and who knows how soon that may happen, you will find yourself in a very forlorn state. At the name of your successor, those crowds, that attend your levee, will vanish like spirits at the dawn of day. None will remain about you, but such as no other administration will condescend to employ: and we may therefore very probably behold you, which would be a pitiful sight indeed, endeavoring to secure a safe retreat with H***** on one side of you, and L****** on the other, two grotesque personages, exactly paired and nearly allied, but surely as little fit to support a minister in his decline, as to adorn his triumph. In such a turn as this, you may depend on my utmost efforts to keep up a spirit for you: and I can make no doubt of being seconded by several of my fellow-writers, since I am certain you will not scruple to share some part of that fortune, which your industry and parsimony have raised, with those who unite to save the whole; and since we shall be reasonable enough not to expect above six pence in the pound out of it, which cannot well amount to more than fifteen or twenty thousand pounds. A trifling sum for so great a service and so weighty a purse!

You may perhaps, after all I have said, be still apt to think that these are wild discourses, which have no other foundation but my desire to render myself necessary. You may refine too much in your reflections on my conduct, and too little in those you make on your present situation; or if you judge rightly of this, it is not impossible but you may depend too much on your own vigilance and dexterity. Should any of those flatterers who often betray their patrons into a fatal security, speak to you much in the same manner, as sleep addresses himself to Palinurus in the fifth book of the Æneis:

> ———Palinure, ferunt ipsa æquora classem,
> Æquatæ spirant auræ, datur hora quieti;
> Pone caput, fessosque oculos furare labori.

You would answer, I am persuaded, as this Pilot did:

> Mene salis placidi vultum, fluctusque quietos
> Ignorare jubes! mene huic confidere monstro!

But Palinurus slept, and you know the consequence.

Be not, therefore, displeased if a sincere and zealous servant rouses you, admonishes you not to trust too much to appearances, and shows you danger when perhaps you least expect it You have sailed long in a smooth sea, with gentle and favorable gales. We believe your courage and your abilities extremely great, but we believe it implicitly; for you have not had foul weather enough to give any considerable proofs of either. These circumstances, which might be abused to inspire security, I urge as reasons why you should be alarmed; for the element which you have to deal with is by the laws of nature inconstant: and therefore the longer you have been without a storm the more reason you have to expect one. There is no surer presage of a hurricane than just such a dead calm as I have observed for some time.

To speak without a figure: I would not have you flatter yourself that the undisturbed quiet you have so long enjoyed is merely owing to your own integrity and political merit, or to the uncommon prosecution of hawkers and pamphleteers, which has been carried on by the direction of one of your principal instruments, and indeed a most vigorous statesman. This quiet, sir, is owing to deep and inveterate designs, which it becomes me to lay before you, without any regard to the censure I may incur, of revealing private conversation, and of breach of trust. Know then, that from the time you came into a fulness of power, many were shocked at the manner in which you seized it, and at the use you made of it. They said that both were hurtful, indecent, and even shameless. They went still farther, and affirmed, that your conduct was foolish with regard to your own interest; since it was foolish for a man to trust to one expedient of government, who had several in his power; and especially to such an expedient as that of money, which would equally serve to support him or to hang him. These persons, however, notwithstanding their discontent, resolved to lie quiet, till your mal-administration should become so glaring as to justify their opposition, even in his majesty's sight: they said they would not follow your example; and upon that occasion they remembered with some sharpness how you did your utmost to distress the king's affairs, upon the first disgust you received; nay they were malicious enough to call to mind some personal reflections,* which the heat of your imagination, and your familiarity with majesty, betrayed you into, and for which they saucily wished what I dare not name. These seditious spirits flattered themselves that you would do your own business when you had the full swing of your power. They were acquainted, they said, with the presumption and distrust, with the boldness and pusillanimity, with the indiscretion and cunning, and with fifty other contradictions, which made up your

---

* See a pamphlet called An Answer to an Infamous Libel, entitled, Sedition and Defamation Displayed. Printed for R. Francklin.

character: and upon these they depended for putting a speedy
end to your administration. This end they imagine to be now
at hand—for thus they reason. A minister, who is attacked on
his management of the public revenue, and has all the advantages of money and authority on his side, may escape, though he
is guilty; but if he is innocent, the proceedings against him in
such a case must necessárily confirm his power, and establish his
reputation: nothing more desirable than such an attack can happen to him. But our present minister, say these malignants,
directly stops all inquiry; in public he evades giving such accounts
as the representatives of the people have a right to demand; in
private he is modest and discreet enough to laugh at those who
think him such a fool as to furnish proofs against himself. Can a
minister keep his ground long, who has no other defence than an
implied confession of his guilt? will such a behaviour be endured
in a nation hitherto free, and where there remain at least some
sparks of honor and of love of the country?

These and many other reflections, which for brevity sake I
omit, upon your particular conduct, and upon our domestic
affairs, are frequently thrown out. But, sir, I confess to you,
that I tremble when I hear the same persons discourse concerning
the state of the nation with regard to her foreign interests. They
affirm, and they offer to demonstrate, that the affairs of Europe
never were in greater confusion, and that the part we take upon
ourselves is such a one, as no nation ever acted which was not
betrayed, or whose ministers were not infatuated. That you
are so, they say, is past dispute, whether you have conducted
these affairs yourself, or have left them to those men of eminent
talents, who are concerned in this part of your administration:
they insist that nothing could have happened to us, if you had
entirely neglected our foreign interests, worse than what you
have brought upon us, by running into the other extreme. For
they ask, what is the fruit of your continual negotiations, supported by a vast expense, and carried on as busily as if the welfare of Great Britain had been at stake in every dispute which
has happened on the continent? They answer for you, and they
defy you to contradict them, that we have made the quarrels of
other people our own; and that we find ourselves engaged as
principals, in some cases where we have but a very remote concern, and in others where we have no concern at all. That our
commerce suffers and runs the risk of being lost, not for a time,
but for ever, in several branches, much more beneficial to us
than the Ostend trade; and that our right to keep those important possessions, which were yielded to us in the most solemn
and authentic manner, is come, by dint of negotiation, from
being indisputable, to be called in question. In a word, that to

restore the public tranquillity, and to settle our own interest, we must engage in a new war and conclude a new peace: that you have contrived to make it impossible for us to do one, without fighting against the very principle for which we have fought ever since the revolution, or to attempt the other without lying under the particular circumstance, that our principal allies will be as much in earnest as our enemies to wrest out of our hands the chief advantages which we obtained by the treaty of Utrecht. At the time when these treaties were made, continue they, your great minister cried aloud and spared not. He complained, as much as any man, that the exorbitant power of France was not sufficiently reduced: and that the barriers of our allies, on the Rhine and in the Netherlands, were left too weak: and is it under his administration that we are to see a pretence given to the French, and an opportunity thrown into their hands, of strengthening their power, and of extending their barriers? When I tell these objectors that your brother answers for the court of France, they laugh in my face, and reply, "Well he may, and so might any of those, who were in the French interest, have done at the time when the triple alliance was broken, and France was encouraged by England to fall upon the Dutch." The ministers, who are answered for, would be as weak as he, who answers for them, if they did not see the advantage in the present juncture, and did not take a secret malicious pleasure in making us, who contributed so much to reduce their power, become the instruments of raising it again. In the case of a war, then, we have, according to this reasoning, which really, sir, has an air of truth, nothing so much to fear as the assistance of our chief ally; and in the case of a treaty, not only France, but Holland likewise, must be against us in that important article of Gibraltar and Port-Mahon, and in all particular advantages of commerce, which we have enjoyed, and may find it reasonable to pretend to. The late Duke of Orleans, as dear a friend as he was to us, insisted strenuously, that we should give up the places before-mentioned; pretended a promise to this effect, and himself obliged in honor to see this promise kept. Every one, who knows any thing of the transactions of those times, knows with how envious an eye the Dutch beheld the separate privileges in trade, and the sole possession of Gibraltar, and of the island of Minorca, which we obtained at the last peace: and what lengths they would have gone to facilitate the negotiations, which at that time they opposed, if they might have been admitted to a share in these advantages.

The danger of an immediate invasion, and the engagements entered into by the emperor and the king of Spain to insult us

with their fleets, and to conquer Great Britain and Ireland for
the Pretender, have been very industriously propagated by those,
who are already in your pay, and by me, who stand a candidate
for this honor, but am hitherto a volunteer in your service. I
am sorry to tell you, sir, but Heaven forbid that I should conceal
so material a circumstance from your knowledge, we do not
succeed. We raise a spirit, but this spirit turns against you.
There are more people than ever against the Pretender; and zeal
for supporting the present establishment never ran higher. But
this zeal is not any longer without knowledge: it is directed to
its proper object, and there is no possibility of leading it hood-
winked to serve any other purposes   Some incredulous wretches
there are, who smile when we talk to them of invasions and the
Pretender, and who content themselves to reply, that the machine
is very seasonably introduced, and according to the rules of art.
The greater number take fire, and lay this new distress, which
we threaten them with, at your door; for, they say, that we disobliged Spain some years ago, to tie the emperor the more firmly
to us, and that we have since that time disobliged the emperor,
by affecting a closer correspondence, and greater union of councils with France than ever was known between the two nations.
They send us to that excellent treatise, " The barrier treaty vindicated," to learn our true and lasting interest in foreign alliances, and there they pretend that we shall find the condemnation of all your measures: they lament the miserable scene,
which they apprehend may soon be opened, his majesty's foreign dominions exposed to all the calamities of war, and perhaps in danger of being lost; we ourselves struggling against
domestic enemies, and defending our coasts against invasions:
these mischiefs brought upon us by a conjunction of the emperor, our old ally, with the king of Spain his rival; a conjunction
so unnatural, that nothing but the highest resentment at our behavior to them both could have brought it about: in short, to
finish up the picture, Great Britain reduced in this distress to
lean solely upon France, and the faith of that court to become
our chief security.

Upon the whole matter, your enemies, sir, the substance of
whose private conversation I have now honestly reported to you,
conclude very insolently that you have filled up the measure of
your iniquity and your folly, and that you must sink, or the
nation must sink under the weight of that calamity which you
have brought and suffered to be brought upon her.

As shocking as this account must be to your ears, I promise
myself that the sincerity and plainness with which I have given
it, will be agreeable to you; and that you will receive into your

bosom a man whose affection for your person and zeal for your service, must be above all suspicion, after giving you intelligence of so high a nature, without any stipulation for the discovery.

I expect to hear from you in eight days from the date hereof; if I do not, you shall hear again from him who is,

Most noble Sir, your honor's most devoted servant,

THE OCCASIONAL WRITER.

From my Garret, Jan. 1726-7.

THE OCCASIONAL WRITER.

_____

Most Noble Sir:—

I think myself obliged in honor to let the world know, that you have treated all my proposals to write in your service with a contempt unusual from one in your station; for I have seen the times when every little paltry prostitute of his pen found countenance and encouragement. These wretches are sure of both, whenever there are any bad measures to be justified, or any bold strokes to be given; and the croaking of these ravens has always, in my imagination, boded some mischief or other to the commonwealth.

For this reason I took upon me the character of a most infamous libeller in my first address to you, that I might be able to make a surer judgment of our present condition, and know better what expectations to entertain; so that I own I am most agreeably disappointed in not receiving any letter or message from you. I own, that instead of biting you, I am fairly bit myself.

Some malicious refiners may pretend, perhaps, that an address of such a nature made in so public a manner, could meet with no other treatment, even from a minister who was willing to accept the proposal. Malice, I say, may refine thus, and endeavor to depreciate a virtuous action, which cannot be denied, by supposing such motives to it as cannot be proved. The practice is too common, and especially where men are divided into parties, where public disputes create and nourish private animosities, and where perpetual feuds irritate the natural malignity of the heart. But far be it from me to judge with so little charity; I am willing to believe, sir, that you declined the offers made you, not on account of the public address, by which they were conveyed, but because you disdained to support a virtuous administration by a venal pen.

When I meet a man with loaded pistols in his pocket, or a

dagger under his cloak, I suspect that he is going upon no very honorable designs. Housebreakers and coiners have been detected, by having their tools found about them. Informers, spies, and hireling scribblers are the tools of an evil statesman; and when I see all such discouraged, and none of them about a minister, I think myself obliged to suppose that his designs are honorable, and his measures directed to the public good.

I take this opportunity therefore of begging your pardon for the trial I presumed to make. The liberty indeed was great; but since it has turned so vastly to your honor, I hope to be the more easily forgiven. Shall I own it, sir? my hopes go still farther; you disdained me under the feigned character which I assumed; from the same principle of honor, from the same consciousness of merit, you will, nay, you must afford me some share of your esteem, when I appear, as I intend to do for the future, under my own. These papers shall breathe nothing but zeal to promote the honor of his majesty, the security of our present happy establishment, and in one word, the good of our country. The same spirit, which animates you and me, shall animate them: and I cannot doubt of your approbation, when I co-operate with you to these purposes; which were certainly the sole inducements you had to enter into business; as it is manifest that you continue at the head of affairs for no other reasons.

The truth is, however, (for I think it becoming a friendship, which is likely to grow as intimate as ours, that I should disguise nothing from you,) two things have lately happened, which gave some little shock to my good opinion of you. The first is an unwillingness you manifested, that the true state of the national debts should be known by the nation; and the severe censure you passed on such persons, as were desirous to give their countrymen a fair account of their condition in a part so essential, that our being a nation, or not a nation depends almost entirely, in this crisis, on our running or not running farther into debt. The other is the publication of a pamphlet supposed to be written by your direction, which is evidently designed to keep us no less in the dark as to all our affairs abroad.

As to the first, that matter has been taken up already; and will, I doubt not, in all places, and in all manners, be so thoroughly sifted, that we shall no longer be at a loss, either as to the revenue, and the real changes upon it, or as to the whole management of it. In which examination, sir, let me advise you, as a friend, to act an ingenuous part, that suspicions may not increase, and that I may not be obliged to write to you in a style, to which I shall turn my pen with reluctance.

As to the latter, I hope, it will be likewise examined; and if I was able to take such a task on myself, I should, I am persuaded, in doing so, but make a second trial of you to your glory, and knit the bands of our friendship the closer, by answering a pamphlet of so pernicious a consequence, and writ with so ill a design. But I know my own unfitness to inform, to instruct, and to rouse our countrymen, some from their lethargy, and some from their golden dreams. I may toll the alarm-bell, but persons of greater strength and skill must be called upon to raise it, and to ring it out in the ears of the nation.

We are grown more easy, nay more willing than ever, to be imposed upon; and we do more than half the work of those who find their account in deluding us. Almost every man considers himself as a single person; those few, who extend their considerations farther, seldom or never carry them beyond the narrow system of a family, or a party. And thus it happens, that private interest is become the criterion, by which judgments are formed upon public affairs. The man, whoever he be, who is at any time in fashion, has nothing to do but to hold out that purse, which the more he empties it, the surer he is to fill. After which let him declaim imperiously, and assert boldly, without regarding proof, or condescending to argue; let one of his tools write a pamphlet in much the same strain, and the work is done, the opinion of mankind is settled, the crowd repeats what the orator has said, and the author writ; the clamor is echoed back on all sides, and these echoes, the reverse of all others, strengthen by repetition. Thus the corrupt lead the blind, and the blind lead one another; the still voice of reason is drowned in popular clamor, and truth is overwhelmed by prejudice.

This is a true account of what happens frequently; it is so far from being a description drawn from imagination, that I could give several instances, and perhaps shall have occasion to quote some, of such gross impositions on the common sense of mankind, offered in this manner, and offered with success, as no one would be bold enough to attempt putting on the weakest man in Britain in private conversation.

There are, therefore, God knows, but too many reasons for him to despond, who entertains a thought of prevailing on the generality of people, to lay aside their prejudices, to check their passions, and to consider the state of the nation in a due extent, and in a true light; and yet such is our condition, such a crisis are we in, that if we do not take and execute this resolution now, it may very probably be out of our power to do it hereafter to any good purpose.

In our senate we hear of great dangers, which we have to apprehend from abroad; and if we believe what is said in a foreign state,* we are exposed to very great ones at home. I am willing to hope, that both one and the other are magnified; but they may grow to be such in reality as they are represented to be, if we do not take more than ordinary care; first, to weigh in a just balance each of the many evils which threaten the nation; and secondly, if we do not penetrate into every one of the causes which have combined to bring them upon us. Should we fail in the first point, we may increase our dangers from abroad; by over-rating those at home, and by applying ourselves solely to prevent the latter. But I believe no one thinks us disposed to run into this extreme; we are much more likely to run into the other, and to increase our dangers at home, by over-rating those which we apprehend from abroad. Should we fail in the second point, and neglect to penetrate into all the causes which combine to bring our present distress upon us, palliative remedies alone will be applied, in the use of which we may very probably expire after a tedious languor, but from which we cannot expect a radical cure.

Convinced, therefore, that if we neglect the present moment, if every man does not think and write, and speak, and act for his country at this time according to his best talents, and according to the opportunities which he has of exerting them, we shall soon be in every sense a ruined nation.

I confess, that I am impatient, however low my hopes of success run, till some abler pen accepts the invitation, which " The Inquirer into the Reasons of the Conduct of Great Britain" gives to every member of this community, till an inquiry is made according to the right which he is pleased to allow, into our present state, and into the measures which have led to it. But then this inquiry must be made upon better principles, and with an honester view than he has, who made this, which lies before me: the person, who accepts his invitation, should be one who would blush to follow his example; for he acts the part of an apologist, where he professes to act that of an impartial inquirer: he seems very zealous for the success of the cause which he pleads, and very indifferent what means he employs to procure this success; many things are disguised, many are concealed, and hardly any are represented in their natural and proper light. Fallacy, sophism, and a puerile declamation, swell the elaborate treatise; but there was a design perhaps, as well as habit, in such a manner of writing upon this occasion, since a bad cause must be defended by such means; and, therefore, by such pens as would disgrace and weaken a good one; since it may possibly appear,

* Vide Letter from Stockholm.

upon a fair examination, that the cause he is retained in is none of the best.

If this should appear, I am apt to believe, that those, who set him at work, will not be much concerned; they could not look on this pamphlet as any thing better than a momentary expedient to mislead and inflame. If it has that effect, if it serves to keep up the delusion till all the jobs, which are to be done, are done; the ends which they proposed to themselves, are perhaps answered. But if this nation should awaken to a sense of their true interest, and if the British spirit should once more revive amongst us, it might very well happen that these persons would have made a faulty reckoning; for surely, after having exercised the justice of the nation, by censuring in one parliament a treaty of peace, which has been approved in another, it will not be thought strange, if we punish, at one time or another, those who have negotiated us out of peace and tranquillity, into war and confusion, although the wisdom of the nation should think fit to support, for the present, the measures of these ministers.

The inquirer supposes the whole face of affairs in Europe to have received the great alteration which he is so much surprised at, within the space of the last year; but I cannot agree with him, that the turn has been so sudden as he represents it. " The calm hardly to be paralleled by any past prospect," as this great master of style expresses himself by a figure of Hibernian rhetoric, was accompanied, as calms frequently are, by many signs of an approaching storm; which signs did not escape the observation of the sailors, and even passengers in our vessel, though they escaped that of our able pilots, who were, it seems, all that while in a most serene security. The particular evils, which we apprehend at present, were known to our ministers above a year ago, if it be true, as the inquirer affirms, that the treaty of Hanover, and negotiations in consequence of it, are " the steps, which the court of Great Britain thought fit to take as soon as possible, after the danger we were in appeared evident beyond all contradiction." But before the particular danger appeared, the general danger was evident enough. When the treaty of Vienna was made, our ship struck; but we had been sailing among rocks and shoals long before, ever since we quitted our port, and launched out to sea, on the wise errand of convoying other people safe to theirs.

He, therefore, who is desirous to make the inquiry proposed, in such a manner as may be of real use to the public, must take up things much higher than this partial writer was instructed to do. Many things happened during the congress of Cambray, which deserve to be explained; and there are treaties both previous and subsequent to the quadruple alliance, which deserve to be commented upon.

Nay, there seems to be a necessity of going farther back than this reign, or even than this century, if we design to be thoroughly acquainted with the original of our present distress. When we have taken a general survey of the conduct of Britain, with relation to the affairs of Europe, for about two hundred years, we shall come much better prepared to discover our true point of interest; and by observing how we have departed from it, we shall learn how to return to it.

This part I will venture to undertake; and what I shall say upon it, may serve at least as an introduction to that work, which, I hope, will be performed by some abler hand.

The foundations of the grandeur of France, and those of the grandeur of the house of Austria, were laid very near at the same period. Ferdinand and Isabella began the latter; and in Charles the Fifth, their grandson, and almost immediate successor, it was carried up to that exorbitant height, which made Europe tremble under his reign, under that of his son, and upon some occasions even later. The progress which France made was not so rapid, but was, perhaps, as sure; she shared with her rival the spoils of the House of Burgundy, by the address and vigor of Louis the Eleventh, who not only extended the bounds, and strengthened the frontier of that close compact body, whose very figure is an addition to the force of it, but assured its inward tranquillity better, and rendered that monarchy more formidable than it had been in the time of his predecessors, when the authority of the prince was less.

The forming of two such powers, in Europe, made it the interest of all other princes and states, to keep as much as possible a balance between them. And here began that principle of English policy to be established, which, however true and wise in itself, has hardly ever been truly and wisely pursued.

We should take things rather too high, if we went up to the reign of King Henry the Seventh, though even there some observations are to be made, which have relation to our present subject.

Frequent and important occasions of acting on this principle presented themselves in the time of Henry the Eighth. Some he took, some he neglected, and some he managed ill; for to say the truth, the whole conduct of this prince was a continued course of extravagance, violence, and levity: his vices glared through the best actions of his life. He exercised the tyranny, and practised the bloody precepts of the Church of Rome, even while he was delivering us from the papal yoke. His deliberations for peace or war seemed often to have a mixture of humor

in them; and his own passions, as well as Wolsey's, made him
hold the balance of Europe, if he did hold it, with an uneven
hand.

The reformation, which began in his time in Germany, and
which was completed by Edward the Sixth, and by Queen Elizabeth, in England, gave occasion to a new division of interests;
and made it of the utmost importance to the welfare of this nation, not only to preserve a balance between the two great powers of Europe, but to support the Protestant cause against them
both.   The first of these was to be done by throwing as much
as the occasion might require of our weight, sometimes into one,
and sometimes into the other of these scales; but the latter could
be effected by nothing less than a constant adherence to that
side which was for a long time the weakest, and which, I doubt
not, is so still.

Both these principles were pursued by Queen Elizabeth, with
the greatest wisdom, and with the greatest success.   To illustrate
this fully, it would be necessary to run through the annals of her
glorious reign.   But a few general observations will suffice for
our present purpose.   When she came to the crown, the nation
was divided between two powerful parties, exasperated by religious zeal; Ireland was papist, Scotland was under the immediate influence of France, and the queen of that kingdom, married
to the Dauphin of France, disputed her title to the crown of
England.   In short, the surest support she had amidst all these
difficulties, besides the firmness of her mind, and the penetration
of her understanding, was in Philip the Second, whom she disobliged by refusing to make him her husband; and who could
not fail of being, on many accounts, as he proved to be, her most
implacable and dangerous enemy.   She kept measures for a
while with him, nay, perhaps, with the court of Rome, and soon
settled her government, and established her power: her own
kingdom was the first and principal object of her care; and she
judged very wisely, that in order to be considerable abroad, she
must begin by making herself so at home.   Her revenue was
administered with the utmost frugality, industry was encouraged,
manufactures improved, and commerce extended: she was far
from neglecting foreign alliances, but her negotiations were conducted with great art and little expense, and the engagements
she took were always necessary, seldom chargeable.   She supported the protestant cause in France, with good offices, with
loans of money; and upon some pressing occasions, with troops.
But she never depended on the gratitude of Henry the Fourth,
and was neither surprised nor unprepared when he made returns
very unworthy of the obligations he had to her.   The Dutch
could not have sustained their revolt from Spain, nor have

formed their commonwealth, without her assistance. She helped them powerfully, but she exacted cautionary towns from them, as a security for her reimbursement, whenever they should be in a condition to pay; and in the mean time, as a check, to keep them under the influence and direction of England. By such methods as these, her own country grew rich and flourishing, while she not only preserved a balance of power abroad, but contributed extremely to reduce Spain from being the terror of Europe, to that low state into which it fell under the successors of king Philip the Second.

The reign of king James the First, is not to be read without a mixture of indignation and contempt. He came to the crown with great advantages; but a bad head, and a worse heart, hindered him from improving any of them. He lost the opportunity of uniting the two kingdoms; he suffered his revenue to be ill administered; his ministers were notoriously corrupt, and he himself very profuse.

Instead of assuaging, he fomented disputes by his pedantry; established such principles of government, and raised such a spirit in the clergy, as could hardly fail to produce the terrible effects which followed in the reign of his son.

Such a management of domestic affairs would have put it out of his power, if it had been his inclination to act a wiser part in foreign affairs; but he had no such inclination. Twelve years he suffered himself to be amused with the Spanish match; he countenanced at least the popish, and he absolutely neglected the protestant interest, both in France and Germany. Instead of helping the dispositions, which appeared, to take the imperial crown out of the house of Austria, he favored the cause of that family, and abandoned his own children to the resentment of the emperor and the popish league. When the thirty years war began in 1618, the liberty of Germany, and the whole protestant interest, were in the utmost peril. The sole measures, which he took for the support of either, consisted in simple embassies, ridiculous letters, and languid negotiations. Queen Elizabeth defeated the ambitious designs of the Spanish branch of the Austrian family; king James favored those of the German branch of the same family.

Over the succeeding reign, and all that followed, to the restoration of king Charles the Second, let us draw a veil.

During this time the decay of the Spanish monarchy increased apace, the liberties of Germany were asserted, and the power of the emperor bounded by the treaties of Westphalia; but another power, that of France, began to rise very fast on the foundations laid long ago. Richelieu and Mazarine had given that crown a great superiority in the affairs of Europe, and the prince who wore it, resolved to maintain and augment this superiority, at the expense of all his neighbors.

The attack which Louis the Fourteenth made upon the Low Countries in 1667, showed, both in the manner of it, and in the pretence taken for it, what Europe had to expect from this prince. On this occasion the triple alliance was made; and happy had it been, if the same principles of policy had continued to prevail. But the king who sat on our throne, with better sense and more courage than his grandfather, was at least as unfit as he to defend the liberties of Europe, and, perhaps, more unfit to defend the protestant interest.

King Charles the Second joined his councils and his arms to those of France; and when he could not openly assist, he privately abetted the usurpations of that crown. He might, by conforming to the desires of his people, who were in his and their true interest, have had the immortal honor of preserving a balance of power in Europe; but he chose the eternal infamy of helping to destroy this balance; and not content to be the ally of a prince, whose enemy he ought to have been, he condescended to be his instrument, and even his pensioner. This conduct, which took so much strength from that side, which was already too weak, and which added so much to that which was already too strong, established the absolute superiority of France, and left Spain, Germany, Italy, and the seventeen provinces, nay and Britain too, in consequence, at her mercy.

This terrible face of things did not mend on the accession of king James the Second to the throne. Whatever his politics were, religion would have got the better of them. Bigotry must have cemented a close union between him and the king of France who was alone able and willing to assist him in the work he had undertaken at home. But the greatness of our danger, as it sometimes happens, saved us; and in saving us, saved all Europe. The revolution in our government caused a total change in our conduct. A prince, who had been long at the head of a weak but resolute opposition to France, mounted our throne; and the principles of maintaining a balance between the great powers of Europe, and of supporting the protestant interest, came once more into fashion in this kingdom, after having been for near a century, either neglected, or acted against.

The body of the nation resumed these principles with warmth, and has supported them ever since with unparalleled spirit and vigor. But let it be said without offence, since it may be said with truth, and since it is necessary that it should be said upon this occasion, we have not pursued them with as much wisdom as zeal. If we have erred in our politics since the revolution, it is sure we have erred on the right side. But errors on the right side are errors still, and may, in time, prove as fatal as errors on the other; and are, in one respect at least, more dangerous, as they are less attended to at first, or guarded against.

Between all extremes there is a certain middle point, which men of genius perceive, and to which men of honor adhere in private and in public life.

Thus avarice and prodigality are at an immense distance; but there is a space marked out by virtue between them, where frugality and generosity reside together. Thus again, to abandon those, whom it is our interest to support, is an excess of folly; and to support the interests of other people, to the ruin of our own, is an excess of folly likewise. But there are lines described by prudence, between these two excesses, within which our common interests meet, and may proceed together.

It would be an invidious as well as tedious task, to go through all the instances which might be produced; wherein we have, under pretence of preserving a balance of power in Europe, gratified the passions of particular men, and served the turns of private interest, till we have rendered that principle, in a reasonable pursuit of which our safety and our glory consist, the occasion of real danger to the interest, and of reproach to the wisdom of our nation. A few of these instances will suffice to deduce the progress of our mistaken policy, to evince the truth of what has been advanced in general, and to fix the application of the whole to the present conjuncture; wherein I apprehend, that we are about to pay the price not only of late errors, but a long series of errors.

The war which began in 1668, was no doubt a very necessary war. It was necessary to extinguish the rebellion in Scotland; it was necessary to reduce Ireland; it was necessary to assert the new establishment of our government. These were our immediate interests; but we had remote interests likewise concerned, which were of themselves sufficient to engage us to enter, at least as allies and friends, into the war. The empire was in danger by the taking of Philipsburgh, and other enterprises of the French; and Holland lay once more open to their invasions, by the seizing of Bonne. In the course of this war, Ireland was reduced; all the efforts against the government in England and Scotland were defeated; and, by the peace, France acknowledged king William.

As unfortunate as we had been on the Rhine and in Flanders, everything, which the French had taken in the course of the war from our allies, was restored at Ryswic; and Luxembourg, which France had usurped before the war, was likewise given up. Thus far all was well. The points, which England had contended for, were carried; and our allies recovered by treaty more than they had lost by war.

If a common guaranty of this treaty had been entered into as soon as those powers acceded who refused to sign when England and Holland did, the tranquillity of Europe would have been better secured than it was at this time, or at the peace of Nimeguen; at least 'England would have engaged, as far as it became her to do, even upon the principle of maintaining the balance of power, and no farther.

But, instead of taking this step, we took another, which proved fatal in its consequences. The death of Charles the Second, king of Spain, without children, was then in prospect. The pretensions of France were known, and its power had been lately felt. Whenever the case should happen, a war seemed to be unavoidable. But this war must have been made by France alone, for the conquest of the Spanish monarchy; which as powerful as we then thought her, and as insolent as she really was, we should not have engaged in lightly. Neither could she have supported it, if she had, since even with Spain on her side, she could not have supported the last, if the mines of Peru had not been unaccountably left open to her.

On the apprehension, however, of such a war, and on the specious pretence of preserving a balance of power in Europe, the partition treaties were made; that is, without the knowledge of the king of Spain, we disposed of his inheritance; without the consent of the emperor, and in concert with his adverse party, we settled the rights contested between the house of Austria and Bourbon; and we engaged to make this partition good by arms.

I do not enter into the reasons for and against this treaty, which may be drawn from the particular stipulations contained in it, but content myself to observe, in general, what impolitic measures we were at this period betrayed into, by an overweening desire to preserve the balance of power; and how much reason we have to be always on our guard against errors of this kind, since a prince, whom genius and experience had rendered the greatest man of his age was not exempt from them, but drew both England and Holland fatally into them.

Whenever this balance is in real danger by the exorbitant growth of one power, or by the union of more, other princes and states will be alarmed of course. All of them ought, and most of them will take measures for their common security. But the wise councils amongst them will, upon every such occasion, proportion their measures, and the engagements they enter into, not according to the nature of the danger considered generally, but according to the immediate or remote relation, which it has to each of them; and according to the strength, situation, or any other circumstance, which may be peculiar to each of them.

To do otherwise, would be to lose sight of our own particular interest in the pursuit of a common interest. It would be nothing better than setting up for the Don Quixotes of the world, and engage to fight the battles of all mankind. The state, which keeps its own particular interest constantly in view, has an invariable rule to go by; and this rule will direct and limit all its proceedings in foreign affairs; so that such a state will frequently take no share, and frequently a small share in the disputes of its neighbors, and will never exert its whole strength, but when its whole is at stake. But a state, who neglects to do this, has no rule at all to go by, and must fight to negotiate, and negotiate to fight again, as long as it is a state; because, as long as it is a state, there will be disputes among its neighbors and some of these will prevail at one time, and some at another, in the perpetual flux and reflux of human affairs.

If the kings of France and Spain and the emperor had made an agreement amongst themselves, about the succession to the dominions of Spain, consistent with the common interest of Europe, and considering the partiality which the court of Spain had, at that time, for the house of Austria, there was little room to fear, that such an agreement would have been too favorable to the house of Bourbon. If any such partition had been made, I say, no objection would have remained, either as to the right or manner of making it, and we might have escaped a war. If these princes had done nothing of this kind, we might have been engaged upon the king of Spain's death, as I said before, in a defensive war, for preserving the dominions of our old allies, and the liberties of Europe, against the usurpations of our ancient enemy. But instead of waiting to be auxiliaries in a defensive war, we put ourselves under a necessity of being principals in an offensive one; and by affecting to secure the balance of power, when we had neither call nor right to meddle, we reduced our affairs to this absurd alternative, that we must either make an offensive war as principals, against the emperor and Spain, in order to conquer for France, which was equally impolitic and unjust, or against France and Spain, in order to conquer for the emperor, under the greatest disadvantages possible; which happened to be the case.

The partition treaties forced the king of Spain to make a will in favor of the house of Bourbon; and the Spaniards threw themselves into the arms of France, to prevent the dismemberment of their monarchy.

Thus was the balance of power lost by our meddling where we had nothing to do, even before it could have been in danger, if we had not meddled at all. We lost it, and the emperor knew that we must restore it for our own sakes, which could be done no otherwise than by conquering for him; and this he left us to do the best we could. While we fought his battles, he lent us the Austrian title, the person of his son, the present emperor; and little else. We neglected everything, and sacrificed everything in the prosecution of this quarrel. But the imperial councils were so far from neglecting anything, or sacrificing anything to it, that they seemed wholly taken up for some years in settling the affairs of Hungary to their satisfaction; and they sacrificed to an idle refinement in politics the greatest opportunity which we ever had, or must ever hope to have; I mean that of destroying the naval force of France, by the taking of Toulon. This they deliberately and almost avowedly hindered.

If ever people were called upon to think of their own immediate interests, we were so at this time. Whether we could then have put an end to the expensive war we were engaged in for the house of Austria, in a manner consistent with the public interest of Europe, I am not able to determine. Certain it is in fact, that far from entertaining any such thoughts, we redoubled our spirit and our efforts in the prosecution of the war. As we acquired new allies, we enlarged our engagements; and as we obtained new victories, we extended our views. The grand alliance formed by king William, for restoring a balance of power in Europe, proposed no other objects than sufficient barriers, security to trade, and reasonable satisfaction to the house of Austria.* These were thought, by that great prince, all the points necessary to be contended for. But instead of confining ourselves to so narrow a plan, we judged that the balance of power could not be effectually restored, unless we wrested the whole Spanish monarchy from the house of Bourbon, to give it to the house of Austria. For this prize we fought, and fought with as little regard to all other interests, as if we had defended our own altars, and our own houses.

Must we not acknowledge, upon this occasion, sir, the shortness of human foresight? The very measure, which we pursued at so great expense of blood and treasure, (because nothing less could secure the balance of power in Europe, and even the trade of this kingdom, and the Protestant succession, against the invasions of France and the Pretender,) that very measure would, it seems, have put all these into the utmost peril.

If we had succeeded in our attempts to set the crown of Spain

* Vide G. Al. Art. 8.

on the head of the present emperor, and his brother the emperor Joseph had lived, would our danger from the union of these two brothers not have been at least as great as that which is apprehended from the union of the present emperor, and of the present king of Spain, rivals almost from their cradles, and by a long course of opposition, such inveterate enemies, that they could hardly be kept, as the inquirer assures us, "within the bounds of common decency towards one another, by all the address of two powerful mediators in a public treaty?" Might not the same address, that threw these enemies into one another's arms, (for it will appear they did not run thither so unaccountably,) and united them in designs destructive to the commerce and rights of other nations, have succeeded equally well between the two brothers, especially since, in this case, there would have been but half the work to do? The union would have been formed to our hands, and our address could only have been shown, in giving such proper provocations, as might have inspired the designs.

Would Charles have been less favorable to the trade of his brother's subjects, at any place in the Austrian dominions, than Philip shows himself to the trade of the subjects of Charles? Would Joseph not have concurred to assist his brother to regain Gibraltar, and the island of Minorca, at least, as zealously as we can suppose that Charles concurs to assist Philip, either by good offices, or, if you please, to have it so, by force of arms? Would not a league between the two brothers have been as much a popish league as that which we are so much alarmed at, between the surviving brother and the present king of Spain? Would not the first have made use of the Pretender, as the latter is said to do, and as every prince or state, with whom we happen to be at variance, may be provoked to do? In short, I may safely challenge the author of the inquiry, as great a casuist as he is, to show any difference between the two cases which I have compared together, except this, that we might have been exposed to greater dangers from that settlement of Europe, which we fought to bring about, than we are, or can probably be exposed to, from that which we were so solicitous to prevent. But the case is still stronger than I have put it. For even after the death of the emperor Joseph, his present imperial majesty continued his claim to the whole Spanish monarchy; and you, and I, and many of us, continued to support his claim, and opposed with all our force the negotiations of peace, which were begun upon a different principle. Happily we failed of success. The many, who remonstrated, "That we were hastening apace to make him a power too great and too formidable; and that we should find in him, at last, the enemy we then dreaded only in another," pre-

vailed.   Had they not, in what a condition should we have been
at this time?   Would the emperor have been more grateful, or
less powerful, with the crown of Spain and the Indies, added to
so many others?   If the union between him and the king of
Spain is so formidable to us, how much more reason should we
have had to apprehend the consequences to our trade, and in the
end, to our liberties and our religion themselves, if these divided
powers had been united in the same ungrateful person, as it is
the mode at present to call the emperor?

If Don Carlos should marry the eldest arch-duchess, if the emperor should die without issue male, if the king of France should
die without issue male, if the prince of Asturias should die without issue male, and the princes of the blood in France and Spain
should not support the validity of the renunciations, all which is
within the bounds of possibility, " Don Carlos may be at once
emperor, king of France, and king of Spain; and have the vast
strength and riches of these powers united and centered in him."
This terrible object stares our speculative inquirer in the face,
and disturbs his head.   It disturbs, very probably, those excellent heads, who set him a scribbling, who can see so far into
futurity at present; and who, not very long ago, were unable to
discern the nearest and most probable events.   Let us consider
now, what consequence of this kind might have happened, if, for
securing a balance of power in Europe, the present emperor had
been likewise king of Spain.   If then the king of France, instead
of marrying the daughter of Stanislaus, had married the eldest
daughter of the emperor, which surely had been within the
bounds of possibility, there would remain but one chance at this
time, viz., the emperor having a son, to save us from the combination of such a power, as would in reality form what we commonly, though improperly, call universal monarchy; since there
would be nothing else, which could hinder Louis the Fifteenth,
from being king of France, of Spain, and of the West Indies,
master of all the Austrian dominions, and, by consequence, emperor.   The truth I would inculcate by what I have said is this,
that as the partition treaty threw too much weight into the scale
of Bourbon, to the destruction of the balance of power in Europe;
so the necessary consequence of the war we made to restore this
balance must have been, if we had succeeded according to our
desires, to destroy it again, by throwing too much weight into
the scale of Austria.   This has been proved by the event, and
the inquirer demonstrates it, or he demonstrates nothing.

As far, therefore, as we have brought this deduction, that is, to
the end of the last war, it is manifest that the notion of preserving
a balance of power in Europe has, for the reasons touched upon
above, and which every man will extend in his own thoughts,

proved to us like an ignis fatuus; in the pursuit of which we have been led from difficulty to difficulty, and from danger to danger.

If we inquire, whether the treaties of Utrecht and Baden did afford us an opportunity of correcting our errors, and of profiting by our experience, it will be found that they did; since all the points, which had been in contest were then settled, and this settlement acquiesced in by all the parties to the war, except the emperor, who kept up still his claim against Philip the Fifth.

But the keeping up this claim could not have endangered the public tranquillity. He was unable to attack Spain for want of a maritime force, or even Sicily, which was covered besides by the guaranty of the neutrality of Italy; and this neutrality served likewise to hinder Spain from attacking him. There might have been a war of the pen, and there could have been no other between them.

At the worst, if the king of Spain had invaded any part of Italy, the guarantees of the neutrality might easily have prevented such an attempt; and in so doing they would have observed the treaties, and kept the peace, far from breaking either one or the other.

In such a state of foreign affairs, we had certainly an opportunity of looking carefully after our own. The king of Spain had no pretence to ask for any alteration in the settlement so lately established with his own consent; and the emperor could not have complained of his majesty for observing treaties, which he would not have made, but which he found made; nor for refusing to enter into a new war on this account.

Whether we improved this opportunity, or not, what our present condition is, and by what steps we have been reduced to it, I leave to the inquiry of some person more capable than myself. Let it suffice, that I have endeavored to remove some delusions, which have affected even men of the best understandings, and the best intentions; and to prepare the minds of my countrymen to consider, at this critical point of time, what our national interest really is, without being biassed in their judgments by what they may have thought of it on any former occasions.

I am, most noble Sir, your honor's most devoted serv't,

THE OCCASIONAL WRITER.

February 3, 1726–7.

POSTSCRIPT.

JUST after I had sent these sheets to the press, a paper entitled, "A letter to the Occasional Writer," was brought to me. I have read this stiff pedantic piece, with more attention than it deserves, tho' I read it cursorily; and notwithstanding the pains which the author takes to pass for you, I am ready to acquit you of the scandal. You would certainly have written better, and your pen at least would not have appeared so near a-kin to that of the Craftsman Extraordinary.

Who this author supposes the Occasional Writer to be, I cannot guess. Such a wretch as he describes is, I believe, to be found nowhere, nor even such an image of guilt and misery anywhere, except in the horrors of his own mind. I shall, therefore, with a decent contempt for this scurrilous scribbler, and without any concern about his imaginary correspondent, continue these inoffensive letters, in great tranquillity and sedateness, as often as occasion invites me, or as I find myself in the humor.

THE OCCASIONAL WRITER.

NUMBER III.

TO THE SAME.

——Quis te, juvenum confidentissime, nostras
Jussit adire domos? Quidve hinc petis? inquit. At ille,
Scis, Proteu, scis ipse; neque est te fallere cuiquam.—Virg.

Most Noble Sir:

When I wrote the postscript to my last letter, I believed firmly that the answer to the Occasional Writer was neither written by you, nor published by your order. Many considerations determined me to this opinion. For instance: I could not think, that in order to vent yourself in a fit of railing, you would draw a picture out of your own imagination, which cannot pass for that of the person who wrote to you, even in the low and vile character he assumed, and which you will hardly venture to own that you meant to be the resemblance of any man in Britain. I could not persuade myself that you would give occasion, as I apprehend very much that you have done, to the drawing of another picture after the life, to which no one will mistake, and which you will not be curious to place in your collection of paintings. I have, with the rest of mankind, a great regard for some of your friends: but I have, with the rest of mankind likewise, a great regard for your particular enemies, among whom it seemed impossible to me that you, who know them so well, should presume to find either slaves or criminals, or insolvent debtors. I dare affirm, that there is not one of them, who ever "mortgaged his estate for more than its value, or reduced himself near the necessity of living by contribution."

These are some of the motives which induced me to acquit you of the scandal, as I then thought it, of writing this paper. But, upon better information, and farther reflection, I have changed my opinion; and I see nothing inconsistent with my respect for you, in believing that you did write it.

As great an advantage as it is in all the affairs of life for a man to keep his temper, it is often excusable, and perhaps sometimes even praiseworthy, to lose it.   When a minister is contradicted in matters relating to his administration, and when busy people shall presume to ask his reasons, instead of submitting to his authority, can we wonder if his passion transports him into rhodomontades, and if he behaves himself a little wildly?   But when the virtue of a minister like you, whose whole life has been one bright example of public and private virtue, shall be suspected, so far as to be tempted to passion, who can refuse him even applause, if his generous soul, transported with a just indignation, breathes forth such expressions, as might, upon a less occasion, pass for indecent ribaldry?

This was your case, most noble sir, in the trial which I presumed lately to make, with too much boldness perhaps, but surely with a very good design.   A man writes to you from his garret, describes himself as a prostitute scribbler, and offers you the service of his pen: this, and this alone, appears to you; upon which a noble indignation seizes you, and you strike boldly, though you strike in the dark.   There is really somewhat fine in this sally of resentment, and it confirms, in the highest degree, the sentiments I have long entertained of your integrity, of your ability, and of a certain grace which accompanies and gives a lustre to every part of your conduct.

The share I had in this adventure affords me great satisfaction. Your anger fell on a feigned character, and hurts me not; but the honor of having drawn an answer from the first minister, and an answer in print, accrues to me, and is such a one as the greatest of our weekly authors could never boast.

Give me leave, therefore, to be transported in my turn, but to be transported with joy, and to insert an abstract of your answer in this paper, as Balzac placed at the head of his works, a letter from the Cardinal de Richelieu.   I consult my own honor, it must be confessed, in doing this; but I consider still more that just applause and admiration which I, with the rest of the world, am obliged on this occasion to give you.

To those parts of the Occasional Writer's letter, which show that you are at this juncture in want of such services as the scoundrel he personated might be fit to do, you make no reply.   The want you seem to admit, but the offer of service you reject: let the public hear in what manner.

ABSTRACT OF THE M——R'S ANSWER TO THE OCCASIONAL WRITER.

Page 1. " Though you have not signed your name, I know you.   Because a man who is without all principles of honesty, who in no one thing can be relied upon, a betrayer of his friend, a traitor to his prince, an enemy to his country, a perjured, ungrateful, unfaithful rascal, must be you; one who is a composition of all these things, can be only you.

Page 2. " You are an infamous fellow, who make a reputation of doing mischief; and Herostratus and Nero were not greater villains than you.

" You are of so profligate a character, that in your prosperity nobody envied you, and in your disgrace nobody pities you.

" You were in the interest of France, and of the Pope, as hath appeared by your writings, and you went out of the way to save yourself from the gallows.

Page 3. " You are a fellow who has no conscience at all, or a damnable complying one: and if you would lend it to me, it would be of no use to me.

" You have no abilities; you are an emancipated slave, a proscribed criminal, and an insolvent debtor: and I am not in such a desperate forlorn condition, to employ a fellow who hath no talents.

Page 4. " You have been a traitor, and should be used like one. And I love my master so well, that I will never advise him to use you, lest you should jostle me out of my employment.

" The majority are of my opinion. One side rails at you, the other dislikes you; and that Palinurus would deserve to be drowned indeed, who would let you have the rudder, if he could help it.

Page 5. " I do not value what you or your company say of me; neither am I to be frighted with a parliamentary scrutiny. You rail at me, because you envy me; and I despise all that a man in the impotence of disgrace can do against me, who could never terrify me in the zenith of his power."

Then follow these admirable arguments.

Page 6, 7, 8. " I. You may talk what you will of France, Spain, and the emperor, power is fluctuating, and perhaps I know who is Britain's enemy as well as another. II. Though we did lend the emperor a helping hand, we are not to let him do what he pleases; and when we set him up, it was good politics, and now it is equally good to take him down. III. I do not question but we shall humble him. IV. I must tell you plainly, you and I, as to foreign affairs, differ widely in opinion. V. When our neighbors grow saucy and encroaching, it is high time to look about us, and not to be taken napping. VI. I know you are like the emperor, because he is like yourself in ingratitude; and you hate our friend France, because you were well received there.

" If any body says any thing of me, pray tell them ALL THESE THINGS. But for all that, I will not give you an employment.

"I know you to be so hot-headed, that when you have read this, you will vent all your malice against me. But I do not value it; for I would rather have you my enemy than my friend.

"Change your names, and be as abusive and scurrilous as you please, I shall find you out. I am Aristæus; you are Proteus. You may change to a flame, a lion, a bull, or a bear, I shall know you, baffle you, conquer you, and contemn you. All your opposition will redound to my honor and glory. And so, sir, I scorn your proffered services. Sir,

"Your most, &c."

How great! how free! how bold! how generous! Well may those who have the honor of a near approach to you, extol the noble openness of your nature, which displays itself in this uncommon manner; and think that temper in a statesman truly admirable, which loses itself so gloriously. Did ever minister speak so plainly, or lay himself so open to any man, and especially to such a man as you supposed yourself writing to at that time? Far from discovering hatred and contempt of such wretches, persons in your situation have generally encouraged, and even feared them. Nay, they have sometimes aspired to be themselves of that class; and Seneca's Apocolocynthosis upon Claudius is not the sole instance of ministers who have dipped their pens in satire, to rail at the memory of a dead prince.

But now, after this honorable declaration which you have made, after this great example which you have given, let every mercenary scribbler, every tool of secret service, tremble and despair. Long may you live, most noble sir, the just model of a minister, who scorns the assistance of flattery, falsehood, artifice, or corruption.

I have devoted myself to your service, and shall certainly attend you through every stage of your fortune: as long as we both draw vital air, you shall feel the effects of my zeal in your cause, and I promise you very solemnly, that from henceforward I will live for no other purpose; so that I am persuaded you will hear with pleasure the three engagements which I think it proper to take with the public and with you.

The first is, that my pen shall constantly preserve decency and good manners, and shall never be stained with any abuse of particular persons. I will chastise vice, I will expose folly, and I will combat error, wherever I find them. But I will never touch upon any unalterable defects in figure, in family, in birth, in any kind whatsoever; much less will I allow myself to hint at any particular scandal, or even to mention any real misfortune, which may equally befall the best and the worst of men; unless I am forced by my subject to it, and unless I can soften the evil by the very manner of recalling it to memory. To attack a vice, a folly, or an error, is correction. To attack the person is defamation. He who writes an invective, does a silly thing, because he loses his end; and the wisest of men has said, " he that uttereth slander is a fool." Even truth loses its force in an invective, as it does in a panegyric; in one, it is thrown into the lump with malice, in the other, with flattery; and he who is guilty of the first, that is, he who writes against the man, not against his crimes, his follies, or his errors, seldom proves any thing more than his own envy, and the other's superiority. To conclude this head, he who writes an invective, does a base and wicked thing; because his design is to disturb the quiet, and destroy the peace of another man, but not to reform him, or to serve the public. The pen of such a writer, like one of those scourges of which the profound Meibomius has written so learnedly, while it chastises the person, serves only to provoke the vice.

The second obligation which I lay myself under, and which equally becomes a man who writes in the cause of truth, is that of entire disinterestedness.

I know the generosity of your nature, I know what places and pensions have been the rewards of some very mean performances in verse and prose; and that R. R. state-writer, of whom we are obliged to ask blessing, is most certainly not at the head of our profession. These examples, and a due consideration of the importance of my services, teach me sufficiently what expectations I might entertain, without any risk of a disappointment. But I have neither ambition of this kind, nor avarice. My fortune is above wanting the necessaries, and my philosophy above wanting the superfluities of life. I therefore discharge you from all obligation of rewarding my services; and I wish, for the sake of your ease, your honor, and your safety, my example was likely to be followed.

When we behold a great man among a crowd of disinterested friends, we know that they follow his virtues, and his merit; when we hear an orator bring over the majority of an unprejudiced audience to his opinion, we must impute it to the force of his eloquence. But surely it is as rare for a minister to have disinterested friends, as an unprejudiced audience; so that a number of followers can be no proof of his personal virtues, or a majority of his eloquence.

The ancients placed great happiness in their inemptæ dapes; I would rather you should place yours in the inempti amici. But alas! sir, as amiable as you are, this happiness will hardly fall to your lot, in our degenerate age; and I know not whether to maintain your power, you may not be forced to tarnish the lustre of your glorious administration. The king has indeed the

hearts of the people; his service will always be supported by a
national concurrence, because his views are always directed to
the national good.   This part is easy and secure, but when once
men come to distinguish between the king's service and yours,
there will arise another part not so easy nor secure.   You have
blended them pretty artfully together hitherto, but I doubt the
discrimination is at hand.   When that comes, you will be reduced to a melancholy alternative; which I beg you to think of,
and to prepare for.   To quit your power and your pretensions,
and to quit them before you have established in your room that
dear brother of yours, who does you so much service at home,
by tiring the ****, and the nation so much honor abroad by diverting the C*** of F***, would indeed be hard.   But on the
other hand, be pleased to consider that this nation has gone very
far into corruption already; that there is a point of corruption, to
which no nation can arrive and recover their liberties, if they
are lost; or even preserve them, if they are not lost, according to
Machiavel's observation; and that whoever is the instrument
of plunging his country irretrievably into this abyss, I use a
word you seem fond of, will fall into a terrible abyss himself, and
have no superiority any where, but where the briber stands
before the bribed, as the devil stands before the sinner.

You see, sir, how my zeal transports me, and carries me upon
the least hint, which may be improved to your honor or service,
even out of my subject.   I return to it, and the third engagement which I take, is to observe a strict impartiality.

To do otherwise, would be to act contrary to my nature, and
to the dictates of my reason.   I have a natural abhorrence of
injustice; and I considered, when I first drew my pen, in how
particular a manner it behooves us political writers to be on our
guard, against falling into any partiality.   The judge is circum-
scribed by forms, to the observance of which he is bound; he has
the law open before him; the parties, on whom he sits in judgment are generally indifferent to him, and far from having any
of his passions awakened, the whole man is sometimes prone to
sleep.   When there is room to suspect a judge of partiality in a
particular case, it is agreeable to the practice of some countries
that he should decline presiding at the trial, or be obliged to
withdraw at the requisition of the party.   With all these, and
many other precautions which wise constitutions have established, it is neither easy nor safe for the venerable sages of the
law to exercise partiality.   But we political writers are not
under the same restraints, and are exposed to strong temptations.
No forms are prescribed to regulate our proceedings; no particular laws adapted to the particular cases which may occur, lie
open before us.   The general law of reason is the only rule we

have to follow; the application of this rule requires the most nice exactness, and we are obliged to make this application often in pronouncing judgment on men and things, when we are the most warmly engaged in those civil contests, which the duty of our profession exposes us to, and even when our tempers are ruffled by opposition. From which consideration the difficulty of preserving a strict impartiality may evidently appear: give me leave, however, to illustrate this matter a little farther.

In the Athenian commonwealth, the citizen who took no side was deemed indifferent to the public good, and was branded for his infamous neutrality. Now, if such an obligation as this lay upon every private citizen in that democratical government, it is certain, that we public persons, at least, ought to think ourselves under the same obligation, even in this limited monarchy of ours. Indifference must be a crime in us, to be ranked but one degree below treachery: for deserting the commonwealth is next to betraying it. Our duty must oblige us in all public disputes to take the best side, and to espouse it with warmth; this warmth will beget warmth; for you know, sir, that the worst side is not always the worst defended. Provocations will multiply daily, and we may be attacked in the most sensible parts. You, sir, yourself, may, for aught I know, be insulted, and your spotless character may be defiled by some saucy scribbler; in this licentious age, nothing is held sacred; under the specious pretence of free-thinking, the providence, and the very being of God, have been openly called in question, and reflections on your administration may possibly steal into the world.

Suppose, for a moment, that anything so monstrous as this should happen, that you should be directly inveighed against, or which perhaps is more poignant, ironically commended; and then consider how difficult it would be for a professed admirer of you, heated in the contest, to keep his temper, and to preserve his impartiality: you must agree with me the task would be extremely difficult.

But I am sure you will agree likewise, that as difficult as it would be, a conscientious man ought to impose it upon himself.

The ill effects of partiality in us political writers, when it carries us to give unjust and false representations of men and things, will not be thought of little moment by you, who labor for fame, and expect a great part of your reward from posterity, as posterity is to receive a great part of the advantages which your wise and virtuous administration procures, in "reviving, supporting and extending credit, in opening so comfortable a prospect of the payment of our debts, in strengthening us abroad by so many beneficial alliances, and above all in amending our morals, by the total discouragement of every kind of artifice and corruption."

The civil magistrate may give away a man's estate, or take away his life; but we can do, and often have done more; we set the general characters and particular actions of men in what light we please, and deliver them down, sometimes very unjustly, under the most amiable or the most hateful colors to future ages; for the rash sentence we pronounce is eagerly received, and as eagerly transmitted by those who are animated with the same passion.

In this manner are unjust, and even false representations established. They become the general opinion of mankind, and then, although our works should grow out of date as fast as a gazette, which it must be confessed happens very frequently: yet still the mischief is done, the historian perpetuates the slander which the politician broached, and triumphs in the cotemporary authority, upon which he writes to serve the present turn, or to satisfy resentment of party; such persons as have no other crime but that of differing in opinion from us, and such events as have no other demerit but our dislike of the persons who bring them about, are loaded with infamy. Posterity is imposed upon as well as the present age, and the children continue the father's vengeance without having the father's provocation.

This faint sketch of some consequences that follow the partiality of political writers, and of the danger wherein we all stand of being transported by our own passions, or hurried by those of other people, so far to be answerable for such consequences, may suffice to show how much reason there is for a man who undertakes the career I am entering upon, to be watchful over himself, and to lay himself under as strong a restraint as I do by this solemn engagement.

Indeed, as the world goes, it is only by running into extremes that a state-writer can effectually please his party, or serve himself; the eye of party sees nothing but quite white, or quite black, observes no degrees between them, and can distinguish no middle color that partakes of both. The greatest genius in writing may be exposed to share the fate of the greatest genie in painting.— Annibal Carache, who followed nature and truth with the utmost exactness, found his noblest works discountenanced and neglected. He thereupon advised Guido and Caravagio, his two favorite scholars, to take quite another manner, to trace nothing faithfully, but to outrage all they represented, the one by painting in the darkest, the other in the lightest manner. By these means both of them were sure of admirers, and both of them grew rich.

To imitate these painters, is all our party writers aim at; whether their manner be black or white, satire or panegyric, no matter. Their principle is to lay their colors on thick, and to be equally in an extreme. But I hope, for my own part, to prove that I am not of this number. On the contrary, I will endeavor to excel in a much more difficult way, in softenings and middle teints; and yet by these to form a manner so strong, as shall be sufficient for my own reputation, and for your service. To you, who have so fine a taste in painting, this attempt will, I flatter myself, be agreeable, and will secure the continuance of your favor to,

Most noble sir, your honor's most devoted servant,

THE OCCASIONAL WRITER.

February 13, 1726–7.

THE FIRST VISION OF CAMILICK.

In Hoc Signo vinces.

HAVING as yet given the reader little besides grave discourses on public matters, and foreseeing that, during the session of parliament, I shall be obliged to continue daily in the same track, I am willing to take this one opportunity of presenting him with something, which has no relation at all to public affairs, but is of a nature purely amusing, and entirely void of reflection upon any person whatsoever.

My friend Alvarez (a man not unknown to many here, by his frequent journeys to England) did some time since make me a present of a Persian manuscript, which he met with while he followed the fortunes of Meriweis. An exact translation of the first chapter has been made, at my request, by the learned Mr. Solomon Negri, and is as follows:

CAMILICK'S VISION.

In the name of God, ever merciful, and of Haly his prophet. I slept in the plains of Bagdad, and I dreamed a dream. I lifted my eyes, and saw a vast field, pitched with the tents of the mighty, and the strong ones of the earth in array of battle. I observed the arms and ensigns of either host. In the banners of the one were pictured a crown and sceptre; and upon the shields of the soldiers were engraven scourges, chains, iron maces, axes, and all kinds of instruments of violence. The standards of the other bore the crown and sceptre also, but the devices on the shields were the balance, the olive wreath, the plough-share, and other emblematical figures of justice, peace, law, and liberty.— Between these two armies I saw a king come forth, and sign a large roll of parchment; at which loud shouts of acclamation were heard from every quarter. The roll itself flew up into the air, and appeared over their heads, encompassed with rays of glory. I observed that wherever the second army moved, this glorious apparition attended them; or rather the army seemed only to move, as that guided or directed. Soon after, I saw both these hosts engaged, and the whole face of the land overspread with blood. I saw the king who had signed and broken that sacred charter, drink out of a golden cup, fall into convulsions, gasp and die.

I then saw another king take his place; who, in the most solemn manner, engaged to make the words contained in the roll the guide of his actions; but notwithstanding this, I saw both armies again encounter. I saw the king a prisoner. I saw his son relieve him, and I saw the chiefs of the other army put to death. Yet that victorious son himself bowed his head to the parchment; which now appeared with fuller lustre than before. Several other battles ensued, with vast slaughter on both sides; during which the celestial volume was sometimes clouded over; but still again exerted its rays, and after every cloud appeared the brighter. I observed those heroes, who fought beneath it, though ever so unfortunate, not once to abate their courage, while they had the least glimpse of that heavenly apparition in their view; and even those, whom I saw overthrown, piêrced with ghastly wounds, and panting in death, resigned their lives in smiles, and with eyes cast up to that glorious object. At last the long contention ceased. I beheld both armies unite and move together under the same influence. I saw one king twelve times bow down before the bright phenomenon, which from thence-forward spread a light over the whole land; and, descending nearer to the earth, the beams of it grew so warm as it approached, that the hearts of the inhabitants leaped for joy. The face of war was no more. The same fields, which had so long been the scene of death and desolation, were now covered with golden harvests. The hills were clothed with sheep. The woods sung with gladness. Plenty laughed in the valleys. Industry, commerce, and liberty danced hand in hand throughout the cities.

While I was delighting myself with this amiable prospect, the scene entirely changed. The fields and armies vanished; and I saw a large and magnificent hall, resembling the great divan or council of the nation. At the upper end of it, under a canopy, I beheld the sacred covenant shining as the sun. The nobles of the land were there assembled. They prostrated themselves before it, and they sung an hymn. "Let the heart of the king be glad; for his people are happy! May the light of the covenant be a lanthorn to the feet of the judges; for by this shall they separate truth from falsehood. O innocence, rejoice! for by this light shalt thou walk in safety; nor shall the oppressor take hold on thee. O justice, be exceeding glad! for by this light all thy judgments shall be decreed with wisdom; nor shall any man say thou hast erred. Let the hearts of all the people be glad! for this have their grandfathers died; in this have their fathers rejoiced; and in this may their posterity rejoice evermore!"

Then all the rulers took a solemn oath to preserve it inviolate and unchanged, and to sacrifice their lives and their fortunes, rather than suffer themselves or their children to be deprived of so invaluable a blessing.

After this, I saw another and larger assembly come forward into the hall, and join the first. These paid the same adorations to the covenant; took the same oath; they sung the same hymn; and added a solemn form of imprecation to this effect. "Let the words of the roll be for ever in our eyes, and graven on our hearts; and accursed be he who layeth hands on the same. Accursed be he, who shall remove this writing from the people; or who shall hide the law thereof from the king. Let that man be cut off from the earth. Let his riches be scattered as the dust. Let his wife be the wife of the people. Let not his first-born be ranked among the nobles. Let his palaces be destroyed. Let his gardens be as a desert, having no water. Let his horses and his horsemen be overthrown; and let his dogs devour their carcases."—In the midst of these execrations entered a man, dressed in a plain habit, with a purse of gold in his hand. He threw himself forward into the room, in a bluff, ruffianly manner. A smile, or rather a sneer, sat on his countenance. His face was bronzed over with a glare of confidence. An arch malignity leered in his eye. Nothing was so extraordinary as the effect of this person's appearance. They no sooner saw him, but they all turned their faces from the canopy, and fell prostrate before him. He trod over their backs, without any ceremony, and marched directly up to the throne. He opened his purse of gold, which he took out in handfuls, and scattered amongst the assembly. While the greater part were engaged in scrambling for these pieces, he seized, to my inexpressible surprise, without the least fear, upon the sacred parchment itself. He rumpled it rudely up, and crammed it into his pocket. Some of the people began to murmur. He threw more gold and they were pacified. No sooner was the parchment taken away, but in an instant I saw half the august assembly in chains. Nothing was heard through the whole divan, but the noise of fetters, and clank of irons. I saw pontiffs in their ecclesiastical habits, and senators clad in ermine, linked together like the most ignominious slaves. Terror and amazement were impressed on every countenance, except on that of some few to whom the man continued dispersing his gold. This he did till his purse became empty. Then he dropt it: but then too, in the very same moment, he himself dropt with it to the ground. That, and the date of his power, at once expired. He sunk, and sunk for ever. The radiant volume again arose; again shone out, and reassumed its

place above the throne; the throne, which had been darkened
all this time, was now filled with the effulgence of the glory
which darted from it.   Every chain dropped off in an instant.
Every face regained its former cheerfulness.   Heaven and earth
resounded with liberty! liberty! and the HEART OF THE
KING WAS GLAD WITHIN HIM.

AN ANSWER TO THE LONDON JOURNAL,*

Of Saturday, December 21, 1728.

THE family of the Publicolæ are surely very numerous. I pretend to no acquaintance with them, and I desire none. Far be it from me therefore to assign to any one of the fraternity his particular lucubration. I do not presume to say, for instance, that such a piece was written by Ben, or such a one by Robin; but I can plainly distinguish, in their productions, a difference of style and character. In some, I feel myself lulled by a regular, mild, and frequently languid harangue; such as often descends upon us from the pulpit. In others, I observe a crude, incoherent, rough, inaccurate, but sometimes sprightly declamation; well enough fitted for popular assemblies, where the majority is already convinced.

The Publicola of the seventh of December quite jaded me. I handled the numb fish till I fancied a torpor seized my imagination; and perhaps you may think, that I am hardly yet recovered from the consequences of that accident. However, I shall venture to play a little with the Publicola of this day; for I think I can go through an answer to his paper. He returns the ball at least, and keeps up the game.

Before I come to this, give me leave to premise a word or two more.

As different as the Publicolæ are in other things, in one they are all alike. They are scurrilous and impatient. They call names, and grow angry at a sneer. Raleigh laid down his pen, rather than continue such a bear-garden contest. I took it up, and answered them for once in their own style; but they must not expect so much complaisance from me any more. The matters we enter upon are serious, and by me they shall be treated seriously and calmly. I shall consider the dignity of the cause I plead for; the cause of truth; the cause of my country; and I shall look down with contempt on the invectives and menaces, which they may throw out; and by which they will suit their style with great propriety to their subject.—But let us come to the point.

---

* This paper was supposed to be then under the direction of Benjamin, Lord Bishop of *****.

The Publicola of this day sets out with stating, in a half light, a question which hath been much debated in the world. No man that I know of, no reasonable man I am sure, did ever find fault that we avoided a war. Our national circumstances are so well known, they are so severely felt, that ministers who maintained peace, and procured to their country the blessings of peace, quiet, improvement of trade, diminution of taxes, decrease of debts, would be almost the objects of public adoration. But the exception taken to our conduct hath been this; that we provoked a war first, and showed a fear of it afterwards. People recall the passages of three years past. They wish we had practised greater caution at that time; but then the same people very consistently wish that we had exerted greater vigor since. If the honor and interest of his late majesty, and of the British nation, say they, were so severely wounded by the public or private treaties of Vienna, that it was fit to keep no longer any measures, even such as have been thought of decency, with the emperor and the king of Spain; why this fear of disobliging them? Why this long forbearance under all the insults offered to us by the Spaniards? If we were in a condition, by our own strength, and by our alliance with France, to enter with a prospect of success into an immediate war; why again have we chosen to defer it, under so many provocations to begin it? Why have we endured some of the worst consequences of a war, without taking those advantages which acting offensively would undeniably have procured to us? But if all this was quite otherwise, continue the same political reasoners; if the honor and interest of his late majesty, and of the British nation, were not so severely wounded; if we were neither, by our own strength, nor by the alliance of France, in a condition to risk a war; nay more, if things were so unfortunately jumbled, that perhaps "this war would have been more to our own detriment than to that of our enemies," as the Publicolæ have more than once insinuated in their papers, what could we mean three years ago, when matters were carried to greater and harsher extremities than it is possible to find any example of among civilised nations, since the quarrels of Charles the Fifth, and Francis the First? If our "principal ally would have been dangerous to our interests in the operations of a war, and is indifferent to them in the negotiations of peace," for this hath been insinuated too from the same quarter, what a treaty was that which procured us this ally? What assurances were those which made us depend upon him? The difficulty of these dilemmas cannot, I think, be solved; and those who attempt it deceive themselves, whilst they mean to deceive the people.

But we are told that we went into a war, as far as the reason of things would give us leave. It seems then that the reason of things would neither give us leave to protect our trade, nor to make reprisals, when our merchants were plundered. If these words are to pass for any thing more than empty sound, it will follow either that Publicola is capable of affirming the grossest untruth in a paper, addressed to the people of England; or that our situation is worse than the least sanguine of our friends ever thought it, or the most malicious of our enemies ever represented it. Very bad indeed must it be, if the reason of things obliged us to bear from the Spaniards, at this low ebb of their maritime power, what would not have been borne when their proud armada covered the seas; what would hardly have been borne, even in the reign of king James the First.

But, God be praised! this is not our case; and therefore Publicola must be content to lie under the imputation which he hath drawn on himself by the boldness of his assertions.

He is frequently guilty of this fault; and the words which immediately follow those I have quoted, afford a strong instance of it. "We did not," says he, "take the galleons and bring them home; but we blocked them up; which as completely answered the true end and design of sending that fleet, as the actual taking of them. The design was to keep the money out of their hands (the Spaniards) and so disable them to carry on the project of the treaty of Vienna." Very well. This matter is brought to a short issue. The blockade of the galleons is over. Our fleet is come back from the West-Indies. The galleons are either come or coming. The Spaniards therefore are, according to Publicola, no longer disabled from carrying on the project of the Vienna treaty. I ask then, have they abandoned, have they renounced these projects? If our fleet blocked up the galleons till this was done, he is in the right. This answered the design of sending it. If they should, after this, break their faith, and renounce the most sacred obligations, none but they are to be complained of.

Publicola would have us believe, indeed, that they have renounced these projects; that they have granted us the main things in dispute; and that the congress is only to settle other affairs of less importance. But this I deny; and he shall be obliged to confess either that he advances, here again, a bold untruth; or that he reckons our keeping Gibraltar not amongst the main things in dispute, but amongst those of less importance. Let him show me, if he can, in the preliminaries, a particular and express confirmation of our right to this place, made by the Spaniards. I will undertake to show him the general words, by which the Spaniards will pretend in the congress, as it is notorious they do every where and on all occasions, that they have still a right to demand the restitution of Gibraltar, and that this right is to be discussed in the congress.

I know it hath been said more than once, in a very public place, and in a very solemn manner, that Gibraltar should not be even mentioned at the congress; but it would be impertinent to lay any stress on the assurances of a person, who hath presumed to give so many groundless ones already; and who either hath been bantered most egregiously himself, or hath made no scruple of bantering his country.

Here then is one main point of our interests, to mention no more, still unsettled; not because the Spaniards have flown off from any agreement they had come to with us about it; but because it was never settled; and yet the galleons are left at liberty to come home.

If asserting our right to Gibraltar, and some other things, which were sounded so high by an acquaintance of yours, Mr. Publicola (the author of the Inquiry), had no share in the ends which were proposed by sending our fleet to the West-Indies, such strange incomprehensible ends may, for aught I know, have been completely answered; but if these points, so essential to Great Britain, were any of the main things in dispute; if they were any of the ends proposed by what is called distressing the Spaniards; then it is false to assert that these ends have been completely answered.

When we consider what numbers of able and useful subjects his majesty hath lost in the expedition to the West-Indies; and that we are, at least, as far off from a settlement of interests with Spain now, as we were before that expedition was undertaken, it is impossible not to feel great and unaffected concern.

If it be asked, what was to be done? I shall answer that, perhaps, it little becomes a private man to determine such great questions; but I will proceed to show that all which Publicola advances against taking the galleons, is trifling.

First then, if blocking up the galleons in the Spanish ports was of such consequence, taking them would have been a more effectual measure to all the same purposes.

Secondly, if we had taken them, as it is certain that Mr. Hosier could have done with ease, and with all their treasures on board, immediately on his first arrival, we should have had a chance the more for taking the flota too, which stole away to Europe, whilst our squadron lay rotting before Porto-Bello.

Thirdly, if we had taken this treasure, we should have had in our hands a sufficient security for indemnifying our merchants, who have been the only sufferers, by the depredations of the Spaniards, whilst the French and Dutch have sailed securely; and to one body of whom, I mean the South Sea company, the king of Spain owes, for former seizures unjustly made, as much perhaps as his proportion in the treasure of the galleons amounts to.

Fourthly, to have taken the galleons would not have been liable to the same inconveniences, as we have severely felt by pursuing another measure. The expedition would have been soon over. The expense of lives and treasure would have been infinitely less. It would have cost little or nothing to have kept the Spaniards out of their money by a seizure, as long as the true reason of things should have required it; whereas it hath cost us more than all that money is worth, to keep them out of it by a blockade only for a time; and for a time, which hath not been sufficient to secure us against their designs, or to make them lay aside their pretensions. " But if we had taken them," says Publicola, " we should have taken the money of other people, as well as of the Spaniards. We should have been pirates." Let us see how this hangs together. If we had restored immediately to the proprietors their respective shares, as he supposes we must have done, the brand of piracy would not have stuck upon us. But suppose we had thought fit not to restore their shares to the Spaniards, till our differences with the court of Madrid had been settled; should we have been pirates in that case? He will be laughed at who affirms it. Would the king of Spain's share in this treasure have been no loss to him? would he not have missed the extravagant indulto, which he is now going to receive on this immense treasure? Should we have been pirates for punishing, in this manner, a prince, who actually besieged one·of our fortresses, who actually detained the ships and seized the estates of our merchants, and whose subjects every day killed, robbed and plundered the subjects of Great Britain?

But I go a step farther; for if we stop with Publicola, it will be always short of the mark, and we shall never exhaust the subject, as I desire to do, because I desire to find the truth,. and to be sure that I find it. What hath been said hitherto, hath been said on the supposition of a seizure only; and I hope the scruples of Publicola's timorous conscience are appeased. I hope he hath found out, by this time, that such a seizure might have been carried on without piracy. But suppose it had been a capture, not a seizure; such a capture as can never be made but in time of open war; such a capture as entitles the captors, by our laws, to the whole profit of the prize. Why then we had commenced a war against Spain by this action, as Spain had done long before against us by a thousand hostilities. Why then vice-admiral Hosier, and the officers and seamen of his squadron, had been in the same case as Sir Charles Wager, and the officers and seamen of his squadron were in the last war; and I do not remember that these gallant men were ever prosecuted as pirates at home; or reputed such abroad, or obliged to refund any part of the treasure they had taken.

Upon the whole matter, Publicola's argument proves nothing in the present case; or it proves that even when we are at war with Spain, we must not presume to attack these sacred galleons. Other nations are always interested in them, as well as the Spaniards. It will therefore be always unlawful, according to this excellent casuist, to make prize of them; and he is defied to distinguish himself out of this absurdity.

Having now gone through what Mr. Publicola calls, I know not why, the subject in general, we will examine the second part of his epistle. I pass over all the Billingsgate with which he ushers in this part; though I could make myself and you too very merry, if I would apply his criticisms on what Raleigh says, concerning one promise, to the interpretation which was given to another promise; by which we might have learned, amongst many other curious distinctions, the difference between a direct promise and a promise ministerially worded: but I shall leave him to his phrenzy, and proceed soberly to show you that he says nothing, or that which is worse than nothing, in every line of this performance; in which he seems to triumph with such vast complacency.

The point he labors is to show that the promise made by the Lord Stanhope to restore Gibraltar, which hath not been complied with, and the destruction of the Spanish fleet on the coast of "Sicily, threw the court of Madrid into the arms of the emperor, and were the true root and real cause of all that thorough hatred and deep malice shown in the treaty of Vienna;" and by consequence that all our present difficulties with Spain proceed from hence; from causes laid many years ago, and when the present ministers were not in power. My business shall not be to blame or to excuse any ministers; but to make a true deduction of facts, and to reason clearly and justly upon them; and I charitably hope, that I may bring Publicola to do so in time; if for no other reason, at least by obliging him to take shame to himself so often: for though I am not so bloody-minded as Publicola, who talks as if he had heads in his power, yet I assure him, that I will not let him alone whilst, amongst other enormities, he makes it his business to bury truth and common sense under such weekly heaps of rubbish.

I shall show immediately that, in whatever terms or manner we suppose Lord Stanhope to have made a promise of restoring Gibraltar to the Spaniards, it will be of no avail to Publicola's purpose. But since he hath told us what he hath heard, and Raleigh hath told us what he hath heard, for neither of them can pretend to speak on their own knowledge concerning this affair, I will likewise take leave to state what I have been informed of, upon better authority than what my adversary hath often written upon in his affirmative style.

I have been informed, then, that Lord Stanhope had been induced, or seduced, call it what you please, by the late regent of France, to make an overture of this kind at the court of Madrid. Lord Stanhope, says our author, might think that Gibraltar was to be "honestly given up for valuable considerations." He might so; and he was so honest a man, so sincere a lover of his country, that if he had thought in another manner, no consideration of private interest, no regard to the service of a ministry, could have prevailed on him to make, nor even to entertain the motion. But have a care of your insinuations, Mr. Publicola; and learn to make them with a little more delicacy. The case is vastly different now. The sense of our august monarch is known. The sense of the whole nation hath been loudly proclaimed; and I believe no minister, how presuming soever, will venture, at this time, to say that Gibraltar may be honorably or advantageously given up; and therefore no virtuous minister will think he can honestly give it up, or conspire in measures which may create the appearance of a necessity so to do. But to return to my narration.

If such an overture was made by Lord Stanhope, it was made to prevail on the court of Spain to desist from the enterprise they then had in hand; an enterprise, which we should have been obliged to prevent, if the treaty of quadruple alliance had never been made, by virtue of our guaranty to the neutrality of Italy. That this overture was not received is evident; since the Spaniards went on with their expedition, which ended in the destruction of their fleet. Now call this an overture, as I do; or call it a promise, as Publicola will affect to do; it was vacated to all intents and purposes by the Spaniards, who refused to comply with the condition on which it was and only could be grounded.

It hath been said by some, that this promise was renewed afterwards, to pacify the Spaniards for the loss of their ships; and for their defeat in Sicily: but this deserves explanation; and will not stand in the light which those who urge it desire it should.

It is, I believe, true, that the French, who first induced us to make this overture, would, on the pretences just now mentioned, and on the pretence of the hopes which the regent had continued to give the Spaniards, have obliged us to acknowledge this vacated promise as a subsisting obligation; but I have been informed, that this was refused flatly to the minister sent over hither upon that occasion, and to the regent himself by our minister abroad. The promise then continued vacated; and we were as much disentangled from the snares which our good allies laid for us, as if no such promise or overture had been ever made.

But farther. If a promise of this kind had been made on our part, even after the expedition to Sicily, which there is no color to affirm, yet that promise must likewise have been void, since it was made so, to all intents and purposes, by the king of Spain's accession to the quadruple alliance.*

That all possessions are mutually confirmed by that treaty, except such as are specified in it, cannot be denied. The possession of Gibraltar was therefore again confirmed to us by the king of Spain, when he acceded to that treaty; unless he can show that our possession of it was excepted, or can produce any private article or declaration, which made a reservation of his right to this place, notwithstanding the cession of it made at Utrecht. But nothing of this can be shown; and it hath been said, I believe truly, that a contrary declaration was made solemnly and publicly by the British minister in Holland, at the very time when the accession was signed.

Thus far then the way is clear before us. When we came mediators to the Congress of Cambray (for such we were at that place, though we have the misfortune to find ourselves principally and almost solely concerned in the disputes to be settled at Soissons), the king of Spain had no right, nor pretence of right to demand of Great Britain the restitution of Gibraltar.   Indeed, if he had then such a pretence; if a promise, on our part, to restore this place to him, which promise we refused to execute, had then subsisted, how could he have accepted of our mediation?

Ay, but (says this poor hunted author, who doubles and shifts and works and tries, at any rate, to save himself) Lord Stanhope, according to Raleigh's own confession, was first in this affair, and laid the foundation of this expectation in the Spaniards.—It is plain the Spaniards had such assurances. It is allowed you, at least for argument's sake, that Lord Stanhope was first in this affair. The Spaniards had such assurances. Make your most of it. These assurances were discharged. These promises were released; and whatever Lord Stanhope can be supposed to have done or said about Gibraltar, hath no more relation to the present dispute, than what was done or said about Gibraltar in the time of king Rodrigue and the Count Julian: so that our author is building up a right for the Spaniards upon foundations which were demolished as soon as laid.   He is building up a right, or he is building up nothing; for to talk, as he does, of expectations, in cases of this nature, without establishing a right, real or plausible, is too frivolous to deserve an answer.

---

* Vide the treaty.

Let me illustrate this by a familiar instance; for things cannot
be made too plain to him. I will suppose him a clergyman. I
will suppose that by merit, of some kind or other, he gets a promise of a bishoprick. After this, he does something inconsistent
with such a promotion. He forfeits all title. He renounces all
pretensions to it. Shall his advocate be admitted to insist that,
notwithstanding all this, he expects to be a bishop still; and instead of grounding his expectations on his right, ground his right
on his expectations? No, certainly, such an advocate would be
hissed out of court, and would deserve at least to have his gown
pulled over his ears.

But the Spaniards are not so chimerical. They ground their
expectations, and what they call their right, on a new engagement taken by us, as they say, since all the transactions, mentioned above, were over; on a private article, in a treaty made
with them in 1721, stipulating the contents of a letter to be written by the late king; and on the letter, written in pursuance of this
article, the original of which they offer to produce; and which they
pretend to be a positive engagement to restore Gibraltar to them.

With what front now could Publicola affirm, that what Raleigh says about the letter is nothing to his purpose; unless this
mysterious letter had been written before this same kind of a verbal promise was made?—If this mysterious or ministerial letter
had been written before Lord Stanhope's promise was made, it
would have been nothing to Raleigh's purpose; because his purpose was to show, that the demand which the Spaniards now
make of Gibraltar, cannot be made on any thing which passed in
lord Stanhope's time; but it was extremely to his purpose to
show that this letter was written after Lord Stanhope's death.
Had Publicola taken upon him to ridicule the plainest and
easiest demonstration in Euclid, he could not have rendered himself more ridiculous than he does upon this occasion.

I am at a loss what words to use. I have debarred myself
from using hard ones; and none but the hardest are equal to what
this writer deserves. Let him pass then without any animadver-
sion from me. Let the reader pronounce sentence upon him.

To sum up the whole on this head. Publicola was to prove
that my Lord Stanhope's promise to restore Gibraltar, is one of
the reasons of the present obstinacy of the Spaniards, and by consequence of our present difficulties. Now it is notorious that in
fact the Spaniards ground their demand on something which
passed whilst he was alive. Publicola says, it never appeared
that the present ministry came into such assurances. If he means
the assurances given by my Lord Stanhope, and long ago made
null, he is most certainly in the right, for a very obvious reason.
But if he means the assurance still insisted upon, I have nothing

to say but this. These assurances, or what the Spaniards call by that name, were given in the year of our Lord 1721.

The second reason assigned, by this profound politician, for the obstinacy of the Spaniards, is the resentment which has lain at their hearts, ever since we destroyed their fleet. Here are no proofs offered; nor can there be any, which are direct; because the assertion relates to what passes, and has passed these many years, in the hearts of the king, queen and ministers of Spain. It is a fact, which we are to take on the bare word of this author, or to reject. I make no scruple of rejecting it, because the probable reasons against it seem to me of much greater weight than his single authority in any case, and especially in a case of this nature. The Spaniards were certainly not very well pleased with us for destroying their fleet. But does it follow from hence, that the resentment which they conceived upon this occasion, operates thus strongly still? How often were the French beaten by us in the last war? Were not whole squadrons of their ships destroyed? How many of their armies were defeated? How many of their towns were taken? Notwithstanding which, we see with pleasure, the most perfect harmony, the most intimate friendship, subsist between their court and ours; even from the time, when their disgraces were recent; and when their resentments against us must have run the highest, it was true that resentment, and not the Ragione di Stato, as the Italians call it, governed the conduct of princes. But the Spaniards are more vindictive than the French. This may be said perhaps by people, who are apt to support one affirmation by another, and to call that proof. But then how came it to pass, that the Spaniards were so soon reconciled to the French, and entered into such close alliances with them immediately after the campaign of 1718. If the British arms beat the Spanish fleet, the French arms took the Spanish towns at the same time. The near relation, and the ancient friendship between the two courts of France and Spain, it may be said again, rendered their reconciliation easy. But this would be to suppose what is quite contrary to the natural course of human passions. According to that, the court of Spain must have been infinitely more piqued against their own family, for joining in opposition to them with the emperor, who had been so long their common enemy, than against the court of Britain, who had not the same ties to them, and who acted for an old ally. This is natural and probable. Nay, when we consider how many marks of the utmost resentment were shown at that time by the Spanish to the French court; how many intrigues the former carried on to subvert the government, and to raise a rebellion in France, I think we may justify affirming that it is true in fact. And yet how soon was all this forgotten at Madrid? How soon was the reunion of the two courts brought about in the closest manner, and cemented by marriages?

The king and queen of Spain might look on the proceedings of the French, in this affair, as a political quarrel, and a national wrong; but they looked on an affair, which happened a few years afterwards, as a personal injury and an affront. I mean the sending back the infanta in so abrupt, so unprepared a manner, without any softening, and with so many aggravating circumstances. Never resentment run higher, nor was expressed in terms of greater passion, than that of the court of Madrid upon this occasion; and yet one or two sacrifices, a little address, and a little management pacified all; united the two courts again; and restored to the French, in a short time, such an influence in Spain, that it is marvellous we, who depend so much upon it, should not yet have found the least effect from it in our favor.

I have dwelt on these observations, in order to show to what poor expedients those writers are reduced, who attribute the present obstinacy of the Spaniards to the beating their fleet nine years ago. Surely it is strange that the Cardinal De Fleury should have been able, in seven or eight months' time, to re-establish a good correspondence and friendship between the two courts of France and Spain, after so great and so sensible an affront as Philip and his queen thought was put upon them by his predecessor in the ministry; and that our ministers should not be able, in the course of as many years, to atone for what their predecessors did; nor to pacify the resentment of the Spaniards, for the loss of their fleet in an action, which they might have avoided; and which they rendered, in some sort, unavoidable to us. It is impossible to believe, that such an incident should produce these effects; which seem to strengthen, rather than to grow weaker, the farther they are removed from the supposed cause of them. There must be something more recent than this anger, at a loss long since sustained and repaired too, as I believe.— Perhaps we may begin to make some discovery of this kind, when we examine the next article; to which I shall proceed as soon as I have made a few reflections more on this head, which Publicola most prudently suggests to me, and which will be of wonderful service to his cause.

" Nor does the quadruple alliance" (says he; but he must mean the king of Spain's accession to the alliance) " being after the promise" (that is, Lord Stanhope's promise or overture, concerning Gibraltar) " prove the Spaniards had given up their expectations founded on that promise; but only that they were not, at that time, in proper circumstances to insist upon it." I have shown how silly it is to talk of expectations, without any right to expect; and how the right of the Spaniards to Gibraltar, acquired by Lord Stanhope's promise, or overture, either real or supposed, was extinguished before the year 1721. But I agree, that if they had then had even a real right, they must have submitted to give it up, as they did at that time, because of the circumstances into which they were fallen. Let me ask Mr. Publicola what reduced them to these circumstances? He must answer, it was beating their fleet. They had been as obstinate before that time as it is possible for them to be now. Alberoni talked at least as high as the Marquis de la Paz. But they grew complying as soon as this hostility was committed. Might not the taking their galleons have had the same effect lately? Would not our incomparable ministers, who run up and down the world negotiating and making treaties, with so much credit to themselves, and so much honor and advantage to the nation, have done better (I speak it with due submission to their approved wisdom) to imitate than to blame the conduct of their predecessors? From 1721 to 1725, we heard of nothing but the happy and flourishing state of our affairs. This must have been owing, according to Publicola, to the circumstances the Spaniards were in; and therefore this must have been owing to the defeat which they received in the Mediterranean. How came we to hear from the very same persons, that all our difficulties and the distresses we are in at present, ought to be dated before the year 1721? Surely, to be in a flourishing state, a nation must be in a secure state; and how could that be true, if, during the four years I have mentioned, a powerful neighbor meditated revenge, and only waited an opportunity of striking home? How could it be declared, even from the throne,* that nothing more than the forms of a congress were wanting to establish the public tranquillity, if the grand quarrel between us and Spain did, in effect, subsist at that time?

There are people so very regardless of truth, and so very indifferent to the shame of being convicted of falsehood, that they never consider, when they affirm a fact, any thing more than the present expediency. Strange, almost incredible instances of this might be quoted. I pass them over in silence for many reasons; and, amongst others, for this reason, that some of them are too recent to be forgot. I stick to the point before me; and shall conclude it by observing, that, when Publicola assigns all the difficulties which we have labored under since the year 1725, to what passed before the year 1721, he is confuted, not only by the reasons I have urged, which seem to me unanswerable, but likewise by an authority which every man will allow to be decisive.

The next article to be considered is this. Raleigh, who was not satisfied with Publicola's way of accounting for our present

---

* Vide the king's speech at the opening of the session, 1721.

difficulties, and for the close alliance between the emperor and
Spain, had ascribed both to our refusal·of the sole mediation at
Cambray. He is accused of maliciously concealing the truth, and
of imputing that to ill management, extraordinary refinement
and great tenderness, which was the result of true reason. Now
I think I can demonstrate that Publicola is ignorant of the truth,
or that he conceals it, I will not say corruptly, but unfairly.

That the treaty of Vienna was actually and in form signed,
before it could be so much as known at Vienna that we had
refused the sole mediation, I might grant in one sense, and, for
the sake of argument, though I do not believe that the fact is just
as he states it, and yet I might safely deny the same thing in the
only sense in which this fact can be of the least use to our author.
I can grant that this treaty might be signed in form at Vienna,
before it could ·be known there, in form, that we had refused the
sole mediation before the couriers from Cambray to London, from
London to Paris, from Paris to Madrid, from Madrid to Vienna,
could perform their journeys, and the several courts could hold
their councils and make their despatches. But the certain knowledge of our refusing this mediation might very well arrive at
Vienna before the treaty was signed; nay, the treaty might be
signed upon this knowledge, by virtue of instructions given with
this contingency specified in them. I say this might be the case;
and, therefore, to affirm this fact, in the terms Publicola affirms
it, is nothing to the purpose. What Raleigh advanced may still
be true.

That full powers were given by Spain to carry on the treaty
of Vienna four months before this offer of the mediation, is most
certainly true: and, therefore, there is as much reason to be asto-
nished that early measures were not taken to prevent it, as there
is that other measures than what we have seen pursued, were
not taken to prevent the effects of such a treaty. Could it be an
absolute secret to our ministers, who ought to be well informed,
since they have had such immense sums for secret service, as
were never heard of before their time, that Spain was negotiating
at Vienna, during these four months? Could it be a secret to
them that, from the death of the Duke of Orleans, and about a
year, at least, before this treaty was concluded, the Spanish ministers were full of fears and jealousies about the completing the
infanta's marriage with the king of France? If these things,
which were not quite unknown to most private persons, who
observed the course of public events, and who sought information about them, did not escape the intelligence of our ministers,
how could a consideration of the circumstances, which the court
of Spain was in at that period, escape their sagacity?

From the time of the accession of the king of Spain to the

quadruple alliance, the whole management of the court of Madrid had been left to the Duke of Orleans and his Cardinal Du Bois; and if we were drawn into the treaty made at Madrid in 1721, by this prince and his minister, as I verily believe we were, it is easy to see who was thanked for this by the Spaniards, and how watchful France had constantly been to seize and improve every occasion of rendering our title to Gibraltar disputable, and of wresting this important place out of our hands.   We came then into the congress of Cambray joint mediators with the French, between the emperor and the king of Spain, but not with equal advantage; not with an equal share in the confidence of one of the parties; and with our share in the confidence of the other, perhaps, a little diminished: for it is not unlikely that the private treaty, made at Madrid with the king of Spain, whilst we were mediators at Cambray between him and the emperor, might give umbrage at least to the latter.   I know not whether this step did not even occasion some complaint, though not in form perhaps, from the imperial ministers.

In this state of things, and in this disposition of all parties, what could it be imagined that the Spaniards should turn themselves to, on the foresight of a rupture of all intimacy, and even correspondence with France?   Could they resolve to leave themselves without any ally with so many enemies, and with their interests still unadjusted?   Could they resolve to run the risk, in this condition, of falling back into a state of war, when they were about to purchase peace at a price which they thought so dear?   Could they resolve to abandon themselves entirely to Great Britain, who had hitherto shown so much partiality to the emperor, still their enemy, and whose principal intercourse with them had been managed hitherto by France, to whom they expected soon to become enemies?   Certainly they could not resolve upon this, even as I have stated the case; much less could they do so, if they had such an inveterate rancor at heart, as Publicola represents.   What then could our ministers imagine the Spaniards should do upon a foresight of the Infanta's being sent back, and by consequence of breaking with France?   I will venture to say, for it is plain and evident, that if they thought anything on this affair, they must think the very thing which the Spaniards did.   The Spaniards began to treat at Vienna, that they might prepare for the worst; and they delayed concluding their treaty, till what they feared happened.   Give me leave to add, that it was easy to see that, whenever the ministers of Philip and the Imperalists should come to examine their master's interest together, they would soon find these interests not so hard to reconcile, nor their want of mediators so hard as they had imagined, whilst rivalship and pique kept them at a distance; and that there were men of great weight in the emperor's court, whose private interest must render them particularly zealous to promote this union. All this happened; and it affords a pregnant instance of what I said above, that reason of state will determine the conduct of princes, not old stale resentments.

From what hath been thus stated I desire to make some inferences, and to recommend them to Publicola's consideration.

First then, It appears more ridiculous than ever to talk of the promise of Gibraltar, and the loss of their fleet as lying at the hearts of the Spaniards, and breaking out upon this occasion. Neither must it be said absolutely, that our refusing the sole mediation at Cambray threw Spain into the arms of the emperor. In what respect this step might contribute to it, will be said presently. But the principal and determining cause of Spain's uniting so closely with the emperor, was the sending back the Infanta.

Secondly, However sudden the immediate resolution for the departure of this princess from France might be; yet this design had been long in agitation; so long, that the suspicion of it had been entertained by the Spaniards, and was even publicly owned by their ministers very many months before they sent their full powers for carrying on a treaty at Vienna.

Thirdly, There was surely, in the whole progress of this affair, notice enough to alarm any reasonable men, and time enough to prepare for the consequences of a breach between France and Spain. During the life of the Duke of Orleans, he had, and it could not well be otherwise, the chief credit at Madrid. But it was obvious enough that, by sending back the Infanta, his successor would furnish us with a fair opportunity of attempting at least to get between France and Spain, as France had stood between Spain and us, and of maintaining ourselves in that post. This indeed was an object of the utmost importance, which deserved more than all our negotiations have cost us, and which it is not impossible might have been accomplished for less. Whenever it shall appear that we took all the measures in our power, in a proper manner and at a proper time, for this great end, infinite honor will accrue to our ministers without dispute.

Fourthly, If we had been as much prepared as one would think we might in so many months have been, we should have had some great advantages, which, if we were unprepared for these events, and even surprised at them, it was impossible we should reap.

The sole mediation could not indeed have been sooner offered than it was; because it could not be offered till Spain had broke with France, and then it was offered to us. Nay, if it had been offered sooner, I agree that we could not have accepted it sooner, for reasons of policy and even of decency. But if we had been prepared for these events, we might have struck a great stroke, as the generality of the world thought, and continue to think, by accepting the mediation in form, as soon as it was offered. In the case supposed of preparatory measures taken by us, on a foresight of such a conjuncture, it is probable that Spain would not have been extravagant enough to precipitate so bad a bargain as she made for herself in the Vienna treaty. Having no mediator nor even ally, she was under the necessity of granting almost any terms to the emperor, provided she secured the main points which she had in view. But, sure of our support, and she might have had assurances sufficient for her to depend upon, it is impossible to think she would have carried her concessions farther than she needed to have done. In this case none of those engagements, which were talked of, but which have never yet appeared so injurious to Britain, could have been taken; and we might have had perhaps the satisfaction of seeing the peace of Europe consummated by the reconciliation of two princes, the adjustment of whose interests had been so long our care, and whose union is, without doubt, in general, and unless some particular circumstances of a very extraordinary nature hinder it, the common advantage of all those who desire to see a balance of power preserved in the western world. But I go farther. I will suppose that we had not been able to soften Spain; or that we had not attempted it, which perhaps was the case; that Spain looked on us with a jealous, and even a revengeful eye; and in short that the mediation was offered to us, without any design that we should concern ourselves in it, and purely for form sake; yet surely, even in this case, some advantage might have been taken by our immediate acceptance of it. Our conduct, at least, would have been free from any objection, and Spain and the emperor would have been left without any color of excuse. Might not such a step have retarded the conclusion of this famous treaty? Might not time have been gained; and would not the least time, in this case, have been of the greatest moment to us?

Fifthly, When the mediation was offered us, we could not know how soon the treaty would be signed. It cannot be pretended that we did. Our refusal of it therefore must have been grounded purely on these two considerations, so often urged in defence of this measure, that the Spaniards were our inveterate enemies, and that we were in alliance with the French. What is meant by being in alliance with the French, and making this a distinction between our relation to them and our relation to the Spaniards, I am at a loss to find. We were surely in alliance with one nation, as well as the other, from the moment the king of Spain acceded to the quadruple alliance, and the matters still unsettled at Cambray were solely relative to him and to the emperor. If it be meant that we thought the French our friends, and knew that the Spaniards waited only for a pretended occasion to break out into enmity with us, I think this reason will prove the very contrary of what it is advanced to prove. Did we suspect that something contrary to our interest, something dangerous to us, was working up in the negotiation of Vienna; and did we for this very reason decline an opportunity of coming at some knowledge of what was in agitation there? did we, for this very reason, refuse the best means we could have hoped for, of keeping our ancient friendship with the imperial court, and of being in a condition to check the court of Spain? Such arguments as these will not pass; and whoever produces them hath too mean an opinion of the rest of mankind, and too presumptuous an opinion of his own sufficiency. On the part of France, no objection could have been made to us, if we had accepted this mediation: for either the points to be mediated upon were pure trifles; such as the titles, and other matters of as little weight, referred to the congress of Cambray; in which case our accepting the sole mediation must have been quite indifferent to the French: or these points were of moment to the general interest; and in this case, the French ought to have desired that we should continue in the mediation, for the same reasons which ought to have determined us to do so. If the friendship and confidence between us and the French was not so strict as it hath been represented, they did not deserve the compliment we made them. If this friendship and confidence were so strict, they might and they would have trusted us with pleasure. Every one knows how concerned and alarmed the French were at the resentment which the king of Spain showed on this occasion.— The first care was to try all possible means of pacifying him.— If we could have been one of these means, their obligations to, and their confidence in us must have increased. We might have treated for them, when they could not treat for themselves. Instead of this, by dint of management, we so disposed affairs, that the French in a short time treated for us with the emperor and the king of Spain, with whom we could not treat for ourselves.

The last inference I shall make, from all that hath been said, is this. As sending back the infanta was the certain and immediate cause of throwing Spain into the arms of the emperor; so our refusal of the sole mediation may justly be deemed an accessory cause of it. This refusal might give occasion to carry the engagements of these two princes farther than it was for our interest that they should go. At least, our acceptance of it was the sole, probable measure, in that instant, of preventing such engagements; for this union of the emperor and the king of Spain is not, in itself, so terrible. Spain might be as well, nay better for us and for all Europe, in the arms of the emperor than of France; and if this union is become formidable to us, we may thank for it our own management, through a long series of business, and through divers revolutions of affairs; our too much neglect of Spain; our too much dependence on France; our being, upon all occasions, indefatigably busy about the interests of other people, and leaving to other people the conduct of our own; of which surely a more strange example cannot be imagined than that which is before our eyes. We would not attempt, nay we would not consent to be mediators, when we stood in that character, and could stand in no other, notwithstanding all the reasons for it in that nice conjuncture. Such was our delicacy. But we have admitted and (may I be allowed to say so?) we have courted France to act as mediator, where she is a party; for France is a party to the treaty of Hanover; and the treaty of Hanover, with the treaty of Vienna, give occasion jointly to the congress of Soissons, and all the present negotiations.

That France is a party in our quarrel, we have been often told; and that she would act as such, we have been often assured. She was to make besieging Gibraltar a *casus fœderis*. She was to march an army into Rousillon. What was she not to do?—But we have seen her act hitherto no part but that of a mediator; a common friend; but unconcerned in the quarrel. No good effect hath yet appeared, even from her offices as mediator. If, by these offices, she hath kept us from acting for ourselves, and made us prefer a precarious dependence to a vigorous war, I am sure the effect of her acting in this character hath been a bad one for Britain.

Nothing can be more plain than that chain of causes and effects, which hath dragged us into our present difficulties; and as these difficulties increased, the obstinacy of Spain must of course increase likewise. If that court had never thought of getting Gibraltar out of our hands, the state we brought ourselves into was sufficient to suggest the design to them. When once Spain had purchased the emperor's alliance, (I may use this expression, the treaty of Vienna will justify it,) she might flatter herself that he would adhere to her, even in unreasonable expectations, since he had no more to expect from us, and had so much to receive from her. As soon as we had sagely declined having to do with her, or for her, unless in concert with France, with whom she would have nothing to do at that time, France employed all possible means to be reconciled to her. Intrigues of every sort, ecclesiastical and secular, were set on foot. They succeeded, and Spain saw she had nothing to apprehend. What she had to hope, I determine not, from this party to the Hanover treaty. The other princes and states, who acceded to this treaty, acceded in such a manner, as it is easy to prove, if Publicola should think fit to deny it, that we could have little to hope and Spain little to apprehend from their engagements, in her disputes with us about our immediate interests.

All other powers softened towards each other by degrees; and by degrees we got deeper into the quarrel. Spain, from having no ally, came to have many; some more, some less to be depended on; none to be feared. From having a multitude of disputes, she came to have none, except with us. We, on the other hand, from having none of our interests in dispute, are come to see hardly any others in controversy. From feeling ourselves backed by several allies, we are come, at least in the points of direct relation to us, to have in effect no ally but one; and with that one we own that we are dissatisfied; nay we own that we are afraid of him. The writer, I am answering, insinuates both; nay, he does it almost in express words. He complains of the indifference of France in support of our interests; and of the danger of engaging in a war, in concert with France. Who would have thought it, Mr. D'Anvers? Here is the London Journal contradicting the Inquiry; and I am able to point out to you many gross instances of his doing the same thing. Here is Publicola accounting for our present difficulties, now they are come upon us, by the very arguments which were urged against the Hanover treaty, and which proved that the natural consequence of that treaty was just what the event hath shown it to be. Those who wrote against the Inquiry foretold what would happen. Publicola justifies the ministry, by complaining that it hath happened!

I will mention but one more instance of this kind; and that shall be with relation to the Ostend company. "The grand quarrel, says Publicola, was between us and Spain. The Ostend trade, about which such a noise hath been made, was more the concern of our neighbors, both by treaty and interest, than our own."—Now I will leave the world to decide by whom all this noise about the Ostend trade hath been made. Did not you, Mr. D'Anvers, and several other writers, maintain that this company was but of little concern to us, in opposition to the whole party on the contrary side, who took all possible pains, both within doors and without, to prove that the Ostend trade was a point of the utmost concern to Britain, and even equal to Gibraltar itself? Nay, the author of the Inquiry, who hath now the mortification to see himself given up, in every material article, by both parties; even by those who set him to work, goes so far, p. 57, of that memorable performance, as to assert that Gibraltar would be of no importance to us, if the Ostend company should be suffered to subsist; and having labored that point, with all his strength, for no less than twenty pages together, concludes it thus: "That not only our own East and West India trade, and that of the Dutch, will be ruined by the Ostend company, which will be the immediate effect of it, or rather is so already in some degree, but also that the contagion will spread to many other branches of the British and Dutch trade; and convey along with it the riches, the strength and the naval power to the same Spanish Netherlands.

"But were it so that Holland alone would be the sufferer by the Ostend trade, which is far from being the case, yet the ruin of Holland must carry along with it, in the end, the ruin of Britain."

Such absurdities as these would provoke merriment in a case of less consequence; but they provoke indignation in a case where the honor and interest of our king and country are so deeply concerned.

Into this state were our foreign affairs brought, when his present majesty came to the crown. I mention this the rather, because they, who now think it for their interest to date the rise of all this mischief so much backwarder than it can consistently with truth be dated, may possibly find it to their interest hereafter, if new and almost unavoidable difficulties should come upon us, in consequence of what they have done in a former reign, to date the rise of them as much too forward. Let it then be remembered that all which hath happened in this reign, is no more than a prolongation of the same scene. The great scenes of the world are not to be shifted at our pleasure. They must be continued sometimes, when we are convinced the most that they are weakly framed. Opportunities must be waited for, and we trust they will happen. We are sure they will be improved by the capacity, the vigor, the experience and valor of our august monarch. A seasonable and powerful effort hath often broke through the most complicated evils. A word hath often effected what the most tedious negotiations, such as we have been accustomed to, could never have brought about.

I have now done with Mr. Publicola for this time; and I hope for good and all. If my letter is grown into a greater length than I designed, this hath been owing principally to an earnest desire of setting these matters (so often and so grossly misrepresented) in a just and clear light. I have advanced no facts but such as are of public notoriety, such as I know to be true, and such as I do verily believe to be so, upon such grounds as reasonable men have always thought sufficient to constitute, in cases of this nature, the highest probability. I have endeavored to push no consequence, nor to strain any argument farther than I judged it would evidently bear; for whatever Publicola may think, which concerns me little, I assure you, Mr. D'Anvers, that I would not have given myself this trouble, small as it is, of answering him for any other reason but this; that, in order to get well out of our present difficulties and dangers, it is necessary to know truly how we came into them; and that he therefore, who contributes to dispel from before the eyes of mankind those mists of error which are so industriously raised at this time, does some service to his king and his country.

I am, Sir, &c.

JOHN TROT.

AN ANSWER

TO THE

DEFENCE OF THE INQUIRY INTO THE REASONS OF THE CONDUCT OF GREAT BRITAIN, &c.

IN A LETTER TO CALEB D'ANVERS, ESQ.

Sir:

As soon as I heard that the author of the Inquiry* had condescended to take notice of a letter which you thought fit to publish in your journal of the fourth of January last, I resolved to make my acknowledgments to him for so great an honor, and to desire you to convey them into the world. This duty should have been discharged immediately, if I had not been diverted from it by avocations of a very different nature; and if I had not observed, on a review of the present dispositions, that there was no reason in force to make a very speedy reply necessary. What I am going to say now will, I think, justify me for what I have said already, in the opinion of mankind; and at least in the secret thoughts even of the author and defender of the Inquiry: and as this effect of the little additional trouble I am about to give myself is the principal, nay, the sole good one which I dare expect, we are in time for that; and by consequence I shall not lose my labor by my delay.

This author hath thrown several matters in my way, to which

* The following was the motto to this Answer to the Defence, &c. viz. "Nor can we conceive a more abject servility of conduct, than for people, so long famed for commerce and bravery, to see their darling good, and their peculiar glory, the pledge of their liberty, and life of all their property, just going to be forcibly and unrighteously torn from them; and tamely to look on without one struggle for so great a blessing, or one hearty effort against the invaders of it. What can we become, if we give our consent to such ruin by our own supine indolence and insensibility, and suffer ourselves to be stript of our boasted strength and ornament at once, by a nation, the most despicable of all nations under heaven; exposed to the contempt and insults of the world about us here below, and rendered utterly unworthy, by our own conduct, of the care of providence above us all?"—Inquiry, p. 86.

it is proper I should say something before I enter into that which
is strictly the subject of our present dispute.

He declares upon this occasion, with all possible seriousness,
that "he hath not written, or dictated, or advanced, or, directly or
indirectly, had the least part in the writing or publishing any
paper which hath appeared in the world, in any form, from the
time of writing the Inquiry, and from some time before that, to
the twentieth of January 1728-9." He makes this declaration,
"and for that space of time, particularly with a view to papers
printed in the London Journal; in all which he had been utterly
unconcerned either directly or indirectly."

Far be it from me to question the truth of so solemn a declaration. I give entire credit to it; and I freely own that he hath
reason to complain of me for insinuating, at least, that he had a
hand in the London Journals. The little share I have had in
the paper war hath not given me many opportunities of knowing
the combatants; and the productions on one side, gave me little
curiosity to inquire after the authors of them. But I found it
universally affirmed, and nowhere contradicted, that this gentleman had a hand in the weekly papers just mentioned. The
persons who recommended these papers, countenanced the opinion; and were glad, perhaps, that so considerable a name should
give them an authority which might supply whatever else they
wanted. Nay, I found amongst those, who were acquainted
with this author, and I profess a particular regard for him, some
who were angry at him on this very account; some who were
sorry for him; but none who doubted the truth of the fact.
What may have given occasion to so general a concurrence, he
can best tell. I urge these circumstances only to show, how I
was led into an error. It was indeed error, not malice. But
still I think myself obliged to take this occasion of asking his
pardon; and I do it with all possible seriousness, as he made his
declaration, and from the bottom of my heart; because I am as
much convinced, that he neither abetted, encouraged, nor paid
the authors of these papers, as I am that he was not himself the
author of them.

It cannot be imputed to me, that I have any thing to answer
for, on account of the personal severities which this author, in a
very pathetic manner complains of. We must acknowledge,
and we ought to lament, that our public papers have abounded
in scurrility. One would be tempted to imagine, that the
Saturnalia were held all the year round in Britain; for those who
can do nothing but rail, have had their encouragement to write;
and I am persuaded that this gentleman's candor will oblige him
to confess, that nothing but a thorough contempt hinders complaints from being made against the writers of his own side,

much better grounded, and supported by much stronger instances, than he can produce against the writers of the opposite
side, in his own, or in any other case. For my part, I should be
extremely sorry to have it said of me, with truth, that I had
railed at any author, instead of answering, or even in answering
his book; and less than any would I be guilty of this crime, for
such it is, towards one who defends, with so much uniformity of
conduct, the liberty of the press, that corner-stone of public liberty. He who will support what hurts himself, because he thinks
it the support of the whole liberty we enjoy, shall meet with nothing from me but that which he deserves from all mankind, the
utmost respect, whenever he leaves me the power of showing
it, consistently with the regard I owe to truth, and to my own
necessary defence.

He will not, I hope, think it inconsistent with this respect for
his person, or with that which I have for some of his writings, if
I cannot bring myself up to have the same for his " Inquiry into
the Reasons of the Conduct of Great Britain;" or for his "Defence
of this Inquiry." He appears to have a paternal fondness for
the first of these treatises, which amounts even to a partiality;
the more surprising, because it is found in one who can boast so
numerous and so fair an offspring. I should not have attempted
to draw him out of an error, which he seems to indulge with so
great a satisfaction, if he had not made it necessary for me. Since
he hath done so, I will offer some observations on the Inquiry
itself, before I come to the Defence.

The circumstance upon which he seems to triumph a little,
(that the Inquiry was not answered,) he will permit me to say is
often a very equivocal proof of the merit of a book. The same
mouths, it seems, which pronounced the Inquiry to be a mean
and despicable performance, " have more than once expressed in
print their earnest desire that some able hand would answer it."
From what mouths he took this, I know not. But surely the
testimony of those who desired some able hand would answer
what they judged to be mean and despicable, is an odd testimony
for him to quote; since it could proceed from nothing but a design
to ridicule him.

Though the Inquiry was not answered in form, yet I believe
that several, perhaps all, the points on which his system leaned,
were occasionally examined, and sufficiently refuted by you, Mr.
D'Anvers, and by others. If no more was done I take the reason to have been plainly this. The ministerial air of authority
and information assumed in it, made even those, on whom this
air did not impose, judge that it was prudent to wait till time and
events should open the scene a little more; and as the scene
opened, they perceived that the Inquiry was daily answered, in

the most effectual manner, to their hands; so that the author might have waited all his life, perhaps, for something more of this sort if he had not thought fit to seize an opportunity of defending it, not more worthy of his notice, than several others before given him; and if my respect for him, and my desire to stand fair in his opinion had not determined me to make him a reply.

As to the effect of the Inquiry, which he thinks so considerable, that it "awakened multitudes out of a dull and languid state into life and vigor; and that it was not found to procure slumbers either to those who liked it, or to those who disliked it;" I, who was most certainly one of those who either liked or disliked it, can affirm with the greatest truth, that if it did not procure me slumbers, it did not keep me awake. Some of the facts advanced in it were strange and surprising; but then they were destitute of any proof, except the strong affirmations of the author, and collections of circumstances so extremely trivial, that they became burlesque as soon as they were seriously applied. A bare exposition of any real danger from the Pretender would have waked multitudes into life and vigor, though the Inquiry had never been written. But I apprehend that so many pages spent on Wharton's rambles, Ripperda's chit-chat, hearsays of what one great man wrote concerning what another great man said, three Muscovite ships coming to Spain, embarkations which were never made, and armies which were never assembled, could have no other effect than to compose multitudes into perfect tranquillity, and to confirm the opinion of their security on this head. Any surmises of an engagement, on the emperor's part, to assist Spain in the recovery of Gibraltar by force, could provoke no indignation, whatever else it might provoke, nor cause any alarm. We knew Gibraltar to be impregnable to the Spaniards, before Ripperda declared it to be so; and what assistance the emperor could give them towards reducing this place, unless he had in his service some of Mr. Waller's winged troops and Pegasean horse, we were not able to discover. As to the emperor's real engagement in this article towards Spain, and as to the engagements of Spain towards the emperor, on the article of trading to the West Indies, we soon knew what they were; and with this knowledge our alarm ceased. What was said in the long dissertations, about the Ostend company, caused likewise little or no emotion in us. Our interest was plainly not that of principals, till the Dutch had the address to make us so, by their accession to the treaty of Hanover; and the conduct of our own court, who beheld, with so much indifference, the rise and progress of this company, had taught us to be indifferent about it. These considerations, and many others which I omit, hindered the Inquiry from having the effect, which this gentleman's paternal fondness makes him believe it had.   The part, if I may have leave to say so, was overacted.   But still I see no reason that he has to be concerned, because one way or other the end of writing it was answered.   The Inquiry was the book of a day, like some little animals on the banks of the river Hypanis, which came to life in the morning, fulfilled all the ends of their creation, and died before night.

There is a point, on which the author and defender of the Inquiry values himself and his book very much; I mean the strict regard to truth which he assures us he observed in writing. Now, though I am ready to agree that this author has always a great regard to truth, yet I affirm that I could write a book as big as the Inquiry, filled with nothing but demonstrations of his errors in matter of fact.   Too much confidence in the informations he received, too much haste in composing, and above all, that fire which is apt to overheat the imagination of polemical writers, must have caused these errors.   It is impossible to account any other way, how a gentleman of nice honor, remarkable sincerity, and even exemplary piety, instead of making his propositions constantly the result of the evidence he found upon a thorough examination, true, should, through a whole book, have constantly suited his evidence to a certain set of propositions; and how facts and dates, as stubborn things as they are in the hands of other men, should grow soft as wax under his touch.

But it is not my design to enter into a disquisition of this sort. It would show ill nature, which I hope I have not; and it would be now of no use whatever.   I must however defend myself, as unwilling as I am to offend him; and therefore since he contradicts what I said, viz. that "he had been given up in every material article of the Inquiry," I think myself obliged to prove it. "How easy are such words as these," says our author, "but how hard to support them?"   Now I do assure him that these words, as far as they may be thought harsh or impolitic, will at no time fall easily from my tongue or pen; but he will find that it is easy for me, upon this occasion, to support them.   I will confine myself to the four great points of danger, arising from the Vienna treaties, and mentioned already.   Let us see whether he has been given up in them or not.

According to the Inquiry, we were in danger of losing not only our East and West India trade, but many other branches of the British trade, by the privileges supposed to be granted to the emperor's subjects, and from the enjoyment of which privileges we are debarred.   Nay, it was very strongly insinuated that even the ruin of Britain was involved in this point.   If this

had been the case, and if the treaty of Vienna had thus settled
the matter, there would have been occasion for all the outcries
which we meet with in the Inquiry, and for still more. But our
most knowing merchants gave up this point, as soon as they read
and considered the several clauses; and it is notorious, that the
contracting powers declared, as soon as they heard of the objection, that their meaning was not to give these privileges to the
imperial subjects above other nations; and that they would explain the text accordingly, if any ambiguity made it necessary.
But in truth there was little or no ambiguity in the matter, except what the representations of it occasioned; for without entering any deeper into it, let us observe that the answers which this
author gives to the objection, which he was forced, from the
notoriety of the thing, to make to himself, are evasive and fallacious; for since the same liberty of entering the Spanish ports
in the West Indies, in case of distress by bad weather, or for re-
freshment, is granted to us by the treaty of 1670, as is granted
to the imperial subjects by the treaty of Vienna, does it follow
that more is granted to them than to us, because the liberty
granted to us hath ceased for many years? If we have not
made use of the liberty, the fact affirmed is nothing to the purpose. If we have been denied it, such denial is an infraction of
the treaty of 1670, and proves that we have had injustice done
us by the practice of the Spaniards; but doth not help to prove
that we have had any done us by their concessions to the emperor, with whom they may keep this article, perhaps, as little
as they have done with us, and who is not likely to have the
same means of obliging them to it as we have in our power,
whenever we please to employ them.

How the eighth article of the treaty of Utrecht came to be
quoted, on this occasion, is to me marvellous. That article is
made general to all nations: but was particularly directed against
the French, who, even at that time, continued to obtain licenses
to send ships to trade in the South Sea, as they had done all the
war. But the treaty of Utrecht confirms the treaty of 1670; and
the stipulation, that "no license, or any permission at all, shall
at any time be given to the French, or any other nation whatsoever—to sail, traffic, &c. to the dominions subject to the crown
of Spain in America," cannot surely be construed to deprive us
of the right of going into those parts, in the cases allowed by the
treaty of 1670. This seems so clear, that I may pronounce the gentleman given up, on this head, by the most knowing merchants,
and by every man who can read and understand what he reads.

But I may go farther, for it appears even from the fifth article
of the provisional treaty itself, which is said to secure us from
the dangerous engagement contained in the treaties of Vienna,

with relation to trade, that the king of Spain "never understood to grant, by the said treaty, any privileges contrary to the treaties confirmed above; nor to give to his imperial majesty any greater advantages than those enjoyed by other nations in their commerce; his imperial majesty adopting for his subjects the above mentioned declaration, made in the name of his catholic majesty." And it is very observable that this article seems to be inserted in the treaty, merely upon the surmises of the ministers of France, Great Britain and Holland, who have pretended, as it is said in the introduction to it, "that in the treaty of commerce, concluded at Vienna on the first of May, 1725—there were divers clauses, which clashed with articles of several treaties of commerce, anterior to the year 1725," &c.

If, therefore, the natural sense of the Vienna treaty itself, as well as the declaration of their imperial and catholic majesties, as soon as the objection was first started, and their offer to remove any supposed ambiguity in this article of the Vienna treaty, were not sufficient to satisfy us, what farther satisfaction shall we receive by the provisional treaty, in case it should be accepted, which contains only the very same declaration?—But this hath been sufficiently explained already by your correspondent Raleigh.

As to the Ostend trade, he thinks that I myself cannot be against him, unless in the degree of the importance of it. Now this is the very point upon which he must be given up, in this case, if he is given up at all. I never heard that any man was wild enough to affirm, that the trade carried on from Ostend, was of no consequence whatever to us. But the question is, whether that trade be of that degree of importance to us which he represents. He asks, "who of those I oppose hath declared against him in this?" I answer, the very person I quoted in the passage he had before his eyes, when he asked this question. He says, in the Inquiry, "that our East and West India trade will be ruined by the Ostend company; that they are so already, in some degree; that the contagion will spread to other branches; in short, that this trade will carry riches, strength, and naval power from us to the Spanish Netherlands." What says Publicola? "The Ostend trade, about which such a noise hath been made," (he must mean by the Inquirer, since the Inquirer made more noise about it than all the other writers put together,) "was more the concern of our neighbors, both by treaty and interest, than our own." I appeal now, in my turn; and I appeal to the Inquirer himself. Is not one of these representations directly contrary to the other? Does not Publicola diminish the consequences of the Ostend trade to us, and treat it even lightly? Does not he magnify it, in the strongest terms, and make our all

depend upon the obstruction of it?   Does not Publicola, an author whom I oppose, give him up?

We are now come to the danger, much insisted upon in the
Inquiry,* " of having Gibraltar wrested out of our hands by
force, if it be possible, unless we will basely yield it up;" and
this danger is grounded on a supposed† mutual engagement
between the emperor and king of Spain, contained in a secret
offensive treaty.   The writer of the Inquiry confesses, " that
the imperial resident read to some of our ministers the words,
which he said were the contents of the article which his master
had entered into, relating to Gibraltar; the which implied, that
his master had engaged to use his good offices for the restitution
of Gibraltar."   Now from hence, because this resident read all
that related to this point, and did not show the whole treaty to
us, any more than we thought ourselves obliged to show to the
imperial ministers the treaties of 1721; which we made at Madrid
with one of the parties between whom we were at that time
mediators, in the congress at Cambray; from hence, I say, the
writer I am answering concludes that the truth of what he imputes to the emperor stands confirmed: but this offensive alliance
hath appeared hitherto nowhere, except in his writings; and the
article relating to Gibraltar, in the defensive alliance between
the emperor and king of Spain, is surely as contrary as possible
to all that he hath advanced.   By that article it appears, that the
Spaniards affirmed a promise on our part to restore Gibraltar.
In consideration of this promise, the emperor declares he will
not oppose this restitution, if it be made amicably; that if it be
necessary, he will employ his good offices, and even his mediation, if the parties desire it.   Till therefore the Inquirer can show
another article between the contracting powers in the Vienna
treaties, about Gibraltar, this must be reputed the sole article of
that kind, and by consequence a flat contradiction to all that he
hath said on this occasion; so that if his own side do not give
him up in this case, both they and he will be given up, I fear, in
the opinion of every other man in Europe; to which I shall add,
since the observation lies fairly in my way, that every man, who
knows anything of the interest of Europe, knows it as much the
interest of the emperor, that Britain should keep Gibraltar, as
it is the interest of one of our allies that we should lose the possession of this place; and yet we have been taught, by some
profound statesmen, to apprehend the emperor's efforts to take
it from us, and to rely on the assistance of France to preserve it
to us.

I have reserved to the last the greatest of all those dangers,

* Page 57.   † Page 34, 35.

which are represented in the Inquiry; and that is the danger of the Pretender.

It is there affirmed,* "that one express article of the alliance between the emperor and Spain, contained an obligation in favor of the Pretender, and a stipulation to make the attempt for him in England, before opening the war in any other parts." Nay, this author was so well informed of all these proceedings, that he gives us the particular engagements which the Pretender, in return, took towards the emperor and Spain. All these things are asserted in the strongest manner, as founded on " positive intelligence; on intelligence from more than one person; on undoubted intelligence; and such as could be entirely depended on." Now I suspect that the Inquirer would think me very impertinent, if I should seem to question the authority of his intelligence; and yet I verily believe, that I have better reasons to do so than he had to depend upon it, when he wrote the words I have quoted. But we will waive saying anything more on a point on which it is proper for neither of us to speak plain. His good opinion of the intelligence communicated to him will not give it the stamp of infallibility; nor will my bad opinion destroy its credit. The world will therefore judge, or rather has judged, of the validity of what he does not explain, by the force or weakness of the other circumstances which he enlarges upon; and by observing whether the course of events hath justified this boasted intelligence or not. I have just mentioned above the chief of these circumstances; and notwithstanding the great respect I have for this author, nothing shall oblige me to treat them more seriously. I will show him, however, that the course of events hath destroyed all the use he pretended to make of these circumstances, and that it has contradicted, instead of confirming his intelligence. He says,† " that the vigorous resolutions taken, and the preparations and dispositions made by Great Britain, suspended the execution of this design. The Spaniards found themselves obliged to send part of their ships from Cadiz and St. Andero to the West Indies, and the Muscovite ships returned home." Very well! The event does not yet justify the intelligence; but that is accounted for. The execution of the design was suspended for the present. The design went on then; and the preparations for an invasion by consequence. It must have been so; for we find in the Inquiry,‡ that the design thus suspended was afterwards prevented by the appearance of a British fleet on the Spanish coast. Now let me desire you, Mr. D'Anvers, to take the trouble of turning to Sir John Jenning's letter, dated August 10, 1726, and made public

* Page 52.   † Page 51.   ‡ Page 97.
x*

here; in which you will find the Spaniards so little prepared to invade us, that when he came on their coast, they seemed to be in the greatest consternation; that all the troops they could assemble did not exceed three thousand men, and that these were in very bad condition.

I ask now, is the intelligence of the Inquirer, upon this head, supported by anything but his own affirmation? Is it not contradicted by the whole course of events? Does there appear the least reason to believe that he had a sure foundation to build upon, when he made such bold assertions, and of such a nature? The secret offensive treaty, which he talks so much of, has never appeared, nor any footsteps of it; and many people are apt to believe that it never existed anywhere but in some people's luxuriant fancy. The several treaties made at Vienna in 1725, between the emperor and Spain, have been long public; and when it was observed, somewhere or other, that nothing was contained in them like what the Inquirer had asserted, the Inquirer was given up. He was said to be mistaken. The article, in favor of the Pretender, was said to be in some other treaty; and afterwards in no formal treaty. It was not a treaty. It was an engagement. This may be called, by some ill-bred people, shuffling: but sure I am that it must pass for a direct giving up of this author; who will find, perhaps, if he pleases to inquire into the particulars of what passed on this occasion, that the person who gave him thus up, had some share in setting him to work.

After this, it is hardly worth notice, that the author of the " Observations on the Conduct of Great Britain," has given him up likewise; for the utmost which this writer ventures to say, when he comes to speak of this engagement, asserted by the Inquirer to be contained in an article of a treaty, is this; " our apprehensions were that there might be engagements in favor of the Pretender." Let the Inquirer consider again, whether I was in the wrong to advance, that he had been given up, even by his own side.

Having justified what I presumed to advance concerning the Inquiry, I come now to the Defence of it.

The gentleman begins this defence by stating the case, so he calls it, as he did in the Inquiry; and then he proceeds to take notice of what hath followed since the date of that book; that is to say, he represents the matter in dispute just as it suits his purpose; leaving out many things necessary to set the whole in a true light; asserting some things which have never been proved, and others, which I think never can be proved; making what insinuations, drawing what conclusions he thinks fit; and, in a word, begging the question in almost every line. It is hard to conceive for what purpose this is done. The reason given, I am sure, is not a good one, since the principal facts and reasonings upon which the strength of all that can be said must be founded, are so far from seeming to be forgot, that they seem to be the only things remembered, or thought of at this time, and are the common topics of almost every conversation. There must therefore be some other reason for this method of proceeding—and I can guess but one. This method may perhaps be thought proper to catch unwary readers, and to give a particular bias to their minds, with which they are to read and to judge of all that follows. I could make use of the same art; and, without being at much pains, draw up a state of the case very contrary to that which he hath drawn, and at least as plausible. But I think the proceeding too unfair to copy after it. I have indeed no reason to do so; since, very different to all other considerations, I seek nothing in this dispute but the discovery of the truth: and, therefore, as I will receive nothing but what is supported by the evidence of fact, and the force of argument, so I will not presume to attempt imposing anything, void of both, upon others. Besides, this gentleman undertakes to " consider what I have advanced, either against anything, in which he can be supposed to be concerned; or upon any subject of debate (of this debate he means) which appears to him to be of importance:" so that if I am able to refute all that he objects to me, in the Defence of this Inquiry, I refute all objections, of any importance, to what I have said in my former letter to you; and then I imagine that his state of the case will do him no great honor, and his cause little good.

The first point on which I am attacked by the defender of the Inquiry is, on the turn, as he so calls it, which I have given to the very beginning of this whole scene. He means the Vienna alliance.

Let us see, therefore, whether it is he or I, for one of us may, perhaps, have done so, who hath endeavored, in treating this subject, to turn everything to the service of some other cause than that of truth.

In the Inquiry he represented the Vienna alliance, as to the manner, and as to the matter of it, to be one of the most astonishing phenomena which ever appeared in the political world. What surprise to see two princes, rivals almost from their infancy, "two powers, that could hardly be kept within the bounds of common decency towards one another, privately running into one another's arms," as he expresses himself? What a suprise to see the emperor abandon the mediation of Great Britain and France; to the first of whom he and his family owed so many obligations; and to the last of whom, in conjunction with the first, he owed the acquisition of Sicily, and the other advantages of the quadruple alliance? What a surprise to see Spain abandon this media-

tion, just in the moment, as my adversary has extremely well
observed, when the interests of the Duke of Parma were in agitation, interests which Spain had extremely at heart, and in the
supporting which, she had reason to think herself sure of success
against the emperor, because the mediators had taken secret engagements with her to favor these interests, by one of the treaties
made at Madrid in 1721? What a surprise to see Spain do this,
and, in doing it, not only forego the advantages which the mediators had procured, and were to procure for her, in many respects;
particularly, in that favorite point, the succession of Don Carlos;
but make so bad a bargain for herself at Vienna, that the emperor, according to this author, and indeed I think according to the
truth, " gained every thing, and particularly the guaranty of his
own succession?"

All this, it must be confessed, appeared wonderful, and excited
a strong curiosity to know what were the springs of so great, and,
according to these representations, so sudden a revolution of counsels and interests. But here we were dropped. The Inquirer
spent much time, and took much pains to show what did not occasion it; but I have not observed, that he pretended to show what
did; unless he meant, that we should take, for causes of it, those
terrible designs which he imputes to the emperor and the king of
Spain. Our ministers, who seem to have foreseen so little that
France and Spain might break, and that the negotiations then on
foot might be thrown into confusion, or take some new course,
by this rupture, grew, it seems, prodigiously alert and sagacious
afterwards. They did not foresee what happened; but they discovered strange mysteries of iniquity concealed under this transaction, when it had happened; and these mysteries we find pomp-
ously unfolded in the Inquiry, with all the improvements and
embellishments which the author's luxuriant fancy could bestow
upon them. Now, supposing these discoveries to have been real,
the things so discovered can be looked upon no otherwise than
as circumstances of the general measure; the measure which the
emperor and Spain took, of treating by themselves and for themselves; and therefore they wanted to be accounted for as much as
the measure itself; but upon this head, I say, the Inquirer gave
us no satisfaction. Far from explaining to us what might induce
Spain to take such a resolution, at that particular point of time,
rather than at any other, he did not afford us the least hint to
guess, why we should take it at all; and yet so strange an effect
must have had some very considerable cause; too considerable
certainly to be absolutely a secret, and even beyond the reach of
conjecture.

This remarkable defect was, I believe, felt by every person
who read the Inquiry; and therefore in the progress of the dis-

pute, the writers of the same side thought it incumbent upon them to assign some cause, which might appear proportionable to such extraordinary effects; and which, at the same time, might be not inconsistent with what their great master, the Inquirer, had advanced. The task was not easy; and indeed they have succeeded accordingly. Some laid the cause of all in that inveterate rancor, which they supposed the court of Spain to have conceived against us, on two accounts; the promise made by Lord Stanhope about Gibraltar, and the defeat of the Spanish fleet in the Mediterranean. When this was exploded, and I think it was so as soon as examined, they had recourse to another system; a very strange one indeed: for it declares that the emperor, France, and Great Britain, the three contracting powers with Spain in the quadruple alliance, acted the most perfidious part imaginable in that whole proceeding; such a part as Ferdinand the Catholic, or Lewis the Eleventh, would have startled at. The succession of Don Carlos, was, it seems,* a point, which all the powers of Europe strenuously opposed; which the emperor, who had already obtained his desires in the affair of Sicily, could not be for; to which the French were averse; which Great Britain had reason to oppose and prevent; and which it was plain that the Spaniards could never carry in a congress, where every party was an enemy to their intentions. Surely nothing so extravagant, nothing so insolent as this was ever yet advanced! If you, Mr. D'Anvers, had presumed even to insinuate anything like it, I believe you would have been prosecuted with all the severity possible; and I am sure you would have been given up by all your friends. Neither can I conceive how the Inquirer, who is so zealous an asserter of our honor in the observation of treaties, could pass by such an imputation as this, without darting his thunder at the impious head who devised the slander; unless he thinks it an irremissible sin to account for anything in contradiction to himself; and a venial fault to accuse Great Britain and France, as well as the emperor, of something worse than a violation of treaties; even of making them with a design to break them; and of obliging a prince, by long negotiations, and by a war, to accept conditions, which they never intended should be made good to him.

Amongst others, I presumed, at last, to account for this great event on principles which I believed to be true, notwithstanding all that I read in the Inquiry; and which I still believe to be true, notwithstanding all that is said against them, in the Defence of the Inquiry.

The defender begins with quoting two or three passages,

* British Journal, Jan. 4.

which relate to the sending back the Infanta, and the point of
the sole mediation, out of my letter to you; and then, without
disproving the facts, or so much as mentioning the argument
grounded upon them, he pretends that the whole is hypothetical;
and thinks it would be a full and sufficient reply to me, to " frame
a scheme on the other side, and to oppose supposition to supposition, and one arbitrary interpretation of appearances to another."
After which he proceeds to frame such a scheme, partly on facts,
which he would have us believe true, and partly, as he says
himself, from his own invention; and this he thinks proper to oppose, in a ludicrous manner, to the account I have given.

Now if it shall appear, on examination, that I have built upon
undeniable facts, and have reasoned justly, instead of building
on suppositions, and giving arbitrary interpretations to appearances, this author's smartness will turn upon himself, and, instead
of showing that I deserved no answer, he will only have shown
that he was unable to give me a good one.

Let us enter into this examination.

I affirmed, and I do still affirm, that from the death of the
Duke of Orleans, the Spanish ministers were full of fears and
jealousies about the completing the Infanta's marriage with the
king of France. Neither do I find any thing urged in the Defence of the Inquiry, to destroy the credibility of this fact.—
Indeed, if it was proper to descend into particulars of so delicate
a nature, it would not be at all difficult to demonstrate, from a
consideration of the change which was made in the French ministry, and of the difference of personal situations, interests and
views, that although there never could have been room for such
fears and jealousies as these, while the Duke of Orleans had
lived, yet there was great room for entertaining them, under the
administration of his successor. But this is not all. These fears
and jealousies increased and strengthened daily, in the minds of
the Spanish ministers; and if this author pleases to inquire, I
believe he will find, or else his prompters deal very unfairly by
him, that the delay and excuses of the court of France, about
performing the cermony of the Fiancialles, which Spain expected should have been performed soon after the time at which the
Duke of Orleans died, confirmed, in the highest degree, the
suspicions already taken. The ceremony of the Fiancialles
would have secured the marriage. What other effect then could
excuses and delays in this affair produce, but that which I have
mentioned?

The Inquiry* says, " that the resolution of the court of France,
relating to the Infanta, did not come, no, not in suspicion to Ma-

* Page 15.

drid, till March 8, N. S. 1724–5." If he means the particular
resolution of sending her back at such a determinate time, that
is nothing to the purpose, how much soever the affirmation
might impose, when it was made use of at first, and before this
matter had been sufficiently canvassed. But if the resolution of
sending the Infanta back, at some time or other; in plain terms
the resolution of not completing her marriage with the king of
France be meant; then, I say, that I might very justly have set
this assertion down in the list of those which are made in the
book without a strict regard to truth; for it is undeniably true,
that the Spanish ministers in foreign courts, entertained this suspicion above a year before that time. It is equally true, that
several months before that time they spoke of this measure as a
thing they expected, and I add, that several private persons, at
least, wrote from Madrid in the same style, to their correspondents
in other countries. Of all this I am as sure as I am sure I now
hold a pen in my hand; or that a pamphlet called " A Defence
of the Inquiry," is now lying before me; and therefore neither
the authority of the Inquiry, nor any better authority can persuade me, that the suspicion of a design to send the Infanta back
from France, did not come to Madrid till March 1724–5; because it would be absurd to believe, that the ministers of that
court were less informed or less jealous about an affair of this
importance, than private persons; or that the repeated advices
which must have come from the Spanish ministers abroad, made
no impression upon those at home.

This fact is, I think pretty well established; and the others I
am to mention will occasion no dispute. They are these. The
Spaniards* first took the resolution of throwing off the mediation,
and of treating at Vienna, in November 1724; and Ripperda's
full powers were signed, according to the Inquiry, on the 22d of
that month; that is, about a year after the death of the Duke of
Orleans. Soon after this, the negotiation was begun; but the
treaties, in which it terminated, were not signed till the last of
April and the first of May, 1725.

These, I presume, are facts, and not suppositions. Let it now
be considered how I argue upon them, and whether my reasoning be nothing more than an arbitrary interpretation of appearances, as the author of the Defence has rashly pronounced, but
not ventured to attempt to prove. The sum of my argument is
this. Since the Spaniards expected that the Infanta would be, a
little sooner or a little later, sent back from France, they expected
to find themselves, a little sooner, or a little later, obliged in honor
to show a due resentment to this affront, to send back the prin-

* Inquiry, p. 15.

cesses of the house of Bourbon from Spain, and to break off that correspondence which had subsisted between the two courts, from Spain's accession to the quadruple alliance, and which had been so intimate during the life of the Duke of Orleans. They could not foresee how long this rupture might last, because they could not foresee how soon a change would be made in the French ministry, and the satisfaction be given them for this affront; but they could not fail to foresee, that if this event should happen during the congress of Cambray, something worse than the affront would follow, and they must remain in the most abandoned condition imaginable; broke with one mediator; not sure of the other; the emperor in the possession of Sicily; and the reciprocal condition, in favor of Don Carlos, not effectually secured to them. These things are so intimately and so necessarily tied together, that I can as little discover how it is possible to allow the first fact which regards the suspicions and expectations of the Spaniards, and deny the consequences which follow, as I can see how it is possible to contradict, with the least appearance of reason, a fact so publicly known, supported by so many circumstances, and justified by so many consequences as the first is. The probable arguments employed in the Defence, and which, it may be pretended, will serve to prove that though the fact were true, and the suspicion I have insisted on was entertained by the court of Madrid, yet that it did not produce the effects of throwing Spain into the engagement she took at Vienna, will be considered presently.

Thus far then, we have a deduction of facts, not of suppositions; so we have a thread of consequential arguments, not a rhapsody of arbitrary interpretations of appearances. The case is fairly stated, and no imaginary scheme is offered to be imposed for truth. The probability, which results from this state, is confirmed, and I think turned into certainty by the event. By the state above mentioned, it was probable that Spain would take measures, in time, against the distress to which she must foresee that she stood exposed. Accordingly, the Spaniards began to treat at Vienna before the Infanta was sent from France, which is a fact allowed on all hands, that they might prepare for the worst; and when I add, that they delayed concluding their treaty, or that the conclusion of their treaty was delayed till what they feared happened, what do I affirm more than what my adversary allows? He had said, at first, that the "treaty of peace was signed at Vienna, before what Spain feared from France was known there." He has corrected this assertion, and has said, "that, as the treaty of peace was agreed to at Vienna before what Spain feared from France was known at Vienna to have happened, so it was signed before the refusal of Britain could be known there;" that is, the refusal of the sole mediation. The first point then is yielded to me. The Spaniards did not actually sign at Vienna, till the news came thither, of the Infanta's being actually sent from France; though they had settled and agreed their terms with the imperialists, on the knowledge that she would be sent away. On the second point, all that I urged, as fact or argument, stands in the same force as it did before; for I desire this author may not be indulged in a liberty I shall never take with him or any one else, the liberty of carrying my affirmations, by strained constructions, farther than the plain and natural import of the terms I employ.

In opposition to Publicola, I showed that the manner in which he affirmed the treaty of Vienna to have been signed before the refusal of the mediation was known there, did not refute Raleigh, on account of some possible circumstances there mentioned. Now this author has been forced to leave the proof, drawn from those possible circumstances, just as he found it. " There is no proof, says he, "but the bare possibility here insisted on." I say no more. The argument is as strong against him, as against Publicola; for even after the advantages taken over Publicola, for not expressing himself clearly, this author has, for reasons easy to be guessed, expressed himself in a manner liable to the same objection. " The peace was signed," he says, " before the refusal of Britain could be known. What! before it could be known by certain and direct intelligence, or before it could be known in form, after the tedious round which this resolution was to take? That is not explained; and yet that was the single point on which anything could be said to the purpose. In short, we pursued with great steadiness, our wise maxims of neglecting Spain, and of adhering closely to France; in so much that those who wished us no good, were perhaps heard, when they insinuated that, far from contributing to ward off a blow so much apprehended by Spain, we privately abetted France, in her design of breaking the match, and imagined by that measure to establish an irreconcilable quarrel between the two courts. The Spaniards, as well as the imperialists, had reason so believe, from our whole conduct, that we should not accept the sole mediation, which had been offered to us; and was it then strange that the former, neglected by us, provoked by France, should press the signing this treaty, without waiting long for our answer; or that the emperor who got so much by the bargain, should consent to it?

Having been thus led to the affair of the sole mediation, which I had hitherto omitted to speak of, in order to avoid confusion, I shall consider it here, as far as this author has made it necessary for me. In my letter to you, Mr. D'Anvers, I dwelt a good deal upon it. I placed it in every light, and debated all the merits of the cause, as well as I was able. Now, if what I urged was absurd and nothing to the purpose, this author should have shown, in general, that it did not deserve a more particular answer. If what I urged was clear and strong, as some people imagine it was, this author, who declares himself, in every point, of a contrary opinion, should have the goodness to examine and refute my arguments. How it happens I know not; but this great master of polemical writing has, in every instance, upon this occasion, avoided to enter into the argument. He has dwelt on the outside of things, and has generally cavilled at circumstances.

I have just now given a strong instance of this; and I lay hold of the opportunity to tell this gentleman, that I am no apologist for Spain, though he endeavors to fix that character upon me by an innuendo, so very fine, that I was for some time at a loss to find out his meaning. I neither sounded to arms against the Spaniards, two years ago; nor am, at present, an advocate for bearing their delays and their insults. I neither aggravated, two years ago, the depredations and hostilities committed in the West Indies by the Spaniards;* "and those violences, by which the whole commerce of Jamaica hath been well nigh destroyed, and the trade of that island reduced to a miserable condition;" nor do I now soften in their favor, and call these outrages and losses by the gentle name of "inconveniences attending a state of uncertainty."†

But to return. Having given an instance of this author's cavilling at circumstances not material in the dispute, I shall now give some instances of his affirming over again, by way of answer, what had been refuted before; and when I have done this, I shall have taken notice of all that he says upon the subject of the sole mediation.

First then he says, that the knowledge of the negotiations going on at Vienna was a just reason to decline this offer, which he supposes to have been a mere piece of mockery. But he does not so much as pretend to say a word, in answer to what I insisted upon, as an advantage in accepting this mediation, even supposing it offered to us without any design that we should concern ourselves in it. He does not pretend so much as to controvert what I urged, to prove that the worse opinion we had of the designs carried on at Vienna, the more reason there was to catch at this offer of the mediation.

Secondly, he insists, that we could not accept this mediation, with a due regard to our alliance with France; and he supposes, that this reason will be thought just by "all those who do not think the breach of faith, and the violation of treaties, matters of no concern." Here again is another charitable innuendo.

---

* Inquiry, page 60.   † Defence, page 13.

But let it pass. It would be easy to strengthen all that was said on this subject, in my letter to you, by showing the difference between such a stipulation as this of a joint mediation, and the covenants which princes and states enter into with one another, about their mutual interests. But there is no need of it, since this author, who thinks fit to insist on this point, hath not thought fit to answer any one of the arguments urged by me, to prove that France could not have complained of us, if we had accepted this mediation; and yet there were some dilemmas laid down, which seemed to deserve a solution.

Lastly, he pretends that I affirmed, against the most public facts, and the plainest appearances, what I said to show that our acceptance of the mediation would have been agreeable to France: and yet what I said was founded on public facts, and the plainest appearances; which he has not touched, because he durst not deny them. It is really very strange, that so considerable an author should continue to write, when he can neither find out new arguments, nor answer the objections made to old ones.

Having now despatched the point of the sole mediation, it remains that I say something to those probable arguments, if they deserve that name, which I have civilly given them, by which this gentleman pretends to destroy what is, I think, established on the solid foundation of fact and reason, concerning the measure taken in France after the death of the late Duke of Orleans, to break the match with the Infanta, and the consequence of that measure, the throwing Spain into the hands of the emperor.

Now the first of these arguments is, that the court of Spain did not mention this affront from France, as any inducement to the transaction at Vienna; and that any such mention would have been inconsistent with other declarations made to Mr. Stanhope at Madrid. Very well. It is then an established rule, that we are not to believe a court has motives for their conduct, which motives they do not own, although we have the strongest reasons imaginable to believe such motives true. Another rule, which this author would do well to establish at the same time, and which is founded on as much reason as the former, is this; that we are to believe all the motives which a court thinks fit to give out, to account for their conduct, although we have the plainest proofs imaginable that these motives are false. Such a logic as this was never introduced into politics, I believe, before; and I am persuaded that you, Mr. D'Anvers, will excuse me, if I spend no time in answering it. Let me desire you, however, before I leave this argument, to turn to the thirteenth and fourteenth pages of the Inquiry, where you will find that the Inquirer says, the imperial ministers at Cambray, at London and at Paris, talked the very language, which the defender of the Inquiry says the Spaniards were always ashamed to make use of.* Nay, the Inquirer adds, that "upon the first public news of the Vienna treaty at Madrid, the discourses of many were taught to run that way, and to dwell upon that same popular topic."

The second of these arguments is this. If the news of sending back the Infanta from France, and of Great Britain's refusing the sole mediation, had both come to Madrid before Ripperda was sent from thence; even this "could not have really been, and would not have been pretended to have been the motive of what was afterwards done at Vienna." And why, pray? Because when the news of our refusing the sole mediation did come, the court of Spain acknowledged it to be a reasonable proceeding. This, you see, is built on the principles laid down in the last article, and deserves no farther notice. But on the news coming to Madrid, that the Infanta was sent home, he confesses that " the court of Spain might, by such circumstances, be induced to try to what honorable terms the emperor would come." This concession goes farther than he is aware of; for I desire to know, if it is reasonable to believe that Spain would have treated with the emperor, when the case had happened, why it is unreasonable to believe that Spain did begin to treat with him on almost a certain prospect that the case would happen, which is the great point we have been contending about? Ay, but Spain would not have treated with the emperor to hurt Holland and Britain, because Spain had been hurt by France; nor would the emperor have entered into a treaty to hurt him, who had no part in the affront to Spain and never injured the emperor. Again; much less would the king of Spain send a minister to Vienna to enter into and finish treaties, which should hurt other nations, upon a suspicion that France would hereafter affront him. I could make several reflections on some of the expressions in this place; and on the turn, which the author takes, of putting some very odd arguments into my mouth; and, what is still more, into the mouths of the emperor and the king of Spain. But I forbear; and content myself with saying two things, which will effectually blunt the point of all the wit employed in this paragraph, and fully answer the whole of what is said farther upon this subject, in the Defence of the Inquiry.

First, then; as far as I am from being, or pretending to be, a master in politics, which degree this writer seems to have taken long ago, I never imagined that the affront, considered merely as an affront, precipitated Spain into all the engagements she took with the emperor; though, by the way, he mistakes very much, if he thinks, as he says, that he may deny new fresh resentments to determine the conduct of princes, exactly upon the same grounds, as I have denied that old stale resentments have this effect. What I imagined, what I said, and what I proved was, that this affront, considered as a necessary breach with France, at least for a time, would throw Spain into such circumstances of distress, as she was to prevent by all possible means; and that therefore reasons of state determined in this case; though no doubt the affront, at the same time, provoked the Spaniards.— Thus I am consistent with myself; and the author might have spared himself the trouble of writing this elaborate paragraph, if he had adverted to my sense, instead of playing with my words.

Secondly; as to the emperor, our author is guilty of begging the question; for the emperor will insist, as he has insisted, that his engagements were not engagements to injure any body; that he entered into no offensive alliance; and that, when he exacted from Spain the guaranty of the Ostend trade, and of his succession, he exacted the guaranty of nothing but of that, which he judges he has an independent right to establish and secure.   As to Spain, it will be likewise said, that when his catholic majesty treated with the emperor, he never meant to hurt other nations, but to secure his own interests; that if his guaranty of the Ostend trade hurts the Dutch or us, he is sorry for it; but could no more avoid that engagement than he could several others extremely disadvantageous to himself, and into which he was however obliged to enter, because he was obliged to purchase the emperor's alliance at any rate; that therefore we must not blame him, who opposed the establishment of the Ostend company, whilst he could do it, without any support from us; who never gave his guaranty to it, till he was forced to do so, by the necessity of his affairs; into which necessity he was falling for above a year together, without seeing the hand of Britain once stretched forth to hinder it.   Such answers as these would certainly be given; and, in the mouths of the imperialists and the Spaniards, they would be just.

If, after all that has been said, this gentleman is unable, upon my notions, to account for the king of Spain's resolute flying from the mediatorship of France, I am sure it is not my fault.— A few sacrifices did indeed help to pacify Spain, and to reconcile her to France; and a few sacrifices might, for aught I know, have reconciled our quarrels; or, which is better, have prevented them.   But as no one can foresee now when such sacrifices will be made here; so neither could Spain, at the time when she sent to Vienna, foresee when such sacrifices would be made in France.

Upon the whole matter, and to conclude this tedious article; if the way in which I have endeavored to account for the resolution taken by Spain to abandon the mediation of Cambray, and to treat at Vienna, be not right, I should be glad to know what the right way is. No other, which this gentleman, or any reasonable man will venture to support, has been yet pointed out. But I apprehend the account I have given to be a just one; because it is built on fact and reason; because the event hath, in every respect, confirmed it; and because it shows not only why Spain broke with France, and applied to the emperor; but why Spain entered into those new measures, after the death of the Duke of Orleans, which it cannot be pretended she ever thought of doing, while that prince was alive. If now this account be a just one, many melancholy but useful truths result from it.

But I need not point out these things. The world will discover them, without any help of mine, and will judge how well the Inquiry hath been vindicated, by the author and defender of it upon this head.

The next point, upon which my reasonings and imputations are to be tried at his tribunal, is that of Gibraltar; and here he sets out, by accusing me, not in terms indeed, but in a manner almost as plain, of lying, of direct, premeditated lying. I will keep my temper, though a field large enough is opened to me, and though the provocation is not a little aggravated by the solemn air with which this accusation is brought, by the pretences to patience and meekness and candor, and by all the appeals to God with which my accuser hath, in several parts of this treatise, endeavored to captivate the good opinion of mankind, and to establish his own reputation, that he might make sure of ruining that of others. He calls to my mind the character of Mopsus in Tasso's Aminta.

> ―――― di quel Mopso
> Ch' a ne la lingua melate parole,
> E ne le labra un' amichevol ghigno,
> ―――――――― e il rasoio
> Tien sotto il manto.

I will have the decency not to translate the verses into English.

It is not necessary that I should say much about the jealousies which this author seems to complain arose at one time, lest Gibraltar would be given up or artfully betrayed into the Spaniards' hands; nor about the vigorous defence of it, which was made afterwards. Thus much however I will say, that when Sir John Jennings was called home, with all the troops embarked on board his squadron, just before the siege, and even from the neighborhood of Gibraltar; when the Spaniards were suffered, under Sir Charles Wager's eyes, to transport by sea many things necessary for the attack of the place; and when it was known that the town wanted almost every thing necessary for the defence of it, people stood a-gaze, and not without reason. The cries of the nation precipitated at last the supplies, and the vigor of the garrison made a glorious use of them.

I come now to the accusation brought against me by this writer. I said, in my letter to you, that the Spaniards ground their present claim to the restitution of Gibraltar, on a " private article in a treaty made with them in 1721, stipulating the contents of a letter to be written by the late king, and on the letter written in pursuance of this article." This is the fact. The accusation is, that there is no such article in the treaty; and many words are employed to cut off all pretences of excuse, and to pin the lie upon me. Now I desire it may be observed, in the first place, how very exact and knowing a critic this gentleman is; who, after pronouncing with so much emphasis, that " he hath read the treaty himself, and finds no one article belonging to it, which hath the least relation to this subject," proceeds to mention the treaty, and quotes a wrong one. No man would have imagined that such a stipulation could have been supposed to be in the defensive alliance between Great Britain, France and Spain, of the thirteenth of June, 1721, who had known that there was a distinct private treaty, of the same date, between Great Britain and Spain. But this, it seems, was a secret to my accuser; though the treaty had appeared printed in the fourth volume of Rousset's collection, when he committed this mistake. It was of this treaty I meant to speak; and the reason why I expressed myself in that manner was this. I have had some years by me an extract of this very treaty, which was long kept a great secret, and for the keeping of which secret there is an express provision in the sixth article of it. When the treaty became public, I found that my extract of the several articles was exact; and therefore I gave the more credit to the separate article, mentioned in the same extract, as belonging to this treaty, and stipulating the contents of a letter to be written by the late king. The letter I never saw; but the account I have had of it by those who have read it, agrees with my extract. All this induced me to think, that there was such a separate and more private article, belonging to this private treaty: nor was I at all surprised to see the treaty come abroad without this article; knowing full well that treaties often appear, when the secret articles belonging to them do not. This is a true state of the case; and will, I believe, sufficiently justify me for what I wrote. But I have not yet done with my accuser. Let it be, that no such private article, as I was led to suppose, does exist, or was ever executed. Will he venture to say that no such article was drawn up, as he expresses himself, about the treaty of pacification? Will he venture to deny that if our ministers were afraid to sign such an article, and therefore did not sign it, the reason on which

the Spaniards were induced to recede from this point, was that
something equivalent should be done; and that this something
was his late majesty's letter to the king of Spain?   I appeal, in
my turn, to the lowest observer, as well as the highest, who
hath gone about to deceive mankind, this author or I: this author
who conceals from the world what he knows, or might know,
with all the means of information which he has in his power,
and what sets the matter in quite another light than he hath
represented it: or I, who, having not the same means of information, fell into an undesigned mistake; which does not alter the
state of the case in favor of my argument, since, if the Spaniards
accepted this letter, which was written in lieu of the article which
was not signed, their pretensions, and nothing but their pretensions are under consideration here, will be still the same.

As to the letter itself, what I affirm about it is, that the
Spaniards pretend it is a positive engagement to restore Gibraltar
to them.   That this should be allowed them, I am as far from
agreeing as this author can possibly be; but that the letter is
sufficient to keep up their pretensions, I affirm: and that in fact
they do keep up their pretension on this foundation, is notorious.
Was this gentleman to dispute the point with the Spaniards, he
might comment as much, and distinguish as subtilely as he pleased,
on the terms of the letter: the others would insist, that it was
given them as an engagement: that if they had not received it
as such, they would not have departed from the article; and I
doubt they would be apt to insinuate, that we could not have
found a more proper casuist than himself, to distinguish us out
of our obligations, amongst their own schoolmen, or amongst all
the sons of Loyola.

To speak seriously; it were to be wished extremely, that the
Spaniards had not had this color for persisting in their demand
of Gibraltar, or that it had been by an express and clear stipulation taken from them; since it is certain, that the right and possession of Gibraltar is nothing less than ascertained to Great
Britain by the preliminaries, as they stand; "and consequently,
that all claim of Spain to it again is not extinguished."

I contradict him in his own words, though none of the properest; and I will prove, in what I am going to say, either that
he does not at all understand the matter he talks so magisterially
about, or that he attempts, in this instance, to deceive the world,
by giving wrong interpretations to some things, and by concealing others.

If, then, although the letter of the late king hath given the
Spaniards a pretence to claim Gibraltar, this claim is effectually
barred, and even extinguished by the first general words of the
second article of the preliminaries; how comes it to pass that

Gibraltar was not specifically mentioned, in order to prevent any
future chicane? It will be said, I know, that, as the king of
Spain's accession to the quadruple alliance vacated any promise
which my Lord Stanhope might have made; so the king of
Spain, by consenting to these preliminaries, has vacated any
engagement of this kind, which the letter may be supposed to
contain; and I, perhaps, shall be quoted again as "one who
must necessarily see the force of this argument." But this
author must not judge of my eye-sight by his own; for I see a
manifest difference between the two cases. My Lord Stanhope's
promise is said to have been conditional; all allow that it was
verbal; and I think it is allowed likewise, that the late king
never confirmed it. The simple accession of the king of Spain
to the quadruple alliance, might therefore be thought very justly
sufficient to put the matter, at that time out of all dispute, for
the reasons given by me, and quoted by this author. But when
the preliminaries were to be settled, the king of Spain's claim
to the restitution of Gibraltar rested on an engagement, or what
he took for an engagement entered into by the late king, and
under his majesty's own hand. Besides, this engagement, or
promise, whether valid or not valid, had been insisted upon as
valid, in a formal treaty, and had been made the foundation of
the second article in the defensive alliance between the emperor
and the king of Spain, which relates to Gibraltar. It required
therefore something more to put an end to a claim founded in
this manner, than to a claim founded on any promise that my
Lord Stanhope could make. These considerations could never
escape the penetration of that most able minister, who negotiated
the preliminaries; and therefore I conclude, first, that the Spaniards would not consent that Gibraltar should be mentioned
specifically in the second article; and, in the next place, that
they could refuse to consent to it on no reason whatever, but
this one; that their pretensions to Gibraltar would be kept alive,
if it was not mentioned specifically, notwithstanding the general
words so much insisted upon by this writer. He has not therefore answered my demand; nor shown "in the preliminaries an
article which is indeed as express and effectual a confirmation
of our right to Gibraltar, as if the word Gibraltar had been put
into it." But he goes on, and observes, "that the latter part of
this second article greatly strengthens the former; because it is
there stipulated, that if any thing shall have been altered with
respect to rights and possessions, or not have been put in execution, the alteration made, or the thing not executed, is to be
discussed in the congress, and decided according to the tenor of
the said treaties and conventions;" that is, in his sense, according
to the tenor of the treaty of Utrecht, and of the quadruple alli-

ance; for he mentions no other, except that of Baden, which
hath nothing to do here.   Now, says he, " nothing, either as to
the right of Great Britain to Gibraltar, or to the possession of it,
hath been at all altered; nor hath there been any non-execution,"
&c.   From whence he infers, that our right to Gibraltar is not
included in this description of points left to be discussed in the
congress.   But how could he avoid seeing that he assumes for
granted the very thing disputed?   No alteration hath been made
in " our right to Gibraltar," says he; " therefore this right cannot
be discussed."   An alteration hath been made in this right, say
the Spaniards, by a private engagement taken with us in 1721;
therefore this alteration is to be discussed at the congress.   Who
doth not see, that whether this right shall be found to have been
altered, and what the alteration imports, are by this preliminary
to be discussed and decided at the congress?

I think I have now shown what I undertook, and what this
gentleman challenges me to show; that is, I have shown those
general words in the preliminaries, upon which the Spaniards
may found a pretence for reviving their demand of Gibraltar; or,
to speak more properly, since they have never ceased to make
it, for continuing this demand.   But I have undertaken something more; and therefore will proceed to show what this gentleman was ignorant of, or what he concealed very unfairly, because it is decisive against him.

I think he could hardly be ignorant that the second article of
the preliminaries, not only recalls the treaties of Utrecht and
Baden, and the quadruple alliance, as he quotes the article, but
likewise all treaties and conventions which preceded the year
1725; which latter words he does not quote.   Perhaps he judged
them unnecessary.   If he did so, he was much mistaken; for by
the fifth article of the treaty of 1721, between Great Britain and
Spain, it is declared, " that all the pretensions of both sides,
touching affairs not exposed in the present treaty, and which
pretensions are not comprehended in the second article of it,"
shall be treated of in the future congress; which was at that time
the congress at Cambray.   Now let it be observed, that the affair
of Gibraltar is not one of the affairs exposed in this treaty.   Let
it be observed also, that the pretensions of the Spaniards to Gibraltar, is not one of the pretensions comprehended in the second
article of it; and then let any man deny, if he can, that, in the
intention of Spain, these words were relative to the pretension,
which she acquired by the private engagement taken in the
letter so often quoted.   If the letter gave her a right, as she insists, it gave her a pretension certainly to claim that right, and this
pretension is carefully preserved by the treaty of 1721.   I do not
say among other pretensions; for I think I may venture to say,

that all other pretensions are specified in the treaty; even that
relating to the free exercise of the Roman catholic religion in
Minorca: and therefore these words seem to have been singly
applied to the pretensions of Spain on Gibraltar. Will not the
Spaniards now insist, upon these foundations, that they enjoyed
in 1721, a right to demand the restitution of Gibraltar, by virtue
of conventions then made; and that the second article of the preliminaries preserves entire, to all the contracting parties, whatever rights, as well as possessions, they had by virtue of any
treaty or conventions, antecedent to the year 1725; and that
therefore the first general words of the second preliminary preserve to them the right of demanding the restitution of Gibraltar,
as a right acquired by conventions made before the year 1725;
whilst the last general words of the same preliminary article preserve this right as an alteration made in the treaty of Utrecht
and in the quadruple alliance?

How little weight soever the defender of the Inquiry may
allow to these observations, which would I doubt have some in a
congress, yet he must allow that they ought not to have escaped
him, or to have been concealed by him; since they do certainly
affect the merits of the cause on which he has so positively pronounced judgment, without any regard to them. But I am almost ready to ask your pardon, Mr. D'Anvers, for saying so
much on this point, when there is another more clear, and more
decisive still behind. Is it possible our author should never have
heard of a certain public instrument, containing a declaration explanatory of the preliminaries made by the French minister at the
Pardo, on the fourth of March 1728, and accepted and confirmed
by himself, and by the Imperial, British, Spanish, and Dutch
ministers on the sixth of the same month? If this instrument
hath ever fallen into his hands, and it is in every body's else,
did he never read these words in it, " that all pretensions, on all
sides, shall be produced, debated, and decided in the same congress?" The disputes about contrabands, and other complaints
made by the Spaniards concerning the ship Prince Frederic, and
the disputes about the restitution of prizes, which articles are
taken notice of in the introduction to this instrument, are, by particular clauses in it, referred to the discussion and decision of the
congress. To what purpose then were these general words inserted? To what purpose was it stipulated that all pretensions
whatsoever (among which the pretension of the Spaniards to the
restitution of Gibraltar must necessarily be included; since,
whether ill or well founded, it is still a pretension on their side)
shall likewise be referred to the congress; and that his " Britannic
majesty shall be obliged to stand to what shall be decided upon
the whole?" But I forbear to press this matter any farther upon

the gentleman; since it would be, in some sort, like stabbing him on the ground.

I proceed to the article of blocking up the galleons; which is the last upon which I am attacked in the defence of the Inquiry. And here I must observe again, that he is very far from entering into a refutation of the arguments advanced by me to prove, that seizing the galleons was a measure liable to no objection, and in every respect preferable to that of blocking them up. He observes indeed, upon Mr. Hosier's letter, that the treasure had been taken from on board the galleons, when our squadron arrived before Porto Bello. Now, without making any reflections on the intelligence brought from on shore to the admiral, and taking it for granted, that all this treasure was in time removed out of his reach; it will still be true, that this circumstance proves nothing in defence of the measure taken to block up the galleons, and not to seize them; since whether they would have the riches on board them or not, when Mr. Hosier should arrive, could not be known when his instructions were drawn. If all these riches had been actually at Porto Bello, when he came thither, he would have had, in effect, nothing more to say to the Spaniards, than what the orders they had received ten days before from Old Spain imported; which was, that they should secure the money in the country.

The single point, insisted upon to justify this measure, and which the writer pronounces to be sufficient, is that the contrary measure, that of seizing the galleons in port, with all their treasure on board, if it had been practicable, would "have put Europe into a flame, by putting all the proprietors of those riches, whether French, Dutch or Spanish, into the greatest uneasiness." At the same time he allows that taking these ships, if they "had attempted, by force or stealth, to come out, had been reasonable." Sure I am it is enough to say in reply to this, that as to the uneasiness which such a seizure might have given the Spanish proprietors, it deserved no consideration; that the French and Dutch proprietors would have believed, or ought to have believed, their effects as secure in our hands, as in the hands of Spain; especially in a point of time, when they were, by treaty at least, engaged on our side in opposition to Spain; and lastly, that the distinction between seizing the galleons at sea, or blocking them up in port, as if one was, and the other was not an hostility, is very manifestly a distinction without a difference; to prove which, I dare appeal to every man in Britain, whether he would not esteem the hostility as great, and the insult greater, if a Spanish squadron should block up Portsmouth, than if it should cruize in the channel, and take our ships at sea. The gentleman cuts the dispute short, by referring us to the observations on the conduct of Great Britain; and I shall readily join issue with him, by referring, on my side, to the Craftsman Extraordinary, in which these observations are fully answered, and treated as they deserved to be.

Having mentioned the galleons, our author could not avoid taking some notice of a question I asked, in answering Publicola, and which he allows to be very material. His answer to it deserves a short reflection or two. " Since the galleons are coming home, hath Spain renounced those designs, which our fleet was sent to the West-Indies to prevent?" Thus he states the question: and his answer is, " Truly I cannot tell; nor can any one in the world, who is not in the secrets of the court of Spain."— A little afterwards he asks the same question; " Has the king of Spain renounced his projects?" that is, those designs which our fleet was sent to the West-Indies to prevent? His answer is, " Yes, undoubtedly, as far as articles ratified by him can bind; and as far as any contracting powers can be bound by treaty to one another." Let us see what is urged between the first and the second asking of the same question, to produce such a wide difference in the answers. The king of Spain hath ratified the preliminaries, in consequence of which the siege of Gibraltar is raised. Orders are sent to restore the South Sea ship; and he has promised that the effects of the galleons shall be delivered. He hath therefore renounced his projects by treaty; but whether he hath renounced them in his heart; " whether he will go on to act an open and honest part," that is more than our author can tell. It is more likewise than any one will desire, that he or those, for whom he is an apologist, should pretend to tell, or be answerable for. But let us see what they are answerable for; what has been really done by treaty; what we have obtained to make us some amends for the rotting of our ships; for the loss of so many thousand lives, and for the depredations and hostilities which this author sounded so high formerly; and which were carried on with redoubled vigor, during the pacific blockade of the galleons—The effects of the galleons are to be delivered. I congratulate the Dutch and the French upon it; but especially the latter, who have such immense wealth on board them. Our share is, I fear, a small one; too small to bear any proportion to the expense we have been at, or the losses we have sustained Orders are sent to restore the South Sea ship; but the claims of the Spaniards either on that ship, or on any account, are preserved to them, and referred to a congress, by whose decision we must abide; and nothing is stipulated, which may secure to our merchants a just recompense for the numberless seizures and captures of their effects and ships.—The siege of Gibraltar is raised; but the right to the possession of that place hath not been

effectually put beyond dispute. The obstinacy and the chicane
of the Spaniards have prevailed so far, 'that they preserve, even
by the preliminaries, a pretence for bringing this right to be decided in the congress; and I shall be glad to hear what ally we
have there, on whose good offices we can depend for securing to
us the right of possessing, and the possession of this important
place. Upon the whole, I am extremely sorry to find, that I was
so much in the right, when I advanced that no man could say,
with truth, that the main things in dispute between us and Spain,
were yielded to us before the return of the galleons; unless he
reckoned our keeping Gibraltar, and I might have added the
procuring satisfaction to our merchants, not among the main
things in dispute, but among those of less importance. I say
very sincerely, that I had much rather have been refuted.

It appears, I think, from what hath been said, that the author
and defender of the Inquiry, has not only been given up by his
own side, but even by himself, in several particulars; and several
other points, which were insisted upon in the Inquiry, and have
been disputed in other writings, are either not mentioned at all in
the Defence, or in such a slight manner as plainly shows the author's consciousness that he cannot support them, though he is
very unwilling to give them entirely up: so that the author gave
a very partial title to his last production, which can be justly
called, at best, a Defence only of some points in the Inquiry, and
is more properly speaking, a " Recantation of it, with a few particular exceptions."

But now, Mr. D'Anvers, what shall I say to you in excuse for
so many and such long letters? The best thing I can say, is to
assure you, and I do it very solemnly, that I will trouble you
with no more of them. The gentleman to whom I have now
replied, may inquire and defend, as much as he pleases, without
any farther molestation from me. When I began to write on
this subject, I meant nothing less than the silly ambition of having
the last word in a dispute. I saw, like every other man, the
public distress. I thought I discerned the true and original cause
of it. The affectation, which I observed to turn us off from this
scent, fortified me in my opinions, and determined me to examine
what was alleged against them. I have done so; and if in doing
it, I have contributed in any degree to open the eyes of my countrymen, on their true, and on their mistaken interests, I have
obtained the sole end which I have proposed to myself. I love
and I hate; I esteem and I despise; but in a case of this moment,
I should abhor myself, if any regard to persons, any consideration, except that of truth, had guided my hand in writing.

I began by asking pardon of this author for an injustice which
I have done him through error, not malice; and I shall conclude

with assuring him, that upon whatever principle he may have treated me, as I think I did not deserve, I lay down my resentment with my pen, and remain in Christian charity with him.

I return to the business of my low profession in life; and if I was worthy to advise him, I would advise him to return to that of his high calling—to feed the flock committed to his charge. That I may the more effectually persuade him to take a resolution so much for his own honor, and for the advantage of the church, I will exhort him to it, in the words of the apostolical constitutions, with some very little variation, in order to render the passage more applicable.

Sit autem episcopis turpis lucri non quæsitor, præsertim de Gentilibus; malitque detrimentum capere, quam inferre. Non sit avarus; non maledicus, non falsus testis, non iracundus, non contentiosus, non negotiis, litibusque secularibus implicitus; non pro alio sponsor, aut in causis pecuniariis advocatus. Non ambitiosus, non duplicis sententiæ, non bilinguis; calumniæ et maledicentiæ non cupidus auditor; non hypocrita, fallaciis vanis non utens. Quia hæc omnia Deo sunt inimica, dæmonibus grata.

Constit. Apostolic. lib. ii, cap. 6.

" Let a bishop then not be fond of making his court for gain, and especially to the Gentiles. Let him rather receive than do an injury. Let him not be given to evil speaking, nor to bear false witness. Let him not be wrathful nor contentious. Let him not be engaged in the business and disputes of the world. Let him not be ready to answer for others. Let him not be the advocate of private interest in public causes. Let him not be ambitious, nor double-minded, nor double-tongued. Let him use neither simulation nor dissimulation in his conduct; nor vain and fallacious sophisms in his discourse. For all these things are hateful to God, and pleasing to the devil."

I am, Mr. D'Anvers, &c.,
JOHN TROT.

REMARKS

ON THE

HISTORY OF ENGLAND.

Written in 1730.

LETTER I.*

SIR:

SINCE the busy scene of the year is over at home, and we may perhaps wait several months before the successful negotiations of France furnish us with new hopes of a general pacification, and give you occasion to carry your speculations forward, it may be proper enough for you to cast your eyes backwards, to reflect on your own conduct, and to call yourself to account before your own tribunal.

I am so much persuaded of the integrity of your intentions, that I do not in the least suspect you will think my advice impertinent; and therefore I shall attempt to lead your thoughts on this subject, by giving you an account of some parts of a conversation at which I happened to be present very lately.

Several of your papers, and several of those which have been written against you, lay before a company, which often meets, rather to live than to drink together; according to that distinction which Tully makes to the advantage of his own nation over the Greeks. They dispute without strife, and examine as dispassionately the events and the characters of the present age, as they reason about those which are found in history. When I came in, a gentleman was saying, that your victories had been cheaply bought; and that he had not seen one champion, able to break a

---

* As the dedication and preface, that stood at the head of these remarks, were written by another and a very inferior hand, they are therefore omitted here.

lance, enter the lists against you, upon which some were ready to observe the inconsistencies of human nature, and how hard it often proves to hire men to avow and defend even that which they are hired to act. Others were willing to hope that corruption had not spread very wide, nor taken root very deep amougst us. All agreed, that if your papers could be suspected to be written in opposition to the present ministers, the feeble and low opposition you have met with would deserve to be looked upon as a very melancholy symptom for them, since it would denote that their cause was deemed universally bad, or that their persons were grown universally odious among men of sense, ingenuity, and knowledge. It would denote their guilt, or their misfortune; perhaps both.

Here one of the company interposed, by observing very prudently, " that any thing so void of probability, as not to fall even under suspicion, was unworthy of farther consideration.   But," sad he, " whatever particular views Mr. D'Anvers may have had, one general effect, which I cannot approve, has followed from his writings.   We must remember that when he began to publish his weekly lucubrations, universal quiet prevailed, if not univeral satisfaction; for in what place, or at what time was the last ever found?   Few people inquired; fewer grumbled; none clamored; all acquiesced.   Now the humor of the nation is altered.   Every man inquires with eagerness, and examines with freedom.   All orders of men are more intent than I ever observed them to be on the course of public affairs, and deliver their judgments with less reserve upon the most important.   From this alteration, for which the Craftsman is chiefly answerable, no good consequence can, I think, proceed; and it is visible that several inconveniences may."

To this many of us could by no means assent.   We apprehend that in a country, circumstanced like ours, and under a government constituted like ours, the people had a right to be informed, and to reason about public affairs; that when wise and honest measures are pursued, and the nation reaps the advantage of them, the exercise of this right will always be agreeable to the men in power; that, indeed, if weak and wicked measures are pursued, the men in power might find the exercise of this right disagreeable, inconvenient, and sometimes dangerous to them; but that, even in this case, there would be no pretence for attempting to deprive the people of this right, or for discouraging the exercise of it: and that to forbid men to complain, when they suffer, would be an instance of tyranny but one degree below that which the triumvirs gave, during the slaughter and terror of the proscriptions, when by edict they commanded all men to be merry upon pain of death.

The person from whom we differed, brought us back to the particular case of your writings, Mr. D'Anvers. He endeavored to support what he had said against them in this manner:

"There was no good reason for raising this spirit, which I dislike, in the nation, when the Craftsman began to write, or there was such a reason. If there was none, why has he given so much alarm? If there was one, how has it come to pass that so great an alarm has produced so little effect? Will you say that he had very good reason to rouse the spirit, but that it has hitherto had no opportunity of exerting itself? Or will you say that his reasons were good and the opportunity fair, but that the minds of men, which had been convinced by the former, have not yet been determined to improve the latter? I observe on all these alternatives, that if there was no good and even pressing reason to raise such a spirit in the nation that I dislike, (because I expect no national benefit, and I fear much inconveniency from it) Mr. D'Anvers has acted a very wicked part, and is little better than a sower of sedition.—If there was such a reason, but no such opportunity, he has acted a very weak part, and is but a shallow politician.—If there was such a reason and such an opportunity, but no disposition in the minds of men to follow their conviction, you may excuse your favorite author, perhaps, by alleging that the minds of men are in the power of God alone; but you will represent our national condition to be more desperate than I ever thought it, or am yet willing to believe it.—Upon this supposition I affirm that Mr. D'Anvers is not to be excused, if he continues to write; for if he cannot raise this disposition by persuasion, what does he aim at farther? I hope that he and you, who defend him, admire as much as I profess to do that divine saying of Plato: 'We may endeavor to persuade our fellow citizens; but it is not lawful to force them even to that which is best for them.' "

Whilst all this passed, I took notice that an ancient venerable gentleman showed more emotion, and greater impatience than I remembered to have seen him ever express before. As soon as the other had concluded, he broke silence in the following manner:

"You have endeavored to prove, sir, that the Craftsman should not have begun to write; or at least that he is inexcusable for continuing. Now I not only differ from you, but I differ from you upon the very foundation on which you have established that whole argument.

"The face of things was, I agree, as calm as you represent it to have been, when my honest contemporary Caleb took up his pen. They were halcyon days truly. We were not only quiet, but we seemed implicit, and dull uniformity of eternal assent prevailed in every place. I agree that, since that time, things are very much altered. A ferment, or spirit, call it which you please, is raised; but, I bless God, it is not the blind and furious spirit of party. It is a spirit, which springs from information and conviction, that has diffused itself not only to all orders of men, as you observed, but to men of all denominations. Even they who act against it, encourage it. You cannot call it toryism, when such numbers of independent whigs avow it. To call it whigism would be improper likewise, when so many tories concur in it. He, who should call it jacobitism, would be too absurd to deserve an answer. What is it then? It is, I think, a revival of the true old English spirit, which prevailed in the days of our fathers, and which must always be national, since it has no direction but to the national interests; ' est jam una vox omnium;' and I hope we shall never have occasion to add, ' magis odio firmata quam præsidio.'

" This spirit the Craftsman has contributed to raise; and I affirm, in my turn, that supposing him to have no other reason for raising and supporting it, than a general observation of the contrary temper into which the nation had fallen, he deserves the acknowledgments of every honest man in Britain, for the part he has acted. The dispute between us is thus reduced to one single proposition; and if I prove this, all your reasoning, sir, falls of course to the ground."

The other assented; the state of the dispute was fixed; and the old gentleman proceeded in his argument to this effect:

" Give me leave to borrow, upon this occasion, an image which my lord Bacon employs, in one of his Essays, upon another. A people, who will maintain their liberties, must pray for the blessing of Judah, to avoid the fate of Issachar, the greatest curse which can befall them. Far from jogging on silently and tamely, like the ass between two burthens, such a people must preserve some of the fierceness of the lion, and even make their roar to be heard like his, whenever they are injured, or so much as threatened.

" I do not mean to recommend your seditious, rebellious spirit, which will create a perpetual scene of tumult and disorder, and expose every state to frequent and dangerous convulsions.— Neither would I be thought to approve even that popular peevishness of temper, which sometimes prevails, so as to discompose the harmony of the several orders of government.— But this I assert, and liberty cannot be long secure, in any country, unless a perpetual jealousy watches over it, and a constant determined resolution protects it in the whole body of the nation. The principle must be permanent and equal. The exercise of it ought to be proportioned to the occasions. The hundred eyes of Argus were not always kept open; but they were never all closed. The whole body of a nation may be as jealous of their liberties, as a private man of his honor. They may be, at all times, animated by a generous resolution of defending these liberties at any risk; as he may, at all times, feel in his heart the courage of venturing his life to maintain his honor. But as there is no necessary consequence from this private character to that of a quarrelsome bully; so neither is there any necessary consequence from the public character I have recommended to that of a factious, rebellious people.

" Liberty is a tender plant, which will not flourish unless the genius of the soil be proper for it; nor will any soil continue to be so long, which is not cultivated with incessant care. ' Variæ illudent pestes; mischiefs of various kinds abound;' and there is no season, in the revolution of the great political year of government, when we can say, with truth, that liberty is entirely free from immediate or remote danger.

" In every kind of government some powers must be lodged in particular men, or particular bodies of men, for the good order and preservation of the whole community. The lines which circumscribe these powers, are the bounds of separation between the prerogatives of the prince, or other magistrate, and the privileges of the people. Every step which the prince, or magistrate makes beyond these bounds, is an encroachment on liberty, and every attempt towards making such a step is a danger to liberty.

" Thus we see how great a trust is reposed in those to whom such powers are committed; and if we look into the heart of man, we shall soon discover how great, though unavoidable a temptation is laid in their way. The love of power is natural; it is insatiable; almost constantly whetted, and never cloyed by possession. If therefore all men will endeavor to increase their power, or at least to prolong and secure the enjoyment of it, according to the uncertain measure of their own passions, and not according to the stated proportion of reason and of law; and if neither one nor the other of these can be attempted without a danger to liberty; it follows undeniably that, in the nature of things, the notion of a perpetual danger to liberty is inseparable from the very notion of government.

" That these principles are true, will appear evident from practice and experience, as well as from speculation. All forms of government suppose them to be so; and in such as are not absolute monarchies we find the utmost precautions, which their several institutions admit, taken against this evil; from hence that rotation of employments in commonwealths; the annual or other more frequent elections of magistrates; and all those checks and controls, which the wisdom of legislators, prompted by experience, has invented.

"In perfect democracies these precautions have been taken in the highest degree; and yet even there they have not been always effectual. They were carried so far in the Athenian form of government, that this people seemed more in danger of falling into anarchy than tyranny; and yet one of their magistrates found means to become their tyrant, and to transmit this power to his successors.

"In mixed governments, the danger must still be greater. Such a one we may justly reckon that of Rome, as well during the regal as republican state; and surely no history can be more fruitful in examples of the danger to which liberty stands exposed from the natural, and therefore constant desire of amplifying and maintaining power, than the Roman history is, from the last of the kings to the first of the emperors.

"A monarchy, limited like ours, may be placed, for aught I know, as it has often been represented, just in the middle point; from whence a deviation leads on one hand to tyranny, and on the other to anarchy; but sure I am that if we are situated just in the middle point, the least deviation is the more cautiously to be guarded against. Liberty would be safer, perhaps, if we inclined a little more than we do to the popular side.

"It may be said, and I would anticipate the objection, that if we are thus placed, our care ought to be exerted equally against deviations on either side; and that I am the more in the wrong to appear so apprehensive of those on one side, and so little apprehensive of those on the other; because even our own history might have shown us, that deviations to the popular side have cost us at least as dear as ever those to the other side can be pretended to have done. But let it be considered;

"First, that as far as these national calamities, hinted at in the objection, have been the unvoidable consequences of methods necessary to secure or retrieve liberty, it is infamous to repine at them, whatever they have cost.

"Secondly, that the cases compared together, and supposed in this objection to be equal, are not so. I may safely appeal to every impartial reader of our history, whether any truth he collected from it ever struck him more strongly than this; that when the disputes between the king and the people have been carried to such extremes, as to draw national calamities after them, it has not been owning primarily to the obstinacy and weak management of the court, and is therefore unjustly charged on the just spirit of liberty. In truth a spirit of liberty will never destroy a free constitution; a spirit of faction may. But I appeal again, whether those of our princes, who have had sense and

virtue enough to encourage the one, have had any thing to fear
from the other.

"Now if experience shows, as I am persuaded it does, that
the prerogative and power of a prince will never be in any real
danger when he invades, neither openly nor insidiously, the
liberties of his people; the same experience will show that the
liberties of a people may be in very real danger, when, far from
invading the prerogative and power of the prince, they submit
to one, and are even so good as to increase the other.   The reason of this difference is plain.   A spirit of faction alone will be
always too weak to cope with the legal power and authority of
the crown; and the spirit of liberty, in the whole body of the
people, which contradistinguishes this case from the other, may
be raised by the fear of losing; but cannot be so raised by the
hopes of acquiring.   The fear is common to all; the hope can
only be particular to a few.   The fear, therefore, may become a
general principle of union: the hope cannot.

"But if a national spirit cannot be any other than a defensive, and therefore unprovoked, an harmless, inoffensive spirit;
that of a prince cannot, without due coercion, be kept within the
same bounds; for here the tables are turned; and the hope of
acquiring, which can never be a common principle among the
multitude, to unite and carry them into action, becomes an almost
irresistible motive to the prince; who, by yielding to it, indulges
the most powerful passions of the soul; who finds many to share
the difficulties and dangers of the enterprise with him; and who
shares the prize with none.

"Generally and abstractedly speaking, therefore, as public
liberty is more exposed under mixed governments, than under
perfect democracies; so it is more exposed under limited monarchies than under any form of mixed government.

"What increases the danger to liberty in this case is, that the
opportunity of invading it, which lies open to a sovereign prince,
suits almost any character.   The powers intrusted to other magistrates, as in a commonwealth, are subject to immediate controls,
the exercise of them is subject to future revisions, and is limited
to a short time; so that if such magistrates invade liberty, with
any prospect of success, it can only happen, when they are able
to compensate for the disadvantages of their political circumstances, by the greatness of their personal qualifications, by superior understanding and superior courage; by a great, if not a
good character, and by the appearance of virtue at least.   Few
men therefore are fit for such an undertaking.

"But the sovereign prince, who rules in a limited monarchy,
has an opportunity open to him for life; and such an opportunity
as requires extraordinary personal qualifications.   He may pos-

sess every vice or weakness, which is opposed to the virtues, or appearances of virtue, requisite in the other case, and yet may destroy the liberty of the bravest people upon earth. The pretences for concealing his designs, and the helps for carrying them on, which his situation affords above that of any magistrate in a commonwealth, will abundantly compensate for the disadvantages arising from his personal character, and will secure his success, if the people are brought, by artifice or accident, to grow remiss in watching over their liberties. Every man is therefore fit for such an undertaking. If these general reflections evince that liberty must always be in some degree of danger under every government; and that this danger must increase in proportion, as the chief powers of the state are intrusted in fewer hands and for longer terms; then liberty is always in some degree of danger; and that not the least, even under our excellent constitution; then the necessity of keeping this jealous spirit, the true guardian of public liberty, always alive and active in this nation, is manifest; then the observation of our being fallen into the contrary temper is alone a sufficient reason to justify Mr. D'Anvers for joining his endeavors to awaken us from our political lethargy; then, sir, my proposition is proved, and your reasoning falls to the ground."

This discourse furnished matter of much reflection to the company; some objections were made; some doubts were proposed; and some explanations asked for. I shall not trouble you with all these particulars, but shall conclude my letter, by relating to you in what manner the old gentleman replied, and by his reply wound up the conversation of the evening.

"I believe, gentlemen," said he, "that we do not differ so much as some of you seem to imagine: for first, though I desire the vessel of the commonwealth may sail safely, yet I desire it may sail smoothly too; and though I must think, till I hear better reasons to the contrary, that public liberty cannot be so easily attacked, and may be more easily defended, in a perfect democracy, or in a mixed republic, than in a limited monarchy; yet it will not follow necessarily from hence, as has been supposed, that I prefer the two first to the last of these forms of government. On either side there are compensations; and if liberty may be better defended in the former, yet still it may be defended, and domestic quiet is perhaps better preserved in the latter.

"Secondly, if I agree with the gentlemen who have insisted so much on the little reason which there was in the late reign, or is in the present, to apprehend any encroachments from the crown on the British liberties; these gentlemen must, I think, agree with me likewise that this will not alter the case; subvert what I have endeavored to establish; or derive any blame on those who have endeavored to revive that public spirit of watchfulness over all national interests, which is the proper and true guardian of liberty, in an age when that public spirit has more than begun to sink and die away.   I hope there will be always men found to preach this doctrine in season and out of season, as the apostles preached the gospel; because if this spirit is not kept at all times in vigor, it may fail us at some particular time, when we shall want to exert it most.   In great and immediate danger, the most sluggish sentinel is alert; but surely they who, in times of apparent security, excite us to be upon our guard, do as real service as they who animate us to our defence when we are actually attacked; and the first is, in my opinion, that kind of service of which we stand the most in need.   I confess freely, that I should not apprehend so much danger to liberty in times of suspicion, if I saw that neither power could subdue, nor artifice divert, nor pusillanimity oblige men to abandon this spirit; as I should apprehend in times of apparent security, if I observed it to be lost.   In a word, no laws, no order of government can effectually secure liberty any longer than this spirit prevails, and gives them vigor; and, therefore, you might argue as reasonably for repealing any law, or abolishing any custom, the most advantageous to liberty, and which you cannot be sure of restoring at your pleasure, because you feel no immediate want of it; as you have argued for letting this spirit die away, which you cannot be sure of reviving at your pleasure, because you perceive no immediate occasion for the exercise of it.

" I hope that I have said enough to give me a right to conclude in this manner; and if I was to descend into particular applications, of the general truths which I nave advanced, I think that no doubt whatever could remain in any of your minds, upon this subject."   After this, our company broke up.   If the same subject is resumed when they meet again, or on any other, which I judge proper to be communicated to you, it is highly probable that you will hear again from

Your admirer, friend and servant, &c.

LETTER II.

Sir:

The same company hath met, and the same subject hath been resumed; so that I think myself under an obligation of writing to you again.

The person who gave occasion to all that was said in your defence the other day, seemed very desirous that the conversation should be pursued at our last meeting; and therefore as soon as we sat down, he addressed himself thus to the old gentleman who had fought your battle.

" Sir," said he, " I own myself a good deal reconciled to the Craftsman by the discourse you held, when we were last together. That some inconveniences must follow from keeping this spirit of jealousy and watchfulness always alive, seems to me very evident; but I begin to think that this evil may be necessary, in order to secure us against greater. Every system of human invention must be liable to some objections; and it would be chimerical in us to expect a form of government liable to none. Even theocracy was attended by some real inconveniences, according to the Jewish histories; and neither the Divine presence in the tabernacle, nor the ambulant oracle, which the priest carried about with him, could preserve entire purity in religion, or good order in the state. We must be content therefore to bear the disorder I apprehend from that ferment, which a perpetual jealousy of the governors in the governed will keep up, rather than abandon that spirit, the life of which is the life of liberty. When the jealousy happens to be ill-placed, we may hope it will not rise to any great and dangerous height. When it happens to be well grounded, it may have the good effect of destroying a wicked minister, of checking a bad, or of reclaiming a misguided prince.

" You see, sir, that my conversion is pretty far advanced; and if you will please to descend into particular applications of the general doctrines you delivered, as you gave us reason to hope that you would, it is very probable that the few doubts I have still may be removed."

The rest of the company seconded this request. The good old gentleman yielded to our common desires, and spoke to the following effect:

" The general truth I am to prove by particular examples is this: that liberty cannot be preserved long by any people, who do not preserve that watchful and jealous spirit of liberty, on the necessity of which I have insisted. If you are once convinced of this truth, you will know what opinion to entertain of those who endeavor to extinguish this spirit, and those who do all they can to keep it alive.

" There are two other general truths relative to this, which I shall establish likewise by particular examples, as I go along.

" One is this: that the spirit of liberty, far from inspiring that rashness and undistinguishing fury which are peculiar to the spirit of faction, is slow to act even against the worst princes, and exerts itself in favor of the best with more effect than any other spirit whatever.

" The second is this: that how slowly soever the spirit of liberty may act in suspicious times and against encroaching governors; yet if it be kept alive, it will act effectually sooner or later, though under the greatest disadvantages, and against the most powerful opposition; in a word, in the most desperate cases.

" The first of these truths will recommend this spirit to every good prince and honest minister. The other will encourage every man who is a friend to liberty, never to abandon the cause through despondency of success, as long as he sees this spirit prevail, or even subsist.

"Having fixed these principal points of view, let us proceed: and though I would not advise you to admit the works of Machiavel into your canon of political writings; yet since in them, as in other apocryphal books, many excellent things are interspersed, let us begin by improving a hint taken from the discourses of the Italian Secretary on the first decade of Livy.

" He observes that, of all governments, those are the best, which by the natural effect of their original constitutions are frequently renewed or drawn back, as he explains his meaning, to their first principles; and that no government can be of a long duration, where this does not happen from time to time, either from the cause just mentioned, or from some accidental cause.

" The reason is obvious. There must be some good in the first principles of every government, or it could not subsist at all; much less could it make any progress. But this good degenerates, according to the natural course of things; and governments, like other mixed bodies, tend to dissolution by the changes which are wrought in the several parts, and by the unaptness and disproportion, which result from hence throughout the whole composition.

" The most effectual, and indeed the sole method of maintaining their health and prolonging their life, must therefore be to bring them back as near and as frequently as possible to those principles, on which their prosperity, strength and duration were originally founded.

" This change, or renewal of the state, hath been sometimes

wrought by external causes, as it happened at Rome, upon the invasion of the Gauls. The Romans had departed from their ancient observances. The ceremonies of religion and the laws of justice were neglected by them. An enemy, whom they despised and provoked, conquered them. The impressions made by this dreadful calamity brought them back to their first institutions and to their primitive spirit. They sprung up from this second original, as Livy calls it, with new vigor, and rose to greater fame, power and dignity than ever.

" But not to dwell on such examples, as point out to us rather the punishment of vice, than the means of reformation, let us observe that this change, or renewal of the state, is oftener and better wrought by internal causes.

" Many excellent institutions were contrived in framing the Roman government, which served to maintain in force the first principles of that political system. Such were the regulations about elections; the laws against bribery; and many other written laws, or confirmed customs. Such again was the constitution of the senate, in whom the majesty of the commonwealth resided, and whose authority controlled the licentiousness of the people. Such was the erection of that sacred, tribunitial power, whose prerogatives served to check the usurpations of the magistrates, and who could arrest with one word, even the proceedings of the senate. Such was the office of the censors, whose inquisitions and lustrations corrected abuses, reformed manners, and purged the senate itself of corrupt and unworthy members.

" These laws, these customs, these different orders, controlling one another, and promoting the general good of the commonwealth, had great effect during some centuries. But this effect could never have followed them at all, if the spirit of liberty, which had enacted these laws, established these customs, and formed these orders, had not continued. The very best laws are a dead letter, nay often a grievance, unless they are strenuously and honestly executed. They never can be so executed, unless the spirit of them possess those to whom the execution of them is committed; and it would be ridiculous to expect to find this spirit in the magistrates, and the several orders of the state, unless it appeared in the body of the people, out of whom these magistrates are chosen, and these orders composed.

" The examples which Machiavel cites to show, that the virtue of particular men among the Romans, did frequently draw that government back to its original principles, are so many proofs that the duration of liberty depends on keeping the spirit of it alive and warm. Such examples were frequent in Rome whilst this spirit flourished. As it decayed, these examples became more rare, and failed at last entirely. The old laws and customs were, for the most part, still in being. The forms of electing magistrates, and of promulgating laws, were in the main observed. There was still a senate. There were still censors and tribunes. But the spirit of liberty being stifled by that of faction and cabal, and the several orders of the government being tainted by the general corruption, these good laws and customs remained without force, or were suspended, or were abrogated, or were perverted to serve the purposes of private ambition and avarice.

" The time-serving flatterers of princes and ministers have no point, amongst all the nauseous drudgery imposed on them, which they are obliged more to labor than that of representing all the effects of a spirit of liberty as so many effects of a spirit of faction. Examples might be found, even without searching long or looking far after them, when this hath been done against the public sense of a whole nation, and sometimes in favor of a cabal, neither numerous nor considerable enough to be called a party. But still it will remain eternally true, that the spirit of liberty and the spirit of faction are not only different, but repugnant and incompatible: so that the life of either is the death or the other.

" We must not imagine that the freedom of the Romans was lost, because one party fought for the maintenance of liberty; another for the establishment of tyranny; and that the latter prevailed. No. The spirit of liberty was dead, and the spirit of faction had taken its place on both sides. As long as the former prevailed, a Roman sacrificed his own, and therefore no doubt every other personal interest, to the interest of the commonwealth. When the latter succeeded, the interest of the commonwealth was considered no otherwise than in subordination to that particular interest which each person had espoused. The principal men, instead of making their grandeur and glory consist, as they formerly had done, in that which the grandeur and glory of the commonwealth reflected on them, considered themselves now as individuals, not as citizens, and each would shine with his own light. To this purpose alone they employed the commands they had of armies, the governments of provinces, and the influence they acquired over the tribes at Rome, and over the allies and subjects of the republic. Upon principles of the same kind, inferior persons attached themselves to these; and that zeal and industry, nay, that courage and magnanimity, which had been exerted formerly in the service of the commonwealth, were exerted by the spirit of faction, for Marius, or Sylla; for Cæsar, or Pompey.

" It is plain, that the liberty of Rome would not have been irretrievably lost, though Cæsar had finished the civil war with absolute success, and was settled in power, if the spirit of liberty

had not been then lost in the whole body of the people; if the
Romans had not been as ripe for slavery, as the Cappadocians
were fond of it; for I think the Cappadocians were the people
who desired that a prince might be set over them, and refused
to be a free people.

"I cannot believe that those who murdered Cæsar, took such
puerile measures as Cicero, who was not let into the secret, pretended that they had taken, when he saw the consequences of
their action. But in this they erred. They killed their bene-
factor, at least, he was such to the greatest part of them; and
renewed the civil war, in order to restore liberty to a people, who
had lost the spirit of liberty, and who would not take it when it
was offered to them. Even in the senate, Octavius had a party;
Antony had a party; but the commonwealth had none. In
short, the freest people upon earth, by suffering the spirit of
liberty to decay, and that of faction to grow up, became slaves
to such a succession of monsters, continued with very few exceptions from the reign of Augustus to the destruction of the
empire, as God never sent in his wrath to execute vengeance on
any other nation.

"Thus I have endeavored to illustrate and confirm the first
general proposition laid down, by a summary application of it to
the Roman story. I have not explained by what degrees, and
by what means one of these spirits gradually decayed, and the
other grew up. The subject is fine, and the task would be
pleasant; but it is unnecessary to our present purpose. We see
enough at this time, if we see that in the greatest revolution of
the greatest government of the world, losing the spirit of liberty
was the cause, and losing liberty was the effect.

"If now we bring these considerations home, we shall find not
only the first general proposition, but the others relative to it,
illustrated and confirmed through the whole course of our annals.
I shall make a deduction of some of these particulars. To deduce
them all would exceed my strength and your patience."

Here one of our company interrupted the old gentleman's discourse, by saying that since we were come to a kind of pause, he
desired leave to make an observation, which he thought pertinent
and material, on what had been said, before we went into any
new matter.—"The difference and opposition between a spirit
of liberty and a spirit of faction," continued he, "hath been justly
stated. A spirit of liberty will be always and wholly concerned
about national interests, and very indifferent about personal and
private interests. On the contrary, a spirit of faction will be
always and wholly concerned about these, and very indifferent
about the others. When they appear, therefore, in their proper

characters, they are distinguished as easily as light and darkness; and the danger I apprehend is over.

"But faction puts on the mask of liberty; and under this false appearance, disputes her being even with liberty herself. Now here, methinks, a great many dangers arise; the danger of mistaking when it is so hard to distinguish; the danger of being bubbles and tools of faction, whilst we fancy ourselves asserters of public liberty; the danger of continuing under this delusion, till it is too late to prevent such mischiefs as we never intended to bring on our country. The spirit of faction may take, and I doubt not hath often taken possession of numbers, who meant to entertain no other spirit than that of liberty; for numbers have not the discernment of spirits. This possession may continue, and in fact, I believe it hath continued very often, till faction hath accomplished, or secured the accomplishment of her ends. I made this observation, which results naturally from what hath been said, and insist upon it, because if faction could not lie latent under the most specious and popular pretences imaginable, there would be no great need of putting us on our guard against it; and because if it can lie thus latent and concealed, we may be exposed to the dangers I have mentioned, which side soever of the question we take in political disputes. At this time, to speak as I think, the case is so clear on one side, that no man who adheres to it, hath the least pretence left him to say that he pursues the public interest, or is directed in his conduct by the generous, disinterested spirit of liberty.

"I could support my assertion by many proofs, if it was necessary in this company. One I will mention for its singularity; and it is this.

"We have seen and heard, in a nation hitherto free, such maxims avowed and pleaded for, as are inconsistent with all the notions of liberty. Corruption hath been defended, nay recommended, as a proper, a necessary, and therefore a reasonable expedient of government; than which there is not, perhaps, any one proposition more repugnant to the common sense of man kind and to universal experience. Both of these demonstrate corruption to be the last deadly symptom of agonizing liberty.— Both of them declare that a people abandoned to it, are abandoned to a reprobate sense, and are lost to all hopes of political salvation.

"The dependence of the legislative on the executive power hath been contended for by the same persons, under the same direction; and yet nothing surely can be more evident than this; that in a constitution like ours, the safety of the whole depends on the balance of the parts, and the balance of the parts on their mutual independency on one another: agreeably to which

Thuanus makes Ferdinand say, in answer to the Castilians, who pressed him to take away the independency of the states of Arragon; 'Equilibrio potentiæ regni regisque salutem publicam contineri; et si contingeret aliquando alterum alteri præponderare, procul, dubio alterius aut utriusque ruinam ex eo secuturam; that the public safety depends on the equal balance of the power of the king, and of the power of the kingdom; and that if ever it should happen that one outweighed the other, the ruin of one, or of both, must undoubtedly follow.'

" On one side then the mask is pulled off. The weak may be seduced to concur; the strongest may be forced to submit; but no man can be any longer deceived.

" On the other, it must be acknowledged that the appearances are extremely fair. True notions of liberty and good government are professed and pursued. Our grievances are complained of; our dangers are foretold; not only those which all men feel or see, but those which are more remote from observation. In short, the spirit of liberty, such as it hath been described, seems to breathe from this quarter, and to diffuse its influences over the nation.

" As I am a lover of my country and of liberty, I have rejoiced in this. I rejoice in it still; and yet I confess freely, that I took some umbrage at a paper, which came out not long ago. The design and tendency of it seemed to me to favor the cause of a faction; and of a faction, however contemptible in its present state, always to be guarded against. The paper I mean is Fog's Journal of the 6th of June; where you have seen a ridiculous speech, supposed to be made by General Monk, and translated, as the author says, from Leti's history of Oliver Cromwell.

" If this wretched production had appeared in Mist's Journal, I should have felt neither surprise nor concern. That writer never wore so much as the mask of liberty; and showed his game so plainly, that whatever he got by faction, faction could get nothing by him. But Fog, who writes incomparably better, hath appeared to write with a much better design. Those who are warmest in the national interest, without regard to persons, and independently of all factions, have made this judgment of him; and therefore I was surprised and concerned to find that he exposed himself even once, or in any degree, to the same reproach that was frequently and justly made to his predecessor."

The gentleman's observation gave occasion to much discourse. Our old sage desired it might be remembered that he had not undertaken the defence of every weekly writer, though he had undertaken yours, Mr. D'Anvers. " The paper," continued he, " which hath been so much mentioned, is a very silly paper, to whatever purpose it was designed.

" If it was designed to inspire a horror of those miseries
from which the restoration delivered the nation, it was a very
superfluous work at this time, when there is no real or pretended
difference of opinion upon that head amongst us. Those who
do not go to church upon the twenty-ninth of May, nor on any
other day, will agree with those who do, in this point, upon
better authority than that of Leti, and for better reasons than
those which are contained in the foolish declamation attributed
to Monk.

" If it was designed to make us commemorate the restoration
of the two brothers, Charles and James, as a national blessing in
itself, and independently of the other consideration, the project
was equally ridiculous. The flattery bestowed upon these princes,
whilst they were in exile, might pass, and many things concurred
to make it pass. But to talk in the same style to mankind at
this time, when they have both sat on our throne, when so many
of us remember both what they did, and what they would have
done, is contemptible to the last degree.

" If it was designed for more modern application, and to raise
a spirit amongst us in favor of the Pretender, the project was
too foolish to have been hatched at home. It must have been
imported from abroad. What jacobite can be sanguine enough
to hope that his cause should revive, when he beholds the
heroical king and queen who fill our throne, auspicious parents
of a numerous progeny of young heroes and heroines, rising up
to emulate their virtues, and to gladden, like them, the British
nation.

" This single consideration might be sufficient to damp the
hopes of any jacobite who lives at home, and is a witness of all
this glory. But however I shall mention another, which ought
to have its weight likewise, and which will have more perhaps
amongst some people. The spirit of jacobitism is not only gone,
but it will appear to be gone in such a manner as to leave no
room to apprehend its return; if we reflect that it hath died
away, whilst all that could be done to keep it alive was doing
by those who professed it, and by those who valued and recommended themselves on their opposition to all the effects of it; if
we consider the numbers of people who have abandoned this
interest, notwithstanding the utmost provocations to the contrary.

" In short, I persuade myself that if the Pretender had no rival
in the throne, instead of having there one so formidable as our
most august monarch, yet his way to the throne would not be
more open to him. The whole bulk of the people hath been
brought by the revolution, and by the present settlement of the
crown, to entertain principles which very few of us defended in
my younger days. The safety and welfare of the nation are

now the first and principal objects of regard. The regard to persons and to families hath been reduced to the second place; and it holds even that but under the direction of the former. Can any man believe that a people brave enough to dispose of their crown for the greatest national advantage, even when the throne was full, will ever dispose of it as long as the spirit of liberty remains among them, for the greatest national mischief, if the throne should be empty?

" There is but one design more, which I can conceive to have given occasion to this silly paper; but one quarter more, from which it could possibly come: and these guesses, perhaps, will not appear the least probable.   Might it not be designed to instil a jealousy of jacobitism, and to prejudice mankind against all writings which those who are offended at them cannot answer? —Might it not be designed to furnish the spruce, pert orator, who strewed some of his flowers in the Daily Courant of the eleventh of June, with a hint, which he hath most happily and modestly improved?   'Fog, says he, avows jacobitism; the Craftsman concurs in the same design; nay, every jacobite in England sinks his master's divine right in the popular topics of debts, taxes and corruption.'   So that jacobitism may now be imputed upon this authority, to ninety-nine in a hundred of the whole nation; for ninety-nine in a hundred do complain of debts, taxes and corruption.   I am sure there is arrogance and impertinence both in such an insinuation too gross to be denied; whereas the Craftsman may destroy the whole proof brought against him of arrogance, by answering three silly questions in the negative.

" If this was the design, I will be bold, for bold it may justly seem, to say that this expedient is, at least, as bungling and likely to prove as ineffectual, as any that have been produced by the same great genius who contrived it; for if we were inclined to believe that the Craftsman, Fog, or any other person, carries on the measures of faction under the mask of liberty; should we believe it on the credit of those who oppose them, and who are notoriously influenced to write, though under specious pretences of promoting loyalty to the king, and an acquiescence in his majesty's measures, yet in reality, for no other service than that of a small number of men; nay, strictly speaking, of a single man? With what face can such writers impute faction to any one living or dead?

" Let them be assured that we can examine and judge for ourselves; and that neither the Craftsman nor Fog would be able, if they went about it, to impose upon us, any more than they themselves have been able to do.

" The pretty author, I just now mentioned, begins his essay with airs of wit, and ends it with airs of wisdom. What pity is it that he should succeed in neither? In his first paragraph he represents the Craftsman, with curious impropriety, as a magician, who conjures up spirits; as a dog, who barks at a distance; as a little insect, who nibbles at a character: and my friend Caleb was all these things, it seems, at the same instant. After this specimen of writing, we may expect to see him compared, in some other production of the same author, to a bird; and made to fly different ways and in different places at once.

"But let us leave the wit and come to the wisdom; which will bring us back to our subject.

"In the last paragraph of this elaborate piece, the author sets the example of my Lord Falkland and others before our eyes; who strengthened, as he says, the republican party so long, that when they found out their designs and forsook them, it was too late to prevent them. After this, he calls most charitably on several well-meaning persons to take warning; for some, whom he allows to be such, he thinks in danger of being drawn in to favor the purposes of those whom he calls opposers of our government.

"Behold this little Gamaliel in cathedra! Observe the scholars he places at his feet for instruction! 'Risum teneatis, amici?' Can the gravest of you forbear laughter?

"When we come to apply the general propositions laid down still more particularly to the English than we have done to the Roman history, I shall show you perhaps that this author, like most other fine men, treasures up in his memory the observations he meets with in history, instead of making his own upon the examination and comparison of the facts and characters he finds there; and that the example he hath chosen will come out against the very purpose he hath applied it to. In the mean time, let us observe that the alarm, which hath been taken by some of this company, and I suppose by others, at the publication of that stupid paper in Fog's Journal, shows how little reason there is to apprehend that those who are actuated by the spirit of liberty, and pursue the national interest, should be imposed upon by the spirit of any faction.

"The spirit of liberty is a jealous spirit; and faction is equally the object of its jealousy, whether the views of faction be directed in favor of the crown, or against it. I make this distinction here, though I shall have occasion to speak more fully upon it hereafter, because I perceive that we are apt to confine our idea of faction to such men and such measures, as are in opposition to the men in power, and to the measures they take; whereas in truth a number of men in power, who exercise it solely for their own private advantage and security, and who treat the nation as their farm, or rather as a country under contribution to them, let them shelter themselves under what authority they please, are as much a faction, as any number of men, who under popular pretences endeavor to ruin, or at least to disturb the government, that they may raise themselves.

" If the spirit of liberty were extinguished, as it is discouraged, the spirit of some faction or other would, no doubt, prevail, but this would not succeed under the mask of liberty. There would be, in such a case, no need of wearing this disguise. Men would avow faction. They would choose that which suited their interest best; and indeed it would be of no great moment which they chose.

" But if the spirit of liberty, which begins to revive in this country, becomes prevalent, there will remain nothing to fear from any faction whatever, whether masked, or unmasked. Whilst it is masked, and the instruments or members of it pursue the national interest, though they intend another, the bad principle is however so far productive of good, and the cause of virtue is so far promoted by vice itself. When it comes to be unmasked, and the instruments or members of it are hurried by indiscretion, or forced by the course of events, as they must be, to show their game, faction is that moment disarmed. The distinction marked, the separation follows of course; and those who espouse the cause of the nation will find themselves doubly strengthened by the assistance which faction gave them at one time, and by the opposition she makes to them at another. In short, gentlemen, the spirit of jacobitism may crawl about and skulk in corners. The spirit of the other faction may roll in gilded spires, and with erected crests in every public place, and hiss and threaten and cast its venom around; but the spirit of liberty, like the divine rod of Aaron, will devour all the serpents of the magicians.

" I see therefore no cause to fear that we may be drawn in to serve the purposes of faction, whilst we pursue the cause of liberty; and if we suffered ourselves to be drawn off from this pursuit by the jealousy which one faction endeavors to give us of another, we should be arrant bubbles indeed. Fog is not to be defended for publishing a paper liable every way to blame, and capable of no excuse; but if he hath hurt any body by it, he hath hurt himself; and the weight which is laid upon it by those on one side, who perhaps wrote it, is as ridiculous as the project of those who thought to advance the jacobite cause by it, if it came from that side."

Here the old gentleman broke off, and though he was pressed to resume the discourse he had begun, when this interruption happened, he desired to be excused, because it was late, and promised to comply with our request upon some other occasion. If he keeps his word, as I am persuaded he will, you shall hear again from, Sir, yours, &c.

LETTER III.

Sir:

Our old gentleman having kept his word with the company, I designed to have kept mine with you; but some business calling me into the country, I send you a few minutes of the conversations which have passed, in hopes that the subject will not be left imperfect for as long a time as my affairs may oblige me to be absent. Throw these minutes into what form and make what use of them you please. They are designed to serve an honest cause, the cause of truth and of liberty. You have espoused it; and I hope will pursue it.

You are able to do this with success, even in opposition to the most plausible writers; and how much more against the cursory observator, who appeared in the Daily Courant, and the London Journalist.

I do not suppose you will think it worth your while to set seriously about answering them; but it may be worth while now and then to show them how little they deserve to be answered.

They complain heavily of the prolixity and dulness of the letters which you have published. Might they not be taught, what they have already taught the world, that an essay of two or three columns may be longer than an essay of five or six? Let them not carp at my words, since they cannot mistake my meaning.

Might they not be convinced that they are the least competent judges in the whole nation, of the dulness of others, for this plain reason: that it is not in the case of dulness, as it is in that of wit and learning; in which he is the best judge of these qualities in others, who possesses them himself in the most eminent degree?

But there is a judge, before whom all productions of this sort are tried, and by whose sentence alone they must stand or fall. This judge is the public; and I am apt to think that these authors may be informed of the sentence pronounced by the public on your papers, Mr. D'Anvers, and on their own, if they will take the trouble to inquire of Messrs. Roberts, Peele, and Francklin.

I am inclined to believe that they have inquired; and that, despairing of success before this tribunal, they have appealed to another, where those whom the public rejects, are pretty sure of being received.

Sure I am that they cannot hope to succeed any where else, whilst they found their merit on Billingsgate, false quotations, gross misrepresentations, and an eternal begging of the question.

That they are guilty of all these may soon be proved. I will point out some instances; as many as the haste I am in allows me time to mention.

The Cursory Observator accuses you and me (for these writers are pleased to suppose us to be the same person who corresponds with himself) of quoting falsely and applying foolishly in every case, whilst he quotes falsely himself and ridicules the application of what it is manifest he never read. His whole charge is built on a lie and a blunder.

Machiavel is made, according to him, in one of my letters, to suppose " that the first destruction of Rome by the Gauls (and I never heard of a second) was a judgment from heaven on the people for their having departed from their ancient observances and religious ceremonies." With this he makes himself wonderfully merry; and having heard that Machiavel did not pass for a very strong believer, he ridicules the imputation of such a supposition to that great politician.

But let this scribbler learn to read before he blots any more paper. Let him learn to speak of what is, or is not in books, after he has looked into those books, and not from his idle imagination of what an author would, or would not have said, agreeably to the character of the author, which his ignorance has taken upon trust.

My old gentleman never said that Machiavel supposed the destruction of Rome by the Gauls was a judgment from heaven; but he reckoned amongst other particulars in which the Romans had begun to degenerate, and to which they were brought back by this great misfortune, that of neglecting the ceremonies of religion and the laws of justice. Now Machiavel does say this in express and strong terms, as this writer would have known, if he had consulted the first chapter of the third book of his discourses on Livy.

But I will tell him something more. This very Machiavel* has written a whole chapter concerning the religion of the Romans, in which he mentions that Rome was more obliged to Numa than to Romulus; in which he shows that her grandeur and felicity were owing to her religion; nay, he asserts in general, that as religion raises commonwealths, so the contempt of it must ruin them. " Good Gods! is this talking like Machiavel?" Why truly it is thus that Machiavel talks; and in talking thus he shows more learning and sense than Observator is master of.

Cast your eye, Mr. D'Anvers, on the next paragraph; in which this able person undertakes to prove from reason, as well as history, a matter of fact. The fact is this: that the destruction of

* L. i, c. 2.

Rome by the Gauls, was owing to the opposition set on foot to the measures and person of the great and much injured Camillus.

It was a great mistake, it seems, to mention this incident in the Roman history, in one of my letters. The Observator shall find that it was a greater blunder in him to dwell upon it.

He knows as little of Livy as he does of Machiavel, or I believe of any other good author. Let him turn to the Roman historian. He will find that Livy, in the transition which he makes from the prosecution of Camillus, to the invasion of the Gauls, says " that if there be anything certain in human affairs, Rome could not have been taken, if that citizen had remained in it." But does he attribute the invasion of the Gauls to this man's banishment? No. He attributes it to the conduct of three rash and foolish brothers, who were sent ambassadors to the Gauls, and who, by breaking the law of nations, justly provoked this people. He attributes it to the force of a faction, which prevailed to screen these criminals, and exposed the state to ruin, rather than give them up to justice.

Thus the fact stands in history. Let the Observator now consider whether it would be very difficult to make certain applications of it, which he would not like. I doubt these applications would appear much more apposite than that which is said to be intended in his paper, of the character of the great and much injured Camillus.

He succeeds, you see, but ill, when he meddles with facts; and I do not find that he pretends much to reason. The rest of his paper contains little more than fool, knave, libeller, incendiary, &c. I shall therefore take notice of but one thing more; and that is the advantage he would make of a mistake in printing.

He must have perceived, or he can perceive nothing, that it was a mistake in printing. If the meaning of my letter had been, that the Craftsman might destroy the whole proof of arrogance brought against him, by answering in the negative all the questions asked in the paragraph referred to, it should have been said, " five silly questions;" for they are five, not four; but the truth is, that no regard was had to the two introductory questions; and that the three main questions which follow, were alone meant. A writer must be reduced very low, by his cause, or be very low in his character, who catches at such an impertinent opportunity of being what he imagines smart.

I should say a word or two to the profound Mr. Osborne, who hath been pleased to let us know that he prefers the absolute monarchy of Augustus to the free state of the Roman commonwealth. He prefers likewise, I suppose, at least his discourse leads one to think so, the violence, the treachery, and the bloody massacres, on which this absolute monarchy was founded, to the

civil disorders, which were occasioned by establishing and maintaining an equal commonwealth. I should desire him to compare
the reigns of a Caligula, a Nero, a Domitian, a Heliogabalus,
which had never happened, if the usurpation of Augustus had
never happened, with the glorious fourth and fifth centuries of
the republic of Rome; but I have not, at present time for this. I
hope you, Mr. D'Anvers, will give him some salutary correction
at your leisure, and make him ashamed of having profaned the
language of a free people in so prostitute a manner, and to such
slavish purposes! Advise him to learn better notions of government from Mr. Gordon's excellent discourses, prefixed to his translation of Tacitus; in which he will find his favorite Augustus set in
a true light, and proved to be an infamous tyrant, though somewhat more artful that his successors. He must certainly acknowledge the obligation, since you cannot be suspected of doing it on
any account, but that of a charitable disposition towards him. If
he was capable of imposing on the dullest quidnunc in any coffee-
house, or of seducing the most raw boy that ever eloped from
school, you might be suspected of some farther and deeper design;
but when you write against so harmless a creature, your efforts
must pass, and ought to pass, for the pure effects of the most disinterested, the most refined charity.

Let me only ask the favor of you to touch three points, amongst
others, whenever you condescend to meddle with squire Osborne.
One is to assure him in my name, and, if you please, in your
own, that a good minister ought not to be abused; nay more, that
he who abuses him is a rogue, a rascal, and an impudent (I had
almost said, for I conform to his dialect, a traitorous) fellow; and
might have justified myself by the authority of a writer on Mr.
Osborne's side, who talked of allegiance to ministers: but let this
important author know, at the same time, that we defy him to
make the least use of these concessions against any one sentence,
any one word in the Craftsman that hath been published.

There are two other things, of which I desire you likewise to
take notice.   One is scandalously impudent; the other infamously
unfair.

When his patron is commended by any honest man in Britain,
it is done most certainly with a sneer.   The "great man" is an
expression which hath undoubtedly occasioned more sneers than
this nation had seen in a century before; but it is saucy and impudent, in Mr. Osborne to suppose that one who speaks of the
king and royal family with all the respect that is due to them,
means a sneer.

The other thing, which I desire you to take notice of, is the
malicious and mean comment made on an expression in my last
letter to you, where I called his present majesty a formidable rival

of the Pretender.   Mr. Osborne is pleased, out of the abundance
of his loyalty, to resent this as an insult on the king.   Now, though
in strictness of fact and propriety of language, his majesty neither
is a rival to any body, nor can have a rival, being our rightful
and lawful king, by the consent of his people in parliament, the
only good title to the crown of these realms, yet in pretension
there is a rivalry; and I may defy Mr. Osborne to give any other
reason for keeping up so large an army in times of peace.

You will observe, Mr. D'Anvers, that the only design of this
letter is to make some short observations on two silly papers
which have been published against my former letters to you. You
are now desired to apply the old gentleman's general positions
to the English history, from the minutes which I have sent you,
and which I believe will be as agreeable to the public as it was
to the company in which he delivered it.

I am, sir, your friend and reader, &c.

LETTER IV.

Few nations have gone through more revolutions, few governments have appeared more unsteady, or fluctuated more between
prerogative and privilege, than this of Great Britain.

If we are freemen, it is because the spirit of liberty has been
never yet quite extinguished among us.

We have been surprised, betrayed, forced, more than once,
into situations little better than that of downright slavery.   But
these usurpations have not become settlements.   They have
disordered the frame, but not destroyed the principles of a free
government.   Like cloudy mornings, they have soon passed
over, and the sun of liberty has broke out again with double
force, and double lustre.

It must be a pleasure to reflect on that uniformity of spirit
which created, and has constantly preserved or retrieved, the
original freedom of the British and Saxon constitutions.

I feel a secret pride in thinking that I was born a Briton;
when I consider that the Romans, those masters of the world,
maintained their liberty little more than seven centuries; and that
Britain, which was a free nation above seventeen hundred years
ago, is so at this hour.

However savage our British ancestors may be represented by
the Romans, whom the luxury of Greece, and the effeminacy of

Asia had already corrupted, they certainly were a people of
spirit and of sense; who knew the ends of government, and
obliged their governors to pursue those ends.

Cæsar himself acknowledges that they fought boldly for their
liberties, when he invaded them; and there is good reason to believe, from his manner of writing, and abrupt way of leaving
this island, that they gave him a warmer reception than he is
willing to own.

But to speak of them after an author, in whose time they were
better known than they were by Cæsar, or even by Tacitus,
Dion Cassius, when he is about to relate the expedition of Severus
into Britain, says "that they held a great part of the government
in their own power."

Their long resistance against the Saxons shows their love of
civil liberty.

Their long resistance against the usurpations of the church of
Rome, begun by Gregory, that flatterer of Phocas and Brune-
hault, under pretence of converting the Saxons, shows their love
of ecclesiastical liberty.

Though the Saxons submitted to the yoke of Rome, in matters
of religion, they were far from giving up the freedom of their
Gothic institutions of government.

The Saxon heretoges, that is, public generals, were chosen
only to conduct them in war, not to rule over them in war and
in peace.

These heretoges, among the German colonies, who settled in
the countries they conquered, and founded new governments,
became kings, and had trappings enough to set off their majesty,
and to enforce their authority; but the supreme power centered
in the micklemote, or wittagenmote, composed of the king, the
lords, and the Saxon freemen, that original sketch of a British
parliament.

Here all important affairs were treated.   The conduct of their
kings was examined in it, and controlled by it.

The rights of the people in those days must have been carried
to a very great height; since they went hand in hand with those
of the church; and since a positive law declared that if the king
did not defend both, he should lose even the name of king.
" Nec nomen regis in eo constabit, verum nomen regis perdit."

The principles of the Saxon commonwealth were therefore
very democratical; and these principles prevailed through all
subsequent changes.

The Danes conquered the crown, but they wore it little; and
the liberties of the Saxon freemen they never conquered; nor
wrought any alteration in the constitution of the government.

Thus much it was thought necessary to premise, concerning

the original constitution of our government. We now come to
that period of history, from whence we propose to deduce our
following remarks.

William, the Norman, is come down to us in history under the
character of a conqueror; and though it may be disputed whether
he was strictly so any more than several other princes who have
supported their titles by their swords, yet we may confess that
he imposed many new laws and customs; that he made very
great alterations in the whole model of government; and that he,
as well as his two sons, ruled, upon many occasions, like absolute, not limited monarchs.

Yet neither he nor they could destroy the old constitution;
because neither he nor they could extinguish the old spirit of
liberty.

On the contrary, the Normans and other strangers, who settled
here, were soon seized with it themselves, instead of inspiring a
spirit of slavery into the Saxons.

They were originally of Celtic,* or Gothic extraction, call it
which you please, as well as the people they subdued. They
came out of the same northern hive; and therefore they naturally
resumed the spirit of their ancestors, when they came into a
country where it prevailed.

Stephen, the fourth king of this race, owed his crown to the
good will of the nation; and he owed this good will to the concessions he made in favor of liberty.

John came to the crown after the death of his father Henry
the Second, and his brother Richard the First, by the election of
the people. His electors, indeed, found themselves deceived in
their expectations; for he governed in the most extravagant manner. But they soon made him feel whose creature he was. The
contests between the laity and an ambitious usurping clergy ran
very high at this time. John had made his advantage of these
divisions. But the spirit of liberty prevailed, and that of faction
vanished before it. Men grew ashamed of being the tools of
private ambition, when public safety was at stake. Those of the
high church and those of the low church united in one common
cause. The king blustered and drew out his army; but it was a
British army. No wonder, therefore, if the king submitted, and
Magna Charta was signed.

It was signed again by his son and successor, Henry the Third,

* We have thought fit to explain the expression in this place, though we
know the word Celtic, as well as Scythian, hath been used in the same large
and general sense, which is made use of here; and we could show, if such a
trifle deserved it, that by the Celtæ antiquity did not always understand the
people inhabiting a part of Gaul, notwithstanding the quotations out of Poly-
bius, Diodorus, &c. which have been urged, by way of cavil, against us.

in full parliament, and with the greatest solemnity.   The people however abated nothing of their jealous, watchful spirit; and it was well for liberty they did not.   The long reign of this prince was one continual struggle between him and them.   The issue of this struggle was favorable to the latter.   By exerting their strength, they increased it under Henry the Third.   They lost no ground under Edward the First, and they gained a great deal under Edward the Second.

Thus was the present constitution of our government forming itself for about two centuries and a half; a rough building raised out of the demolitions which the Normans had made, and upon the solid foundations laid by the Saxons.   The whole fabric was cemented by the blood of our fathers; for the British liberties are not the grants of princes.   They are original rights, conditions of original contracts, co-equal with prerogative, and coeval with our government.   As such, in the days we speak of, they were claimed; as such they were asserted by force of arms; as such they were acknowledged; and as such they were constantly maintained afterwards by that pertinacious spirit, which no difficulties nor dangers could discourage, nor any authority abate; not even that of the pope, as impudently as it was exercised, and as foolishly as it was revered in those superstitious ages.

Had this spirit relaxed in the course of so many years, our government must have settled in an absolute monarchy, or tyrannical aristocracy.

The Norman kings, of imperious tempers, assumed great power.   The barons did the same.   The people groaned under the oppression of both.   This union was unnatural, and could not last.   The barons, enjoying a sort of feudatory sovereignty, were often partners, and sometimes rivals of the kings.   They had opposite interests, and they soon clashed.

Thus was the opportunity created of re-establishing a more equal free government than that which had prevailed after the Norman invasion.

The kings, the barons, and the clergy, not less ambitious or avaricious than either of the others, had powerful means of promoting their usurpations.   The commonalty had little or no share in the legislature; made no figure in the government; and it is hard to conceive how they could act, as the others might, and certainly did by particular concerts, to the advancement of their particular interests.

All these disadvantages were supplied by that spirit of liberty which diffused itself through the whole mass.   Numbers were on the side of the commons.   In all disputes, therefore, it was necessary to apply to them.   They made the proper use of such conjunctures. Whoever lost, they were sure to be gainers; for so they deemed themselves, when they suffered all the hardships of war, and even laid down their lives, in the quarrel, if they left liberty more improved and better secured to their posterity.

By concessions to the commons, our kings maintained and extended their prerogatives over the barons. By espousing the national interest, the barons continued able to cope with the crown, till they broke among themselves. Nay, even the church, notwithstanding that ancient and close alliance between secular and ecclesiastical tyranny, was forced, on some few occasions, to be a friend to the liberties of the people.

The king, the barons and the clergy were all, in reality, enemies to public liberty. Their party were so many factions in the nation; yet they all helped, in their turns, to establish liberty.

So true it is, that every thing, even the vices of mankind, and the misfortunes of a country, will turn to the advantage of liberty, where the spirit of it is maintained in vigor; as every thing, even the good qualities of mankind and the prosperity of a country, may operate a contrary effect, where this spirit is suffered to decline.

As losing the spirit of liberty lost the liberties of Rome, even while the laws and constitutions, made for the preservation of them, remained entire; so we see that our ancestors, by keeping this spirit alive and warm, regained all the advantages of a free government, though a foreign invasion had destroyed them, in great measure, and had imposed a very tyrannical yoke on the nation.

LETTER V.

We are now come to the reign of Edward the Third. We must desire our readers to stop here, and at the reign of his successor a little; since no reigns can furnish us with more memorable and pertinent examples, to show how the spirit of liberty exerts itself in favor of good princes; how slow it is to act even against the worst; and yet how effectually it is able to act even in the most desperate cases.

Old Froissart says,* that the English had an opinion, grounded on observations made from the days of good king Arthur, that between two valiant and able princes in this nation, there al-

* Vol. i, c. 2.

ways intervenes a king "moins suffisant de sens et de prouesse; of less sense and courage." I shall not warrant the exact truth of this observation. The proportion, I fear, is much greater on the worst side in all kingdoms. But certainly Edward the Third, whose story gave occasion to Froissart to broach this anecdote, stands between his father Edward the Second, and his grandson Richard the Second, a bright instance of this truth, that "great and good princes are favorers of liberty, and find their account in promoting the spirit of it; whilst the weakest and the worst princes chiefly affect absolute power, and often meet with the fate they deserve for such attempts."

The former know that they have nothing to apprehend from this spirit; and they wisely prefer the generous efforts of good-will and affection to the reluctant compliances of such as obey by force.

The latter, conscious that they are unable to lead, endeavor to drive their people. Unworthy to be kings, they struggle to be tyrants.

Few were the blemishes which may be thought to tarnish the lustre of this reign of Edward the Third. Few and short were the struggles between him and his people; for as he was fierce and terrible to his enemies, he was amiable and indulgent to his subjects. He not only observed the laws, but he made the sense of the nation, in some measure, a law to him. On this principle, in which, to a considering mind, there will appear as much wis-don as goodness, he removed a son, nay a favorite mistress from court.

Henry the Fourth, if I mistake not, did something of the same kind; and which of their successors, after such examples, could presume to think it below his dignity to consult the inclination of his people, and make them the rule of his conduct?

Under this great prince, the constitution of our parliaments, and the whole frame of our government became reduced into a better form. A spirit of liberty breathes in the laws of this glorious king; and the power and duty of parliaments are set forth, in some of them, with such terms as would never have been passed by a prince who had put the least pedantry, or the least foppery, into his notions of kingship.

The spirit of liberty was not idle in this reign, though it had little or no occasion of exercise against the crown. The usurpations of the church were many and grievous. They had been long murmured against; but a false respect for religion had hitherto maintained them. This delusion began now to be removed. Wickliffe arose to dispel this magic charm; to undraw the veil of this pretended sanctuary; and to expose the horrors and trifles which lurked behind it, to public view, indignation and contempt. The axe was now first aimed at the root of popery; and prelates were taught the first lessons of moderation. Parliaments sat and proceeded on business, even on ecclesiastical business, without the intervention of mitres. There was, I believe, one parliament held, to which few or none of the prelates were summoned; in order, perhaps, to teach them how little their concurrence was essential to give due weight to the counsels; or full authority to the acts of parliament.

As this prince loved, instead of hating, as he encouraged, instead of discountenancing, the spirit of liberty in his people; so he was strengthened and supported by it in such a manner, and in such circumstances as cannot be paralleled.

The nation had been miserably harassed by civil wars and oppressions of various kinds, when he came to the crown. The burthen of personal service, and the taxes raised to defend the dominions which his predecessors held on the continent, had exhausted all degrees of people. This mischief was so much resented by them, that foreign interest and foreign counsels may be justly reckoned among the principal causes of all the disputes, and even wars, between them and their former kings.

In this situation, and in this temper of mind was the nation, when Edward the Third, by laying claim to the crown, and undertaking the conquest of France, opened to his subjects the terrible prospect of being worse than ever oppressed by the same grievances; and yet his nobility and commonalty seconded him in all these enterprises, with fewer complaints than could have been expected. These men, so apt to complain of grievances, and so little patient under them, carried him triumphantly through all his wars abroad, though they struggled with want, pestilence and famine at home.

What principle produced this wonderful change? Did higher notions of prerogative prevail? Had the doctrines of a slavish submission at once possessed our ancestors? By no means. It was not the power, it was not the authority of the king, which forced; but it was the character of the man, which invited to these compliances. The spirit of liberty exerted itself in favor of the patron of liberty.

A corrupt parliament, a degenerate nobility, a servile commonalty, will sacrifice anything to any prince; to a Richard the Second or an Edward the Third, equally and discriminately. But a free, a generous, a virtuous people, such as we may boast our ancestors were in those days, will sacrifice everything, except liberty, to a prince like Edward the Third, and liberty is a sacrifice which a prince like him will never require at their hands. To him who would require it, they would sacrifice nothing. Such a people may be well governed with ease; and it ought to be hard to govern them ill. They will do more for a prince whom they love and esteem, than he has a right to expect from them. If they do less for a prince whom they despise or hate, they are surely very excusable.

In order to render this example still stronger and more useful, it may be proper to point out, besides his general character, some of those particulars in the conduct of Edward the Third, which probably induced his people to sacrifice their estates, and their lives too, so cheerfully in a cause, to which, under other princes, they had been so averse.

In the first place, as his father Edward the Second lost his crown and his life, in the most miserable manner, by suffering himself to be governed by his ministers, and protecting them from the resentments of the people; so his son very early exerted his own authority, and freed himself from the guardianship, or rather subjection, of the queen and Mortimer, who had long oppressed the nation, and dishonored the young king by their scandalous conduct.

The next reason seems to have been this: Though he was magnificent in his court, yet he limited, with great care, the exactions of his purveyors, kept a severe hand over them, and suffered no more to be levied on his people, than what the necessary expense of his household required. He saved for his people, not for himself.

Thirdly, The taxes laid in his time, were laid for visible and important services, wherein the honor at least of the nation was concerned; which every man knew and approved.

Fourthly, The expenses were lessened by that double economy, which is so rarely found, or even understood. I mean not only that inferior economy, which consists in the management of the receipts and issues of the public revenue; but that superior economy, which consists in contriving the great schemes of negotiation and action. When the talents for this economy are wanting in those who govern, the public pays for their want of genius; and the prince's, or minister's errors are so many additional taxes on the people. When these talents are wanting, the very reverse happens. The genius of the prince, or minister, comes in aid of the public charge. Much is saved; and art and management supply it all.

Edward the Third began his war against France, in conjunction with German allies. He saw no better expedient at that time. But as soon as fortune and intrigue had procured it for him, he took another, shorter, cheaper, and more effectual method. He supported the Earl of Monfort, competitor with Charles of Blois, for the Dutchy of Brittany. "Avecques les Allemans, et les Brabançons," says Froissart, "il n'avoit riens fait,

sors despendre grossement; et l'avoit mené et demené les sieg-
neurs de l' empire, qui avoient prints son or et son argent, ainsy
qu'ils avoient voulu, et riens fait. Si descendit à la requeste du
comte joyeusement," &c. That is, " with the Germans and the
Brabançons, all he had been able to do was to spend great sums
of money. The princes of the empire, who had taken as much
as they would of his gold and his silver, and had done nothing
for it, were accustomed to amuse him, and to tire him out. He
condescended therefore to the request of the earl very joyfully."

Fifthly, It was not owing to his success that the people had a
good opinion of his enterprises, and promised themselves a
happy issue, how difficult, or dangerous soever these enterprises
might appear. Their confidence was placed, and very justly, in
those qualities, and that tenor of conduct, which they observed
in their king, and to which his prodigious success was owing.
No man contrived, prepared, resolved with more phlegm, or
acted with greater fire; the reverse of his successor, who resolved
rashly, and executed irresolutely. He waited sometimes for
opportunities, but he always improved them when they happened; and those accidents which govern or dictate the measures, and perpetually shift the fluctuating schemes of weak
governments, were bent by this great prince to serve the wisest
and most steady purposes!

Sixthly, If he drained away some of the national wealth by
taxes, he restored it very amply again, by the great care he took
of extending and improving trade; by which he opened new
mines of treasure; and, for a few temporary contributions, enriched his people to future generations. A prince, who adds to
the national stock, has a right to share the advantage he procures, and may demand supplies from his people without blush-
ing. But a prince who lives a rent-charge on the nation he
governs, who sits on his throne, like a monstrous drone in the
middle of a hive, draining all the combs of their honey, and neither making nor assisting the industrious bees to make any; such
a prince, I say, ought to blush at every grant he receives from a
people, who never received any benefit from him. The Duke of
Gloucester told Richard the Second, on his restoring Brest to the
Duke of Brittany, that he should have taken a town by his own
valor and conduct, before he resigned what his ancestors had left
him. Much to the same purpose might an oppressed people
justly answer a craving prince. When you have increased the
riches and advanced the prosperity of the nation, you will have
some right to make these demands upon us; but till then we
shall think that you have none.

LETTER VI.*

THE glorious scene of government which displayed itself in the reign of Edward the Third, was strangely altered on the succession of Richard the Second; a violent, haughty, obstinate and weak prince; whose reign, as one of our historians observes, "affords but little matter that may shine in history; and cannot boast of any one great and distinguished captain; any one memorable battle, or important siege; but prorogations of truces, abstinences, sufferances, patiences, tolerances, were the language and amusement of the times; and treaties were all the while kept on foot for a perpetual peace; treaties," says he, "hitherto fruitless, illusory, and impracticable."

It must be confessed that the reins of government hung pretty loose in the hands of Edward the Third, towards the latter end of his reign; from whence proceeded the growth of those factions which disturbed the beginning of his grandson's reign. Some part of this was owing, very probably, to the abuse of Wickliffe's doctrines: more to the cruel treatment which the inferior part of the commonalty received. The lords grew tyrants, and the commons rebels. But these commotions were soon suppressed by the united force of the rest of the nation; much sooner, and with consequences less fatal than in other countries, where rebellion and popular insurrections seem to have been the epidemical distempers of that age.

If the spirit of faction was soon quelled among the commons, it prevailed openly, scandalously, and dangerously in the court. Something of it might be discerned, perhaps, among the lords, who opposed the court: even in the Duke of Gloucester, the favorite of the people; in the Duke of Lancaster, a wise prince, and who acted long the moderating part; in Arundel and others.— Nothing of it was to be observed in the general proceedings of parliament, and in the national conduct.

The justness of the character given before of Richard the Second, discovered itself very early in his actions. He had a brutality, and a good opinion of himself; one of which might have betrayed him into a discovery of what it was his interest to conceal, if the other had not made him capable of doing it, even on reflection. Hence came those famous and foolish sayings of this prince, which history has preserved, and which gave his people

---

* Mr. Francklin was taken up for printing this paper and the preceding one, on the reign of Edward the Third; but no farther prosecution hath been yet commenced against him on that account.

timely warning what they had to expect from him.   Of his commons he said, "that slaves they were, and slaves they should
be."   Upon an address from parliament to remove his chancellor
and treasurer, his answer was, "that he would not remove, at
their request, the meanest scullion out of his kitchen."

However, he found men, as all princes may easily do, who flattered him in his vices and follies; such men, for instance, as Nevil,
Vere, Poole, Tressilian, and others; who, to fasten him to themselves, made the nation odious to him, as they made him odious
to the nation, by their rapine, their insolence, and by a weak administration, which exposed the kingdom to be invaded by the
Scots, and threatened and insulted by the French.

During all this time, parliaments met frequently, and gave necessary supplies; some grievances they redressed, but bore the
mal-administration of the court faction till the tenth year of this
king, when they prosecuted the favorites with great justice, with
temper, and yet with vigor.   They spared nothing to provide for
the defence of the kingdom by sea and land; and having put the
administration, for a time, into the hands of persons chosen by
themselves, gave the king such a warning as might have taught
him to abandon a faction, and to throw himself on his people—
but it proved in vain.   His favorite ministers persuaded him that
they suffered for his sake; that the aim of their enemies was to
dethrone him by disgracing them; and whilst all the troubles of
his reign were due to his support of them, they made him believe
that they suffered for executing his orders, and maintaining his
authority.—Nay, they represented to him that, by accusing the
counsellors, a man plainly shows that he believes the sovereign
incapable of governing; and that the readiest way to discredit a
prince is, persuading his subjects that he makes use of ill ministers.   These arguments and artifices, ridiculous as they seem,
succeeded, and had their effect for some time longer.

The deluded king entered into a closer conjunction than ever
with his ministers.   He took their iniquities on himself; made
their cause his own; was privy to their plots of poisoning their
enemies; of packing juries; of corrupting the judges to give opinions against law; and to all that dirty work which they wanted,
not he.   Nay, by his encouragement they raised troops, and a
battle was fought in their quarrel; but they were defeated, and
the fourteenth parliament, called the wonder-working parliament
having punished the judges and ministers with proper severity,
endeavored to reconcile the king and his people.   They gave him
great subsidies, and renewed their homage and fealty to him.

Even all this still proved in vain.   No experience was sufficient
to reclaim Richard the Second.   He governed tyrannically at
home, and took a wife, and bought a peace from France.   It is

remarkable, that the peace cost him four hundred thousand pounds, much more than he got by his wife. His favorite ministers had before this time endeavored to persuade him to give up Calais, and purchase the friendship of France, to assist him against the lords and others who opposed him. This is not the last, nor least instance of conducting foreign affairs purely with regard to the interest of ministers, and without any to the honor and interest of the nation.

The factions among the great men were of double advantage to the king for a time.

First, the body of the people, who showed themselves sufficiently animated with a spirit of liberty, grew cool in espousing the quarrels of the lords, after they thought liberty secured by the proceedings of parliament, in the tenth year of this king; and though many particular actions of violence, of treachery, and of cruelty, were committed by Richard the Second, they bore all with the greatest patience for several years.

In the next place these factions among the great men enabled the king to divide them, to play one against the other, and to build up his tyranny on the ruins of both. His uncle, the Duke of Gloucester, was basely betrayed, and barbarously murdered by him. He procured a packed parliament, consisting of men imposed on the shires and towns by the king's authority, wholly managed by court favorites, and which bent all its endeavors to destroy the liberties and privileges of the people. With the help of such a parliament, he wreaked vengeance on those who had opposed him; got his authority exalted above all law, and exercised a most cruel tyranny.

The people still bore, and it is probable that the king, and others as well as he, imagined that they would be obliged to bear on, since the whole legislature united in their oppression. But in this he was deceived. When the parliament took the part of the people, the people followed the motions of parliament. When they had no hopes from parliament, they followed the first standard which was set up against the king. The same spirit of liberty, which had been so slow to act under so many provocations, acted with the greatest vigor when it was least expected. The king, at the head of an army in Ireland, the Duke of York at the head of another in England, and the Earl of Salisbury at the head of a third, could do the king no service. The armies would not fight for the king against their country. The whole nation abandoned him, or acted against him. Some of his ministers were hanged; particularly those who had been the great instruments of taxing and oppressing the people. He was, at length, forced to resign, and to subscribe an instrument with his own hands, by which he confessed himself unworthy to govern the kingdom any longer. This instrument of resignation was not only unanimously approved of in parliament, but articles of accusation were ordered to be drawn up against him, to justify their resolution of deposing him. These articles were thirty-five in number, setting forth the particulars of his misgovernment; two of which are to this effect:

"That he had put the administration of the public affairs in the hands of unexperienced· and ill-designing persons, to the. great damage of the people, who were loaded with excessive taxes.

"That in his negotiations with foreign princes, he had made use of so many equivocations and sophistries, that none would take his word any more."

It is very observable, that these extremities fell upon Richard the Second, at a time when every thing seemed to contribute to his support, in the exercise of that arbitrary power which he had assumed. Those whom he had most reason to fear, were removed either by violent death, or banishment; and others were secured in his interest by places, or favors at court. The great offices of the crown, and the magistracy of the whole kingdom, were put into such hands as were fit for his designs; besides which, he had a parliament entirely at his devotion: but all these advantageous circumstances served only to prove that a prince can have no real security against the just resentments of an injured and exasperated nation; for, as Rapin observes upon the sad catastrophe of this reign, and that of Edward the Second, "in such governments as that of England, all endeavors used by the king to make himself absolute, are but so many steps towards his own downfall.

It is farther observed by another eminent writer upon this reign, which he justly calls a reign of favorites, "that the king in his distress saw himself forsaken by those whom he should have forsaken before; the very men, who had so much flattered him with their excessive love and loyalty; and like those mean insects, which live with a little warmth, but shrink at any change of weather, they who had contributed to all his errors in his prosperity, transplanted their zeal into the new sunshine, as soon as his successor demanded the crown."

LETTER VII.

From the reigns of Edward the Third, and Richard the Second, we shall hasten downwards, as fast as some necessary observation will permit. Those of the princes of York and

Lancaster, form a period of more than eighty years, which passed in foreign and civil wars, in frequent revolutions of government, and in all those disorders which usually accompany and follow such revolutions.

The party of Richard the Second, even after the death of that unhappy prince, broke out into open rebellion against Henry the Fourth: but their efforts were vain. He held the crown fast which the parliament had given him; and the chief of his opposers perished in their attempts. Happy had it been, if they alone had suffered; but here we must observe a necessary and cruel consequence of faction. As it oppresseth the whole community, if it succeeds; so it often draws oppression, not on itself alone, but on the whole community, when it fails. The attempts to dethrone Henry the Fourth, justified him, no doubt, in supporting himself by a military force. They excused him likewise; very probably, in the eyes of many, for governing with a severe hand; for doing several illegal and tyrannical actions; for invading the privileges of parliament, at least in the point of elections, and for obtaining, by these means, frequent and heavy taxes on the people: for as all this might appear the harder, because it happened in the reign of a king who had no title to his crown but the good-will of the people, and the free gift of parliament; so it might appear, on the other hand, the less grievous because some part of it was rendered necessary by the opposition which a faction made to a parliamentary establishment; and because the rest of it was represented, perhaps, under that umbrage, to be so likewise, by the court logic of that age.

A people may be persuaded to bear patiently a great deal of oppression, as long as they can be persuaded that they bear it only to defend their own choice, and to maintain their acts; but if they discover this to be nothing more than a pretence, by which such powers are kept up as are unnecessary to their security, and dangerous to their liberty; by which the wealth of the whole nation is drained into the coffers of a few; and by which, in one word, they become exposed to ruin by the very means which they took to avoid it; it cannot be expected that they will be patient very long.

It deserves particular notice, that although Henry the Fourth was willing to show his clemency, at the beginning of his reign, by inflicting a very slight punishment on the wicked and hated ministers of the late king; yet it being alleged in their excuse, that Richard had compelled them to act, the parliament took occasion from thence to pass an act, by which it was declared that, for the future, compulsion should be no legal excuse to justify actions contrary to law. The reasonableness and expediency of this act are very manifest; for it is the indispensable duty of a good minister to dissuade his majesty from all illegal measures; or, if he cannot prevail, to quit his service, rather than suffer himself to be made the instrument of them; and if the commands of the prince were to be allowed a sufficient justification, the prerogative of doing no wrong would be extended to ministers, and nobody would be left accountable for maladministration.

In the short, but triumphant reign of Henry the Fifth, the spirit of faction was awed; and the spirit of liberty had no occasion of exerting itself, at least with struggle and in any signal manner, under a prince just, moderate and pious, according to the religion of those times.

The reign of his son was the reign of faction; and it discloses an horrid scene of iniquity, folly, madness. The scandalous management of the public affairs, which brought infinite loss and dishonor to the nation, gave real occasion, as well as pretence, to commotions and insurrections. The contemptible character of the man who sat on the throne, revived the hopes of the faction of York. The faction of Lancaster took the alarm. Most of the great and active men were attached to one side or to the other, by obligation, by resentment, by hopes, or by fears. The national interest was sunk, to the shame of the nation, in the particular interest of two families.

In the civil wars, which happened a century and a half, or two centuries before this time, the point in dispute was how the people should be governed. In these we are speaking of, the point in dispute was who should govern. The first was worth contending for, and deserved all the blood which was shed in the quarrel. But this cannot be said of the last, which ought always to be looked upon with great indifference; except in cases where it has so immediate and necessary a relation to the first, that securing the first depends, in a great measure, on settling the last. Such cases have happened; and particular instances may be easily found; but the contrary cases, where men have fought for governors without regard to government, are easy to be found likewise; and that was plainly the case of the two factions of York and Lancaster.

The parliaments in those days seemed to be in another temper; very little concerned who was king, and very much to preserve the constitution. In the many revolutions which happened, each side would have the parliament for them. Whatever titles they set up, they were glad to hold the crown by the grant, or by the confirmation of parliament. The parliament wisely complied, whoever prevailed. The chance of war determined who should be king; at one time Henry the Sixth, at another Edward the Fourth, and the parliament accordingly placed them on the throne, and settled their government.

There is another observation which ought to be made, before we leave this period of time.   The reigns of Richard the Second and Henry the Fourth had shown the dangerous consequences of that influence which the crown had obtained in the elections of members of parliament.   The watchful spirit of liberty was soon alarmed, and prevailed to make such regulations about elections, and about the qualifications of the electors and the elected, as seemed at that time sufficient to prevent this influence for the future.   These regulations appear in several laws, made during the reigns of the three Lancastrian princes; and our elections proceed, in a great measure, upon them to this very day.   These regulations have required, and must, in the nature of things, require to be altered, as the course of accidents, or the change of national circumstances shall suggest reasons for so doing.   But then such alterations have been, and ought always to be contrived so as to adapt them better, and to enforce them more strongly; because the principle on which they are founded, can never vary, and is so essential to the preservation of liberty, that if it be lost, and if a practice in opposition to it should ever prevail, the balance of our government would be that moment lost, and the British constitution left at the mercy of any ambitious prince, or wicked minister.

For this reason Mr. Rapin observes very justly, " that there are but two ways of depriving the English of their liberties; either by laying aside parliaments, or by bribing them." And in another place he says, "that the English freedom will be at an end whenever the court invades the free election of parliaments."

It is necessary to insist upon this observation a little; because it hath been ridiculed, though dully, and great pains have been taken to explode the doctrine contained in it, which was laid down in these words: " In a constitution like ours, the safety of the whole depends on the balance of the parts; and the balance of the parts on their mutual independency on each other." These words, it seems, even with those of Thuanus to explain them, convey no idea to the London Journalist; but this will be found, as I apprehend, to be his fault, or his defect, not Oldcastle's.   A man born without the sense of hearing, or stopping his ears, and determined at any rate not to hear, may be deaf to the voice of Stentor himself.

I shall not enter into any altercations with the London Journalist, nor go out of the road to have the honor of such company.   But when I meet him in my way, I shall encounter him frankly, without the least fear of being crushed by the weight of his arguments; or, which is more, by the power of his patron.

To say, like this author, that the " carrying on of business, and maintaining government by powers absolutely distinct, and absolutely independent, is a mere Utopian scheme, must proceed from ignorance or folly." Have not powers, absolutely distinct and independent, been joined by federal unions? Are no such examples to be found, even at this day? Has not this been brought about by the very reason given to prove that it can never happen; because men agree when they see reason for agreement; and they see reason for agreement, when they see their interest in agreeing? Osborne could not have been in earnest, when he let such stuff fall from his pen. He meant to elude the argument, and to perplex his readers, or he meant nothing. But this shall not pass. The matter is too important. He shall be talked to as he desires, without a metaphor; and what has been advanced shall be applied to our government.

A king of Great Britain is that supreme magistrate who has a negative voice in the legislature. He is entrusted with the executive power, and several other powers and privileges, which we call prerogatives, are annexed to this trust. The two houses of parliament have their rights and privileges; some of which are common to both, others particular to each. They prepare, they pass bills, or they refuse to pass such as are sent to them. They address, represent, advise, remonstrate. The supreme judicature resides in the lords. The commons are the grand inquest of the nation, and to them it belongs likewise to judge of national expenses, and to give supplies accordingly.

If the legislative as well as the executive power, was wholly in the king, as in some countries, he would be absolute; if in the lords, our government would be an aristocracy; if in the commons, a democracy. It is this division of power, these distinct privileges attributed to the king, to the lords, and to the commons, which constitute a limited monarchy.

Again: as they constitute a limited monarchy, so the wisdom of our government has provided, as far as human wisdom can provide for the preservation of it, by this division of power, and by these distinct privileges. If any one part of the three which compose our government, should at any time usurp more power than the law gives, or make an ill use of a legal power, the other two parts may, by uniting their strength, reduce this power into its proper bounds, or correct the abuse of it; nay, if at any time two of these parts should concur in usurping, or abusing power, the weight of the third may, at least, retard the mischief, and give time and chance for preventing it.

This is that balance which has been so much talked of, and this is the use of it. Both are plain to common sense, and to experience; as will appear farther in the course of these remarks, where we shall have occasion to show, how often the proper use of this balance has saved our constitution; and to what misfortunes we have been exposed by the neglect, or improper use of it. Since this division of power, and these distinct privileges constitute and maintain our government, it follows that the confusion of them tends to destroy it. This proposition is therefore true; that, in a constitution like ours, the safety of the whole depends on the balance of the parts. Let us see whether it be true, that the balance of the parts consists in their mutual independency.

To speak again without any metaphor, the power, which the several parts of our government have of controlling and checking one another, may be called a dependency on one another, and may be argued for by those who want to throw darkness round them, as the dependency opposed to the independency, mentioned in the proposition. But the fallacy is gross. We have shown that this power of control in each, which results from the division of power amongst all the parts of our government, is necessary to the preservation of it: and thus a sort of constitutional dependency, if I may have leave to express myself in that manner, is created among them; but this mutual dependency cannot be opposed to the independency pleaded for. On the contrary, this mutual dependency cannot subsist without such an independency; for whenever this independency is lost, the mutual dependency is that moment changed into a particular, constant dependency of one part on two; or, which is still more unreasonable, of two parts on one. The constitutional dependency, as I have called it for distinction's sake, consists in this; that the proceedings of each part of the government, when they come forth into action and affect the whole, are liable to be examined and controlled by the other parts. The independency pleaded for consists in this; that the resolutions of each part, which direct these proceedings, be taken independently and without any influence, direct or indirect, on the others. Without the first, each part would be at liberty to attempt destroying the balance, by usurping or abusing power; but without the last, there can be no balance at all. I will illustrate this, by supposing a prince, who claims and exercises a right of levying money without consent of parliament. He could not be opposed effectually, if the two houses of parliament had not a right to oppose him, to call his ministers to account; and to make him feel that, far from being absolute, he was under this constitutional dependency; but he would not be opposed at all, if the two houses of parliament were under his influence, and incapable of directing their proceedings independently of him. One would be ashamed to insist thus much on a point so very clear, if some men were not

so hardened to all sense of shame, as to maintain the contrary;
and that there are men capable of doing this, is one of those melancholy symptoms which characterise the present age. I could
almost appeal to the cool thoughts, and the private reflections of
some of these writers, whether any thing can be more scandalous than the task they have undertaken. To screen their patrons,
they endeavor to distinguish us out of our greatest national advantages; as was observed in the case of Dunkirk. To reconcile
the minds of men to such measures as their patrons may want,
and as no honest man will take, they endeavor to demolish the
very corner stones on which the whole fabric of liberty rests.—
Their iniquity, it must be confessed, is very systematical. When
they write for corruption, they write for the means. When they
write for the dependency of the parliament on the court, they
write for the end. Well might Oldcastle say of these writers,
their patrons and abettors, " that the mask was pulled off on one
side." Let me conjure them, in the name of modesty, to call
themselves Whigs no longer. It is time they should lay that
appellation aside, since it will not be hard to prove, from the
general tenor of their writings, that the maxims they advance,
the doctrines they inculcate, and the conduct they recommend,
lead to the destruction of civil liberty, as much as the political
lessons of Sibthorpe, Manwaring, or archbishop Laud himself.
They and their followers declared themselves directly against
liberty. To plead for it was almost blasphemy; and to assert it
little less than the sin against the Holy Ghost, according to the
doctrines taught by those divines. Such absurdities made few
converts in those days; and the preachers of them would meet
with the utmost contempt in these. But the writers, of whom
we now complain, affect to maintain the cause of liberty, whilst
they betray it. They assert the principles of liberty in general,
and sometimes reason upon them well enough; but when they
apply them to particular cases, they prevaricate, evade, and exert
all their poor endeavors to turn the cannon of liberty against
herself. The others had fænum in cornu. They put mankind
on their guard against them, and were the true promoters of all
the mischief and confusion which followed, when the nation run
into the utmost extremes, in opposition to them. These men insinuate themselves as friends to liberty. They are looked upon
as such by some few persons, who mean well to liberty, even at
this time; and yet they are almost wholly employed in promoting that which is destructive of liberty, and inconsistent with it,
corruption and dependency. Laud and the others endeavored
openly to lop the branches and cut down the tree; but these men
are privately poisoning the root of liberty. The power of the
court, and the authority of the lawyers could not make the levy-

ing ship-money pass for law, nor prevail on the nation to bear it. But if it were possible to suppose a house of commons as dependent as these lawyers, (and they would be as dependent, if the doctrines which we oppose prevailed amongst them,) the nation might then be loaded with taxes, oppressed with debts, and reduced to the greatest misery by law. Our liberties, as well as our estates, might be taken from us. We might be legally undone. These are possible consequences of such doctrines. If they are not probable, we owe no thanks to the weekly preachers of them. The nature of our present settlement, which is built on the foundation of liberty, the interest and honor of the prince now on the throne, as well as of all his illustrious posterity, are our security against these dangers; but still I say, we owe no thanks to the writers on the side of the ministry.

I have dwelt pretty much upon this point, to show what is the real design of these remarks; and I will venture to add that those persons who oppose such doctrines as we have been opposing, will appear at last to be the truest friends to his majesty king George, and the Protestant succession; which can subsist only upon those principles upon which it was originally established.

LETTER VIII.

IF the reign of Henry the Sixth was a reign of faction, those of the house of York were so likewise. The popularity, bravery, cruelty, rashness, uxoriousness, incontinence of Edward the Fourth; in short, his good and his bad qualities worked the different effects of supporting, exasperating and increasing factions. The characters of Henry the Sixth's queen and of the Earl of Warwick, to mention no more of the principal actors on that bloody stage, conspired to maintain and aggravate this national calamity.

In these long continued struggles, the whole nation became involved, and the factions of York and Lancaster growing every day more animated and better disciplined, we are not to wonder that they fought usque ad internecionem; at least, till the field of battle, the scaffold, and some theatres of clandestine murders had left no man on one side alive, who was in a condition to oppose or give jealousy to the other. But that which may very justly raise our wonder is, that Edward the Fourth, having secured to himself and his family the possession of the throne, by the murder of Henry the Sixth, and his son, and by the total defeat of the whole

Lancastrian party, should suffer two new factions to be nursed up, which divided his own party, occasioned the murder of his sons, and by establishing the short-lived tyranny of his brother, brought the Earl of Richmond to the throne, and sunk for ever the house of York in that of Lancaster.

Edward the Fourth's queen was the original cause of all this mischief, and a principal sufferer herself in the course of it. She was resolved to govern at any rate; and Rapin observes, " that as her being queen gave her no manner of title to meddle with the affairs of the public, she knew how to manage that matter another way; namely, by the influence she had over the king. Though Edward often proved false to her, she bore it very patiently, and never showed her uneasiness at it. Edward, charmed to find himself at liberty to pursue his inclinations, without danger of continual reproaches, repaid her moderation with the most obliging and condescending behaviour; of which she knew how to make a good use." She maintained this ascendant over her husband to the last, and for a little complaisance, which cost her nothing in present, she purchased a degree of power in the state, which cost her dear in consequence, by alienating the affections of the people from her husband during his life, and ruining his family afterwards, as I have hinted before.

" Her aim was, according to Rapin, to secure her power during the king's life, and in case she survived him, to make sure of the government of the kingdom, in the name of the prince her son, when he should come to be on the throne; but by a fatality, not unusual to the best laid projects, this very thing proved the occasion of her own, and her family's ruin."

I cannot think, as Rapin seems to do, that her project deserved to be ranked amogst those which are the best laid. It appears to be the narrow project of a woman, who had cunning, insinuation, and the spirit of intrigue; with much pride and ambition; but wanted that extensive knowledge, and that superior genius, such as Catherine of Medicis, and our queen Elizabeth possessed, which is necessary to conduct so great a design as her passion prompted her to undertake; for what was her project? Was it to acquire an interest in the nation by deserving well of it? Nothing less. It was singly this; to form a faction at court, by raising her relations and immediate dependants, which should be wholly her own, and into whose hands she might throw all the power and profit which the king had to bestow. She had the good luck to compass this design, and triumphed, no doubt very wisely, in her great success. Surrounded by her creatures, she looked no farther than that circle, and either took no notice of the temper of the nation, or judged of it by the temper of the court. But the rise of this faction immediately formed

another, and established the distinction of ancient and new nobility. The former had the true natural strength, which great
estates in land and established credit in the nation gave them.
The latter had no strength of their own, none but that adventitious strength, which arose from employments and favor at court.
They brought nothing to court, which could make the court
amends for the envy and discontent which their elevation
created. To supply this, two things were done; which served,
perhaps, to fortify the queen in her delusion, and thereby made
the ruin of her ambitious projects the surer. All those who were
not in the good graces of her faction, were disgraced at court,
and in effect banished from it. Nay they were persecuted by
the power of it; as the Duke of Clarence, the king's own brother,
was even to death. The names of the parties of York and Lancaster might subsist and be made use of on proper occasions;
but in reality, the being for or against the party of the queen,
was the sole distinction which prevailed; and even the friends of
the house of York, whom the queen did not affect, were debarred
from the king's ear, excepting only three of his old and most
faithful servants, who maintained themselves against her and
her faction. I mean Stafford Duke of Buckingham, Hastings
and Stanley.

Another method which this queen took to strengthen herself
and her faction, was by raking up money by illegal and oppressive means; particularly by setting prosecutions on foot against
the rich men of the kingdom, several of whom were arraigned
for high treason, and encouraging the judges to get them found
guilty at any rate. Habington observes, in his history of this
king, " that as their wealth was the principal evidence against
them, though their persons were acquitted, their estates were
found guilty."

The same historian observes farther, "that the memory of these
carriages hithertofore, in a business that concerned the life of a
man reputed innocent, drew the world into much fear that he
would now decline to rigor. Neither was the king totally excused, although this cruel avarice was laid to the queen, who
having a numerous issue and kindred, by favor raised up to the
highest titles, was almost necessitated, for supportance of their
honors, to rack the kingdom."

Edward seemed sensible before his death, of the mischievous
consequences which this conduct, and the clashing of two factions might produce. He endeavored to prevent them, by "re-
conciling the two parties; a poor expedient!" as Rapin justly observes, " which could not easily produce the effect he expected."

The Duke of Gloucester, who concealed his design till his
brother's death, took advantage of these factions. He made his

court publicly to the queen, and held a private correspondence with the opposite party. Nay he found means, by fomenting it, to raise a third for himself.

I have dwelt the longer in this place, on the strange turns and cruel effects of faction; because I believe, no example can be produced out of any history, which sets them in a stronger light; and because this period of time affording but small matter to recommend the spirit of liberty, which had little to do in the transactions of it, I imagine that pointing out the fatal consequences of the contrary spirit, which then prevailed, may answer the same end, as exposing of vice is frequently the strongest recommendation of virtue.

But we must not imagine, notwithstanding all the contrary appearances in this period, that the spirit of liberty was absolutely extinguished. Though that flame was lost, for the most part, in the constant glare of faction, yet it was still alive; and by living, preserved the constitution of our government during the whole course of these civil wars.

If we look closely into these scenes of confusion, we may discover many particular instances of the operations of this spirit. Such were the difficulties and delays opposed to the grant of tonnage and poundage, for nine years together; and the many restrictions added to this grant, when it was at last obtained by Edward the Fourth. Other instances to the same purpose might be quoted; but we choose to insist on a more general observation, already mentioned by us, which runs through the whole period, and is so strongly vouched by history as to admit of no cavil.

The observation we are going to make, contains a memorable exception to this proposition, which is but too generally true, that the spirit of liberty and the spirit of faction are incompatible, and cannot long subsist together. The virtue of our ancestors made this exception; and if it hath been remembered to their shame, that they sunk the national interest in the particular interest of two families; it ought to be remembered to their honor, that they did so in this single point only, who should reign, and in no other. We took notice, in a former paper, that upon every revolution, each side engaged the parliament for them, and that whoever prevailed, the parliament wisely complied. This conduct, which lasted from Richard the Second down to Richard the Third, preserved our liberties; but it could not have been pursued, nor could our liberties by consequence have been preserved, if the spirit of liberty had not been latent in the hearts of those very men who seem to breathe nothing but faction. How could it have happened that the sole title of conquest was ever established in so many revolutions brought about by the sword, if the actors in them had not been strongly affected with a love and reverence for the free constitution of our government? The princes of York and Lancaster themselves were willing, nay desirous to have a parliamentary confirmation of their titles, real or pretended. But how came they to be so desirous of it? How came they to think it necessary? The case is plain. The temper of their parties and of their armies begot this necessity. The spirit of liberty prevailed enough in the whole body of the nation, out of which these parties and armies were composed, to preserve the principles of public freedom, though not enough to preserve the public peace. Each side contended to have a king of their own party; but neither side would have a tyrant. They sacrificed their lives to faction; but would not give up their liberties. The victorious armies led their kings to the foot of the throne; but carried them no farther.

The author of the Short History of standing armies observes that, "in all the wars of York and Lancaster, whatever party prevailed, we do not find they ever attempted to keep up a standing army. Such was the virtue of those times," says he, " that they would rather run the hazard of forfeiting their heads and estates to the rage of the opposite party, than certainly enslave their country, though they themselves were to be the tyrants." This remark is just, as far as it goes; and it goes as far as that author wanted to carry it; but it is not so full, nor carried so far as history will warrant. That the princes, who obtained the crown by their armies, did not attempt to govern by their armies afterwards, is most true, and may reflect some honor on those princes, and on the heads of their parties. But there is something more than this remarkable in the conduct of those times; for even in the heat of victory, in the raptures of a successful revolution, and before the armies could be disbanded, we see these princes obliged to ascend the steps of the throne in such a manner, and under such conditions, as the parliament thought fit to prescribe, and as were not always agreeable to them. This, I am sure, reflects great honor on the parliaments, who were actors in the last scenes of all these revolutions; and on the armies, who contented themselves to become spectators in such conjunctures. We will take the first example which presents itself in these wars.

The Duke of Lancaster was at the head of an army of sixty thousand men, when he came to the crown. The proclamation which he published the very day he was crowned, showed how very unwilling he was to seem to hold his crown purely by right of election. He would gladly have set up that of conquest; or a title derived from Richard the Second's resignation; or a title by blood; or any title but the true one. Notwithstanding this, he was obliged when nothing could have obliged him but the sense of his own party and army, to submit to as formal an election as ever was made. The two houses took notice of the blind claim of right which he entered. They chose him to be king, upon the question put to them, after having given their negative to the Duke of York, to his sons, and to others, who were severally proposed in the same manner to them. They seem industriously to have contrived and pursued, on this occasion, a method of proceeding as opposite as possible to the views and inclination of this prince, whose army attended him, and whose rival was his prisoner.

Again; to take another example from the latter end of these wars. The battle of Northampton being won, and Henry the Sixth taken, the Duke of York hastens out of Ireland to put himself at the head of his party and his army. The parliament meets. The duke asserts his undoubted right, by descent, to the crown, which he demands as due to him, without any interposition of parliament. He shows the utmost, and even an indecent impatience to take possession of it. He is supported by his own party. He is opposed by others. But the matter is by all submitted to the debate and decision of parliament. The debate itself must have been grievous enough to a prince so fond of a crown, and so much warmed with the notion of his hereditary right. But the decision of this affair must have wounded him to the quick. So little regard was paid to his right, that he was forced to content himself with leaving the crown on the head of Henry the Sixth during that prince's life, and not to have the prospect of succeeding to it, till after that prince's decease; which, by the way, was a point of the less value to him, because he was older than Henry the Sixth, and could not hope to be the better for it, according to the course of nature. He submitted to all these mortifications; and a very judicious historian attributes his submission to his moderation; but I believe those who fully consider his former conduct, and his passionate behavior at this time, will hardly subscribe to such a judgment. His submission, like that of Henry the Fourth, in the case before cited, was a submission, which the temper of his party rendered necessary. They would not force the resolutions of the two houses; and why the two houses would go no farther in his favor, at that juncture, might easily be accounted for, if this were a proper place for that disquisition.—After the battle of Wakefield, where the Duke of York was killed, and that of St. Albans, where the Earl of Warwick was beaten, the faction of York were determined, by the dangers they had run, and by the losses they had sustained, to balance no longer, but to set the crown on the head of the Earl of March; and yet they proceeded no otherwise than under the authority of parliament, which had ratified the agreement made between the late Duke of York and Henry the Sixth. By one article of this agreement it was stipulated, that if King Henry broke it in any point, the crown and royal dignity should immediately devolve on the Duke of York, if alive; or, in failure of him, on his next heir.   The Earl of Warwick therefore, in a kind of military assembly, (for a part of the army, at least, was there,) proceeded to the election of Edward the Fourth; but he proceeded on this foundation.   The great efforts made to break this agreement and to defeat the effect of it, by king Henry's queen, and the Lancastrian party, were interpreted, and not without color, as so many infractions of it.   By consequence, Edward the Fourth had an immediate right to the crown, by virtue of the act of parliament made in confirmation of this convention, which act and convention were produced by Warwick, who caused them to be publicly read.   The proceeding of this assembly, which hath a tumultuous air in history, was therefore in reality a proclamation of a king, made by authority of parliament, and not of an election of a king, without that authority.

Let us conclude, that if the spirit of faction hath, on some occasions, prevailed over the spirit of liberty, so far as to defeat and even pervert the designs of the latter; the spirit of liberty hath likewise revived, in its turn, on other occasions, and prevented the consummation of that misery which faction would naturally and of course have produced.   Let us conclude that all standing armies, for whatsoever purpose instituted, or in whatsoever habit clothed, may be easily made the instruments of faction; because a body of men separated, in many respects, from the rest of the nation, constrained to different customs, and in some measure subjected to different laws, may be easily persuaded that they have a different interest.   Let us conclude that these casuists in red, are the most dangerous in this respect, that having swords by their sides, they are able at once to cut those Gordian knots which others must untie by degrees.   But let us conclude, at the same time, that if a spirit of liberty be kept up in a free nation, it will be kept up in the army of that nation; and that when it is thus kept up, though the spirit of faction may do great hurt, it cannot complete the public ruin.   We see the truth of this observation exemplified near three centuries ago; and let us remember with gratitude, that the same truth was again confirmed to us no longer ago than two-and-forty years.

LETTER IX.

One of the historians of Brittany, if I remember right, and I
think it is Argentre, says the people of that duchy grew so much
tired with the disputes between Charles of Blois and the Mon-
forts, that the two parties agreed, just before a battle, to make
an end of the quarrel at once, by taking off that prince, against
whom the fortune of the day should declare itself.—Our ancestors
were very far from following this example; but they seized the
opportunity which was presented to them, after Richard the
Third had usurped the throne, and murdered his nephews, of
abolishing tyranny, and extinguishing faction.

The princes of York and Lancaster butchered one another in
such a manner, that the right of the former centered in Elizabeth,
eldest daughter of Edward the Fourth, and the pretensions of
the latter were allowed, by the whole Lancastrian party, to
belong to the Earl of Richmond.—This was the state of the
families.

The faction of York detested Richard for his usurpation and
cruelties.—The faction of Lancaster hated him for his name; and
neither the great qualities which he really had, nor the good
qualities which he affected, could reconcile mankind to his bar-
barity.—This was the temper of the nation.

The opportunity thus formed, was improved by the universal
concurrence, which a spirit of liberty and a regard to the public
good, independent of party, inspired.   The faction of York became willing to receive a king of the house of Lancaster; and
the party of Lancaster a queen of the house of York. All parties
labored to unite the two roses; and faction itself was bent, in this
fortunate conjuncture, to extirpate faction.

The deposition of Richard, and the advancement of the Earl
of Richmond to the throne, upon this express condition, that he
should marry the Princess Elizabeth, were pursued with success,
even when Richard thought himself most secure; when the parliament had been obliged to confirm his usurpation; to declare
the children of Edward bastards; and to attaint the Earl of
Richmond.

What a scene of national peace and prosperity was opened
by this revolution and new settlement!   But how soon was it
shifted?   How soon were the wise and honest views of the
many defeated by the cunning and iniquity of the few?—Henry
the Seventh, a creature of the people, if ever any prince was
such, had been raised to the throne, in order to cut up the roots
of faction; to restore public tranquillity; and to establish a legal

government on the ruins of tyranny.—He did the very reverse
of all this.   His reign and that of his son have been two of the
severest under which our country hath groaned since the conquest; and yet, in these very reigns, the foundations of liberty
were laid much broader and stronger than ever.—How this came
about, it must be useful, and perhaps it may be entertaining, to
consider.

Henry the Seventh, who would have been glad a little before
to have assured himself of the crown on any terms, grew difficult
as soon as he had obtained it.   He durst not avow a title by
conquest; but he evaded the appearances of a parliamentary title
very industriously, and made the ceremony of his coronation
precede the meeting of his parliament.   He evaded, in the same
manner, the appearances of any communication of right from the
Princess Elizabeth, by deferring his marriage till an act had
passed to settle the crown on him and his posterity, without any
mention of the house of York.   In short, his whole skill, credit
and power were employed to get the act of settlement so generally and so ambiguously penned, as to leave him room to assert
afterwards a right inherent in himself, and independent of the
authority of parliament.   Nay, he went farther; for, in the bull
of confirmation, which he obtained from the pope, and in which
he affected to have all sorts of titles enumerated, he took particular care to have that of conquest inserted.

Such a conduct gave sufficient reason for alarm; but we do not
find that it was taken.   The tyrant was dead, and the new establishment was made.   The nation was overjoyed; and the work
of liberty was done by halves.   The new king found a compliance with all his measures, as new kings generally do.   But little
reflection was made, perhaps, at that time, on these proceedings
of the court; or if a just reflection was made, we may easily believe that it was soon stifled by that adulation, which represents
the most necessary precautions, the most just complaints, and the
assertion of the clearest rights, as proofs of disaffection.

The whole course of Henry the Seventh's reign was answerable to these beginnings; and he seems to have established himself in the power of pursuing principles of government, evidently
repugnant to those upon which he had been raised to the throne,
before the nation was well aware of what he intended.   He
planted faction anew, and was the true cause of all the disturbances which followed from it, and which began even in the first
year of his reign.   Many of the York party had signalised themselves in his cause.   All of them submitted to his government;
and that small branch of this party, which had supported Richard
the Third, was too inconsiderable to hurt him; but he soon made

it considerable, by driving almost the whole York party into that interest. " He had conceived," says Rapin, " so mortal a hatred for the whole house of York, that he let slip no opportunity to humble the Yorkists; behaving always towards them not as a just king, but like the head of a party."

That some of his ministers, of the Lancastrian party, might find their private account in such a measure, and sacrifice to it both the interest of their master and their country, is obvious enough; but how the king, who was certainly an able man, could prefer dividing, instead of uniting his people in affection and obedience, would appear very marvellous, if experience had not taught us that men of the greatest genius fall sometimes into the same errors, as men of the least genius would be apt to commit in the same circumstances.—How this happens we are not, in this place, to inquire.

Henry the Seventh proceeded as he had been suffered to set out, and established by degrees, and those not slow, a power almost absolute. His jealousy, his pride, and his insatiable sordid avarice had their full swing. He became hated even by his own party, and might very probably have lost his crown, if many circumstances, both at home and abroad, had not conspired in his favor, and if he had not improved them all with the utmost ability of council and dexterity of management. The chief of these circumstances, and it well deserves to be remarked, was this—they who ventured their estates and lives in several insurrections against him, and they who privately fomented these insurrections, instead of uniting on a national principle, and bending their endeavors to a reformation of government, united on a principle of faction: for the king's behavior had revived this spirit; as we observed above; but still this spirit, though revived, had not attained its former strength. The nation in general was tired of faction; dreaded a relapse into the consequences of it, and would not engage for a Simnel, a Warbeck, or even a real prince of the house of York. A national coolness on one side, and vigilance and vigor on the king's part, defeated all these enterprises as fast as they were formed. Every one of these defeats gave Henry additional strength and increase of reputation, which is strength in its effects. Thus it happened in this case; and thus it hath happened in many others. By making an ill use of his power, the king was the real author of all the disorders in the state, and of all the attempts against his government; and yet, the better to prevent such disorders, and to resist such attempts, farther powers were intrusted to him. Because he had governed ill, it was put in his power to govern worse; and liberty was undermined, for fear it should be overthrown. It hath fared sometimes with monarchy as with the church of Rome.   Both have acquired greater wealth and power by the abuse of what they had, and mankind have been egregiously the bubbles of both.

We must not however conclude that this king made force the sole, though he made it the principal expedient of his government. He was wise enough to consider that his court was not the nation; and that however he might command with a nod in one, he must captivate, at least in some degree, the good-will of mankind, to make himself secure of being long obeyed in the other; nay more, that he must make his people some amends for the oppressions which his avarice particularly exposed them to suffer.   For these reasons, as he strained his prerogative on some occasions very high, so he let it down again upon others; and affected to show to his parliaments much condescension, notwithstanding his pride, as well as much communication of counsels, notwithstanding his reserve.

To attribute to this Solomon of Great Britain the sole merit of the laws made in his time, as some have done, seems unreasonable; but it was certainly great merit in him, and we may add rare merit, instead of opposing, or refusing, constantly to remunerate his people, by promoting and passing of " good laws, which evermore were his retribution for treasure."   These are my Lord Bacon's words, and better than his cannot be found to express the general character of the laws which the wisdom of those times produced.   " They were deep and not vulgar; not made upon the spur of a particular occasion for the present; but out of providence of the future, to make the estate of the people still more and more happy, after the manner of the legislators in ancient and heroical times."   Husbandry, manufactures, general commerce, and increase of useful people were carefully attended to, and considerably advanced; so that whilst the weight of taxes and the vexations of Empson, Dudley, and their subordinate harpies were severely felt, every man felt likewise the particular benefit which he received in the general advantages procured to the nation.   These drops of manna, which fell from the throne, softened the murmurs of the people.   They could not make the king beloved, but they made him less hated: and the middle and lower ranks of men, who felt less the rigor of his government, felt more immediately the effects of his care and his wisdom.

We will not refine so much as to say that the commons were patient under the pressures of this reign, because they foresaw the consequences of those measures which the king took to lessen the power of his nobility.   He did not, perhaps, himself discern these consequences in their full extent; but surely if this part of his conduct was politic, it was no less popular at that time; since the same exorbitant power of the peers, which had been so formidable to the crown, had not been less oppressive to the commons. The weight of personal service had been terribly felt during the wars of York and Lancaster, and the obligation of that tenure had, no doubt, contributed to prolong them. The tenant, therefore, who found this service commuted into a rent, could not but think his condition mended, and be extremely pleased with this alteration, though he did not see the consequences of the other, which, by opening a way to the lords to alienate their lands, opened a way to the commons to increase their property, and consequently their power in the state, as may be very easily observed in the succeeding reigns.

LETTER X.

HENRY the Eighth came to the crown with very great advantages. Whatever objections had been made to his father's title, there remained no pretence of objecting to his; and if any pretence had remained, the disposition to make use of it would not have been found. The nation was grown weary of faction; fond of tranquillity; and every day more and more attentive to the arts of peace. The prerogative had been extended wide and carried high; and the means employed to acquire and maintain this authority, had been established by a reign of twenty-four years. The treasures which Henry the Seventh had accumulated and left to his son, were immense; and in leaving him these treasures he left him that which was more valuable than all of them. He left him an opportunity of gaining the affections of his people, on his accession to the throne, by putting a stop to that public rapine which had been so long exercised, and by disgracing and punishing those who had been the principal instruments of it. Henry the Eighth seized the opportunity and improved it. He confirmed, in the first moments of his reign, that pardon which his father had granted in the last of his life, and when he could hope for no farther profit by not pardoning. He invited, by proclamation, such as had been wronged to complain, and promised them satisfaction.

If Henry the Eighth had been avaricious, or weak enough to prefer wealth to popularity, he would have observed another conduct. He would have thought those men fittest to serve him, who had signalised themselves most in fleecing the people, and without any regard to their ability in playing the game of statesmen, he would have chosen them purely for their skill in packing the cards. Empson and Dudley would have continued in power, and have risen in favor. But he was too wise, or too honestly counselled in these beginnings of his government, to pursue such measures, or to employ such ministers. He kept some in his council, who were of approved abilities; but far from loading his own administration with the principal guilt of the former; far from grieving and provoking his people, by countenancing the most hated, and the most justly hated, men of the whole kingdom, he threw those criminals out of the sanctuary of the court, and exposed them to that national vengeance, under the weight of which they perished. The manner in which their lives were taken away seems liable to great objection, and I would not be thought to approve it; for a spirit of liberty can never approve such proceedings even against the worst and most guilty of men, as may be applied to destroy the best and the most innocent. All I mean to commend is the wisdom of Henry the Eighth, in abandoning these ministers, in gaining the affections of his subjects, and in making such impressions of gratitude on their minds, as lasted long and were of service to him, even when he oppressed the people in his turn.

Vanity and presumption were reigning qualities in the character of this prince. The first betrayed him into continual errors. The last made him persist in them. Pride is observed to defeat its own end, by bringing the man who seeks esteem and reverence into contempt. Vanity, self-sufficiency, presumption, the offspring of pride, have much the same effect; since no one is so liable to be deceived and governed, as he who imagines that he is capable of neither.

The characters of the princes and popes of this age, rendered the scene of foreign affairs very important. Henry the Eighth was happy enough to have no interest of his own abroad worth engaging him in the broils of the continent. He was free from guaranties of foreign dominions, and from all engagements to foreign princes, which could in the least incumber him. In this state he might have kept himself with equal dignity and advantage. He might have increased his strength, whilst other princes wasted theirs. He might have been applied to as the mediator, or arbitrator of the Christian world, and have found his account in all the wars and negotiations, without being a party in them. He did the very contrary. A rose, blessed by the pope, an emperor serving in his army, and taking his pay, a whimsical project of conquests never designed to be made, and impossible to be kept, if they had been made, were sufficient to draw him into the most extravagant engagements, in which he always played gold against counters with allies, who generally played counters against gold. His engagements of this kind became numberless, frequently inconsistent, and so very rash and unadvised, that

whilst his aim, or his pretence, was to keep a balance between
the great powers of Europe, he more than once assisted the
strongest to oppress the weakest.   The spring of all this strange
conduct lay in the private interests and passions of Wolsey, who
became his first minister very early, and was his favorite earlier.
If Henry the Eighth negotiated perpetually, and was perpetually
the bubble of those with whom and for whom he negotiated, this
happened chiefly because he was, in the first place, the bubble of
his minister.   Wolsey's avarice was fed and his ambition flattered by the emperor, by the court of France, and by that of
Rome, in their turns.   He supported himself, in a great measure,
at home, by the opinion of his credit abroad; and his master's
favor to him was strengthened by the art of those whom he served
at his master's and his country's expense.   In short, the success
or disappointment of his private schemes were the hinges on
which the whole policy of this nation turned for twenty years:
and the grossest mismanagement, obstinately pursued, by the
minister, in the midst of universal disapprobation, was sanctified
by the king.

The king, no doubt, thought himself infallible in the choice of
men as in the choice of measures; and, therefore, when he had
once given his confidence to Wolsey, no matter by what inducements, his presumption screened the minister from his suspicion.

It was easy for Wolsey to keep his master from hearkening to
particular advice, or to the general voice of the people; because
it was easy to persuade him that he wanted no advice; that he
could not be deceived, though his people might; and, perhaps,
that it was unbecoming a great prince to alter his measures, or
withdraw his favor, on the clamors of the public.   At the same
time, we may fairly suppose (for the monuments of history will
justify us in supposing) that the butcher's son was not such a
bungler, nor rendered by a low education so void of address, as
not to know how to insinuate without the air of advising; and
how to receive all his own suggestions back from his master, in
the style of orders, with the utmost demonstration of implicit
submission to his judgment, and absolute resignation to his will.

But however blind the king might be, the eyes of the people
continued open to his and their true interest.   The discontent
grew general; and to this general discontent were owing the
principal difficulties which Henry the Eighth met with, during
the first half of his reign.—As much complaisance as he had
been used to find in his parliaments, he durst not always demand money of them, for the support of his enterprises.   His
minister soon put him upon the expedient of raising it by his
own authority.   But these attempts were resented warmly, and
opposed so sturdily, even when the rough name of a tax was

changed into the softer sound of a benevolence, that the king was obliged to retract; to compound; to excuse himself; to disavow his minister; and to pardon all those who had been concerned in particular insurrections, from a fear of one which might become universal.

No prince could be more firmly seated on his throne. No prince could be less framed to brook opposition. No prince could be less susceptible of fear. And yet to this point of distress did Henry the Eighth bring himself, by trusting his first minister too much, and regarding the sense of his people too little.—All orders of men concurred on these occasions; and the merchants signalised themselves. Neither the flattery, nor the menaces of Wolsey could prevail on them to be silent, when they felt that their own and the national interests were sacrificed or neglected, at every turn. Much less could they be cozened so far as to expose their fortunes in trade, the only fortunes which merchants acquired in those days, in order to conceal the blunder of a minister, or to stop the clamor against him. We find a remarkable instance of this behavior of the merchants in the year 1528; when the commerce of the Low Countries, on which our woollen trade depended principally at that time, was interrupted by a war with the emperor, which evidently took its rise from no other motive than a pique of the minister.

The ill success of these illegal methods, obliged the king to have recourse to his parliament: but his parliament thought like his people; and the opposition given in the house of commons was such as became the representative body of the nation. That which happened in the year 1523, is worthy of particular observation. It was not grounded only on the exorbitancy of the sum demanded, but likewise on the nature of the service for which the demand was made. As high as prerogative was carried at this time, and as undisputed a point as the power of the crown to make war or peace might be, yet it is undeniable that the commons would not give money without knowing how it was to be employed; and that they proportioned their grants to the judgment they made of the reasonableness or unreasonableness of the employment designed.—Wolsey, the most insolent minister our nation had seen at that time, was, however, so far from objecting to this method of proceeding in the house of commons, that he opened to that house, in a long discourse, the reasons of the king's measures, as he affected to call his own measures; and endeavored to prove the necessity of supporting them. Nay, when neither his rhetoric could persuade, nor his authority influence, he offered to debate the whole matter, and to answer the objections of those who opposed the king's desires. The house rejected his offer; observed their forms; maintained their dignity. They disapproved a war, wantonly undertaken, and in which the interests of the nation were not concerned. They showed, however, their regard to the king, by giving some part of the subsidy, and their regard to the kingdom, by refusing, to the last, to give the whole.

As for the minister, he received the mortification which he deserved.—These frequent oppositions, on the part of the people and the parliament, were really made to the minister. Henry the Eighth seemed, on some occasions, to desire that they should be so understood, even before Wolsey's favor began to be in its wane; and yet we shall have no reason to be surprised, if we consider the true character of this prince, that these very oppositions prepared his mind for receiving those lessons which Wolsey was ready to give him, against liberty, and in favor of arbitrary power.—A wicked minister, who neither gains, nor deserves to gain the good-will of a nation, must secure and will endeavor to revenge himself, by persuading his master to neglect it. Force and corruption being the sole means, by which he can maintain his power, and preserve his ill-gotten wealth, it is necessary for him that the prince whom he serves, should look upon those as the sole expedients by which government can be supported. Wolsey pursued this abominable scheme. "He looked upon the king's subjects," says Rapin, "as so many slaves; and unfortunately for them, he inspired the king by degrees with the same principles; and insinuated to him, that he ought to consider the parliament only as an instrument to execute his will."—These were the seeds he sowed, which fell on a rank soil, and produced in the latter half of Henry's reign, such bitter fruit as this nation never tasted before, nor since.—Wolsey had been the scandal and the scourge of his country, whilst he lived: and he continued to be so even in the grave.

LETTER XI.

THE divorce of Henry the Eighth and Catharine of Arragon begins a new and most memorable era in the general history of England; and indeed of all Europe. It is the beginning likewise of a new period in the particular reign of which we are speaking.—A king, who had been till now the great assertor of the authority of the pope, and the great defender of the doctrine of the church of Rome, undertakes to destroy the former in his dominions, and gives several incurable wounds to the latter.—A king, whose whole attention had been employed abroad, and in whose time "there was no treaty and almost conventicle in Christendom, wherein he had not his particular agent and interest," as my Lord Herbert expresses himself, becomes wholly taken up with domestic affairs; and if he looks abroad, during the rest of his life, it is chiefly on account of what passes at home. He, who had connived at seditions and pardoned insurrections, grows impatient of the least contradiction.—He, who had often compounded with his parliaments, and submitted to them on many occasions, dictates all their proceedings; and the voice of the law is little else than the echo of the voice of the king.—In short, he who had been led, amused, governed by his minister, drives, overbears, tyrannizes; butchers his servants and his wives, his commons and his nobility.

When Henry the Eighth first engaged in the affair of the divorce, he could not foresee the consequences of it; because he certainly did not expect the difficulties which gave occasion to them. He went on during the first two years, in the beaten road, by which so many others had gone before to the same end; and he seemed to have no view besides that of employing the authority of one pope to undo what the authority of another pope had done. Nay, after Cranmer had begun to open other views to him, he seemed still to cling to Rome, resolved to succeed any way; but desirous to succeed that way.—Happy was it that he took his measures no better, and that he was no better served on this occasion than on many others!—He suffered himself to be amused by Clement the Seventh, the least scrupulous man alive; and who would have divorced him, or have done any other pontifical job for him, if the league formed to reduce the emperor's power in Italy had succeeded. But the emperor's power there continuing to prevail, the pope concluded his treaty with this prince on the most advantageous terms. He obtained that favorite point, for which he would have sacrificed not only the interest of Henry the Eighth, but even those of the papacy itself. I mean the re-establishment of the family of Medicis on the ruins of the Florentine liberty. The loss of Genoa, the total destruction of the French army in the kingdom of Naples, and several other considerations induced Francis the First to make his peace with the emperor likewise, and to submit to the treaty of Cambray.

Thus did Henry the Eighth find himself at once disappointed in the expectations he had been made to entertain from the court of Rome, and destitute of all foreign assistance; Francis being the only ally, of whom he could avail himself to influence the councils of Rome, in opposition to the emperor.

In this state of affairs, Henry resorted to that which will be

always the best and surest reserve of a king of Great Britain;
the inclinations and affections of his people. He had not the
trouble of disposing them, for he found them already disposed to
his purposes. The spirit raised by Wickliffe about two centuries
before, against the usurpations of the pope and the clergy, was
still alive. The sufferings of the Lollards, as his followers were
called, had not abated it. The art of printing had been propagated; and the late success of Luther had encouraged it. There
were multitudes, therefore, in all parts of the kingdom, who desired a complete reformation of the church, both in doctrine and
in discipline. Others again were content that the papal authority,
grievous in its nature, and scandalous in its exercise, as well as
the extravagant power and impertinent immunities of the clergy
should be taken away. But they meant to go no farther. Many
would not go even so far as this; but were still slaves to all
their prejudices; and remained in the midst of this defection,
attached to the pope as well as to the corrupted doctrine, and the
depraved discipline of the church.

Whilst the divorce was solicited at Rome, and the proceedings
relating to it were carried on by the direction, and under the
authority of the pope, it was the king's affair; it was the affair
of his ministers. But when it appeared impracticable in this
method, and Henry resolved, in order to accomplish it in another
to deliver himself and his people from the yoke of Rome; the
affair of the divorce became a national affair, and the cause of
the king became the cause of his subjects. As he proceeded in
it, he was encouraged to proceed. The concurrence of his people
grew every day more general, and he was supported with the
greatest warmth. He soon held the clergy at his mercy, and the
popish party was broken and terrified, if not entirely crushed.

During this eager pursuit after ecclesiastical liberty, a power
very dangerous to civil liberty was erected. We observed before that the prerogative had been carried high, and extended
wide in the reign of Henry the Seventh, who obtained much by
law, and obtained more by his manner of construing and executing the law. His son, parting with none of his authority,
and improving the conjuncture so as to acquire a great deal
more, acquired so much at last, that the power of the crown
exceeded by far that proportion, which is consistent with the
security of public liberty and private property. It is true, indeed, that he always took care to have the law on his side; and
would neither venture on the exercise of acts of power against
it, or without it. His experience in the former part of his reign,
had taught him the danger of such a conduct; and in the latter
part, he had no occasion to pursue it. The opinion of the nation
went along with him now; and, as exorbitant as his demands

frequently were, his parliaments refused him nothing. At one time they gave up to him, in a great degree, the legislative authority: and his proclamations were made, under some restrictions, equivalent to acts of parliament. At another time, they ascribed to him a sort of infallibility; and letters patent, under the great seal, were made necessary to determine the articles of faith, which men were to believe fully, and the doctrines, rites and ceremonies, which they were to observe and practice under several penalties.—The suspicious state of affairs abroad was amplified to give a pretence to one of these laws; and the confused state of religion at home, and the clashing of parties about it, might afford some color to the other.—The truth is, that any pretence served, at this time to grant whatever the king desired; a stronger instance of which cannot be imagined than that of the subsidy, obtained in the year 1540. Henry had got immense riches by the first and second suppression of monasteries. A principal inducement to the last, which was likewise the greatest, was this; that the king might be enabled, without taxing the people, to defend them against such invasions, as the court had been pleased to suppose; and with the rumors of which the nation had been purposely alarmed. These invasions did not happen. Henry continued in peace with all his neighbors: and yet, the very next year, he not only accepted from the clergy of the province of Canterbury, with the approbation of parliament, a grant of the fifth part of their revenue; but he demanded a subsidy likewise of the house of commons. So extravagant a demand could not but meet with some opposition. The subsidy however was granted in as large a proportion, as if the nation had been engaged in a dangerous war. The reasons for granting it were almost burlesque. It was affirmed, by the king's party, that he had laid out vast sums in securing the coasts; and that the keeping his subjects in peace and plenty cost him more than the most burthensome war.—Thus a precedent was made of converting into ordinary aids of the government those heavy taxes, which ought never to be felt by the people, unless upon the most extraordinary occasions. That they ought to be laid in time of war neither was, nor ever could be doubted. That they were equally necessary in time of peace, was now established by the logic of the court; and we may be sure that the argument would have been urged with still more force and effect, if the nation had fallen, by the management of the courtiers in that age, into such a situation as could neither be called properly a state of war, or a state of peace.

The absolute power which Henry the Eighth exercised over the purses, lives, liberties, and consciences of his people, was due to the entire influence which he had gained over the parliament; and this dependency of the two houses on the king did, in effect, establish tyranny by law.—If we look for the true cause of this dependency, we shall find it, as Rapin hath very judiciously observed, in those divisions of the nation concerning religion, which I have mentioned above. The party, which opposed all reformation, by a bigoted attachment to the discipline, as well as doctrine of the church of Rome, furnished the king with as many pretences for grasping at power, and squeezing money out of his people, as ambition could wish, or profusion require. The other two parties concurred with the king, and went together to a certain point: that is, to throw off the papal yoke, and to lessen the power of the clergy. But here they separated, and went different ways; one to carry the reformation forward, and the other to stop it where it then stood; whilst the king seemed to keep in a middle way between them both. Sometimes, he seemed to favor those whose principles led them to an entire reformation, and he touched the doctrine, though with a gentler hand than the discipline of the church.— Sometimes he appeared zealous for the doctrine, and even for some part of the discipline; and the manner in which he often executed that bloody statute, the law of the six articles, would incline one to think that he joined to his political considerations a tincture of religious prejudice on these heads. But however that was, certain it is that the hopes which each of these two parties entertained of the king, and the fears which they entertained of one another, occasioned their continual bidding for him, if I may be allowed to use such an expression. This emulation formed then, what it always must form, the most dangerous conjuncture to which liberty can be exposed. When the motives of contending parties are founded on private ambition and avarice, the danger is great. How much greater must it be, when those motives are founded on religion likewise; when the heads and hearts of both sides are heated even to enthusiasm; when this spirit mingles itself with the spirit of faction; so that some through folly, and some through knavery, are ready to sacrifice public liberty to their particular schemes of religion?

In such circumstances as these was this nation, when Henry the Eighth died; and if he had left a son and successor, of full age, and bold and enterprising like himself, our liberties had been irretrievably lost, according to all appearances. Henry the Eighth, by applying to his parliaments for the extraordinary powers which he exercised, and by taking these powers for such terms, and under such restrictions as the parliament imposed, owned indeed sufficiently that they did not belong of right to the crown. He owned likewise, in effect, more than any prince who went before him, how absolutely the disposition of the crown of England belongs to the people of England, by procuring so many different and opposite settlements of it to be made in parliament, and yet tyranny was actually established. The freedom of our government might flourish in speculation; but certainly it did not subsist in practice. In the case therefore supposed above, our forefathers would very soon have found how fatal it is, in any circumstances, by any means, or under any pretences, to admit encroachments on the constitution; and how vain it is, when these encroachments are once admitted, for the service of some present turn, to prescribe limitations to the exercise or duration of them.

But Providence directed the course of things better, and broke those shackles which we had forged for ourselves. A minority followed this turbulent reign; the government was weak; the governors divided; and the temper of the people such as made it prudent to soothe them. This the Duke of Somerset did out of inclination, and the Duke of Northumberland out of policy. To the former we owe not only the complete establishment of the church of England on the ruins of popery, but the first and great steps which were made to restore a free government. In the very first year of his administration, several acts which had passed in the reign of Henry the Eighth, and in some preceding reigns, grievous to the people, and destructive of liberty, were repealed; and among others that absurd act, which gave to proclamations the force of laws. The law of the six articles was likewise repealed. Others were explained, and several new laws were made in favor of civil, as well as ecclesiastical liberty; both of which got so much strength, in the reign of Edward the Sixth, that they were able to stand the short but violent shock of Queen Mary's reign. This princess lived long enough to confirm, not to destroy our religion by persecution. The ill-concerted insurrection of Wyatt gave strength to the faction which prevailed at court, and discouraged, for some time, all opposition; nay, the methods taken to influence the elections, and to gain by corruption the members who were chosen, were carried on so openly, that the price for which each man sold himself was publicly known. No wonder, then, if the papal authority was restored, and the queen's marriage with Philip the Second approved. But this state of things could not last long, nor was the nation disposed to bear a continual sacrifice of her interest to Rome and Spain.

The parliament, corrupt as it was, began to revolt against the court. The spirit of liberty revived; and that spirit, and the spirit of reformation in religion, had made more progess than was readily perceived. This progress had been made principally among the commons; and therefore, though the authority of the crown, of the council, and of the great lords kept up other appearances, yet there was a secret fire burning, which must and would have broke out.   The effects of the causes, laid in the reign of Henry the Seventh, began now to appear.   The lands of the nobility were lessened, and those of the commons increased.   Trade had been encouraged for several years.   We see that some care had been taken of it, even in the troublesome times of Edward the Fourth, and very much was done towards the advancement of it in the reigns of Henry the Seventh and Henry the Eighth.   The West Indies had been discovered about half a century before; and part of the immense treasures, which flowed from thence into Europe, began to increase the profits, and, increasing the profits, to increase the industry of our merchants. Henry the Eighth had sold a very great part of the church lands at low prices, on purpose to engage the body of the nation in one common interest against the Romish clergy.   The commons had made their use of this strain of policy, and had got into very great estates in lands, by these as well as by other means: so that the king, the lords, and the church, who had formerly held so great an overbalance of property in land, had now little more than one-third of the whole belonging to them; the consequences of which were not foreseen by Queen Mary; neither did she live long enough to feel them in any great degree.   They did not escape the penetration of her sister.   She foresaw them, and the great glory and happiness of her reign may justly be attributed to this first principle; that she had the wisdom to discern not only the actual alteration, which was already made, but the growing alteration, which would every day increase in the state of property; that she accommodated at once the whole system of her government to this great change; and instead of depending upon expedients, which were now no longer of season, chose the sole expedient that remained, for making herself and her people happy; which was to place the whole strength and security of her government in the affections of her people, and in her superior credit with them.

LETTER XII.

WE have now brought these remarks on the English history not only down to times little remote from our own; but to a period, when the monarchy settled on a new foundation; upon which it still continues and rests more firmly than ever at this hour. The observations, therefore, which remain to be made, in order to illustrate what hath been advanced, concerning the spirit of liberty and the spirit of faction, will for these reasons be the more apposite, the more affecting, and by consequence the more useful; but, for these very reasons likewise, it is probable that they will become the occasions of louder complaints, and of more impertinent clamor. We shall be sincerely sorry for this; because we look on the alarm, which hath been taken at our endeavors to revive the spirit, and to confirm and propagate the doctrines of liberty, in a country where liberty is still avowed, and under a government established on the principles of liberty, as a most suspicious and melancholy symptom. But the stronger this symptom appears, the more incumbent we shall think it upon us to pursue the honest design, to which we have devoted ourselves with constancy and vigor.

The shameless crew, who write against their country, as they would write against their God, for hire, shall have little regard from us. The scandalous license with which they have presumed to draw odious parallels, and the impudence with which they have imputed these parallels to us, have been abundantly exposed already. The few, the very few things, which they have alleged in point of fact, or arguments, have been often answered; perhaps too often, considering how little weight they carried with them, and how little impression they were capable of making on the understanding, even of those, who had other reasons for inclining to that side of the question. The ribaldry which these scribblers employ, hath been and will continue to be despised, not answered. It cannot be expected that we should take notice of every little frivolous, childish declamation, which appears in public, however some persons may demean themselves by pretending to admire them. The menaces affectedly and insolently thrown out on one side; and the flattery, servilely offered on the other, are equally objects of our contempt; and if we take a little notice of the former, once for all, before we proceed any farther in these remarks, it is purely because we cannot understand them to be the language of these writers. When they talk in this style, they speak the language of him who guides their pens, and who is known to reward their labors. To him, therefore, it may not be improper to address ourselves in the following manner:

"The persons, whom you threaten, sir, neither value your favor, nor fear your anger. Whenever you attempt any act of power against any of them, you shall find that you have to do with men who know they have not offended the law; and therefore trust they have not offended the king; who know they are safe, as long as the laws and liberties of their country are so; and who are so little desirous of being safe any longer, that they would be the first to bury themselves in the ruins of the British constitution, if you, or any minister as desperate as you, should be able to destroy it.   But let us ask, on this occasion, what you are, who thus presume to threaten?   Are you not one, whose measure of folly and iniquity is full; who can neither hold nor quit his power with impunity; and over whose head the long-gathering cloud of national vengeance is ready to burst?   Is it not time for you, sir, instead of threatening to attack others, to consider how soon you may be attacked yourself?   How many crimes may be charged upon you and yours, which almost every man can prove; and how many more are ready to start into light, as soon as the power, by which you now conceal them, shall determine?   When next you meditate revenge on your adversaries, remember this truth: the laws must be destroyed before they can suffer, or you escape."

Let us now return to our subject.—In the early days of our government, after the Norman invasion, the commons of England were rather formidable in their collective, than considerable in their representative body; by their numbers in extraordinary emergencies, rather than by their weight in the ordinary course of government.   In later days, they began to acquire some of this weight by degrees.   They represented grievances; they gave, or refused subsidies; and they exercised, in a regular, senatorial manner, the powers lodged in them by the constitution; but still they did not obtain the entire weight, till they were wholly emancipated; and they were not so till the great change, which we are speaking of, happened.   Before this time, they had too much of the dependency of tenants, and the king, the nobility and the clergy had too much of the superiority of landlords. This dependency of the commons added to that, which the crown frequently found means of creating, either by influencing their elections, or by corrupting their representatives, notwithstanding all the provisions made against it, which we have touched in a former paper,* kept this part of the legislature in such a state, as made it unable fully to answer the end of its institution; and the system of our government was by consequence, in this respect, defective.

Could Henry the Seventh have found means, as he reduced the nobility lower, to have hindered the commons from rising higher; could he have opened a way to the diminution of the property of the lords, and have prevented that increase of the same property amongst the commons, to which, on the contrary,

* See the Craftsman, No. 225.

he gave occasion, and which time and accidents conspired to bring about; the balance of this government would have been totally lost, though the outward forms of it had been preserved. Our liberty would have been lost by consequence; and our kings, with a house of lords and a house of commons, and all the appearances of limited monarchs, might have been as arbitrary as those princes are, who govern countries, where no such constitution prevails. The reason of this will appear plain to those who remember what hath been observed, in some of our former papers, that a dependent exercise of the powers, lodged in the two houses of parliament, will endanger, and may, more effectually than any other expedient, destroy liberty; and that the preservation of our freedom is no way to be secured but by a free and independent exercise of these powers. Now such an exercise could not have continued, much less have been improved, if Henry the Seventh had been able, at the same time, to weaken his nobility, and to keep his commons from acquiring new strength. But this was impracticable. At least, it was not attempted. Henry the Seventh hastened to the cure of that evil which pressed him most, the power of the nobility, as his son soon afterwards effectually reduced the exorbitant power of the clergy; and in pulling down these powers, which, as they were constituted and had been exercised, hurt the crown more than they served the people, these princes, became the instruments of raising another power, which is the best, if not the sole effectual barrier against usurpations of illegal, and abuses of legal prerogatives; and which, at the same time, can never be applied to do any real hurt to the crown, unless in cases where it is bent and forced to do this hurt by the crown itself, in the first place, against the natural tendency and direction of it.

This increase of the property of the commons, by taking off from them a constant dependency of one sort, and by rendering them less obnoxious to an occasional dependency of another, gave greater dignity, and added greater weight in the balance of government, to their representative body. The house of commons became more powerful, without the attribution of any new powers, and purely by the different manner in which their independency, the effect of their property, enabled them to exercise the same powers, which they enjoyed before. A concert with a few great lords, and a few leading prelates, was now no longer sufficient to guide the sense of parliament, and to establish the measures of government; no, not even in cases, where this concert might be extended to some of the commons themselves.— Intrigue and cabal became unnecessary, when the national interest was wisely pursued; and ineffectual, when it was not. The way was opened to gain the parliament, by gaining the nation; but to impose on the nation, by gaining the parliament was hard; for the weight without doors determined, in those days, the weight within. The same causes, which rendered the house of commons more considerable to the court, to the nobility, to the clergy, to the commons themselves, rendered likewise the whole body of the commons of more importance to those who were chosen to represent them. Besides which, the frequency of new elections, which was deemed an advantage, as long as the service was deemed an honorable burthen, gave the nation frequent opportunities of modelling the representative body, according to the interests and inclinations of the collective body. From hence it followed, that that credit and influence in the nation, which can only be acquired and preserved by adhering to the national interest, became the sole means of maintaining a lasting credit and influence in the house of commons; upon which the harmony of government, and the happiness of prince and people depended more than ever.

Thus were we brought back, in times very distant and in circumstances very different, to the principles of government, which had prevailed amongst our Saxon ancestors, before they left Germany. Whatever particular pre-eminences, or powers, were vested in the principal men, the great affairs of state were directed by the whole body of the nation.—De minoribus principes, de majoribus omnes.

Such were the natural effects of this new settlement; and thus our limited monarchy became capable of as much perfection, as wisdom and favorable accidents can communicate to any human institution; for can we raise our ideas of this kind of perfection higher than ordering the distribution of property and power in such a manner, that the privileges of the people and the prerogative of the crown cannot be taken away, unless with their own consent, or by their own fault? Now to this point of perfection was the constitution of our government brought, and farther it could not be brought; because it is impossible to secure either prince or people against themselves, or against the effects of their own conduct.

One part of what hath been said upon this subject, will not, I think, be disputed. The other, perhaps, may seem a paradox; and a settlement, which rendered our government more democratical, will not be readily allowed to have been advantageous to the crown, though it must be allowed to have been so to the people. Let us examine, therefore, whether it was really so or not.

In all limited monarchies, and we are not speaking of any other, the power of preserving these limitations must be placed somewhere. The question therefore is, whether it can be placed more advantageously, even for the crown as well as the people, than in the whole body of the nation.

Whilst the commons had not property enough to have any share in this power, the sole check which could be opposed to the encroachments of the crown was the power of the barons and of the clergy. But these two orders of men had their particular interests, frequently opposite to each other, and to those of the people, as well as to those of the crown; so that they were not only very incapable of forming a secure barrier to liberty, but their power became terrible and dangerous to the crown itself.— They slided easily into faction. They often encroached on the prince's authority, whilst they resisted his encroachments, real or pretended, on their own privileges; and under the plausible veil of law, or gospel, private ambition had a greater share than public liberty in their contests. It is true that during these contests Magna Charta was signed and confirmed, and the condition of the people, in point of liberty, very much improved. But this was the accidental effect of the contest between the kings, the barons, and the clergy, as we have remarked, in speaking of those times, and not the natural effect of the property and power lodged in the barons and the clergy. The commons were courted by all sides, because they were wanted by all. Had they been bubbles enough to look on the nobility and clergy as the proper guardians of liberty, and to have adhered to them accordingly, they might indeed have avoided being slaves to their kings, but they would have rendered both their kings and themselves little less than slaves to their temporal and spiritual lords.

After the reigns of Edward the First and Edward the Third, power came to be better poised; and government took a more regular form. The prerogatives of our kings, and the privileges of our nobility, the authority and immunity of the church, and the rights of the people were more ascertained; and yet, after this time, the same observations will hold good in a very great degree. It is certain that the vast over-balance of property and power, which still continued in the nobility and clergy, instead of preventing, softening, or shortening the calamities which followed, helped to form and maintain those factions, which began, renewed, fomented the civil wars of York and Lancaster, as well as the wicked conduct of Richard the Second, and the weak conduct of Henry the Sixth. Redress of grievances and sufficient security against them for the future might have satisfied the people, if they had been left to themselves; but nothing less than revolutions of government could satisfy the factions, into which the great men were divided, and into which they divided the nation, by their influence over the people, and by the advantages which the ill conduct of the Yorkists and Lancastrians gave to each other.

Thus we see how unsafely for the crown, as well as insecurely for the people, that property and power, which is necessary to preserve the limitations of our monarchy, was placed before the time, when that great change in one and the other happened, which makes the subject of this discourse. But as soon as this change did happen, the crown was no longer exposed to the same mischiefs.

When the little power which Henry the Fourth of France had in the town of Rochelle, was subjected to him, he made an answer worthy of his heroic spirit. "I do," said he, "all I desire to do there, in doing nothing but what I ought." This moderation of temper is, in all governments, the best; and, in limited monarchies, the only sure and durable foundation of power. By preventing jealousy in the people of the prince, it takes away all advantage against his government from faction; and the more watchful the people are over their liberties, the more sensible will they be of this moderation, and the more grateful for it. Faction proceeds always without reason; but it can hardly ever succeed without pretence, and sufficient pretence will hardly be found under such a government.

When a prince, who manifests this moderation of temper, pursues the true interests of his people, and suffers no other interest to come into any degree of competition with it, far from being the object of their jealousy, he will be the principal object of their affection; and if he joins to this character of goodness that of ability, he will be the principal object of their confidence likewise. These are the strongest chains by which a people can be bound to their prince; easier indeed, but far stronger than those of adamant, by which Dionysius the elder boasted that he had secured the tyranny of Syracuse to his son; force, fear, a multitude of troops, and a guard of ten thousand barbarians. A prince, who establishes his government on the principles of affection, hath every thing to hope, and nothing to fear from his people. A prince, who establishes his government on any other principles, acts in contradiction to the very end of the institution. What objection, therefore, could be made, even on the part of the crown, to a settlement of property and power, which put the guardianship of liberty into such hands as never did, nor ever will invade the prerogative and authority of the crown, whilst they are employed to those purposes, for which alone they were entrusted? It is confessed, that if a prince should attempt to establish his government on any other principle than these, if he should choose to depend rather on deceiving, corrupting, or forcing his people, than on gaining their affection and confidence, he might feel the weight of their property and power very heavy in the scale against him. But then it must be confessed likewise, that, in such a case, this opposition of the people would be just; and that the prince, not the people, would be answerable to himself and his family, to God and to man, for all the ill consequences which might follow.

We hope that we have said nothing, in order to show the excellency of our constitution, as it settled about the time of queen Elizabeth, which is not agreeable to reason; and sure we are that the truth of these general propositions will be confirmed by the particular examples which are to follow. The reign of queen Elizabeth will be one continued proof that the power of preserving the limitations of a monarchy cannot be placed better, for a good and wise prince, than in the whole body of the people; and that the spirit of liberty will give greater strength, as well as procure greater ease, to the government of such a prince, than any absolute monarch can hope to find in the most abject spirit, which principles of blind submission and passive obedience are capable of inspiring. The reigns immediately succeeding this, will be one continued proof, that whenever the power of the people hath been exercised against the crown, it hath been owing primarily to the weak management and obstinacy of the court, and to the unhappy choice which those princes made of governing by factions, in opposition to the sense and interest of the nation. From whence it will follow, that the great calamities which befel our country, in the middle of the last century, are unjustly charged on the spirit of liberty, or on the nature of the British constitution of government.

LETTER XIII.

There is no part of our annals, nor perhaps of the annals of any other country, which deserves to be more studied, or to be oftener called to remembrance both by those who govern, and by those who are governed, than the reign of queen Elizabeth. We shall not however descend into all the observations which it affords; nor even into all those which might properly serve to our present purpose.

In some papers* we made a few remarks on this reign, and on that of king James the First. We apprehend that the contrast

* See the Craftsman, No. 137, 138, 139.

between them appeared very strong on that occasion. This contrast will probably appear still much stronger, and by consequence be the more instructive, when those remarks and these we are going to make come to centre in one single point; to show that the conduct of queen Elizabeth, under great disadvantages, produced all the good effects, which prince or people could desire; because it was wisely suited to the nature of our government: whereas the conduct of king James the First, who had many great advantages which his predecessor wanted, made his reign grievous to the people, uneasy to himself, and accessory to those misfortunes which befel his son; because it was ill-suited to the nature of our government, and founded on principles destructive of liberty.

Few princes, no not even her cotemporary Henry the Fourth of France, have been ever raised to a throne under more disadvantageous circumstances, or have been surrounded in it with more complicated difficulties than queen Elizabeth.—Let us take a general survey of them.

The division and animosity of parties had been carried to the height of religious rage. The cruelty of queen Mary's reign, in which much protestant blood had been shed, and even that of her sister with difficulty spared, rendered of course the persecuting side more desperate; and the other more exasperated. It is hard to imagine that queen Elizabeth had been able to cultivate many personal attachments to herself, before she came to the crown; except that of Sir William Cecil, afterwards Lord Burleigh, and perhaps one or two more. Her imprisonment for a time, and the great constraint under which she lived, during her sister's whole reign, gave her little opportunity for it; and the jealous eye, with which Gardiner and other ecclesiastical zealots observed her conduct, made it dangerous to attempt it.

In general, the protestants desired her succession: and the papists feared it. But the former were under oppression, and even a kind of proscription. The latter had the whole authority of the church and the state in their hands, in this kingdom; and that of Ireland, bigoted to popery and prone to rebellion, was at their devotion.—The protestants themselves were divided, and those who meant equally a reformation, fell into the utmost asperity against each other, concerning the manner of making it, and the point to which it ought to be carried, on account of religion as well as of policy.

In this divided state, and in the ferment which such divisions must necessarily cause, queen Elizabeth found the people whom she came to govern. Surely, a more nice and perilous state can hardly be imagined; especially for her, who was led by inclination and determined by particular circumstances of interest to establish the reformation; that is, to declare for the weakest, though not the least numerous party.

It is observed, I think by Nathaniel Bacon in his historical and political discourses, that the methods taken by Henry the Seventh to accumulate treasure, made a rich king indeed, but did not enrich the crown. His son had several opportunities of doing both; instead of which he impoverished himself, the crown, and the people, by all the methods which the most wanton profusion could invent. He exhausted the wealth of the nation. He did more. He debased the coin, by mingling it with copper, and loaded the public with debts. These again were considerably increased in the reign of Edward the Sixth. Queen Mary was so far from diminishing them, that one of the principal complaints against her administration, next to the cruelty she exercised, was the great dissipation of the revenue, occasioned by her restitutions to the church, and by her new foundations of monasteries. In this low, incumbered state queen Elizabeth found the revenues of the crown, and the wealth of the nation.

Her situation abroad was still worse than her situation at home. Calais, and the other English possessions in Picardy, had been lost in a quarrel, where the interest of England had no concern. For the sake of Spain, we had war with France. The war with Scotland still continued; and queen Elizabeth had no one ally, on whose assistance she could depend.

Such distressed situations are rare; and when they have happened, they have been often rendered less difficult in reality, than in appearance, by some particular circumstances which have attended them. But when Elizabeth began her reign, no such circumstances existed in her favor. On the contrary, almost every circumstance aggravated her distress. The thrones of France and Spain were filled neither by old men, worn out with age and cares; nor by weak men, unequal to their rank and business; nor by children, under the tuition of regents. Henry the Second reigned in France; Philip the Second in Spain; princes, in the vigor of their age; of great ambition, of great talents; and seconded by the ablest ministers and generals in Europe. The French monarchy had been growing up from the time of Louis the Eleventh, towards that fulness of power and affluence of wealth, at which the Spanish monarchy was already arrived. Both these princes were, by bigotry and by policy, attached to the court of Rome; implacable enemies to the reformation; and such by consequence to queen Elizabeth. Henry the Second had a farther reason for being so. He grasped, in his ambitious views, the crown of England, as well as that of Scotland; and looked on queen Elizabeth as the usurper of a right, belonging to his daughter-in-law. Philip, indeed, kept some faint and affected measures with Elizabeth, as long as he apprehended the union of so many crowns in the house of Valois: but this apprehension was soon at an end; and even his shows of friendship with it. Henry the Second, and his eldest son, Francis the Second, died in about two years. The deaths of these princes did, perhaps, diminish the difficulties and dangers to which queen Elizabeth stood exposed on one hand; but then they increased these difficulties and dangers on the other; since they took off all restraint from Philip in pursuit of his enterprises against her. His life lasted almost as long as hers, and his inveterate enmity as long as his life.

Another source, from which difficulties and dangers were incessantly arising to queen Elizabeth, lay in the objections which the papists made to her title, on a principle of religion; and which were but too really, though indirectly, abetted by some protestants, on a principle of faction. Whilst disputes about the succession to the crown were confined to England, and turned on maxims of our own growth, if I may use that expression, we have seen how little regard was paid to the titles, and to the pretended divine, indefeasible right of princes. But when foreign nations came to be interested in the succession of our crown, they reasoned and they proceeded on other notions; not on those which both custom and law had established here.

The attacks of this kind, made on queen Elizabeth, were the more grievous to her, because they not only united the Roman catholic powers against her; but they made the divisions wider and more irreconcilable at home, where she placed the chief strength and security of her government.

Mary queen of Scotland was a pretender, neither abjured in England, nor disavowed and unsupported in other countries. Sovereign of one part of the island, she had a powerful party in the other; wife of the dauphin, and after that queen of France; encouraged and assisted by her uncles, who possessed more than regal power in that kingdom; by Spain and by the whole popish interest; she was justly formidable to queen Elizabeth, as long as she lived. Another circumstance made her so still more. The success of the reformation seemed to increase the zeal of those who continued in the communion of the church of Rome. The influence of the court of Rome became consequently stronger at this point of time. It appeared both in France and in England too as powerful, though not as successful, here at least, as it had appeared in the eleventh century, in the days of the brave, but unfortunate emperor, Henry the Fourth, and of that insolent friar, Gregory the Seventh. Even this circumstance may justly seem to have been enforced by another; by the establishment of the order of Jesuits. This order, the offspring of a mad Spaniard, has had·the principal honor, though other religious orders have endeavored to share it, of giving to the pope an authority like that which was exercised by the king of the assassins or the old man of the mountain, as he is called by some of the French historians; an authority, which proved fatal to Henry the Third, and Henry the Fourth of France; and which had like to have proved so to queen Elizabeth, and even to her successor.

Such were the difficulties and dangers which encompassed this princess. The situation of England, in her time, resembled that of a town powerfully besieged without, and exposed to treachery and sedition within. That a town in such circumstances, should defend itself, and even force the enemy, by its own strength, to raise the siege, hardly falls within the bounds of probability. But that all this should happen, and the inhabitants feel none of the inconveniences of a long and obstinate siege, nay, that they should grow opulent during the continuance of it, and find themselves at last better able to offend the enemy than they were at first to defend their walls, seems an adventure of some extravagant romance. But it conveys a true image of this reign. Unallied and alone, queen Elizabeth maintained a glorious and successful war against the greatest power and the richest potentate in Europe. She distressed him in the West Indies. She insulted him in Spain. She took from him the empire of the sea. She fixed it in herself. She rendered all the projects of universal monarchy vain; and shook to the foundations the most exorbitant power which ever disturbed the peace, or threatened the liberties of Europe. She supported the oppressed people of the Netherlands, against the tyranny of their prince. She supported the protestant subjects of France, against Catherine of Medicis and her sons, those execrable butchers of their people. She supported the kings of France, Henry the Third and Fourth, against the ambition of the princes of the house of Lorraine, and the rebellious league of their popish subjects. She, who seemed to have every thing to fear in the beginning of her reign, became in the progress of it terrible to her enemies. The Pretender to her crown lost her own. The English, who appeared at first so favorable to the queen of Scotland, became at last as desirous to sacrifice the life of that unfortunate princess to the security of queen Elizabeth. Whilst war, confusion, and the miseries which attend them, raged in the dominions of those who bent their aim at the disturbance of her government, she preserved her subjects in peace and in plenty. Whilst the glory of the nation was carried high by achievements in war, the riches and the strength of it were raised by the arts of peace to such a degree, as former ages had never seen, and as we of this age feel in the consequences. Well, therefore, might my Lord Bacon, speaking of queen Elizabeth, say,* "as for her government, I assure myself I shall not exceed, if I do affirm that this part of the island never had forty-five years of better times; and yet not through the calmness of the season, but through the wisdom of her regiment."

Having made these remarks on the difficulties and on the success which attended queen Elizabeth, it is time to consider the cause, which produced the stupendous effects of her reign. Now this cause is, I think, very plain. She was wise enough to see clearly into the nature of that government, at the head of which she was placed; and to know that " the supreme head of such a government owes a supreme service to the whole."† She was wise enough to know that to be powerful, she must either usurp on her people, deceive them, or gain them. The first two, she saw, were hard, dangerous and dishonorable. The last, she saw, was easy, safe and glorious. Her head and her heart concurred to determine her choice. She made herself very soon the most popular person in the kingdom. In her reign, the sense of the court, the sense of the parliament and the sense of the people were the same; and whenever she exerted her own strength, she exerted the whole strength of the nation. Nothing she asked was ever refused by parliament; because she asked nothing which would have been refused by the people. She threw herself so entirely on the affections of her subjects, that she seemed to decline all other tenure of the crown. At least, she was not very solicitous about clearing her title to it by descent. An act, declaring her right according to the order of succession settled in parliament thirty-five Henry the Eighth contented her; and she neglected the precaution, which her sister had taken, in getting the act, which excluded them both from the crown, repealed, as far as it related to herself. The particular reasons of her conduct, in this case, might perhaps be guessed at with more probability than they have been; but certainly one general reason outweighed them all in the mind of this heroical princess. She knew that however the subtlety of lawyers and political casuists might influence opinions, nothing but her own conduct could give her the hearts of her people. These she deemed her great security. These she acquired; and the little glosses, which might have been put on her title, she despised. The being not only tied, but knit to her people was her aim; and she pursued this great point of view on all occasions; the least, as well as the greatest; and even on those, where she thought it necessary to

* Advancement of Learning, lib. i.
† See Nath. Bacon's Hist. and Pol. Discourse.

refuse or to reprimand.   Nature, as well as art, fitted her for this conduct.   She had dignity without pride.   She was affable, without sinking into low familiarity; and when she courted her people, she courted them like a queen.   This popularity was sometimes carried so far, both in her manners, and in her expressions, that her enemies have endeavored to make it pass for gross and fulsome affectation, and for such, indeed, it ought to have passed if it had gone alone.   It might have shocked, instead of alluring, if it had not been seconded by every action of her life, and contradicted by none.   Let us now consider, therefore, in some instances, what that conduct was, which convinced her people so entirely of her goodness and her wisdom; and which procured her such large returns of gratitude, of duty, of affection and zeal.

LETTER XIV.

A FIRST and essential condition, towards obtaining the love and confidence of a free people, is to be neither feared nor despised by them.   Queen Elizabeth was, at no time, in any danger of the latter; and she soon put herself above all the suspicions, which might have exposed her to the former.   The only difference between her and her parliament, which carried any passion or unkindness with it, happened in the ninth year of her reign.   It was founded on the apprehensions of the dangers which would arise after her death, if the succession was not fixed during her life.   But we do not find the least insinuation of any jealousy of her government; though the heat of both houses, at that moment, was too great to have concealed any uneasiness, which had lain at their hearts.   That she was fond enough of her prerogative is certain; but then she took care that she should never be grievous; or that if it was so, on some occasions, to particular persons, it should appear, by the occasions themselves, and by the manner of exercising it, specious to the public.—The prerogative certainly run high in those days.   Her grandfather had raised it by cunning, and her father by violence.   The power of the privy council in civil affairs, and the censorial power of the star-chamber in criminal affairs, as my Lord Bacon very properly styles it, took too much of the pleas of the crown and of the common pleas out of their proper channels, and " served rather to scare men from doing wrong, than to do any man right."*—But the exercise of these powers having continued in four preceding reigns, the people were accustomed to it; and care being taken to give no flagrant occasion of clamor against it, we are not to wonder if it was borne, without opposition or murmur, in a reign as popular as this.

The high-commission court, that we may quote another instance, had no doubt very extraordinary powers. The bishops, who held the principal sway in it, exercised by these means two very great authorities at the same time; one, as ordinaries in their dioceses; the other, as judges in this court; so that they might fine and imprison, as well as excommunicate and deprive. Now, it is not very probable, that the parliament, who thought the first of these powers too much, as may be seen by the attempts made against it, in the twenty-eighth year of this reign, were very well pleased to see the second in the same hands. However, the steadiness of the queen, in maintaining this part of the prerogative, which had been given her, was the less unpopular, on account of the unsettled state of religion at this time; of the great moderation of the bishops in these early days of the reformation; and of the prudent manner in which the jurisdiction of the high-commission court was executed.

The effects of a bare-faced prerogative are not the most dangerous to liberty, for this reason: because they are open; because the alarm they give is commonly greater than the progress they make; and whilst a particular man or two are crushed by them, a whole nation is put on its guard.—The most dangerous attacks on liberty are those which surprise, or undermine; which are owing to powers given under pretence of some urgent necessity; to powers, popular and reasonable, perhaps, at first; but such as ought not to become settled and confirmed by a long exercise; and yet are rendered perpetual by art and management; and, in a great degree, by the nature of these powers themselves. Examples of this kind might be produced from the Spanish and other histories. But queen Elizabeth was far from setting any such examples. She showed her moderation, in desiring no suspicious powers, as well as in the exercise of her prerogative; and this moderation was the more remarkable, because no prince ever had the pretence of necessity to urge on stronger appearances. Her whole reign may be almost called a state of defensive and offensive war, in England, as well as in Ireland; in the Indies, as well as in Europe. She ventured to go through this state, if it was a venture, without the help of a standing army. The people

* Bac. Hist. and Pol. Disc.

of England had seen none, from the days of Richard the Second; and this cautious queen might perhaps imagine, that the example of his reign, and those of other countries, where standing armies were established, would beget jealousies in the minds of her people, and diminish that affection, which she esteemed and found to be the greatest security of her person, and the greatest strength of her government. Whenever she wanted troops, her subjects flocked to her standard; and her reign affords most illustrious proofs, that all the ends of security, and of glory too, may be answered in this island, without the charge and danger of the expedient just mentioned.

This assertion will not be contradicted by those, who recollect in how many places, and on how many occasions, her forces fought and conquered the best disciplined veteran troops in Europe. Other examples might be brought to show how careful queen Elizabeth was to avoid every thing which might give the least umbrage to her people. But we have said enough on this head. Let us proceed to another.

The conduct she held, with respect to parties, deserves to be remarked; because the moderation, the wisdom, and the equity, which she showed in it, contributed very much to cool the ferment in the beginning of her reign; by which she had time to captivate the good will of her people; to settle her government; to establish her authority; and even to change the national religion, with little contradiction, and without any disturbance.

Notwithstanding all the indignities she had suffered, and all the dangers she had run, before her accession, several persons were restored, and not a man was attainted in her first parliament. The steps I have mentioned being once made, she stood on firmer ground, and had less to fear from the spirit of faction. This clemency once shown, she could, more safely, and with greater reason, exercise severity, when the preservation of the public peace made it necessary.

The peace of the kingdom was the standard, to which she proportioned her conduct. She was far from casting herself with precipitation and violence even into that party which she favored, and on which alone she resolved to depend. She was far from inflaming their spirits against the adverse party; and farther still from pushing any sort of men, puritans, and even papists, into despair; or provoking them to deserve punishment, that she might have a pretence to inflict it. She pursued her own scheme steadily; but she pursued it gradually; and accompanied it with all the artful circumstances which could soften the minds of men, and induce those, who were the most averse to her measures, to bear them at least patiently. On these principles she proceeded, in the whole course of her reign.

To the papists she used great lenity; till the bull of Pius
Quintus, and the rebellion, and other attempts, consequent upon
it, obliged her to procure new laws, and execute more rigor.
Yet even then she distinguished "papists in conscience from
papists in faction."* She made the same distinction with regard
to the puritans. "Their zeal was not condemned; only their
violence was sometimes censured," until they attempted to set
up their own discipline, in opposition to that which had been
established by national authority; until their motives appeared
to be "no more zeal, no more conscience," says secretary Walsingham, "but mere faction and division."

Thus cautious and steady was the conduct of queen Elizabeth towards parties; steady to the principle, and therefore varied
in the application, as the behavior of parties towards her government varied; not as success abroad, or the change of servants at
home, might have influenced that of a prince of inferior abilities.
What has been said relates to parties in the nation; for as to
parties at court, the conduct of this queen, though directed to
the same general end, seems to have been different. In the
nation she chose one party. She rendered the system of that
party, the system of the whole. By this establishment the
other parties became so many factions; and by the conduct we
have described, she defeated and disarmed these factions. At
court, she countenanced and perhaps fomented the parties, which
different characters and different interests created. But however
that was, she found means to attach them all to herself; and she
found this benefit by keeping her ear open to them all, that the
truth could not be concealed from her by the most powerful of
her ministers; as we have explained in a former letter on this
subject. On her accession to the throne, she retained thirteen of
her sister's counsellors, and balanced them by no more than eight
of her own religion. "On those, as well as on all others, which
she afterwards admitted into the ministry," says Camden, "she
bestowed her favors with so much caution, and so little distinction, as to prevent either party from gaining the ascendant over
her, whereby she remained mistress of herself, and preserved
both their affections and her own power and authority entire."

The favors, by which she distinguished the Earls of Leicester
and Essex, are not exceptions, in the course of so long a reign,
sufficient to destroy the truth of this general observation. Besides, both these lords felt the weight of her displeasure, nay one
of them, the rigor of her justice, when they presumed too much
on her favor, and swerved from their duty. The singular confidence which she placed in Cecil and some others of her minis-

* Walsingham's Letter.

ters, cannot be quoted in opposition to it; for if she distinguished them, it was rather by the labors, than the favors she heaped on them. She supported them indeed against their enemies; but then the merit of these men was far from being problematical. Their works testified daily for them, in bold and well-concerted enterprises; in wise and well-conducted negotiations. The people reaped the benefit of their services, as well as the prince. They were justified in the nation, as well as supported at court. In short, by this discernment of spirits, by this skilful management of parties, without the help of military force, unless in actual rebellions, queen Elizabeth preserved her people in tranquillity; though there passed not an hour in her whole reign, without some intrigue against her life and the public peace.

This moderation, in assuming and exercising power, might have been illustrated more, and evinced against all the little cavils made, and to be made, if we had not avoided too great prolixity. But it is time to hasten to the consideration of some other parts of her conduct.

Queen Elizabeth was accused of avarice by her enemies; and perhaps she was so by some of her friends. Among that hungry crew, which attends all courts for the loaves and the fishes, she could not escape this charge. But surely the nation had reason to applaud her frugality. Her grandfather hoarded up riches. Her father dissipated them. The consequence under both these princes was, that every slight occasion became a sufficient pretence to ask for subsidies; nay, they were asked and granted too, when even the slightest occasion did not exist. They were asked by Henry the Seventh for wars which he never intended to make; and by Henry the Eighth for resisting invasions which were never designed against him. Thus was the nation equally oppressed by the avarice of one, and by the profusion of the other.

But queen Elizabeth neither hoarded up nor lavished away; and it is justly to be questioned whether any example of prudent economy in private life, can be produced equal to that which she practised in the whole management of her affairs. The famous Burleigh used to say, that "he never cared to see the treasury swell like a disordered spleen, when the other parts of the commonwealth were in a consumption;" and his mistress thought that "money, in the pockets of her subjects, was better placed than in her own exchequer." Surely, these maxims were wise as well as popular. If a prince amasses wealth, to hoard it up like Henry the Seventh, it is useless to himself and lost to the public. If he squanders it away, like Henry the Eighth, he will enrich particular men, and impoverish the state. But whilst these treasures remain in the purse of the subject, they circulate in commerce; they increase the common stock; and they increase by consequence the riches of a princess like queen Elizabeth; for to such a princess this purse will be always open.

As immense as the expenses were, which she found herself obliged to make from the moment she ascended the throne, she received nothing in taxes from her people till the sixth year of her reign. The taxes then given, were given by way of retribu tion; which was generally the method in her time. In former reigns, the people granted aids, not without a general communi cation at least of the uses, to which they were to be applied; but often without a sufficient assurance that they should be so applied. In this reign that method of proceeding was inverted.

The prince in the world who deserved to be trusted most, desired to be so the least. The aids which she had from her people were not so properly grants as reimbursements of money advanced for national services. And for what services? For establishing the protestant religion; for defending England; for rescuing Scotland; for carrying on a successful war against an opulent and potent enemy; for assisting the subjects and even the kings of France; for supporting the people of the Netherlands; for refining the debased coin; for paying all the debts, and restoring the credit of the crown; for providing ammunition at home, which before this time we had been always obliged to purchase abroad; for improving both home and foreign trade; for rebuilding and augmenting the navy; and for doing all this, without any burthensome imposition on the people; as the parliament more than once acknowledged.

It was so much a maxim of queen Elizabeth, to save for the public, not for herself; and to measure her riches by the riches of the nation, not by the treasures she had in her coffers; that she refused supplies offered, and remitted payments of supplies granted, when she found that she was able to carry on the public service without them. The two great principles of that economy, which enabled her to do so much for her people, and to oppress them so little, seem to have been these. First, she made the most of her revenues; not by tormenting, and racking her subjects, like Henry the Seventh, but by keeping a strict hand over her officers, and hindering them from enriching themselves, either by direct fraud, or by a clandestine management, which may be justly termed indirect fraud, and is often more pernicious than the other.—Secondly, she practised that superior economy, of which we have spoken in a former paper, with the utmost ability. What could be done by wisdom, or courage, she never attempted by money; nor expected that her subjects should buy her out of difficulties. Strong at home, she affected little to lean on foreign help. As her alliance was often courted, and she seldom courted that of others, it was in her power, and she took the advantage, to engage in no expense, but such as the interest of her kingdom rendered immediately necessary. To this interest alone she proportioned her expense. This was the sole rule of her conduct. The Huguenots, whom she assisted in their first war, made their peace without her, and assisted to retake from her the places she had bargained for with them; yet she helped them, in the wars which followed, with her troops, her ships, and her money. The Dutch had given her no cause to complain of their behavior. Yet when France abandoned them at the treaty of Vervins, and they had no support but hers remaining, she made a new bargain with them, and lessened her own charge; because she knew they were able, at that time, to supply the deficiency.

In all these expenses, she was careful neither to starve nor overfeed the cause, while it lasted; and she frequently stipulated a repayment; which she might exact afterwards, if she found reason so to do; or which she might remit, and thereby create a second obligation to her, if she found her account in such an instance of generosity. Queen Elizabeth was not only thus frugal for her people, but perpetually attentive to the methods of enriching them. In the very first parliament which she held, amidst the most important affairs; such as the settlement of the crown on her own head; the change of religion, and the establishment of the church, regulations for the improvement of trade and increase of shipping were not forgot.

We might pursue the same observation through the whole course of her reign, both in parliament, and out of it; and show, in numberless instances, how she rose to the highest, and descended even to the lowest circumstances, which in any degree affected the trade and navigation of her subjects. We might show the advantages she took in these respects, not only of the faults committed by other governments, but of the misfortunes of other countries. In a word, we might show how war itself, one of the greatest public calamities, instead of impoverishing, became a source of riches to this nation, by the manner in which she made it.

But these particulars would carry us beyond the bounds we have prescribed to ourselves. In general, it will not be denied that, besides the spirit of industry, which exercised itself at home, queen Elizabeth raised and pushed to the highest degree, by the protection and encouragement she gave, a spirit of discovering new countries; making new settlements; and opening new veins of trade. The force of this first impression has lasted long amongst us. Commerce has thrived under neglects and discouragement. It has subsisted under oppressions and obstructions; and the spirit of it is not yet extinguished by that of stockjobbing; though the spirit of stockjobbing be to that of trade, what the spirit of faction is to that of liberty. The tendency of both is to advance the interest of a few worthless individuals, at the expense of the whole community. The consequence of both, if ever they prevail to the ruin of trade and liberty, must be, that the harpies will starve in the midst of imaginary wealth; and that the children of faction, like the iron race of Cadmus, will destroy one another.

Before queen Elizabeth's reign, the commerce of England was confined and poor. In her reign, it extended itself over all the known, and even into the unknown parts of the world. We traded to the north, and opened our passage into Muscovy. We carried our merchandise up the Duina, down the Volga, and across the Caspian Sea into Persia.

Our merchants visited the coasts of Africa; all the countries of the Grand Seignior; and following the tracks of the Venetians into the East Indies, they soon followed the Portuguese thither by the Cape of Good Hope. They went thither through the South Sea, and sailed round the world. In the West Indies, they not only traded, but established themselves, in spite of all the power of Spain.

Before queen Elizabeth's reign, the fleet of England was so inconsiderable, that even in the days of her father, if I mistake not, we were forced to borrow, or hire ships of Hamburg, Lubec, Dantzick, and other places.

In her reign, it soon grew to such a number and strength, that it became terrible to the greatest maritime powers of Europe.

On such foundations were the riches and power of this kingdom laid by queen Elizabeth; and these were some of the means she employed to gain the affections of her subjects. Can we be surprised if she succeeded?

LETTER XV.

QUEEN ELIZABETH succeeded in gaining the affections of her subjects, not only by the conduct which she held at home, but by that which she held in the management of the national interest abroad.

We have endeavored to explain some particulars of the former. It remains that we give the least imperfect ideas we are able of the latter, and that we apply the whole great example of this reign, to confirm the doctrines we have advanced.

Queen Elizabeth could not have established and preserved, as she did, the tranquillity of her people in the midst of disturbance, nor their security in the midst of danger, if she had not taken some share in the general affairs of Europe. She took therefore such a share as the interest of England necessarily required at that time; and she conducted herself in the management of it with wisdom and address superior to any of her predecessors.

Her sister had been rendered by bigotry an egregious bubble to the court of Rome. Persuaded by her husband, and deceived by her ministers, she was so likewise very fatally in the quarrel, which broke out between France and Spain. The parliament, in assenting to her marriage with a foreign prince, had imposed such conditions, as were judged sufficient to preserve the constitution of the government, and the independency of the kingdom.

Philip had sworn to the observation of these conditions. Such of them, as he had not either time, or opportunity, or temptation to break, were observed; but the others proved too weak to hold him. Thus, for instance, we do not find that he enriched himself at the expense of England. He is said, on the contrary, to have brought hither very great treasures: and his father had trusted the distribution of an immense sum to Gardiner: so that if he bribed the nation, it was with his own money, not theirs; but he engaged the nation in a war with France because France broke with Spain; notwithstanding the express condition made by parliament,* "that the match should not at all derogate from the league lately concluded betwixt the queen of England and the king of France, but the peace should remain inviolate between the English and the French."

This sacrifice of the national to a foreign interest cost us Calais; a conquest, which the French looked upon as a compensation for near two hundred other places, which they were obliged by the treaty of Cambray, to give up to Philip. Boulogne had been sacrificed in the preceding reign, not to a foreign interest, but to that of the minister, Dudley, Earl of Warwick, afterwards Duke of Northumberland. The people were willing and able to assert their right, and to defend their possession; but the situation of the minister, and the schemes of private interest, which he was carrying on at home, required that he should avoid, at any rate, a war, even a defensive war. In short, Boulogne, for which France had engaged to give two millions, was delivered up for four hundred thousand crowns; and the very same minister, who had opposed with violence all the public considerations, urged by the protector for yielding this place, yielded it to

* Cambden.

purchase a treaty necessary for himself, detrimental and dishonorable to the nation.

We have said enough, in a former letter, concerning the wild
conduct of Henry the Eighth, in foreign affairs; and there is no
need of going any farther back. These examples are sufficient
to show the opposition between that of queen Elizabeth and
that of her predecessors. She was neither deceived, like them,
by her ministers; nor betrayed by her passions, to serve any
other interest at the expense of England.

It would be easy to prove, from many instances, how careful
she was to avoid every thing which might even warp the steady
tenor of her conduct in this respect. As long as she had no real
interest distinct from that of the country she governed, she knew
that no fictitious interest could be imposed on her. She kept
herself, therefore, clear of any such real interest, and thought
that the crown of England deserved her sole, her undivided care.

Much has been said of her behavior in all the treaties of
marriage proposed to her. We shall not engage in that disquisition. But this, we think, cannot be controverted; that if ever
she was in earnest resolved to marry, she was so when the articles of marriage between her and the Duke of Anjou were
signed. It is hardly possible, as Rapin observes, to account for
her conduct on this occasion by any other principle. Now upon
this supposition, what motive could determine her to break this
match in so abrupt a manner? The reasons urged by Cambden,
and other writers in general, prove too much. They serve rather
to prove that she should not have entered into those engagements at all, than to account for her breaking them as she did.
But among the reasons, on which Walsingham insisted, when
he was sent into France on this occasion, we may observe one
in particular, founded on a fact, which happened after the signing of the articles; and which accounts for the queen's conduct
in this case agreeably to principles, on which she proceeded in
all others. The Duke of Anjou had accepted the sovereignty of
the Low Countries. By this step, he had engaged himself in a
war with Spain; and the queen would not, on his account, engage
her people in it,* "desiring nothing more than that by this marriage the realm might be preserved in peace and tranquillity."

She might incline to marry this prince, under all the limitations and reserves contained in the articles, whilst he had no
dominions on the Continent; and yet start backwards and resolve
to break the match, as soon as she saw him actually possessed of
the sovereignty of the Low Countries.

* Cambden.

Nay, if we should suppose, against historical probability, that she never designed to consummate her marriage, though she entered into articles, yet there will still remain no reasonable way of accounting for the sudden resolution she took of breaking at this precise point of time; unless we suppose that she thought this reason the strongest and the most unanswerable of all those which could be urged in excuse of a measure liable to several objections, and some very inconvenient contingencies.

There were few things, which she had more at heart than rescuing the Netherlands from the Spanish yoke; and there was nothing in the whole extent of foreign affairs, to which she gave greater attention. Even at this time she supplied the Duke of Anjou with very considerable sums, for the support of his enterprise; and about four years afterwards, she espoused more openly the cause of these provinces, by making a treaty with the states, and by sending an army to their assistance. But as she would not marry a prince who was their sovereign, so she would not accept this sovereignty, when it was offered directly to her. She persisted in avoiding an engagement, which might in its consequence carry her farther than the interest of England required; or oblige her to make greater efforts than were consistent with that easy and flourishing state in which she resolved to preserve her own people.

Much more might be said; but this may suffice to show what the first and fundamental principle was, by which queen Elizabeth governed herself in all foreign affairs. She considered the interest of no kingdom, no state, nor people, no, not even the general interest of the reformation, as zealous a protestant as she was, nor the preservation of a balance of power in Europe as great a heroine as she was, in any other light than relatively to the interest of England. She assisted, or opposed, she defended or attacked, just as this interest directed; and the degree to which it was concerned, was the exact and constant measure to which she proportioned her good, and her ill offices, her friendship, and her enmity. She was diverted from this principle of conduct neither by weakness nor strength of mind; neither by fear nor hope; neither by pusillanimity nor courage; neither by moderation nor ambition.

We may conclude this head, by venturing to affirm that, in the whole course of her reign, there was not a penny of English money spent, nor a drop of English blood spilled, except where it was necessary to keep off from this nation some real, visible disadvantage.

Queen Elizabeth's policy was deep; and the means she employed were often very secret; but the ends to which this policy and these means are directed, were never equivocal. Let us now descend into some particular instances of the wisdom and address, with which she pursued this great principle.

These particulars may be reduced properly, we think, under two general heads. The first is this: " she watched the ebbs and flows of the power and interest of Europe; the vicissitudes and fluctuations in the affairs of peace and war." We use the words of a late writer,* but shall make a very different application of them.

This uncertain, varied, shifting scene was so far from being the cause of bad measures, or the excuse for bad success, at the time we are speaking of, that it was the very source from whence queen Elizabeth derived those opportunities, which she improved so gloriously. A weaker council than hers might have been puzzled, and weaker heads might have been turned by so confused a state of affairs. Unable to steer steadily through so many difficulties, every current would have carried such men along with it. Every blast of wind would have driven them before it. Perpetually tossed about, at the mercy of every event, they must have lived from day to day, or from hour to hour.

If the kingdom had escaped entire destruction in this forlorn condition, it must have been by miracle, and without any merit on the part of those who governed; but this entire destruction would much more probably have followed, after a long series of calamities; without any other excuse on their part, than that of charging the catastrophe to the account of fortune, the common scape-goat of unskilful ministers.

The conduct and the success of queen Elizabeth and her ministers were very different. She managed France, until she had taken such measures, as left her less to fear from Scotland; and she managed Spain, until she had nothing left to fear from France.

She knew what designs Henry the Second built on the pretensions of his daughter-in-law, Mary queen of Scotland; and no one, who considers the history of this time, nay, even as he finds it deduced by Rapin himself, will be of his mind, that she expected to " enjoy great tranquillity by the peace," which she made soon after her accession to the throne, with France and Scotland.

But the making this treaty gave her time, which was of the utmost importance to her to gain, abroad as well as at home, in the beginning of her reign. The manner in which she made it, gave her reputation likewise; and she was wise enough to know of what real advantage reputation is, and how much that of a prince depends on the first steps he makes in government.

She practised in this negotiation a rule, which she observed to the last. How much soever Philip resented her proceedings at

* Vide Observations on the Writings of the Craftsman.

home, it was plain he could not abandon, at that time, her interests abroad. The point of honor, drawn from the consideration that England had entered into the war for the sake of Spain, did not probably weigh much with him; but the pretensions of France gave him a just alarm; and the same reasons, which are said to have induced him to save her life, when she was princess, stood in force to make him support her, now she was queen, against the power of France. Notwithstanding this plausible consideration, queen Elizabeth resolved to treat for herself, and by herself. " She was of opinion," says Cambden, "that it would not redound to the honor of England, or herself, to be reduced to the necessity of supporting her interests by a dependence on Spain." She exerted the same spirit, and behaved herself with the same dignity, on a very remarkable occasion, and in a very nice conjuncture, at the latter end of her reign; at the treaty of Vervins.

She despised the offers made by Henry the Fourth. She resolved to continue the war, and to support alone the states of the Low Countries, rather than to suffer the man in the world, who had the greatest obligations to her, to treat for her.—True it is, that she had reason to be dissatisfied with his behavior; but besides that, the good understanding between this prince and Philip the Second being promoted by the court of Rome; it is possible queen Elizabeth might think such negotiators, as were devoted to that court, not quite so proper to be trusted with the interests of her kingdom.

As soon as Henry the Second was dead, and his son Francis the Second, a young and in every sense a weak prince, was on the throne of France, she acted with less reserve and caution. The treaty, which had been privately negotiated before with the malcontents of Scotland, was now signed; her army marched to their assistance; the French were driven out of that kingdom; the reformation was solemnly and legally established there, and queen Elizabeth was the avowed defender of the liberties, privileges, and religion of the Scotish nation.—Francis the Second lived a very short time, and died without leaving any children. The fear, therefore, of an union of the crowns of England and Scotland with that of France, terrified Philip the Second no longer. Queen Elizabeth had, therefore, the more to fear. The court of France had still the same bigotry, and the same hatred to her; though not the same pretensions. The court of Spain could be now no more restrained, by any political consideration, from pursuing those designs against her, even in conjunction with France, which no other consideration had hitherto retarded.

The projects formed and the engagements taken between these powers, at the congress at Bayonne, were not absolute secrets. She felt the effects of them every day, in conspiracies against her

government, and even her life. Too weak to defend herself by
force on so many sides, she defended' herself by stratagem;
improved every incident; and took some advantage of every
turn. She contented herself to countermine the intrigues of the
courts of Rome, of France, and of Spain. With the first she
kept no measures, because she could have no war. With the
two last she kept all measures to prevent one. Though queen
Elizabeth's whole reign was properly a state of war, and there
was no point of time in it, where she was free from all attacks,
private as well as public, indirect as well as direct; yet the first
twenty-five years of her reign may be said, in one sense, to have
been neither a state of war, nor a state of peace; because both
sides pretended to look on the treaties of peace as subsisting; and
either disavowed, or excused the hostilities reciprocally committed, not constantly, but occasionally committed. If she had fallen
into this state from that of a settled peace, disentangled from all
pretensions, either of her own upon others, or of others upon
her, there would be no occasion to admire her conduct. But that
she should be able, when she neither had, nor could have a settled, secure peace with her neighbors, to stand so long on the
slippery verge of war, and avoid the necessity of engaging directly in it, till she was in a condition of doing so with success,
is justly matter of the greatest admiration. If she had only
aimed to keep off the evil day, it might at last have come upon
her with a double weight of misfortune. If she had only gained
time to prolong suspense, she might have lost opportunities;
wasted her strength; tired, jaded and exhausted her people.—
But this was far from being the case. She was in this state by
good, not by bad policy; and she made the use she designed of
it. She disappointed, divided, and weakened her enemies. She
prepared the opportunities which she afterwards improved. She
united, animated, and enriched her people; and, as difficult as
that may seem to be for a prince in such a situation, she maintained her own dignity, and supported the honor of the nation.
To exemplify all these particulars, would be to write her history;
but it is necessary to say something upon them.

Of the two powers abroad, from whom alone she had any
thing to apprehend, and with whom she was principally concerned, France gave her the least and the shortest trouble.—
Charles the Ninth came a minor to the crown. Two factions,
drunk with religious enthusiasm, and headed by men of the most
desperate ambition, desolated the kingdom. The queen mother
blew up the flames first; and tried in vain afterwards to extinguish them, by a deluge of blood. Queen Elizabeth, who had
probably encouraged the famous conspiracy of Amboise, which
broke out just before the death of Francis the Second, continued

to abet and support the Protestant party; but still subordinately to such measures, as her situation, relatively to Scotland, or Ireland, or Spain, obliged her to keep with Charles the Ninth.— These measures were sometimes such, and even after the massacre of St. Bartholomew, as the zeal of the Huguenots could hardly forgive her.   But she went wisely and steadily on to her own purposes.

"Non ponebat enim rumores ante salutem."

When Henry the Third came to the crown, and the league was once formed, the crown of France wanted her assistance, and had it; and as powerful as the princes of the house of Lorraine were, they could give her little open disturbance, unless they prevailed in their wicked, and almost chimerical projects in France. With these princes and their faction, therefore, she never kept any measures—as they never kept any with her.   As politic a prince as Philip the Second is esteemed to have been, he was amused by the regard which queen Elizabeth affected sometimes for his person, and always for the treaties subsisting between them; and he lost the opportunities in which he might have attacked her with advantage. The slow councils of Spain, and the slower execution of them, produced opportunities which her sagacity and vigor improved.   The support she gave to the Huguenots made the Spaniards afraid of provoking her, by too hasty and direct attacks, to give the same support to the people of the Low Countries.— She turned their game against them, and acted in the Low Countries in the same manner as they acted in Ireland, and even in England, but with better effect.   From the year 1577 she began to favor this revolt, and in the year 1585 she made a formal treaty with the States.   Such of these measures as could be concealed, she concealed.   Such of them as could not be concealed, she excused, or endeavored to justify and reconcile with the treaties between Spain and England.

As the time she gained, and the diversion she gave by this management, put it quite out of the power of France, and made Spain less able to hurt her; so they alone put it in her power to settle her government, and to do all the great things at home, of which we have spoken in other papers.*   We shall not repeat them here; but shall conclude this head by observing, in an example or two, how she maintained her own dignity in other cases, besides that of treating, which is taken notice of above, and how she supported the honor of the nation. and the interests of her subjects.

During the time she was the most careful to avoid a war with

* Vide the first seven volumes of the Craftsman, printed for R. Francklin.

Spain, and had the most reason to be so, even in the year 1568, whilst those revolutions, which broke out soon afterwards, were preparing, she would not suffer the least injury to be offered to any of her subjects with impunity. Some vessels and effects, belonging to an English merchant, had been seized by the Spaniards in the West Indies. She did not make war upon this; but she soon found and seized an opportunity of resenting the insult. She laid hands on very great sums of money, claimed indeed by Genoese merchants, but sent to the Low Countries, and designed, no doubt, for the Spanish service there. The Duke of Alva seized, in return, the persons and effects of the subjects of England; and she immediately made reprisals on those of the Flemmings. What composition was made with the Genoese, does not, I think, appear; but as the seizure was to the disappointment and loss of Spain, so the composition was probably to the advantage of England, since, at this very time, queen Elizabeth discharged the debts contracted by her father and brother to foreigners. As to the effects of the Netherlands, she returned the overplus of the value, after having repaid to her own subjects the full amount of their losses. She carved for her people; and would not leave it to a dispute, what reparation they should have; much less whether they should have any reparation or not.

Such a conduct as this, which she held, even whilst she kept measures with Spain, and avoided a war, foretold what might be expected from her, and what she actually performed, when she thought it no longer expedient to keep the same measures. But this will come, with other reflections, more properly under the next general head; to which we think that the particular instances of queen Elizabeth's wisdom and address, in the management of foreign affairs, may be reduced.

LETTER XVI.

If queen Elizabeth considered every former interest relatively to the interest of England, she considered likewise every measure to be taken in foreign affairs relatively to the situation of England. This we establish as the second general head, to which the particular instances of her wisdom and address, in the management of foreign affairs, may be properly reduced.

She considered herself as queen of a country cut off from the Continent, and separated by the sea from all other countries, except Scotland. Her conduct, therefore, towards Scotland was very different, in many respects, from that which she held towards every other nation. A due observation of these different principles, on which queen Elizabeth proceeded in the divided state of our island, may serve to set, in a stronger and clearer light, that single principle which remains to be followed in our united state.

The situation of an island affords great advantages, when they are wisely improved; and when they are neglected, as great disadvantages may result from this very situation. The reign, now before us, is a glorious and unanswerable proof that the halcyon days, so much boasted of, and so seldom found, days of prosperity, as well as peace, may be enjoyed in an island, whilst all the neighboring continent is filled with alarms, and even laid waste by war. But our own histories will show us likewise, how an island may approach, as it were, too near the continent, and be fatally drawn into that great vortex. Lest we should ramble too widely in the large field which opens itself, let us confine our reflections to some of those different means and objects, either of defence, or offence, which nature, improved by art, presents to people who inhabit islands, or to people who inhabit the continent, according to their different situations. A powerful navy is of indispensable necessity to the former of these. Without it, they must be poor and exposed. With it, they may be rich and secure. Barriers of fortified towns, and great standing armies are of the same necessity to the latter. Without this security, they lie open to every inroad, and at the mercy of every neighbor. With it, they may be safe from foreign danger, and even terrible to those who live round them. But then, as the sea is a barrier of no expense, and as a maritime force carries no domestic danger along with it, but enriches the community it defends, so a fortified barrier, and a regular army, which are necessary to secure a nation situate on the continent against foreign danger, carry great domestic inconveniences, and even dangers, too, along with them. Both of them, like armor, too heavy to be borne, waste the strength of those who are covered by them; and an army, like a sword, which recoils on the blow, may wound the constitution it was meant to defend. But farther: as particular families, by uniting together, formed larger societies, for their common defence, and gave rise to the kingdoms, and states, which have appeared in the world; so these larger societies have, ever since, found it necessary, or advantageous, to unite together in various manners; sometimes by an entire union, or an incorporation of different people into one body politic; sometimes by a partial, or federal union of distinct states in one common cause; and at all times by alliances, made on particular occasions, and suggested by a real or seeming conformity of interests. This occasional union, by alliances with other states, of which alone we are to speak in this place, is so necessary to all the nations on the continent, that even the most powerful cannot subsist without it; and those who manage it best, are accounted wisest. Their several interests are the objects of their alliances; and as the former are subject to change, the latter must vary with them. Such variations, whether occasioned by the course of accidents, or by the passions of men, though made by a few, will affect many; because there always are, and always must be, systems of alliances subsisting among these nations; and therefore, as a change in some of the parts of one system necessarily requires a change in all the rest; so the alteration of one system necessarily requires an alteration of the others.

Thus are they always tossed from peace to war, and from war to peace. Perpetual negotiation is the life and soul of their governments. Their well-being, nay their safety at home, requires that they should always be busy abroad. It is necessary for them to be mediators, arbitrators, or, which is infinitely worse, guaranties; to be contracting parties in preliminary, provisional, or explanatory treaties; in defensive, or offensive alliances; by which means they get over daily difficulties, by the multiplication of lasting incumbrances.

The interfering and clashing of their rights and pretensions, and the various obligations, by which they stand bound to one another, appear to be and are the immediate causes of all these disputes and contentions. But the principal and remote cause arises from the proximity and other circumstances of their situations. That necessity, or advantage, which gave occasion to the original engagements, has maintained and multiplied them since; and the last would not be reasonable, if the first had not been necessary.

Here then arises an essential difference between those objects, which are proper to the policy of an island, and those which are so to the policy of the continent; a difference greatly to the advantage of the former; the circumstances of whose situation not requiring so constant and intimate an union with other states, either for defence or offence, render unnecessary a great part of the engagements which prove such heavy and lasting incumbrances on the latter.

An island under one government, advantageously situated, rich in itself, richer by its commerce, can have no necessity, in the ordinary course of affairs, to take up the policy of the continent to enter into the system of alliances we have been speaking of; or, in short, to act any other part than that of a friendly neighbor and a fair trader. If an extraordinary crisis happens on the continent, which may endanger the safety even of those who are separated from it, such as we saw at the beginning of the present century, self preservation will no doubt determine men, as it ought, to unite by stricter alliances with those powers with whom they are occasionally united by a more immediate interest; but even in this case, neither will self-preservation require, nor good policy suffer, that such a people should enter deep into the quarrels, or involve themselves intricately, much less continually, in the political schemes of the continent. We pass over offensive cases, because it is manifest that the people of an island can have no interest in making foreign acquisitions; and that therefore it would be absurd in them to spend their blood and treasure in acquiring only for others; or to attack any farther than is necessary to defend.

We confine ourselves to the case of defence before mentioned; and upon that we say, a people on the continent may have reason to engage as deeply in defence of another country, as if they defended the walls of their own towns, or the doors of their own houses; because another country may be the sole barrier of their own. But this can never be reasonably done by the people of an island, who have another, and a better barrier than any the continent can form for them. Such a people are to look on their engagements with other countries, as on outworks cast up in haste, which may serve to defeat a weak attack, or to delay and disappoint a strong one. But it would be the height of folly in them, even in one of those extraordinary conjunctures, which we now suppose, to lay the whole stress of their defence here; to spend their strength improperly; and to forego those advantages which nature has given them.

The nations on the continent might teach them another lesson. They are careful to employ every advantage of their situation; a river; a lake; a ridge of mountains; and shall the inhabitants of an island neglect the sea? Shall they do by choice all which other nations are obliged to do by necessity? Surely not, and if at any time such a conduct can be proved necessary to certain purposes, we think it will result from this proof, that such purposes should be laid aside, not that such measures should be pursued.

These reflections, with others of the same kind, present themselves naturally to those who consider the conduct of queen Elizabeth, and the events of her reign. We may therefore conclude that they were, at least, some of the principles of her government.

How she formed, or rather how she protected, and aided a party, already formed in Scotland, on principles of religion and liberty, has been observed; as well as the success of this mea-

sure, by which the troops of France were driven out of that
kingdom, and the influence of France on the government was
either removed, or guarded against.   To maintain and improve
this advantage, was the great affair of her life.   England was,
with respect to Scotland, like a kingdom on the continent, and
queen Elizabeth employed, with respect to Scotland, all the
policy of the continent. ·

We find her busy on that side in almost every page of her
history; almost always negotiating, and always intriguing.   A
friend, an enemy, a mediatrix, an umpire, a guarantee, she
played every part, which might keep others from hurting Scotland, and Scotland from hurting her.   Her armies were at all
times ready to march, and her fleets to sail thither.   As strict
an economy as she practised everywhere else, she was profuse
there; but her profusion turned to account, and therefore deserves
another name.   There may be such schemes, such management,
and such success, as may render even the smallest expense, profusion; but those of queen Elizabeth were sufficient to justify the
greatest.   The secret service of her reign was private in transaction and public in effect; not equally inscrutable in both.

About the fourteenth year of her reign, she had brought the
affairs of Scotland to such a pass, that she seemed to have nothing to fear from that quarter.   The plots, in favor of queen
Mary, had been discovered; the insurrections defeated; and the
Duke of Norfolk executed in England.   In Scotland, the same
party was broken.   The Earl of Morton, a man absolutely devoted to queen Elizabeth, was regent; the castle of Edinburgh
was taken; the civil war was finished with complete success,
and she enjoyed great tranquillity; because, according to Rapin's
observation, she could now be only attacked by sea; that is, she
had now the whole advantage of an island.

This happy state did not continue long without interruption.
Morton lost, and reassumed his power, was disgraced, prosecuted, and at last beheaded.   King James had taken very young
the government of this kingdom; and young, as well as old, was
governed by his favorites.   The party of his mother in Scotland
did not indeed rise again, so as to give queen Elizabeth any
umbrage.   But his general character, and his behavior on some
particular occasions, the character of his favorites, and the intrigues they were known to carry on, obliged her to reassume,
if she had ever laid it aside, and to pursue her ancient conduct
towards Scotland.   She pursued it to the end of her reign; and
although king James, when he had more experience, and was
better advised, kept such measures with her, as were necessary
to secure and to facilitate his succession; yet this wise queen continued to give quite another attention to the affairs of Scotland,

than she gave to those of any other country; or would have given to these, if Scotland had been divided from England by the sea.

It is impossible to make these reflections, and not to reflect, at the same time, on that happy change which the union of the two kingdoms has brought about. We are now one nation under one government; and must, therefore, always have one common interest; the same friends, the same foes, the same principles of security, and of danger. It is by consequence now in our power, to take the entire advantage of our situation; an advantage, which would make us ample amends for several which we want, and which some of our neighbors possess; an advantage which, constantly attended to, and wisely improved, would place the British nation in such circumstances of happiness and glory, as the greatest empires could never boast. Far from being alarmed at every motion on the continent; far from being oppressed for the support of foreign schemes; we might enjoy the securest peace, and the most unenvied plenty. Far from courting, or purchasing the alliances of other nations, we might see them suing for ours. Far from being hated or despised, for involving ourselves in all the little wrangles of the continent, we might be loved and respected by all those who maintain the just balance of Europe, and be formidable to those alone who should endeavor to break it.

Having made these few reflections on that part of queen Elizabeth's policy which regarded Scotland, it is necessary that we should say something of that which regarded the nations on the continent. Now with these it is plain she took the fewest engagements she possibly could, and shunned as industriously the occasions of mingling her interests and counsels with theirs, as she sought the occasions of mingling both with those of Scotland.

We believe, upon very good grounds, that periods of four or five years might be pointed out, in which this nation had been a party to more treaties than were made by queen Elizabeth in the course of forty-five years; and yet we presume it will not be easy to show, that this nation had more imminent dangers to avoid and more formidable powers to resist; or that such ends were attained with greater glory and success at these, or any other periods, than in the reign of queen Elizabeth. Let us descend into some particulars.

With the northern crowns she kept in terms of amity, and good correspondence; and had some negotiations with that of Denmark, concerning the interests of her subjects in trade. The same interests drew her into negotiations with the Muscovite, and she found means to conduct them to her great advantage.

The settlement made in Germany, a little before the abdication of Charles the Fifth, continued. The protestants were quiet there, and desirous to remain so. The general interest of religion did not call upon her to look that way; and it is evident, by the whole conduct of her reign, that she thought the particular interests of her kingdom very little concerned in those of the empire.

How attentive soever she might be to penetrate into the councils of the court of Rome, and to trace the intrigues of the Vatican from their source; she bore no part whatever in the affairs of Italy.

In short, as all the measures she took in foreign affairs were considered relatively to the situation of England, she had nothing to do in the much greater part of the business of the continent; and she was so far from entering into engagements by treaty, that she was scarce ever concerned in negotiations about it. In France, Spain, and the Low Countries she had more to do; but even there the part she took was strictly no more than the security and welfare of her own kingdoms required; and she acted it in no other manner than was suitable to the situation of England.

The state of Scotland, of Ireland, and for some time of England itself, gave her just reason to apprehend that the French, or Spaniards, or both, might get footing there. Each of these had, at different times, pretensions of their own to her crown. The cause of Mary queen of Scotland afforded them, for a long time, both pretence and opportunity; and the united force of the Roman catholic party was, at all times, ready to support their enterprises. Spain was the greatest maritime power in Europe, and able to attempt the invasion of England, even when queen Elizabeth had been above thirty years on the throne, and had raised her navy from the low condition in which she found it. In a word, the whole coast, from the strait of Gibraltar almost to Jutland, belonged to France and Spain. Such circumstances formed a conjuncture, wherein these two powers had advantages against her, which they could have had in no other; and if she was obliged to act towards them in a different manner from what she did towards the other powers of the continent, it was because she stood exposed to lose, at least in part, with respect to them, the advantages of her situation.

How she acted towards them, has been observed already. She amused them and eluded their designs, by the most artful series of management. She sought no alliances against them with other nations; and though she did not fail to abet and support the insurrections of their subjects; yet even with these she was cautious of entering into engagements by treaty. She did it with the Huguenots by a treaty signed in 1562, which the vidame of

Chartres had negotiated. The success of the treaty, and the ungrateful behavior of the Huguenots to her, confirmed her in the principle of depending little on allies, and much on herself. She chose rather to assist when and where she thought fit, and to assist gratis, than to be tied down to the consequences of constant obligations, for the notional advantage of reciprocal engagements.

In the year 1577 she began to take so intimate a concern in the affairs of the Low Countries, that the most important counsels and resolutions of those states were communicated to her; and she lent them a hundred thousand pounds; yet it does not seem probable, that she entered so soon into a formal alliance with them, though such an alliance be mentioned by Meteren, as well as Cambden, and inserted from the former in the collection of treaties.

In the year 1585 the clouds gathered on every side, and threatened queen Elizabeth with that terrible storm, part of which fell upon her, and part of which she averted. She beheld Philip master of Portugal as well as Spain. She beheld the Duke of Guise growing apace to be master of France. She saw these two princes closely united by principles, which might continue in force long enough to complete her ruin. She saw the Low Countries almost quite reduced by the arms of Spain; and the Protestants of France in the utmost danger of being so by the league. Dangers from Ireland, and dangers from Scotland impended over her.

In such a crisis, more terrible, as we apprehend, than any which has threatened this nation since that time, what was the conduct of our heroic queen? Did she immediately prepare to oppose these dangers, by making alliances on the continent?— Did she purchase accessions to these alliances? Did she raise armies, and pay subsidies abroad? Did she give guaranties to every prince and state who asked them; and, in order to ward against one danger, sow the seeds of many? By no means. She sent indeed Sir Thomas Bodley, to the king of Denmark, as well as to the landgrave of Hesse, and other Protestant princes of the empire, " to procure a league for defence of their religion," says Cambden. But this league does not appear, nor any other effect of these negotiations. "As she was very saving of her money, it is likely," says Rapin, " that she did not employ the most proper means to bring the princes of Germany into her interests." She secured herself by a great deal of management on the side of Scotland. She assisted the king of Navarre, and the prince of Condé, with money and ships; and the sole treaty she made on the continent was that with the states of the Low Countries, concluded the tenth of August 1585, at Nonesuch. Her chief dependence was upon her own ability and courage; upon the affection and zeal of her people. Neither failed her. Sure of being attacked, she began the attack. Whilst Cavendish pillaged the coasts of Chili and Peru, she sent Drake to the coasts of Spain, with orders to burn all the Spanish ships he should meet. Her orders were executed with the spirit with which they were given. More than a hundred vessels, loaded with provision and ammunition, were burnt at Gibraltar. The Spanish admiral was insulted at the mouth of the Tagus, and the Spaniards were taken, or destroyed, even under his eyes; an infamy so great, that the suffering of it was scarce in example before that time. The riches coming from the Indies to Spain, fell into the hands of the English. The projects of Philip were disappointed in the year 1587; and when the invasion was attempted in the year 1588, his army was blocked up in the ports of the Low Countries, and his invincible armada was beaten, scattered, and destroyed.

We have now gone through all we propose to say at this time concerning the conduct of queen Elizabeth, both at home and abroad; concerning that conduct, which, by convincing her people of her goodness and her wisdom, procured from them those large returns of gratitude, of duty, of affection and zeal, the sole foundations on which she rested her authority and her security; and the sole foundations on which they can be rested, suitably to the nature of our government. The limitations, necessary to render monarchy consistent with public liberty, must be many and great; for which reason it has been objected to them, that they took off from that weight of authority, and restrained that fulness of power, which are many times necessary to be exerted, even for the good of the whole community. If this objection was well founded, it would be a sufficient answer to say, that a few accidental inconveniences, which may happen, and which may be recompensed too, in government, deserve not to be prevented, at the expense of leaving liberty perpetually exposed. But the reign of queen Elizabeth proves, beyond contradiction, that a prince like her will enjoy, at the head of the freest people on earth, all the authority, and all the power necessary to promote the joint security, prosperity and glory of prince and people. So that all the objections which can be raised on this side to the British constitution of government, will centre here; that it has not provided for strengthening and enlarging the authority and power of a weak or a wicked prince.

A prince who never separates the interests just mentioned, and who pursues them wisely, will have absolute power in the most limited monarchy. A prince who separates these interests, turns government itself into faction; and the spirit of liberty will rise against him.   An arbitrary government is suited to any character. A free government requires a great, at least a good one.   In the former, all kinds and degrees of power are in the prince, or flow from him.   In the latter, his powers are limited and confined. When he wants to increase, or extend them, he must derive the faculty of doing so from his people; and from hence it follows, that as long as such a constitution remains entire and uncorrupt- ed, the prosperity, nay, the ease, and even the security of the go- vernment, will depend on the disposition of the people towards the prince—as the disposition of the people will always depend on the behaviour of the prince towards the people.   Queen Eli- zabeth saw these truths in all their force.   She was both willing and able to proportion her conduct to them.   She never felt, therefore, any want of power.   She was supported by the spirit of liberty, and she overcame that of faction.   Some of her suc- cessors either did not see these truths in all their force, or were unable to proportion their conduct to them.   These princes, there- fore, felt the limitations of our monarchy like shackles upon them. The spirit of liberty either opposed, or did not support them; and they nursed up a spirit of faction to the ruin of themselves, of their families, and almost of the nation.

LETTER XVII.

THE scene we are now going to open will appear vastly dif- ferent from that which we have just closed.   Instead of an unin- terrupted, pleasing harmony of government, we shall meet with a perpetual, jarring dissonance; instead of success and glory abroad, disappointment and contempt; instead of satisfaction, prosperity and union at home, discontent, distress, and at last civil war, will present themselves to us in all their horrors.

To consider this melancholy change, and to show from whence it proceeded, whether from the prince or from the people, is our present business.   That it was brought about and carried on by faction, must not be denied.   The sole question will therefore be, which was the factious side?   Now to determine this, we need only inquire, which side was for usurping on the other; which was for preserving and which for altering the established consti- tution of government.   On this point the question will turn; for in a country of liberty, in a limited monarchy, whatever some persons may think, or desire to have believed, it is certain that there may be faction for the crown, as well as against the crown.

The reason is plain.   There may be conspiracies against liberty, as well as against prerogative.   Private interest may screen or defend a bad administration, as well as attack or undermine a good one.   In short, conspiring against any one part of the constitution in favor of another, or perverting, to the support of national grievances, the very means which were instituted to redress them, are destructive of the whole frame of such a government, and are the proper characteristics of faction.

On which side faction, thus defined, is likely to be found the oftenest, and to act the most effectually, we shall not stay to examine here.   They, who have read the first of these letters, may remember what is there said, to show the difference between the motives and the means, which a prince hath of usurping on his people; and those which the people have of encroaching on their prince.   We shall only observe, to our present purpose, that as he, who confines his notions of faction to oppositions made to the crown, reasons, in an absolute monarchy, in favor of the constitution; so he, who confines them thus, reasons, in a limited monarchy, against the constitution; is weak enough to deceive himself, or wicked enough to attempt deceiving others; and, in either case, is thus far a betrayer of public liberty.—On such principles as these we said, in our last paper, that government itself might be turned into faction; and that some of Queen Elizabeth's successors had nursed up a spirit of faction, to the ruin of themselves, of their families, and almost of the nation.—We presume that this will appear, in the course of our inquiries, to be undeniably true; and that there will be as little room to doubt whether the factious conduct of the court, in the reigns of king James and king Charles the First, gave a rise to all the struggles between them and their people, as there is room to deny that the destruction of our constitution in church and state, was the dreadful consequence of these struggles.   The spirit of liberty and the British constitution of government, whose cause we are pleading, and whose cause we are sorry there should be so much occasion to plead, will therefore, we hope, remain clear of all imputations.

We wish that this justice could be done without opening wounds which are hardly yet entirely healed, and without arraigning the conduct of princes, whose memories have been held in great veneration by many worthy persons: but since this cannot be; nay, since the opening of these wounds may contribute to the more effectual healing of them; and since arraigning the conduct of these princes hath been rendered the more necessary by the accounts which have been given of it, and by the principles on which it hath been defended; we must speak with the same liberty of them, as we have used in speaking of those who reigned before them.

The Ægyptians paid so much respect to their very limited monarchs that when they went to warn these princes against particular vices, they commended them for opposite virtues. We cannot persuade ourselves that this method of reforming, or instructing, by panegyric, the usual and most deadly poison of other princes, had a good effect on those of Ægypt. But however this might be, when these princes were dead, notwithstanding the respect shown to them living,* they underwent the same trial as the custom of the kingdom had established for all private persons, and funeral honors were equally denied to them, and to the meanest and most guilty of their subjects, when their memories were condemned, on a solemn and strict examination of the conduct they had held in life.

Though we propose to inquire with all this freedom; and though we are persuaded that the result of these inquiries will be a confirmation of what hath been advanced by us; yet are we very far from admitting many of the objections which have been made to the conduct of king James and king Charles the First. Much less do we approve those cruel insinuations against them which are to be found in several invectives, not histories, dictated by a spirit of faction, not by the spirit of liberty. The spirit of liberty reflects on the errors of princes with sorrow, not with triumph, and is unwilling to aggravate what it wishes had never happened. In the temper which this spirit inspires therefore, we shall proceed. We shall dwell on no facts, but such as we think uncontroverted; and shall make no reflections, nor draw any consequences from them, but such as arise naturally and without the least force.—The truth would not be so evident, as we presume it is in this case, if any thing more was necessary to the illustration of it.

Amongst the many advantages which king James had on his accession to the throne of England, we might very justly reckon the recent example of his predecessor. Her penetration discovered the consequences of that great change in the balance of property, of which we have spoken in letters XI and XII; and she accommodated at once the whole system of her government to it, as we have there observed.—Whatever doubts she might have entertained, concerning the success of her own measures, before she had experienced the happy effects of them, king James could reasonably entertain none. Experience, as well as reason, pointed out to him the sole principle on which he could establish his government with advantage, or even with safety; and queen Elizabeth's reign had every year afforded him fresh proofs that this principle of government, which is easy in the

* Diodor. Sic. lib. 2, c. 3.

pursuit, is effectual in the end to all the purposes which a good
man and a just prince can desire to obtain. But king James
paid as little regard to her example as he did to her memory.
In the last respect he was indecent; in the other, unwise. He
boasted most ridiculously of an influence which he never had
over her councils. Happy would it have been for him, for his
family, and for this whole nation, if her example had really had
a due influence over his conduct; or, at least, if his example had
obtained less influence over the conduct of his successors.—
Fraught with learning, not with knowledge; ignorant of the true
principles of government; more a stranger to our constitution by
his notions and his habits of thinking, than to our country by his
birth; obstinate, though not steady; misled by self-opinion, and
confirmed in error by superlative pedantry, king James the
First seemed to expect the love, and to demand the obedience of
his subjects, purely because the crown had dropped on his head.
Whereas queen Elizabeth seemed, both by her declarations and
her actions, to think herself entitled to the first, and secure of
the last, for no other reason than this; because she wore the
crown to the greatest advantage of her people. Her good sense
taught her what he had not found in his books; that the ties
between prince and people are not the same with those between
particular persons in private life. These persons converse and
live familiarly together. Natural sympathies, therefore, more
easily to be felt than described, may unite them without the
motives of gratitude or expectation. Those common good
offices, which the heart alone suggests, are often sufficient to
maintain such unions; and a man, who is neither a saint nor a
hero, may hope to find and keep a friend. But public, or political, or state friendship, by which we mean an intimate and affectionate union between the governors and the governed, cannot
be contracted without gratitude, or expectation, nor maintained
without both. If it could, if subjects were attached to their
prince by a kind of instinct, as hard to be accounted for, and
yet as prevalent as the sympathies we have mentioned; the
assertors of the divine right of princes, and of the universal
obedience due to them, would have had long ago a more plausible argument than they have yet produced in favor of their
doctrines. They would have been able to stop the mouths of
all gainsayers; even of him who required a miracle to become
their convert; and who resolved never to believe that slavery
was of divine institution, till he beheld "subjects born with
bunches on their backs, like camels, and kings with combs on
their heads like cocks;" from which marks it might be collected
that the former were designed to labor and to suffer, and the
latter to strut and crow. But till some such miracle is wrought,

or the instinct supposed above is born with men, we think it will remain true that the union we speak of, between prince and people, neither can, nor ought to subsist on any other terms, than those of good government on one part, and of gratitude and expectation on the other.—This union may be, and hath been maintained by absolute princes with their people; because it is not impossible that an absolute prince should be a wise and good man; and because some such there have been. But here lies a difference. The absolute monarch may exert the whole power of the state. He may govern easily, safely, and with all other advantages, though he neglects to cultivate this union; or, which is worse, though he breaks it. But the case of a limited monarch is not the same, for the reasons which we touched upon at the end of our last letter. It is, therefore, the immediate, the personal, the highest interest of such a prince, as it is the duty of every prince, to contract this union, and to maintain it inviolate. The wisdom of our constitution hath made it so; and, in making it so, hath imitated that divine wisdom, which appears in the constitution of the moral world. In this, it may be easily proved from a consideration of the circumstances in which we stand as individuals, that the general good of society is the particular interest of every member. Our Creator designed, therefore, that we should promote this general good. It is by consequence our duty to do so; and every man who believes a wise, all-directing mind, and who knows that proportioning of means to ends is essential to wisdom, must subscribe to this opinion.— and yet, determined by false appearances of good, or attracted by the force of immediate objects, men may, and they frequently do, imagine that they pursue their particular and separate interests, whilst they neglect, or act against the general and common interest of society.

In like manner, king James the First, and those princes who have trod in his steps, imagined no doubt that they pursued a particular, separate interest of their own, whilst they neglected an union with their people, and even made such an union impracticable, by transgressing, in pretensions and in fact, the bounds which our constitution prescribed to them. But the mistake is equal in both cases; for in both cases, interest and duty remain indivisibly united, however they may be separated in opinion; and he who sins against one, sins most certainly against the other; though the natural consequences of his actions do not appear immediately, nor on every occasion, to follow.

These consequences followed in a signal and terrible manner upon the occasions which we have mentioned, and into the particulars of which we shall descend some other time. These examples, therefore, are complete. The causes and the effects come together under one view, and if we carry our observations forward to later times, we shall see causes of the same kind laid again, and producing effects of the same nature; effects always proportionable to them; sometimes jealousy, discontent, tumult; sometimes open resistance, and deposition of the prince; for though, in all these cases, the people have suffered, as well as the prince; yet in some, the prince alone hath been undone; and thus, by an equal distribution of justice, the principal share of the common calamity hath fallen on him, without whom no part of it could have happened.

Though these general reflections, which we have premised, may appear long to some of our readers, and may seem too nearly allied to reflections already made; yet we hope for indulgence, on account of the importance of the matter. It must surely be of use to explain very clearly, and very fully, from whence the weakness of our government, at some times, and the disorders and revolutions of it at others, have proceeded since that era, when our liberties became better secured, and our constitution capable of greater improvements, by a new settlement of the balance of property and power. No point hath been more mistaken. None hath been more artfully misrepresented.

LETTER XVIII.

WE have observed already of how great advantage the example of queen Elizabeth might have been to king James the First. It might have taught him to struggle through the most intricate difficulties. But he had none such to encounter, till he created them by his own management. On the contrary, his accession to the throne of England was accompanied with all the favorable circumstances of ease and security, which were necessary to form a conjuncture proper for him; so that with abilities, much too inferior to those of his predecessor, he might have reigned as gloriously abroad, and as happily at home. Many of the difficulties and dangers which surrounded her, were personal to her. They arose from her birth; from her title; and from that which Mary queen of Scotland pretended. They therefore ceased with her. Many others she had conquered by a wise and steady administration. Many had been worn out by length of time; and many had been so changed by the course of events, that king James was safe, where she was most in danger; and strong, where she was weakest. His title was not contested;

nor any opposition, either open or secret, given to his succession. They who had sounded so high the right of his mother, could not refuse to acknowledge the same right in him; and the rest of the nation submitted to it; for how little regard soever many of them might pay to his right in their hearts, or how great suspicion soever of his future conduct might be justly infused into them by his past behavior, the people would have a king, and there was no other prince, in whom the protestant interest could unite at that time. That riddle of a plot, in which Sir Walter Raleigh was involved, does not deserve to be mentioned, as an exception to the national unanimity we speak of. —True it is, that, in other respects, the nation was far from being united, either by a conformity of opinion, or by an acquiescence of those who differed from the establishment.—It was, no doubt, a severe misfortune, and such it continnes to this very hour, that the great and glorious work of the reformation, being carried on at different times, and in different places, was carried on likewise without a general concert. The several churches reformed themselves, according to the different circumstances they were in, and according to the different characters of the few, who led the many in each of them. The separation of them all from the church of Rome was entire; but in some, it was thought proper to reform; in others, to alter the whole model; in some, many things were retained, which had been in practice before the reformation; in others, a total opposition to every instance of conformity with the church of Rome seemed to be the sole standard of Christian purity.—This variety of opinions and establishments amongst the reformed was a great evil in itself; but this evil was aggravated by a circumstance of the most fatal consequence. The reformers, and especially those who came latest, as our excellent Mr. Hooker* observes, by enforcing too peremptorily their particular modes of reformation, brought the people in many cases to receive and respect, as divine laws, even those orders and that discipline, which expediency or other political motives had suggested. Now, the natural tendency of this persuasion was not only to render all comprehension or reconciliation amongst the reformed churches impracticable: but to make the divisions, in any particular church, incurable.—Thus, when queen Elizabeth completed that establishment of a church, which Edward the Sixth had begun, many dissented from it; and the scruples of private conscience were pleaded against submission to the public authority of the state.—If regard had been paid to all who petitioned the queen, or admonished the parliament, in the heat of these times, it seems probable that no establishment at all could have been made; and

* Eccl. Polity, Pref.

if none had been made, an ecclesiastical anarchy must have
ensued.—How far the number of separatists might have been
lessened by more compliances with the learned and moderate
amongst them, for such there certainly were, we shall neither
presume to determine, nor go about to inquire. It is sufficient
for our present purpose to observe, that, although these seeds of
disturbance had been sowed before the accession of king James,
yet no disturbance had happened, nor was any likely to happen
at that time. The measures which had been pursued, and the
temper which had been observed in queen Elizabeth's reign,
tended to diminish the religious opposition by a slow, a gentle,
and for that very reason an effectual progression; and, in the
mean while, to prevent such consequences of it as might disorder or weaken the government.—By the laws which were
made, the several dissenting sects were discouraged and kept in
awe; but by the execution of these laws, they were not exasperated. They were punished, not provoked. They felt the weight
of the government, as often as they attempted to disturb it, but
they never felt the oppression of party; and when they were
treated like factions, they had not the pretence to complain that
they were treated so by a faction.—Upon this foot there was
even room to hope, that when the first fire of these men's zeal
was spent, reasonable terms of union with the established church
might be accepted by such of them as were not intoxicated with
fanaticism. Such as these were friends to order, though they
disputed about it, and could have the less pretence to reject with
obstinacy that which had been settled by queen Elizabeth, because they knew that their own discipline had been established
where it prevailed, as the church of England had been by the
supreme authority; that it had been made a law of the country;
that the people had been bound by oath to the maintenance of
it; and that Calvin himself had been a most rigorous exactor of
conformity to it.—If such as these had been once incorporated
with the established church, the remaining sectaries would have
been of little moment, either for numbers, or reputation; and the
very means, which were proper to gain these, were likewise the
most effectual to hinder the increase of them, and of the other
sectaries in the mean time.—Upon the whole matter, we think
it very plain that king James the First, besides the advantage
of coming to the crown after all the difficulties and dangers of
completing the reformation and establishing a new church were
over, had an easy and secure opportunity of preventing any bad
consequences, which might be apprehended from the divisions
of his protestant subjects; and that the improvement of this opportunity, consisted in giving neither alarm to the well-affected,
nor pretence to the factious.

The designs of the Roman catholic party, against the constitution in church and state, were carried on with as much rage,
but not with as much strength as ever. The hydra-heads, which
sprouted continually out of that body in the former reign, had
been lopt so often, that they appeared more rarely; and if the
venom of that principle which produced them, was not abated,
yet many of the springs, which fed and nourished it, were exhausted. The Guises, Mary queen of Scotland, Philip the
Second, were dead. The reformation was established; not only
in outward form, but in the hearts of men. It was grown up to
be a part, and a favorite part, of the constitution. The spirit of
liberty had blended our civil and religious rights together, and
was become equally jealous of both. Let us add, for we may
add it with great justice, that the church of England was, by
the sobriety, wisdom and sanctity of her institution, established
on a rock; that this rock was defended by the greatest number
of excellent men, which any Christian church could boast of; and
from all this let us conclude, that as she was able to resist the
attacks of those sects, which private conceit, mistaken zeal, some
enthusiasm, and perhaps some faction had nursed up in her own
bosom; so she was better able than any other protestant church
to defend herself, and the state too, against the fallacies, the se-
ductions, and the violence of Rome. The policy of this court
saw it, and neglected nothing to prevent the consequences. Seminaries had been erected at Doway and other places abroad,
for the education of English youth in popery. Gregory the
Thirteenth had given the direction of that, which was erected at
Rome, to the Jesuits; and upon that occasion these incendiaries
crept into England. If we may believe some accounts, they
mingled themselves amongst the clergy of the church of England
and the puritan ministers. That they took all methods to foment
our divisions is probable; and that they were not men, who
would stick at any, may be certainly collected from that account
of their conduct here, and of the doctrines they taught, which is
contained in the complaints exhibited against them by the rest
of the popish clergy.*

Thus was the spirit of the church and court of Rome kept up
here, even at the time of the accession of king James; a spirit,
which might serve to bring about an assassination, or any barbarous and desperate stroke, like that of the gun-powder-treason,
which a few enthusiasts were capable of executing; but not to
subvert the reformation, and introduce popery anew. The efforts
of this party now were like the last convulsions of a strong body,
mortally wounded; frightful to behold; sufficient to hurt others;

* Thuan, lib. 126.

but tokens of death, not symptoms of recovery. King James had it therefore in his power to keep down with ease a party, which queen Elizabeth had subdued with pain; and, whatever impression the bloody designs they had often formed, and sometime brought to effect, might make on his mind, certain it was, and the event made that certainty undeniable, that no degree of favor to them, except the utmost, could effectually secure him against their attempts; and that the least degree of favor shown, or encouragement given them, would be productive of the greatest national mischief.

We have dwelt longer on these points of religious divisions, because we think a clear and just notion of them absolutely necessary to fix a right opinion, concerning one of the principal causes which were laid in this reign, of all the national calamities that followed. We shall mention the other advantages which attended king Jamss the First, as briefly as we can; not because they were small, for, on the contrary, they were exceedingly great; but because they are more notorious, and have no need of being so much developed, in order to be made sensible.

Thus, for instance, the different conditions in which he found the navy, the commerce, and the wealth of the nation, as well as the revenues of the crown, from that in which queen Elizabeth had found them all at her accession, is known in general of every one who hath dipped into history. Without entering into more particulars, therefore, than we have done already, we may venture to conclude that he reaped the benefit of her economy, and was a rich, as well as a powerful king. We know very well that when the session of parliament was opened by commission in 1610, by the Earls of Suffolk and Salisbury, one of the reasons urged, for demanding money of the commons, was grounded on a debt of queen Elizabeth, which was said to have absorbed three hundred and fifty thousand pounds, due on the last subsidies granted to her. If this fact was true, all that resulted from it is, first, that queen Elizabeth left a mortgage on the lands of the crown, and money enough to discharge it; secondly, that king James parted with his money to recover his lands; and we shall not oppose any person who will charitably believe that that prince would have paid the debts of his predecessor, though they had not been thus secured, out of the money she left in her coffers; because to have done otherwise, would have been a manifest violation of all the rules of religion, honor, and common morality. But we much doubt whether even this averment of the lords, who opened the session, will have any great weight when it shall be considered that their whole discourse was too ministerial to be sincere; and that some of the reasons by which they accounted for the king's want of money, such, for instance, as the charge of protecting his wife and children from being robbed on the road to London, were really burlesque.

The advantages which this prince had in the situation of foreign affairs, both at his accession to the throne, and during the greatest part of his reign, were remarkably great; and we doubt whether it is possible to find more than one conjuncture equally favorable since that time. Philip the Third was on the throne of Spain; a prince of small capacity, and less application; governed by his favorite, and his favorite detested by the people. Before the end of king James's reign he died; and Philip the Fourth, his son, succeeded; a youth of sixteen years old, and governed as absolutely by Olivarez as his father had been by the Duke of Lerma. The declension of the Spanish monarchy hastened on apace, under these princes. It is said that Philip the Third refused to support the Roman catholic party, in the beginning of the reign of king James; which is the more probable, on account of the early and precipitate steps made by this prince, towards a peace with Spain. The defeat of Don John d'Aquila in Ireland, and the entire reduction of Tyrone, which happened a little before the death of queen Elizabeth, discouraged the Spaniards from making any more attempts of that kind. They turned their eyes from these islands to the continent; to the Low Countries and to Germany, where they continued, during the course of many years, to consume the remains of strength, in abetting the ambitious projects of that branch of the house of Austria.

As king James had nothing to apprehend from the enmity of Spain, so he was secure of the friendship of France. Henry the Fourth was now established on that throne. He was in peace indeed with Spain, but intended not to be so long. We are very far from believing that this prince could seriously entertain so chimerical a project as that of making an entire new settlement of Europe, by dividing it into fifteen states, which Parefixe and other authors have related, upon the faith of the compilers of Sully's memoirs; but, without doubt, he had great views of checking the ambition, and reducing the power of the house of Austria. It was therefore his interest to live well with the king of Great Britain; and accordingly he sent the Marquis of Rosny, afterwards Duke of Sully, to renew the treaties with king James, as soon almost as this prince was seated on the throne of England. When Henry the Fourth was stabbed by Ravaillac, a minority followed in France, and the counsels of that court were, for many years, chiefly employed about their own affairs: so that nothing could happen on that side, even after this great change, to give the least disturbance to king James.

The states of the Low Countries were no longer in the same

distressed condition. Their commonwealth had taken form; their naval force was increasing; and their commerce extending itself every day. Ostend kept the Spanish forces at bay for more than three years; and when Spinola made himself master of that heap of ruins, the Dutch thought themselves sufficiently recompensed by the acquisition which they had made, in the mean time, of Sluyce and other important places. The truce of eight months between Spain and the States was signed in 1607. It was prolonged afterwards; and in the year 1609, the truce of twelve years was concluded at Antwerp; by which the king of Spain was forced to acknowledge the liberty and independency of the United Provinces. Thus was that commonwealth established, to be a great and lasting accession of strength to the Protestant interest; and king James might have reaped the benefit of an useful alliance, where queen Elizabeth had no other advantage than that of defending the oppressed, and diverting the forces of a common enemy.

The affairs of the North, indeed were in great confusion about the same time. The crown of Sweden belonged to Sigismund in course of descent; but Sigismund was a Papist, and king of Poland. For both these reasons, he had been excluded, and his uncle Charles preferred to the throne by the states of Sweden; who provided, by the act of settlement, not only that their kings should be of the religion of the country, but that none of the princes of the royal family should accept another crown, nor any foreign dominions. Their experience. it seems, had shown them the necessity of such limitations. This gave occasion to those long and cruel wars, which followed between Sweden and Poland. Others succeeded between Sweden and Denmark; but the scene of them all was so remote, and the interests of this country so absolutely unconcerned in the events of them, that he, who should have advised king James to take any part in them, would have passed, in those days, for a very bad politician.

The indolent Rodolphus slept on the throne of the empire till the year 1614. His brother Matthias succeeded him; and their cousin Ferdinand succeeded Matthias. During the reign of Rodolphus, there were troubles in Hungary, in Transylvania, in Bohemia, and in several parts of the empire. Most of them were caused, all of them were fomented, by religious divisions. During the reign of Matthias, these troubles increased. They grew up to maturity, as the accession of Ferdinand to the empire approached. The Bohemians, long oppressed, and long provoked, took arms at last in 1618. Many causes conspired to render all accommodation impracticable. Amongst the principal were the designs, which all the branches of the house of Austria had laid and begun to execute against liberty and the protestant religion

in Gemany; the character of Ferdinand, violent, cruel, a bigot,
though artful; and, to speak impartially, the ambition of Frederic,
elector Palatine. If this ambition had been the sole motive to
engage king James in these quarrels, we must think that he
could not have answered to his own people the engaging in
them, as popular as the Palatine, his wife, and his cause were
in England. But these quarrels were of another importance.
Frederic lost not only the crown of Bohemia, but his own patrimony. The protestant religion, and the liberty of Germany
were well nigh sacrificed to the bigotry and ambition of the emperor; so that the interest of this nation, as well as the king's
family interest, was very much concerned to prevent these consequences; and yet, even upon this foot, we must likewise think
that it would not have been long popular in those days, when
the memory of queen Elizabeth's policy was fresh in the minds
of men, to have maintained great armies on the continent, and
to have fed with subsidies so many hungry princes, who had, at
least in the beginning, nothing less at heart than the common
interest.

This difficult and dangerous situation of affairs on the continent, in which we allow that king James ought to have taken
some part, may be thought, perhaps, to form an exception to
what hath been said, concerning those circumstances of advantage, of ease, and security, which accompanied the reign of this
prince; but there will be room to think so no longer, when it shall
be considered that king James had time and means to prepare
for this critical conjuncture. The distress in foreign affairs began with queen Elizabeth's reign; and she was in danger abroad,
before she was settled on her throne at home; but he had reigned
near eighteen years before any thing happened on the continent,
which could give him a just occasion of acting vigorously in that
scene. Besides, when this occasion did happen, he had it in his
power to have acted with great glory to himself, and effectually
for the service of those whom it was his interest to support,
without taking any other part than that which becomes a king
of England, in opposition to that which becomes a prince on the
continent, and agreeably to the principles of his predecessor's
conduct. This will appear evidently true, when we come to
consider the part he did take; and we shall insist upon it the
rather, because we observe with how much affectation the case
we are now speaking of, hath been quoted as parallel to the
present situation of affairs; and how impertinently it hath been
taken for granted, that king James the First was condemned in
his own time, and hath been condemned since, for not doing
what these time-serving politicians recommend; that is, for en-
tangling himself in the affairs of the empire, as if he had been a

prince of the empire; and for not acting on every appearance of danger, or even of inconveniency to any little state of Germany, in such a manner as is agreeable neither to the interest, nor situation of our island.

What hath been said may be sufficient to show how few the difficulties were, compared with the advantages, which king James had to encounter both at home and abroad; and how fortunate a conjuncture was prepared for him by the wisdom of his predecessor, and by a happy combination of circumstances.— What use he made of these advantages, what conduct he held, and what consequences it had, must be the subject of another discourse.

LETTER XIX.

By what hath been said, in former letters, we think it appears, that from the time our constitution settled on the foundation on which it remains still, there hath been not only no possibility of governing this nation with strength and dignity; without the concurrence of the people in their representative body; nor with ease and safety without their concurrence in their collective body; but that this concurrence hath depended, and does and must always depend, on the union of interest and affection between the king and his subjects.

We beg leave to repeat that queen Elizabeth saw this to be a sure, and the only sure principle, on which she could establish her government under such a constitution; that she very wisely took the government on the terms of the constitution, and the constitution as she found it; that instead of struggling through trouble and danger to bend the constitution to any particular notions or views of her own, she accommodated her notions, her views, and her whole character to it. Let us observe, by the way, that this is no more than what every prince ought to do; and what every free people will expect and exact too, if need be, that he should do. He is made for their sakes, not they for his. He is raised to maintain, not to alter the constitution.

Now king James begun and continued, through the whole course of his reign, to govern without any regard to this principle; nay, in absolute defiance of it. He chose other expedients of government, and trusted to so many broken reeds. Without any talents ·to procure the esteem, he awakened the jealousy and never courted the good-will of his people; but, instead of it, en-

deavored to instil into their minds what was rooted in his own,
a very good opinion of himself, and a very mean opinion of
them. He endeavored to persuade men, who felt that the balance of property was on their side, and that they held a great
share of the supreme power in their hands, that though they had
this property, yet they had no right, or a very precarious one, to
this power. He meant, by the force of new-fangled opinions, to
attach the nation to him, as queen Elizabeth had done by the ties
of affection and confidence; or he meant to govern without the
concurrence of the nation; or he meant nothing. The first was
chimerical, the second was wicked, and the third was stupid.—
Elizabeth had been jealous of her prerogative, but moderate in
the exercise of it. Wiser James imagined that the higher he
carried it, and the more rigorously he exerted it, the more strongly
he should be seated on his throne. He mistook the weight for
the strength of a sceptre; and did not consider that it is never so
likely to slip, or be wrenched out of a prince's hands, as when
it is heaviest. He never reflected that prerogative is of the nature of a spring, which by much straining will certainly relax
and often break; that in one case it becomes of little, and in the
other of no use at all.

As absurd as the notions and principles of government were,
by which king James hoped to establish his authority, he found
numbers to adopt them; for numbers are at all times liable to be
deceived, ready to be tempted, and prone to be corrupted.—New
systems of law and policy were not only received, but propagated. Some men were heated by opposition. Others were
educated in prejudice. The plainest rights of the people were
called iu question. The least justifiable pretensions of the crown
were established as true axioms of government, and certain principles of the English constitution. What Father Paul observes
to have happened in the church, happened here in the state. Our
court, like that of Rome, by affirming and denying boldly, and
by insisting peremptorily, brought many things to be received as
certain, which had been never proved, and many others to be
looked on as problematical, which had been often demonstrated.
Thus were those divisions created, which could alone render the
other fatal. Disputes about the use of the surplice, or the cross
in baptism, would not have unsheathed all the swords in the
nation. Puritanism neither did, nor could make such deadly
wounds; but when they were once made, puritanism festered in
the sore, and rendered them mortal. King James conjured up,
by using tricks of government, that storm in which his successor
perished. His successor, for we will finish the sketch we have
begun, a religious and a just prince, came a party man to the
throne. His prejudices, confirmed by habit, fortified by the

flattery of his courtiers, and provoked by the opposition which his father and he met with, carried him to continue an invasion of the people's rights, whilst he imagined himself only concerned in the defence of his own. The faction of the court tainted the nation, and gave life and strength, if it did not give being, to the factions in the state. If the spirit of liberty could have prevailed in time against the first, there had been no danger from the others. But the long and obstinate resistance of the first gave time and opportunity, and even assistance to the others to extinguish this spirit. Cavaliers and Roundheads divided the nation, like Yorkists and Lancastrians. No other option was left at last. To reconcile these disputes by treaty became impracticable, when neither side would trust the other. To terminate them by the sword, was to fight, not for preserving the constitution, but for the manner of destroying it. The constitution might have been destroyed, under pretence of prerogative. It was destroyed under pretence of liberty. We might have fallen under absolute monarchy. We fell into absolute anarchy. The sum of all is this. We were destroyed by faction; but faction prevailed at court near forty years before it prevailed amongst the people. It was the original principle on one side. It was an accident on the other. Churchmen and royalists attacked the constitution. Puritans and commonwealthsmen, and, above all, a motley race of precise knaves and enthusiastic madmen ruined it. But the last could never have happened, if the first had not; and whoever will dispassionately trace the causes of that detestable civil war, will find them laid in the conduct of king James the First, as early as his accession to the throne of England.

Having given this general idea of the two reigns which followed that of queen Elizabeth, it is time to examine whether this idea of them can be supported by a series of uncontroverted facts.—Let us descend into some particulars.

"A prince that is invited, or comes newly to a kingdom," says Wilson, "must have his chariot wheels smooth shod;" and surely if ever prince had motives and an opportunity to render himself popular, king James had both. Essex, Southampton and others, even Cecil, a principal minister of the late queen had held a correspondence with him, for their own private interest; but the millions who submitted to his accession, submitted to it upon trust, and were determined by the nature of the conjuncture, not by any knowledge of the persons who composed this new royal family. It was not therefore enough for them to be placed in and about the throne. Their true interest required that the hearts of the people should be gained to them; and that popularity should supply that spirit in their favor, which seldom fails to operate in favor of those princes, who are born and bred amongst the people they are to govern. The opportunity of doing this lay fairly before king James. He was received with transports of joy, and all ranks of men made their court to him. —If he looked on this national behavior, for so it was, to be the effect of a desire in the people to endear themselves to him, and to unite closely with him, this should have suggested to his mind the ease with which he might acquire popularity, by improving the disposition, and captivate the good-will of a people, so desirous to be pleased with their king. If he looked on this national behavior as the effect of levity, inconstancy and love of change, it should have taught him to apprehend how soon this honey-moon would pass away; how soon the stream of popular favor might turn against him; and how soon they, who seemed to have forgotten queen Elizabeth, might return to regret her.— But that which a Scotsman foretold, happened, This behavior of the English spoiled a good king; or made a bad king worse. It was natural for a vain man to believe what his flatterers told him, and what he, his own greatest flatterer, told himself; that these applauses and transports of the people were due to his eminent merit, and were an homage paid for the honor he did them in accepting their crown.—He took therefore much state. He did not indeed make his journey, as Henry the Seventh made his entry into London, in a close chariot; but he forbid by proclamation the concourse of the people to him.* "He dispersed them with frowns, that we may not say with curses."—Such different turns of thought can vanity inspire. Some will be respected, like eastern monarchs, unseen within the shrine of their court. Others grow fond of public triumphs; delight in noisy acclamations; and are pleased to drive, like Indian pagods, over a prostrate crowd.

As much as king James neglected to gain the public, even at the cheap price of affability, he sunk into low familiarity with his favorites, and was profuse of riches and honors to particular men. He bestowed, at first on a few, and afterwards on one man, that affection which he had promised the whole nation, in some of the plausible, commonplace discourses which he held at certain times. There is no need of mentioning the particular instances of a profusion he acknowledged himself. The estates he gave to his courtiers impoverished the crown; and, as it always happens, the people were forced to pay for those very grants, at which they murmured. Honors he bestowed in so lavish a manner, and with so little distinction, that they ceased,

* Wilson.

in some sense, to be honors. To know the British nobility, it was become almost necessary to have nomenclators, like those who attended the candidates at Rome, to tell them the names of the citizens. The jest went so far that an advertisement of " an art to help weak memories to a competent knowledge of the names of the nobility,"* was pasted up at Paul's.

Thus king James began, and thus he continued his reign. That experience, which he said in his first speech to his parliament, would teach him not to be so easily and lightly moved in granting, taught him nothing. What a contrast does this conduct make with the affibility of queen Elizabeth; with the economy and reserve she used, in disposing of her treasure, and in conferring honors? But king James stood in need of helps, to the want of which she was superior. " A good government," says one of our writers, " makes a good people." When a prince hath turned the spirit of a nation in his favor, he need not be solicitous about gaining particular men; but when he hath turned this spirit against him, he must employ all arts, even the lowest, to detach particular men from the body of the people, and to make them act by motives of private interest against the public sense. This is faction; and therefore whenever a court is industrious to seduce, to inveigle, to corrupt particular men, we may securely conclude, without waiting for any other sign, that such an administration stands on a factious, not on a national bottom. But to return to king James.

Whilst he neglected the affection and sought the reverence of the public, he lost one, and was disappointed of the other. His private and public character both fell into contempt. Learning was the part upon which he valued himself. This he affected more than became a king, and broached, on every occasion, in such a manner as would have misbecome a schoolmaster. His pedantry was too much even for the age in which he lived. It would be tedious to quote the part he took in the conference at Hampton Court; and in the theological wrangles between the Gomarists and Arminians; or to go about to prove, by some instances, what appeared in all his words and actions; what is universally allowed; and what the unkingly volume he left behind him testifies. Let us only observe, that the ridicule which arose from hence, and which fixed on him, was just; because the merit of a chief governor is wisely to superintend the whole, and not to shine in any inferior class; because different, and, in some cases perhaps, opposite talents, both natural and acquired, are necessary to move, and to regulate the movements of the machine of government; in short, because as a good adjutant may

* Wilson.

make a very bad general, so a great reader, and writer too, may be a very ignorant king.

There are many other circumstances which concurred to lessen this prince in the eyes of his subjects and of all mankind, as we shall have occasion to observe frequently in the course of these remarks. In the mean time, we shall observe here, that the state he affected, and the pompous titles he was fond of, served to render his pusillanimity, which, with his vanity, made up the main of his character, more conspicuous, and his person by consequence more contemptible.   The hostilities between the English and Spaniards continued, when queen Elizabeth died.   This great queen, not content to have done herself and her subjects justice, on many signal occasions, put it likewise into their power to do themselves justice, by granting letters of reprisal on the subjects of Spain.   King James was so fond of peace, that is, so afraid of war, that, without staying to be solicited on this head, or to be complimented on his accession to the throne by the king of Spain, he revoked these letters in a few weeks after he came into England.   He disarmed his subjects before he had provided for their better security.   He stopped them in the course of doing themselves justice, before he was sure of obtaining reparation for their past losses.   The impressions which such a proceeding must make on the minds of a trading people are easily felt.   He who had revoked these letters in such a manner, was not likely to grant them on any other occasion.   What protection, therefore, and, much less, what encouragement to trade could be expected from a prince who began his reign by sacrificing this, the most valuable interest of his people, to a foreign and hostile nation; to the mean arts of false policy, and even to his fears?   Again; one of the first embassies which king James sent abroad, was that of the Earl of Hertford to Brussels.   A Dutch man-of-war meeting the ship which carried the ambassador, refused to strike;* and hav-

---

* N. B. This fact stands in history, as it is here related; but having looked into Sir William Monson's naval tracts, we find it differently told.   He says nothing of striking, or not striking the flag; but confesses that an affront was offered by two Dutch men-of-war.   He adds, that he sent for the captains on board his ship; that he threatened to right himself upon them; but that he dismissed them at the entreaty of my Lord Hertford, on their excusing themselves, and promising to punish the offenders.   How severely these offenders were punished may be collected from hence.   "One of these captains," says Sir William Monson, "was he, who since that time committed a foul murder upon his majesty's subjects in Ireland, that were under protection."   If we had no other proofs of the indignities offered to our nation by the Dutch, from the time of the accession of king James the First, than the memorials of this gentleman, they would be sufficient.   He complains of these indignities very much, and mentions several.   In this very tract he affirms that the Hollanders took and burned our ships, and murdered our men for trading to the ports of Flanders,

ing offered this affront to the united crosses, which had never been offered to that of St. George, went off with impunity. It is said that the ambassador hindered the captain from asserting the honor of the British flag. But two things are certain; one, that queen Elizabeth would have severly punished her officer, and have exacted ample reparation from the States General; the other, that king James did neither. This commonwealth had been raised by queen Elizabeth, and was still in want of the support of England. The sovereignty of her state had not been yet acknowledged by any of the powers of Europe. How much the pacific temper of king James was capable of bearing had not yet become so apparent, as he made it in the course of his reign. From all which it is easy to collect, that if he had demanded satisfaction, he must and would have received it. But the good prince was afraid, where no fear was, and bore dishonorably what he might have resented safely: nay, what he ought to have resented in any circumstances, and at any hazard. We are not to wonder if so poor a conduct as this soon brought king James into contempt, mingled with indignation, amongst a people, eagerly bent on commerce, and in whom high notions of honor and a gallant spirit had been infused, by the example of queen Elizabeth, and encouraged during the whole course of a long reign.

These things, and several others of the same kind, which I omit, might however have been borne. The ridicule might have appeared less in the eyes of men accustomed to it. The other faults might have been excused, or softened at least, by hopes of amendment. But there are some things behind, which no excuse would alleviate, nor any patience endure. We shall now bring them forward, and shall speak of them under three heads. The pretensions set up, and the attempts made against the freedom of this constitution. The management of parties. The conduct of our national interests abroad, against the sense of the nation.

whilst they suffered their own countrymen, even in our sight, to trade thither. The truth is, that our nation was insulted with impunity, during this pacific reign, not only in Europe, but in every other part of the world; not only by the Dutch, but by other nations; and that our government fell from the highest esteem into the lowest contempt. If, therefore, the instance we have quoted should be disputed, on the representation of this fact by Sir William Monson, an hundred others, and several of them more flagrant, might be soon produced.

LETTER XX.

A FUNDAMENTAL principle, on which king James affected to establish his authority, was that of an hereditary right to the crown. This sacred right, according to the political creed which he imposed, was not to be contested, much less to be set aside; and yet this sacred right was a mere chimera; contradicted by the general tenor of custom from the Norman invasion to his time; by the declared sense of his immediate predecessors; by many solemn proceedings of parliament; and by the express terms of law. Two families (for the race of Plantagenet was grafted on the Norman race, and they may be reckoned properly as one) had furnished, indeed, all our kings; but this constituted no hereditary right. When a prince of the royal family, but in a degree remote from the succession, comes to the crown, in prejudice of the next heir, hereditary right is violated as really as it would be, if an absolute stranger to this family succeeded. Such a prince may have another, and we think a better right; that, for instance which is derived from a settlement of the crown, made by the authority of parliament; but to say he hath an hereditary right, is the grossest abuse of words imaginable. This we think so plain, that we should be ashamed to go about to prove it; and yet there are men, in this age of paradoxes, either dull enough, or prostitute enough, to assert hereditary right, even in the case above mentioned.

Our kings of the Norman race, were so far from succeeding as next heirs to one another, and in a regular course of descent, that no instance can be produced of the next heir's succeeding, which is not preceded and followed by instances of the next heir's being set aside. Thus Edward the First succeeded his father Henry the Third; but his father Henry the Third and his grandfather John had both been raised to the throne, in plain defiance of hereditary right; the right of Arthur, nephew to John, and the right of Arthur's sister, cousin-german to Henry. Edward the Second succeeded his father Edward the First; but Edward the Third deposed Edward the Second; the parliament renounced all allegiance to him; and Edward the Third held the crown by a parliamentary title, as much as William the Third. If we go up higher than this era, or descend lower, we shall find the examples uniform. Examples, sufficient to countenance this pretension of hereditary right to the crown of England, are to be found nowhere. But we hasten to king James; who raised, or, if you please, revived this pretension, so needlessly for himself, and so very unprofitably for his posterity.

The British race began in Henry the Seventh; and from him alone king James derived that right, which he asserted in such pompous terms; that undoubted right to the throne, as he called it in his first speech to parliament, which God, by birthright and lineal descent, had in fulness of time, provided for him. Now surely, if ever any prince came to the crown without the least color of hereditary right, it was Henry the Seventh. He had no pretence to it, even as heir of the house of Lancaster. His wife might have some, as heir of the house of York; though her hereditary title was not free from objections, which the character of Edward the Fourth rendered probable; but the title of his wife had no regard paid to it either by him, or the parliament, in making this new settlement. He gained the crown by the good will of the people. He kept it by the confirmation of parliament, and by his own ability. The notional union of the two roses was a much better expedient for quiet than foundation of right. It took place in Henry the Eighth; it was continued in his successors; and this nation was willing it should continue in king James and his family. But neither Henry the Eighth, nor his son, Edward the Sixth, who might have done so with much better grace, laid the same stress on hereditary right as king James did. One of them had recourse to parliament on every occasion, where the succession to the crown was concerned; and the other made no scruple of giving the crown by will to his cousin, in prejudice of his sister's right. This right, however, such as it was, prevailed; but the authority of parliament was called in aid by Mary, to remove the objection of illegitimacy, which lay against it. Elizabeth had so little concern about hereditary right, that she neither held, nor desired to hold her crown by any other tenure than the statute of the thirty-fifth of her father's reign. In the thirteenth of her own reign, she declared it by law high treason, during her life, and a præmunire, after her decease, to deny the power of parliament, in limiting and binding the descent and inheritance of the crown, or the claims to it, and whatever private motives there were for putting to death Mary, queen of Scotland, her claiming a right, in opposition to an act of parliament, was the foundation of the public proceedings against her.   •

Such examples, as we have quoted, ought to have some weight with king James. A prince, who had worn the crown of Scotland, under so many restraints, and in so great penury, might have contented himself, one would think, to hold that of England, whose pensioner he had been, by the same tenure, and to establish his authority on the same principles that had contented the best and greatest of his predecessors; but his designs were as bad as those of the very worst princes who went before him.

Happily for Great Britain, he wanted the capacity of Henry the Seventh; the resolution of Henry the Eighth; and the favorable opportunities which they had the luck to find, or the art to contrive, of raising prerogative, acquiring wealth, and encroaching on liberty.

We observed, in discoursing on the reign of Henry the Seventh, that he had laid the foundations of an exorbitant power, before the nation was well aware of what he intended.—King James, on the contrary, showed his whole game from the first. Besides the pleasure, which his vanity found in boasting of an absolute, independent right to the crown, inherent in himself, he imagined that the transition would be easy, and so indeed it proved amongst many, from this to some other useful apophthegms. He hoped to get, and he did get, an act of recognition of his right of succession; for we cannot persuade ourselves, with Rapin, that he was indifferent on this point: and though this act, as well as the oath of supremacy, which had been established long before, and that of allegiance, which was established soon after, is in itself, as it hath proved in effect, but a feeble prop to support the pretence of hereditary right; yet king James certainly looked on it as an admission of his claim, and meant a real advantage, where the parliament very probably meant nothing more than a compliment.—This prince brought with him the true spirit of a missionary; and, by preaching a new doctrine, endeavored to establish a new power. From the notion of independent right was deduced the notion of independent authority; a right superior to law; an authority unbounded by it; a right, which could not be proved; an authority, which might not be defined. The inference from both these was obvious. This independent king must be accountable to God alone. He could not be accountable to man.

If this excellent system of policy could have been generally imposed, his sacred majesty might have battened, with great ease and delight, in the full sunshine of arbitrary power; and that he should succeed in imposing it, his own vanity and the servile flattery of his ministers had made him to expect. True it is, that the language he held was not so plain, nor the efforts he made so direct and violent, in the beginning of his reign, as they grew soon afterwards; but yet, if we consider the multitude of his proclamations; the nature of some; the style of all; the obedience he exacted to them; the acts of power which he exercised; those which he essayed, and many other particulars of his conduct, which, for brevity, we omit; we must of course conclude, that he thought himself sure, at that time, of laying the foundations, since he prepared to erect so great a superstructure. He was deceived. Instead of making his impositions pass on the people, he only awakened their jealousy. He had, in his own age, and he hath, in ours, the demerit of beginning a struggle between prerogative and privilege; and of establishing a sort of warfare between the prince and the people. But the spirit of liberty baffled all his designs. The spirit of liberty was not enervated by luxury in those days. It was not only alive, but vigorous and active. It rose in the nation, as that of faction rose at court. The same principle which complied with queen Elizabeth, resisted king James. The opposition began as soon as the invasions; and tyranny was, at least, nipped in the bud.

King James made one attempt, indeed, in the beginning of his reign, which bid fairer for success than any of those which he made afterwards; and which, if it had succeeded, would have done the great work of his reign, by means more silent and more dangerous; more soft in appearance, and more deadly in effect. We mean the attempt he made on the privileges of the house of commons, in the case of elections. In the proclamation for calling his first parliament, he assumed a new and unjustifiable prerogative, by his manner of prescribing to the electors and to the elected; and by subjecting both to severe penalties, if they failed, not only against the laws and statutes, but against the purport, effect and true meaning of his proclamation. In the course of the session, he endeavored to put this prerogative in execution, by insisting first, that the commons should confer with the lords; and when this was refused, that they should confer with the judges, on the merits of an election and return for the county of Buckingham, which they had already heard and decided. If the king had prevailed in this attempt of garbling the house of commons, he would have prevailed very probably in that which he made some time afterwards, of imprisoning and punishing the members of it. Thus he might have intimidated those by one prerogative, whom he could not exclude by the other. Such an influence as must have resulted from hence, joined to that which the executive power gives unavoidably to every king, would soon have rendered the house of commons as dependent upon him, as the house of lords at that time appeared to be; for if money gets money, which will not, we suppose, be denied in this stock-jobbing age, it is no less true, and perhaps no less visible, that influence begets influence. Now we apprehend that, in this case, the barrier of liberty had been totally destroyed, and that king James would have virtually been in possession of arbitrary power; for whether the will of the prince becomes a law, by force of prerogative, and independently of parliament; or whether it is made so, upon every occasion, by the concurrence of parliament, arbitrary power is alike established. The only difference lies here. Every degree of this power, which is obtained without parliament, is obtained against the forms, as well as against the spirit of the constitution; and must therefore be obtained with difficulty, and possessed with danger. Whereas in the other method of obtaining and exercising this power, by and with parliament, if it can be obtained at all, the progress is easy and short; and the possession of it is so far from being dangerous, that liberty is disarmed, as well as oppressed, by this method; that part of the constitution, which was instituted to oppose the encroachments of the crown, the mal-administration of men in power, and every other grievance, being influenced to abet these encroachments, to support this mal-administration, and even to concur in imposing the grievances.—National concurrence can be acquired only by a good prince, and for good purposes; because public good alone can be a national motive. But king James was not ignorant that private good may be rendered a superior motive to particular men, and that it is morally possible to make even parliaments subservient to the worst purposes of a court. Richard the Second, by influencing the elections, and queen Mary, by corrupting the members, had created such a dependence of the parliament on the court, that the first had well nigh established, in spite of all other opposition, his absolute power; and that the latter was able to subvert what her father and her brother had done; to govern with the utmost cruelty; and to sacrifice the interests of the nation to those of a husband, whom she took against the general inclination of her people.— If therefore king James could have created the same dependence, he might have promised himself the same success. He might have governed in great quiet and safety, with the concurrence of parliament, tyrannically at home, and ignominiously abroad.— He might have beggared the nation, as he beggared himself, and have given an absolute dominion over both to one insolent and incapable minister. But this concurrence could not be obtained; because the dependence of parliaments upon the king could not be created. By asserting their privileges, they prevented any direct and open influence of the crown. Had king James been rich, and it was in his power to have been so; had luxury and the offspring of luxury, corruption, both which he introduced, prevailed in the body of the people, an indirect and private influence might have been established; this nation might have been enslaved by the least beloved and most despised of all her kings. But the king continued poor, and the nation honest; this indirect and private influence was either not attempted, or attempted without effect; and we are persuaded that no advocate for it could have been found, even in this reign, or the next. There were men wicked enough to ascribe such powers to the king, as would

have destroyed effectually the powers of parliament; but there
was no man absurd, as well as wicked enough, to allow those
powers which are given to parliament by the constitution, and to
argue for an expedient, which must of course render them ineffectual, or pervert them to purposes opposite to those for which
they were instituted.   Thus liberty was preserved, by preserving
the independency of parliaments.   The proceedings of the commons, in the whole course of the affair we have mentioned, were
extremely moderate.   They went farther, not only in expressions and outward demonstrations of respect and submission, but
in real compliances, than could have been expected, or than was
perhaps strictly right; and when an expedient was fallen upon
to draw the king, with some reputation out of the contest, they
gave way to it, although by admitting a writ for the election of
a member, in the room of one whose election they had allowed,
they suffered a precedent to be established, which might be turned
against them.   But the spirit of liberty, though easily alarmed,
is slow to resent even great provocations, and to act with violence, even against the worst princes.   Repeated injuries, imminent and extreme danger can alone bring things to such a pass;
and no king of this nation was ever distressed by his people,
without receiving frequent warnings, as well as accumulating insupportable grievances.   King James felt some part of this distress in process of time.   He deserved it perhaps already.   The
commons however contented themselves in an address to him, to
assert their privileges, and to complain of this invasion of them,
amongst other grievances.—The proceedings of parliament were
carried on in subsequent sessions, with the same moderation and
temper.   In that which followed the discovery of the gunpowder
treason, the oath of allegiance was imposed; and this pledge of
fidelity, for the future, was the sole hardship, for such the court
of Rome and a great number of that communion esteemed it,
which the Roman catholic party drew on themselves by so execrable an attempt.   The parliament complied, on this occasion,
with the king, probably against their own sentiments; since nothing could be more different than his notions and theirs, concerning the conduct to be held with papists, and even concerning
popery itself; and since the favor he showed, not to say the court
he made to this party, had already created great uneasiness, and
began to be a most unpopular part of his government.—He had
no war on his hands, and his revenues were at least as considerable as those of the late queen.   The commons however gave
him one of the greatest supplies which had ever been given in
parliament; and upon this occasion it may not be improper to
observe, in confirmation of what we have advanced already, that
the natural bent of the people to live well with their kings, is so

strong, that parliaments under no other influence than this, will neglect nothing to gain them; nay, that a prince like king James, disliked, distrusted, despised, may prevail on his parliament for a time, and till all hopes of gaining him are lost, to do as well as bear in his favor, what would not be attempted in a better reign, nor succeed, perhaps, if it was attempted.

His design of uniting the two kingdoms of England and Scotland failed. It was too great an undertaking for so bad a workman. We must think that the general arguments against it were grounded on prejudice; on false and narrow notions. But there were other reasons, drawn from the jealousies of that time, and from the conduct of the king, who had beforehand declared all the post-nati, or persons born since his accession to the English throne, naturalised in the two kingdoms; and these were, without doubt, the true reasons which prevailed against the union —The next time the parliament assembled, to proceed on business, was in the year 1610, and by that time the general discontent of the nation began to show itself in loud and universal murmurs. Some monopolies, the rigid and impolitic proceedings of the high-commission court and star-chamber, and many other causes, combined to raise them. But no particular grievance either had, or deserved to have, so great an effect as the continual endeavors which were used to establish practices and principles, absolutely destructive of the general constitution of the English government.—Such was the attempt made by Bancroft, Archbishop of Canterbury, when he presented the twenty-five articles, commonly called the Articuli cleri, and petitioned the king to grant prohibitions upon them.—Such again were the books published by Cowel and Blackwood, asserting that the king is neither bound by the laws, nor by his coronation-oath; that he hath a right to make laws and impose taxes, without the consent of parliament; and that the nation was reduced to a state of slavery by the Norman conquest.—Such, to conclude this head, were the many acts which the king himself had done, and the many declarations which he had made; nay, such was the declaration he made in this very parliament, when he affirmed that although "all kings, who are not tyrants, or perjured, will bound themselves within the limits of their laws; yet as it is plasphemy to dispute what God may do, so it is sedition in subjects to dispute what a king may do in the height of his power."—These doctrines were new, ungrateful and shocking to English ears; yet the parliament kept in temper, and bore such language from this fearful, bullying prince, as the fiercest of his predecessors, since Richard the Second, had never presumed to hold. They took no notice of Bancroft, nor pursued any farther measures against Cowel and Blackwood, after these libels had been called in by proclamation, and the reading of them had been forbid. Nay, there was a subsidy granted in this very session, with as little pretence as there had been for granting the former.—All this temper, submission, and generosity of the parliament were lost on the king. They would not connive at grievances, nor sacrifice liberty; and those were the only terms, upon which an union with him was to be obtained.—From the year 1610 to 1614, he held no parliament; and it is evident, that he would never have called another, if his ministers could have supplied his profusion by all the illegal and oppressive means, which they used to raise money on the people, and which we forbear to enumerate, because the most partial writers, who have endeavored to excuse them, have not presumed to deny them.—Even under this necessity, he did not take the resolution of calling a new parliament, till he was prevailed on by his favorite, Somerset, who had formed a scheme for influencing the election, and, at the head of several other undertakers, flattered himself and his master, that he could get such members chosen, " as should comply solely to the king's desires."* But this project proved abortive. " The English freedom cannot be lost," says Wilson; and may his saying prove true to all future generations! " by a few base and tame spirits, that would unmake themselves and their posterity, to aggrandise one man." It happened to king James, as it happened to his son. Disgrace at court proved a recommendation in the country; and the faces which appeared in this new parliament, made the countenance of the court to droop.

From this time began that conduct, on the part of the court, and on the part of the parliament, which continued to be held, with very fatal uniformity, till it ended in a civil war. That the people had reason to be jealous of the designs of the court, hath appeared, and will appear still more flagrantly in the sequel; but that the court had at this time, nay even in the month of May 1640, when king Charles dissolved the last parliament he had it in his power to dissolve, any reason to be jealous of the parliament, or the people, we deny; and are able to justify our denial by fact and authority; even the authority of my Lord Clarendon. But the father and the son, and especially the former, having no end in calling their parliaments but to get money from their people, and to evade rather than refuse the redress of grievances; the art of the court was constantly employed, under the pretence of the urgency of affairs, and in the parliament of 1614, without any pretence at all, to get the subsidies first despatched. The commons, on the other side, who knew for what they were called together, and who expected that little time would be allowed

* Wilson.

them to inquire into mal-administration and to represent grievances, when they had once given the money, insisted for the most part, for there happened occasions, in which they did not insist, that the consideration of grievances should precede, or at least go an equal pace with that of the supply. This was the rock on which so many parliaments split. This alone occasioned the dissolution of that we are speaking of, and made king James resolve, tnough he could not support his resolution to the end of his reign, to govern by his prerogative alone, and without the assistance of his parliament; that is, to avow absolute power.

LETTER XXI.

In our last discourse, concerning the pretensions set up, and the attempts made by king James against the freedom of the English constitution, we carried these remarks down to the year 1614. We chose to stop there, because it seems to be the very diametrical point of opposition, or a point very near to that, between the government of this prince and the government of queen Elizabeth, which we have so largely insisted upon.—The distrust between him and his people was now entirely formed. His offensive, and their defensive pretensions were now fully explained. A union of affection between him and his people, which the latter still desired and had long courted, was now grown desperate. A union, unworthy of a free people, a factious union between the parliament and the court, founded in the dependence and submission of the former, and so much affected by the latter, was after many trials become evidently impracticable. The king, as he had managed affairs, could never govern with parliament, nor without it; and those powers, which are designed to be mutual helps, were turned to be mutual clogs on one another; not by any deviation on the side of the people, or of their representatives, from the true line of government; but by a manifest and almost continual deviation from it, on the side of the crown.

Thus were those great disorders in government and that national confusion raised, which in a few years more destroyed the whole constitution. In short, that melancholy scene, which had been preparing ever since the accession of king James, was opened about this time, and continued open with few variations, every one of which was for the worse, till that tragedy began, wherein the noblest as well as the meanest blood in the nation was shed so profusely, and with the beginning of which we purpose to conclude these remarks.

We have charged the whole, and we think very justly, to the account of king James; who attempted to govern England by foreign, not by English maxims; nay, by such as he was unable to govern his own country. Sure we are, that no part of it can be laid to the constitution, or people of England. The constitution was the same in his time as in the time of queen Elizabeth; and the people claimed under him no other privileges, nor powers, than they had enjoyed under her. It was his fault, not theirs, if by treading in the same path, which had kept them united with her, they were divided from him. These are points on which we think it proper to insist a little more in this place, in order to cast a greater light on the particulars which follow, and to avoid any prolix repetitions, when we come to wind up the whole.

King James had opened the parliament, which met in 1614, by asking money for the portion and other expenses of his daughter's marriage to the elector Palatine, and promised the commons leave and leisure to inquire into grievances, when they had complied with this demand; but distrust, the bane of all harmony, prevailed amongst them, as it is plain even from this conditional promise that it prevailed with him, and they resolved to begin the work of the session by a representation of grievances.

A principal article in this roll was the growth of popery, encouraged, no doubt, by several passages in the conduct of king James, and particularly by two; his employing not only suspected, but known Roman catholics, in offices of the highest trust and consequence; and his avowed design of marrying his son to some princess of that religion. Shall we say, in the style of king James, that it was presumption in the commons to meddle in such deep matters of state? Shall we not rather think it was presumption in the prince to determine a matter of this importance to the public welfare, to the present and to future generations, without the advice, nay against the opinion of the great council of the nation? Shall we not rather applaud the wisdom and foresight, as well as the virtue of those men, who discovered the fruit in the seed; whose minds foreboded all the mischievous consequences of such an alliance, and who did their utmost to prevent the true, original cause of our greatest misfortunes?

Under another head of grievances, complained of at this time, were the monopolies, and many illegal exactions of money from the people. The parliament had the more reason to lose no time, and to spare no endeavors in putting a stop to these encroachments on liberty, because the longer they lasted, the more familiar they grew. The court improved in the practice of them. The people, who submitted to them by force, might have been brought to submit to them by custom, and the king might become able in time to supply his wants without the assistance of parliament; a case almost as desperate as that of his being able to supply them when, in what manner, and in what proportions he thought fit, by the assistance of parliament. We say almost as desperate, on the principles touched in our last letter; for, in the first place, if king James could have supplied his wants without parliaments, he would certainly have called none, and the condition of this nation had been worse than that of Spain, of France, and of other nations, whose examples have been absurdly enough quoted, to justify these arbitrary methods of raising money, and to induce mankind to submit to them. In France, for instance, the people must suffer; but they may complain. Their mouths are open; that is, their parliaments may represent, and even remonstrate; nay, they have gone so far as to refuse with success to register and give the necessary forms of a law to an edict of the prince, which they judged oppressive to the people. But if king James had prevailed, he would have governed without even these shadows of a parliament. The people must have suffered, and could not have complained. Their sole mouth, the mouth of parliament, would have been stopped, and redress of grievances being no longer attainable by the applications of their representative body, which would no longer have existed, they must have submitted tamely and silently, or have sought a remedy in their collective body, which can only act by resistance and force. This situation would have been bad enough, God knows; yet not so bad as the other; for, in the second place, if the parliament had been made dependent on the crown, no matter by what kind of influence; whether by the distribution of honors; the translation of bishops, the corrupting the electors and the elected, or the other methods king James took, the mouth of the people had not been stopped indeed; but it had been formed to speak another language than that of the heart. The people must have suffered, and the parliament must have rejoiced. If they had felt an increasing load of debt, the parliament must have testified great satisfaction at the diminution of it. If they had felt the decay of trade, and the growth of national poverty, the parliament must have boasted of the wealth and flourishing state of the kingdom. If they had seen the interest and honor of the nation, as they saw it too often, neglected or sacrificed, the parliament must have exulted in the triumphs of both. In short, such a depending parliament must not only have connived at the grievances of their country, but have sanctified them too. They must not only have borne the rod, but have kissed it too; not only the rod of their prince, but the rod of some upstart minister, who owed his elevation to his dishonor, and his favor to his shame. But as the integrity of parliament secured the nation from any danger of this kind; so the necessities of the king were the great security against any danger of the other. Was the parliament therefore to blame, who opposed strenuously every innovation set on foot, to lessen this security?

A third grievance, which the parliament desired to have redressed, was that incredible waste, which king James made of the revenues of the crown. These revenues were, at that time, so much more than sufficient for all the ordinary occasions of the government, that queen Elizabeth, who had so many extraordinary occasions of expense, who paid so many old debts, without contracting new, and achieved such glorious enterprises abroad, as well as at home, did not receive in grants from her people above four millions* in more than forty years. If king James, who had no extraordinary occasions of expense, who paid no debts, who achieved no glorious enterprises any where, had neither asked money, nor raised it without asking, the squandering his revenue had not probably come under debate in parliament; but, since he expected that the people could provide for his debts, and supply his necessities, it was just that the representatives of the people should examine how they were contracted. The immense estates, which were made in these days at court, the known corruption not only of inferior agents, but of principal ministers, and even of those who were at the head of the treasury, made such an examination the more necessary, and provoked and excited the more to it. The house of commons would have thought that they had betrayed their trust, if they had neglected so important a part of it. By the proceedings, as well as declarations of the parliaments in these times, it is plain that they thought they had not an arbitrary, but only a conditional power, over the purse of the nation, though the strings of it were in their hands; that they were to tax the people in no greater proportion than was strictly necessary to support the honor and interest of the nation, and the dignity of the crown; that they could make no judgment concerning this proportion, if they had not a full communication of the nature of the service, for which extraordinary aids were demanded; and if they did not examine before they granted these aids, how the ordinary

---

* We do not want to be told that the value of money was very different at that time from what it is now; but though we admit of the highest calculations, this sum will appear surprisingly small for so many years when compared with the profusion and extravagance of some later reigns.

revenues and any precedent extraordinary grants had been applied. Such maxims as these will not be condemned, we presume. They have been always professed and frequently pursued, from the time we speak of, down to the age in which we live. Since the reign of king William the Third, our princes have indeed stood on a different foot. They have had a distinct revenue assigned to them for their particular use. The annual expenses and the debts of the nation have been separately provided for by parliament; and yet not only the management and application of these annual grants, but also the immense property of the creditors of the public have been left to the crown, as the management and application of those revenues were, which belonged properly to the crown, and by deficiencies, on which the crown, not the nation, was immediately affected. It is no wonder therefore if our parliaments have thought themselves obliged, since this great alteration, sometimes by committees, and sometimes by extraordinary commissions, to inspect more narrowly into revenues, which are still managed by the officers of the crown, though they make no longer any part of the estate of the crown; and we persuade ourselves that no honest man would be sorry, if the wisdom of our present representatives should think fit to make any inquisitions of the same nature; but even before this alteration, before the settlement of a civil list, and when our princes stood on the same foot as king James the First, with respect to their private and public revenue, the maxims we speak of were pursued on many occasions, and always with the universal applause of the people. In the reign of king Charles the Second, for instance, our whig patriots endeavored not only to detect and punish frauds and abuses, by inquiries into the management of the public money, but to prevent them likewise, by appropriating what they gave to the uses for which it was given; and thus much we think may suffice, to clear the conduct of the parliament of 1614 from any imputations on this head.

Let us mention, in this place, one grievance more, which we have touched upon in another. A former parliament had taken some notice of it, and this parliament would probably have taken more, if the king had allowed them time. The doctrines which established the unbounded and ineffable prerogative of the king; which reduced the privileges of parliament to be no longer an ancient and undoubted right and inheritance, but derived them from the permission and toleration of the crown, and declared them liable to be retrenched at the will of the prince; and which by necessary consequence changed at once the nature of the English constitution, from that of a free to that of an arbitrary government; all these doctrines, we say, or the principles, on which they were established, had been already publicly and

frequently asserted by king James. They were the language of
the court; and a party had been formed in the nation, who made
profession of them. They were maintained in conversation.
They were pleaded for in print; and they became soon afterwards the disgrace and profanation of the pulpit.

We have sometimes compared, in our thoughts, these usurpations of king James over the privileges of his people to those of
the popes, which gave that prince so much offence, over the
rights of the emperors, and indeed over the civil rights of mankind. Charlemagne had made these priests princes. They continued for about two hundred and sixty years, to submit, in the
main, to those rules, which the imperial constitutions and ecclesiastical customs had established; after which they started, at
once, out of these bounds. They would be limited pontiffs no
longer, but arbitrary high priests, like the dairo of Japan, something more than human, and civil as well as ecclesiastical tyrants.
They scorned to go to tyranny by degrees, but carried their usurpations at one leap to the utmost pitch of extravagance. Alexander the Second denied the right of the emperors to choose, or to
confirm the election of a pope. His successor took the investi-
tures from them. Henry the Fourth asserted the imperial rights,
in opposition to this invasion, but Gregory the Seventh asserted,
in opposition to him, that Rome was the capital of the world;
that the pope was independent of all powers on earth; that
kings and emperors were liable to be deposed by the plenitude
of his authority. The pope was believed by many, on his word;
and there were more, who found their private account in seeming to believe him. Factions were raised to maintain these
principles. They were consecrated by the church. They prevailed in those days. More than five centuries were not sufficient to abolish the practice, and more than six have not been
sufficient to extirpate the principle. True it is, that these popes
had several advantages, which king James had not; and, amongst
others, the minority of Henry the Fourth at the time when they
began this monstrous usurpation; whereas when king James set
up his pretensions, and talked, and wrote of prerogative, in terms
as ridiculous and full of as much bombast as those which the
briefs and other public acts of Hildebrand contained, the commons of England were grown up to a full maturity of property
and power. Shall we condemn them for endeavoring to preserve the principles of liberty, that they might preserve the spirit
of it; and by preserving the spirit, deserve and secure the continuance of so great a blessing? Should an English parliament
have sat quiet and silent, in humble dependence on the prince,
whilst slavery in speculation, as well as practice, was making
such large advances; whilst the laws of the land, the laws of na-

ture, and those of God himself were perverted to impose a yoke of base and servile prejudices on the understandings and consciences of mankind? We think not. Sure we are that our parliaments have been always watchful to censure and explode, in time, such doctrines as might, even by induction and consequence, weaken the foundation of liberty. The instances of this kind are so well known, and some of them so recent, that we need not quote them. But, in order to justify still farther the sense and conduct of our forefathers, let us appeal even to the present sense of mankind. We all know that there are mercenary and abandoned wretches amongst us, who have dared to plead for a dependence of the parliament on the crown; not for that dependence of the several parts of the government on one another, which our constitution hath formed, and on the preservation of which the freedom of our government entirely rests; but for the most indirect, the most iniquitous, as well as dangerous dependence imaginable; for a dependence, to be created by corruption, which must always produce effects as infamous as its cause. Corruption, we say, hath been defended, nay, recommended, for we will repeat the assertion, as a necessary expedient of government. The representation of the country by the independent gentlemen of the country, hath been saucily and awkwardly ridiculed; as if a bill, to prevent all persons, who have neither places nor pensions, from sitting in parliament, was proper to be passed, and those salutary laws, which are in force for preventing persons who have places and pensions from sitting there, were as proper to be repealed. Nay, these incendiaries, who go about to destroy our constitution, have not blushed in the same breath to admit, that standing armies have been generally the instruments of overturning free governments, and to affirm that a standing army is necessary to be kept up in ours; if you ask them against whom, they answer you very frankly, against the people; if you ask them why, they answer you with the same frankness, because of the levity and inconstancy of the people. This is the evil; an army is the remedy. Our army is not designed, according to these doctors of slavery, against the enemies of the nation, but against the nation. We are confident that the present army is incapable of being employed to such purposes, and abhors an imputation, which might have been justly cast on Cromwell's army, but is very unjustly insinuated against the present.

Now let us suppose that the time was come, when the parliament should think fit to censure and put a stop to the influence of such writings as these; would any honest man, if he laid his hand upon his heart, disapprove their proceedings? On the contrary, would not every man, who wished that the constitution of this government might be preserved, applaud such measures and bless the representatives of his country for their zeal against the betrayers of it?

Upon the whole matter, we think it very plain that the alarm, which was taken at the propagation of those infamous doctrines, in the reign of king James the First, is abundantly justified not only by the examples of other parliaments, but by the general sense of mankind in all ages.

Whenever the fundamentals of a free government are attacked, or any other schemes, ruinous to the general interest of a nation, are pursued; the best service that can be done to such a nation, and even to the prince, is to commence an early and vigorous opposition to them; for the event will always show, as we shall soon see in the present case, that those who form an opposition in this manner, are the truest friends to both, however they may be stigmatised at first with odious names, which belong more properly to those who throw the dirt at them.

If the opposition begin late, or be carried on more faintly, than the exigency requires, the evil will grow; nay it will grow the more by such an opposition, till it becomes at length too inveterate for the ordinary methods of cure; and whenever that happens; whenever usurpations on natural liberty are grown too strong to be checked by these ordinary methods, the people are reduced to this alternative: they must either submit to slavery and beggary, the worst of all political evils; or they must endeavor to prevent the impending mischief by open force and resistance, which is an evil but one degree less eligible than the other. But when the opposition is begun early and carried on vigorously, there is time to obtain redress of grievances, and put a stop to such usurpations by those gentle and safe methods, which their constitution hath provided; methods, which may and have often proved fatal to wicked ministers, but can never prove fatal to the prince himself.—He is never in danger but when these methods, which all arbitrary courts dislike, are too long delayed.

The most plausible objection to such proceedings, and by which well-meaning men are frequently made the bubbles of those who have the worst designs, arises from a false notion of moderation. True political moderation consists in not opposing the measures of government, except when great and national interests are at stake; and when that is the case, in opposing them with such a degree of warmth, as is adequate to the nature of the evil, to the circumstances of danger attending it, and even to those of opportunity. To oppose upon any other foot; to oppose things which are not blame-worthy, or which are of no material consequence to the national interest, with such violence as may disorder the harmony of government, is certainly faction; but it is likewise faction, and faction of the worst kind, either not to oppose at all, or not to oppose in earnest, when points of the greatest importance to the nation are concerned.

The truth of all this reasoning will be confirmed by what remains to be said of king James and king Charles the First.—If there had not been an early and honest opposition, in defence of national liberty, against king James, his reign would have sufficed to establish him in the seat of arbitrary power.—If the opposition had been more generally backed with the weight of the nation in due time; if the court had not been able to divide men against their general interest, upon principles of prerogative and liberty, king James must have complied in time; the constitution would have been preserved; all our national calamities would have been prevented; and the sins of the court might have been expiated by the punishment of one or two of the ministers.—But a prerogative party having been nursed up from the beginning, and gained strength in the whole course of king James's reign, the strength of the nation was divided, and the contest continued so long between the king and the people, that resentment and passion and prejudice and faction took place on all sides.   The soft and gentle methods of cure, which our constitution had provided, became impracticable.   A provoked people sought their remedy in resistance.   A civil war followed.   The English government was subverted, instead of being reformed.

What hath been said will serve to justify the conduct of the parliament, as well as the general alarm, which the nation had taken in 1614.   These were the crimes, the heinous, unpardonable crimes, for which king James dissolved this parliament, with so much indignation, after they had sat but a few weeks, and had not time given them to pass even one law.   These were the crimes, for which he confined to the Tower and other prisons, and punished in other ways, so many of the most active members.   Lastly, these were the crimes which made him resolve, what he had before attempted, to govern without parliament.— The particular consequences of these measures will appear in our next letter, when we come to consider his conduct of our national interests abroad, against the sense of the nation; in which period of time, the foreign affairs are so intermixed with parliamentary and domestic affairs, that we shall not divide them, but speak of them together, having first very briefly made our observations on his management of parties.

LETTER XXII.

In Letter XVIII, we have spoken of the state of parties at the
accession of king James. We are now to make our observations
on his management of them. It is necessary we should do this,
in order to give a complete and just idea of his government; and
yet so much hath been said on the subject by writers of all
denominations, and even by ourselves, that there remains but
very little to be added, either for curiosity, or instruction.

We might observe how he drew himself into some trouble, if
not danger, and exposed himself to the necessity of shedding
some blood, in the very first months of his reign, by espousing
the passions of a party; by disgracing and proscribing men, who
had no crime at that time towards him but their attachment to
the late queen; by avowing the cause of the Earl of Essex, whose
designs had been, no doubt, as treasonable, at least, and as chimerical too, as those into which he drove Grey, Cobham, and
Raleigh, or which were imputed to them.

Several other anecdotes, concerning factions at court and parties
in the nation, might be collected and remarked upon. But we
shall pass them over, and confine ourselves to observe, in a very
few instances, how he adapted his particular management of
parties to the general and main design of his policy; what strength
he acquired; what strength he lost by this conduct; and what contests he entailed on posterity.

There were no parties, at this time, in the nation, but such as
were formed on religious differences; and it had been a great
object of the policy of queen Elizabeth, to keep all parties within
these bounds. We know the maxims on which she proceeded,
by a letter of Sir Francis Walsingham, wrote expressly on this
subject. She thought that "consciences were not to be forced,
but won and reduced by truth, time, instruction and persuasion;
and that causes of conscience lose their nature, when they exceed
their bounds and grow matter of faction."—By keeping to these
maxims, she succeeded. The parties in the church made none
in the state. They were obliged to live in due subjection to
laws, wisely made and moderately exercised. They were never
punished, whilst they continued in this subjection, much less
were they provoked or encouraged to go out of it. The powers
of the church were applied to the support of the establishment,
not rendered subservient to any factious designs of the court;
and ecclesiastical violence was restrained from confirming the
obstinacy of those who dissented, by persecution of them, or from
increasing their numbers, by persecution of others.

Directly opposite to this conduct was that of king James.—In haste to show his parts, he had a conference between the bishops and the puritan ministers at Hampton-court, in a few months after his accession; where he made himself a principal party in the dispute. His courtiers flattered him, and Archbishop Whitgift, who died soon afterwards, and probably doated then, declared himself "verily persuaded that the king spake by the spirit of God." But surely such a confidence, however it might frighten and silence, could neither instruct nor persuade; and the king was so far from trusting, like his predecessor, to the force of truth and the aid of time, that in this very conference he threatened to employ another kind of force, if he did not meet with compliance in a time to be limited. The bishops were at first to admonish paternally and to confer amicably; but lest they should not succeed by preaching, writing and living men into conformity, the sole means they ought to desire; or, if they desired others, the sole means they ought to be suffered to employ, they were to have recourse to compulsion afterwards.—The same spirit reigned in the first speech which this prince made to his parliament; for there he not only massed together, imprudently as well as unjustly, all the dissenters from the established church, under the general denomination of puritans and novelists, but he declared them all "insufferable in any well-governed commonwealth:" so that he put them all out of his protection, even though they confined themselves within those bounds, to which causes of conscience may reasonably extend, and proscribed them for their opinions, not their practices.

On these principles he proceeded, and what we have said here may suffice, upon this head, for his whole reign.—The consequence of this conduct was that those sects, who were not dangerous at first, became so at last. They became so, in some degree, from the moment the declarations we have mentioned were made: for nothing is found more true in nature and experience than this, that they who are oppressed by governments, will endeavor to change them; and that he who makes himself terrible to multitudes, will have multitudes to fear.—But this was not all.—As he made these sects his enemies, so he gave them great advantages of popularity and strength.—The first of these advantages which we shall take notice of, arose from the great indulgence he showed to the Roman catholics, and the favorable sentiments of that religion, which he expressed on all private and many public occasions. We need not descend into the particular instances; for though we give little credit to Deageant's memoirs in general, and none to what he says of a letter, written by king James to the pope, acknowledging him vicar of Christ and head of the church; yet there is a multitude of other proofs, too notorious and too well supported to be denied.—We think it plain, upon the whole matter, that several passages in his conduct, both before and after his coming into England, were unworthy of a protestant king at any time, and were equally impolitic at this time, when the zeal of papists to attack, and of protestants to defend the reformation was at the highest pitch; and when even the least condescension on either side; would have been thought little less than apostacy.   Fear for his person, and little notions of policy, were probably the motives which determined this part of his conduct; but whatever the motives were, the effect was certainly this.   He made the cause of the court to pass amongst many for the cause of popery; and it was not hard by consequence of the puritans, who were oppressed by the court, to make their cause pass for that of the reformation. We are far from thinking that this was properly the case on either side; but the appearances were strong enough to fix such prejudices in the minds of men, already prepared by jealousy and suspicion.   This advantage, so foolishly given, operated strongly against the court, both in this reign and the next.   In this it was applied to no ill purposes.   In the next, it was very wickedly improved; but they who gave it first, and who continued to give it afterwards, are justly to be reputed the accomplices of those who improved it so wickedly, how much soever they stood in opposition to one another.

A second advantage of popularity and strength, which king James gave to the puritans, was this: He ranked amongst their party, nay he drove into that party, as much as he was able by severe usage, all those who stood up in defence even of civil liberty.   The aversion which he expressed to the puritans, formed a kind of league between him and the warmest of the established clergy; and when these were once become a court party, we are not to wonder if others grew as warm as these, and if the greatest part of that body of men united in a cause which flattered their passions, and opened the road of preferment to them.   No king no bishop, was the language of the court. No bishop no king, was that of the church.   Had the monarchy and the hierarchy been attacked, this united zeal in a common cause would have been commendable and successful too; for the nation was not now, nor for a long time afterwards, so distempered, that any faction could raise its head with effect against the just prerogative of the crown and the established rights of the church.   But the truth requires we should say, that this union was formed to offend and invade, and to extend both beyond the bounds prescribed to them by the English constitution.   It was great blindness in the clergy not to see that to enlarge the bottom of the court, they narrowed their own; that they fixed a centre of union, wherein all their divided enemies would meet and unite with many, who were then friends to the church, but might come, as it happened afterwards, from being against the clergy to be against the·church itself. It was a great misfortune to the nation, that the clergy did not see these truths in time; since, if they had seen them, they might have been happy instruments of preventing that mischief which followed soon after the time we speak of, and that division of interests between the crown and the people, which was created by king James, and hath proved so fatal to his posterity.—But to return. By a contrary conduct, by espousing and sanctifying the principles and by promoting the measures of king James, the clergy became part of the faction of the court, and shared very unjustly the imputation of favoring popery, but very justly that of advancing tyranny. This was a second advantage, which king James gave to the Puritans. He varnished their cause with popularity, and he increased their numbers. He made puritans in his time, as Jansenists have been since made in France, and Jacobites in Britain, by calling men so and by treating them as such.—They must have been sharp-sighted, indeed, of whom my Lord Clarendon speaks, and who could discern " the rebellion contriving from, if not before, the death of queen Elizabeth;" but they must be quite blind, who do not discern the seeds of rebellion sowing in every part of the conduct of king James, and particularly in this which we have now touched, the management of parties.

These evils were aggravated, and the consequences of them were precipitated by his conducting our national interests abroad against the sense of the nation.

During the first period, into which we divide this reign, that is, to the year 1614, king James meddled little, and, to say the truth, had little occasion to meddle in foreign affairs.—The treaty which he made with Spain in 1604, had been much censured, and Sir C. Cornwallis, in a letter to the Lord Cranburne, asserts "that England never lost such an opportunity of winning honor and wealth unto it, as by relinquishing the war against an exhausted kingdom and a prince held in little veneration for suffering himself to be wholly governed by a man generally hated." This treaty, however, was not probably so bad as it had been represented, and the commerce opened with Spain became a source of inexhaustible riches to our nation; but still there was something preposterous and mean in the conduct of king James abroad, even whilst he had so little to do there, and so safe a part to act. He courted that very power, the power of Spain, whom queen Elizabeth had broke, and who would have courted him, if he had known how to put so much as dignity in his pro-

ceedings. He disobliged the Dutch, whose power had been
raised by queen Elizabeth, and who must have continued to depend on him, if he had known how to be either a friend or an
enemy; and yet he bore most ignominiously from this very
people the greatest injuries and affronts imaginable. He had
neither the courage to chastise this infant state, nor the sense to
protect it. Their treaty with their old masters, the Spaniards,
began in the year 1607; was continued in 1608; and ended in
1609, in a truce of twelve years. During the whole course of
this long negotiation, king James showed his partiality in favor
of the Spaniards; and though he signed, about this time, two
treaties with the states as sovereigns; yet he made no scruple,
upon some occasions, of declaring them rebels.—The death of
the Duke of Cleves, and the disputes about that succession, presented to Henry the Fourth an opportunity he waited for; and
he was ready, when Ravaillac stabbed him, to attack the house
of Austria, whose power in Germany began once more to give
umbrage, though Rodolphus the Second was still on the imperial
throne. King James left his troops with the Dutch, notwithstanding the truce. They were employed in this quarrel; and
we cannot think him to blame for taking no farther part in the
hostilities. His views were, and they ought to have been, at
this time, and in this respect, very different from those of that
heroical king of France. But in the new scene of German
affairs, which opened a few years afterwards, and which continued, during the last period of his reign, that is, from the year
1614, nothing could be more scandalous than his taking no part
at all, except his taking the part he did take.—That he should
have made himself a principal in that terrible war, which broke
out in Germany in 1618, and which lasted thirty years, we cannot persuade ourselves; neither do we believe that any man,
who does not take up his opinions on trust, but examines this
intricate and perplexed part of the history of the last century
with care, will be of another mind; and yet king James must
have made himself a principal in this war, if he had engaged in
it, as he was advised by some to engage, and as he hath been
blamed by many for not engaging. The censures, under which
he hath passed on this occasion, would have been juster, if those
who have made them, had distinguished better between the
patrimony of his children, by defending the Palatinate, and promoting their grandeur, by seconding their ambition; between
contributing to support the protestant interest abroad, and taking
on his shoulders a load which it was neither reasonable nor possible that he should bear; between that conduct, which he ought
to have held, as king of this island, and that which he might
have been obliged to hold, if his dominions had laid on the con-

tinent. Our writings will not pass, we believe, for apologies in favor of king James; and yet we shall explain this point a little less to his disadvantage, perhaps, than it hath been usually taken.

If king James had followed the advice of those who would have had him enter into an immediate war to maintain the elector Palatine on the throne of Bohemia, he must have exhausted and ruined this nation to support it. He must have furnished subsidies to Bethlehem Gabor and the prince of Anspach; he must have fed the war in Hungary; fomented the revolt in Austria; paid the army of the princes of the union; opposed the Duke of Bavaria in Bohemia, and Spinola in the Palatinate. Let us consider in opposition to whom, and in concert with whom, he must have carried on this vast undertaking. On one side, the whole popish interest in the empire was closely united, and the cause of Ferdinand was the common cause of the party. The popish interest out of the empire conspired in the same cause. The king of Poland assisted the emperor in Hungary. Troops from Italy and a great army from the Netherlands acted for him in Germany. The purse of the pope and that of the king of Spain were open to him. Even France, who ought in good policy to have opposed the house of Austria, was induced, by the bigotry of her court, and, perhaps, by the private interest of Luines, to declare for the emperor against the king of Bohemia. On the other side, the protestant interest in the empire was far from being closely united, and farther still from making the cause of Frederic the common cause of the party. Even the princes of the union had different views; many of them leaned to the emperor; none of them could be entirely depended upon; and the elector of Saxony, the most powerful of the protestant princes of the empire, was so far from uniting with the others, that he was first privately, and afterwards openly, but all along very steadily on the side of Ferdinand. Out of the empire, some assistance might have been expected from the king of Denmark and the Dutch; but even their accession must have been purchased; at least, it must have been made useful at the expense of Britain. What other allies could king James have hoped for; and who can see, without smiling, in that goodly prelate, Archbishop Abbot's letter to Sir Robert Naunton, the name of the Duke of Bouillon, together with Tremouille, a rich prince in France, mentioned upon such an occasion? Short and imperfect as the account we have given is, those who know the state of Europe at the time we speak of, know that it is true; and if we were to look no farther than the representations made by Juliana of Nassau to her son, against his accepting the crown of Bohemia, we should discover in them, with the true and fatal reasons why king James did not assist Frederic at all, unanswerable reasons why he ought not to have taken

upon him the Bohemian quarrel, in the manner he must have
taken it, if he had taken it upon him at that time.   That king
James should have prepared for this storm, which was long in
gathering, that he should have labored to unite and fortify the
protestants of Germany before it happened, and to comfort, and
succor. and protect them, after it happened; that he had many
fair opportunities of doing this, without engaging farther than the
interest of Britain allowed, and that he neglected them all, we
admit and are able to show.   He might have put himself on such
a foot in Europe, as to have mediated at least, which was the
only part he attempted to act, successfully for the Bohemians,
and to have screened his son-in-law from the vengeance of the
emperor, and the ambition of the Duke of Bavaria.   But he put
himself on such a foot, and he acquired such a character, that he
had no credit among the protestants, nor much influence over his
son-in-law, and that the Roman catholic party, sure of amusing
him, neglected and despised him.   He might have declined taking
the Bohemian quarrel upon him, and yet not have made his court
to the emperor and the king of Spain, by disavowing and con-
demning Frederic, and even by suffering them not only to drive
this prince out of Bohemia, but to take the Palatinate from him
and his family, and give a wound, almost mortal, to the whole
protestant cause in Germany.   Nay, he did worse.   By foolish
embassies and ridiculous negotiations, he gave time and furnished
advantages, which could not have been had without his assistance to the popish party.   By the same means he checked, he
weakened, he discouraged, and more than once disarmed the
protestant party.   In short, not only the principles of his conduct
were wrong, but the measures of it composed such a series of
blunders as we seldom find in history; because it is hardly
possible, in the course of nature, that such characters, in such
situations, should appear above once in a century.

It may be objected, perhaps, by some of the writers, who
adorn and instruct the present age, that king James was universally and justly condemned for not taking the Bohemian quarrel
upon him, as well as for not defending the Palatinate; and that
he must have pursued, in the last case, the same measures as we
think him justified for not pursuing in the former.   We shall
not refute this objection by showing, as it would be easy for us
to do, in various particulars, the prodigious difference between
the two cases; the insuperable difficulties he would have encoun-
tered in one, and the many facilities he would have had in the
other.   The deduction would be too long and extensive for the
narrow limits of these essays.   But we shall content ourselves
with making two observations, sufficient to satisfy any reasonable man, and which will show, at the same time, what different

notions of the part this nation ought to take in foreign affairs, were entertained by our forefathers, from those which we, their wiser offspring, have pursued. When king James took the resolution of calling the parliament, which sat in 1621, the battle of Prague was lost, and Bohemia too with it. The affections* of the people were raised, but it was for the recovery of the Palatinate; and in this point the sense of the parliament went along with the affections of the people. On the other point, the sense of the parliament had not been expressed, there having been no parliament held from the year 1614 till this time. But what this sense would have been, may be easily collected, from the advice given in the petition and remonstrance of the commons at this time. As zealous as they were to engage even in a war, for recovering the Palatinate, they were not enough transported by their zeal, or enough biassed in favor of any foreign interest, to forget the true interest of Britain. They advised the king to a war; but they advised him not to rest upon a war in those parts only which would consume his treasure and discourage his people. They advised that the bent of this war might be against that prince, the king of Spain, whose armies and treasures had first diverted and since maintained the war in the Palatinate. On which side now was the sense of the nation; and how impertinent are they who have quoted this sense, to authorise our taking part in every German quarrel, by paying subsidies, maintaining armies, and involving ourselves in all the affairs of the continent? How monstrous is the absurdity and impudence† of those who have asserted that the case of the people of the Palatinate, invaded by a powerful enemy, who pretended to nothing less than the conquest of them, is parallel to that of the people of Hanover, invaded by no body, and over whom no foreign power pretends to any dominion!—The parliament pointed out to king James a measure effectual for supporting the protestant interest abroad; but such a measure as this nation might pursue by exerting her natural strength. The power of Spain supported the emperor and the popish league; an army of Spain conquered the Palatinate; and yet the artifices of that court deluded king James to such a degree, that he dreamed of recovering the patrimony of his children by the good offices of the Spaniards, and was incapable of pursuing in earnest any other measures, even at the time when Spinola was stripping them of this patrimony, and reducing them to seek their bread in another country. To this dependence in Spain he sacrificed not only them, but his own honor, the affection of his subjects, the prosperity of his

* See Rush. Coll.
† See Observations on the Present State of Affairs.

kingdoms, and the security of the protestant religion. It was this magic charm which the parliament endeavored in vain to dissolve, by pressing him to a war with Spain, which his maritime force could have carried on principally; which would have stopped that source from whence the popish party in Germany derived so many supplies; and which would have rendered the protestant party, by consequence, a more equal match for the emperor. But this was not the sole wise and honest view which the parliament proposed, by pointing out and insisting on this measure. There was another, which touched them more nearly, and which they had more at heart. We shall mention it in our next discourse, and it will lead us from our observations on this reign to those few on the next, with which we intend to close, at least for the present, all our remarks on the history of England.

LETTER XXIII.

ANOTHER object besides recovering the Palatinate, which the parliament had in view when they pressed king James to break with Spain, was preventing the marriage of the Prince of Wales to the Infanta. He had been bantered and abused by the Spaniards, when he treated of a marriage between his eldest son, Prince Henry and Anne of Austria; and yet no sooner did the Duke of Lerma, in the year 1616, make some overtures of marrying the Infanta Mary, second daughter of Philip the Third, to Prince Charles, but this Solomon of ours caught at the bait which was thrown out to him, and hung fast on the hook for seven years together.

The scheme of farther usurpations in Germany was already laid by the house of Austria; and the character of Ferdinand, who was to succeed Matthias, and who did succeed him three years afterwards, gave hopes of pushing these usurpations with vigor and advantage.—The part of Spain had been great in promoting these designs. It was essential to their success that it should be so likewise in the execution of them. No opposition of any moment was to be apprehended from France, where the principles of despotism and of bigot-popery prevailed more than ever, and who had concluded, in the year 1615, a double marriage with Spain. The truce of twelve years, made with the Dutch in 1609, would enable the Spaniards to support the popish league from the Low Countries, as in all cases they might do from Italy; and if they could keep the king of Great Britain from

diverting the forces of Spain in the mean time, there was reason
to hope that these united powers might conquer both the Pala-
tinates, as well as Bohemia, and break the force of the protestant
league in Germany, before the expiration of the truce and the
renewal of the war with the united provinces of the Low Counties should create another diversion. This was a principal part
of the plan laid by the house of Austria and the other Roman
catholic princes, for oppressing the protestants and invading the
liberties of Germany. To the eternal infamy of king James, it
succeeded even beyond the hopes of those who laid it. The
hints which Digby gave him in the very beginning of this negotiation, might have put him on his guard, and a thousand things
which happened in the course of it, would have undeceived,
provoked and determined any other man. His presumption, his
fear, and, above all, his perverse system of policy prevented any
effects of these kinds. We forbear entering into the particulars
of what he did for Spain; of what he suffered Spain to do; and
of all the indignities which he received from every branch of
the house of Austria, during these transactions. Most of them
have been observed, and are sufficiently known; and it would
be an unnecessary work to point out some few instances more,
which have not been, perhaps, taken notice of, or explained as
much as they deserved. We shall spare ourselves and our
readers this disagreeable recollection, and only observe in general the plan upon which king James appears to have acted; as
we have observed what the plan was of those who made so
fatal a use of his weakness. His silly pride could not be satisfied, unless he matched his son with a daughter of Spain, or
France. He had been disappointed formerly on that side, and
lately on this. He was resolved at any rate not to be disappointed a third time. The immense sum which had been promised for the Infanta's portion tempted him the more, because
for several years he would call no parliament to grant him supplies, and he found it hard to raise them, even in small proportions, without a parliament. He imagined vainly that this
alliance with Spain would give him great consideration abroad;
and wickedly, that it would afford him means of raising and
extending his prerogative at home. He saw the mischiefs which
accrued to the protestant interest abroad, either as immediate, or
as remote effects of his conduct; either in consequence of what
he did, or in consequence of what he neglected; and we are
willing to believe that he felt, in some degree, those which fell
on the family into which he had married his daughter. But the
interest of the protestants in general touched him little. Abroad,
as well as at home, he chose rather by condescensions and sub-
missions to court his enemies, than to unite his friends among

one another, and to attach them to himself. In his zeal for the
imaginary rights of princes, he could not forgive the elector
Palatine for taking arms against the emperor; and whilst he
looked on him as a rebel, forgot that he was his son. If he remembered it at any time, and felt any concern, the sentiment
was surely very faint; since we find that the distant and uncertain prospect of making some tolerable composition for this
unhappy prince, by the intercession of Spain, was always sufficient to calm his paternal solicitude. He saw, without doubt,
at least during the life of Philip the Third, who did not die till
the year 1621, that Spain was not much in earnest to give him
the Infanta; but he seemed resolved to overcome all difficulties,
and to determine the councils of Spain, and even of Rome, in
his favor, by dint of concessions. The truth is, he went so far
in his concessions at last, that these councils seemed to be determined. Those of Spain, at least, were so most certainly in the
year 1623, even before the voyage of the prince into Spain; and
the articles sworn to both by him when he was there, and by his
father here, amounted to little less than a direct establishment of
popery. That this charge is just will, we think, appear evident,
when it shall be remembered, without entering into more particulars, that by these articles the king and Prince of Wales engaged for the suspension, and even abrogation of all laws made
against Roman catholics; that they engaged never to consent to
the making any new laws of the same kind; and that, as the
children to be born of this marriage were to be educated by
their mother, till ten years of age, in compliance with the king of
Spain's demands; so the prince was prevailed on to promise that
he would lengthen this term till twelve years, according to the
desire of the pope.

Thus was king James amused till the beginning of the year
1623, when the Upper Palatinate and the dignity of elector were
taken from Frederic and conferred on the Duke of Bavaria, by
the diet of Ratisbon: or, to speak more properly, by the prerogative of Ferdinand, who acted in the diet as dogmatically and
as absolutely as king James endeavored to act in his parliaments.
When this point was gained by amusing king James, and the
protestant interest was broken in Germany; the next point was
to be carried by concluding with him and making the match on
such terms, as might secure an immediate toleration, and open
the prospect of a future establishment of popery in this kingdom.
—The parliament of 1621, beheld part of this scene, and apprehended, upon very just grounds, the sequel. They saw the fatal
consequences of the negotiation, whilst it was in suspense, and
they dreaded those which would follow the conclusion of it. To
stop the first, and to prevent the last, there was but one expe-

dient; the forcing king James into a war, for recovering the Palatinate. This they endeavored with all their might; but he meant nothing less, and he called a parliament purely to get money from his people, on pretence of a war he was resolved not to make. Some money he got by this trick; but when he had it squandered away in trifling negotiations and a ridiculous show of war, he could get no more: so that this parliament ended as others had done, and even with greater dissatisfaction between the king and the people, both on account of his conducting foreign affairs against the interest and sense of the nation, and of his attacking more openly than ever the privileges of parliament. The parliament remonstrated, petitioned, protested. The king dissolved the parliament in a rage; imprisoned several members of the house of commons, and even some of the house of lords. He resumed his project of governing without parliaments, since he could not govern as ill as he had a mind to govern with them. But this project was not pursued above two years; for what his parliament could not obtain from him an unworthy favorite did obtain. Motives of private interest, and, perhaps, of a worse nature, made that great turn in affairs, which so many motives of a public nature and of national interest had never been able to make. In short, a cabal at court prevailed on this prince to alter his conduct in those very points, on which the parliament, seconded by the clamors of the whole nation, had never been able to prevail.—We shall not attempt to guess, as many have done, at the secret reasons, which determined Buckingham, nor at those by which he determined the Prince of Wales to undertake the romantic and, in every light, ridiculous journey into Spain, to carry the treaty of marriage to a conclusion; then to break it off again in so abrupt and ungracious a manner; and to become so earnest for engaging in a war with Spain. Whatever these reasons were, the reason given for breaking the match was not the true one. The restitution of the Palatinate had been very coolly pressed, not to say neglected, even whilst the prince was at Madrid; and yet after he came from thence, the king of Spain had signed an act, by which he engaged for this restitution: so that on the principles on which this negotiation had been conducted, there seemed to be no reason for breaking it off given by Spain at the time when it was broken. But the parliament which king James called upon this occasion, proceeded like the last, on other principles than the court had done, and was therefore, very consistently with these principles, ready to seize the opportunity offered, by advising the king to break the match, and enter into a war for recovering the Palatinate, and by giving him very large supplies for this purpose.—We cannot, upon this occasion, subscribe to the censure passed by my Lord Clarendon, how much soever we esteem his history, and honor the memory of that noble historian; for in the first place, the supplies given by this last parliament of king James, were not only very large, as we have just now said, but they were such as the king was contented with, and thanked the parliament for, in his answer to the speaker of the house of commons. Secondly, we cannot agree that it was the parliament, properly speaking, who prevailed on the king, and engaged him in the war. The parliament advised him to it indeed; but nothing can be more manifest than this, even by my Lord Clarendon's own account, that the measure was resolved on before, and that it was the measure of the prince and of Buckingham, which the king, however unwillingly, adopted.— The parliament in truth did no more than advise him to break a treaty which he had already broken; and those who reflect on precedent passages, will easily concur with us, that if this had not been the case, it would not have been in the power of the parliament to break the match; much less to engage the king in the war. Thirdly, if subsequent parliaments did not support those great mountains of promises, as they are called, which this parliament raised, we shall venture to affirm that it was the fault of the court, not of the parliament.

This last article requires to be set in a very clear light, because it opens to us a source of causes, from whence a great part of the mischiefs, which followed in the next reign, arose; or by which, at least, they were aggravated and precipitated.—First, therefore, we observe that the measures of the court were so foolishly taken for pushing the war, that if parliaments had given by millions, and given with as little stint in those days, as they have given since, their grants must have been ineffectual to any good purpose. Just before the death of king James, an army had been raised for the Palatinate war, under the command of the famous Mansfeldt. The French first and the Dutch afterwards refused passage to these troops, or even to suffer them to land. The cry of the court was loud against the perfidy of France, as it had been against the emperor and Spain in their turns. This will be always the case, when silly ministers bungle themselves into difficulties, of which others make their profit; or when they knavishly engage a national quarrel for some private, indirect interest, and inflame the people to resent imaginary injuries. But the truth is, that king James had nobody to blame but himself, when he took general and ambiguous answers for sufficient engagements, and did not see that France would refuse passage to these troops for the same reasons as made her decline entering, at that time, into a league against the house of Austria.

Another blunder committed about the same time, by this wise

king, and that wise minister, his scholar, Buckingham, must be mentioned.   He was to take possession of Frankendal, which had been deposited in the hands of the Infanta Isabella.   The Infanta agreed to yield the place to him, and to give passage to his troops, who were to compose the garrison, according to her engagements; but refused to answer for their passage over the lands of the empire, to which she was not engaged.   Then, and not till then, he made this discovery in geography, that his troops must march over the lands of the empire to get from the Low Countries into the Palatinate.   Such blunders as these were sufficient to disgust the parliaments of that age, and to make them backward in supplying a war thus managed.   Much more reason had they to be so, when they saw the same managers and the same management continue in the next reign.   This disgust at the management of the war, however, would not have produced so many fatal consequences, if it had stood alone.   But we observe, in the second place, that the parliaments, which met after the accession of king Charles, became incensed, as they discovered more and more that the account given by the Duke of Buckingham, in the reign of king James, and on which the resolutions of that parliament had been taken, was false in almost every point.   A system of lies dressed up to deceive the nation, and imposed on the parliament, could neither remain undiscovered nor escape the resentment and indignation it deserved, when discovered.   Besides, that parliament and the nation too, when they expressed so much joy at the breach with Spain, flattered themselves that, by preventing the marriage with the Infanta, they had prevented all the dangers, which they apprehended from that marriage; whereas it appeared soon afterwards that they stood exposed to the very same dangers by the marriage concluded with France; nay, to greater; since the education of the children by the mother, that is in popery, had been confined to ten years by the former treaty, and was extended to thirteen by the latter.   In short, it cannot be denied, and my Lord Clarendon owns, that as the insolence of Buckingham caused the war with Spain, so his lust and his vanity alone threw the nation into another with France.   Spain was courted first without reason, and affronted afterwards without provocation.   Ships were lent to the king of France against his protestant subjects; and the persecution of his protestant subjects was made the pretence of a rupture with him.   Thus was the nation led from one extravagant project to another, at an immense charge, with great diminution of honor and infinite loss to trade, by the ignorance, private interest, and passion of one man.   The conduct therefore of the parliament, who attacked this man, was perfectly consistent with the conduct of that parliament, who had so much applauded him; and one cannot observe without astonishment the slip made by the noble historian we have just quoted, when he affirms that the same men who had applauded him, attacked him without imputing the least crime to him, that was not as much known when they applauded him, as when they attacked him. Now it is plain that many of the crimes imputed to him, in the reign of king Charles, when he was attacked, could not be known, and that many others had not been even committed in the reign of king James, when he was, upon one single occasion, applauded.

To the disgusts taken at the management of foreign affairs, must be added those which were daily given by the court in the management of domestic affairs. Real, not imaginary, grievances arose and were continued in every part of the administration. Some of these king Charles, like his father, was obstinately bent to maintain, and his right of imposing them was asserted. Others were disguised and excused rather than defended; but in redressing even these, he showed such a reluctance, that he complied without obliging, and increased the disgust of his people, even whilst he granted their requests. We have said in a former discourse, that king Charles came a party man to the throne, and that he continued an invasion on the people's rights, whilst he imagined himself only concerned in the defence of his own. In advancing this proposition, we were far from meaning a compliment at the expense of truth. We avow it as an opinion we have formed on reading the relations published on all sides, and to which, it seems to us, that all the authentic anecdotes of those times may be reconciled. This prince had sucked in with his milk those absurd principles of government, which his father was so industrious and, unhappily for king and people, so successful in propagating. He found them espoused, as true principles both of religion and policy, by a whole party in the nation, whom he esteemed friends to the constitution in church and state. He found them opposed by a party, whom he looked on indiscriminately as enemies to the church and to monarchy. Can we wonder that he grew zealous in a cause, which he understood to concern him so nearly, and in which he saw so many men, who had not the same interest, and might therefore be supposed to act on a principle of conscience, equally zealous? Let any one, who hath been deeply and long engaged in the contests of party, ask himself on cool reflection, whether prejudices concerning men and things, have not grown up and strengthened with him, and obtained an uncontrolable influence over his conduct. We dare appeal to the inward sentiments of every such person.—With this habitual bias upon him king Charles came to the throne; and, to complete the misfortune, he had given all his confidence to a mad man. An honest minister might have shown him how wrong his measures were; a wise one how ill-timed. Buckingham was incapable of either. The violence and haughtiness of his temper confirmed his master in the pursuit of these measures; and the character of the first minister became that of the administration. Other circumstances, which often happen, happened likewise in this case. The minister was universally hated; the king was not. To support the minister, it was necessary that the prerogative should be strained, and violent and unpopular means should be employed. To support the government, nothing of this sort was necessary. Nay, the very contrary measures were necessary to reconcile the king to his people, and to stop in time that alienation of their minds from him; which began even then to appear. In this difference of interests, those of the crown were sacrificed to those of the minister. King Charles, who had encouraged parliamentary prosecutions, in his father's reign, would not suffer them in his own. He dissolved his parliaments, and broke almost all the few ties of union, which remained between himself and the nation, that he might screen some of the most unworthy men who ever disserved a prince, or dishonored a court.—Before the death of Buckingham, irreparable mischief was done. "The distemper of the nation was so universal," according to my Lord Clarendon, "that all wise men looked upon it as the prediction of the destruction and dissolution that would follow." This prediction was soon verified. The king executed what he had often threatened. Parliaments were laid aside.— The very mention of them was forbid; and he continued to govern without any for twelve years. During this interval, the distemper lurked indeed; but it grew more malignant; and if a national serenity appeared about the time when the king went into Scotland, it appeared just when the poison worked most effectually and began to seize the heart. Jealousies about religion and liberty were now at their height. The former, as far as they affected the king and his protestant ministers, were ill-founded; but for that very reason, it would have been easy to cure them; and if they had been cured in time, as we think, on my Lord Clarendon's authority, that nothing could have led the Scotch nation into rebellion, so are we persuaded that a great motive and spur to the rebellion in England would have been taken away. The latter were but certainly too well founded.— The king had, in a manner, renounced the constitution; and instead of governing with the assistance and concurrence of a parliament, he governed by illegal acts of power, which the council, the star-chamber and the high commission exercised. There was something still more dangerous to liberty in practice. Not only the government was carried on without law, or against law, but the judges were become the instruments of arbitrary power, and that law, which should have been the protection of property, was rendered, by their corrupt interpretations of it, so great a grievance that "the foundations of right were, to the apprehension and understanding of wise men," says my Lord Clarendon, "never more in danger to be destroyed."

Whilst things were in this situation here, king Charles lighted up another fire in Scotland, by resuming the project of modelling that church, which king James had begun. Archbishop Laud, who had neither temper nor knowledge of the world enough to be intrusted with the government of a private college, conducted this enterprise and precipitated the public ruin. The puritans of England soon united in a common cause with the puritans of Scotland; and the army, which the latter had raised, marched into England. Many of those who had appeared against the court, and even some of those who were on the side of the court, favored, in different manners, the Scots, and hoped to apply this force and to improve this incident so as to restrain the prerogative within known, perhaps narrower bounds, and to strengthen the barriers of public liberty.—That this might have been brought about, and that the civil war which followed, might have been prevented, appeared very manifestly in the temper and proceedings of the parliament, which met in April 1640, when all had been done, which could be done, to destroy the constitution; for if the king had been able to continue to govern without parliaments, the constitution had been destroyed; and when calling a parliament was visibly the effect of necessity and fear, not choice, the parliament, which was called, showed wonderful order and sobriety in their whole behavior. If some passion had appeared in their debates, it might have been well excused in a house of commons assembled at such a time; and yet scarce an angry word was thrown out. The few, that escaped from some, were either silently disliked, or openly disapproved. The king, even in this crisis of affairs, preserved the same carriage he had formerly used towards them, and showed too plainly that he regarded them only as tax-layers. In a word, about a month after their meeting, he dissolved them, and as soon as he had dissolved them, he repented, but he repented too late, of his rashness. Well might he repent; for the vessel was now full, and this last drop made the waters of bitterness overflow.—Here we draw the curtain, and put an end to our remarks, by observing, first, that if the spirit of liberty had once relaxed in the space of almost forty years, liberty must have been swallowed up by prerogative; secondly, that after these long contests between the king and the people, and when the latter had received the utmost provocations, the spirit of liberty was not transported into any excess; determined to defend the people, but unwilling to offend the king.

The king, and he alone could have done it, forced the affairs of the nation, as he had put his own long before, into the hands of a faction. The true friends of the constitution were divided; and divided, were too weak to prevail on either side. The spirit of faction, not the spirit of liberty, is answerable for all which followed; and who is answerable for reducing the contest, on both sides, to be the contest of faction may, we think, be sufficiently collected from what hath been said in these discourses.

LETTER XXIV.

SIR:

SINCE you have gone through the task, which you undertook at my desire, and have carried your remarks on the History of England, as far as you judge them necessary at this time, I think myself obliged to return you thanks for your trouble, and to say something to you, concerning the clamor raised and the conduct held upon this occasion, by those, who, not content with the merit of being your adversaries, have declared themselves such at last to the very being of the British constitution, and to the principles on which the present establishment is built, and on which alone it can stand secure.

Before I left the town, nay as soon as my first letter to you appeared, the whole posse of ministerial scribblers was summoned. Their numbers were augmented; perhaps their pensions. Their strength, indeed, continued much the same; but their fury redoubled. At my return to London, I am informed that these weekly swarms have continued to buzz about ever since; that the insects have been dispersed by every flap of your pen; but, that, like true insects, they have still gathered again and renewed their din.—I say, that I am informed of this; because, among other circumstances, which compose the ease and quiet of a country life, we are sure of not being infested there by these mighty swarms of little creatures. As their lives are short, the extent in which they ramble is narrow, and few of them take their flight beyond the bills of mortality.

The manner in which these writers have supported the dispute between you and them, and the explanations to which they have been pushed, confirm all the suspicions which it was natural to entertain, when so great an alarm was taken at the first direct avowal of an attempt to revive the spirit of liberty, and to recall to the minds of men the true notions of the British constitution. They were so earnest to discourage the prosecution of such a design; they were so eager to find fault, where so little fault was to be found, that they caught at every word, in which they imagined the least slip had been made, though the subject would not have been affected, nor the merits of the cause have been altered, if these slips had been real, and had proceeded from my ignorance, as the objections proceeded from theirs.

I should not so much as mention this, if it was not necessary to show that your real crime, as well as mine, towards the persons who encourage and direct these authors, is our starting the subject, not our manner of treating it.   Their anger appeared, the clamor of their party was raised, and all the powers of scurrility and calumny were called forth to their aid, before any of those pretences were found out, which they afterwards so meanly and so immorally employed against us. To prove this beyond the contradiction of any man of sense and candor, it will be only necessary to appeal to the whole scope of my first letters to you, which raised the storm; for what do those letters contain besides general and inoffensive reflections on the nature of liberty and of faction, and on the necessity of keeping the spirit of liberty alive and active, even in times of apparent security?   Your writings were justified, indeed, in these letters; but so they had been in others, and on many precedent occasions.   The charge of Jacobitism was refuted, indeed, with the contempt it deserved, and factious designs of another kind were pointed out; but factious designs had been imputed to the same persons before and upon the same grounds.   It remains, then, that this new alarm was taken, as I just now said, at the general design of those papers; and if that was sufficient to give such an alarm, sure I am that you are more than justified for all you wrote before this dispute begun, and for all you have published in the course of it.

The old gentleman, who defended you in the former letters, thought you deserved the acknowledgments of every honest man for attempting to revive this spirit, even supposing you to have no other reason than your observation that a contrary temper prevailed.   How much is this reason enforced, how much more do you deserve the acknowledgments of every honest man, if it is become evident not only that a supine temper, contrary to the activity of this spirit had prevailed; but that a contrary spirit hath been raised, and that principles, destructive of all liberty, and particularly adapted to destroy that of the British government, are avowed, taught, and propagated?   If I pronounced too hastily, in my second letter, that the mask was pulled off, surely we may now say, upon knowledge, not belief, that the mask is fallen off from your adversaries in the scuffle. I shall not repeat what is said in your discourses, nor add any thing to them.   You have there quoted the doctrines of slavery.

You have showed the direct and indirect tendency of them all; and you have remarked that some of them have been taught even by those who have in the same breath admitted the consequences of them. Nothing less, therefore, than a constant and vigorous opposition, of which you have set us the example, will be able to stop the progress of those pernicious doctrines. The principles which king James the first established, were not more absurd than these. Their tendency was more obvious; but, for that reason, they were less dangerous. If those principles prevailed very far by time and encouragement, and had like to have prevailed farther, why should not these have the same or greater success? It may be said, perhaps, that the authority of the crown helped the progress of the former, which is not our present case. To this distinction I shall submit very readily; but if these principles have gained some ground already, and that they have gained some cannot be denied, without this authority to enforce them, is there not reason to fear that they may gain more, and is not every degree they gain a degree more of danger to this constitution of government? Surely, sir, there can remain no doubt in the breast of any man, who hath given the least attention to the disputes between you and your adversaries, whether they or you are on the side of liberty; and therefore it is an aggravation of their guilt, that they have endeavored to make your writings pass for an opposition to the present happy establishment, and their cause for that of the crown. You and I have sufficiently declared ourselves, and answered them, on the first head. If they had been able to produce an instance where, departing from your subject, you had given occasion to draw any odious parallel, the intention of drawing such a parallel might, with some color, have been imputed to you; but since they have not been able to do this, and have been defied to do it, the reproach and infamy of making such parallels, as well as the scandalous immorality of imputing them to others, must lie at their door. Let us see how well their pretensions are supported on the second head, and whether we cannot prove, without any forced constructions of their words, or arbitrary interpretations of their meaning, that the open and secret abettors of these writers are either enemies of the present establishment, or have some private interest more at heart than the true interest of this establishment.

This establishment is founded on the principles of liberty—on the very principles you have maintained. It was made by the people of Great Britain to secure the possession of their liberty as well as their religion. Had contrary principles prevailed, either those which tend to subvert the constitution, by raising prerogative, and which were justly objected to some of the tories formerly, or those which tend to subvert it, by undermining liberty, and which are as justly objected to some of the whigs now, this establishment could never have been made. Who are enemies and who are friends, therefore, to public liberty and to the present establishment? Are you their enemy, who defend not only the general principles of liberty, but the particular principles and the particular ends on which and for which this establishment was made? Are your adversaries friends to either, when they only seem to admit some general notions of liberty, that they may promote with greater effect, on particular occasions, the doctrines of slavery, and when they endeavor to destroy the principles and to defeat the ends of the present establishment? The revolution and the acts of settlement have secured us against the dangers which were formerly apprehended from prerogative. To what purpose are measures and principles of policy daily pleaded for, which would expose us to greater dangers than these? Why are such incessant pains taken to show by what means liberty may be undermined, and our constitution destroyed, even now, after all we have done and all we have suffered to secure one, and to improve the other? I shall not give particular answers to these questions, nor offer to assign the private interest which the persons who are guilty of this may have at heart; for I will upon no occasion even seem to follow the example of your adversaries, nor presume to deliver my suspicions, though real and well-grounded, as the intentions of other men. This alone I will repeat; that they who argue, and hire others to argue in this manner, do in fact promote some interest, which is repugnant to the ends for which the people of this nation established the protestant succession and the present settlement of the crown. They have not yet attacked the religion, but they manifestly attack the liberty of their country; and as much as these two are interwoven together, though it be true that whenever our religion is in danger our civil liberty must be so likewise; yet it is as true that religion may be safe and civil liberty in danger.

I have nothing more to add upon this head, before I proceed to that which shall conclude my letter, except my desires that you will persist; and my hopes that you will succeed in the cause you have undertaken—the cause of your country, the cause of truth and liberty. The means you employ are those of argument and persuasion; the lawful, and the sole lawful means, which can be employed to rouse an indolent, to inform a deceived, to reclaim a corrupt, or to reconcile a divided people. Let the factious continue to assert, as they have had already the impudence and the folly to do, in one of their ministerial pamphlets, that the faults they are pleased to ascribe to the people of Great

Britain render an army necessary.*   Instead of endeavoring to persuade and to win, let them endeavor to force and corrupt their countrymen.   The spirit of liberty abhors such means, and the cause of liberty would be dishonored by them.   If this nation was as corrupt and depraved as it is said to be by those who do their utmost to corrupt and deprave it, if our country was in that declining state, and the freedom of our government as near its period as they affirm, there would remain no part for any honest man to take, except that of sitting silently down and perishing in the common shipwreck: but surely this is not yet our case, unless we are induced to believe it so; unless we make our ruin irretrievable by struggling no longer against it.   There are men, many, we think, who have not bowed the knee to Baal, nor worshipped the brazen image.   We may therefore hope that there is still a blessing in store for us.   In all events, Mr. D'Anvers, you are sure of one advantage, which no violence, no injustice can take from you; the inward satisfaction of having served your country to the utmost of your power, by those lawful means which the constitution of its government allows, and by no others.

If I hear in that retreat, to which age, the circumstances of fortune, and above all, the temper of my mind determine me, that you succeed, I shall rejoice in the common joy.   If I hear that you fail, my concern for you will be lost in the common calamity.

The article with which I propose to conclude my letter, is of such a nature that I cannot omit it, on this occasion, with any regard to truth, justice, honor, and the sentiments of a most reasonable indignation.   The writers, who are employed against you, have received, with an unlimited commission to rail, particular instructions to direct their Billingsgate chiefly at two gentlemen. The art of blackening characters, by private closet-whispers, hath been always practised, when power and confidence have been given to the insolent and the base.   Perhaps it may have been thought proper, at this time, to confirm the effect of such insinuations by an echo from the press, and to prevent a general national clamor from sounding in some ears, by raising an artificial clamor round about them: but whatever the design may have been, sure I am that this strain of malice could not have been employed against men, who value it less, or who hold in greater contempt both the contrivance and the contrivers.   This they may do, because they are falsely and maliciously accused; but he, who is the object of a just clamor and of national hatred, and who cannot turn his eyes on himself, without confessing to himself that he is a principal cause of the grievances of his country, must tremble

* See Observations on the Present State of Affairs.

at a clamor which he knows ought, and which he hath reason to fear will, sooner or later, prevail against him.

The calumny against one of the gentlemen, mentioned above, is confined to two heads; that he hath left his friends and party, and that he is urged to oppose the minister by the stings of disappointed ambition. How ridiculous is the charge, and on whom can such stuff impose? Hath he changed his notions of right and wrong in matters of government? Hath he renounced the principles of good policy, which he formerly professed? His greatest enemy is defied to show that he hath; and yet, unless this can be shown, nothing can be more impertinent, or more silly, than the imputation of leaving his friends and party. If he pursues the same general principles of conduct, with which he first set out, and is in opposition now to some few of those, with whom he concurred then, they have left him, because they have left the principles they professed. He left neither. For instance, he inveighs against public profusion and private corruption. He combats both with a constant inflexibility, which might have done honor to a Roman citizen, in the best times of that commonwealth. Hath he left his friends in doing this? No; they who oppose him in it, have left both him and virtue; and such men, though they have sometimes had the honor to concur with him, could never be his friends.

Is the latter part of the charge better founded? Is it not a manifest begging of the question, and a begging of it on the least probable side? He assisted a minister to rise to power. He opposes this minister in power. Ergo, spite and resentment are his motives. May not the abuse, which he apprehends this minister makes of his power, may not measures, which he fears are wicked, knows are weak, and sees obstinately pursued, be his motives? May not dangerous ambition, insatiable avarice and insolent behavior be his provocations? May not this gentleman think himself the more obliged to contribute to this minister's fall, for having contributed so much to his elevation? Let me ask farther, whom we shall soonest suspect to have been actuated by sentiments of private interest; the person accused, or his accuser? Whose circumstances most demanded, whose family most required an increase of wealth and fortune; those of the accused, or those of the accuser? Who hath given greater proofs of avarice to gather, and profusion to squander; the accused or the accuser? In whom have we seen stronger evidences of that vindictive temper, which prompts to personal spite and resentment; in the accused or the accuser?—If we may form any judgment of the gentleman accused, there is not the least color of reason to suppose that his opposition proceeds from a spirit of ambition, or a design of pushing himself into the administration.

He hath already possessed two very considerable employments in the state; one of which he voluntarily laid down, as by his conduct in parliament, against some measures of the court, he forced the ministers to take the other way, having behaved with unspotted integrity in both; and if I am rightly informed of his resolution by those who seem to know him very well, it will hardly be ever in the power of the greatest man in England, or of the best friend he has in the world, to persuade him to accept of a third.—There is an ambition, with which these spreaders of calumny and their masters are entirely unacquainted; the ambition of doing good and the receiving the reward in fame. He who hath this ambition, can never be disappointed in the other; and if any man, in our age and country, hath reason to be satisfied with his success in the pursuit of this ambition, it is the gentleman of whom we speak.

Whenever the defamation, which hath been displayed against the other gentleman is examined with the least knowledge of facts, or the least impartiality of judgment, it will appear equally false, and perhaps still more scandalous; for, in this case, the slanderers take an ungenerous and mean advantage, which they have not in the other; the advantage, which his singular situation gives them. They, who would have declined a contest with him, whilst he was in a condition to answer for himself, have not blushed to declaim against him in another condition. They have experienced, in his case, that the unfortunate are not friendless.

They may live, perhaps, to experience, in their own, that the guilty are so. Another advantage, which these slanderers take against this gentleman, arises from the various scenes of life, through which he hath passed; some distant in place; some secret in their nature. Here calumny hath more room to assert, and innocence less opportunity to defend. Common honesty, in some cases, and even decency, in others, shut the mouth of the man who carries these qualities about him; and even more in his own cause than in that of another person; but calumny is subject to none of these controls; and we speak on our own knowledge, when we affirm that, in the present case, the false imputations, which the accusers bring, are screened from absolute detection by nothing but the honor of the accused.

Let us take notice of some of the crimes, (for crimes and heinous crimes they would be, if the facts were, in any degree, true,) which are laid to the charge of this gentleman.

His ingratitude and treachery to the late Duke of Marlborough and the Earl of Godolphin stand first in the roll. I believe no man acknowledges more sincerely than he the superior merit of these two illustrious men, or wishes more ardently that they were now alive, and had the conduct of the affairs of Great Britain;

but I know no obligation of gratitude or honor, which he lay under to continue in their administration, when the measures of it were altered. They might have reasons, perhaps good reasons, for altering their measures. He could have none in point of honor, whatever he might have had in point of interest, for complying with that alteration. Some of the enemies of this gentleman came into the world on such a foot, that they might think it preferment to be the creatures of any men in power. He who came into it upon another foot, was the friend, but not the creature of these great men; and he hath had the satisfaction of proving himself such on different occasions and without ostentation, at least to one of them, at a time, when the creatures of great men usually renounce them; at a time, when they could do him neither good nor hurt. That he came to court, on the call of the late queen, in opposition to them, and exerted himself in her service, when they served her no longer, will not be objected to him by any man, who thinks more allegiance due to the prince than to the minister. If the present minister hath a mind to avow a contrary doctrine, he hath my consent; but then let those who engage with him, remember on what terms they engage. On the same false principle is another accusation brought. This gentleman had no patron, or patroness, but the late queen. He neither projected, nor procured the disgrace of her last minister, nor knew that it was resolved, whatever he might suspect, till he heard from herself that it was so. Much more might be said on this article; but we choose to pass it over for many reasons, and, among others, for this; that whilst we defend the living, we are unwilling to say anything which might be drawn by these slanderers into an insult on the dead.

The last charge of ingratitude, brought against this gentleman, is hard to be answered seriously. Thus much, however, shall be said truly and seriously. He acknowledged, with the deepest sense of gratitude possible, the clemency and goodness of his late majesty; but sure he hath reason, if ever man had reason, to disclaim all obligation to the minister. The mercy of the late king was extended to him unasked and unearned. What followed many years afterwards, in part of his majesty's gracious intentions, was due solely to the king. That they were not fulfilled, was due solely to the minister. His ambition, his causeless jealousy and private interest continued a sort of proscription, with much cruelty to the persons concerned, and little regard to the declarations which his royal master had been pleased so frequently to make.

That this gentleman was engaged in the cause of the Pretender, is true. That he served him unfaithfully, is false. He never entered into these engagements, or any commerce with him, till he had been attainted, and cut off from the body of his majesty's subjects.   He never had any commerce, either direct or indirect, which was inconsistent with these engagements, whilst he continued in them; and since he was out of them, he hath had no commerce, either direct or indirect, in favor of that cause.   On such an occasion as this it is decent, not arrogant, to challenge all mankind.   I do it, therefore, in the behalf of this gentleman, to produce one single proof, in contradiction of any one of these general affirmations.   For the truth of some, I may appeal even to these who have been in the service of his late, and are in that of his present majesty; and particularly to a noble lord,* who by the post he was in, when most of these transactions passed, must have had the best opportunities of knowing the truth of them, and by whose testimony I am willing that the gentleman I defend should stand or fall; a decision to which, I am sure, he will himself be ready to submit his life, and, what is more, his honor.

I make you no excuse for the length of my letter.   The justice I have done, or endeavored to do, to those, who have been vilely calumniated, and particularly on the occasion of your writings and of mine, will be a sufficient excuse of itself.

I am, sir, &c.

* The late marshal Earl of Stair.

A FINAL ANSWEF

REMARKS ON THE CRAFTSMAN'S VINDICATION;

And to all the Libels, which have come, or may come from the same quarter
against the person last mentioned in the Craftsman of the twenty-second
of May, 1731.

IT is impossible to have read the papers, which have been
published against the writings of the Craftsman, and not have
observed that one principal point hath been labored with constant application, and sometimes with a little art. The point I
mean hath been this; to make all the disputes about national
affairs, and our most important interests, to pass for nothing more
than cavils, which have been raised by the pique and resentment of one man, and by the iniquity and dangerous designs of
another. Nothing ,which could be said or done to inculcate this
belief, hath been neglected. The same charges have been
repeated almost every week, and the public hath been modestly
desired to pay no regard to undeniable facts, to unanswered and
unanswerable arguments, because these facts and these arguments were supposed, by the ministerial writers, to come from
men, to whom these hirelings ascribed, against all probability,
the worst motives, and whose characters they endeavored to
blacken without proof. Surely this proceeding rendered it necessary, at least not improper, at the end of those remarks, which
were to conclude the collection of the Craftsman, to say something concerning the persons, who had been so particularly
attacked on account of the part which they, who railed at them,
were pleased to suppose that these gentlemen had in the writings
contained in that collection. This, I say, was necessary; at least
proper; not in order to raise a spirit, as it is impertinently sug-

gested in the libel which lies before me; but to refute calumny, and to remove at least some of those prejudices, which had been raised, or renewed, on the occasion of these writings, and which were employed to weaken the effect of them; an effect, which may be said with truth to have been aimed at the noble pair of brothers; since it keeps up a national spirit of inquiry and watchfulness, which it is the interest of these persons, as it hath been their endeavor, to stifle; and which it is the interest of every other man in Britain to preserve in himself, and to nourish in others; an effect, which cannot be said, without the greatest untruth, to have been aimed against the present settlement; since the highest insolence which can be offered to his majesty, is to attempt to blend his interest and his cause with those of his unworthy servants, as the tools of these unworthy servants are every day employed to do, and probably at his majesty's expense.

Something was said therefore by the Craftsman, in his journal of the twenty-second of May, to the purpose I have mentioned. If he went out of his way, (for he ought most certainly to confine himself to things, and meddle with persons as little as possible) he went out of it on great provocation. He carried truth and reason along with him; and he used a moderation and a decency, to which his adversaries are strangers.

To set this matter in a full light, let us consider what he said; let us consider how he hath been answered; and by fairly comparing both, let us put the whole merits of this cause upon one short but decisive issue. It will be time afterwards to make a few observations on the clamor raised; on the reasons and designs of it; in a word, to detect the mean artifice and silly expedients to which the two honorable patrons of the remarker are reduced. In doing this, I shall neither affect to declaim, nor to inveigh, though I have before me an inexhaustible fund of matter for both, and the law of retaliation to bear me out. As I am persuaded, the men I have to do with, can raise no passion in the person concerned, so have I no need of endeavoring to raise the passions of others.—But to proceed.

The Craftsman took notice of those accusations which are brought against the gentleman he mentions in the second place. —I meddle not with the defence of the other, which hath been undertaken by an abler pen. Some of these he answered in general only; and yet he answered them as particularly as he ought to have done for reasons of honor, which are touched upon by him, and which shall be a little more opened by me.

But there were other points, not at all affected by these reasons, on which no explanation was necessary to be given by the accused, and on which the Craftsman had a right to demand proofs from the accusers. They were points of a more determined nature; such as admitted of no different constructions; such as could not be altered by circumstances. They were of a more public nature; such as the men, who brought the accusations must have it in their power to prove, if they were true; and such therefore as must be false, if the men, who brought the accusations, were not able and ready to prove them.

On these the Craftsman insisted. He affirmed propositions directly contrary to the accusations brought. He appealed to unquestionable authority for the truth of what he affirmed; and to one in particular, which should have been treated with more respect by the remarker, since it will outweigh, at home and abroad, a thousand such authorities as those of his patrons. He challenged all mankind to produce one single proof in contradiction of any one of the general affirmations.

Was there any thing unfair, or indecent in this proceeding?—Was there any thing in it, which could provoke the choler of those who are friends to truth and justice? If they, who brought these accusations, had been such, an opportunity was presented to them of convicting the guilty man at the very tribunal before which his cause had been pleaded. By producing proof on these heads, they had it in their power to condemn him upon all the rest; and if this part of the charge was made good, the opinion of mankind would have been fairly enough decided as to the other.

Issue being joined therefore in this manner, the accused person must be found guilty of all the crimes laid to his charge; or his accusers must be found guilty of slander, of calumny, and of the worst sort of assassination.

Thus the Craftsman left the matter. Let us see what hath been said in answer to him.

I pass over the many scurrilous productions of those weekly ministerial scolds, who are hired to call names, and are capable of little more. The elaborate libel, entitled " Remarks on the Craftsman's Vindication," seems to be the utmost effort of their and their patron's collected strength; and though I have waited several days to see if they had any more scandal to throw out, yet I never doubted an instant from what quarter this remarkable piece came into the world.

The whole pamphlet is one continued invective, and deserves no more to be called Remarks on the Craftsman, or an answer to him, than the railing and raving and throwing of filth by a madman deserve to be called an answer to those who unwarily pass too near his cell. All that malice could ever invent, or the credulity of parties, inflamed by opposition, receive, is assembled. Truth is disguised by misrepresentation, and even many things which the noble pair know to be false, are affirmed as true.

But you will ask, perhaps, whether the challenge is not accepted, and whether proofs are not brought to contradict the plain and positive affirmations made by the Craftsman? I answer, the challenge is accepted, and the remarker assures us that he hath brought proof in numerous instances against these affirmations; which is the more generous, because the Craftsman exacted but one single proof in contradiction of any of them.

The first of these affirmations was, that the gentleman concerned never entered into engagements, or any commerce with the Pretender, till he had been attainted and cut off from the body of his majesty's subjects.—Let us examine the facts, which we find scattered up and down in the remarks, which may be applied to prove, in opposition to this affirmation, what hath been so often asserted, that this gentleman was a zealous jacobite and an agent of the Pretender, even in the reign of the late queen.

The first fact of this kind is this. He left the kingdom. His high treason, among other crimes, was confessed by his shameful flight.

Had the libeller proved this high treason, I might agree that the gentleman's leaving his country was a consequence; but I can never admit that it is a proof of his guilt. Could no other reason for leaving his country be given, except his guilt, his leaving his country would be a strong presumption against him. But many other reasons will soon occur to those who remember the passages of that time; and reasons there are of a more private nature still, which would be very far, to say no more, from reflecting dishonor on a step, which is called, by these foulmouthed advocates of power, shameful and ignominious. One thing it may be proper to assure them of, that they may pretend to mistake the Craftsman, and to misapply his words no more. It is this. The gentleman never declined a contest with the two honorable patrons of this libel. One of them was, in those days, below his notice; and he never found, upon trial, that he had reason to apprehend being foiled by the other. But we must not yet dismiss this article.

If the proof we are examining proved any thing, it would prove too much. If to decline, in certain circumstances, a trial; if to go into voluntary exile, either before a trial, or even after condemnation, were absolute proofs of guilt, the conduct of many greater and better men than the person now accused would deserve our censure, and that of calumniators, as vile as these libellers, would merit our approbation. Metellus and Rutilius must be condemned. Apuleius and Apicius must be justified.

This sort of proof therefore not appearing sufficient to make good the charge, that this gentleman was engaged with the Pre-

tender before his attainder, great pains are taken, and much
rhetoric is employed to show, what we shall not presume to contradict, that he ought not to have engaged in that cause after his
attainder. Neither did the Craftsman insist on this circumstance
as a defence of the person accused. He fixed this date of the
engagements mentioned, in contradiction to those who had falsely affirmed that these engagements were much more ancient.
But he neither urged it as a defence, nor pleaded it as an excuse;
and yet I am persuaded that this very circumstance had some
weight with his late majesty, when that excellent prince, the
mildness of whose temper, and the clemency of whose nature,
would have rendered him amiable in the most private station,
and made him almost adorable in that great elevation, to which
the providence of God had raised him; when that excellent
prince, I say, was pleased, on his own motion, and without any
application from the person here spoken of, to extend his present,
and promise his future favor to him.

Though the Craftsman did neither say nor intend what has
been objected by the remarker to him, yet he might perhaps
mean something more than hath been observed; and if he did
mean it, he meant to inculcate upon this occasion, a very useful,
general truth. Let us grant that the man, who engages against
his country, even when he has been oppressed in it, or driven out
of it by violence, is not to be defended; that these are occasions,
wherein we ought to kiss the rod, which scourges us, and reverence that authority, which we think has been unjustly exercised
against us. But then let it be granted likewise, that human
passions are so strong, and human reason so weak, that men,
who suffer persecution or who imagine they suffer it, are seldom
able to keep within these bounds of heroical moderation. They
will be apt to seize the opportunities which may be offered, of
resisting, or of attempting to repair the injuries done them.
They will flatter themselves, that they do not vow their revenge
against the people, the innocent and collective body of their
countrymen, nor go about to subvert the constitution of the government. They will persuade others, nay they will persuade
themselves, that they do not seek revenge, but redress; nor aim
to destroy the law, which punishes, but to prevent the abuse of
it, which persecutes. Thus will men, who actually suffer, be apt
to reason; and if the case be common to numbers, they will be
apt to proceed from reasoning on such principles, to act upon
them. Wise governments therefore have been careful to distinguish between punishment and persecution; have never suffered
the former, however just, necessary, or severe, to carry the least
appearance of the latter. Ludlow was justly punished. My
Lord Clarendon, whom the remarker hath so strangely yoked

with the regicide, was unjustly, ungratefully and cruelly persecuted. We may pronounce, without uncharitableness, that the
former would have taken any opportunity of subverting a second
time the constitution of his country; not from resentment alone,
but from principle. The latter would have been moved by no
resentments to disturb that frame of government, which he had
contributed so much to restore. The former example therefore
hath nothing to do in this place; and if I admit the latter, it will
only serve to show us how men should act, not how they do act.
It will be one example of virtue, opposed to innumerable instances of frailty. Innumerable, indeed, are the instances of men
in all ages, who, having been driven out of their country by violence, have endeavored, even by violence, to return to it. This
is the general and known course of nature; depraved indeed, but
human: and since it is so, if we allow that they, who disturb a
government, because they think themselves persecuted, deserve
no excuse, we must allow that those, who give occasion to this
disturbance by persecution, deserve very little.

I hope I may deserve some for this digression, into which the
remarker led me; and I return to my subject, by saying that neither the Craftsman had pretended, nor do I here pretend, to
excuse the engagements which this gentleman took, after his
attainder, and which his late majesty so graciously pardoned;
but that his taking these engagements, after his attainder, is no
proof that he was under them before; and that his going out of
the kingdom, in the late king's reign, is no proof that he was a
zealous jacobite, and an agent of the Pretender in the late queen's
reign.

The libeller, finding himself unable to make this charge good,
lessens the charge that he may suit his proof to it. If he cannot
prove that the gentleman was in the interests of the Pretender,
before his attainder, he will prove at least that he had a strong
propension to those interests; and how does he prove even this?
He asserts that in the year 1702, this gentleman was "one of
the virtuous one hundred and seventeen, who gave their votes to
throw out the bill for settling the protestant succession," &c.—
False and impudent assertion! A few pages before he pretends
to have the journal book of the house of commons before him.
Had he it before him now? if he had, how can he affirm, in
direct contradiction to it? If he had not, how could he venture
to affirm anything, concerning this matter? The bill for settling
the protestant succession, in the present royal family, passed the
house of commons in the month of May 1701, not in 1702; and
it passed, nemine contradicente, to bring in a bill "for the farther
security of his majesty's person and the succession of the crown
in the protestant line, and extinguishing the hopes of the pre-

tended Prince of Wales, and all other pretenders, and their open and secret abettors." This bill was accordingly brought in, and the persons who, by order of the house, prepared and brought it in, were Sir Charles Hedges and one Mr. St. John. In the progress of this bill through the house, it appears that there were some debates and divisions about particular clauses and amendments; but the bill was passed without any division: so infamously false is the assertion made by this libeller, that there was no division of an hundred and seventeen, or of any other number, for throwing out either the bill which settled the succession; or the bill, which was made for the farther security of it. There was a division indeed, of a hundred and seventeen against a hundred and eighteen, upon a clause added by the lords to a bill for enlarging the time for taking the oath of abjuration, &c., and this happened in the year 1702; but what relation hath this fact to the fact asserted? Whether the gentleman voted against this clause, or not, I am unable to say; and it is to no purpose to inquire; for the clause regarded only such persons as had neglected to take the abjuration oath in time, and provided that if such persons had forfeited any office, benefice, &c., to which any other persons had been preferred, the former should not be restored by taking the advantage of this act. If this pretended proof is not another instance of the vilest calumniation, the libeller himself confesses that the Craftsman's challenge was properly made; and that there is not one proof in the world against his general affirmations.

Another fact, which is advanced and most pathetically declaimed upon, for reasons not hard to be discovered, is likewise applied to maintain the same charge. "This gentleman," says the libeller, "had the impudence to oppose his present most sacred majesty, when he demanded a writ of right—The writ of summons to parliament. He afterwards caused the elector of Hanover's minister to be forbid the court, for no other crime than having demanded that writ." And did this gentleman oppose this writ? Nay, did any other servant of the late queen oppose it? False and impudent is the assertion. It was ordered to be made out the very day* it was demanded. If the minister, who demanded the writ, was forbid the court, was this gentleman the cause of it? Is every disagreeable circumstance to be ascribed to him in an affair, which was too important not to be laid, by the proper minister, that is by the chancellor, not the secretary, before her late majesty and her council; and in which it may be supposed that her majesty's resentments were alone sufficient to determine such a resolution? Besides, if the minis-

* Vide Annals of the Reign of Queen Anne.

ter received the affront mentioned, was it singly and abstractedly for demanding the writ; or was it founded on the manner of demanding, and on many other circumstances, some expressed and some hinted at in the letters, written soon afterwards by the late queen to her late electoral highness the princess Sophia and to his present majesty, which lie before me in the printed annals of queen Anne's reign? Was the reception, given by his late majesty, then elector, to the minister, who made this demand, at his return home, such a one as showed his majesty's approbation of this measure, and his disapprobation of what had happened here upon it?—I say no more.

We have now gone through all I can find in this libel, which seems not so much as to aim at making good the first head of accusation, on which the Craftsman made his challenge.

On the second head, the Craftsman affirmed that the "same gentleman never had any commerce, either direct or indirect, inconsistent with the engagements he took after his attainder, whilst he continued in them." Now this affirmation, instead of being disproved, is evaded. "It is foreign to me," says the remarker—Is it so?—Have not all his scribbling associates charged this gentleman over and over for being treacherous to the Pretender; for being engaged with him; and at the same time a spy and a partisan, such is the language they use, of the late king? Is not the flat contradiction given to this lie a part of the challenge made by the Craftsman? Hath not this libeller accepted the challenge? Hath he not called it a weak, a foolish, and a slavish defence? May he evade it after all his boasting? Is he not bound to make it good in every part, or to own the charge of calumny, which I make on him, on the whole scribbling crew, and on those who pay them? What he, or they will own I neither know nor care. What the public will determine is evident.

On a third head of accusation against this gentleman, the Craftsman affirmed, that since he was "out of the engagements last mentioned, he hath had no commerce, either direct or indirect, in favor of that cause." Now, upon this head, though the accusation be not given up in terms, yet is it as little maintained, or supported by proof as the last. The libeller, indeed, calls the gentleman a leviathan of treason; displays the terrible dangers which would have attended the reinstating him; presumes to call it a libel on the late king's memory to say that he had such intentions; and yet dares not deny that his majesty signified his having such intentions. In short, with much bombast, he makes the panegyric of his patron, for defeating these intentions. I shall not condescend to make one single remark on this rhapsody of scurrility and adulation. Such poison carries its antidote along with it into the world; and no man will be at a loss to judge whether public or private motives determined the servant, in this case, to defeat the intentions of the master. Whichever they were, he who can believe that the gentleman so often mentioned has upon him any of that obligation, which the Craftsman disclaims for him, deserves to be pitied; and he, who can bring himself up to affirm it, deserves to be despised. But before I leave this article, it may not be improper, nor unseasonable to inquire, by what criterion good subjects to his majesty and faithful friends to the present establishment are to be distinguished and known. Are all those to be reputed such who assumed the greatest zeal for the protestant succession formerly? This cannot be; for many of the tories have this title; and all, who ever wore that name, are proscribed by the system we have advanced. Are all these to be reputed such, who were alike zealous for the protestant succession, and who have besides made constant profession of the principles of whigism? This cannot be neither; since many such as these are daily stigmatised with the reproachful names of malcontents and incendiaries; and since endeavors are used, by false deductions and by arbitrary interpretations, to prove them enemies to the government, and in effect, arrant traitors.— What is this criterion then? I am able to discover but one, and it is this; being for, or being against the noble pair of brothers, the two honorable patrons of the remarker. Without the merit of approving their conduct, no man is to be reputed a faithful subject, or a friend to his country. With this merit, and with that of a blind submission, even they, who have been the most obnoxious, may be received; and they, who have been called enemies to the government as loudly as any others, may be enrolled among its friends. This practice of endeavoring to confine the interest of the government to as narrow a bottom as that of two ministers, has been of late most audaciously pursued. It has been said in direct terms that "if his late majesty had put the administration into any other hands, he would have been unjust to those brave men who had done and suffered much to serve him; and that he would not have deserved to wear the crown if he had not employed the men whom he did employ."* Here, again, there might be room for some particular reflections, if I was disposed to make them. But I avoid this invidious part as much as my subject will allow me to do; and shall therefore content myself with desiring these bold writers, their inspectors and patrons, to consider what the necessary consequences of such positions are. If they dare to assert that his late majesty would have been unjust; that he would not have

* London Journal, May 15, 1731.

deserved to wear the crown, if he had not employed the men he did employ: what might they not assert if his present majesty should, at any time, think fit, in his great wisdom and goodness to his people, to remove some of those very men, whom his royal father did employ? The assertion is not even extended to party. It would have been still indecent if it had. But it is confined to a certain number of particular men; as if the zeal for the protestant succession in the present royal family had not been directed, as it most certainly was, to the national advantage; but had been intended, as to be sure it was not, for the advantage of particular men, and to perpetuate the administration in a private family. This is such language, as, I believe, was never held before, and as no man would presume to hold now, if the encouragement to it did not proceed from those, by whom it should be discountenanced and punished.

There is another fact, which I must not omit to take notice of in this place; because, though it is not one of those on which the Craftsman made his challenge, yet it hath been positively asserted by him, and half of it at least as positively denied by the remarker.

The Craftsman said " that the mercy of the late king was extended to the gentleman we speak of, unasked and unearned." That it was unearned the remarker thinks probable; and in thinking so he gives the lie to all his fellow-scribblers, who have so often affirmed the contrary. That it was unasked, he says, is a downright falsehood. He hath the journal-book of the house of commons before him; and there he finds "that the house was acquainted, by his late majesty's command, in April, 1725, that this gentleman had, about seven years before, made his humble application and submission, &c., which his majesty so far accepted as to give encouragement to hope for some future mark of his majesty's favor and goodness."—In this he exults; but here again the effrontery and falsehood which he charges on others, will recoil on himself. Who drew this ministerial message I know not; nor how far the style of it may be necessary, according to the forms usual on such occasions; but the remarker might have known, if he had consulted even his patrons, that his majesty's mercy had been extended to this gentleman two years before the seven there mentioned; and that his mercy did not consist in encouragement to hope for some future mark of his majesty's favor and goodness, but in a gracious and absolute promise of his favor in the full extent, which the circumstances of that gentleman required. I may be the more bold in affirming this fact, because the noble lord,* who delivered the message

* The present Earl of Winchelsea.

I quote, is still alive, as some other persons are, to whom his late majesty was pleased to own that this message had been delivered by his order, and to express his gracious intentions conformably to it.—But to proceed.

It appears most undeniably, that of the three heads, on which the Craftsman gave, and the remarker accepted the challenge, the remarker hath shown himself unable to prove the first by any true facts, and hath scandalously attempted to do it by false ones; that he hath given up the second; and that he hath not so much as attempted to prove the third.

Let us ask now, shall men, thus plainly convicted of calumny on accusations brought so often and charged so peremptorily by them, expect belief, when they endeavor to defame in any other case?   Shall they; who are convicted of accusing falsely in cases, which are plain in their nature, where no proof can be wanting, and where no pretence can be alleged for not producing it, expect that the public should condemn any man, and especially a man who is under so many circumstances of disadvantage, peculiar to his singular and unexampled situation, because they affirm him guilty in cases, which are intricate in their nature, and where reasons of honor, of prudence, and of decency, may all concur to impose silence?   How often have the noble pair defended themselves, and been defended by others, on this principle; that no man ought to charge another, unless he is able and ready to prove the charge?   How often have they called for proof on this principle, and triumphed that it was not immediately brought? Now, although this defence may not be sufficient in every case, where matters of present transaction are concerned, and where the persons attacked are in actual possession of the greatest power; yet surely it may be thought, with reason, to be a sufficient defence, when matters long ago transacted, and long ago censured too, are concerned; when the persons, who attack, are in actual possession of the greatest power; and the person who is attacked, hath none of those offensive or defensive weapons at his command, which power furnishes in so abundant a manner.

The remarker thinks that no "reasons of honor, prudence, or decency ought to shut the mouth of innocence; that shame and guilt alone are silent in the day of inquiry." When this day of inquiry is to come, and who is to be the subject of it, I know not; but let him learn that there are many cases, wherein it is not honest, and many others may occur wherein it is not prudent, to say all that might be said either in defence or in excuse; that is, when the defence or excuse of ourselves must affect others, not concerned in the debate.   In such cases the most innocent will rather bear the imputation of imaginary crimes, by keeping silence, than be guilty of a real crime, by breaking it; and to carry this as far as it can be carried, instances might be produced of men who have died, rather than accuse others, whose blood was thirsted after more than theirs.

Much hath been said, and great complaints have been made, of the torture, as it is called in this libel, given to another gentleman's actions. If, by this, be meant ransacking into all the private and public passages of his life, and wresting every one into a crime, far be it from me to approve, in his case, what I abhor this libeller for doing in the case of another. But is it really so? Have we seen accusations of treachery and ingratitude towards several, who are dead, and towards any, who are living, insisted upon in the former case? Has it been reproached to the patrons of the remarker, that they wormed out of power a person, to whom they were nearly allied, and ought to have been firmly attached by gratitude and friendship? And yet is that a subject which affords nothing to be said? Are there no circumstances which might be aggravated at least? Are there no strong colors which might be laid? Even I should not be at a loss to do it, if I thought it fair to do it; if I thought it honest to push any man to a silence, of which I might take a seeming advantage, or to a necessity of justifying or excusing himself by saying what, supposing him innocent, he ought not to say. Are there no facts relating to former transactions of great importance not commonly known, and yet not absolutely secrets, which remain still unmentioned? In short, is it not apparent that there are men who accuse, indeed, when the immediate subject of debate leads, and provokes them necessarily and unwillingly to it, whilst there are others, who wait for no such necessity, but accuse merely to defame.

It would be tedious, not difficult, to go through this whole invective; to deny with truth many things which are falsely affirmed; and, by giving a just turn to others, to set them in a very different light from that wherein the author exposes them to public view; to explain what he perplexes; to distinguish what he confounds. But I shall not take this task upon me, for the reasons I have given, and for others which I am going to give.

As to the conduct which the person against whom such torrents of ribaldry are poured forth, held towards those who were at the head of affairs, whilst he was in business, I shall only add to what hath been said already, what no man of candor will deny; that the heat and animosity which perpetual contests and frequent turns of party raise, have carried many, perhaps the person who is blamed, perhaps the persons who blame him, to do what, in any other situation or temper of mind, they would carefully avoid: in a word, that the just man hath been, on such occasions sometimes unjust; the good-natured man ill-natured; and the friendly man unfriendly. Few there are, I fear, who could with a safe conscience take up the first stone upon such a trial. Few there are who are blameless. But here is the difference. The just, the good-natured, the friendly man returns to the character out of which he started. The unjust, the ill-natured, the unfriendly man persists. The first reflects with sorrow on what the last reflects with triumph; and whilst one wishes undone what the heat of party carried him to do, the other is glad of the excuse of party, such as it is, to indulge the viciousness of his own nature, and to repeat unjust, ill-natured, and unfriendly actions to the living and even to the dead.

There is an example before us, which may serve to illustrate what I have said. Great advantage is taken of a memorial sent to the late queen, by the late Earl of Oxford, wherein many hard reflections are made on others; but the hardest of all on the person here referred to. He is painted in the worst colors, and accused to the queen of the greatest faults. Should I descend into the particulars, I might show that the accusations were groundless, and point out, perhaps, the unjust causes of suspicion which were taken, as well as the motives to the writing that memorial, which I wish had never been written, for a reason very different from that which the remarker would be ready to assign. But I shall not descend into any such particulars, nor give a double advantage to the malicious, who would be just as well pleased to have any handle given them by the living, of inveighing against the dead, as they are ready to seize, on every occasion, that which was given them, so many years ago, by one who is now dead, of inveighing against the living.

The persons who had the honor to serve the late queen, in the last period of her life, have been these twenty years the subjects of great clamor. If the differences which happened amongst them so long ago, gave, in some measure, as I apprehend that they did, both occasion and force to this clamor, it would be strange conduct, indeed, in those of them who remain alive, and in the relations and friends of those of them who are dead, to preserve the spirit of difference, and to assist in reviving this clamor.

The day will come when authentic history will relate the passages of those times, without regard to the partial views of any party, or the particular defence of any man. Till this day does come, every one must decide, or suspend his judgment, as he sees reason to do; and they, who may suffer by these judgments, must bear it with that temper and respect which is due from every private man to public censures—nay, even to public prejudices.

But what hath all this to do with the characters and conduct of the noble pair? Suppose the men in power two reigns ago to

have been angels of darkness, will it follow that the two honorable patrons of the remarker are angels of light? What then is
the meaning of so great a clamor, affectedly raised on so slender
an occasion as the Craftsman of the twenty-second of May gave;
wherein little was said, and that little with much moderation,
after much provocation? Why are so many pens employed, and
so great pains taken, to divert the attention of the public from
present to past transactions, from national considerations to personal altercations? The reason is obvious; and no other reason
in nature can be assigned. The noble pair have been hard pushed, on their management of public affairs, both at home and
abroad. Not only their errors have been pointed out, gross, pal-
pable errors, but a long series of error; a whole system of cool,
deliberate, conducted, defended, expensive error, hath been laid
open to public view. What I believe never to have happened
before, hath happened on these occasions. The noble pair have
been admonished in time, and shown the precipice, into which,
whoever led, they were both falling. The consequences of their
measures have been foretold as early as possible, and even whilst
the causes were laying. Surely this conduct, on the part of their
adversaries, savors more of public spirit than of private resentment; and yet, when they have taken advantage of it, they have
stopped short, and triumphed in their escape, as they did in the
case of the Irish recruits. These very admonitions, which gave
them time and opportunity to do so, have been modestly attributed to private resentment alone, though nothing can be more
manifest than this; that private resentment would have found its
account better in silence, would have preferred accusations to
admonitions, and would have waited longer to have struck more
home.

Sometimes, instead of stopping short, they have gone on, answering for and being answered for, till the events have justified
the predictions; till the inconveniences, disadvantages and difficulties, against which the noble pair had been warned in vain,
have followed and increased upon them; till even their apologists
have been forced to allow some errors, and till they themselves
have confessed their boasted system to be wrong, by changing it,
and by boasting of the change. Even after all this, they have
complained of clamor; and they still complain, as if there had
never been the least occasion for it given by them. How their
new schemes are planned, and how they will be pursued; whether these able men have failed hitherto, because they set out on
mistaken principles of policy, or whether they have failed for
want of skill to conduct the rightest, we shall soon see.

But these are not the only circumstances, which have borne,
and still bear hard upon them. In the course of these and other

disputes, it seems to have been plainly and fully proved, that such principles have been established, and such doctrines have been taught by the ministerial writers, as tend manifestly to destroy the freedom of the British government. Such are, the dependency, I mean the corrupt dependency, of parliaments on the crown; the necessity of standing armies, notwithstanding the danger of them to liberty; and some other points, which I need not recapitulate. It is sufficiently known how much, and with how much reason, the far greater part of mankind have been alarmed at these attempts; which, if they succeed, must hurt not only the inferior and temporary interests, but the greatest and most permanent political interest, which a Briton can have at heart; that of the constitution of this government.

As these things have been objected strongly on one side, so endeavors have been used on the other, to disguise and to palliate them, or to evade the consequences drawn from them. But these endeavors have not succeeded. How, indeed, should they succeed? As well might those, who make them, expect to persuade mankind that slavery and beggary are preferable to liberty and wealth, as to make the world believe that these blessings can be preserved to Britain by the very means, by which they have been lost in so many other free countries.

Since this therefore cannot be imposed; since the minds of men cannot be convinced of such absurdities, they must be diverted, if possible, from the subject. A new cry is, therefore, raised, or an old one rather is revived. Disputes, which inflamed the minds of men, whilst the affairs they relate to were transacting, and the conflict of parties was the most fierce, are renewed at a time, when they can be of no benefit to the public, and when the same motives of party subsist no longer. One man, in particular, is made the subject of new invective. Nothing, which malice can suggest, and ill-nature and ill-manners utter, is omitted to render his person odious, and to represent his designs as dangerous. In the same breath, we are told that this odious, this dangerous man is endeavoring to come into power once more. He stands again "a candidate for grace and trust. He would again administer the public, abandon its allies, and sacrifice its honor. Nothing will satisfy him but the power, which he once abused and would again abuse; the trusts, which he once betrayed and would again betray." These are represented, with equal modesty and fairness, to be his requests; and the hero of the remarker, that is, the remarker's paymaster, who administers the public so righteously; who never abandoned its allies; neither the emperor nor France; who never sacrificed its honor to one, nor its interest to both; who never abused his power, nor betrayed his trust, through ambition, through pride, through private interest, or private pique; this person is applauded for his opposition to such requests, for his just and fatal discernment.

What fatality there may be in his discernment, I know not; but surely there is a fatality, which attends those who indulge themselves in speaking and writing, without any regard to truth. How could it happen else that the remarker should so egregiously contradict himself, and destroy in his fortieth page the whole drift of his thirty-ninth? This bold and rash scribbler takes upon him to marshal and to characterise insolently the friends of the man he rails at. If I was not of that number myself, I should probably say more on the subject. This however I am under an obligation to say; that the friends of this gentleman must be such to his person. They cannot be so to his power. That he takes it as the greatest compliment, which can be made to him, to have a sympathy of nature and a conformity of principles and designs with them attributed to him; that he thinks their friendship an honor to him; such an honor as the warmest of his enemies have cause to envy, and do envy; such an honor as the highest of his enemies would be heartily proud to obtain, and have not been able to obtain.

The friends now of this gentleman, whom he is sometimes said to lead, and who are sometimes said to employ him as their tool, just as it suits the present purpose of scandal to say; these very friends, it seems, the very men, who defend him, " would never raise him above his present low condition, nor make him the partner of their success." However they may employ him, the remarker and his patrons know how they mean to reward him. Since this is the case, since they know it to be so; for what reason, in the name of wonder, is all this bustle made about so insignificant a tool? Why so many endeavors to raise a jealousy, and give an alarm, as if this man was aiming again at power? Why so much merit ascribed to the noble pair, for keeping him out of it? His own friends would not raise him to it. How ridiculous then is the affectation of his enemies, who value themselves on their opposition to him?

Let the noble pair stand or fall by their own merits, or demerits. I dare answer to them and to the world, upon better foundations than those of the remarker's laying, that their continuance in power will never break the spirit of this man, nor their fall from it excite his ambition. His ambition, whatever may have been said or thought about it, hath been long since dead. A man must be dead himself, who is utterly insensible of all that happens, either to the public or to himself; but he who seeks nothing but retreat, and that stability of situation, which is essential to the quiet of it, hath surely no ambition. Now that this is the case, and hath been long the case of the gentleman, concern-

ing whom I speak, I know to be true, and I affirm boldly. He
never had the least, I say more, he never would have the greatest
obligations to any country, except his own; and yet so desirous
was this man of rest and quiet, that he was contented to enjoy
them where fortune had presented them to him. A little frankness might have kept him abroad all his life, without complaint.
Much art has been employed to confine him at home, and to
teaze him there. If, forgetting all former persecutions, he resented the last, would he be much to blame?

I am not conscious of having said, in this paper, a word against
the truth; and I am sure that I have the same truth on my side,
when I assert that this man, whom the libeller represents to be
so turbulent, so outrageous, and of such pertinacious ambition,
however he might have been willing formerly to have had the
obligation to the noble pair, of enjoying, by their assistance, the
full measure of his late majesty's intended goodness, would decline with scorn, after all that has passed, to be reinstated in his
former situation, at the intolerable expense of having the least
appearance of an obligation to them. Neither they, nor their
advocates, can be half so solicitous to keep him out of power,
and even out of a state of aspiring after power, as he is determined against the first, and indifferent about the last.

I am sensible that all this may appear a little improbable to
the persons I oppose. It will be hard for them to conceive that
the man, who has once tasted power, can ever renounce it in
earnest. No wonder they should think in this manner. Those
who find nothing in themselves to rest upon with satisfaction,
must lean on power, on riches, or both, and on other external
objects. Nay, those who have of the two vices, ambition and
avarice, the meanest in the most eminent degree; and who would
be glad to quit their power, and to retire with their gains, may
be afraid to quit it, because they have abused it. They may be
so miserable as to see no security out of power, nor any other in
it, except that precarious, that temporary security, which is the
last and useful refuge of desperate men; the continuing the same
violences to maintain, by which they acquired, their power; the
keeping up of dissensions, and the embroiling of affairs; those
noble arts, by which they rose.

But there are men in the world, who know that there is something in life better than power, and riches; and such men may
prefer the low condition, as it is called by the remarker, of one
man to the high condition of another. There are men who see
that dignity may be disgraced, and who feel that disgrace may
be dignified. Of this number is the gentleman whom I have
undertaken to defend; who possesses his soul without hopes or
fears, and enjoys his retreat without any desires beyond it. In

that retreat he is obedient to the laws, dutiful to his prince, and true to his oaths. If he fails in these respects, let him be publicly attacked; let public vengeance pursue and overtake him; let the noble pair indulge for once their passions in a just cause. If they have no complaints, of this nature, to make against him, from whence does this particular animosity proceed? Have they complaints of any other kind to make, and of a private nature? If they have, why is the public troubled on this account? I hope the remarker's mask is now taken off; that the true drift of all this personal railing is enough exposed; and that the attention of mankind will be brought back to those more important subjects, which have been already started, and to those which every day may furnish.

After what has been here said, the gentleman, in whose defence I have appeared, can have no reason of honor to enter by himself, or his friends, into these altercations; and if my opinion can prevail, should these libellers continue to scold, and to call names, they should be left to do it, without reproof or notice. The answer now given should stand as a "Final answer to all they have said and to all they may think fit to say hereafter."

ON LUXURY.

A DISCOURSE on Operas, and the gayer pleasures of the town, may seem to be too trifling for the important scene of affairs, in which we are at present engaged; but I must own my fears, that they will bear too great a part in the success of a war, to make the consideration of them foreign to it. A very little reflection on history will suggest this observation, that every nation has made either a great or inconsiderable figure in the world, as it has fallen into luxury or resisted its temptations. What people are more distinguished than the Persians under Cyrus, nursed up in virtue, and inured to labor and toil? Yet (in the short space of 220 years*) they became so contemptible under Darius, as scarce to give honor to the conqueror's sword. The Spartans, and the long-rulers of the world, the Romans, speak the same language; and I wish future history may not furnish more modern examples.

When the mind is enervated by luxury, the body soon falls an easy victim to it; for how is it possible to imagine, that a man can be capable of the great and generous sentiments, which virtue inspires, whose mind is filled with the soft ideas, and wanton delicacies that pleasure must infuse? And were it possible to be warmed with such notions, could it ever put them in execution? For toils and fatigues would be difficulties unsurmountable to a soul dissolved in ease. Nor are these imaginary, speculative ideas of a closet; but such as have been the guide and policies of the wisest states. Of this we have the most remarkable instance in Herodotus. "The Persians, after their great and extended conquests, desired Cyrus to give them leave to remove out of their own barren and mountainous country into one more blest by the indulgence of Providence. But that great and wise prince, revolving the effect in his mind, bid them do as they would; telling them at the same time, that for the future they must not expect to command, but obey; for Providence had so

* Liv. lib. 9, cap. 19.

ordered it, that an effeminate race of people were the certain produce of a delicious country." What regard the great historian had to this opinion, may be easily collected from his reserving it for the conclusion of this excellent piece. And the case is directly the same, whether pleasures are the natural product of a country, or adventitious exotics. They will have the same effect, and cause the same extended ruin. How often have they revenged the captive's cause and made the conqueror's sword the instrument of his own undoing? Capua destroyed the bravest army which Italy ever saw, flushed with conquest, and commanded by Hannibal. The moment Capua was taken, that moment the walls of Carthage trembled. What was it that destroyed the republic of Athens, but the conduct of Pericles;* who by his pernicious politics first debauched the people's minds with shows and festivals, and all the studied arts of ease and luxury; that he might, in the mean time, securely guide the reins of empire, and riot in dominion? He first laid the foundation of Philip's power; nor had a man of Macedon ever thought of enslaving Greece, if Pericles had not first made them slaves to pleasure. That great statesman Tiberius† clearly saw what was the surest instrument of arbitrary power; and therefore refused to have luxury redressed, when application was made to him in the senate for that purpose. Artful princes have frequently introduced it with that very view. Davila tells us, that in an interview and semblance of treaty with the king of Navar, Catharine of Medicis broke the prince's power more with the insidious gaieties of her court, than many battles before had done. But there is a single passage in Herodotus,‡ which will supply the place of more quotations. "When Cyrus had received an account that the Lydians had revolted from him, he told Crœsus, with a good deal of emotion, that he had almost determined to make them all slaves. Crœsus begged him to pardon them; but, says he, that they may no more rebel, or be troublesome to you, command them to lay aside their arms, to wear long vests and buskins. Order them to sing and play on the harp; to drink and debauch; and you will soon see their spirits broken, and themselves changed from men into women; so that they will no more rebel, or be uneasy to you for the future." And the event answered the advice. They are puny politicians, who attack a people's liberty directly. The means are dangerous, and the success precarious. Notions of liberty are interwoven with our very being; and the least suspicion of its being in danger fires the soul with a generous indignation. But he is the statesman formed for ruin and

* Plut. in Peric., and Demost. Orat.   † Tac. An. lib. 2, cap. 33.
‡ Herod. lib. 1, cap. 155.

destruction, whose wily head knows how to disguise the fatal hook with baits of pleasure, which his artful ambition dispenses with a lavish hand, and makes himself popular in undoing. Thus are the easy, thoughtless crowd made the instruments of their own slavery; nor do they know the fatal mine is laid till they feel the goodly pile come tumbling on their heads. This is the finished politician:·the darling son of Tacitus and Machiavel.

But, thanks to Providence, the sacred monuments of history extend the short contracted span of human life, and give us years in books. These point out the glorious landmarks for our safety; and bid us be wise in time, before luxury has made too great a progress among us. Operas and masquerades, with all the politer elegances of a wanton age, are much less to be regarded for their expense (great as it is) than for the tendency which they have to deprave our manners. Music has something so peculiar in it, that it exerts a willing tyranny over the mind; and forms the ductile soul into whatever shape the melody directs. Wise nations have observed its influence, and have therefore kept it under proper regulations. The Spartans,* vigilantly provident for the people's safety, took from the famed Timotheus's harp the additional strings, as giving his music a degree of softness inconsistent with their discipline. The divine Plato is expressly of opinion, that the music of a country cannot be changed, and the public laws remain unaffected. Heroes will be heroes, even in their music. Soft and wanton are the warbled songs of Paris;† but Achilles‡ sings the godlike deeds of heroes. A noble, manly music will place virtue in its most beautiful light, and be the most engaging incentive to it. A well wrought story, attended with its prevailing charms, will transport the soul out of itself; fire it with glorious emulation; and lift the man into a hero; but the soft Italian music relaxes and unnerves the soul, and sinks it into weakness; so that while we receive their music, we at the same time are adopting their manners. The effects of it will appear in the strongest light from the fate of the people of Sybaris; a town in Italy, strong and wealthy; blessed with all the goods of fortune, and skilled in all the arts of luxury and ease; which they carried to so great an excess, that their very horses were taught to move and form themselves as the music directed. Their constant enemies, the people of Crotona, observing this, brought a great number of harps and

---

* Cicero, lib. 2, de leg. cap. 39.
† Hor. lib. 1. Od. 15.
———————Grataque fœminis
Imbelli cithara, carmina divides.
‡ Hom. Iliad. 9, 189.

pipes into the field, and when the battle began, the music played; upon which these well-bred horses immediately began to dance; which so disconcerted the whole army, that 300,000 were killed, and the whole people destroyed. Though this story seems a little fabulous, yet it contains at least a very good moral.— What effect Italian music might have on our polite warriors at Gibraltar, I cannot take upon me to say; but I wish our luxury at home may not influence our courage abroad.

REMARKS

ON A LATE PAMPHLET,

ENTITLED, OBSERVATIONS ON THE CONDUCT OF GREAT BRITAIN, &c.

IN A LETTER TO CALEB D'ANVERS, ESQ.

Written in the year 1729.

THE late pamphlet, entitled, " Observations on the Conduct of Great Britain, &c.," being chiefly designed as an answer to my first letter on the pretended project of a truce, it may be thought incumbent on me to justify what I have written; for though this piece (which consists of nothing but inconsistencies, contradictions, prevarications, and downright falsehoods), is already sunk into that contempt which it deserves; yet when a private person launches into politics, it is his duty to pay some regard to an adversary, who produces the least marks of authority, however mean and despicable his performance may be thought.

The shortness of time will, I hope, excuse any little inaccuracies of style, or trivial mistakes, that I may happen to fall into through the course of these remarks, which every body will perceive required haste.

I shall pass over all his little sophistry on the freedom of writing, as well as his dirty imputations of libelling, disaffection, and ill designs against the government, (those trite, worn-out topics of every wretched scribbler against you for above these two years past,) and come directly to the points, upon which the whole stress of his arguments, such as they are, depends.

The first objection which he undertakes to confute, is the supposed inactivity of our squadrons, and the depredations committed by the Spaniards, upon our merchants in the West Indies.

In order to do this, he hath given us, what he calls, the instructions to Admiral Hosier, and the other commanders of our squadrons in those parts.

I shall not inquire from whom he received these lights; though it seems very extraordinary that a little, obscure pamphleteer should be favored with papers of such a private nature, as have been sometimes refused, even upon applications in parliament.

Neither will I offer to dispute whether these instructions are genuine and authentic; though there are several things in them which have a suspicious aspect. By the first orders, given to Admiral Hosier, it looks as if those who sent him did not understand the service they sent him upon; for they direct him to block up the flota and galleons in the port of Carthagena; which is indeed a proper port to look for the galleons in; but the flota was never there since the Spaniards traded to that country. By the second instructions, they seem to be sensible of their mistake, by giving him distinct orders to take care of the flota, which makes it probable that, at first, they took the flota and galleons to be the same fleet, and did not know that one came from Peru, and the other from Mexico.

Neither can I find out the reason for preferring the galleons, in these instructions, to the flota; for if keeping the Spanish treasure from going home was the intent of that expedition, the flota was as material an attention as the galleons, having as much money aboard them; and both might have been intercepted, had our fleet been rightly stationed at first, viz. in the bay of Matanzas, in the island of Cuba, where they might have stayed much more conveniently than at the Bastimentos.

Indeed, stopping the flota is made the next point to stopping the galleons; but considering the port from whence it comes, and the course it steers, it was almost impossible that a squadron, lying at the Bastimentos, should intercept them, or gain any intelligence of them.

In another part of these orders, Admiral Hosier is instructed to persuade the Spaniards to let him take them; which I confess looks, at first sight, somewhat romantic and ridiculous.

These particulars, I say, might render the whole liable to suspicion; but though I could not help taking some notice of them, I would not be thought to infer from hence the impossibility of their being authentic, for though I have a very bad opinion of the pamphleteer, I cannot think that he would dare to impose upon the world in a matter of such consequence; but since it was thought necessary to give the public some satisfaction in this affair, I could wish he had favored us with all these instructions

at length and entire, (for this does not appear to be the case,) that
we might have been able to form a true judgment, upon a view
of the whole, which cannot be so well done by scraps and
extracts.

However, it appears from these orders themselves (as he hath
thought fit to publish them) that stopping the galleons was to be
their chief care; and that they were not to risk the success of it
upon any account.   I will, therefore, leave it to the judgment of
mankind, whether any prudent officer, under such a strict and
particular injunction, would run the least hazard of failing in that
main point, by endeavoring to protect our merchants.   It is certain, at least, that the Spaniards did, and do still continue their
outrages with very little molestation, and without any considerable reprisals made on our parts.   Nay, the commanders of our
squadrons were so far from giving any assistance to our merchants of those seas, that it is well known the exigencies of the
public service obliged them to make such an impress on their
ships (to supply the great loss and destruction of the men, on
board our squadrons) as rendered them unable to perform their
voyages.

His reasoning, therefore, on this head, is reduced to one of
these points; either first, that the naval force sent to those parts
was not sufficient to perform such different services; or secondly,
that our admiral and commanders did apprehend themselves to
be confined or embarrassed by some cautions and limitations; or
thirdly, that they either neglected, or did not understand their
duty; which would be such a reflection upon the skill, courage
and integrity of those excellent officers, as will not easily pass
upon the world.

The pamphleteer hath produced part of one letter from Admiral Hosier; in which he gives an account, contrary to the
general opinion here till this time, that the Spaniards had dis-
embarked their treasure, and sent it back to Panama, before he
arrived at the Bastimentos; upon which this writer observes, that
he could not have taken any thing but empty hulks; and then
seems to think himself very smart in asking, whether such a
pledge would have had much influence on the counsels of Spain?
To which I reply, first, that this is nothing to the purpose,
because it is plain, that the admiral had no power to seize the
galleons, in case they had not been unloaded; so that his arrival
could have no other effect than that of their own advice-boat, to
make them secure their treasure.   Secondly, I do not think it
would have been such bad policy to have taken even the empty
hulks, or burnt them in the port, (so that the Spaniards could
have made no farther use of them,) and to have sailed immediately to Vera Cruz and seized the flota, instead of lying so long

to watch empty hulks, till our own ships became rotten, and almost empty hulks themselves.

I could wish, for the farther information and satisfaction of the public, that the pamphleteer had found it convenient to give us the sight of Admiral Hosier's letters; for no doubt he must have sent several, during his long and disastrous continuance on that station; from whence perhaps we might have had some farther light into this affair, or collected at least what his opinion was of the nature of his instructions, and the conduct of that expedition. However, it is well known in what manner he expressed himself upon several occasions, both at Jamaica, and in letters to his friends in England.

I am ready to subscribe, with the greatest pleasure and sincerity, to all the encomiums which this writer makes on Sir Charles Wager; whom I know to be a gentleman of the most amiable character, both in public and private life. I am confident that no difficulties or dangers could deter him from doing his duty; that no temptations could prevail upon him to betray his trust; and that he did not want the greatest skill and abilities to execute it. I have the same good opinion of Sir John Jennings, and other commanders, who were sent upon those services; and when the pamphleteer was in his panegyrical strain, I could wish that he had done justice to their characters; and likewise paid some small tribute of gratitude to the memory of those brave officers, who had the misfortune to perish (I was going to say, were sacrificed) in the service of their country.— But they are dead, and have it not now in their power to justify themselves, or to accuse others.

But to return.—I do not find by the orders given to Sir Charles Wager, the 22d of December, 1726, that he was empowered to intercept any ships, with stores, ammunition, or provisions bound for the Spanish camp, then in sight of Gibraltar, in order to besiege it; nor instructed, even by the soft endeavors of persuasion, or otherwise to get them or their cargoes into his possession, to disable them from beginning hostilities; notwithstanding the same orders directed him to reinforce the garrison of Gibraltar, which was then going to be besieged, by sending the land forces then on board Admiral Hopson's squadron, and, in case of need, to give all the relief and assistance he was able to the said garrison; though I have been credibly informed the Spaniards were permitted to pass by our squadron, even under the stern of the admiral, and safely landed stores, provisions, ammunition, and other necessaries for the siege of that place.

If this be true, as I am assured it is, I should be glad to know for what reason his instructions ran in that soft strain; or why so much complaisance was shown to the Spaniards, upon the occasion of such an undisguised design against that important fortress. I am the more desirous to know this, because I am sure it could not proceed from any want of vigilance or zeal in that brave and excellent officer, who is a man of too established a character to suffer in any body's opinion, by the oblique and ungenerous insinuation of this writer, after all his compliments, that he was not attended with his former good fortune.

The pamphleteer having thus refuted the objections against the supposed inactivity of our squadrons, by producing some parts of the instructions to the commanders of them; and shown, as he tells us, that the losses of our merchants have not been owing to any want of that care, which the government ought always to take for the protection of our trade; he proceeds in the next place, to give us some account of those captures, which he says are not near so considerable as they have been represented; and having prefaced this part likewise with a great many angry reflections, he produces a list of twenty-six ships, which he would have us believe to be all, that we have really lost.—His address in cooking up this account is very remarkable.

1. We are told this is an exact list of all such ships as have been taken by the Spaniards in the West Indies, since the conclusion of the treaty of Hanover.   But why should he confine it thus to place and time?   I mentioned indeed, only three years past, by reason of the frequency of the captures during that time; but if I had undertaken to give the public an account of all our losses, I should certainly have begun my account a great deal farther back; much less should I have limited it to the West Indies; since I presume that ships taken in the ocean and other seas, are as much losses to our merchants as those taken in America, and that they have the same right to expect reparation for them.

2. This is a list of such captures only, as have been, at any time, conveyed to the knowledge of the government, either by the immediate complaints of the merchants concerned in those captures; their representations to the commissioners for trade and plantations; or the account transmitted by his majesty's ministers and consuls abroad, which is what I suppose he means by the most authentic testimonies.   But is it to be inferred from hence, as he seems to do, that no more losses have been sustained than what have been thus formally complained of?   I grant, indeed, that no merchant can expect reparation, who does not give in the particulars of his losses; but it is well known that many of these sufferers did not do this; which might proceed from different causes.   Several merchants, who reside in our plantations and settlements abroad, might not have opportunity to transmit the

particulars of their losses, and authorise their agents to make a
regular complaint; for, if I am not misinformed, some complaints
were actually brought in, after the account was closed, and therefore not inserted in it.   Others might neglect to do it, by despairing of success; and thinking, perhaps, that the prospect of reparation would not answer the trouble of complaining.

The public, I believe, will soon seee a true account of our
losses, by the depredations of the Spaniards, both in the West
Indies and in other seas, from a proper period of time; which will
more fully show the fallacy of this partial list, which ought to be
resented with the utmost indignation, as an insult on the misfortunes and calamities of the British merchants.

I am told that the pamphleteer had a design to oblige us likewise, in this piece, with a counter-list of those ships, which we
have taken from the Spaniards, during the late disturbances; and
that this was actually printed, but afterwards cancelled and suppressed.   I am sorry to hear that any motives could induce so
impartial a writer to rob us of this catalogue, which was not only
very proper, but would no doubt give great satisfaction to the
public.

The only objection, says the pamphleteer, that remains to be
answered upon this point of the Spanish depredations, is with
regard to letters of marque and reprisal; by which the traders
might have been authorised to make themselves reparation.   He
acknowledges that the merchants, in the situation we were then
in with regard to Spain, had a right, both by our own law and
that of nations, to demand such letters.   He then proceeds to
justify the ministry, (which I hope wants no justification,) by
showing that such letters were not refused.   Those are his
words.   But how does he show it?   Why, he gives us two
instances of owners of ships, who did apply for them, upon an
order published in the Gazette, and were actually refused; and
does not produce one instance of any man whatsoever, to whom
they were granted.

He tells us, indeed, by way of apology for this refusal, that the
preliminary treaty having been for some time negotiating at
Paris, his late majesty thought proper to defer issuing these commissions, till he should see the success of that negotiation.   He
adds, that the preliminary articles were signed at Paris, the 20th
of May, and that draughts of instructions to the lords of the
admiralty for granting letters of marque, were signed by his late
majesty, after the 21st of April.   As, therefore, the preliminary
treaty had been some time negotiating at Paris, the question is
whether it was not actually negotiating at the time, when this
order was published in the Gazette; and if it was, why was the
order published at all; since it could only tend to putting the

merchants upon equipping ships for this service (as I am told several did at Bristol) to no purpose, and at a great expense.

This therefore is such a justification of the ministry, as I am sure you Mr. D'Anvers, would be afraid to publish.

He proceeds, in the last place, to expose the clamor that hath been raised against the negotiations at Soissons, and the project of accommodation, which hath caused so much disquiet.

I confess it gives me some pleasure to find that I was right in my conjecture, that if any such project was really in agitation, it would not bear the name of a truce; for lo! it is not called a truce; it is a provisional treaty; though, for my part, I am not able to discover any difference between them, unless it be in the sound; for a provisional treaty does not seem to imply, any more than a truce, a final determination of all the differences, which is so much wanted, but only a suspension of them for a time.

The preliminary treaty was, properly speaking, a provisional treaty, as it was to provide for something farther at the congress; but that the negotiations at this assembly should end in a provisional treaty only, is not what we had reason to expect from the assurances so often given us.

I cannot forbear observing in this place, the various denominations under which this treaty hath passed. At first, we were promised a full, formal, and established peace; but soon after the conclusion of the last session, it was called, in the foreign prints, a pacification; and after that an idea of a pacification; then it was a truce, and bore that name in all papers, foreign and domestic, for several months together; at last, according to this writer, it is neither a peace, nor a pacification, nor an idea of a pacification, nor a truce, but a provisional treaty.

Well! if a peace could not be obtained, and a truce would not go down; e'en let it be a provisional treaty; or what else they please. I scorn to insist upon names with these gentlemen, but will examine the treaty itself, as it is given us by the pamphleteer.

It is somewhat strange that a writer, who takes upon himself such an air of authority, should condescend to borrow his materials from the Post-Boy; and more strange, that he should charge me with affecting to call this treaty a truce; when he cannot be ignorant that the Post-Boy, from which he quotes the articles, as well as the Dutch prints, from whence the Post-Boy translated them, and all papers, for at least two months before I wrote my first letter, called it constantly by that name.

When I first undertook this examination of the pretended project of a truce, I treated it as chimerical, or the invention of ill designing men, and argued from the defects of the articles, that I could not believe them to be genuine. What therefore could induce this writer to affirm, that we have not so much as pretended to show that this project is deficient, in not providing for all those points, that have been the subject of the late disputes between Great Britain and foreign powers; when the whole tenor of that letter was to prove the defects of it, by a very circumstantial induction of particulars?——But in this he not only advances a falsehood, but contradicts himself, as such writers are apt to do; for in the very page before this assertion, that we have not so much as pretended to show that this project is deficient, he tells us, that he shall make some observations on the objections, which these writers have made to it.

Neither can it surely be forgot, that the author of the British Journal represented this project, and these very articles, in the same manner, as chimerical, and charged me with trumping them up, in order to asperse the ministers with odious designs. He called them besides unintelligible projects, dark things, and ill meant reports, which bear no sign of credibility, and do not deserve the name of intelligence; so that when these articles had been given up, in this manner, by a writer (who, I was informed, had access to a person in authority,) it would have been ridiculous to enter into a farther detail of the defects of them.—But now (according to the usual inconsistency of these men, and their desultory method of reasoning) we are to unbelieve everything which we were taught to believe about six weeks ago. These unintelligible projects, which it was faction at that time even to mention, are now acknowledged to be really genuine; the whole success of our negotiations is put upon them; and they are made the basis of our future settlement.—Some farther observations, therefore, are now become seasonable and requisite.

He tells us that by this treaty we obtain the plainest and most direct acknowledgment and confirmation of our right to all our possessions, and to all our privileges in trade; even those which had been disputed, in opposition to preceding treaties. But in what manner is this acknowledgment and confirmation obtained? The pamphleteer proves it thus. By the second article, the treaties of Utrecht, Rastad, and Baden, the treaty of the Hague in 1717, together with the quadruple alliance, and all the treaties and conventions, antecedent to 1725, the preliminary articles, and the convention signed at the Pardo, are made the basis and foundation of the present treaty; and being expressly confirmed by it, without any restriction of time, whatever hath been stipulated in our favor, in any of those treaties and conventions, receives a new and perpetual sanction by this.—Upon which I observe,

1. That I cannot comprehend how a temporary treaty, which

I take a provisional treaty to be, can give a perpetual sanction to any thing.

2. Can a treaty be properly called perpetual, (though not expressly limited to any time,) or be said to give a perpetual sanction, which does not finally adjust one point in dispute, but leaves them to the determination of commissioners, and consequently subject to future debates?

3. Supposing this treaty leaves us upon the foot of former treaties; is it not well known that the sense of some of those treaties hath been disputed; and may they not be disputed again, and occasion the same disturbances?

I will instance only in the case of Gibraltar. As the second article of this treaty is to the very same effect as the second article of the preliminary treaty, (both of which relate to our possessions in general; for Gibraltar is not particularly mentioned in either,) I cannot see how we are better secured against the pretensions of Spain to this place, than we were by the preliminary articles; and is it not notorious that the Spaniards have insisted, and yet do insist, that their pretensions, founded upon a promise under the hand of his late majesty, in the year 1721, are confirmed by the said preliminaries? As they insist therefore to have this pretended promise cleared and adjusted in the Congress in their favor; so, as we maintain, on the other hand, that these pretensions to Gibraltar, however founded, are given up by this second article, it is equally incumbent upon us to insist that the preliminaries should be so explained in our favor, as to exclude all doubts and questions upon them for the future; for as this is the most important point with relation to Great Britain, it is reasonable that it should be secured to us, in this treaty, by a particular article to explain it; as some other things of less consequence have been, which seem to require no explanation, and are as fully and clearly provided for, in the second article of this treaty.

It must be farther observed, says the pamphleteer, that by this article, and by the third and fifth, we are effectually secured from all the dangerous engagements, contained in the public and private treaties of Vienna.—Those dangerous engagements were, as he tells us,

1. That the trading subjects of the emperor should be treated in the dominions of Spain more favorably than those of Great Britain. But this appears to be false from the treaty itself, which mentions only that they should be treated as the most favored nations, which other treaties provide for us, who are to be always looked upon as *gens amicissima;* and consequently whatever privileges the emperor, or any other prince, may obtain for their subjects, from his catholic majesty, must be conceded to us, at

the same time, by virtue of those former treaties. But how are we now secured from the dangerous engagements of the Vienna treaty, unless by a declaration of his catholic majesty, that he never understood to grant, by the said treaty of Vienna, any privilege contrary to the treaties confirmed with us, nor to give to the subjects of his imperial majesty any greater advantages than those enjoyed by any other nations?   This is no more than what both the courts of Vienna and Madrid have from the beginning declared.   Yet as this hath been a labored point, and strenuously asserted by us, as well in Parliament as elsewhere, and made the basis of the Hanover treaty, as of the utmost importance to this kingdom; a declaration only in this case, can be of no more force and virtue than it hath hitherto been, whilst the Vienna treaty subsists in every part, as much as it did the first day it was made.

2. That the emperor, in case his good offices were ineffectual, would assist his catholic majesty to recover Gibraltar by force.— This likewise does not appear by the treaty; nor did his imperial majesty, as far as I ever heard, give the Spaniards the least assistance, when they actually besieged that fortress.

3. That Spain would by arms assist the emperor in carrying on the Ostend trade, which is to be suspended by this treaty.   It must be owned indeed, that the Dutch are extremely happy, if this provision content them, in having such advocates, or rather champions, to support their quarrels; whilst our fleets and armies, at the expense of our treasure, and the lives of so many brave men, have procured them these concessions, and they remain unactive in all parts, reaping the benefit of our quarrels, and driving on the trade of the whole world; and are at the same time courted, to say no more, to espouse their own interest.

And here it must be repeated, that though it has been disputed whether the Ostend charter is an infraction of former treaties; yet since it is made a point, and insisted upon to be prejudicial to our commerce, and we are bound by treaties to support the Dutch in these pretensions; it might seem perhaps absolutely necessary to have this affair finally adjusted, so as never to break out again; or at least to be revived in any short time; by which Europe may be engaged in the like quarrel; in which England must bear the greatest part, if she is not made the only principal; and therefore it is not so absurd to expect that the emperor should put an end to this dispute by revoking his charter.

But it is pretty extraordinary that, considering the great interest we have in this affair, (as it is affirmed,) and the point we have made of it, there should be no notice taken of us in the article, which provides for its suspension, nor so much as a compliment made to us for our generous interposition.

4. And lastly, (pray observe him!) our apprehensions were, that there might be engagements in favor of the Pretender.— Alas! how do the observations fall short of that spirit, which appeared in the Inquiry? There we see the author rousing up the nation to a just resentment of those dangerous engagements in favor of the Pretender. We see him affirming, with the greatest confidence, that soon after the publication of the Vienna treaties of peace and commerce, they had positive intelligence, and intelligence from more than one person, and such as could be entirely depended on, that one express article of this alliance between the emperor and Spain contained an obligation in favor of the Pretender. We have not his authority for it only; but the assurance of a certain gentleman in parliament that he knew, and was absolutely convinced of the truth of this. We had the addresses of the whole kingdom justly inflamed on this occasion. We had his excellency Mr. Issac Leheup's vigorous remonstrances at the diet of Ratisbon, in the very teeth of the emperor, concurring in, and affirming the same charge. Nay, we had still much greater authority, even authority from the throne; for did not his late majesty declare that he had certain and undoubted intelligence that it was resolved to attempt an invasion of these kingdoms, in consequence of a secret article to this purpose?* And, was not the imperial minister ordered to depart the kingdom, in a very abrupt manner, for denying any such engagement or design in his master's name? And after all these repeated assurances, after all these extraordinary steps, are we fallen so low as to acknowledge that we had apprehensions only that there might be such engagements?—If this scribbler takes upon him to advance facts of less consequence, he may depart from them (as he generally does when expedients are wanting) without hurting anybody; but in affairs of this high nature he ought not to meddle, let who will be his instructor, without good grounds and sufficient authority.

For my part, I was always willing to believe (for the honor of his late majesty and the British nation, as well as out of regard to those who drew, or advised, or approved that speech) that he had something more than bare apprehensions to justify us in such declarations and extraordinary proceedings; for the honor of the crown is a thing of a very sacred nature, and ought not to be trifled with on any occasion, or made an instrument to serve ministerial purposes.

King James the First observes very justly (in a speech to his parliament, in the first year of his reign; which is, perhaps, the best he ever made,) that speeches from the throne should be plain

---

* Vide his speech at the opening of the session in 1727.

and sincere. By sincerity, says he, I mean that uprightness and honesty which ought to be in a king's whole speeches and actions; that as far as a king is, in honor, above his subjects, so far should he strive, in sincerity, to be above them all; and that his tongue should be the true messenger of his heart.

Yet this king, at the latter end of his reign, was drawn in by Buckingham to make a false representation of the Spanish affair to his parliament; which had its effect so far as to make Buckingham a little popular for the present, at his majesty's expense; but as soon as the people found themselves imposed upon, they gave no credit to the assertions and assurances of this lying minister any more.

Nay, we have a much later and more remarkable instance of the effect of any supposed endeavors to prostitute the honor of the crown; for it cannot be forgot that a certain gentleman thought fit to make it an article of impeachment against the late Earl of Oxford, that he had corrupted the sacred fountain of truth, and put falsehoods into the mouth of majesty, in order to obtain the sanction of parliament to his traitorous proceedings.

I hope this digression, upon so important a point, will not be thought unseasonable. But I now return to the provisional treaty.

If it is really true, that the emperor and the king of Spain did enter into all, or any of these dangerous engagements, I could wish to see them formally renounced and annihilated; for I still think that a solemn cassation of the treaties of Vienna would secure these our most important interests more effectually than is done by the before-mentioned articles, that leave them upon the precarious foot of former treaties, which we have already found ineffectual to these ends.

For, when different interpretations have been put upon the same treaties by different powers; when objections have been started on both sides; when contrary claims and pretensions have been made, and embroiled Europe for several years; what other effectual method can be used to secure us against the like disputes and disturbances for the future, than finally to adjust the sense of such treaties, and confirm the respective rights, privileges and possessions of the powers concerned in the plainest, most direct, and explicit manner?

And if the powers, with whom we are concerned, do really understand these articles in the same sense which the pamphleteer hath put upon them, why should they refuse to make us easy by a particular explanation? Or, if they do actually refuse this, is there any room to doubt that they have some reasons for preferring dark and ambiguous terms?

But it may be objected, says the pamphleteer, that I have

misspent my time and labor, in endeavoring to silence the clamors which have been raised against that particular form of peace, which hath been the object of our late negotiations, since it does not appear that the king of Spain is disposed to accept even of these terms. Why truly that is a very material objection, and may arise perhaps from a determined resolution of his catholic majesty not to come to any terms with us, after what hath passed without obtaining his favorite ends.

He tells us indeed but two lines before, in his usual self-contradicting style, that none of the powers concerned have hitherto given just cause to conclude that they will reject it. Now, methinks, where there is an apparent disposition not to accept it, there is some cause to conclude that they will reject it; but whatever reasons there may be against it abroad, I am sure there are many at home.

It is, at best, by his own confession, only a plan or project, which is not yet accepted. But let us suppose it accepted, for argument sake. Nay let us go farther, and for argument sake likewise, suppose it to be a good one; the question will still return, whether we have taken the shortest, the least dangerous, or the least expensive methods to accomplish it. But to glory in measures, which have not succeeded, whether commendable or not, and have only a bare probability of success, is certainly very extraordinary.

Lastly, let us examine this affair with respect to the time we have been about it. The pamphleteer indeed says, and seems to triumph upon it, that this progress towards the establishment of a general peace hath been made in a few months, after the opening of the congress. But how much time, as well as money, did we spend in expeditions, embassies, negotiations, preliminaries, and ratifications, before the congress was opened? Nay, though we date the present disturbances but three years back, it is certain that we have not been in a state of perfect amity, and free commerce with Spain for above these seven years past; but by the great sagacity and penetration of certain gentlemen, (to say nothing of secret service-money,) we have at last, according to this writer, some hopes of being, one time or another, in almost as good a condtion as we were in, before our affairs were thus embroiled.

This puts me in mind of Sir Epicure Mammon, in the Alchymist; who, when he had spent his whole estate in search of the philosopher's stone, was comforted after all his cost, though disappointed of his main end, with the hopes of getting a little something to cure the itch.

He tells us, at the conclusion, that this nation never acted a part more suitable to its dignity and character; and that to the firmness and fidelity of our allies, and to these measures we owe our present tranquillity. I shall say nothing of that glorious part, which we have been lately acting; nor of the firmness and fidelity of our allies. I neither know what they engaged to do, nor what they have actually done for us. But to boast of the present tranquillity, when we are at best only in a state of political purgatory, between peace and war; when our ships are every week taken, as in time of war; when we are at all the expenses, and under almost all the inconveniences of a war; to talk and boast of tranquillity, I say, at such a time, must either be an egregious banter on the ministry, or an insult on the nation; and let the pamphleteer take his choice.

I have but one thing more to mention, before I conclude; which is, that the author of this wretched pamphlet hath the insolence to make the regal character subservient to his designs. Whatever measures, or whatever conduct he finds it necessary to approve, are the king's measures, and the king's conduct. This is a mean artifice, which hath been constantly practised of late by these men, when other arguments are wanting. But I hope it will not put a stop to your inquiries; for every Englishman hath a right, by our laws, to judge and debate these affairs; and I am sure his majesty will abhor the thoughts of abridging this liberty, though weak and wicked men endeavor to screen themselves under the protection of his sacred name.

I am, sir, &c.

ON GOOD AND BAD MINISTERS.

WHILST a wicked and corrupt minister is weighing out pane-gyrics and dedications against just satires and invectives; or, perhaps, is numbering his creatures, and teaching them their implicit monosyllables; whilst he is drawing out his screen, and providing for a safe and decent elopement; or, it may be, comforts himself with the hopes that the public joy, at his removal, will drown all future inquiries; or that he shall keep sweet a good while longer, till the worm seizes his carcass, and posterity preys upon his memory; it may not be improper to turn your thoughts upon the reverse of his character, and to inquire by what marks a good minister may be found out and distinguished; or, since he is only a creature, by what arts, and in what method, he may be formed and brought into being. A people who are running the hazard of a death-bed repentance, want nothing so much as a good minister; and a bad one dreads nothing more than an honest successor, who comes after him without treading in his steps; takes his place without giving into his secrets; and will not be won by a share of his rapine to partake, at the same time, of his crimes and corruptions.

We know the mighty hand that is to form this creature, and that the breath of our nostrils is to give him being; but it is no presumption, no infringement of the right of election, to trace out a general character of many just and worthy candidates. It is no nomination, no designation to a particular office, to describe a good officer at large with all his qualifications and endowments. Neither the honest laborer, who discovers the mine, or digs out the ore; nor the skilful artificer, who purifies, refines, and weighs it, can in any sense be said to encroach upon the authority of those above him, who are appointed to make the last essay; to shape and mould it; and all these are friends to Cæsar, who finishes the work, and gives it his own image and superscription.

Let us then imagine a number of men, scattered up and down a great, wise, and discerning nation; in their descent noble and generous; full of the virtues of their ancestors; in their temper affable and sweet-natured; educated in the knowledge and study of our constitution, its laws, settlements, dependences, and interests; always faithful to the crown, when consistent with their duty to their country; fonder of the substance, than the outside of religion; easy in their fortunes; lovers of mankind; more careful to preserve, than to aggrandise a family; making virtue the foundation of their friendship, and merit the title to their favor; preservers of the freedom of others, as well as of their own; delighting rather to be thought good than great; pleased with any opportunity of making their fellow creatures happy; just in all their dealings; moderate in their pleasures; true to the several trusts, which have been reposed in them; watchful over the accounts of others, and ready to submit their own to a full and impartial inspection; not servile when out of power, nor imperious when in it; studying more the propriety of oratory, than its ornaments and garniture; and speaking rather to the good sense of others, than to their passions or interests; not solicitous for a place, because they want it, but because the place wants them; so keen in their resentments for the public, that they have no room for those which are personal; well acquainted with the most noted characters and transactions of late years; indifferent in their choice of public or private life, but careful to adorn both; and looking on the revenue of an office to be so far public money, as it is intended for the support and dignity of that office, to which it is appropriated.—Men of this character, stars of this lustre, are still stuck in good plenty up and down our hemisphere. The changes of the weather may sometimes hide, but cannot extinguish them. Their short-lived obscurity is indeed their advantage; for by this we know what it is to want them, and their influence. Their brightness is tried, and distinguished from meteors and false fires. The regularity of their courses is more observed; and their glory, when it breaks out again, becomes doubly recommended.

Imagine now a man, of this order and character, advanced to the ministry. Suppose him not well acquainted with the course and dependence of many of the offices and branches of trust under his direction; and for that very reason not over-forward to prescribe for abuses, or admit of corruptions upon the plea of custom; yet whilst it is natural for him to find out, or to place in these offices such men as most nearly resemble himself; he could never want good intelligence both at home and abroad; clear and faithful accounts. The eyes, hands, and feet, which he borrowed from others, would be so much like his own, that he could not fail to see clearly, act fairly, and walk uprightly. Such a minister would with pleasure meet a senate, chosen as himself was, by the same marks and qualifications. He would encourage such a choice as his best security; and when the *boni et legales viri de vicineto* are returned to parliament, as well as upon juries, the electors do alike consult their own honor and interest. A triennial, or septennial bribe, as ill-spent as it is ill-gotten, makes no amends for the loss of credit and reputation, which are the support of commerce; and it is as easy to prove, that the corruption of some boroughs is the cause of their poverty; as to prove that their poverty is the cause of their corruption. But to resume my former subject.—The marks I have pointed out, and the rules I have laid down, are of such use to the public in the choice of a good minister, that where only one of them (the character of common honesty) hath been attended to, and the rest have been barely guessed at, or left to wild chance; such a choice has very often been more beneficial to a country than a choice made upon the very brink, or even from the bottom of that horrible and dreadful gulf, commonly called profound policy.—I shall illustrate this truth by one remarkable instance, which I hope is too remote and far-fetched, to be hauled and wrenched into modern application. The Grand Seignior is said to walk abroad very often incognito, and to have his outlets and conveniences, both in the camp and seraglio, where he can oversee the assemblies of his domestics and officers, and be his own spy upon their actions and conversation. Listening one day to the grand minister of his kitchen, in a full assembly of his own culinary subalterns, closely debating the present juncture and posture of affairs, (when discontents ran high, and the general voice laid the whole blame upon the prime vizier,) he heard the grand master, then in the chair, sometimes threatening justice, and denouncing vengeance; brandishing his long knife at the close of every period, sometimes shaking his stew-pan with —Oh! he could toss up such a dish of politics!—And every menace, every period concluded with a wish—that he was prime vizier but for one month only.—The Grand Seignior took him at his word; and, in a few days advanced him to that high post next himself. Where all are slaves, this advancement was by no means surprising. It was a mere despotic humor and frolic; and perhaps done with a design to punish his vassal's presumption, by setting his own knife to his throat, upon the first false step, or mismanagement in his conduct. But the man was honest, and the master agreeably disappointed. No minister ever filled that station, for many years, with greater honor and reputation; or was better beloved both by prince and people. He fed the empire as he had done the emperor, with good, wholesome diet, well cooked and garnished. He strewed plenty every where, and seemed by his conduct to understand perfectly well that fine maxim of Cæsar, which deserves a whole physical, moral, and political essay, fully to explain it—" Let me have men about me that are fat."

If chance and incident, or caprice and humor, can go thus far in the choice of a good minister, who at first setting out only stumbled upon good sense, and common honesty; what will not good sense and common honesty do, when joined with those other noble qualifications of which I have given a detail, and when marked out and distinguished by a regular and judicious choice? They have made the reigns of minors, and of monarchs, never out of their minority, glorious and flourishing. They have transformed queens into amazons, and confined the faults of a soft and vicious prince to a few apartments; made them darlings of their people, and their people happy under their government. But where a prince, truly wise and great, and good in himself, is surrounded by a multitude of such counsellors, to how amazing a height, and to how many generations may he extend his grandeur and the public felicity?—Such ministers, under a monarch, the father of his country, will consequently consider all his subjects as princes of the blood, (so a merry writer of the last age called them,) or, in the inspired, royal style, as flesh of his flesh, and bone of his bone; not in a natural sense; for adoption is better than nature. Such ministers will put out the revenues of their master to interest in the pockets of his subjects; then, with a—*non rapui sed recepi,* recall them upon a real necessity. Such ministers will raise a standing force, so very numerous, that it shall take in all the landed gentry and trading commons of a nation; and perhaps 5d. a day is not so good encouragement, as when men fight for their all; for they fight for their all when they fight for a prince with whom they have but one common safety and interest. Such ministers will not suffer the law to be made the back-sword of justice, which cuts only on one side. They will not score up a war to the reckoning, when the good company have not had it in; nor palm a truce upon us, with all its accidents, for the real body of a solid and lasting peace, by a new political trans-or-consubstantiation. In short, they will not, like some old Roman minions and favorites, make a statue of their master, and then fly to it for refuge.

POLICY OF THE ATHENIANS.

Hoc illud est præcipuè in cognitione rerum salubre, ac frugiferum, omnis te exempli documenta in illustri posita monumento intueri; inde tibi, tuæque reipublicæ quod imitere capias; inde fœdum inceptu, fœdum excitu quod vites.

SIR:—It is so common a failing to think that every thing, which particularly affects us in reading, will equally please and entertain others, that I hope you will excuse the fondness of a young student for an old story, which I have lately met with in the history of Greece; and I fancy it may prove as agreeable an amusement to others as it hath been to myself; but if you think otherwise, the use it will be of to you in lighting your pipe will make you some amends for the trouble of reading it.

Darius Hystaspis is the first, I think, who is mentioned in history to have been possessed with the wild ambition of universal empire; and in order to carry on this chimerical design, he made several unsuccessful expeditions into Europe; where he was informed that Greece, which then made a very considerable figure in the world, would probably give him no small opposition in his projected conquests; particularly the Athenians, who with some of the islanders, their confederates, had given him a mortifying instance of their boldness and resolution, by daring to assist their colonies in the lesser Asia in their endeavors to shake off the Persian yoke, and recover their ancient liberties. This was looked upon as such an affront to the power of the grand monarch, (as he is styled by the historians of those times,) that nothing would satisfy him but the entire conquest of Greece; to which he was likewise continually solicited by Hippias, son of the famous tyrant Pisistratus, who, upon being expelled by the Athenians for invading their laws and liberties, had fled to Darius for protection and assistance to recover his tyranny.

The monarch, however, to give some color to his quarrel with the Grecians, sent to the sevaral states to demand earth and water from them, as an acknowledgment of their homage and subjection to him; requiring, at the same time, that the Athenians should restore Hippias.

Athens and Sparta, the most considerable states in Greece, fired with a just resentment at this haughty demand from a free people, took his messengers and threw them into deep pits; telling them that there they might find earth and water for their king Darius; who, being enraged at this new provocation, sent his generals Datis and Artaphernes, with an army of above one hundred thousand men, to revenge such an open defiance and contempt of his power, with orders to bring the Athenians prisoners.

It is well known that Miltiades with a very small number of men, animated with the glorious love of liberty, routed these numerous forces at the famous battle of Marathon, and for some time secured the liberties of Greece.

Darius, being very desirous to recover this disgrace, employed all his endeavors, with the power and riches of the Persian empire, to make preparations for a second attempt; but dying before they were completed, he left the prosecution of this design to his son Xerxes; who, having raised the greatest army that ever appeared upon the stage of the world, (being said to be some millions,) marched with them into Europe over a bridge made across the Hellespont; but before he entered Greece, he again experienced the courage and bravery of the Grecians, by the stop that was put to the progress of this incredible multitude, with a very inconsiderable number of men, under Leonidas, at the pass of Thermopylæ; which the Persians gained at last, by the treachery of a fugitive Greek, who led them a private way over the mountains to surround the Grecians.

The unexpected success of this small body, with the victory which the Athenians singly gained soon after over Xerxes' fleet, would, they hoped, have been a sufficient encouragement to the confederated Grecians, who had entered into a grand alliance against the Persians, to have continued firm to them, in the defence of their common liberties; but when the Athenians proposed to attack the Persians, in order to prevent their marching into Attica, the Spartans with their other allies, either from treachery or cowardice, or a mixture of both, in a very shameful and infamous manner refused to march, and deserted the Athenians, leaving them to struggle with those unequal numbers, which it was impossible for them alone to resist; yet placing their happiness in their liberty, and their liberty in their valor, (as Thucydides expresses it,) they did not even in this extremity despair; but their virtue and courage taking new force from their distress, they abandoned Athens to the fury of the Persians, having first transported their wives and children to their friends in the neighboring islands, and resolved with their fleet, without any other assistance, to conquer or die in the defence of their liberties.

This glorious resolution, with their knowledge and skill in naval affairs, which they had very happily cultivated, enabled them to gain an entire victory over the Persian fleet. This so terrified the haughty Xerxes, that he fled with the utmost precipitation and confusion to the Hellespont, and passed into Asia in a little boat; and the forces he left under his general Mardonius, to continue the war, being some time afterwards entirely routed at Platea, Greece was absolutely freed from all farther fears of the Persians, solely by the virtue and valor of the Athenians; who, forgetting the former ill treatment of their allies, had besides the additional merit of leaving Athens a second time exposed to the plunder of the enemy under Mardonius, rather than make a separate peace with the Persian, who offered to render them full satisfaction for all their losses in the war; to pay them a vast sum of money; and make them sovereigns of all Greece; but they generously refused to be instrumental in enslaving that country which they had so bravely defended, and preferred the glorious title of the deliverers of Greece, to all other considerations.

We may now look upon Athens in the height of its glory and prosperity; and they would, in all probability, have continued to be the last flourishing state in Greece, if they had been masters of any prudence, and improved the advantages which now lay open to them; but such is the uncertainty of all human felicity, that we soon find them, by their foolish conduct, gradually losing all the benefits of their amazing successes in the war, till they at last fell under the power of that state which owed its being and preservation to them. Athens, therefore, may be truly said to date its ruin from the day of its triumph over the Persians; for presuming upon her great merits and signal services in defending and preserving the common liberties of Greece, they grew haughty and insolent to all the neighboring states; and wholly neglecting the care of their own affairs, they took all occasions of intermeddling with those of their neighbors; too often promoting differences, in order to make themselves the sole arbitrators and umpires of them; by which means they were generally so unfortunate as to increase the number of their enemies, instead of making new friends. But that which raised the greatest resentment against them was their pretending to prescribe laws to the trade of all Greece, and endeavoring to exclude the Megareans from any share in it. This was made the ground of the war between them and Sparta, which was not a little offended at the imperious manner in which Athens claimed the right of holding the balance of power in Greece, which they were certainly in possession of, and might have long and easily kept, if they could have been content with the thing, without affecting to make a vain show of it, and thereby shocking the other powers of Greece, equally independent with themselves; for nothing would have more effectually secured the superiority they aimed at, than making use of the great reputation and credit which they had deservedly gained, by interposing their good offices to reconcile the frequent differences which arose amongst the several states of Greece, ever jealous of their own authorities; but whilst the Athenians kept within the bounds of moderation, the other states showed upon all occasions the greatest deference and respect to their mediation; and the whole of their policy consisted in interposing their force in cases of necessity only, to prevent the weak from being unjustly oppressed by their more powerful neighbor; and in avoiding, as much as possible, to make themselves parties, much less principals in their quarrels.

Such a wise conduct would have given them leisure and opportunity to enjoy the fruits of that peace which they wanted to recover the losses and ease the burdens of a long and heavy war, supported chiefly by them, and carried on at a much greater expense of blood and treasure than they had suffered at any time since the foundation of their state.

It is certain that they were under the happiest circumstances to have effected this, soon after the war; for their great naval power, which made them the undisputed masters of the sea, made them likewise equally esteemed and feared by their neighbors. To this we may add the advantages of their situation, and knowledge in all maritime affairs, with their numerous ships, and the benefits of their colonies abroad; which might have enabled them to improve and extend their trade, the only true source of riches, beyond any other nation, and would have soon put them into such a flourishing condition, as would have deterred the most powerful of their neighbors from entertaining any thoughts of disturbing their tranquillity; and much more from entering into projects of humbling or subduing them.

But they had the misfortune for several years, to groan under the government of a set of ministers, who were too intent upon their own interest to have any serious regard for the welfare of the public; though that was the constant subject of their own praises; and the better to carry on their selfish and mischievous designs, and divert the people of Athens from looking into their conduct, they not only promoted continual dissensions amongst them, under the different distinctions of favorers or opposers of the former tyranny of Pisistratus; but they likewise engaged them, on one side or the other, in every quarrel that arose, not only in Greece, but in Asia and places at the greatest distance, upon the smallest pretences of ancient alliances, or kindred with their ancestors; by which means they wasted their strength and riches in many fruitless and unnecessary foreign expeditions, for no other purpose than to make a parade of their power at sea; and which had no other effect than to increase the envy and jealousy of their neighbors.

To support such extraordinary and extravagant expenses, they were obliged to raise almost as great and heavy impositions as they did in the time of the Persian war, to the great decay of trade and impoverishment of the people; and though this was colored with the specious pretences of extinguishing all remains of the former war, and settling a solid and lasting peace; yet it did not prevent the frequent murmurs and complaints of the public; nor were there wanting persons who vigorously and honestly opposed measures which were so visibly destructive of the true interest and safety of Athens; measures which it would have been impossible to have continued, if the heads of the faction who got possession of the government, had not found means to delude the people, from time to time, with the great advantages they were every day to receive from an universal, established peace, by which they were to be delivered from all apprehensions of the return of Hippias, or any of his descendants; and the balance of power was for ever to be secured to the Athenians; a notion which had been so successfully propagated in Athens, and so much intoxicated the minds of the people, that there was no imposition so gross which their leaders could not pass upon them under this pretence; and it was the never-failing argument for silencing all oppositions, and removing all objections to the most chimerical projects, or unreasonable propositions in their public assemblies.

Athens was daily languishing under this unhappy management, which would have brought certain ruin upon her in the end, without the calamity of the Peloponesian war; for nothing prevented it but the continual struggles of her great men to supplant one another. This kept them in some awe, and restrained them from doing all the mischief which they had both in their inclination and power; so that the preservation of Athens for some time, may be said to be owing, in a great measure, to the short continuance of those in the administration.

But Cimon, Aristides and Tolmidas, with several other considerable men of real merit and abilities, who, notwithstanding some failings, had done their country very great and eminent services; these men, I say, happening to go off the stage very near one another, left the field open to Pericles, who first subverted their constitution, and then erected to himself an arbitrary power, which ended in the destruction of Athens.

He was a gentleman of a private fortune, but unmeasurable ambition, which made him stick at nothing to advance himself in the state. For this purpose he set out on the foot of liberty, and courted the affections of the people, by pretending a zeal for their interest upon all occasions; but when he had once made himself considerable by these methods, he threw off the mask, and treated them with the utmost insolence; by turns betraying all those who trusted him, and knowing no friendships or enmities, but such as favored or opposed his corrupt purposes. He gave a very remarkable instance of this, with regard to Cimon, a noble Athenian of great parts and integrity, but one whom Pericles hated and constantly opposed, for keeping him under that subordination which became his station and character. Yet Cimon afterwards falling under a prosecution from the people, he screened him in the public assembly, and then made a bargain with him to share the government between them; but took an opportunity to revenge himself in the ruin of his son Lacedæmonius, after his father's death.

As he was master of great volubility of tongue, with a knack of speaking plausibly in public, and had joined to this a very daring and consummate assurance; so he knew perfectly well how to improve them to his own advantage in supporting any proposition, right or wrong, as it best suited his present purpose; for nothing was more common than to see him in one assembly with great zeal confuting his own arguments in a former one; and he never scrupled to contradict the most certain truths, or to assert the most notorious falsehoods in order to carry his point, though sure to be discovered a few hours afterwards, having always an evasion ready at hand.

But notwithstanding the great opinion which he seemed to entertain of his own eloquence and cunning, he was convinced they would prove but a very feeble and short-lived support to him, without some better assistance. He therefore made use of all his art and contrivance to work himself into the administration of the public revenues, in which he had the good luck to succeed, after the death of Aristides; who, having been long treasurer of Greece, did not leave money enough behind him to defray the expenses of his funeral.—Happy had it been for Athens, if Pericles had succeeded him in his noble qualities, as well as employment. But his character was the reverse of the good Aristides, and his administration one continued scene of rapine and profusion. Thus did he establish his power on a much more lasting foundation than his predecessors, by applying himself to the foibles and vices of mankind, which are too often the surest hold upon them; for though it is not to be imagined but that many corruptions had sprung up during the former disorders and weakness of the government; yet some remains of the modesty and virtue of their ancestors had hitherto restrained the Athenians from an open and avowed prostitution of their integrity; but Pericles, by the licentious distribution of bribes and bounties amongst the people, soon extinguished all sentiments of their former honesty and love of their country, which he treated as the most ridiculous fanaticism; and all the endeavors of a few to oppose this torrent of iniquity were the public and standing jest of his conversation.

This extravagant and unnatural flow of the public money by degrees introduced that spirit of expense and luxury amongst all ranks of men, under the mistaken notion of politeness, which consumed the estates of the best families in Athens, and soon made them so necessitous, that forgetting their ancient honors and the dignity of their birth, they were not ashamed to become the known pensioners of Pericles, living in as abject a dependence upon him as the meanest of the people.

Thus was universal corruption spread over the whole state; and, to complete their misfortune, the very money which was reserved for the necessities of war only, was spent in debauching the minds of the people, and what was designed for their preservation, turned to their destruction.

As Pericles was not qualified by his rank to be of the assembly of the Areopagus; (the great and supreme judicature of Athens;) so to remove every obstacle to his ambition, he employed all his art to undermine their authority, and by degrees drew all public business of consequence to the popular assemblies; where, by the assistance of bribes, pensions, and employments, which were all at his disposal, he was secure of carrying every thing almost without opposition.

This, together with the scandalous disrespect with which Pericles affected to treat them upon all occasions, and their slavish submission at the same time, to all his orders, falling in with the general depravation of the times, soon brought them into the lowest contempt with the people, and destroyed all regard for that ancient and august assembly, which had for so many ages been the bulwark and defence of the constitution.

After this fatal blow to a state which made the proudest boast of its liberties, and had ever showed the greatest jealousy of any encroachments upon them, Pericles obtained almost as absolute and uncontrolled a power as the tyrant Pisistratus himself; which gave occasion to the calling him and his creatures the new Pisistratides; for though it is well known that the Archons had the exercise of the regal power, yet we scarce read of any thing but their names, during the whole ministry of Pericles; to whom all applications, both at home and abroad, were constantly made; and he scarce left them the shadow of sovereignty.

But in the height of this prosperity, he was not a little disturbed with the threats of a war from Sparta; the seeds of which, as is before observed, were sown soon after the end of the Persian war, and ripened into action by the monstrous conduct of Pericles, who by turns provoked their resentment, and courted their friendship, in the most ignominious manner.

It would be tedious and unnecessary to enlarge upon the particular differences which had, from time to time, arisen between them, and increased the animosities of the two states.

Many endeavors had been used to put an end to this uneasy situation of affairs; in which both states were under the inconveniences and expenses of an actual war, though no formal declaration had been made of one, and the interruptions the Athenians found in their trade, with the continuance of very severe taxes, occasioned many loud complaints amongst the people; to quiet which a sort of cessation was agreed upon for five years. This, however, lasted but a very short time, the old grudges breaking out again into new hostilities; in the pursuit of which both parties being tired, a peace was made between them for thirty years, though it lasted between five and six years only, which were chiefly employed in forming new alliances in order to be prepared for war; each side being very sensible that the articles of the treaty were only patched up for the present, but were not a sufficient foundation for a lasting peace; and accordingly they were very negligently observed on both sides; but it was the misfortune of Athens always to lose ground by these short intervals of truce; for their unhappy behavior had irritated many of their neighbors against them; and their confederated subjects took the first opportunity to choose new protectors, and free themselves from the grievous impositions which the Athenians had laid upon them, under the pretence of raising supplies for the war.

Pericles, well foreseeing the fatal consequences which an open rupture with Sparta would be to his affairs, neglected no endeavors to prevent it; and it is not improperly said, that the age of negotiation then began in Greece. Ministers and ambassadors were seen continually posting not only over all Greece, but even in the adjoining kingdoms of Macedon, Thessaly, and Thrace; both sides endeavoring to engage them in new alliances in their favor; and Pericles was not ashamed to court the friendship even of the Persians, to whom he had formerly professed so much enmity and hatred, by putting the balance of power in their hands.

He did not make a much better bargain for his country with some other of their allies, who owed their preservation to Athens, and pretended the greatest friendship for them; yet being in hopes of an addition of power and wealth, by the diminution of the trade of Athens, and the decrease of their naval strength, in consequence of it, they very faintly supported the interests of the Athenians, and remissly discharged the obligations of their alliances.

Pericles, to remedy these growing mischiefs, endeavored to gain over to his interest some of the neighboring powers, by the proposition of certain wild and impracticable projects; such as joining the forces of Athens to theirs, and making new accessions to their dominions, by altering the dependencies of some of the lesser principalities of Greece; but this scheme gained him nothing but shame and contempt; so that after much time and labor had been spent in these fruitless negotiations, he had recourse to the same methods abroad which he had found so very successful at home, and backed all his foreign transactions with the offers of a round sum of money; by which means he engaged many of the lesser states of Greece to lend their names, at least, to his new alliances, and kept some of the favorite ones in constant pay, under the pretence of making good their expenses, in keeping troops to assist Athens upon occasion, though they never raised one man more for their service.

As he could not treat in the same manner with the greater powers, he made his application to their ministers, whom he judged by himself, and endeavored that way to gain them to his interest. Most of them took his money; and perhaps excused themselves by their intentions of neither doing him any good, nor their country any harm; for they only amused him with intelligences of pretended secrets, many falsehoods, and things of little or no consequence.

By this infamous management, Athens was made the common tributary of all Greece and the neighboring powers; not only to the great waste of the public treasure; but, what was worse, these mean condescensions from a state, which had for many ages made so considerable a figure in that part of the world, lost them all their former authority, and brought Athens into the utmost contempt.

However Pericles endeavored, from time to time, to varnish over the present state of affairs; continually amusing the people with assurances of the successes of his negotiations abroad; and even the perplexity of them was of benefit to him; for it helped to divert the public from looking into his conduct; his creatures, upon the least offer at it, crying out that divisions at home would give the greatest encouragement to the common enemy.

The present uncertainties gave him likewise some pretence for supplying his vast expenses, either to carry on engagements to prevent a war, or for making the necessary preparations to begin one; and thus arguments were never wanting to fleece the people, who in vain complained of the great profusion of the public money, without any account having been given of it by one, who had for so many years the sole and absolute disposition of their revenues; whereas it had ever been usual before his time for the prytanis, who were a committee of the senate, annually to examine the public accounts, in the most solemn manner, being sworn upon the altar, before they entered upon that office, to discharge their duty with the utmost impartiality, fidelity and justice to their country.—So careful have all wise governments ever been to preserve this branch of the administration from corruption; well knowing that without it all other precautions would be vain and ineffectual to support the liberties of a free people.

As Pericles fell under the general censure of the people, on this account, so he did not escape being several times charged in the public assemblies with the visible corruption of his management; which once went so far that Dracontides, as Plutarch informs us, carried a resolution, or decree, for impeaching him of embezzling the public treasure; but Agnon, one of his creatures, by the alteration of some words, rendered it ineffectual; and by these little arts and shifts, which too many of his dependents in the senate were always ready to countenance and support, he baffled all endeavors to obtain any account of the immense sums, which he had spent, during his administration.

But it would have been impossible for him to have stood the general clamor and demand of the people for bringing him to justice, if he had not had recourse to a new artifice, which no minister before him had the assurance to attempt. This was a proposal for allowing him ten talents for secret service-money; which, though no very great sum, yet as it was understood, and even acknowledged by himself, to be the wages of iniquity, it was giving a public sanction to corruption, and was a precedent, that at once quite overturned all the ancient checks and controls, by which their ancestors had, in the strictest manner, guarded against the embezzlement of public money; the disposal of which was, by this stroke, put into the absolute power of him, who was at the head of the treasury; for, under this cover, he had the most unlimited scope to supply any expenses, under pretence of the public service.

One would think that nothing more could have been desired

to gratify the most insatiable thirst of power and dominion; but such were the extravagant expenses of Pericles, in unprofitable negotiations abroad, and satisfying the craving importunities of his dependents at home, who always rose in their demands in proportion to the difficulties, in which they saw him engaged, and the want he had of their service, that though he feared no repulse to the most unreasonable demand of new supplies, yet being conscious himself of his exorbitant expenses, he began to be ashamed that the people should see what money he consumed. He therefore resolved to make one bold step more, to secure himself of a fund, which would at once fully answer his purposes and conceal his profusions. This he put in execution, by seizing upon the sacred treasure at Delos, which was deposited there by the common consent of the states of Greece, to be kept inviolable, never to be touched but in case of the utmost extremity, and that not without their unanimous advice and consent.

Such an open violation of the public faith raised the clamors of all Greece upon Pericles; which he endeavored to palliate at first with the pretence of its being in greater safety, and the advantages, that might be made of it, by employing it for the benefit of the public; but when he saw how few there were, who had the virtue or courage to oppose him, even in this extreme act of violence, he grew bolder, in a little time, and being pressed upon this article, openly defied them in the public assemblies, and with the most assuming arrogance declared, that the money, when it was once granted, was no longer theirs who gave it, but theirs who received it.

He soon after followed this with another declaration; that the necessities of the state, of which he was to be the judge himself, were above all laws, and that nothing was so sacred but that even the plate and riches of the temples might be seized, and restitution made afterwards; well knowing that it would not be in his time, nor any part of his concern.

This great treasure being now wholly in the possession of Pericles, he had no farther trouble than to give such account of it to the public as he thought fit; for any proposal of appointing persons (as was the ancient custom) to examine his books, or count the talents remaining, was opposed with the old cant of distrusting so virtuous an administration, as his creatures had the impudence to call it, and forwarding the designs of the enemy, by raising divisions at home; the constant artifice of those, who are engaged in measures destructive to their country, and are sensible that their actions will not bear examination; whereas, in truth, no enemy is so dangerous to a free people as these domestic spoilers; for though nations may, and often have been, laid waste by foreign invaders; yet many of them have recovered their ancient freedom and prosperity, as Athens itself had lately done, after all the malice of the Persians; whereas history affords us no example of any nation, that ever regained their liberties, when they had tamely consented to the loss of them, or infamously sold them to their governors for the present supply of their luxury and vices; but their unhappy posterity have for ever groaned under the inheritance of slavery, delivered down to them by their forefathers. But to return to Pericles:—

His success, which even exceeded his own expectations, struck every honest Athenian dumb with astonishment at the continued, abject compliances of their fellow citizens. Pericles now flattered himself that his authority and power were so firmly established, as to be out of the reach of all accidents. This made him so haughty and insolent, that he became grievous to his own creatures, and the object of universal odium; which was not a little heightened by the growing necessities of the state, and the poverty of the people; so that the former clamors were again renewed with great warmth and violence for an account of the disposition of the money which had been dissipated during his long and expensive administration. This roused his apprehensions and threw him into great perplexities; which his relation Alcibiades taking notice of one day, when he was more melancholy than usual, he asked him the reason of it. Pericles told him that he was considering how to make up his accounts with the public; to which this young profligate (who gave such an early instance of the mischiefs he was one day to bring upon his country) replied that he had much better consider how to avoid giving any account. Unhappily for Athens, he took his kinsman's advice, and seeing no other way to escape and divert the impending storm from bursting upon himself, he chose to turn it upon his country, by plunging them into a war with Sparta.

The Spartans, notwithstanding the inclination they had shown to begin the war, yet when things came near to an extremity, still expressed a desire of continuing the peace; and at last offered to desist from it, in case the Athenians would consent to take off the restraint from the trade of the Megareans.

Pericles, in a long speech, dissuaded them from accepting the conditions offered, by telling them that though this was a matter of no great consequence, (as, in truth, it was not,) yet the manner, in which it was asked, made it necessary for the commonwealth to show their firmness on this occasion, in order to support their honor, and prevent the attempts of future impositions upon them, in matters of greater concern.

This determined the venal assembly for war, which was soon after begun by the siege of Platea, a strong town of great importance, and the only acquisition of the Athenians by all their glorious successes over the Persian; which however, in the course of the war, was scandalously neglected by the Athenians, and fell a sacrifice to Sparta.

Some endeavors were used to terminate the war soon after it begun by a truce made for a year, in order to agree upon preliminary articles of peace; but they were never settled in such a manner as to take effect; and a peace, that was afterwards concluded between them, had little better success, the articles being never put in execution, or complied with on either side; but the short time it lasted was spent in breaking and renewing alliances with their neighbors in such a manner, that it would require copying out the fifth book of Thucydides to repeat the mutual infidelities and treacheries practised by Athens and Sparta, during this cessation, which both sides were more tired with than the war; and all Greece, with the neighboring powers, being now one way or other engaged, it was soon renewed with the greatest animosity, and at last ended in the entire reduction of Athens to the subjection of Sparta; a fate, which they might in all probability have escaped, if Pericles had either had the honesty to have preserved the peace, by forbearing to intermeddle, where he had nothing to do, or the spirit to have begun the war sooner, before Athens was quite exhausted, and had lost all credit abroad by his wretched management.

It ought, however, to be remembered, for the honor of that learned state, that the most celebrated wits and poets of Athens endeavored to open the eyes of their countrymen, and animate them against Pericles, by exposing his conduct in satirical poems and invectives, but they were too far gone in luxury and corruption to recover their ancient spirit, being continually soothed in their vices by a set of profligate writers, whom Pericles had picked up and employed in his service. These fellows were so abandoned, that they not only made a jest of liberty, and justified all the methods of arbitrary government, but put their patron in competition with Jupiter himself, and flattered him with the appellation of Olympius, at the same time that he was precipitating the destruction of their country.

Thus we see that the overgrown power, ambition and corruption of one man brought ruin upon the most flourishing state in the universe; and there are not wanting instances of the like kind in history to convince us that the same conduct will have the same consequences in all ages and all nations.

I am, sir, &c.

                                        PHIL-ATHENUS.

ON THE

POWER OF THE PRINCE,

AND THE

FREEDOM OF THE PEOPLE.

Furono veramente tutti i rè principio capi, e non rè, di republiche, e non di
regni. Ma poi il lungo uso hà fatto che i populi si siano disposti et anuez-
zati all' habito dell' intiera ubbidienza, come apunto suole assuefarsi una
pianta, & un corpo humano a viuere, in terreno, e sotto clime diuerso dal
suo naturale.
CARD. BENTIVOGLIO, *Relatione delle Prov. unite de Fiandra. Lib. 3.*

CARDINAL BENTIVOGLIO, from whose writings I have taken
the motto to this paper, was a man on all accounts little to be
suspected of favoring the cause of liberty; much less of writing
strongly and boldly for it. But the love of it is innate in the
mind of every man; and however we may be depraved by bad
education, however inflamed by party, interest, or the spirit of
opposition, yet whenever we grow cool, and are not immediately
agitated by our passions, that spirit breaks out, and shows itself
even in those, who are the greatest abettors of arbitrary power.

Thus the cardinal, borne down by the force of reason, and the
influence of this principle of nature, expresses in this sentence
not only his own opinion, but that of all mankind, though private
reasons may induce many to profess themselves of contrary sentiments; nor is it impossible for some men, weak in their natures
and warm in their tempers, to be either so far seduced by the
arguments of designing men, or so heated by political contentions, as even to become in some manner convinced, that they
have no natural right to liberty; and that their princes are born
with a just title to that arbitrary power, which is always the
child of fraud, or usurpation.

It is our great happiness that his present majesty's dominion is founded upon a better title than either the *jus divinum*, or hereditary right. He owes it purely to the voice of the people in parliament. He got it by their favor, and will keep it by their affection; nor is it less for the advantage of his family, or for that of the nation, that he came to the throne upon these terms. The limitations and conditions, by the due observance of which he is entitled to it, will serve as a certain rule to his posterity, by which if they guide themselves, they may depend upon the hearts and purses of their subjects to all eternity. His predecessors had not the same advantages. They were bred up in a notion that their prerogative entitled them to do what they pleased; nor were the privileges of the people so firmly ascertained. This occasioned perpetual jealousies, gave opportunities for evil ministers to impose upon the prince, and for seditious persons to inflame the people. It often gave rise to unwarrantable acts of power; and thus frequently exposed both the royal family and the nation to the utmost confusion.

Machiavel, in his political discourses, lays down this position; that no government can long enjoy liberty, unless it be frequently brought back to its first principles. It is the nature of all government to degenerate. As it grows older, it gradually deviates and flies farther from its first intention, which is singly the advantage of society; till at last it attains such a degree of corruption, that its order becomes entirely inverted; and that institution, by which the prince was first only the servant of the public, obliges the public to be slaves to the prince. For this reason he recommends a frequent renewal of the constitution. The various revolutions in this kingdom have, in a great measure, answered this end. They have purged off the luxuriances of power; and though few of them have gone so deep as to bring us back to the primitive purity of our constitution, yet they have still preserved us a free people, when liberty is lost in almost every other part of Europe.

The last revolution has done more for us than any of the rest. I would not be understood to speak of that, which was brought about in favor of our great deliverer the prince of Orange. I mean that, by which the present royal family were seated upon the throne. This happy change in our government, though it is not marked out by any such appellation, is the most important we have had. It has amounted within a few degrees of that reduction to the first principles of government, which Machiavel recommends. Our constitution has received a new spring from it; and had we taken care to guard against a few inconveniences, as we might have done, or used the same caution to prevent new dangers, as to redress old grievances, our liberties had been delivered down to our posterity, after a thousand years, more secure and with a greater prospect of long duration, than at the very beginning of the commonwealth.

The sentence prefixed to this paper contains an account of the first powers, with which princes were invested. It alleges, that the present power of unlimited monarchs owes its rise only to an abuse of the first trust reposed in them; to which (though repugnant to human nature) by gradual steps and long use, men were insensibly habituated. The original state of monarchy is justly described very different from what it is now in all arbitrary governments. Kings were then no more than chiefs, or principal magistrates, in states republican and free.

It ought to give every Englishman the greatest satisfaction to find the constitution we now live under, since its last renewal, bearing so near a resemblance to primitive liberty. Our princes are now, in a great measure, upon the same foot with these chiefs, or principal magistrates of old. They have authority given them to defend the laws of the land, but not to break them. They have too lately received their crown from the hands of the nation to forget that it is to them only they owe it, and that consequently they can be entitled to no powers but what are granted by them. The people must still remember that their own hands adorned the temples of their kings, and can have recourse to known and positive laws, if privilege and prerogative should ever clash. They are no longer to be abused by the sound of words; nor will they suffer themselves any longer to be duped into an opinion, because most of those, who have enjoyed the title of king, have also enjoyed an arbitrary sway, that therefore regal authority must inevitably import an absolute dominion. They justly look upon this word as one of the many, which have different meanings; and signifies with us no other than a third estate, superior to every individual, yet inferior to the collective body of the people, whose advantage and prosperity were the only causes of its existence.

The act of settlement has obtained all these great advantages for us. That compact between prince and people, which has been formerly treated by some persons as a mere chimera, is now no longer to be disputed. In that act are contained certain stipulations and conditions, under which the prince has consented to accept, and by which tenure only he holds his crown. By these means every subject in the nation may know the precise extent of his prince's power, and the measures of his own allegiance; how far and how long he is bound to obey.

It would be tedious to enumerate the many wise and prudent restrictions of this our second magna charta. I shall only mention two of the fundamental points of this public act, which suffi

ciently evince the care and zeal, with which the parliament, on
this occasion, pursued the interest of the nation. They even
seem, if we may judge from what has since happened, to have
carried their caution beyond the bounds of absolute necessity, or
prudence. Being apprised that the dominions of the present
royal family were very considerable abroad, and not knowing
how far their tenderness for their native country might carry
them to the prejudice of this kingdom, they made these two
points the principal conditions of their government; first, that the
king should never leave his British dominions without consent
of parliament; and secondly, that he should never engage England in any broils relating to his foreign territories. I think I
may venture to say, without any reflection upon the prudence
of the parliament, who insisted upon these conditions, that they
were upon this occasion, a little deficient in good manners; but
this error may be forgiven, as it proceeded from their zeal, and
we have since corrected it, by abandoning those two points, of
which I have been speaking; the first soon after his late majesty's
accession to the throne; the other not long ago, in that just,
honorable, and ever memorable resolution of the house of commons, by which we engaged to support and maintain his majesty's German dominions, with the utmost efforts of Great
Britain.

The remaining articles of the act of settlement are of such a
nature, that we have no reason to fear they will be dispensed
with. I have already shown how much it is the interest of the
prince, as well as the people, to maintain them. I have mentioned many advantages arising from a settlement established on
the foot of liberty. They are such, that I think any man, who
endeavors to raise the prerogative one step higher than it stands
at present, or even argues in favor of such conduct, either with
a view to seduce the people, or to ingratiate himself with his
prince, is the worst of traitors, and deserves the curse and hatred
of the whole community.

Sir William Temple, in his observations upon the Dutch
republic, made this judicious remark:—" That this stomachful
people, who could not endure the least exercise of arbitrary
power, or impositions, under the Spanish government, have been
since inured to digest them in the highest degree, under their
own popular magistrates; bridled with hard laws; terrified with
severe executions; environed with foreign forces; and oppressed
with the most cruel hardships, and variety of taxes, that was
ever known under any government."

The reason of this great and general content, under the most
severe oppression, was only this; that they found every one subject to the same law. The persons in the administration could

make no advantage from the public calamities. On the contrary, they felt the weight of the public misfortunes more heavily than those, who had less interest in the general welfare. It was never observed in that country, that the principal men in the commonwealth increased in riches, in proportion as the country grew poorer, or the public labored under heavier taxes. These evils were well guarded against by their constitution; and therefore they considered all their misfortunes as a wise and just regulation of Providence for some important ends, which consequently they never repined at.

The Hanover succession under the limitations, which I have mentioned, and on which it is founded, has obtained, in a great measure, these advantages for us. The prince himself is now subject to the law, and the act of settlement binds him equally with the meanest peasant.

The benefits of this excellent establishment are not so easily discovered, until some abuses happen. But if ever a weak and corrupt administration should arise; if an evil minister should embezzle the public treasure; if he should load the nation, in times of peace, with taxes greater than would be necessary to defray the charge of an expensive war; if the money thus raised should be expended, under the pretence of secret services, to line his own pockets; to stop the mouths of his hungry dependents; to bribe some future parliament to approve his measures; and to patch up an ill-digested, base, dishonorable peace with foreign powers, whom he shall have offended by a continued series of provocations and blunders; if he should advise his sovereign to make it a maxim, that his security consisted in the continuance, or increase of the public debts, and that his grandeur was founded on the poverty of his subjects; if he he should hazard the affections of the people, by procuring greater revenues for the crown, than they should be able to spend, or the people be well able to raise; and after this engage his prince to demand still farther sums as his right, which all men should be sensible were not his due; I say, if the nation should ever fall under these unhappy circumstances, they will then find the excellence of a free constitution. The public discontent, which upon such occasions has formerly burst forth in a torrent of blood, of universal confusion and desolation, will make itself known only in faint murmurs, and dutiful general complaints. The nation will wait long, before they engage in any desperate measures, that may endanger a constitution, which they justly adore, and from which they confidently expect a sure, though perhaps a dilatory justice, upon such an enormous offender.

These are the inestimable advantages of our present, happy settlement. Let us prize it as we ought. Let us not have the

worse opinion of the thing itself, because it may, in some instances, be abused.   But let us retain the highest veneration for
it.   Let us remember how much it is our right, and let us resolve
to preserve it untainted and inviolable.   Thus shall we truly
serve our king; we shall do our duty to our country; and preserve ourselves in the condition, for which all men were
originally designed; that is, of a free people.

END OF VOL. I.